INTRODUCTION
to
THE ANALYSIS
of
POLITICAL DATA

SUSAN ANN KAY

Miami University, Oxford, Ohio

PRENTICE HALL, Englewood Cliffs, New Jersey 07632

Library of Congress Cataloging-in-Publication Data

Kay, Susan Ann.
   Introduction to the analysis of political data / Susan Ann Kay.
     p. cm.
   Includes bibliographical references and index.
   ISBN 0-13-488594-5
   1. Political science—Statistical methods—Data processing.
 I. Title.
JA73.K39   1991
326′.028′5—dc20   90-7725
                                                                    CIP

Editorial/production supervision and
  interior design: Serena Hoffman
Cover design: Bruce Kenselaar
Pre-press buyer: Debbie Kesar
Manufacturing buyer: Mary Ann Gloriande

 © 1991 by Prentice-Hall, Inc.
A Division of Simon & Schuster
Englewood Cliffs, New Jersey 07632

*All rights reserved. No part of this book may be
reproduced, in any form or by any means,
without permission in writing from the publisher.*

Printed in the United States of America

10 9 8 7 6 5 4 3 2 1

ISBN 0-13-488594-5

Prentice-Hall International (UK) Limited, *London*
Prentice-Hall of Australia Pty. Limited, *Sydney*
Prentice-Hall Canada Inc., *Toronto*
Prentice-Hall Hispanoamericana, S.A., *Mexico*
Prentice-Hall of India Private Limited, *New Delhi*
Prentice-Hall of Japan, Inc., *Tokyo*
Simon & Schuster Asia Pte. Ltd., *Singapore*
Editora Prentice-Hall do Brasil, Ltda., *Rio de Janeiro*

for my father

CONTENTS

Formulae xv
Preface xvii

CHAPTER **1**

**STARTING OUT: WHAT POLITICAL SCIENTISTS DO
WHEN THEY DO RESEARCH** 1

Explaining Phenomena 1
    Exercise 1 Phenomenon to Be Explained 2
Explaining Variation in Phenomena 2
    Exercise 2 Variation in the Dependent Variable 3
Using Independent Variables to Form Relationships 3
    Exercise 3 The Independent Variable(s) 4
Stating and Evaluating Tentative Explanations (Hypotheses) 4
    Exercise 4 Evaluating Hypotheses 6
Operationalizing the Variables 7
    Exercise 5 Operationalizations 10
Measuring 10
    Exercise 6 Measurement Levels 11
Cases 11
    Exercise 7 Cases for Analysis 12
Sampling 12
    Exercise 8 Sampling 12
Collecting Data 12
    Exercise 9 Data Collection Techniques 12
Analyzing Data 12
    Exercise 10 Data Analysis 13
Looking Back and Looking Ahead 13
SUGGESTED READINGS 13
ARTICLES 14

CHAPTER 2
DESCRIBING THE DISTRIBUTION OF CASES ON A VARIABLE 16

Why Do Univariate Analysis? 16
The Arithmetic Mean to Describe the Typical Case 18
    Exercise 1 Calculating the Mean 18
Plotting the Dispersion around the Typical Case 19
    Exercise 2 Drawing the Distributions and Locating the Means 19
The Median to Describe the Typical Case 20
    Exercise 3 Locating the Median on the Distributions 21
Using the Difference between the Mean and Median
to Begin to Visualize Skewed Distributions 22
    Exercise 4 Skewness 22
The Mode to Describe the Typical Case 22
Which Measure of Typicality to Use When 23
More Discussion of the Mean 23
Describing Distributions with the Standard Deviation or Variance 24
    Exercise 5 Visualizing the Distributions 24
    Exercise 6 Calculating the Variation 25
    Exercise 7 Calculating the Variance 26
    Exercise 8 Calculating the Standard Deviation 26
    Exercise 9 Locating the Standard Deviations on the Distributions 27
EXERCISES 28
SUGGESTED READINGS 29
ARTICLES 30

CHAPTER 3
USING A COMPUTER TO GET UNIVARIATE DESCRIPTIVE STATISTICS 31

Computer Packages 31
Preparing Data for Computer Processing 32
Setting Up the SPSS File 33
SPSS 34
    Exercise 1 Setting up an SPSS Job and Submitting It 34
Running the Job 37
Interpreting What You Get 38
    Exercise 2 Examining the Output 38
Visualizing A Distribution 39
    Exercise 3 Sketching an Approximate Distribution 39
Going On with These Procedures 40
SUGGESTED READINGS 41

CONTENTS vii

CHAPTER 4
RELATIONSHIPS BETWEEN INTERVAL LEVEL VARIABLES 42

Explaining Variation 42
Plotting the Cases on Two Variables at Once 43
    Exercise 1   Plotting a Positive Relationship 43
    Exercise 2   Plotting a Negative Relationship 44
    Exercise 3   A Plot of Scores That Are Not Related 45
Measuring the Strength of Relationship between Two Variables 45
    Exercise 4   Determining the Amount of Error Making Best Guess from Mean 45
    Exercise 5   Drawing the Lines for the Best Guess from the Independent Variable 46
    Exercise 6   Determining the Amount of Error Making the Best Guess from the Line 47
Calculating and Interpreting a Statistic to Measure the Relationship 48
    Exercise 7   Calculating the Measure of Association 48
Residuals 50
Uses of the Measure of Association and Limitations 51
    Exercise 8   Problems with Curved Relationships 51
EXERCISES 53
SUGGESTED READINGS 54

CHAPTER 5
CALCULATING PEARSON'S r^2 AND RELATED STATISTICS 55

Interpreting Pearson's r^2 55
Calculating Pearson's r^2 56
    Exercise 1   Calculating r^2 from the Formula 57
More on Interpreting Pearson's r^2 58
Interpreting Pearson's r, the Correlation Coefficient 59
Calculating the Regression Coefficient (Slope) and Intercept 60
    Exercise 2   Calculating the Regression Statistics 60
Visual Presentations of the Best-Fitting Line 61
    Exercise 3   Drawing Slopes from the Statistics 61
Interpreting the Intercept and Slope 61
    Exercise 4   Locating Predicted Values of Y 61
Some Characteristics of a, b, and r 62
SUGGESTED READINGS 65
ARTICLES 65

CHAPTER 6
USING PEARSON'S r WITH REAL DATA: HYPOTHESES, INDICES, AND THE RELIABILITY OF MEASURES 67

About Previously Constructed SPSS Files 67
    Exercise 1   Testing a Hypothesis with PLOT 68
COUNT and CORRELATIONS Procedures 71

Exercise 2 Uses of Pearson's Correlation in Assessing Inter-item Reliability 71
Exercise 3 Another Kind of Reliability Test Using CORRELATIONS 78
EXERCISES 79
SUGGESTED READINGS 80

CHAPTER 7

EXPLAINING VARIATION IN AN INTERVAL DEPENDENT VARIABLE WITH A NOMINAL/ORDINAL INDEPENDENT VARIABLE 81

Analysis of Variance 85
    Exercise 1 Computing E^2 89
    Exercise 2 Comparing r^2 and E^2 92
    Exercise 3 Making the Computer Do the Work 92
    Exercise 4 Analysis of Variance on Real Data 94
EXERCISES 96
SUGGESTED READINGS 97
ARTICLES 97

CHAPTER 8

READING TABULAR DATA 98

Relationships between Ordinal Variables 98
Review: Similarities between Types of Analyses 98
Describing Distributions of Ordinal Variables 101
    Exercise 1a Describing the Overall Distributions of Ordinal Variables 102
    Exercise 1b Describing Conditional Distributions of Ordinal Variables 103
    Exercise 2 Building and Interpreting Tables 104
    Exercise 3 Reading Tables for Strength and Form of the Relationship 105
Help in Reading Tables 105
SPSS Table Construction 107
    Exercise 4 CROSSTABS 107
Recoding for Crosstabular Analysis 107
EXERCISES 110
SUGGESTED READINGS 112
ARTICLES 112

CHAPTER 9

MEASURES OF THE STRENGTH OF ASSOCIATION BETWEEN ORDINAL VARIABLES 114

Understanding the Logic of the Measures of Association Based on Pairs of Cases 114
    Exercise 1 Counting Concordant and Discordant Pairs of Cases 115
Gamma 116
    Exercise 2 Calculating Gamma 118

Kendall's Tau$_b$ 119
    Exercise 3   Computing Tau$_b$ 120
Somer's d_{yx} 120
    Exercise 4   Calculating d$_{yx}$ 122
Deciding Which Statistic to Use   122
Tau$_c$ 123
Monotonicity and Linearity   124
Communicating the Form of the Relationship   125
SPSS Ordinal Measure of Association   125
    Exercise 5   Computer Generated Statistics   125
SUGGESTED READINGS   126
ARTICLES   126

CHAPTER 10
MEASURES OF RELATIONSHIP FOR NOMINAL VARIABLES   128

Two PRE Measures of Association   128
    Exercise 1   Calculating Lambda   130
    Exercise 2   Lambda on Misleading Data   131
    Exercise 3   Calculating Goodman and Kruskal's Tau   132
    Exercise 4   Tau as It Reflects Strong and Weak Relationships   133
    Exercise 5   Calculating Tau, Treating Row Variable as Independent   133
Measures of Association Based on Chi Square   134
    Exercise 6   Calculating Expected Frequencies in Chi Square   135
    Exercise 7   Calculating the Chi-Square-Based Measures of Association   136
Interpreting the Chi-Square-Based Measures of Association   136
The Form of Relationships between Nominal Variables   137
Gamma for Nominal Variables   137
    Exercise 8   Computing Yule's *Q*   138
SPSS and Nominal Measures of Association   138
    Exercise 9   Using the Computer for Tables and Nominal Measures of Association   138
Preparation for the Next Step   138
Measurement Validity   138
SUGGESTED READINGS   139
ARTICLES   140

CHAPTER 11
INTRODUCTION TO CONTROL VARIABLES   141

Goals of Multivariate Analysis   141
    Exercise 1   Trying Out Multivariate Hypotheses   149
Experimental versus Statistical Control   150
SUGGESTED READINGS   155
ARTICLES   155

CHAPTER 12
MULTIPLE CORRELATION AND REGRESSION I: MULTIVARIATE ANALYSIS WITH INTERVAL INDEPENDENT AND DEPENDENT VARIABLES 156

Controlling the Effects of a Third Variable: The Partial Correlation Coefficient 156
    Exercise 1 Calculating the Partial Correlation Using the Residuals and the Formula for Pearson's r (bivariate) 160
    Exercise 2 Computing Formula for the Partial 161
    Exercise 3 Using the Computer for Partial Correlations 162
    Exercise 4 Interpreting the Partial r 164
EXERCISES 166
SUGGESTED READINGS 168
ARTICLES 168

CHAPTER 13
MULTIPLE CORRELATION AND REGRESSION II: MULTIVARIATE ANALYSIS WITH INTERNAL INDEPENDENT AND DEPENDENT VARIABLES 170

The Prediction Equation and the Proportion of Explained Variation 170
    Exercise 1 The Multivariate Model 172
Interpreting the Partial Slopes (Regression Coefficients) 172
The Multiple R^2 177
    Exercise 2 The Multiple R^2 178
    Exercise 3 Multiple R^2, Computing Formula 179
Using the Computer for Multiple Regression 180
    Exercise 4 The REGRESSION Procedure 180
SUGGESTED READINGS 183
ARTICLES 184

CHAPTER 14
MULTIPLE REGRESSION III: NEW OPERATIONALIZATIONS AND STANDARD SLOPES 186

Operationalizing with Standardized Variables 186
Standard Scores and Standardized Slopes 190
    Exercise 1 Creating and Using Multi-indicator Indices Composed of Standardized Variables 191
SUGGESTED READINGS 194
ARTICLES 195

CHAPTER 15
TWO-WAY ANALYSIS OF VARIANCE 196

Analysis of Variance with Uncorrelated Independent Variables 196
Statistical Interaction 202
The ANOVA Procedure in SPSS 207
    Exercise 1 Uncorrelated Independent Variables 209
ANOVA with Correlated Independent Variables: Multicollinearity Revisited 211
Multicollinearity and Interaction Compared 215
Other Comments and Reminders about Analysis of Variance 216
    Exercise 2 Analysis of Variance on Real Data 216
EXERCISES 218
SUGGESTED READINGS 221
ARTICLES 221

CHAPTER 16
DUMMY VARIABLE REGRESSION AND AN INTRODUCTION TO ANALYSIS OF COVARIANCE 223

Dummy Variables 223
    Exercise 1 One-Way Analysis of Variance; Dummy Variable Regression 225
Two-Way Analysis of Variance with Dummy Variables 227
    Exercise 2 Two-Way Analysis of Variance with Dummy Variables 228
Combining Interval and Noninterval Independent Variables 230
    Exercise 3 Combining Interval and Noninterval Independent Variables 235
SUGGESTED READINGS 237
ARTICLES 237

CHAPTER 17
READING MULTIVARIATE TABLES AND CALCULATING PARTIALS FOR NOMINAL AND ORDINAL DATA 240

An Example 240
    Exercise 1 Table Construction 240
Interpreting the Tables 242
    Exercise 2 Bivariate Correlations on the Example Table 245
    Exercise 3 Multivariate Associations on the Example Table 248
Measures of Association 248
    Exercise 4 Measures of Association for Control Tables 248
Getting SPSS to Do Multivariate Tables 249
    Exercise 5 SPSS Table Construction 249
EXERCISES 251
SUGGESTED READINGS 253
ARTICLES 253

CHAPTER 18

INFERENTIAL STATISTICS 255

Inference 255
A Test Based on the Normal Distribution 256
    Exercise 1 Using the Normal Distribution to Test Significance 260
A Slightly More Formal Statement of the Inference Procedures Outlined Above 261
Some Tests Based on the F Distribution 263
    Exercise 2 Using the F Test Statistic 266
    Exercise 3 Using the t Statistic 267
Statistical versus Substantive Significance 267
Other Tests Based on the F Distribution 268
    Exercise 4 Using F Tests in Analysis of Variance 269
Another F Test 270
Summary of F Tests 270
    Exercise 5 Using Significance Tests on Other Output 271
Inference without Population Assumptions 271
    Exercise 6 Using the Chi-Square Table and Output 273
SUGGESTED READINGS 274
ARTICLES 274

CHAPTER 19

A BRIEF INTRODUCTION TO SAMPLING 275

Sampling and Inference 275
Goal of Sampling 276
Size of Sample 276
Kinds of Sample 278
A Type of Sample to Avoid 279
Defining the Population and Its Elements 279
Controversies in Sampling 280
SUGGESTED READINGS 281

CHAPTER 20

FORMULATING YOUR OWN RESEARCH DESIGN 282

Reasons for Research Designs 282
The Beginning 282
Hypotheses 284
Secondary Hypotheses 285
Ideal Design 286
Proposed Design 287
Finishing the Design 290
SUGGESTED READINGS 291

APPENDIX A
A SAMPLE OF CASES AND A SELECTION OF VARIABLES FROM THE AMERICAN NATIONAL ELECTION STUDY, 1980 PRE- AND POST-ELECTION WAVES   292

Pre-election Questions   292
Post-election Questions   298

APPENDIX B
A DATA SET BASED ON *THE COUNTY AND CITY DATA BOOK (UNITED STATES), 1983*   302

APPENDIX C
A LEGISLATIVE DATA SET   306

The Senate File   307
The House File   314

APPENDIX D
STATISTICAL TABLES   319

Table A.1   The Standard Normal Distribution   320
Table A.2   Critical Values of F at .01 and .05   323
Table A.3   The Chi-square Distribution   325

INDEX   326

FORMULAE

Formula 2.1	The Arithmetic Mean 18	Formula 10.2	PRE Measure of Association (Goodman and Truskal's Tau) 133
Formula 2.2	Error in Guessing Case's Scores from Their Means (Temporary Definition) 24	Formula 10.3	Chi Square 135
Formula 2.3	Variation 25	Formula 10.4	Phi 136
Formula 2.4	Variance 26	Formula 10.5	Cramer's V 136
Formula 2.5	Standard Deviation 26	Formula 10.6	Yule's Q 137
Formula 4.1	Squared Deviations of Scores from the Mean (error 1) 46	Formula 12.1	Pearson's Correlation (r) 161
Formula 4.2	Squared Deviation of Scores from the Line (error 2) 48	Formula 12.2	Computing Formula for First-order Partial Correlation Coefficient 161
Formula 4.3	Proportionate Reduction of Error Statistic 48	Formula 12.2	The Partial Correlation Coefficient 163
Formula 4.4	A PRE Measure for Interval Data 49	Formula 13.1	The Partial Slope for Y Dependent on X with Z Controlled 171
Formula 5.1	Pearson's r^2 55		
Formula 5.2	The Regression Coefficient (slope) 60	Formula 13.2	The Partial Slope for Y Dependent on Z with X Controlled 171
Formula 5.3	The Intercept 60		
Formula 7.1	The PRE Measure of Association 86	Formula 13.3	The Intercept in the Multivariate Prediction Model 172
Formula 7.2	E^2 a PRE Measure of Association, Interval Dependent Variable and Categorized Independent Variable 87	Formula 13.4	Error Guessing Dependent with No Knowledge of Independent (Error by Definition 1) 177
Formula 9.1	Gamma 116	Formula 13.5	Error Guessing Dependent from Knowledge of Independents (Error by Definition 2) 177
Formula 9.2	Tau_b 119		
Formula 9.3	Somer's d_{yx} 121		
Formula 9.4	Tau_c 123	Formula 13.6	PRE Formula: Multiple R^2 178
Formula 10.1	PRE Measure of Association (Lambda) 130	Formula 13.7	Multiple R^2: Uncorrelated Independent Variables 178

XV

Formula 13.8	Multiple R^2: Correlated Independent Variables 179	Formula 18.1	The Formula for a Z Score Based on Gamma 258
Formula 13.9	The Partial Correlation Coefficient: The Relationship Between Z and Y with X Controlled 180	Formula 18.2	F for Testing the Significance of a Correlation or Slope 265
		Formula 18.3	F Test for the Significance of Interaction 268
Formula 14.1	Standardized Partial Slopes 190	Formula 18.4	F for the Significance of E^2 269
		Formula 18.5	F Test for Curvilinearity 270
Formula 15.1	Partial E^2 for the Relationship between X and Y with Z controlled 214	Formula 18.6	The Chi-square Statistic 272

PREFACE

Many political science students spend their whole undergraduate careers reading textbooks full of conclusions about politics without ever having a chance to challenge those conclusions. Research papers, if they are simply strings of apparently authoritative quotations, may reinforce this practice of accepting conclusions without developing the ability to criticize the methods through which the conclusions were reached.

This text is designed to provide some of the skills you need to criticize conclusions arrived at by political scientists and to begin to conduct your own research as well. In the process of formulating your own questions and finding your own answers by applying some of the techniques used by political scientists, you will become familiar with elements of research design, statistics, and computers.

No one text can cover everything you need to know about conducting research. This text is organized on the basis of how political scientists use various statistics to help them explain the subjects they are interested in. Research design, data collection, and other aspects of methodology are covered only in passing. The bibliographies at the end of most chapters will lead you to other sources for more detail on topics that can't be covered in full in this text. These bibliographies are not intended to be exhaustive; they will merely get you started seeking out material on your own. The goal is to make you increasingly independent of the text.

This text asks you to participate actively in learning from the very beginning. Proceeding in a semiprogrammed way, you will do exercises that help you practice each part of the text, rather than just reading passively. The data sets that accompany this text represent some of the different kinds of data used frequently by political scientists, so that you can become accustomed to practicing on real political data and can learn some of the special problems and pitfalls of various data types.

If you examine the journal articles suggested at the end of most chapters, you will see each technique in the context of actual political science research. Since these articles are drawn from different subfields of political science, you can choose those which interest you most and can begin to learn some aspects of research design and data analysis within the context of different areas of the discipline.

These articles were chosen because they use the techniques under discussion and because they cover questions of research design, data collection, and measurement (and also because they are interesting, I hope). They aren't necessarily classic exemplars in the field, so don't feel intimidated about criticizing them. The more you try to take them apart and take them to task, the more you will learn about applying the information in this text.

As you go along, you'll find it useful to compare notes with others in your class who have used a different data set or selected different articles to read. That way you can find out how the methods and statistics can remain the same, yet the problems and interpretations in the various subfields can be different.

In fact, the more you talk with other students, the more you will learn. Frequently, one of you will catch on faster and be able to help the others, who will later be able to return the favor. Do your own work. You won't learn anything if you just copy what someone else has done. But do talk about ideas, procedures, problems, and pitfalls. Talk about which readings are most or least accessible. Talk about shortcuts you discover for computer programs.

As you go along, remember that knowledge is cumulative. What you learn in one chapter will be used over and over in later chapters. Don't assume that your task is just to "get through" each chapter and then forget it. Get each chapter down thoroughly before proceeding. If you find you aren't sure of material in later chapters, look back and rework the exercises. In this kind of course the burden is on *you* to learn. Instructors can help, but they can only teach—not learn for you.

All research and data analysis texts face one common problem, namely that the planning of a research project, collection of data, analysis of data, and presentation of results constitute a *circular* process. To understand how to plan a project, you really have to understand what kinds of data analyses are possible. The kinds of data analyses you end up doing are determined by decisions you made at the planning and collection stages. You will find that your understanding of each step is enhanced by your understanding of every other step. Unfortunately, you have to start somewhere.

As nearly as possible, this text gets you involved in this circular process all at once, and then repeats parts of the process as each new kind of data analysis is introduced. The first chapter attempts to show you everything at once. If it seems a bit overwhelming, try to remember this is just the initial plunge into material you will be covering repeatedly. From the first chapter on, you may be focusing on an analysis technique, but you may also be required to think about the measurement decisions that led up to that analysis or about other aspects of research. As much as possible, each form of data analysis is discussed within the overall research context, and you should pay attention to that context as you focus on the analysis. Also try to remember that each aspect of research design needs further elaboration from other texts. This text's organizational focus on statistics as a tool for explanation necessarily short changes important aspects of the overall process.

ACKNOWLEDGMENTS

In writing a text such as this, an author amasses serious debts. I am especially grateful to SPSS, Inc., for permission to rely on its analysis packages, and to the Inter-University Consortium for Political and Social Research for permission to use excerpts from its data sets.

I am most grateful to the secretary who typed numerous drafts of the work, Dorothy Pierson. Colleagues Clyde Brown and Philip Russo of my own department at Miami University and Joe Simpson of Miami Academic Computer Service provided advice and technical assistance. Bret Billet and Peter Bishop, my graduate assistants, tested the data sets and computer commands and helped locate some of the articles for applications. The Miami University Audio-Visual Service provided the illustrations.

Three reviewers made remarkably thorough comments on earlier drafts of this work: Diana Owen, Rutgers University; E. Terrance Jones, University of Missouri-St. Louis; and Stephen Percy, University of Virginia. I am grateful to them, as well as to all the students who repeatedly pointed out where things could be clearer. Of course, all errors are mine, but I do acknowledge my debt and appreciation.

Finally, special thanks to Anita and Roy for patience and moral support.

Susan Kay

CHAPTER

1

STARTING OUT: WHAT POLITICAL SCIENTISTS DO WHEN THEY DO RESEARCH

Let's start by taking a look at the results of research that are typically published in one of the professional journals. Seeing the end product will give you an overview, and we'll break the process down into steps using that end product to provide examples. Read one of the articles listed at the end of this chapter. At first, just read it quickly to get an idea of the whole thing. Then reread it carefully as you work through the material and questions that follow.

EXPLAINING PHENOMENA

Although very basic research may set out only to *describe* something very carefully—to list its characteristics—more sophisticated research is usually an attempt to *explain* something—to tell why it occurs as it does. In the kind of research we are dealing with, the thing to be explained is something that can somehow be observed either directly or indirectly, an *empirical phenomenon*. Research reports, such as the one you've been reading, usually start off with a statement about precisely what the researcher wants to explain.

Why do researchers select a particular phenomenon for explanation? For some researchers, it's just a matter of simple curiosity; they stumble across some odd fact while reading a newspaper or observing politics, and they wonder about it. Usually they then try to find previous explanations of the phenomenon and decide whether those explanations satisfy their curiosity. They might, for example, go to *Political Science Abstracts*, check entries for the phenomenon and related phenomena, and use the brief description of research reports given there to lead them to the whole articles that report previous explanations. If they find no satisfactory explanations, they design research that will yield new explanations. Maybe someone in the field has explained related phenomena, and the researchers decide to test whether that explanation will also apply to the phenomenon they are interested in. Maybe the researchers decide to test some common-sense explanation. This may sound a little hit or miss for a systematic approach, but good science can often begin with a hunch or a sense of wondering about what one sees.

A more formal approach to deciding what phenomenon you want to explain is to read widely in your field. The more you read the research reports of others, the more you can see the questions that have not been answered, the problems in approaches or methods that may have led others to misleading conclusions, and the questions that follow logically from the work done by others.

The most formal approach of all in deciding what phenomenon you want to explain is to start from a theory about some aspect of politics. Theories are sets of interrelated explanations, at least some of which have previously been tested. Using a theory as a guide, you can work logically to create a tentative explanation about some related aspect of politics. That tentative explanation can then be tested.

Most of the things political scientists try to explain have something to do with politics and government. Definitions of politics, which indicate the range of phenomena potentially explicable by political scientists, are material for a whole course. For our present purposes, a few selected definitions will suffice: Easton's (1960) "the authoritative allocation of values for an entire society" and Lasswell's (1958) "who gets what, when, and how" seem to blend into Isaak's (1985) "the use of power to reconcile conflicts over the distribution of goods and values, typically through the institutions of government." Working within such definitions, political scientists have attempted to explain such phenomena as political participation, support for government, political violence, legislative voting, selection of leaders, judicial decision making, military arms buildups, success in implementation of policies, and probably several thousand other topics.

EXERCISE 1   Phenomenon To Be Explained

Now, go back to the article you read and see if you can determine the phenomenon the author is trying to explain. Usually there is just one thing being explained. Everything in the article is directed at one or more explanations of that topic. And why did the author(s) pick this particular phenomenon? Was it a matter of simple curiosity, readings from the literature of the field, or a more formal theory? The authors may not come right out and tell you, but you should be able to infer the reason from their introductory material, which usually locates this piece of research in the larger field of political science or its subfields. What evidence can you cite from the article to substantiate your answer?

EXPLAINING VARIATION IN PHENOMENA

The phenomenon to be explained is sometimes called the *dependent variable*, especially when we are talking about observing it systematically. When we observe the phenomenon, we see that it is not always the same across all the cases that we look at. Sometimes it is present, and sometimes it isn't. Sometimes it is more intense than at other times. Since it is not always the same for all cases, we say that it *varies*. As we observe it, we can label its different appearances by assigning different *values* to represent each one. Thus, variables are observations of the phenomenon in which we are interested that have different values for the different cases we observe.

For example, a political scientist may be trying to explain the phenomenon of political ideology as it appears among individuals in a country. On the survey questions about ideology that the political scientist presents to people, some people are found to be more conservative, some are found to be middle-of-the-road, and some are found to be more liberal. In this instance, the *variable* is political ideology, and the *values* on that variable are "liberal" for some cases, "middle-of-the-road" for some cases, and "conservative" for others. The *cases* under consideration are the people who responded to the survey.

Another political scientist may be examining political instability and find that in one country there were ninety-five occurrences of antigovernment demonstrations and riots in one year; in another, there were only thirty-five such activities; while in yet another country, there were only five. In this example, the variable is political instability, and the values on that variable are the number of incidents: 95, 35, and 5. The cases under consideration are the countries that are examined.

As another example, imagine that you are trying to study why judges decide as they do, and you observe that one judge delivers more decisions for the defendant and that another delivers more decisions for the prosecution. The variable you would be explaining is judicial decisions, which could have one of two values: (1) decides more for the defendant; or (2) decides more for the prosecution. The cases in your study are the judges.

Why cases have different values on the dependent variable is what we want to explain. For more examples, we may want to explain why some people participate in politics more than others; the degree of political participation is the variable. We might want to explain why some members of Congress vote more conservatively than others; the level of conservatism is the variable. We might want to explain why some countries spend a higher percentage of their gross national products on defense than do others; the percentage of their gross national product spent on defense is the variable. We might want to explain why some states spend more on welfare programs than do others; the percentage of state budget spent on welfare programs is the variable. Or we might want to explain why some countries have parliamentary rather than presidential systems; parliamentary or nonparliamentary system is the variable.

If all cases were alike on the phenomenon, there would be nothing to explain—no differences to account for. We would have no way to test our explanations of the phenomenon because there would be no different cases for purposes of comparison. In order to test explanations, we have to *compare*. For example, we can't answer the question: Why do nation states have governments? They all do; in fact, that's part of the definition of what nation states are. Since no nation states are without governments, we just have to leave such questions as unanswerable or turn to philosophy or speculation for answers. The techniques you will learn here cannot deal with unvarying phenomena. You *can* deal, however, with the question of why nation states have the *kinds* of government they do. Kind of government varies and is explicable.

EXERCISE 2   Variation in the Dependent Variable

Turn back to the article again and see whether you can begin to get an idea of how the dependent variable varies. What are the possible values that the variable can have?

USING INDEPENDENT VARIABLES TO FORM RELATIONSHIPS

Once we are sure that we have a dependent variable that varies, we can proceed with the explanation of the phenomenon in which we are interested. We will explain the *dependent* variable by relating it to an *independent* variable. We will test whether different levels or conditions of the independent variable are *associated* with different levels or conditions of the dependent variable. If they are, and if we can't rule out other reasons for finding that *relationship*, we will say we have explained the dependent variable. An explanation, then, is simply showing that, when cases have a certain value on the independent variable, they are more likely to have a certain value on the dependent variable than those cases that have a different value on the independent variable.

Notice that, like the dependent variable, the independent variable must vary; it must be different for different cases, or we will not have the comparison necessary for a test. We need to be able to demonstrate that cases which have different values on the independent variable are likely to have different values on the dependent variables.

For example, we might show that the higher their social class, the more likely people are to participate in politics. In this case, high values on the independent variable (class) predict higher values on the dependent variable (participation), while low values on the independent variable predict lower values on the dependent variable. We might also show that parliamentary forms lead to greater enactment of public opinion into law than presidential forms do. In this case, the parliamentary value on the independent variable predicts greater enactment of public opinion than the presidential value does.

This will become clearer with practice. Right now, the important concepts to get straight are—

1. Political scientists try to explain phenomena called dependent variables.
2. The explanations are constructed by showing that independent variables are related to or associated with those dependent variables.
3. Relation or association simply means that cases which differ on the independent variable are likely also to differ in systematic ways on the dependent variable.

It is very tempting to think of the independent variable as the "cause" of the dependent variable, and it may be. But even though we find an independent variable associated with a dependent variable, we never know whether we have isolated "the" cause. There are so many possible causes of the phenomena with which we will be dealing that we may simply have found one of them. Or we may only have found some independent variable that itself is associated with the "real" causes that we have not examined.

And we can't *prove* causation anyway because it isn't itself a phenomenon we can observe. Although we can think in terms of causation and theorize about causes, we are really only making inferences about what we think we see in the real world. When two phenomena vary together in predictable ways, when one precedes the other in time, and when we can't find any other reasons for the association of the two, we sometimes infer that one is causing the other.

Political scientists, therefore, sometimes avoid talking or writing about causation and use words like "association," "relation," "linkage," etc. At this stage, it will probably help you keep the independent and dependent variables straight if you *do* think in causal terms. Remember the dependent variable *depends* on something else. It depends on the independent variable that precedes it in time, was acquired earlier, or is somehow "more basic."

Researchers decide which independent variables may be associated with dependent variables for many of the same reasons that they pick the phenomenon to be explained in the first place. They may, from experience, have hunches about what explains what. They may be testing common-sense explanations. They may have searched the literature to see what has been used to explain related phenomena. They may have deduced from theory what independent variables will explain the dependent variable they are examining.

EXERCISE 3 The Independent Variable(s)

Now, go back to the article you read and see if you can determine the independent variables the author is using to explain the dependent variable. There may be several. Try to determine why those particular variables were picked as potentially explanatory.

As you write these names down or just think about them, try to get into the habit of phrasing the names of variables so that the fact that they vary is communicated both to you and to those listening to you. To go back to our earlier examples, say, "the level of conservatism" rather than "conservatism"; say, "percentage spent on defense" rather than "defense spending"; say, "presidential/nonpresidential" rather than "presidency." This way of speaking will emphasize that you are looking at variables.

STATING AND EVALUATING TENTATIVE EXPLANATIONS (HYPOTHESES)

Empirical

The explanation of the dependent variable by the independent variable is usually written in the form of a tentative explanation, a *hy-*

pothesis, that can be subjected to an empirical test. (Remember that empirical simply refers to sense experience—seeing, hearing, touching. So the test will be something we can do by actually looking at—sensing—concrete evidence rather than appealing to authority or intuiting or speculating.)

Falsifiable

The hypothesis indicates what the researcher expects the relationship between the independent and dependent variable to look like, and it is stated in such a way that it can be rejected when subjected to tests with the evidence. We never know if we have enough evidence to say that the hypothesis is *right*; we can only know if it is wrong (and even that is complicated, as you will learn later).

Since we can only falsify and never prove the truth of hypotheses, they have to be stated in such a form that they are *capable of being rejected*. Thus, it is very important that the independent and dependent variables be *distinct* from each other. They must be distinctly different ideas; that is, they must be conceptually distinct. And they must be different in the data gathered that we will use to test the hypothesis; that is, they must be operationally distinct—more on that, later. If they aren't distinct but are merely two ways of stating the same or similar ideas, if they aren't based in different data, we can't test the hypothesis because we have something true by definition—a tautology.

You would never make a hypothesis such as the following one: "As an object increases in size, its measurement in inches increases." This hypotheses cannot be rejected, regardless of data, because it is true by definition. Sometimes, however, we do see political scientists making equivalent statements; for example, "The more liberally a judge has voted in the past, the more likely he is to vote for the left-leaning side of a case." And that's practically, if not truly, tautological. Make sure, therefore, that the independent and dependent variables of the hypothesis you are reading (or making up yourself) are distinct.

Explicit in Form

Hypotheses usually take such forms as the following: "As the independent variable increases, the dependent variable increases"; "Specific values of the independent variable will be associated with specific values of the dependent variable." Stating the hypothesis without specifying or implying values (e.g., "The independent variable is associated with/related to/affects the dependent variable") is ambiguous and should be avoided. Such phrasing doesn't say *how* the two variables are expected to be associated or related. If you have a clear statement of how the two variables are expected to fit together, it is much easier to select the proper statistics for analyzing the data in a test of the hypothesis; and it is easier to decide if the hypothesis has failed the test.

Let's take an obvious example. When you say, "SAT scores are associated with success in college," you haven't said whether higher or lower SAT scores suggest higher or lower success. A better phrasing would be "The higher their SAT scores, the more likely students are to experience success in college."

Plural

While it's not a major concern, notice that the hypothesis given just above is stated in the plural. It's done that way for a reason (although you shouldn't expect all authors in political science to do it). The types of explanations political scientists make apply to groups of cases—not to singular, individual incidents or cases; that is, our explanations are, in effect, meant to say that we can generally explain what is happening but not in every single instance. Even when we state our explanations absolutely, we *mean* that there are exceptions and errors. We might say, "A person in the upper social class participates more in politics than a person in the lower social class." What we *mean* is "Generally speaking, people in higher social classes tend to participate more in politics than do people in lower social classes; nevertheless, some lower class people may be more participant than some upper class people."

It is logically incorrect to apply the kind of statistical explanations we have been discussing to a single case when the explanation *admits* of exceptions and admits the possibility of other independent variables not explicitly stated (both of which all political science explanations do). By writing hypotheses in the plural, we can keep ourselves and our readers alert to this limitation on our explanations. We explain tendencies, trends, probabilities—not single incidences.

Grammatical

It's a good idea to keep the English phrasing of the hypothesis as close as possible to what is expected. Notice in the phrasing above that the independent variable comes first. To say, "The higher their SAT scores, the more likely students are to experience success," is completely different than to say, "The more successful the students, the higher their SAT scores." In the former, you are implying (correctly) that SAT scores are *independent*; that is, they explain success and are not dependent on success. In the latter phrasing, you are implying (incorrectly) that they are *dependent*—that somehow success comes first and influences SAT scores—or you may be implying that all you wish to do is to describe more successful students rather than explain their success. A correctly phrased hypothesis will make selection of the proper test of the hypothesis much easier later on.

Consistent with Data

It's usually a good idea to keep the hypothesis as close as possible to the data as well. We deal with various kinds of data. For example, we sometimes have *longitudinal data* in which we are collecting the information on the same cases over time. At other times, we have *cross-sectional data* in which we gather information on many cases at the same time. It is logically incorrect to assert from a cross-section that differences can be attributed to the passage of time; for attributing differences to change over time, we technically need longitudinal data.

For example, if you are examining first-year students, sophomores, juniors, and seniors in order to assess the effects of college on their political attitudes, it is probably best not to imply in the phrasing of the hypothesis that you are following the *same* students from their first through their fourth years in order to watch the individuals change. Thus, "The higher the academic class of the students, the more conservative they are" is a better cross-sectional phrasing than, "Students become more conservative the longer they are in college," which implies that you watched them over time. Although we sometimes settle for cross-sections because we don't have the resources for longitudinal studies even though we want to study change, careful phrasing of the hypotheses can keep us from thinking that we have better data than we do.

Similarly, it is logically incorrect to assert that you know how individuals behave when you only have information on groups of individuals; that is, you technically cannot explain *individual-level* behavior with *aggregate-level* data. And to keep yourself and your reader straight on what, exactly, you are doing, it is probably better to have the hypothesis reflect the kind of data rather than leading yourself to think that you are testing something that you don't really have the data to test. If, for example, you have data on counties for a test of the relationship between educational level and voting for Democrats, you probably should say, "The higher the median educational level, the lower the Democratic percentage of the vote." To say, "The higher their educational level, the less likely people are to vote Democratic," implies that you have examined individual people.

EXERCISE 4   Evaluating Hypotheses

You are now ready to make a first effort at evaluating hypotheses. Look for the statements of the hypotheses in the article you have read. See if you can determine whether they are:

1. Empirical
2. Falsifiable
3. Explicit in form
4. Plural
5. Grammatical
6. Consistent with the data

Sometimes you will find hypotheses stated in the "null" form, which means that the authors write that they expect *no relationship* between the independent and dependent variables. The reason for this is that each test of a hypothesis really involves testing two hypotheses simultaneously, even though both of them are rarely stated. There is the hypothesis that two variables are unrelated (*null hypothesis*) and the hypothesis that the two are related (*alternative hypothesis*). Remember that we can only falsify hypotheses; we can never prove them to be true. When we find a relationship between two variables, we falsify the null hypothesis but do not falsify the alternative hypothesis. When we find no relationship between two variables, we falsify the alternative hypothesis but do not falsify the null hypothesis. The more times an alternative hypothesis fails to be falsified, the surer we feel about the explanation it represents; but we are never completely sure. Remembering this keeps us humble. It reminds us that we can never prove that we are correct in our interpretations of events. (You will find much more about null hypotheses in Chapter 18.)

Once hypotheses are tested (and retested), they take on the status of *explanations* and are sometimes called *generalizations*. Whether they are any good as explanations depends, in part, on whether they stand up to repeated empirical tests. Their value as explanations also depends on whether they stand up to challenges and criticisms by the professional community and whether the researcher finds that the explanation satisfies curiosity. You would not likely be very satisfied if "region" were the variable used to explain political participation in the United States: Southerners participate less than Northerners, who participate less than Westerners. You would probably still want to ask why that was so. You would probably be more satisfied with an explanation that substituted economic circumstances, available avenues for participation, party competition, and regional traditions for the simple variable "region." The latter, then, would be a better explanation; but both are considered explanations.

These tested generalizations then form the basis of theories that explain whole classes of political phenomena. The theories are linked sets of generalizations, definitions, and methods. They are what we are both trying to build and test when we do research.

OPERATIONALIZING THE VARIABLES

Theories exist at the level of ideas; they are mental constructions. They are tested on an empirical level, however, with data gathered through observation of the phenomena in which we are interested. We have to get the ideas at the theoretical level—concepts which are defined and related to each other through words—into a form that can be applied, objectively and systematically, at the empirical level.

Before researchers begin tests of hypotheses, they must determine ways to operationalize the variables that have previously been discussed only conceptually. They must define the variables in terms of observable characteristics. An *operationalization* (sometimes called an *operational definition*) spells out precisely how to observe the case in order to determine what value it has on each variable. In other words, an operational definition spells out the operations that are performed by the researcher in describing a case on a particular variable. Some concepts are operationalized directly, while others are operationalized indirectly; but they all come down either way to observable phenomena.

What we mean by direct observation is that we can look at a case and simply see what its characteristics are on a specific variable. Take, for example, the concept "voting participation," which conceptually has two values: the person did or did not vote. The researcher can observe a person casting a ballot; or the researcher can examine voting records in which a county election official observed the person taking a ballot and recorded the information in public records. Thus, voting in an election is (if we ignore such things as secretly spoiled ballots for the moment) directly observable.

Indirectly observable phenomena, however, are a little more complicated. If we can't observe something directly, we have to come up with *indicators* of it. Thus, although we cannot see the phenomenon itself, we use things we can observe—those that we believe are parts of or consequences of the phenomenon in which we are interested—to get a sense of the phenomenon. For example, we cannot see "attitudes," but we can argue that, if people hold certain attitudes, they will answer sets of survey questions in certain ways. We can use those responses on surveys as indirect indicators of their attitudes.*

Sometimes an operationalization of a concept will include several separate indicators rather than just one. When that is the case, each separate indicator has to be operationally defined; *and* the ways in which the indicators are to be combined in order to yield an operationalization of the overall concept have to be spelled out as well. Generally speaking, we usually argue that multiple indicators make for better operationalizations, as you will see in subsequent chapters.

Some examples may help to clarify this notion of operationalization for you. Let's imagine that we have a variable which at the conceptual level has been called "level of democratization." When we conceptualize "level of democratization," we think in terms of various levels of democracy, for example, not democratic, progressing toward democracy, fully democratic. Thus, the variable, "level of democracy," has three values, at least at the conceptual level: low (not democratic), medium (progressing toward democracy), and high (fully democratic).

An operationalization is necessary to spell out precisely how we can observe countries and decide whether any given country is low, medium, or high. Our operationalization can be something as simple as the following: we will hire three experts and ask each, independently, to rate each country as high, medium, or low; when two of the three experts agree, we will assign that value to the country; when they disagree, we will discard the case.

We can, however, also use multiple indicators to operationalize the level of democracy. Perhaps we argue that a country can be considered more or less democratic to the extent that it possesses multiple attributes from the following list: peaceful turnover of office-holders; an unregulated press; regular elections; competing political parties. Each of those separate attributes will have to be operationalized separately, spelling out just what we consider evidence of "peaceful turnover of office-holders," or "unregulated press," etc. Then, "the level of democracy" can, itself, be operationalized as "the number of attributes from the stated list possessed by the country." Each country will end up with a value on the democracy variable of 0 to 4 depending on how many of those attributes it has; we may also need another value to indicate that the country under consideration cannot be classified for one reason or another. In this example, the separate indicators are reasonably directly ob-

---

*An eagle-eyed student of logic should recognize immediately on what thin ice we tread when we operationalize concepts indirectly. We are dangerously close to "the fallacy of affirming the consequent"—observing the consequences and asserting that the cause occurred. Nevertheless, if our definitions are grounded in the literature, if we spell them out clearly enough so that others can criticize them and use them in other contexts, and if we worry about the quality of our definitions enough to keep trying to improve them, we don't usually let ourselves be deterred. We know that scientific explanations are always tentative and always open to being rejected in subsequent tests. Therefore, we tend to acknowledge that our operationalizations may be a reason that our findings are later discounted; but we do the best we can and get on with it.

servable, even if the overall concept is only indirectly observable.

For another example, let's assume that a person can feel some sense of affinity for a political party. Conceptually, we can discuss this as "party identification" and assume that people who are attached to one party will be at the opposite end of a spectrum from those who feel attached to the other party. We may also assume there are degrees of intensity in such feelings. An operationalization is necessary to spell out precisely how we are to determine whether any given respondent is a strong Republican, weak Republican, independent leaning Republican, independent, independent leaning Democrat, weak Democrat, or strong Democrat. The operationalization indicates which of the seven values on this scale to assign as the appropriate description of any given respondent.

Here the operationalization we use would probably be that of the Center for Political Studies, Institute for Social Research, since it is the established one in the field. It uses the responses to survey questions as indirect indicators of the "party identification" attitude.

Ask respondent:

> "Generally speaking, do you usually think of yourself as a Republican, a Democrat, an independent, or what?"
>
> (*If Republican or Democrat*): "Would you call yourself a strong or a not very strong (Republican/Democrat)?"
>
> (*If independent*): "Do you think of yourself as closer to the Republican or the Democratic Party?"
>
> On the basis of the answers to the three questions, determine whether the respondent is a strong Republican, weak Republican, independent leaning Republican, etc.
>
> If respondent does not fit any of the seven categories clearly, assign another value that indicates that the respondent could not be classified.

In another example, a case might be determined to be "nonpresidential" on our previously mentioned presidential/nonpresidential variable if executive offices were routinely filled by vote of a legislative body, whether or not an office designated "president" happened to exist. The case might be determined to be "presidential" on that same variable if the main executive office were filled by a vote of the people (however indirectly) independently of the vote for legislative offices. This is an instance of an operationalization for a rather directly observable phenomenon.

Take another example. In operationalizing the percentage of the gross national product spent on defense, the researcher would have to specify a precise definition of gross national product (Are services as well as goods to be included?), as well as exact categories of spending to be considered defense (e.g., Is the Coast Guard for defense or not?). Then the rest of the operationalization would say something like the following: to determine the value for each country on the variable "defense spending," divide the total expenditures for defense (as defined) by the total gross national product (as defined).

Or another example. To operationalize the percentage of a state budget spent on welfare, the researcher would have to list precisely what categories of spending constitute "welfare," total the expenditures in the "welfare" sections of the budget, and divide by total budget expenditures.

The values on each variable must be mutually exclusive. The range of values on each variable must be exhaustive. *Mutually exclusive* means that each case cannot have more than one value assigned; once a case has been determined to have one value, no other value will fit it, given the operational definition. *Exhaustive* means that each case must have some value. No case is left without some value on that variable, even if you have to create a special value to stand for "missing data." The value for missing data is used whenever a case cannot be described on a variable because the data are unavailable for some reason.

Sometimes the values on a variable are called scores or categories. These are just other words for the same values we have been describing. Typically, *score* implies that numbers have been chosen to represent the values in some meaningful way, as you will see below under the section on measurement. *Category* usually implies that we only have rough groupings of cases on the values of the variable. The usage of these terms is not strictly observed, however.

Researchers seek operationalizations that are both reliable and valid. A *reliable* operationalization has little error in it, although some error is almost inevitable. We tend not to worry too much about small amounts of error as long as they don't bias the outcome of the tests. Reliable operationalizations are also consistent; they classify the same characteristics the same way repeatedly. *Valid* operationalizations are those that "get at" what we hope they will get at. A valid operationalization lets us feel fairly sure that what we have observed is a fair representation of the concept we want to be dealing with, even if there is some error in how we have classified some cases. Criteria for assessing reliability and validity will be discussed at greater length in later chapters.

Operationalization is a tricky business. For some variables that have been used a long time in political science, operationalizations are relatively standard. For other variables, no precise operationalizations have been accepted, and it is up to the researcher to determine what to do. You will discover which is which as you read more and more in the field.

In either case, biased or invalid operationalizations can contribute to apparently falsified hypotheses. When a researcher is trying to determine why a hypothesis failed, there are at least two possible reasons: it didn't fit what was really going on in the world; or the operationalizations were faulty. Repeating the tests is usually the only way to determine whether a failed hypothesis is the result of the former or the latter. This is a chief reason why researchers ought to spell out the operationalizations very clearly. Another experienced researcher should be able to repeat the tests *exactly* with newly collected data or be able to criticize and modify the operationalization for new tests.

EXERCISE 5 Operationalizations

Now that you know a bit about operationalization, go back to the article you have been reading and see if you can find the operationalizations of the dependent variable and the independent variable(s). Don't worry if this seems hard now. It does for almost everyone. Just plunge in and give it a try. This isn't the last time you'll see explanations of operationalization. And later you will have a chance to learn more by doing your own.

MEASURING

Operationalization usually involves *measurement*, which means the assigning of numbers to cases on the basis of procedures specified in the operational definition. In the example of presidential/nonpresidential systems, you might be told to assign a "1" if the country being examined fits the definition of presidential and a "0" if it does not. (Or, if no computer analysis that requires numeric values is anticipated, the values might just as well be left in the non-numeric form of presidential/nonpresidential; they are still considered to be the values a case has on the variable, even if they aren't assigned numbers.)

In the example of the percentage of gross national product spent on defense, you might be told to count up all the dollars spent on all the categories determined to represent defense, divide by the dollars that represent the total gross national product, and assign the resulting number to the case being examined. (In this sample, foreign currencies would have to be converted to dollars for consistency in measurement across cases.) The numbers assigned to the cases represent the *values* on that variable.

Variables can be measured in several ways. Our presidential/nonpresidential variable is an example of nominal measurement. In *nominal measurement*, the numbers that represent values on the variable simply represent attributes and have no intrinsic meaning as numbers. The cases that are scored "1" are different from the cases that are scored "0," but 1 is not interpreted to be more than or less than 0; the numbers simply stand for longer concepts. The two categories might just as easily have been labeled 99 and 42, or P and Q.

Another kind of measurement is called ordinal measurement. In *ordinal measurement*, the numbers are related to each other by order; 1 is less than 2, which is less than 3, which is less than 4, etc. While the numbers represent relative position in an order, they do not indicate any particular distance between 1 and 2, or between 2 and 3; that is, with ordinal measurement, we don't have a sense of how much less 1 is than 2. The democracy variable given above that was operationalized by asking a panel of experts could represent this kind of measurement. If we assign a 1 to any country the experts agree is "low" on democracy, a 2 to any country the experts agree is progressing toward democracy, and a 3 to any country the experts agree is fully democratic, we might then argue that countries scored 1 are "less democratic" than countries scored 2; that countries scored 2 are "more democratic" than countries scored 1; that countries scored 3 are "more democratic" than countries scored 1 or 2, etc. However, we could not say that those scored 3 are 3 times more democratic than those scored 1; the numbers don't stand for quantities related in that way.

Another kind of measurement is called *interval measurement*. Our variable above, percentage of the state budget spent on welfare, is that kind of variable. The numbers not only mean more/less but also the intervals between numbers are all equal. The distance between 22 and 25 is the same as the distance between 30 and 33. This fact allows us to add and subtract the values. Not only can we say that a state that spends 55 percent on welfare spends *more* than a state that spends 51 percent but also we can say exactly how much more—4 percent.

A fourth kind of measurement is called *ratio measurement*; it has all the characteristics of interval measurement *and* a real zero. If a country could really spend nothing—zero percent of its gross national product—on defense, the example above of "percentage of the gross national product spent on defense" could be labeled a ratio measurement. Similarly, if a state could conceivably spend nothing on welfare, the variable mentioned above, "percent of the budget spent on welfare," could be considered ratio measurement. A better example, although not without problems, might be "years of formal education" on which a person more reasonably could be imagined to have no years of such education. It is the real zero in ratio measures that allows us to multiply and divide those scores.

The distinctions between different kinds of measurement are important in determining which statistics to apply in tests of hypotheses, and the distinctions will become clearer as the statistics are examined. In short, separate statistics to indicate the relationships between variables have been constructed for variables measured at each level of measurement.

EXERCISE 6 Measurement Levels

For now, you just need to begin recognizing the level of measurement of the variables you are reading about. Turn back to your article and see if you can specify the level of measurement for the variables you have already identified.

CASES

Notice that variables are characteristics of cases. Each case is assigned a number that represents its value on a variable. In effect, operationalization and measurement together represent a means of describing a case on that variable. It is important to keep straight in your mind just what a case is in your analysis. All variables in the analysis will be measured for each case. If you have several independent variables and a dependent variable in the analysis, each case must have a value for each of those variables. Sometimes when you cannot, for one reason or another, find out what value a case has on a particular variable, you will consider that case "missing" for any analysis which uses that variable. Usually you designate some otherwise meaningless number to represent the value "unknown" for each variable. This will become clearer as you work with actual data later.

Remember that cases may be individual people, counties, countries, legislators, etc. It depends on the unit on which you observe the variables for your analysis.

EXERCISE 7 Cases for Analysis

Make sure you know what the cases are in the analysis you are reading. Go back to the article, if necessary, to determine what constitutes a case in that particular instance.

SAMPLING

Whenever there are too many cases for a researcher to examine each one, because either of cost considerations or simple practicality of time considerations, a sample is drawn. A *sample* is a smaller group of cases designed to represent the population of cases from which it came. With good sampling techniques, a researcher can be relatively sure that the findings based on observing a sample of cases would be very similar to those that would have been obtained from observing the whole population.

EXERCISE 8 Sampling

You will learn a bit more about sampling later in Chapter 19. Mentioning it here will just alert you to another step in the research process. But do look at your article and see whether a sample was drawn. Does the author indicate what kind?

COLLECTING DATA

The techniques for collecting data are not really covered in this text. You will begin to understand some of the various ways of getting data—from experiments, from surveys, from government documents, from Congressional roll calls, from periodical sources, from participant observation—as you read the articles indicated from the subfields. You should be warned, however, that some data collection methods are arts, if not sciences, in themselves. Promise yourself that you won't limit your reading about the techniques to what can be covered here in this text. The suggested readings will give you a mere hint at where to start reading on this subject; in addition to the data collection texts listed, look at chapters on specific techniques in the general methodology books listed.

EXERCISE 9 Data Collection Techniques

As a start right now, at least find in the article you have been reading what techniques the authors used to gather data. Did they use surveys that they constructed? Or did they analyze surveys that had been conducted for another purpose? Did they use data collected by governments? Did they systematically examine documents? Did they collect data on events reported by newspapers? Or what?

ANALYZING DATA

The next step in the research process involves the analysis of the data and the drawing of conclusions from those analyses—the process around which the subsequent chapters of this text are organized. Now that you have an overview of what political scientists must do before they start actually testing hypotheses, you are almost ready to start testing hypotheses through analyzing data yourself, and, in the process, you will get some practice with all of the ideas we have gone over so far. You will see again and again the notions of independent and dependent variables, hypotheses, operationalizations, and measurement.

EXERCISE 10 Data Analysis

Although you aren't expected to be able to read the data analysis sections of the article very thoroughly at this point, do turn to those sections and see if you can determine what statistics the researchers are using to analyze the relationships between the independent and dependent variables.

LOOKING BACK AND LOOKING AHEAD

It may be a good idea to stop here before you go on and compare notes with your colleagues. See if you agree on what the major variables are in the various articles, what is wrong with the statement of the hypotheses, how the variables are operationalized, what the cases were, etc.

You are now on your way to understanding the process of research and some of the language associated with doing research. The references below and later in the text at the end of each chapter can provide you with leads to further information on any point about which you feel the need to learn more. After each chapter, it's a good idea to look those references over for three other reasons as well: (1) they will reinforce what you've learned in each chapter; (2) they will alert you if you are misinterpreting something in one resource; and (3) sometimes one author will say something in a way that "clicks" with you, while another author just can't quite get through.

If you are going to be designing your own research soon, rather than just reading that of other political scientists, you may want to turn to Chapter 20. It has rather detailed instructions for preparing a research design. Reading it now may reinforce some of the ideas in this chapter and may give you a clearer picture of how a political scientist approaches the construction of a project such as the one you have been reading about in the articles.

SUGGESTED READINGS

AGNEW, NEAL MCK., and SANDRA W. PYKE. *The Science Game*, 4th ed. (Englewood Cliffs, NJ: Prentice Hall, 1987). Part I is on the nature and language of science; Chapter 11 is on measurement. Designed to educate consumers of social scientific writing, this book is clearly written, and emphasizes a no-nonsense approach. The measurement chapter, especially, may help clear up some concepts from the chapter you have just finished.

ANDERSON, LEE F., MEREDITH W. WATTS, Jr., and ALLEN R. WILCOX. *Legislative Roll-Call Analysis* (Evanston, IL: Northwestern University Press, 1966). A useful beginning to one form of data collection, this book is in the same series as the Backstrom book listed below, *Handbooks for Research in Political Behavior*.

BABBIE, EARL R. *The Practice of Social Research*, 3rd ed. (Belmont, CA: Wadsworth, 1983). Chapters 1, 2, and 3 are on the nature of social sciences. Chapters 5 and 6 are on measurement and operationalization.

BACKSTROM, CHARLES H., and GERALD D. HURSH. *Survey Research* (Evanston, IL: Northwestern University Press, 1963). This is a place to start reading about one of the most useful forms of data collection in political science. The series to which this book belongs is getting old, but it still provides useful introductions.

BLALOCK, HUBERT M., JR. Social Statistics (New York: McGraw-Hill, 1972). Chapter 2 is on operationalization and measurement.

BOWEN, BRUCE D., and HERBERT F. WEISBERG. *An Introduction to Data Analysis* (San Francisco: Freeman, 1980). It wouldn't hurt to look over the first three chapters of this. The coverage is broader than that of Chapter 1 in this book, but the clear, crisp presentation may help you see what's happening.

HOOVER, KENNETH R. *The Elements of Social Sci-*

entific Thinking, 3rd ed. (New York: St. Martin's, 1984). Chapter 2 covers, in an introductory way, many of the concepts in this chapter. You might also want to look at Chapter 4, which has more depth on hypotheses and variables.

JOHNSON, JANET BUTTOLPH, and RICHARD A. JOSLYN. *Political Science Research Methods* (Washington, D.C.: Congressional Quarterly Press, 1986), Ch. 1–4. Chapters 1 and 2 are a good introduction to the scientific study of politics; 3 introduces concepts and hypotheses; 4 is on measurement.

KIDDER, LOUISE. *Sellitz, Wrightman and Cook's Research Methods in Social Relations*, 4th ed. (New York: Holt, Rinehart and Winston, 1981). Chapter 1 is an introduction that includes notions of theory, hypotheses, validity, and reliability.

NACHMIAS, DAVID, and CHAVA NACHMIAS. *Research Methods in the Social Sciences*, 3rd ed. (New York: St. Martin's, 1984). See Chapter 3 for the "Basic Elements of Research." Chapter 1 gives background on the nature of science. Chapter 7 is on measurement.

OTT, LYMAN, WM. MENDENHALL, and RICHARD LARSON. *Statistics: A Tool for the Social Sciences*, 2nd ed. (North Scituate, Mass.: Duxbury, 1978), Ch. 2. This is on measurement. Useful here and as introduction to the next chapter.

PLANO, JACK C., ROBERT E. RIGGS, HELENA S. ROBIN. *The Dictionary of Political Analysis*, 2nd ed. (Santa Barbara: ABC-CLIO, 1982). This is a handy source of definitions of various concepts and statistics used in data analysis.

SHIVELY, W. PHILLIPS. *The Craft of Political Research*, 2nd ed. (Englewood Cliffs, NJ: Prentice Hall, 1980). Chapters 4 and 5 are on measurement. Shively's book is a straightforward, nononsense, *clear*, easy-to-read and comprehend primer of research.

ZISK, BETTY H. *Political Research: A Methodological Sampler* (Lexington, MA: D.C. Heath, 1981). Chapter 2 is on the process of research and similar in form to the outline of the chapter that you have just finished.

Reviews of Basic Math

If you are feeling unsure about high school algebra skills, you may want to consult one of these books early on.

EDWARDS, ALLEN L. *Statistical Methods*, 2nd ed. (NY: Holt, Rinehart and Winston, 1967), Appendix A.

MCCALL, ROBERT B. *Fundamental Statistics for Behavioral Sciences*, 4th ed. (San Diego: Harcourt Brace Jovanovich, 1986), Appendix 1.

Definitions of Politics

EASTON, DAVID. *The Political System* (N.Y.: Alfred A. Knopf, 1960).

ISAAK, ALAN. *Scope and Methods of Political Science* (Pacific Grove, CA: Brooks-Cole, 1985).

LASSWELL, HAROLD. *Politics: Who Gets What, When, and How* (Cleveland: The World Publishing Company, 1958).

ARTICLES

JOHNSON, DONALD BRUCE, and JAMES R. GIBSON. "The Divisive Primary Revisited: Party Activists in Iowa," *American Political Science Review*, 68 (March 1974), 67–77. Mailed survey of party activists analyzed with percentage differences, chi square, and gamma. Based both in theory and practical politics. Easy to read and understand.

MUNDT, ROBERT J., and PEGGY HEILIG. "District Representation: Demands and Effects in the Urban South," *Journal of Politics*, 44 (1982), 1035–1047. Based on data for 209 Southern cities, populations over 10,000, and at least 15 percent black. Census data on demographic and socioeconomic variables, information on attempts to establish district representation on city councils, and success of previous minority candidates. Crosstabulation tables and chi-square, Cramer's V.

THOMAS, MARTIN. "Election Proximity and Senatorial Roll Call Voting," *American Journal of Political Science* (February 1985), 96–111. Using nothing more complicated than simple averages (except significance measures, which can be ignored until later), this article examines the roll-call voting of U.S. Senators. Clear statements of hypotheses drawn from theory. Clear operationalizations.

WALLACE, MICHAEL D., and PETER SUEDFELD. "Leadership Performance in Crisis: The Longevity-Complexity Link," *International Studies Quarterly*, 32 (December 1988), 439–451. Measures the "integrative complexity" of decision makers from archival material; tests for decline in complexity during and after crisis compared to precrisis period. Compares first sample of leaders to sample selected for high degree of involvement, importance of nation, accessibility of data. Difference of means.

CHAPTER 2

DESCRIBING THE DISTRIBUTION OF CASES ON A VARIABLE

One of the most important things you do in data analysis comes before you start examining the relationships between variables. First, you describe the "typical" case on a single variable and determine how typical it really is. This is called *describing the distribution of cases on the variable*. Sometimes it is called "examining the marginals" or checking the "marginal distribution." Using "marginals" as a word for the distribution of a single variable probably comes from analysis of tables where, as you will see later, a distribution of a single variable can be found in the margins of a table.

A more useful term may be *univariate analysis*. That phrase makes it clear that we are examining one variable at a time, not one variable in relation to another variable (bivariate analysis).

WHY DO UNIVARIATE ANALYSIS?

Sometimes univariate analysis is done as an end in itself. You are probably already familiar with one widely publicized form of univariate analysis—public-opinion polling. Numerous firms do surveys in order to determine how the public feels on particular questions, whether the public prefers one candidate or another, whether the public recognizes the name of potential candidates, what issues the public feels are important, and so forth. These surveys are important enough these days that they have become news items in themselves. Most often, these surveys are just univariate analysis: the distribution of the opinion of the respondents on one question at a time.

If the presentation of the results goes beyond simple univariate analysis, it is most often to compare the distribution of opinion in one group to that in another: comparing the way women and men feel about a topic; whether Southerners differ from the rest of the nation on their responses to questions; whether those with high education differ in their opinions from those with low education. That kind of simple bivariate analysis with two variables (group and opinion) we will save for other chapters, as we focus now on how to describe one variable at a time.

You can probably think of univariate analyses that are somewhat less grandiose than trying to describe what the nation thinks about a particular question. You may want to say, for example, that the typical voter in a particular district is a certain number of years old; or that the typical wage-earner in an area makes a certain amount in a year; or that the typical country spends a certain percentage of its gross national product on defense. In these cases, you would probably also want to know whether the voters were clustered around a typical age or spread out over a wide age-range, whether the wage-earners in an area were much alike or very different, and whether the amount one country spends for defense is close to the amount spent by other countries or is very different.

Stop and think about these examples in purely practical terms for a minute. If you knew how old the typical voter in a district was, you could arrange a campaign directed at the needs or interests of that age group. If the typical voter were 25, you would arrange different campaign event attractions than you would if the typical voter were 60. You'd probably be less likely, for example, to have a rock band as rally entertainment in the latter case.

Just knowing how old the typical person is, however, won't tell you enough. If you don't know whether the voters in a district are almost all roughly the same age or whether they are spread out over a wide age-range, you won't know whether scheduling a rock band will draw many or just a few voters to the rally. Two districts could both have their typical voter at age 27. One district might be a university environment in which a large majority of people are 18–30. The other, however, might have very few people right around the typical case; the ages of people could be quite diverse and still have the representative or typical case at 27. In the first district (homogeneous), the rock band could be expected to appeal to many voters. In the second (heterogenous), the same band might appeal to very few. It is crucial to know the range and spread of the single variable, age, within each district and also to know the typical value on that variable, age.

Now think about the example of the typical wage-earner in an area. The income in the middle of the range of incomes for two areas might be identical at $20,000 per year. However, you would hardly consider the two areas to be alike if, in one area, there were large numbers of both very high and very low incomes, while in another area almost everybody had roughly the same lower middle-class income. In purely practical terms, you'd have to know more than just which income represents the middle of the range of incomes for the district in order to know how well a product was likely to sell. You would also have to know whether that mid-range income came from a homogeneous or heterogeneous area.

Consider the third example about defense spending. Think through the difference between two different distributions of the "defense spending" variable. In one world, almost every country spends between 3 and 4 percent of its gross national product on defense. In percent spent on defense, the middle country spends about 3.5 percent. In another world, the middle country also spends about 3.5 percent, but about half the countries spend almost nothing, and the other half spend 7–8 percent. The practical consequences of the two different distributions might be in the realm of decision making about how much a country has to spend in order to feel secure; surely, it would be a lot less, given the first rather than the second distribution.

Sometimes the examination of the distribution of a variable is not an end in itself; it is preliminary to examining relationships. As we said in the first chapter, the variables (whether dependent or independent) must vary before we can tell anything about the relationship between variables. To analyze relationships, we need cases that are fairly heterogeneous on the variables—not all alike. We need cases all along the possible *range* (difference between highest and lowest possible scores) in order to tell whether high scores on one variable go with high scores on another variable, or vice versa, i.e., whether there is a relationship.

When we get to the process of interpreting whatever relationships we find, our interpretations may depend, in part, on whether the variables have sufficient variation in them. When our variables turn out to have low variation and the cases we have to work with are relatively homogeneous on those variables, we may not be able to discern relationships that, in fact, actually exist. Or we may be misled by seeing a relationship that is different in the limited range of the variable that happens to show up in our data from what it would be elsewhere.

These univariate distributions are also important when we try to make statements about the population from which our sample was drawn, but we are getting ahead of ourselves. Such inferences to populations don't come up until Chapter 18.

Prior to Chapter 18, in subsequent chapters, we will focus on the consequences of low variation for interpreting relationships as we cover the statistics that measure the relationships. When we begin to interpret the statistics, the kinds of univariate analyses discussed in this chapter are considered just a first step, but it is an important first step.

Here, we will deal with measures of the typical case and measures of the homogeneity of the cases primarily at the level of interval measurement. Still, you will be able to see parallels to other levels of measurement and to apply similar principles to analysis of those kinds of data in later chapters.

THE ARITHMETIC MEAN TO DESCRIBE THE TYPICAL CASE

One way of describing the typical case is to calculate an *arithmetic mean*. This is the kind of average you've been calculating for years. You simply add up the values of all the cases on a variable and divide by the number of cases.

Even though you hardly need a formula for the mean, let's show Formula 2.1 for the mean, so you can start getting used to one variety of statistical notation.

FORMULA 2.1
The Arithmetic Mean

$$\bar{X} = \frac{\Sigma X_i}{N}$$

For the mean, the formula is read: "X bar equals the sum of the X sub-i divided by N." X bar ($\bar{X}$) is the designation for the mean of the X variable. *Sum* is indicated by the Greek capital letter sigma (Σ) and simply means add up what follows. X_i refers to the scores of individual cases (i) on any variable (X). N refers to the total number of cases. Therefore, to calculate an arithmetic mean following the formula, you simply add up all the scores of the cases on a particular variable and divide by the total number of cases.

In some texts, you will find two different formulae for each statistic. One is a *defining formula* that gives a clear statement of the meaning of a statistic, and the other is a *computational formula* that gives equivalent results with a slightly easier method of calculation. In this text, you will be computing each statistic once by hand in order to get a feel for what that statistic is doing; then, you will turn to the computer. Since definitional formulas give you a clearer handle on what is going on in the statistic, you will be using only these throughout the text. Should you ever need to compute these statistics on large quantities of data by hand, the computing formulas are available in most statistics books.

EXERCISE 1 Calculating the Mean

Now is a good time to start trying your hand at computation as we go along. In the exercises at the end of the chapter, you will find several cases with their values on three variables. Calculate a mean for variable 1. You will also find it helpful to your own interpretation if you write out a sentence that describes the typical case in words.

As you work on each problem from now on, try to think about what you are doing at each step. Let the process of working through each statistic teach you about what that statistic is doing for you. Don't just blindly press keys on a calculator; anticipate what a reasonable result would be, and compare the answer you get to that estimate. Compare answers from one exercise to those from another. Ask yourself what each means, and what differences and similarities mean. For example, if you get an answer for an arithmetic mean that is higher than any score of any case, you know you've calculated incorrectly and should go over the work again. Or, if you get a mean for one

DESCRIBING THE DISTRIBUTION OF CASES ON A VARIABLE **19**

group of cases that is higher on a variable than the mean of the same variable for another group of cases, stop and ask yourself why that difference might have occurred.

Get in the habit of writing down all of your work even on simple problems, so that an instructor can see how to give you corrections if you should happen to go wrong. For your own sake, be neat. More problems have been missed because columns of numbers didn't line up or because work wasn't clear enough to check than because of misunderstanding.

When you write out your sentence to describe the typical case in words, refer clearly and explicitly to the variable being measured. Don't just say, "The typical case is 4.5." Say, "The typical case does 4.5 political activities per year." It's also important to refer to the possible range on the scale of measurement: "The typical case does 4.5 out of a possible 10 activities per year." Both are important if you are to communicate in words precisely what it is you are doing in data analysis. In data analysis, numbers are meaningless except in the context of the operational definition of a concept; thus, the variable must be named along with the numeric score. Stating the range of measurement keeps both researcher and reader aware of the limitations and characteristics of the measurement devices being used. Such precise communication is imperative. Get into the habit now.

When you get to the final answer in your calculations, round it off to one or two decimal places. Although you will keep more decimal places than these in intermediate steps to preserve exactness, you should not report an answer with any more than one or two decimal places. More decimal places than one or two communicates too much precision to you and to your reader—the kind of precision that measurement in political science rarely has. As a rule of thumb, don't let your final answer communicate too much more precision than the measurements on which it was calculated.

Now do the same thing for the second and third variables. Calculate the means and write out sentences that describe the typical case on each variable.

PLOTTING THE DISPERSION AROUND THE TYPICAL CASE

As you discovered above in the discussion of how atypical the typical case can be, there are times when the mean doesn't tell us much about what the average case looks like. That happens when the cases are very heterogeneous and do not cluster around the mean. As you will see in the next exercise, the mean can also be distorted and, as a result, tell us less than it might otherwise about the typical case.

EXERCISE 2 Drawing the Distributions and Locating the Means

Examine Figure 2.1 below, which shows the distribution of the cases on the first variable in the exercise section at the end of this chapter. In that example, the mean does seem to communicate something to you about the typical case. Most of the cases are relatively close to the mean, and although they are spread out on either side of the mean, the cases are much fewer in number as you move away from the mean.

You can begin to see instances of both ways the mean can give limited or misleading information about the typical case by constructing and filling in two diagrams similar to Figure 2.1 for the other two variables in the exercises. One of the diagrams you construct will be of a

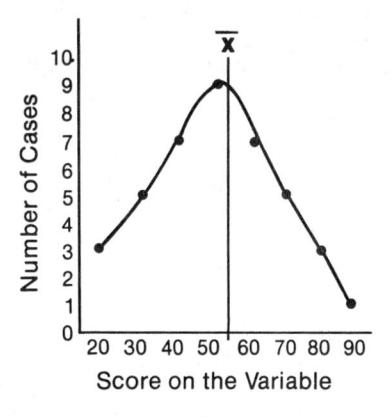

FIGURE 2.1 A Frequency Distribution

very heterogeneous distribution in which the mean doesn't communicate much because the cases are so spread out. The other diagram will be of a very homogeneous distribution but one in which a few cases distort the mean and make it somewhat less precise than it might be of what the average case looks like.

For each diagram you are constructing, draw two lines at right angles. On the vertical lines, indicate the number of cases, as the example in Figure 2.1 does. Make sure that the horizontal lines are the same length as that in the example. Only by keeping the lines on which you are going to place the scores visually the same (regardless of the actual numbers on them) can you readily compare the distributions at this point. In effect, you are making all three scales of measurement the same in order to be able to compare the distributions by looking at them. You will learn an arithmetical way of accomplishing what you are here doing only visually in Chapter 13, where you will find out about standard scores.

On the first diagram you draw, fill in the low and high values of the scores on the second variable at the beginning or end, respectively, of the horizontal line. Divide that bottom line into segments that represent the various scores on the second variable. Above each score, at the height specified on the vertical scale on the side of the diagram, place a dot representing how many cases share that score on the second variable. When no cases share that score, just leave a blank column above it. Connect the dots so that you can get a good look at the distribution as it appears for the cases you have (and as you can imagine it would appear if you had many more cases to work with that were distributed similarly).

Draw a vertical line at the point on the value scale for the variable that represents the mean of that variable. Label it $\overline{X}$, as in the example. Now repeat the process of drawing the distribution and labeling the mean for the third variable.

Notice that in the distribution of variable 3, the mean falls in what seems to be about the middle of the distribution. Even so, the cases are so spread out on either side of the mean that you can't really communicate much about the characteristics of all the cases by just reporting the mean.

Notice that in the distribution of variable 2, the mean doesn't fall in the middle of the area in which most of the cases lie in a cluster. There are a few cases with relatively extreme scores, and their scores pull the mean in their direction away from the greater number of cases, distorting the information that is usually conveyed by a mean. This is an example of a distribution that is said to be *skewed*—one that doesn't have mirror-image halves but, instead, has a cluster of cases on one side and a "tail" of relatively few cases on the other. When the few extreme cases in a skewed distribution have very high values on the variable, the distribution is said to be "skewed high" or "skewed to the right." When the extreme scores are low ones, the distribution is said to be "skewed low" or "skewed to the left."

In the example on which you are working, there are so few cases in the area where the scores are clustered and such a narrow range of scores that the difference between the group of cases and the mean is not very great. The point remains, however, that the mean is "pulled" toward the few extreme cases and away from the cluster of cases we would consider more typical.

THE MEDIAN TO DESCRIBE THE TYPICAL CASE

Since the mean is sensitive to these extreme scores and is pulled in their direction, we sometimes need a better measure to describe the "typical" case. In these instances, we can use the *median*. The median is that value on the variable below and above which 50 percent of the cases lie. The easiest way to find the approximate value for the median is to figure out how many cases constitute half the cases, and then to count up the number of cases at each value on the diagram until you get to the score above and below which 50 percent of them fall. Even if no score exists for that point, you can create one. For example, if 20 cases have scores at 5 or below and 20 cases have scores at 6 or above, we'd say the median is 5.5, creating a score that doesn't really exist in the data, which are in whole numbers.

When there's an odd number of cases, the score on the middle case is the median. There's a problem when several cases share the middle case's score. In such a situation, the best you can do for a rough estimate is to call the score of the middle case the median score, regardless of how many cases share it. You should have roughly the same number of cases above and below that score, but the number on each side won't necessarily be even and will represent less than 50 percent of the cases. Ordinarily, you won't need much more precision than this when you are estimating a median from data in which several cases share the same middle score. If you do, the Kohout book listed in the readings can help.

EXERCISE 3   Locating the Median on the Distributions

For each of your diagrams, figure out the approximate value of the median and draw another vertical line on each diagram to represent it. Label the line representing the median, "Md."

Notice how the mean and the median almost coincide when the two halves of the distribution are similar. Also notice how the median is closer to the more typical cluster of scores than is the mean in the most skewed distribution. That makes it a clearer description of what is typical in such instances.

For example, if you wanted to discuss the typical income in the United States, you probably wouldn't want to average the incomes of people like the Rockefellers into a mean and call that result the "typical" United States income (unless you were trying to convince someone that all people in the United States were quite wealthy). You'd use a median income figure because that is closer to what we think of as the "average American."

Since the actual scores do not enter into the calculation of the median, it cannot be affected by extreme scores the way that the mean can. For the median, you are just looking for the score that separates the top half from the bottom half of the scores; you aren't adding the actual scores themselves or, in any other way, manipulating their actual values.

However, that positive attribute of the median—that it does not manipulate actual scores and is, therefore, unaffected by them—also means that the median turns out to be not a very reliable statistic. It is susceptible to considerable error. Consider the easy situation when each case has a different score. You can just put them in order like this: 1 4 6 8 10 12 14 16 19 and count up or down to the middle (5th) case to find that the median score—the score of the middle case—is 10. However, with just a little error in recording the data or in entering the data into a computer, that case could have been scored 9 or 11, and the median would shift as well. Consider also the easy case when you calculate a median by averaging the two middle cases of an even number with fully ranked scores. In this instance, 1 4 6 8 10 12 14 16 19 20, the median is the average of the scores on the two middle (5th and 6th) cases, or 11. Here, had there been error in either the 5th or the 6th case, the median would shift. You should be able to see that, even when the median is clear, it may not be a very exact statistic for indicating the typical case.

The mean, however, is generally considered less susceptible to error, even if it is distorted by extreme scores. It is based on all the scores; each case's score enters into the calculation—not just one or two middle scores. Scoring error is, therefore, averaged out. If some cases have error in the measurement of their variables that makes their scores a bit high, others probably have error that makes them a bit low. Over many cases, you get a fairly good estimate of what the mean ought to be. It is a fairly reliable statistic.

You can see that even simple statistics such as means and medians need to be understood before they are used and interpreted. The choice of which to use is not always a clear-cut decision, and they rarely interpret themselves.

You have to know how they behave so that you can shape your interpretations accordingly.

USING THE DIFFERENCE BETWEEN THE MEAN AND MEDIAN TO BEGIN TO VISUALIZE SKEWED DISTRIBUTIONS

There is a statistic that measures skewness, but we needn't bother with calculating it at the moment. The statistic takes on a value of zero when the distribution is perfectly symmetrical (when the distribution of cases is identical on both sides of the mean so that one-half of the distribution is just a mirror image of the other half). Positive values on the skewness statistic indicate that there are extreme scores to the right of the mean (that cases are clustered to the left and there are the few, extreme cases distributed on the right). Negative scores on the skewness statistic indicate that there are extreme scores to the left of the mean and the major cluster of cases to the right.

Although the statistic that measures skewness is more complicated, you can remember how to get the sign of it, at least, by subtracting the median from the mean: mean - median. If the result is positive, the mean is higher than the median—representing the pull of the mean to the right extreme. If the result is negative, the median is higher than the mean—representing the pull of the mean to the left. If the result is near zero, the mean and the median coincide—representing the conjunction of the two in the middle of a distribution that is the same on both sides.

EXERCISE 4 Skewness

You can use this simplified version of skewness for each of the variables you plotted above. Just subtract the median from the mean for each example. Is the skew positive or negative for each distribution?

Later on, we will worry about skewness when we use the statistics in Chapter 18 for generalizing from a sample to a population. In the meantime, you will see questions of skewness again as we examine relationships between variables. There will be questions of whether those cases in the skew are numerous enough for us to understand anything about the cases that have such extreme scores, or whether they may be distorting our measures of relationships. There will be times when extreme scores make us think that we have a relationship between two variables when, in fact, we do not. There will be times when we will just have to discard the cases with the extreme scores in order to get true pictures of the relationship for the vast majority of cases.

THE MODE TO DESCRIBE THE TYPICAL CASE

There is one final measure of a typical case to consider. The score that more cases have than any other is called the *mode*. All you have to do to determine the mode of your distributions is to look at the number of cases on each score and find the score with the largest number of cases.

As a description of the typical case, the mode leaves a lot to be desired because information about only one score enters into its "calculation." It doesn't tell us a whole lot. But if we were working with nominal data, it would at least tell us the category that had the most cases. For example, if we had a variable that measured religion and it had the following values (1 = Protestant, 2 = Catholic, 3 = Jew, 4 = Other/None, 5 = Not answered), knowing that the mode was 1 would at least let us know there were more Protestants than any other single grouping in the sample.

When we are working with interval data, the mode allows us to describe the numbers of clusters of cases. For example, on some kinds of survey data, we might expect people to respond both rather positively and rather negatively. If we had a distribution in which roughly equal numbers of cases shared the positive and negative scores, as suggested in Figure 2.2, we would say that the distribution is *bimodal* (has two modes). When cases are dis-

FIGURE 2.2 A Bimodal Distribution

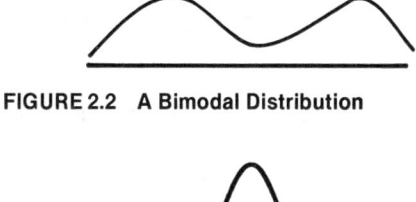

FIGURE 2.3 A Unimodal Distribution

tributed so that there is only one large grouping of cases around the mean, as in Figure 2.3, we say that the distribution is *unimodal*.

WHICH MEASURE OF TYPICALITY TO USE WHEN

Notice that the variables you have been working on are almost interval measurements. (If you're having trouble remembering what "interval" means, check back to Chapter 1.) When you calculate a mean, you have to add values on the variable together. In order for addition to have any meaning, the distance between any two adjacent whole numbers (3 and 4, for example) has to be the same as the distance between any other two adjacent whole numbers (101 and 102, for example). If you just have ordinal measurement and try to add values up, the result will be meaningless because the distances between numbers aren't the same. If a value scale is interval, you can say that 3 + 2 = 5 and 1 + 4 = 5; if it is ordinal and you don't know whether the distances from 2 to 3 and from 1 to 2 are the same, you can't do those additions and expect them to have any meaning.

Because you have to add scores to calculate a mean, the mean is an appropriate statistic to describe the typical case only if your values are on an interval scale. (Later, as you get to know more about measurement, this rule can be relaxed a bit; but right now, it's better to learn it in its most rigid form.)

When values are on an ordinal scale, the median is appropriate as a measure of typicality because you don't have to manipulate the values of the variable with addition or subtraction. You just use the values to order the cases from lowest to highest.

When the variable is a nominal one, the appropriate measure is the mode because for a nominal statistic you only have to count cases that share a value. The value itself is not used to order cases or for arithmetic manipulations.

Although you must have at least a certain level of measurement for each statistic, lower-level statistics may always be applied to higher-level data. Thus, while you must have interval-level data in order to calculate a mean, a median may be constructed for those same interval data. Sometimes, such as when you have badly skewed distributions, you will often consider the median preferable to a mean, even though you could appropriately calculate a mean on those data. Similarly, although you must have at least ordinal data for a median, a lower-level statistic—the mode—may be useful to describe aspects of a distribution of ordinal data as well. And, as the diagrams above suggested, sometimes the mode is even useful in describing interval distributions.

Thus, when deciding *what* statistic to use *when*, an important consideration is the measurement level of the data. Not all data can meet the demands of the arithmetic operations that have to be performed in order to calculate the statistic.

Another consideration, however, is whether the statistic communicates to a reader what you want it to communicate. Frequently, you will find that a lower-level statistic can help you communicate a description of what is going on better than a higher-level statistic can.

MORE DISCUSSION OF THE MEAN

The mean has some properties that we will be using later. Let's examine one of them briefly. If you knew the mean of a variable for a set of cases and were asked to guess the scores for each case without knowing the exact scores for any cases, what would your best guess be?

Now we have to define "best" before we can go on. "Best guess" would be the guess that left you with the least amount of total error. This, of course, then depends on how error is defined. Here we will say, for the moment, that error is the distance of the guess from the true score of a case on a variable. In this case, your best guess—the guess with which you would make the least amount of error—is to guess the mean for each case.

In the formula notation shown in Formula 2.2, error, as we are temporarily defining it, is the sum of the differences between each case's score and the mean.

FORMULA 2.2
Error in Guessing Cases' Scores from Their Mean (Temporary Definition)

$$\text{Error} = \Sigma (X_i - \bar{X})$$

Were you calculating this, you would follow these steps: take the score on case 1, and subtract from that score the mean of the variable; take the score on case 2, and subtract from that score the mean of the variable; and so forth, to the last case, n. Sum all those differences, one difference for each case.

When the guess about each score is the value of the mean, the sum of the differences between the scores and the mean will always be zero. To guess any value other than the mean increases the amount of error in the guess. (If you don't believe it, take the mean and go through the calculations to come up with zero; then take any value other than the mean and go through the calculations again to prove to yourself the answer is not zero. Use the first variable in the exercises.)

Given the definition of error above, you make zero error guessing the mean. Anything other than the mean as a guess would leave you with a greater absolute value for the error. (*Absolute value* means the value disregarding the plus or minus sign.)

DESCRIBING DISTRIBUTIONS WITH THE STANDARD DEVIATION OR VARIANCE

We can use this characteristic of the mean to construct a statistic that will help us describe a distribution when the measure of the typical case (the mean or median or mode) is not enough to describe the distribution because the cases are heterogeneous.

As you can see from examining the variables you plotted, the average cases on some distributions are more typical of the cases in those distributions than are the average cases on other distributions, even when there is no skewness to worry about. On some variables, the cases are clustered so that the mean and the median give a pretty good description of many of the cases. The cases are generally pretty much alike—fairly homogeneous. On some variables, the cases are so spread out that the mean and the median don't communicate much. The cases are very diverse—heterogenous.

EXERCISE 5 Visualizing the Distributions

Before going on, review quickly to make sure you know which distribution is the most homogeneous and which is the most heterogeneous. The statistic you are about to learn will help you to communicate that heterogeneity, but it helps if you can visualize what is going on. On which of the three variables in the exercises are the cases the most homogeneous? On which of the three are the cases the least homogeneous? Write out your answers.

This statistic, which will help you describe how typical the typical case is, will be small when the distribution is relatively homogeneous and the typical case is close to many of the others. When you have a relatively heterogeneous distribution of cases on the same variable and the typical case is not so close to many of the others, the statistic will be larger. To reiterate, the statistic will be smaller when the cases are closer together and larger when the cases are more spread out—as long as you are comparing distributions on the same measurement scale. Unfortunately, as you will see, you won't be able to take the statistics from the three examples you have been working with and compare just the statistics in order to see which has the most homogeneous distribution. The three distributions are for different variables with different scales of measurement. You will still have to visualize the distributions as you did in Exercise 5 to answer that question; but the statistic here will help you to visualize distributions you haven't actually seen.

This statistic is based on a notion, similar to that used above, of how much error you would make if you guessed that each case in your data set had the mean score on a variable or how far you would be off the real scores for all those cases. We are going to end up with a statistic that gets bigger as our error gets bigger and smaller as our error gets smaller.

When the mean represents the other cases fairly well, as it would in a homogeneous distribution, the error will be low, and the statistic will be small. When the mean doesn't represent the other cases very well, as in a heterogeneous distribution, the error will be high, and the statistic will be large.

We won't use exactly that same procedure as before because it will always give us a zero when we subtract the mean from each score and add the results. Nor will we take the absolute value of the differences between the scores and the mean and average them. (That is called the *average deviation*; inasmuch as it doesn't fit as well with the statistics you will learn later, you will almost never see it.)

We will, instead, square the differences between the scores and the mean to get rid of the sign, and then sum the squared differences. We will then have a measure of the total of the squared distances of the scores from the mean.

We are just changing the definition of error we used above a bit. Now, instead of measuring error as the difference between the guess (the mean) and the true score of that case on a variable, we are measuring error as the squared difference between the guess and the true score. This measure is called *variation*, and it can be written as shown in Formula 2.3.

FORMULA 2.3
Variation

$$\text{Variation} = \Sigma \, (X_i - \overline{X})^2$$

This can be read in English as, "Variation equals the sum of the squared differences between the true scores and the mean."

EXERCISE 6 Calculating the Variation

You calculate the variation by following these steps:

1. Subtract the mean from the score of case 1 on the variable, $(X_1 - \overline{X})$.
2. Square the resulting difference, $(X_1 - \overline{X})^2$.
3. Repeat steps 1 and 2 for each case.
4. Add up the squared differences, $\Sigma \, (X_i - \overline{X})^2$.

Do this now for the three variables in the exercises at the end of the chapter so that you can be sure you have grasped the idea before going on.

While you're at it, notice how the scores that are farthest off the mean seem to add in more than their fair share of the total variation. The squaring seems to give the contribution of the extremes much more weight in the overall total, especially if you compare this result to what happens when you square very small differences from the mean. This fact will always plague you in interpreting statistics based on variation; so note it now. You will frequently have to ask whether a few extreme scores are distorting your statistics. Remember, however, that looking at the skewness in the univariate analysis can help you figure out whether this may be the case; those few extreme scores become important when they start adding so heavily into other statistics.

As you can see, this measure of variation is not easy to interpret by itself. You are left looking at a number, perhaps wondering what it could possibly mean in and of itself. It will be useful later on in other contexts, but a bit of manipulation here can make it easier to interpret.

Instead of using the variation statistic itself to describe the distribution of the cases, we will transform it into the *variance*, which is a measure of the average squared error in guessing the mean. On average across all the cases, how much error would you make if you guessed the mean and compared it to the true score? The answer is given by Formula 2.4.*

FORMULA 2.4
Variance

$$\text{Variance} = \frac{\Sigma(X_i - \bar{X})^2}{N}$$

EXERCISE 7 Calculating the Variance

Simply take the variation and divide it by the total number of cases. Do that now for the three variables in the exercises. Like the variation, the variance will be larger for a group of cases that are more spread out and smaller for a group of cases that are more tightly clustered. The variance is the average error made in guessing the cases.

The variance statistic doesn't help you to visualize and describe the distribution, however, unless you also know the possible scores of the variable on which the variance has been calculated. You have to have some sense of what the range can be. Look again at the distributions you plotted for the three variables. Look at the variance you have calculated for each. Notice that the absolute value of the variance doesn't communicate how clustered up the cases are unless you know the scale on which the scores are laid out. To interpret the average error, you have to know the meaning of the scores and what the differences between them stand for.

Another manipulation of the variation is more commonly used in research reports to describe how clustered up the cases are, and it is a bit more meaningful in its interpretation. This is the *standard deviation*, which is defined as the square root of the variance, as in Formula 2.5.

FORMULA 2.5
Standard Deviation

$$\text{Standard Deviation} = \sqrt{\frac{\Sigma(X_i - \bar{X})^2}{N}}$$

EXERCISE 8 Calculating the Standard Deviation

Just take the square root of the variance. You can stop and do that now for the variables in the exercises. There should be a square root key on your calculator (or on one you can borrow from a friend). There's no need to remember how to do this from junior high math.

Now look at how we can visualize what the standard deviation is doing. If we take a distribution where the scores are clustered up, as in Figure 2.4, the standard deviation gets smaller. However, if the cases are spread out, as in Figure 2.5, the standard deviation gets bigger.

Because the measurement scale is the same for these two distributions and for the one you were given earlier in Figure 2.1, you can compare the standard deviations on them. The standard deviation for first variable in the exercises, which you were given as the example in Figure 2.1, works out to 17.58. (Use this answer to check your own calculations to see that you are doing them correctly.) For the more clustered distribution in Figure 2.4, the standard deviation is 8.79. For the more spread out distribution in Figure 2.5, it is 22.88.

In these examples, the number of cases at

---

*In many statistics books, the formula for variance shows N - 1 in the denominator. That is the formula you would use when you are trying to figure out from the sample data what the variance probably is in the population from which the sample is drawn. (More on these kinds of analyses in Chapter 18.) Basically, the idea is that the sample will have a smaller variance than the population from which it is drawn so you have to correct the sample data (N-1) to get the estimate for the population. For now, use the formula for describing the sample since that is what we are doing. With a large sample it makes practically no difference which one you use.

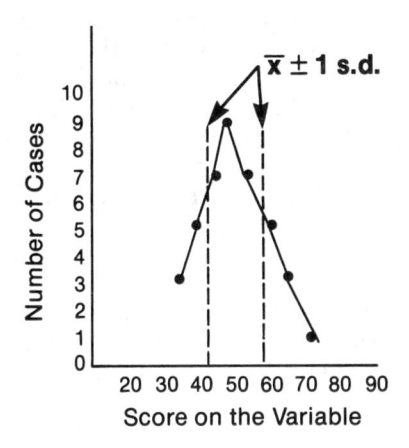

FIGURE 2.4 Distribution with Small Standard Deviation

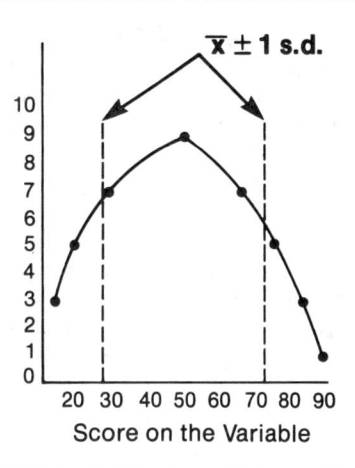

FIGURE 2.5 Distribution with Large Standard Deviation

each point doesn't change; there are always 3 at the first point, 5 at the second, 7 at the third, 9 at the fourth, and so on. They are just being shown as more or less like the cases at other points. In the most homogeneous distribution (Figure 2.4), a majority of the cases fall in a range of about 9 points (1 standard deviation) on either side of the mean. To take in that many cases in the most heterogeneous of the three distributions (Figure 2.5), you have to go about 23 points (1 standard deviation) above and below the mean.

EXERCISE 9 Locating the Standard Deviations on the Distributions

Now take the values you calculated for the standard deviations of the second and third variables in the exercises. Turn back to your distributions of the two variables. Count up from the mean the value of the standard deviation, and put a mark on the horizontal line where it falls for each variable. Do the same thing counting down from the mean. Draw dashed vertical lines on each distribution to represent 1 standard deviation above and below the mean.

Although you still have to know the scale of measurement (and whether there is a skew) before you can interpret it, the standard devia-tion (s.d.) does begin to give you an interpretable notion of how spread out the cases are. For reasons we don't need to go into here, the range represented by ±1 s.d. from the mean will usually cover roughly two-thirds of the cases in a distribution. This is precisely so only for distributions that are the same on either side of the mean (symmetrical) that also have certain degrees of peakedness as well. And, as you can see from the diagram of the second variable in the exercises, that guideline doesn't hold very well for very odd distributions. The standard deviation below the mean of that very skewed distribution even runs below the scale of measurement.

Now, if you will count how many cases fall into the range of the mean plus or minus one standard deviation for each variable you've been working on, you'll see that, excepting the oddest distribution, roughly two-thirds of the cases fall within + or -1 standard deviation of the mean. Soon you will begin to visualize a scale for any variable you are using and mentally add and subtract the value of the standard deviation to or from the mean. The wider that range relative to the scale of potential scores, the flatter the distribution and the more heterogeneous will be the cases on the variable. The narrower that range of the mean plus or minus one standard deviation, the more peaked the distribution and the more homogeneous will be the cases on the variable. (You can also use the fact that one standard deviation below or above the mean runs off the measurement scale in certain instances; this fact will help you visualize skewed distributions.)

As you can tell, by knowing the possible range of scores, the mean, and the standard deviation, you can begin to get a pretty good notion of what the distribution looks like without ever plotting out the cases, as you did earlier in this chapter. If you also know the skewness, you can get an even better impression without looking at the distribution itself.

(For a complete description of a distribution, you also usually need a statistic that we haven't discussed; it measures how peaked or flat the distribution is.) As we said before, the distribution of scores on a variable is useful to know simply for descriptive purposes, but it is also useful later on in interpreting measures of relationships between variables.

Our next step is to make the computer do these calculations for you. When you have more than a small number of cases, you don't want to spend your valuable research time adding and subtracting scores by hand.

EXERCISES

For the exercises in this chapter, you will be working with 40 cases and their scores on three variables. The data given below are hypothetical, but sometimes it helps to imagine what they might really represent. To help in your interpretations, therefore, some imaginary operationalizations of the three variables—age, participation, and efficacy—are provided.

Hypothetical Data for Calculating Measures of Central Tendency and Measures of Dispersion

Case Number	Age Variable 1	Participation Variable 2	Efficacy Variable 3	Case Number	Age Variable 1	Participation Variable 2	Efficacy Variable 3
1	20	0	0	21	50	1	4
2	20	0	3	22	50	1	4
3	20	0	8	23	50	3	7
4	30	1	0	24	50	2	9
5	30	1	8	25	60	1	9
6	30	0	1	26	60	3	5
7	30	1	6	27	60	3	5
8	30	0	9	28	60	2	10
9	40	1	7	29	60	3	12
10	40	2	3	30	60	1	8
11	40	0	1	31	60	2	10
12	40	15	7	32	70	2	5
13	40	1	7	33	70	4	8
14	40	0	2	34	70	4	8
15	40	2	4	35	70	13	6
16	50	2	3	36	70	12	10
17	50	1	7	37	80	0	9
18	50	1	2	38	80	3	6
19	50	4	2	39	80	14	11
20	50	4	6	40	90	0	11

Imaginary Operationalizations for the Three Variables

Age. Imagine we asked our sample of forty people, "Are you in your 20s, your 30s, your 40s, your 50s, or what?" Technically, for interval data we would probably have asked, "In what year were you born?" (People tend to give an answer such as, "In my fifties," if you ask them, "How old are you?"; they respond more exactly—more reliably—if asked the year of their birth.) For this example, however, we need the numbers of cases that result when we cluster cases by decades.

Participation. Imagine we had asked our sample: "Please tell me which of these things you have done in the past: (1) voted in a general election, (2) worn a campaign button, (3) put a bumper sticker on your car, (4) given money to a party, (5) given money to a candidate, (6) written a letter to a newspaper or magazine, (7) written a letter to someone in government, (8) attended a campaign rally, (9) attended a party meeting, (10) participated in a demonstration, (11) voted in a primary election, (12) attended a city council meeting, (13) given money to an interest group, (14) held an office in a party, and (15) run for public office." Then imagine we gave a person one point for each activity. We'd have a participation scale which ran from 0 to 15—zero for no participation at all to 15 for having done everything we mentioned. (See questions from the Election Study, Appendix A.)

Efficacy. This concept refers to the feeling that a person can influence the government if he or she wants to. Imagine we asked our sample six questions, giving each person zero points for a non-efficacious answer, one point for a partially efficacious answer, and two points for a completely efficacious answer to each question. If we then summed each person's responses for the six questions, the person would have an efficacy score with a value somewhere between zero for total inefficacy to 12 for total efficacy.

Political scientists frequently use such indices (an *index* is a single scale made up from more than one question that measure a single concept) because they increase the reliability of the measurement. One question might have a lot of error in it for many reasons, but that error is likely to be averaged out when several items are used to measure the same thing.

Some argue that such indices aren't really interval data, but, for our purposes here, these indices are close enough to interval.

SUGGESTED READINGS

AGNEW, NEIL MCK., and SANDRA W. PYKE. *The Science Game*, 4th ed. (Englewood Cliffs, NJ: Prentice Hall, 1987), pp. 174–180. Note that you don't need the material on the normal curve or *z* scores yet.

BABBIE, EARL R. *The Practice of Social Research*, 3rd ed. (Belmont, CA: Wadsworth, 1983), pp. 351–356.

BLALOCK, HUBERT. *Social Statistics*, 2nd ed. (New York: McGraw-Hill, 1972), Part 2, pp. 31–93 (i.e., not Section 7).

BOWEN, BRUCE D., and HERBERT F. WEISBERG. *An Introduction to Data Analysis* (San Francisco: Freeman, 1980), Ch. 5, except pp. 55–57.

JOHNSON, JANET BUTTOLPH, and RICHARD A. JOSLYN. *Political Science Research Methods* (Washington, D.C.: Congressional Quarterly Press, 1986), Ch. 11. For the time being, don't worry about pp. 260–263 on the normal distribution.

KIDDER, LOUISE H. *Selltiz, Wrightsman, and Cook's Research Methods in Social Relations*, 4th ed. (New York: Holt, Rinehart, and Winston, 1981), pp. 314–323.

KOHOUT, FRANK J. *Statistics for Social Scientists: A Coordinated Learning System* (N.Y.: John Wiley and Sons, 1974), pp. 41–43. He makes a clear statement of how to estimate a median when many cases share the middle score in a distribution.

OTT, LYMAN, WM. MENDENHALL, and RICHARD LARSON. *Statistics: A Tool for the Social Sciences*, 2nd ed. (North Scituate, MA: Duxbury, 1978), Ch. 3-4. Chapter 3 presents many ways to display data graphically; Chapter 4 is on measures of central tendency and dispersion.

ZISK, BETTY. *Political Research* (Lexington, MA: D.C. Heath, 1981), pp. 215-229.

ARTICLES

CAPUTO, DAVID A. "New Perspectives on the Public Policy Implications of Defense and Welfare Expenditures in Four Modern Democracies: 1950-1970" *Policy Sciences*, 6 (1975), 423-446.

FRASER, JOHN. "Validating a Measure of National Political Legitimacy," *American Journal of Political Science*, 18 (1974), 117-133. Table 1 can be considered a univariate analysis (percentage distribution) to demonstrate enough variation in the measures to proceed.

JACOBSON, GARY C. "The Marginals Never Vanished: Incumbency and Competition in Elections to the U.S. House of Representatives, 1952-82," *American Journal of Political Science*, 31 (February 1987), 126-141. Table 1 is means and medians of percentage of votes won by incumbent candidates; Tables 2 and 3 are percentages of incumbents defeated. After these presentations, the article sometimes uses more advanced statistics but should still be understandable at this point. Table 4 uses means and standard deviations to measure vote swings from election to election. *See also*: Monica Bauer and John R. Hibbing. "Which Incumbents Lose in House Elections: A Response to Jacobson's 'The Marginals Never Vanished,'" *American Journal of Political Science*, 33 (February 1989), 262-271.

PALUMBO, DENNIS, and RICHARD A. STYSKAL. "Professionalism and Receptivity to Change," *American Journal of Political Science*, 18 (1974), 385-394. Tables 1 and 2 can be looked at as examples of univariate analysis. Even though they compare school-board members and principals or different classes of respondents, they are basically just percentage distributions and differences of means.

REMP, RICHARD. "The Efficacy of Electronic Group Meetings," *Policy Sciences*, 5 (1974), 101-115. Part of a project to develop a mass participatory decision-making system, this article analyzes results of 16 conference phone calls with nine participants each, who are paid volunteers from the university community. Simple percentage distributions of subjects responses to questions about the session.

ROTHGEB, JOHN M., JR. "Contagion at the Sub-War Stage: Siding in the Cold War, 1959-63," *Conflict Management and Peace Science*, 6 (Spring 1982-83), 39-58. Tables I and II are rankings of countries on two different operationalizations of their joining in international conflicts. Table III examines means and standard deviations of those two scores in order to compare members of alliance blocs with non-members on their joining of conflicts. Article continues with bivariate and partial r—statistics you will learn in Chapters 5 and 12.

SAVAGE, JAMES. "Postmaterialism of the Left and Right: Political Conflict in Postindustrial Society," *Comparative Political Studies*, 17 (January 1985), 431-451. Tables 1a - 1c (combined sample, pre- and post-1945 groups) can be read as univariate distributions of postmaterialist values in each of nine countries. To understand the tables, you will only need to know means and standard deviations.

SHIN, EUI HANG, and IK KI KIM. "Variations in the Duration of Reign of Monarchs," *Comparative Political Studies*, 18 (April 1985), 104-122. Table 1 is univariate distributions of duration of reign and life, age at ascent to the throne (with mean, medians, and standard deviations), causes of removal, and kinship type.

THOMAS, MARTIN. "Election Proximity and Senatorial Roll-Call Voting," *American Journal of Political Science* (February 1985), 96-111. Look back to the means discussed in this article (mentioned in Chapter 1) now that you are getting more used to the numbers than when this was first mentioned.

CHAPTER

3

USING A COMPUTER TO GET UNIVARIATE DESCRIPTIVE STATISTICS

COMPUTER PACKAGES

Although this text will always have you doing examples by hand in order to get a feel for each statistic, from now on you will also be using a computer to do much of the calculating for you. Even if you've never used a computer for statistical analysis before, there really isn't a lot to learn at first. You won't really have to program the computer; you'll use a prewritten set of computer programs. Thus, you won't have to worry about using a computer language, which sometimes can seem foreign, to instruct the computer to perform each operation step by step; you can use a variant of ordinary English to instruct the computer to find the prewritten instructions that it has stored for the operations.

Outlines of instructions are included here for the *Statistical Package for the Social Sciences* SPSS-X Data Analysis System Release 3, which requires a large computer, and for SPSS/PC+ Base Package, the version that runs on smaller personal computers.* Both of these sets of prewritten instructions have many statistical procedures you will eventually need. You will be communicating with SPSS in fairly simple commands. Through a programming language, it will then communicate with the computer for you.

Generally speaking, you will want to use SPSS-X when you have very large data sets with many cases and variables or when you need to do the kinds of sophisticated analyses that are available in this package but not in the basic PC version. The PC version is more useful for somewhat smaller data sets, and it can be upgraded for more sophisticated applications. SPSS/PC+ does require a rather large personal computer with a hard disk drive, however. When all you have access to is a smaller computer, you may want to investigate other statistical packages, including the *Studentware* version of SPSS/PC+.** The principles you learn in this text ought to be readily transportable, regardless of the package you use.

For anything other than the most basic applications, you will want to consult the manuals for the SPSS-X and SPSS/PC+ packages,

---

*SPSS is a trademark of SPSS, Inc., of Chicago, IL, for its proprietary software. No materials describing such software may be produced or distributed without the written permission of SPSS, Inc. The SPSS-X and SPSS/PC+ commands are used here with the permission of the publisher.

**There is brand-new PC version of SPSS (for OS/2) that has all the advantages of SPSS-X and that runs with similar commands. See Barry Simon, "First Looks," *PC Magazine*, 9 (January 30, 1990), 44.

as well as this text. References in each chapter's Suggested Readings direct you to specific places in the various manuals. The sooner you get used to using the manuals, the easier you will find it to learn variations and elaborations on the many available procedures, to find corrections for mistakes, and to uncover easier and faster ways of doing your work. In fact, in this text, the commands for the computer are not spelled out repeatedly for the same procedures in order to encourage you to look them up when you don't remember the form precisely. This will help you become familiar with the manuals more quickly.

Regardless of what package you are using, you first need to get the data into a shape that can be utilized by the computer. It makes sense to consider this process, called *coding*, before you turn to the analysis package, and it will make parts of the package make more sense as well.

PREPARING DATA FOR COMPUTER PROCESSING

Whenever you are coding data, you are transforming the information you have collected into a form (here numeric) that can be used by the computer. In effect, you are assigning numbers to represent the values on the variables for each case in your data.

The same numbers have to mean the same thing on all the cases. For example, if you have the variable "sex" and have decided that the three values are male/female/undetermined (remembering that measurement categories must be mutually exclusive and exhaustive—see Chapter 1 if the reminder is not ringing bells), you may decide to assign a 1 to stand for the value "male," a 2 to stand for the value "female," and a 0 to stand for the value "undetermined." Once you have made that decision, you must follow it for all the cases you are examining.

In addition to transforming the values of the variables into numbers, data coding involves placing those numbers in consistent locations where the computer can find them for all the cases. The easiest way to code data (and the most usual one for computer processing, although there are others) is to place the same variable in the same location for each case you are using.

Imagine that you are typing lines of numbers across a page, with each line representing one of your cases. Envision putting the information on the variable "sex" in the first place on a line. For the first case, the number 1 would go in the first place on the line if the case were a male. For the second case, a number 1 would go in the first place on the line if the case were a male. For the third case, a number 2 would go in the first place on the line if the case were a female, etc. You always put the information on a variable in the same relative location for each case. Each space (sometimes called a *column*) across the line can take one bit of information—a single digit of a number, a single symbol, a single space, etc. The total number of spaces that it takes to code the values on a single variable is sometimes called the *field* for that variable.

Think back to the data you used to calculate means and standard deviation in Chapter 2. Those data there are presented in a form that can be used by the computer. There are 40 lines of information, one line per case, and the numeric values for the variables are lined up in columns.

If you were planning to enter the data into the computer, you would first notice that the largest number of digits for any value on the first variable is 2. That means you can get the information on the first variable into the first two spaces of a line for each case. Thus, two spaces is the field of the first variable. If the biggest value on a particular variable for any case is three digits, each and every case will have the same three-space field reserved for that variable—even if no other case has a value that exceeds two digits.

When not all cases have values with the same number of digits, the values are *right-justified* in the field. Basically, this means that the ones go in the far right column of a field, the tens go in the next-to-last column, the hundreds go in the third-to-last column, etc.—just like your grade school teacher insisted you keep the ones in the ones' place, the tens in the tens' place, etc.

Decide now how many spaces need to be reserved for each of the three variables you have been using from the exercises in Chapter 2. (You can also decide to reserve some columns with nothing in them in order to make coding easier. For example, you might plan to leave a blank space between the values for the first and second variables.)

You may find it useful to write the values on the variables for the first case on one line of paper, write the values on the variables for the second case under them, and then do the values for the third case, etc., until you have written out all 40 cases. Or you may find that you prefer to just look at the variables printed in the exercises and imagine typing those values directly from there. There are data-coding sheets that have 80 blanks across each line, which make it easier to see the columns and keep the fields straight. You may be able to find them at your bookstore or computer supply store.

Don't think that you can only have the amount of information on a case that you can get onto one line. You can imagine using several lines per case. The only trick to using multiple lines is that you have to have the same variable in the same field on the same line for each case. For example, if "political party identification" is in the fifth space of the second line for the first case, in this method of coding, it has to be in the fifth space of the second line for the second case as well.*

Also don't get the idea that the only way to code data is by looking at the source (the interview, the roll call, the judicial decision, the census, etc.), writing the variables for each case line-by-line the way they appear in the exercises, and typing the variables on a keyboard into the computer. This can all be done by the use of scanner forms (much like those you see with standardized tests and those that you may use for objective exams), and there are newer ways of preparing data for computer analysis as well. When you have large projects, you will want to consult the computer staff on your campus.

Now that you know something about preparing data for the computer, we can look at the commands that are necessary to get the computer to use the data. You will probably want to take a clean sheet of paper (coding sheets if you have been able to find them) and set up the commands necessary for your job as we go through the chapter; that way, you can just copy the information into your computer file later, rather than having to go through the chapter again.

Essentially, you will be typing out the commands necessary to run your job and the data on which you want the computer to operate. All these commands and data, which are typed into a form the computer can read (called a *file*), will be stored in a way that you will be able to get to the information later to change or to use it again. When you have another job to do with the same data, you can recall your file, change some of the commands, refile it, and submit it—all without having to type the data a second time.

When the computer finishes with your job, it will file the results so that you can examine them. You will also be able to have your results printed so that you will have a copy of them.

SETTING UP THE SPSS FILE

The file you will be setting up consists of a few commands to instruct the computer on where the data are, the data themselves, and a few commands for what the computer is to do. Here I will show you just the SPSS part of the file. Unless I indicate otherwise, assume the

---

*In some instances, you can also imagine an almost infinite line for each case. You might, for example, have the information on political party identification in the 1,257th space on each case. Most often, you will find such notation when you are analyzing data that have been stored for you on magnetic tape.

commands for SPSS-X and SPSS/PC+ are identical.* For your location, there may be a line or two at the beginning of the file for communicating with your specific computer.

Just to let you see how simple this is going to be, let me give you a sample of what one file might look like before explaining each of its elements in greater detail.

```
DATA LIST / AGE 1-2 PARTYID 6
   POLPARTI 10-11.
BEGIN DATA.
18    2    10
25    4     5
27    7    12
46    6     9
54    3    15
60    5    11
32    7     8
41    6     7
39    3     4
53    4     2
END DATA.
DESCRIPTIVES VARIABLES = AGE,
   POLPARTI/
   STATISTICS = 1 6.   (SPSS/PC+)
DESCRIPTIVES VARIABLES = AGE,
   POLPARTI/ STATISTICS = MEAN
   VARIANCE.           (SPSS-X)
FREQUENCIES VARIABLES =
   PARTYID.
```

Sometimes you will need one more line with the word FINISH on it, but this short set of commands and data is all you need to get the mean and variance for two variables (age and political participation) on ten cases and a distribution of those cases on another variable (political party identification). The listing given above is the simplest possible setup for a file. There are many other commands you will learn to add to it as you go along, but these commands are really all you need to be able to start. We now can examine each piece of the setup in more detail.

---

*Sometimes things are optional in some uses of one of the two packages but mandatory in the other. I have opted to present only one version where possible, in order to give you maximum movement between the two versions and to keep things simple.

SPSS

For your first exercise in SPSS, I will take you line by line through setting up a job that will get the same statistics for you that you calculated in Chapter 2. As I explain each line of the SPSS job, you will begin to get a feel for how other kinds of SPSS jobs might work.

For this first time through, you'll be copying many things exactly as I print them below. (What you are to copy exactly appears in capital letters.) In some instances, you will be asked to substitute information unique to your situation. (You are to make such substitutions when lower case letters appear in examples.) Later on, you can branch out into variations on your own.

Let me warn you before you start that SPSS is fussy about spelling. It expects all of its recognized commands and subcommands to be spelled correctly. SPSS makes the same demand for variable names; once you have told it that you are going to refer to a variable by a certain name, it wants that name to be spelled exactly the same way whenever it encounters it.

EXERCISE 1 Setting up an SPSS Job and Submitting It

SPSS requires that data be set up with certain information about where the data are located, characteristics of the variables, certain labeling information, and so forth. Your first task, therefore, is to spell out the requisite information. For the simple tasks we are doing here, this takes only one command, DATA LIST.

The DATA LIST Command

For the first line of the job, you will have a DATA LIST command. Here you will tell SPSS what the names of your variables are and where the values on a variable are located on each case.

You get to make up a name for each variable. Variable names may be up to eight characters and must begin with a letter (rather than a number). Later on, we want to be able to tell SPSS to give us a statistic on a particular variable. We'll tell it which variable by using a name for it that we have assigned on this DATA LIST command. The computer will look back to this command and find the name.

Along with the name, you will indicate where the values on that variable are to be found by indicating the name of each variable followed by the beginning column and ending column—separated by a dash—of the field in which the computer will find the values of each case for that variable. If the values on the variable need only a single column, you can just indicate the beginning column.

Here's an example of what a completed DATA LIST command looks like:

```
DATA LIST / VARNO1 1-4 VARNO2
 6-9  VARNO3 10-13.
```

You can see another completed DATA LIST command in the example setup given above. (When you are actually working on the computer, be sure to distinguish the letter "O" from the number zero, "0." There will be two different keys for them on the keyboard you are using. Also be sure to distinguish a slash—slanted line leaning to the right—from a perpendicular line.)

In this example, we have assumed that the data for each case will be found on just one line (*record*). If the data for each case took more than one line, we'd just have to adjust this format slightly. We have begun defining the data by use of the slash. We have named three variables (VARNO1, VARNO2, VARNO3) and told the package where it will find the values on each variable for each case. 1-4 means that the values on variable VARNO1 will begin in space 1 and end in space 4 on each case; 6-9 means that the values on variable VARNO2 will begin in space 6 and end in space 9 on each case; 10-13 means that the values on variable VARNO3 will begin in space 10 and end in space 13 on each case.

Basically, we're telling the package that it will later on find, in lines reserved for data, three variables; the biggest number any of those variables will have is four characters;

and the entries on each case for each variable will be separated by a space between the first and second variable (i.e., space 5 will be blank). Such data lines might look something like this for the first three cases:

```
7509 21576542
6891 35782490
2319 47355801
```

On these lines, the value of VARNO1 on the first case is 7509; the value of VARNO2 on the second case is 3578; the value of VARNO3 on the third case is 5801.

From the DATA LIST command, the computer will know that, whenever you later ask it to do something with, say, VARNO2, it will have to look in spaces 6-9 on each case to find the values for that variable. When you ask it to do something with VARNO3, it will have to look in the field from spaces 10 through 13, etc.

VARNO1, VARNO2, and VARNO3 are acceptable SPSS variable names; they are less than eight characters, and each starts with an alphabetic character. You will usually find it more convenient to give names to variables that are easier to remember and more descriptive of what they are, for example, INCOME for the median income for a county, AGE for a person's age, or GNP for a country's gross national product.

If you are faced with a situation in which you have many variable names, you will need more than one line for the DATA LIST command. That's ok. Whenever *any* command needs more than one line, we indicate to SPSS that we are simply continuing onto another line (rather than starting a new command) by indenting the second line one or more spaces like this:

```
DATA LIST / name x-x name x-x
 name x-x name x-x name x-x
 name x-x.
```

Examine that format again before we go on. You would fill in the names of the variables (in the space typed "name" above), and the spaces/columns in which the values for those variables will be found (in place of the x-x typed above).

Now finish your DATA LIST command on your blank sheet. Make sure you have started with the words DATA LIST, continued with a slash, given each variable a unique name that meets the requirements for naming variables, and indicated the fields in which those variables are to be found.

The Data

Next you put in the data themselves—either by typing them directly from the source or from your coding sheets—right below one line that reads:

BEGIN DATA.

After you have typed a line of data for each and every case and have checked that the values on the variables are in the columns you identified on the DATA LIST command, you type:

END DATA.

Using Procedure Commands

You are now ready to give SPSS its first command to do a procedure (calculations) for you. The procedure command tells SPSS which subpart of the package you want to use.

You want to get the same statistics you learned in the second chapter. Most of them are available with a procedure called DESCRIPTIVES. For this procedure, you simply write DESCRIPTIVES on the next available line and follow it, on the same line, with the subcommand VARIABLES = and the names of the variables on which you want the procedure performed. Here's an example:

DESCRIPTIVES VARIABLES =
    VARNO1, VARNO2, VARNO3/

To get the mean, the standard deviation, the variance, and the skewness, continue with the SPSS/PC+ subcommand:

    STATISTICS = 1 5 6 8.

Or with the SPSS-X subcommand:

STATISTICS = MEAN STDEV
VARIANCE SKEWNESS.

The numbers that represent the various statistics are from the list in the manual that accompanies each procedure, but you don't have to worry about this yet. There are other subcommands for this procedure that are listed in the manual; you don't yet have to worry about these, either.

On your paper where you are writing out your setup and on the line that follows the END DATA command, write out the DESCRIPTIVES command and the names of the three variables on which you want the calculations performed. Make sure you spell the variable names exactly as you spelled them on the DATA LIST you have already written.

Additional Procedures

You may have noticed above that you didn't tell the computer to calculate a median for you. Since DESCRIPTIVES works on interval data, and since medians require the kinds of calculations usually done on ordinal data, it takes another procedure to get a median. On the next line of your setup, create another procedure. Follow the example given below:

FREQUENCIES VARIABLES = name
    TO name/FORMAT=NOTABLE/
    STATISTICS=
    MEDIAN MINIMUM MAXIMUM.

Fill in your variable names where I have typed "name." Because all your variables are right next to each other on DATA LIST, you can simply type the first and last variable names in the list you want, separated by the word "TO" as in:

FREQUENCIES VARIABLES = VARNO1
    TO VARNO3.

Since you are asking for the statistic on all the variables in the file defined on DATA LIST in this case, you can simply use the word "ALL" in place of the variable names, as in:

```
FREQUENCIES VARIABLES = ALL.
```

Finishing the Setup

When you get to the very end of what you want SPSS to do, you only need one more line, and that consists only of one word:

```
FINISH.
```

Summary of SPSS Setup

A summary of a setup to get means, standard deviations, variances, skewness, and medians for the three variables in Chapter 2 follows:

```
DATA LIST / name x-x name x-x
     name   x-x.
BEGIN DATA.
    ... Here you will have data lines, one for
        each case, containing the values on
        each of three variables for each
        case ...
END DATA.
DESCRIPTIVES VARIABLES = name
    name name/STATISTICS =
    1 5 6 8.            (SPSS/PC+)*
DESCRIPTIVES VARIABLES =
    name name name/
    STATISTICS = MEAN STDDEV
    VARIANCE SKEWNESS.   (SPSS-X)
FREQUENCIES VARIABLES =
    name TO name/
    FORMAT=NOTABLE/STATISTICS =
    MEDIAN MINIMUM MAXIMUM.
```

In this SPSS setup, I have had you blindly follow what I've told you to do. This should give you a feeling for what you are doing before you start reading the manuals for SPSS. It's important to learn to read the guides that accompany statistical packages, and you soon will. But sometimes having done it once in simple form makes understanding the guides a bit easier. (If, however, you feel completely lost at this point, turn now to the Suggested Readings at the end of this chapter. Some of them may "click" better than the presentation here.)

RUNNING THE JOB

You're now almost ready to go to the computer for SPSS/PC+ or to the terminal for SPSS-X and begin to run your first job. You will need to learn a few things before you start—like how to get the terminal to connect with the mainframe, how to type a setup and correct mistakes in it, how to get into SPSS-X, and how to print your results; or how to get the personal computer to get you into SPSS/PC+, how to make corrections, run your job, and print the outcome.

SPSS/PC+ has a good tutorial that your instructor may want you to use after he or she introduces you to the personal computer. Some computer installations may have something similar for their mainframes. These preparatory steps, however, may vary so much that this text cannot cover them. Here, we'll stick to the SPSS segments of the jobs. Your instructor will be able to help with the rest.

Your instructor may ask you to work either interactively or in batch-processing mode. At most installations, both SPSS-X (Release 3) and SPSS/PC+ allow you to type your commands to the computer in either way. When you are communicating *interactively*, you give a single command at a time, which the computer checks for accuracy and tells you how to correct before prompting you to give it the next command. Any analysis you ask for is done while you wait. If you are using SPSS-X interactively on a large computer (usually called a *mainframe*), the work probably has a relatively high cost, and you may need to use interactive computing sparingly.

In *batch processing*, you assemble all your commands, file them, and submit them at one time to the computer. The computer does the

---

*Don't copy the SPSS/PC+ or the SPSS-X in parentheses. They are there to guide you in selecting which form to use.

job and files either the results or a set of error messages that you can read. If you have errors, you have to retrieve your set of commands, fix the errors, and file it again, before resubmitting the job. With batch processing, you don't have to wait around to give instructions. You can go do something else while the job runs. With SPSS-X on the mainframe, you may be able to do batch processing more cheaply. When you have to work with data sets stored on tape, you will need to know about batch processing.

There are three things to keep in mind about using SPSS in batch and interactive mode. First, in interactive processing, every command ends with a period. If you don't put the period in, SPSS thinks you are still typing part of the same command and tells you to continue. The period (called *command terminator*) isn't required in SPSS-X batch mode, but it won't hurt to use it, so I have put it in throughout the text in the examples.

Second, in batch processing, anything associated with a single command has to be indented if it takes more than one line. The indentation is what tells SPSS that you are continuing. Indentation isn't required in interactive processing (where periods end commands), but it won't hurt anything. I have chosen to show examples with the indentation.

Third, FINISH works somewhat differently in the two modes. In batch, you put it at the end of your job to indicate that you are asking for no more commands to be executed for any single job. In interactive processing (where commands are executed one at a time), it gets you out of SPSS altogether. I've put it in, but be careful with it if you use interactive processing.

INTERPRETING WHAT YOU GET

EXERCISE 2 Examining the Output

Now run your job on the computer. When you get your output, examine it, and answer the questions below. If you've set up your job interactively, you've corrected errors as you've gone along. Remember, however, that the SPSS package can only correct you if you're asking it to do the impossible. It cannot correct you if you are just asking it to do something illogical.

If you've run your job in batch, don't worry if it has errors the first time around. One nice thing about SPSS is its relatively clear indications of what you have done wrong—once you figure out its few quirks. One thing you may need to learn quickly is that, if there is a mistake in the form of the DATA LIST command, the computer will see all references to any of the variables listed on that DATA LIST as errors. SPSS output will tell you that the variable you are interested in is "undefined." That probably means that there's an error on your DATA LIST, so the computer cannot put that variable name together with data in a specific location. Sometimes, if you correct the error on the DATA LIST, all the other errors will correct themselves.

You will eventually get used to the logic of SPSS error messages. You will find more detail on some of them in the SPSS manuals. If you can't figure out the problem, you may wish to see your instructor, but give it a try first. You can only learn how to deal with SPSS error messages by working with the package.

Once you have your output, the first thing to look for is a message at the end of it: "NORMAL END OF JOB; 0 ERRORS ENCOUNTERED." If you don't find this message, there's a mistake somewhere in your file, and the job will have to be resubmitted; SPSS tells you how many errors there are, what they are, and where.

If you do find NORMAL END OF JOB; 0 ERRORS ENCOUNTERED, it means that the package did everything you told it to do. It does not mean you told it correctly; there may still be logic errors or mistakes in the data, for example.

The next thing to do is to scan the output, looking for the number of cases for each variable on each procedure. Make sure the right number of cases is reported on each variable. If it isn't, chances are you didn't get all the data lines in correctly.

Also check the output itself for where SPSS tells you the beginning and ending columns it has read to find the data. Compare what's printed there to your input. When you find errors, correct them and resubmit the job.

When you are satisfied that the job has run perfectly, use the information on the output to write out the same statistics that you computed in Chapter 2 for each variable. Write out the name of the variable, its mean, median, skewness, variance, and standard deviation. (But note: SPSS uses a more complicated definition of skewness than the one you calculated by just comparing median and mean. This more formal measure tells a researcher more than you need to know at the moment, but you can read just the sign and use either "positive" or "negative" to indicate whether the skew is toward the high or low values.)

Compare the values from the computer with those you got in Chapter 2 doing the calculations by hand. Are they the same? If so, everything is going as it should. If they are only off a few decimal places, it's probably because you and the package used different methods of rounding or slightly different formulae. (For example, SPSS uses the $N - 1$ version of the formula for the variance and standard deviation.) If the values are off a great deal, try to find the problem. Either your calculations were off earlier, or you entered the data incorrectly for the computer. You can bet that the computer's calculations aren't wrong—for the data you typed in.

VISUALIZING A DISTRIBUTION

EXERCISE 3 Sketching an Approximate Distribution

Without looking back at the diagrams you drew for Chapter 2, try to imagine, just using the output before you, what the distribution on each variable looks like. Just as you drew distributions in the second chapter, sketch out what you think the distributions on the three variables look like.

It won't be possible to be exact because you have neither any measure yet of how high to draw the distribution nor how many cases are above each value. (Moreover, you don't have enough cases really to expect a nice, smooth distribution.) You do know, nevertheless, that all three distributions have the same number of cases. You can show this by making the vertical line on your diagrams indicate the same numbers and also by having the flatter distributions lower and the more peaked distributions higher on that scale. Your computer printout also has the lowest and highest scores (you got these results from FREQUENCIES, almost without knowing it, by asking for MINIMUM and MAXIMUM on the STATISTICS subcommand), so you can label a horizontal line to indicate the scale of values properly. Make those horizontal lines the same length so that you can visually compare the distributions.

You have the median, so you know where the cases are divided in half. You have the mean, so you know, by comparing it to the median, whether there is a skew and in which direction; or you can look at the skewness statistic to know the direction of the skew. Remember that the mean is pulled in the direction of the skew. And you have the standard deviation, so you know the range between which roughly two-thirds of the cases will fall (except on badly skewed distributions).

Try it. Indicate the scale, the mean, the median, the standard deviation, and then draw a curve that represents the probable number of cases at each point on the scale, paying attention to the skewness. Now remember what your diagrams looked like in Chapter 2. The ones here should be pretty similar, but don't expect exactness; you are simply learning to get a rough idea of what a distribution looks like from the statistical measures. You aren't learning to lay out what one looks like exactly.

It is probably a good idea to compare notes with someone else in the class so that each of you can make sure the other is on the right track. Are you beginning to get the idea of what a distribution looks like? If not, consult the instructor.

It is usually a good idea to keep a printout and your exercises after you have completed them (and after your instructor has checked them over, if that is the procedure you are following). They may be useful in later chapters.

You are now beginning to be able to make the computer work for you. The more you deal with it, the easier it will become. Right now, it may seem easier to do things by hand rather than to fool with an obstinate machine. That feeling will pass. Just keep working at it.

GOING ON WITH THESE PROCEDURES

In case you're deciding you rather like manipulating the computer, you may find it interesting to do some further exercises with FREQUENCIES. For example, FREQUENCIES will construct a picture of a distribution very similar to those you have been drawing when you have data (similar to those you have been using) in which several cases share the same value on the variable. Usually these are ordinal or nominal, even though in the exercises we have been treating them as if they were interval.

After you've done all the exercises above, go back to your SPSS setup file. For the first procedure command (DESCRIPTIVES), substitute the following (for "name," put in the name of a variable on which there are only a few possible scores and on which many cases share the same score):

```
FREQUENCIES VARIABLES = name/
   FORMAT = NOTABLE/BARCHART.
```

Delete the second procedure command (the earlier version of FREQUENCIES). Now run the new job (storing it first, if necessary).

Compare your output to the diagram you drew in for the same variable in Chapter 2 and to the sketch you made above. In both of those diagrams, you were trying to approximate the kind of distribution you would have with a large number of cases and interval data. Here you can see a way to draw a distribution with nominal or ordinal data. Let the length of the bar indicate the number of cases for any single score, rather than letting the height of the curve above any single score indicate the number of cases, as you have been doing in the previous examples.

More? How about taking one of your variables, breaking it into three or four categories, and seeing how many cases fall into each category? (This is another way of looking at the distribution.) You will actually be making a nearly interval variable ordinal in this exercise and seeing how many cases fall into the lowest category, middle category, and highest category.

Pick out the variable that has the widest range but not the one you used before. Look back at the minimum and maximum scores you obtained from the run of the first FREQUENCIES to figure out the range (maximum score - minimum score). Looking at the range, if you wanted 3 or 4 categories, evenly spaced along the range of scores, what interval of scores would give you 3 or 4 catgories? For example, with a range of scores from 1 to 20, an interval of 10 would give you 2 categories; an interval of 4 would give you 5 categories. Using this procedure, the interval has to be the same all along the range, and it has to be a whole number.

Once you know what interval you want, you'll substitute it in place of the "n" on the following procedure command. Substitute the resulting procedure for the first procedure in your SPSS setup file, and submit the job again (storing it first, if necessary).

```
FREQUENCIES VARIABLES = name/
   FORMAT = NOTABLE/
   HISTOGRAM = INCREMENT(n).
```

The FREQUENCIES procedure is useful for lots of things. When I have nominal or ordinal data or interval data in which many cases share the same value and in which the range is limited, I often use FREQUENCIES as a check on whether I've typed in all the data correctly. FREQUENCIES will print out all the values on a variable and how many cases have that value. I can spot quickly whether there are any codes (values) that look wrong. If there's a code for which there is no meaning in my coding scheme, I assume I've typed in the values on that variable incorrectly somewhere along the line, and I go back and look over all the cases to see if it can be fixed. (If it can't be fixed, I tell the computer to ignore that case when computing the statistics with a MISSING VALUES command; but more of that, later.)

Why don't you try this? Take the variable you found on which many cases share the same value. Enter its name on the following command. Put this procedure in place of the first procedure command and run the job again:

FREQUENCIES VARIABLES = name.

FREQUENCIES will also calculate all those interval statistics we obtained using DESCRIPTIVES; but it takes more computer time and space to do it. Therefore, for efficiency's sake, it is probably better to use DESCRIPTIVES whenever you want interval statistics.

SUGGESTED READINGS

BABBIE, EARL R. *The Practice of Social Research*, 3rd ed. (Belmont, CA: Wadsworth, 1983), Ch. 13.

BERENSON, MARK L., DAVID M. LEVINE, and MATTHEW GOLDSTEIN. *Intermediate Statistical Methods and Applications: A Computer Package Approach* (Englewood Cliffs, NJ: Prentice-Hall, 1983), Ch. 2. This chapter is an introduction to computer packages.

BOWEN, BRUCE D., and HERBERT F. WEISBERG. *An Introduction to Data Analysis* (San Francisco: Freeman, 1980), Ch. 4.

NORUSIS, MARIJA J. *SPSS/PC+ V2.0 Base Manual* (Chicago: SPSS Inc., 1988). Section A is a good introduction to the system. Part B, Chapter 8, is on DESCRIPTIVES and FREQUENCIES as statistics. C50–53 and C65–69 are on the commands for the two procedures. The statistical descriptions in Part B are clear and may help you get a better handle on what's going on here.

SPSS-X User's Guide, 3rd ed. (New York: McGraw-Hill, 1988). Part I is "An Introduction to the System." Chapter 5 is on "Defining Data." Chapters 26 and 29 are on the DESCRIPTIVES and FREQUENCIES procedures. The sooner you can venture into this manual, the better.

CHAPTER 4

RELATIONSHIPS BETWEEN INTERVAL LEVEL VARIABLES

EXPLAINING VARIATION

Now you're ready to start explaining some of that variation around the mean. What you will be doing is asking, "Why aren't all the cases just alike and at the mean on this variable? Is there some way I can explain why some cases are high compared to the mean, some low compared to the mean, and some closer around the mean?"

Remember that in Chapter 2, when we were working with only one variable, we asked what the best guess would be if we had to guess the score for each case on a variable, knowing only the mean and not the true score for each case? (If not, review Chapter 2 at this point.) That spread of scores around the mean could be considered the amount of error we made in our guesses. Thinking along those lines allowed us to develop statistics such as variation that measured how spread out the cases were around the mean.

Now we are going to use a similar procedure to develop a statistic that will tell us how related two variables are. We are going to try to reduce the error in guessing the scores on the dependent variable by finding an *independent* variable that will help us in guessing the score of the dependent variable. The better that independent variable helps us guess the score on the dependent variable, the more we will reduce our error, and the more the statistic that we are developing will show us that the two variables are related. If knowing the value that a case has on the independent variable improves our guesses on the dependent variable, we will say that we have *explained* part of the variation of the dependent variable. The statistic will indicate the strength of the relationship between the independent and dependent variables.

Any systematic pattern in which the independent variable is related to the dependent variable may improve our guesses. In this chapter, however, we will be focusing on just the simplest systematic patterns. We want to create a statistic that measures how strongly related two variables are in these simple patterns, and we want to discover a way to communicate what the pattern or form of the relationship is.

For example, consider the pattern in which cases with *high* scores on the independent variable are more likely than other cases to have *high* scores on the dependent variable, and cases with *low* scores on the independent variable are more likely to have *low* scores on the dependent variable. In effect, we will examine a case for its score on the independent variable; and, if we see a *high* independent variable score, we will guess it to be *high* on the dependent variable. If we see a *low* independent vari-

42

able score, we will guess it to be *low* on the dependent variable. If we see an in-between score on the independent variable, we will guess the case to be in between on the dependent variable.

The more our guesses are improved, as compared to when we were just guessing the mean, the more the statistic that measures the strength of the relationship will indicate that we have explained variation in the dependent variable. The form of the relationship will, for now, just be described as positive; high scores on the independent variable lead us to guess high scores on the dependent variable, while low scores on the independent variable lead us to guess low scores on the dependent variable.

Or consider another pattern. If cases that have *high* scores on the independent variable are more likely than other cases to have *low* scores on the dependent variable, and cases that have *low* scores on the independent variable are more likely to have *high* scores on the dependent variable, we can use this pattern to improve our guesses. We examine the case's independent variable score and guess high, low, or in-between on the dependent variable based on what we see.

The better our guesses are compared to when we were just guessing the mean, the more the strength measure will indicate that the variables are related. The form of this relationship for this pattern will be described as negative; high scores on the independent variable lead us to guess low scores on the dependent variable, while low scores on the independent variable lead us to guess high scores on the dependent variable.

To summarize, when the independent variable helps us guess whether cases are high, low, or in the middle on the dependent variable that we are seeking to explain, we can say that the independent and dependent variables are related. How strongly related they are will be communicated in a statistic that we are about to create. (In what pattern they are related will be communicated in another statistic that we will examine in Chapter 5; for now, the form will be described simply as positive or negative.)

Since we will be working with interval data in this chapter, we will be able to be much more precise than high/medium/low when we examine cases for their scores on the independent variable and when we guess their scores on the dependent variable. We will have interval scores to work from rather than just the order implied by high/medium/low. This kind of data will also allow us later to be more exact in describing the pattern of the relationship than just saying that it is positive or negative. We will be using a straight line to describe the relationship, and the statistic you will learn in the next chapter will help you locate the best straight line for describing the relationship between the variables.

PLOTTING THE CASES ON TWO VARIABLES AT ONCE

EXERCISE 1   Plotting a Positive Relationship

Instead of speaking in the abstract, let's plunge right in and start by plotting several cases on two variables. Notice, in the following exercise, the difference between plotting the cases in the space delineated by the values of two variables and the exercise in Chapter 2 of describing a single variable. In Chapter 2, you were indicating how many cases were scored with each value of a single variable. Here you are indicating cases and their scores on two variables simultaneously.

At the end of this chapter in the exercise section, you will find twelve cases and their scores on five variables. One variable is designated as the dependent variable for all four relationships. Each of the other variables is indicated as the independent variable for one relationship. If you can find some sheets of graph paper with one-quarter inch squares, it will help you in the following exercises; otherwise, you can draw your own grid by covering pages with light lines one-quarter inch apart vertically and horizontally.

Use the first sheet of graph paper and start with the independent and dependent variables indicated for relationship 1. Draw a horizontal line to represent the scores on the independent variable (from zero to highest) and a vertical line to represent the scores on the dependent variable (from zero to highest). Make both the vertical and horizontal axes start at the point that represents zero for both. Consider each block on the paper equal to one point.

For each case in relationship 1, find the point on the horizontal axis that corresponds to the score for that case on the independent variable. Go up vertically from that point to the height on the vertical axis that corresponds to the dependent variable score for that case. Place a point at that location. Now go on to the second case and do the same thing. Repeat until all the cases have been plotted. You will have as many points as you have cases. Each point will represent the scores on both the independent and dependent variables for that case.

Figure 4.1 provides an example to help you in filling in the blank graph paper. (The dotted lines, however, are to help you see how to plot the scores. Don't put such dotted lines on your graph; just plot the points.)

As you can see by looking at your own *scatterplot* for relationship 1, the cases here that have higher scores on the *independent* variable (usually, but completely arbitrarily, designated "*X*") also tend to have higher scores on the *dependent* variable (usually, but equally arbitrarily, designated "*Y*"). This is an example of a positive relationship. Such a relationship is usually read something like: The higher cases are on the independent variable, the higher they are likely to be on the dependent variable.

Before going any further, try your hand for practice at stating a hypothesis that indicates the relationship between these two variables. Write your answer below your scatterplot for relationship 1. (Remember the criteria for good hypotheses that were covered in Chapter 1 and review the materials, if necessary.)

EXERCISE 2 Plotting a Negative Relationship

Now let's look at a scatterplot of a different kind of relationship. Again using the cases at the end of the chapter, plot the values of the independent and dependent variables indicated for relationship 2, using a second sheet of graph paper.

Here you can see by examining your scatterplot that cases that have high scores on the independent variable tend to have low scores on the dependent variable. This is an example of a *negative* relationship. It is usually read something like: The higher the cases are on the independent variable, the lower they are likely to be on the dependent variable.

Write a good hypothesis below the scatterplot that describes the relationship between the two variables. (Remember to check your phrasing against the criteria for good hypotheses in Chapter 1.)

Sometimes students have trouble with the concept of a negative relationship. Perhaps it will help you to think of how some higher scores on some independent variables could lead to lower scores on some dependent variables. Consider some examples. The larger the share of countries' budgets spent on national defense, the lower the sense of security felt by their populations. The more alienated from their government citizens feel, the less likely they are to participate in political actions. The more authoritarian the attitudes of city manag-

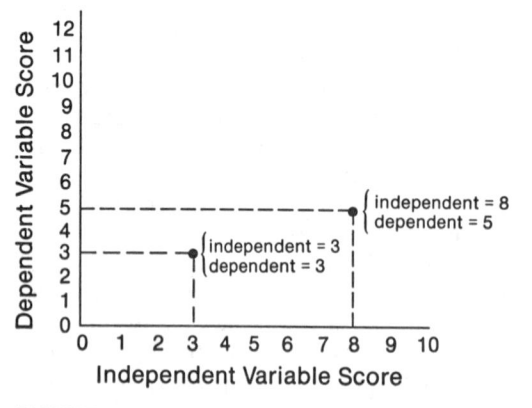

FIGURE 4.1 Example Plot of Cases on Two Variables

ers, the less productive the employees of the city government, and so forth.

EXERCISE 3 A Plot of Scores that Are Not Related

Perhaps it will help you to see what is going on if you also plot two variables that do not have any relationship. In such a case, there is no systematic tendency for high scores on the independent variable to be associated with either high or low scores on the dependent variable. Look at cases at the end of the chapter again and plot, on a third sheet of graph paper, the cases' values on the two variables indicated for relationship 3. Write out a hypothesis that indicates a relationship between the two variables but is disconfirmed by this test.

As you can see on this third scatterplot, the cases are scattered all over the place with no discernible pattern. Knowing that a case is high/low on the independent variable doesn't help you at all in trying to guess its value on the dependent variable. This, then, is an example of no relationship between the two variables.

MEASURING THE STRENGTH OF RELATIONSHIP BETWEEN TWO VARIABLES

We can now talk about measuring how strong the relationship is between the variables. What we want to end up with is a single number that will communicate—to ourselves as researchers and to those who read our research reports—how much we have explained the variation around the mean of a dependent variable using the independent variable.

In Chapter 2, you used the mean of a variable as the best guess of values on that variable and measured the sum of the squared distances between the true values and the mean in order to find out how much variation there was in the variable—how much error you would make in guessing the mean for all the cases. You came up with a single number that indicated how much variation there was in the variable.

We now want to see how much of that variation we can explain—how much less error we make in using a second variable to guess the values on the first. We want a measure of how much the independent variable improves our guesses. To the extent that two variables are related, we will make less error using the second variable as a guide in guessing than we did by guessing the mean. If two variables are unrelated, we will make just as much error.

EXERCISE 4 Determining the Amount of Error Making Best Guess from Mean

The first step in examining possible relationships between variables is to determine what the variation is on the dependent variables. Rather than calculating variation as you did in Chapter 2, do it a slightly different way, which is equivalent to what you did before, but which will make seeing the process easier.

First, calculate the mean of the dependent variable for the first relationship in the usual way. Add up the scores on the dependent variable and divide by the number of cases. Then find the point on the vertical axis of the first graph that represents the value of the mean; put a mark there and label it.

Now on the vertical axis of the same graph, mark each case's score on the dependent variable (disregarding the independent variable value), just as you marked the dependent variable mean; that is, find the point on the vertical line that represents the score of each case on the variable represented by the vertical line. Put a mark at that point; you will have as many marks as cases. (In case of two or more cases sharing the same score, put the marks close together on either side of the line.)

Third, still on that same graph, do the following: (1) count the number of squares between the mean and each case's actual value; (2) square the count; and (3) add the squared counts together. Remember, from calculating the variation in Chapter 2, that you square the distance between the score and the mean because your total distance would be zero if you did not; the scores are equally above and below the mean in distance. Just to add up the positive and negative differences between them and the mean would give you a zero.

As you are figuring out the variation this way, you don't have to be completely exact—just come close. You only have to figure out the variation in the dependent variable once because the dependent variable is the same on all three relationships. Enter the result on each page of the graph paper and label it as the error in guessing from the mean.

The result of summing the squared counts of distances from the mean is *roughly* the same result as you would have gotten from calculating the variation according to the formula for the variation which is repeated in Formula 4.1.

FORMULA 4.1 Squared Deviations of Scores from the Mean (error 1)

$$\text{Variation} = \sum (Y_i - \overline{Y})^2$$

Formula 4.1 is the same formula you used in Chapter 2 to calculate the variation except that "X" is changed to "Y," as the indication of the variable here, because we need to indicate that we are working on a *dependent* variable. The number represents how much variation there is in the dependent variable to be explained or, in equivalent terms, how much error there is in guessing the mean for each case. (We hope to explain this error by using the independent variable.)

EXERCISE 5 Drawing the Lines for the Best Guess from the Independent Variable

Now look back at each scatterplot you have done for this chapter. On the first, take a ruler and draw a straight line through the scatter of points. The straight line you draw should come as close as your eye can make it to all of the points, even if none of them is exactly on the line, and the line should intersect the vertical axis of the graph.

Your eye has already told you that the first relationship is positive. The line that represents a positive relationship starts lower on the left and goes up as it crosses the page to the right. The angle at which it goes up depends on the location of the points. Just try to make the angle of increase the one that will result in the line's being as close as possible to all the points. You can't be exact at this stage; just draw the line that best fits the points according to what you see. Figure 4.2 will give you an example.

Now draw lines for the second and third graphs. On the second, you have already decided the relationship is negative. Represent this by a line that is higher up the Y axis on the left side of the page where the X values are lower. The line will go down across the page so that at the right side, where X values are high, the line will represent low Y values.

On the third graph, you have decided that there is no relationship—that you can't guess any better knowing the independent variable value than you can by just knowing the mean. The line that comes closest to all the points on graph 3, therefore, is a line at the mean of Y—flat across the page. (Remember from Chapter 2 that the mean comes closer than any other value to all the scores on a single variable; here, if there is no relationship between X and Y, you don't improve your guesses any knowing the independent score, and so you might as well be guessing the mean.)

The lines you have drawn represent the pattern or form of the relationship between the

FIGURE 4.2 Scatterplot of a Positive Relationship

two variables. The height of the line above any score on the independent variable indicates a kind of mean of the dependent variable scores of all cases which share that score on the independent variable.*

We can, therefore, use the line to define what the "best guess" is that we can now make about a variable. Comparing the error we made when our best guess was the dependent variable mean to our best guess from the line will give us a measure of how much better we do knowing the independent variable. That measure will be our statistic of how strongly the two variables are related.

If we were handed a case and told the score that case had on the independent variable, we would locate that score on the horizontal axis, where the values are represented for the independent variable. We would then go up vertically from that point to the line and read across to the vertical axis (at the same height as the line) what score on the dependent variable we had reached. That score on Y would now be our best guess on that case. Examine Figure 4.3, where you are told that the independent variable has a score of 5. Go up from the 5 on the independent variable until you hit the line. Then read across to determine that the "best guess" score for Y on that case is 7. Still using Figure 4.3, notice that if $X = 4$, the "best guess" for Y is 6, etc. What is the "best guess" for Y if $X = 3$? If you said 5, you are ready to go on.

We also need a definition of the error we would make in our best guess comparable to our definition of the error that we would make from guessing the mean. When the mean was our best guess, error was defined as the squared distance from the mean to the true value of each case summed for all the cases. Now, using the line as our best guess, we define error as the difference between our best guess (the point on the line) and the real, true score

---

*Even if, theoretically, we don't have the cases immediately on hand to work with, we can say that we are using the cases we do have to estimate what the mean would be if we had more cases that had the same score on the independent variable.

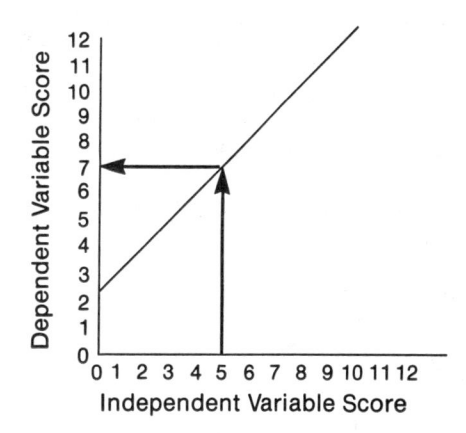

FIGURE 4.3 Reading Expected Dependent Variable Scores from Independent Variable Scores

of each case on the dependent variable, squared, and summed for all the cases.

We square the distance from the line to the actual score for much the same reason that we squared the distance from the mean to the actual score in the earlier definition of error. If we just added up the differences between the scores and the points on the line, we would get a zero. The line is the best guess precisely because it, like the mean, represents the guess for which we will make the least error—the guess that is closest to all the points. When the line has that property, the distance of all the points above it will equal the distance of all the points below it.

EXERCISE 6 Determining the Amount of Error Making the Best Guess from the Line

To find the error we would make when we know a case's score on the independent variable and guess its score on the dependent variable, go back to each scatterplot you've done in the exercises for this chapter. For each scatterplot, take each case and figure out the difference between the Y score represented by the line and the actual plotted Y score for that case, square that difference, and sum the squared differences for all the cases. For the moment, just come close; you don't have to be exact for the purposes of this exercise. In fact, you can just count the squares or fractions of squares vertically from the line to the point, square the count, and sum the results. Enter your result on each graph and label it the error in guessing from the line.

We can symbolize this operation as shown in Formula 4.2.

FORMULA 4.2 Squared Deviations of Scores from the Line (error 2)

$$\text{Error from the Line} = \Sigma(Y_i - Y_p)^2$$

Formula 4.2 means: (1) Take the actual score on the dependent variable for a case (Y_i); (2) subtract the score (Y_p) that is predicted by the line (use the independent variable score to tell you how far out the horizontal line to start for that case, go up vertically until you hit the line, and read across to the Y axis to find the score of Y predicted by the line); (3) square the difference; (4) do the same thing for each case; (5) sum the results. The result of this is the error you make when using the line as your best guess.

CALCULATING AND INTERPRETING A STATISTIC TO MEASURE THE RELATIONSHIP

Now we can use the two calculations of error to construct a measure that will communicate how much of the variation in the dependent variable we can explain using the independent variable, assuming that their relationship can be represented by a straight line like the ones we have drawn in over the points in the plot. The first calculation of error was *variation*—error made when our best guess was the mean. The second calculation of error was the error made when our best guess was from the position on a line determined by the value of a case on the independent variable. The measure that communicates how much we have reduced error knowing the independent variable is expressed simply in Formula 4.3.

FORMULA 4.3 Proportionate Reduction of Error Statistic

$$\text{PRE} = \frac{\text{Error by definition 1} - \text{Error by definition 2}}{\text{Error by definition 1}}$$

Notice how the *numerator* compares our error when we knew only the mean (definition 1), which is the same as variation, to the error we make when we know each case's value on another variable (definition 2). The statistic is measuring how much of that *variation* around the mean can be explained by the other variable.

If there's just as much error the second way of calculating it as the first, the numerator will equal zero. We reduce error by zero when the error doesn't go down. If there's much less error or even no error the second way of calculating it, the numerator approaches the value of the error by the first definition. We've reduced error by as much error as there was to begin with, or, in other words, we've explained all that variation.

However, how well we're doing in explaining variation depends, in part, on how much variation there was to explain. This is the denominator—the measure of overall variation. By dividing the amount of variation explained that is in the numerator by the total variation, we get the *proportion of variation explained*— a measure of how associated/related the two variables are.

EXERCISE 7 Calculating the Measure of Association

Before we go through this again (don't worry if you find you have to think it through several times), let's put the formula for the statistic in terms closer to the notation we've been using. Stop and examine it before going on. The steps for calculating this measure, which is equivalent to a formula you will see later for Pearson's r^2, are just below Formula 4.4. The given steps will help you think through the formula.

FORMULA 4.4 A PRE Measure for Interval Data

$$\text{PRE} = \frac{[\sum(Y_i - \bar{Y})^2] - [\sum(Y_i - Y_p)^2]}{\sum(Y_i - \bar{Y}_p)^2}$$

In order to calculate the measure of association yourself, use the numbers you have already written on each graph:

1. Take the variation you calculated. This is the amount of error in guessing you would make if you knew only the mean and tried to guess the score on the dependent variable for each case by guessing the mean. (For this exercise, you "computed" it by counting the squares between cases and the mean on the vertical axis, squaring the counts, and summing the results.)

$$\sum(Y_i - \bar{Y})^2$$

2. Subtract from that the error you had when you used the line as your best guess. This is the amount of error in guessing you would make if you knew the score of a case on the independent variable and knew the line and tried to make your best guess from knowing the independent variable's score. (For this exercise, you "computed" it by counting squares between cases and the line, squaring the counts, and summing the results.)

$$\sum(Y_i - Y_p)^2$$

3. Divide the difference by the variation.

$$\sum(Y_i - \bar{Y})^2$$

4. Write your result on each of the graphs and label it "measure of association."

You would interpret this statistic as the proportion of variation in the dependent variable explained by the independent variable and a linear relationship. In effect, the *numerator* of the statistic is the amount of variation explained (i.e., the *overall* variation *minus* the *remaining* variation—the remaining variation that cannot be attributed to the independent variable "causing" the variation and must be attributed to other "causes" or error, which we don't know). The *denominator* is the overall variation. Thus, dividing the two gives you the *proportion* of explained variation.

Another way of thinking about it is the *proportionate reduction of error* knowing the independent variable as compared to not knowing it. Statistics that have this interpretation are known as PRE statistics, and you will be seeing others as we progress through later chapters.

By moving the decimal in the statistic two places to the right, you change *proportion* into *percentage*. You can then interpret the statistic as the percentage of variation explained or the percentage by which error was reduced. The statistic will never exceed 1.0. You cannot explain a proportion greater than 1.0 or a percentage greater than 100%. The statistic will never be lower than zero because you can never explain a negative proportion or percentage. You cannot do worse in your explanation than guessing the mean. (If you did get a minus in your calculations on Exercise 3, it's because the flat line wasn't located exactly at the mean; in real calculations that won't happen.)

You will quickly see that if two variables are unrelated, as in the case of the third scatterplot, the amount of error around the line is almost the same as the amount of error around the mean. You can see this by comparing your plot on the vertical axis alone to the plot in both the horizontal and vertical space. The scatter of scores up and down around the mean or up and down around the line looks roughly the same. The numerator of the statistic becomes zero (or near that), indicating that you have not reduced your error in guessing the dependent variable scores when you know the independent variable as compared to when you do not know it. To put it another way, you have not explained any of the variation in the dependent variable. The independent variable does not help at all in explaining why some cases are above the mean and why some are below it. The independent variable does not help us understand why all cases are not alike on the dependent variable.

You will also see that the more closely related the two variables are, the higher the proportion of explained variation, and the higher the r^2 statistic is. The closer the cases are to the line we have used to describe the relationship, the higher the r^2. The independent variable does a pretty good job of telling us what to guess on the dependent variable; i.e., the relationship between the two variables is pretty strong, and there is not much error in our guesses. Cases still lie above or below where they are predicted to be but not by very far.

Conversely, the further cases are from the line—the less clustered about the line—the lower the r^2. As cases are scattered, we can think that there remains a lot of variation we haven't explained. We don't know why some cases are above and some are below where they are predicted to be. It may be just error, or it may be variation that might be explained by other independent variables which we have not examined in the analysis at hand.

Visualize the closeness of the relationship by thinking about how far from the line most of the cases fall. Imagine lines drawn parallel to the line you have been using for prediction. In your imagination, visualize these lines taking in most of the cases even if a few extreme cases lie outside this boundary.

Now imagine how far from the mean the scores were as you sketched them on the vertical axis of the graphs. (Even here you may want to think about how far most of the scores are from the mean, eliminating any that are terribly extreme.) Think about how much closer the scores are to the line than they were to the mean, especially as they were in the first example. They were less so in the second. Think about how there is no difference between the scatter around the mean and the scatter around the line when two variables are not related. The difference between the width of the scatter on the vertical axis around the mean and the width of the scatter about the line is analogous to how much variation we have explained. Remember that this is not at all mathematically exact; it is just a way to help you see what is going on.

If you can imagine an analysis where all the cases fall exactly on the line, where our best guess for a case's score would be exactly the same as the true score of the case on the dependent variable, you can see that the proportion of explained variation would be 1.00, as in Figure 4.4.

In Figure 4.4, the difference between the predicted dependent variable scores and the actual scores on the dependent variable would be zero. Thus, the $\Sigma (Y_i - Y_p)^2$ element of the numerator would be zero, leaving the numerator and denominator identical at $\Sigma (Y_i - \overline{Y})^2$. The fraction that represents the statistic would then be 1.00.

RESIDUALS

Later on in the text, we will reconsider the question of how far cases lie off the straight line that we have used to describe the relationship between X and Y. The vertical distance off the line is called the *residual* because it represents the part of the score of a case on the dependent variable that is left over—that part which the independent variable cannot explain. As indicated above, the distance between the true Y score of a case and its predicted Y score may just be error, perhaps some kind of error in our measurement of the variable. That distance between the true score on Y and the Y score predicted by X, however, may represent variation in Y that can be explained by other independent variables. Later on, we will be adding independent variables to the analysis to see if we can explain those resid-

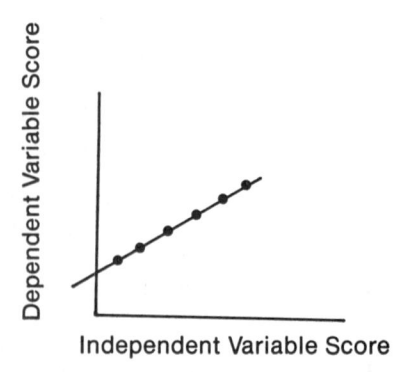

FIGURE 4.4 Scatterplot of a Perfect Relationship

uals that the initial independent variable could not.

USES OF THE MEASURE OF ASSOCIATION AND LIMITATIONS

In social sciences, you will rarely see a relationship as perfect as the one in Figure 4.4. Because we deal with phenomena with many different causes, because we cannot measure as exactly as we would like to and have to deal with error in our measurement as well as in the relationships we describe, we generally cannot explain 100% of the variation in any dependent variable. The closer we come to 1.00 in our PRE statistic, however, the more we can argue that we have explained the variation in our dependent variables. (Keep in mind, though, that whether an explanation is good or bad depends on much more than how closely related the two variables are. You may want to review Chapter 1 now for some of the criteria for a good hypothesis and explanation.)

One of the advantages of this statistic is that it allows you to communicate to yourself and a reader just what the relationship between the variables (the bivariate distribution) looks like without plotting it out on a scatterplot, just as knowing the mean and standard deviation allows communication about the distribution of a single variable (the univariate distribution). You know that numbers closer to 1.0 represent cases closely clustered around a straight line; all other things being equal, numbers closer to 0 represent cases scattered farther. The closer to 1.0, the stronger the *linear* relationship between the two variables; the closer to 0, the weaker the relationship between the two variables.

EXERCISE 8 Problems with Curved Relationships

It is important to note that we have been measuring the distance of cases off a *straight* line. If the relationship between X and Y is not a straight-line relationship, the r^2 statistic will give you misleading results.

Look at an example in order to see what we mean. Use the data in the exercise section for the fourth relationship. On another piece of graph paper, draw your axes and indicate the scales of measurement on each. Plot the cases on the two variables. You will be able to see that X and Y are very clearly, systematically related to each other. Think about stating a hypothesis that might predict such a relationship between the two variables.

Try to draw a straight line that comes as close as possible to all the points. You will be forced to draw an almost flat line that falls almost at the mean of the dependent variable; and that flat line suggests that there is no relationship between the variables, even though you can clearly see one—a curved one.

Notice that the r^2 statistic has the same problem as the line you have drawn. Figure out the proportionate reduction of error just as you did for your other graphs. Count the squares between each case's true Y score and the Y score predicted for it by the straight line. Square the difference. Sum the squared differences for all the cases. Subtract that from the overall variation. Divide the difference by the overall variation. You will see that the r^2 is nearly zero. That would suggest to a reader that there is no relationship between the two variables, but you would not want to report such a misleading description of the relationship.

Theoretically, we could plot our cases, look at the scatter, draw a *curved* line that comes closest to all the points, figure distance of true values from that line, square the distance, and sum it. Think, for a minute, about some other relationships that might logically be curved.

Imagine trying to explain the feeling that citizens can influence the government (efficacy) by a measure of party identification that may have values from zero for the strongest Democrat, through 50 for independents, to 100 for the strongest Republican. We might expect the Republicans to be more efficacious than the Democrats but also expect party identifiers to be more efficacious than indepen-

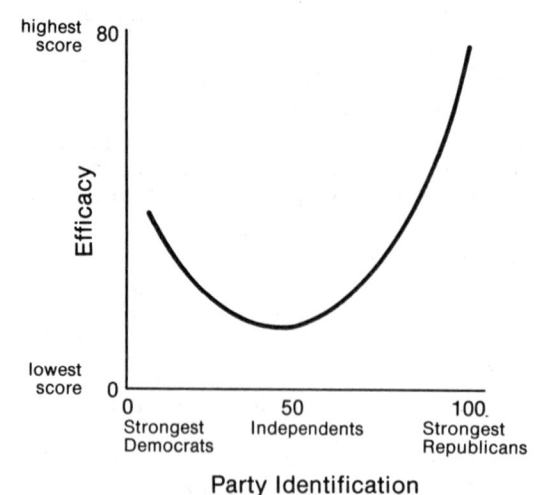

FIGURE 4.5 A Hypothetical Curved Relationship

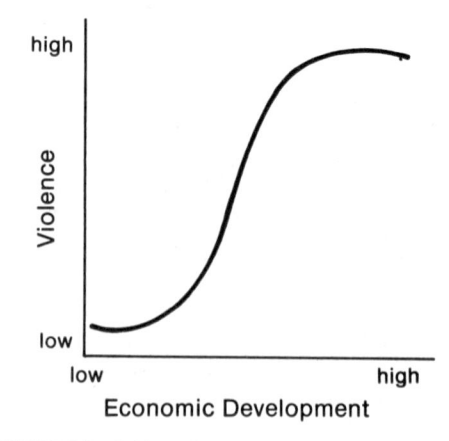

FIGURE 4.6 A Hypothetical Curved Relationship

dents. If that were the case, the relationship would look something like that shown in Figure 4.5.

Theoretically, we could figure out how much we've reduced our error—just as you did on the graph paper plots—by comparing the real scores to those that fit the curved line we draw which seems to fit the data.

Similarly, we could imagine a kind of "threshold effect." Perhaps we could hypothesize that violence in a country will remain low until a certain level of economic development is reached; violence would then increase as economic development increased up to a certain point of development; and then it would level off. Such a relationship would look something like that shown in Figure 4.6.

Again, it is logical that we could measure our error in prediction off the curved line just as you measured error off the straight lines you drew on your scatterplots. We could then see how much of the variation we explained by the independent variable and the curved line representing the relationship.

The problem with dealing with anything other than straight lines, however, is getting some precision in locating the line where it provides the best possible fit to all the points. There are relatively simple methods of locating the best fitting *straight* line, as you will see shortly, but curves are much harder to work with. Therefore, we often use straight lines to describe relationships that have some small amount of curve to them. There is more error around a straight than a curved line when the values themselves lie in something of a curve. If the additional error is not too great, however, we often just tolerate it.

One criterion for a good explanation of a phenomenon is that it be simple. (We know we are never going to explain each and every little difference across cases. What we are after is a generalization that encompasses many cases.) If the curve in a relationship is not so great as to discredit a straight-line explanation, we sometimes go for the simpler straight line in the name of parsimony. You will also learn another way to deal with curved relationships in Chapter 7.

Sometimes there are modifications of the scores themselves that we can do which have the effect of straightening out a curved-line relationship. That, however, is a topic for a more advanced text than this one.

Before going on, be sure to note that the PRE statistic we have discussed here is for *interval* data. We need interval measurement because calculating the statistic requires that we subtract the mean or the predicted value from the true value. To get the mean, we have to add values on the variable. Those arithmetic operations logically require interval data. To apply this statistic to lower-level data can give you misleading results unless you know what you are doing.

Now you need a more precise way to locate the line that best describes the relationship between X and Y, and you need a better measure of just how strong that relationship is. It is to those tasks that we will turn in Chapter 5.

EXERCISES

In Exercise 1, you will treat efficacy (variable 1) as the dependent variable and the number of years involved (variable 2) as the independent variable. For Exercise 2, you will again use efficacy as the dependent variable and social distance (variable 3) as the independent variable. For Exercise 3, you will use efficacy again as the dependent variable and income (variable 4) as the independent variable. Later on in the chapter, in Exercise 8, you will again use efficacy as the dependent variable and knowledge (variable 5) as the independent variable.

Hypothetical operationalizations of all the variables follow. These may make what you are doing seem a bit more realistic. You will need to refer to them for writing your hypotheses.

Operationalizations (Hypothetical) for Variable 1 through Variable 5

Variable 1 is efficacy in affecting the activities of a political party, i.e., whether a person feels he or she has power to influence decisions. Imagine now we had six questions designed to indicate whether a person felt he or she could have influence on party activities. We gave the person one point for a nonefficacious answer, two points for a partially efficacious answer, and three points for a totally efficacious answer. (Remember that for interval data we merely need equal intervals; zero isn't necessary.) We then summed the points in order to get one measure of efficacy. Therefore, 14 might represent two nonefficacious answers, zero partially efficacious answers, and four totally efficacious answers:

Hypothetical Data from a Hypothetical Group of Active Political Party Members to Be Used in Examining Relationships among Variables

Case Number	Variable 1 Efficacy	Variable 2 Years Involved	Variable 3 Social Distance	Variable 4 Income	Variable 5 Knowledge
1	6	3	13	4	1
2	9	5	8	7	23
3	6	2	19	22	25
4	9	6	22	14	3
5	11	12	1	9	6
6	8	9	15	12	2
7	12	14	4	13	8
8	9	12	19	19	24
9	14	18	3	5	12
10	11	19	11	2	20
11	14	20	9	21	14
12	13	23	6	16	17

$(2 \times 1) + (0 \times 2) + (4 \times 3)$.

Or 11 might represent two nonefficacious answers, three partially efficacious answers, and one totally efficacious answer:

$(2 \times 1) + (3 \times 2) + (1 \times 3)$, etc.

Variable 2 is, hypothetically, a measure of the number of years a person has been actively involved in a political party organization.

Variable 3 is, hypothetically, a measure of social distance between the respondent and the chair of the political party organization. Imagine that for good theoretical reasons we assigned points to each respondent according to the following scheme and summed the points to get a measure of social distance from the chair.

> 1 point for each five years of age respondent is removed from chair
> 1 point for each $5,000 income discrepancy between respondent and chair
> 1 point for each observed disagreement over procedural or issue questions between respondent and chair—six-month period
> 1 point for each monthly meeting respondent has missed in six-month period
> 1 point for each year of formal education that separates the respondent from chair
> 2 points for different sex—respondent and chair
> 1 point for each five years of difference in county residency between respondent and chair
> 1 point if respondent and chair are from two different towns within the county
> 2 points for different race—respondent and chair
> −1 point for each committee respondent serves on with chair
> −1 point for each committee respondent chairs
> −1 point for party office held by respondent
> −1 point for each special meeting called by chair that respondent attends

Variable 4 is, hypothetically, a measure of income. Imagine that the lowest income among our respondents was $18,000 and we assigned that case a 1. For incomes above $18,000, we assigned one additional point per $1,000 extra. (Notice no case has a score of 1 in this example. Pretend it was "missing data" on the dependent variable. Sometimes, when we don't have data on a case for one variable or another, we have to drop that case from analysis.)

Variable 5 is, hypothetically, a measure of knowledge about the affairs of the party. Let us assume that we cannot measure knowledge directly, so we therefore use the *surrogate* measure of the number of hours the respondent has spent in special party-education sessions. (A surrogate is a measure that, while not ideal, is probably associated with a better measure of the same concept were we able to find and use one.) Here, then, we have measured the total number of hours each respondent has spent in meetings that were designed to instruct the respondent in the workings of the party.

SUGGESTED READINGS

Those listed for chapter 5 are also appropriate here.

CHAPTER 5

CALCULATING PEARSON'S r^2 AND RELATED STATISTICS

Now that you're beginning to get a feel for measuring the strength of a straight-line relationship and the problems of dealing with curved ones, you need to learn a more precise way of calculating the linear PRE statistic for measuring the strength of a relationship and a more exact way of locating the best-fitting straight line so that you can more precisely (than by just eyeballing the data) report the form of the relationship. It may seem more complicated at first, but the logic is similar to what you've already done.

INTERPRETING PEARSON'S r^2

The PRE statistic that you've already calculated, by counting and squaring the number of squares on graph paper, is a rough estimation equivalent to Pearson's r^2, Formula 5.1.

FORMULA 5.1   Pearson's r^2

$$r^2 = \frac{[\Sigma(X_i - \overline{X})(Y_i - \overline{Y})]^2}{[\Sigma(X_i - \overline{X})^2][\Sigma(Y_i - \overline{Y})^2]}$$

The different way of writing the formula here may give you a better intuitive grasp of what the statistic measures if you examine it bit by bit.

In the numerator, you see that the independent variable score is compared to the mean of the independent variable for each case ($X_i - \overline{X}$). That difference is multiplied by the dependent variable score compared to its mean ($Y_i - \overline{Y}$). If X is above the mean on the same case for which Y is above the mean, the two large positive numbers will give you a large positive product for that case. Extending that same situation, if X is below the mean on the same case for which Y is below the mean, the multiplication of the two negatives will give you a large positive product for that case. Therefore, the more cases you have in which X and Y are high together or low together, the larger that numerator will be when the products are summed across all the cases.

There's another way to get a large numerator for this statistic. If the X scores are consistently above the mean on cases whose Y scores are below the mean, you'll get a large numerator when the products for the cases are summed (but with a negative sign). And remember the extension: when X scores are consistently below the mean on cases whose Y scores are above the mean, you'll get a large numerator with a negative sign when the products are summed for all the cases. Notice that the negative sign disappears when the summation of the products is itself squared. (A negative multiplied by a negative gives a positive.) r^2 cannot be negative.

Any *linear* way (either positively or negatively) that X and Y vary, together and systematically, will give you a large absolute (disregarding the sign) value on that numerator. This is equivalent to saying that anytime knowing the score of X helps you predict the score of Y in a linear relationship, the numerator is bigger.

If scores on X don't relate systematically to scores on Y in a linear fashion, however, you'll get a low or, perhaps, zero numerator; that is, if on many cases X is above its mean and Y is above its mean, but on as many cases X is above its mean and Y is below its mean, the score on X doesn't link systematically with any particular scores on Y. In such a situation, the numerator will be near zero. This is equivalent to saying that anytime knowing the score on X does not help you predict the score on Y, the numerator is smaller.

Notice that when *both* low and high scores on the independent variable link with high scores of the dependent variable, and medium values of the independent link with low values of the dependent, as in the party identification/efficacy example in Chapter 4, you will also get a near zero numerator with this formula. Cases on which X is above its mean and Y is above its mean, yielding a large positive product, will be canceled out by cases on which X is below its mean and Y is above its mean, yielding a large negative product; cases where both X and Y are near their means will yield a near zero product and contribute nothing to the summation.

You will also get a low numerator if one of the variables is very homogeneous. The distance off the mean will be very small for all the cases in such a distribution, and those deviations won't contribute much to the numerator.

You can see that there are three ways to get a low or near zero numerator: (1) no systematic relationship between the values of X and Y; (2) a systematic but curved relationship between X and Y; and (3) a variable with little variation in it.

The quantities that make up the denominator should be familiar to you by now. The first is just the variation in X, that is, $\Sigma (X_i - \overline{X})^2$. The second is the variation in Y, that is, $\Sigma (Y_i - \overline{Y})^2$.

Pearson's r^2 can be interpreted, therefore, as the *linear covariation* between X and Y relative to the *product of the variations* in X and Y. *Covariation* is the numerator (how much X and Y *co*vary systematically and linearly); the product of X's and Y's *separate variations* is in the denominator.

We're back to something very similar to the "how much of the variation in Y is *explained* variation?" question used in Chapter 4, phrased now as "how much (what fraction) of the variation in X and Y is shared (co)variation?" The earlier formulation—error not knowing the independent minus error knowing the independent, and the result divided by error not knowing the independent—gives exactly the same answer as this formula for Pearson's r^2 if, in figuring error, a precise prediction of the dependent variable has been used. Thus, your earlier work (were it exact) would give you identical results to calculating with this formula. And the interpretations are exactly equivalent, if a bit differently phrased.

CALCULATING PEARSON'S r^2

To use this formula above to calculate r^2, go through the following steps:

1. Calculate the mean of the X scores and, beginning with the first case, subtract that mean of X from the score on the independent variable for each case, $(X_i - \overline{X})$.
2. Next, calculate the mean of the Y scores, and subtract that mean of Y from the score on the dependent variable for each case, $(Y_i - \overline{Y})$.
3. Next, multiply the two differences (the result of step 1 for each case and the result of step 2 for each case) together for each case.

$$(X_i - \overline{X})(Y_i - \overline{Y})$$

4. Sum the products (the result of step 3 for each case) of all the cases.

$$\Sigma (X_i - \overline{X})(Y_i - \overline{Y})$$

5. Square the result of step 4.

$$[\Sigma (X_i - \overline{X})(Y_i - \overline{Y})]^2$$

6. Figure the variation in X and, separately, the variation in Y as you did in Chapter 2.

$$\Sigma (X_i - \overline{X})^2; \ \Sigma (Y_i - \overline{Y})^2$$

7. Multiply the two variations from step 6 together.

$$[\Sigma (X_i - \overline{X})^2][\Sigma (Y_i - \overline{Y})^2]$$

8. Divide the result of step 5 by the result of step 7. Round off the answer to no more than two decimal places.

$$\frac{[\Sigma (X_i - \overline{X})(Y_i - \overline{Y})]^2}{[\Sigma (X_i - \overline{X})^2][\Sigma (Y_i - \overline{Y})^2]}$$

Take a minute to look over those steps. Compare them to Formula 5.1 to help you in reading it. (Note: do the operation inside the innermost parentheses first, working out.)

EXERCISE 1 Calculating r^2 from the Formula

You really need to do a few of these r^2 statistics by hand to get a good grasp of what's going on, so work with the same data you used in Chapter 4 for the scatterplots. Calculate r^2 for at least two of the relationships in the Chapter 4 exercises. Just work slowly through each step of the formula. Show each step of the work as you go along. Remember that neatness will, in the long run, save you time and errors. There are many different figures here, so it's important for you to keep columns straight and clearly labeled. Also be sure to indicate which relationships you are working on.

As you work these statistics out, *notice* what's happening. Remember that relationship 1 is a positive relationship. Notice, as you are working on that one, how those cases that have high X scores tend to have high Y scores, and those cases that have low X scores tend to have low Y scores. Notice how such cases contribute heavily to the numerator and how high the proportion of variance explained is for cases as tightly scattered about the line as these are.

Remember that relationship 2 is a negative one. While you are working on this exercise, notice how those cases on which X is high and Y is low, along with those cases on which X is low and Y is high, contribute greatly to the size of the numerator. Notice that the sum of the products is negative before you square it. Notice that the proportion of variation explained is pretty high but (remember how scattered those points were) not close to 1.0.

Remember that relationship 3 is near zero. Here, notice how little each case contributes to the sum in the numerator. There is no pattern to the XY product, so each case generally contributes relatively little to the sum of the products. Even when you do see high absolute numbers in those products, you soon find that positive ones are canceled out by negative ones.

Remember that relationship 4 is also near zero but for a different reason. Notice how the pattern you can see when you look at the scatterplot is canceled out in the calculation of a statistic that is based on the degree to which X and Y covary linearly.

As you work, remember what it felt like to plot those values. On the first two scatterplots, you probably began to feel, after only four or five cases, where to move your hand just by looking at the score on the independent variable. On scatterplot 1, you probably felt your hand moving up and to the right when you saw a high X value or down and to the left when you saw a low X value. On scatterplot 2, the negative relationship, you probably felt your hand moving down and to the right when you saw a high X score or up and to the left when you saw a low X score. On scatterplot 3, you probably had to go more slowly because you couldn't guess, even after half the cases, where to move your hand when you saw particular X scores. On scatterplot 4, you might have felt that the Y score was likely to be low when X was either high or low.

Pay attention while you work on the calculations, too, so the feel of the statistic becomes clear to you. Once you have finished the calculations, compare your results to those you estimated earlier for the same data. They should be in the same ball park, at least, even though the estimates were far less precise than the calculations from the formula.

MORE ON INTERPRETING PEARSON'S r^2

Remember that r^2 is read as the proportion of variation in Y explained by X or as the proportion of the variation in X and Y that is covariation. When the r^2 you get is high, you can be fairly sure that there is a strong linear relationship between the two variables.

There are exceptions to which you should be alert. The most likely is that a few extreme cases can inflate the value of r^2 and make you think you have a much stronger relationship than you do. Remember the skewed distributions in Chapter 2? We mentioned there that extreme scores had an effect on the variance out of proportion to their numbers. And we suggested the same problems would face us with all variance-based statistics. Here we see the problem again if there are extreme cases on both of the variables in the relationship. If you have a few cases that are way above the means of both variables (or way below the means of both variables), they can have an impact on the total amount of measured covariation far out of proportion to their numbers. Analogous to the effect that squaring the difference between the true score and mean has in inflating calculations of the variance, the effect of multiplying two large differences together in the measure of covariation is to indicate a very large amount of covariation for those few cases and, as a consequence, to inflate r^2.

Consider this example shown in Figure 5.1. There is practically no relation between X and Y in the large group of cases on the left of the illustration. An r^2 calculated on just those cases would be near zero. But the two extreme cases, *outliers*, will distort, and inflate, the r^2.

In such a circumstance, you could be misled

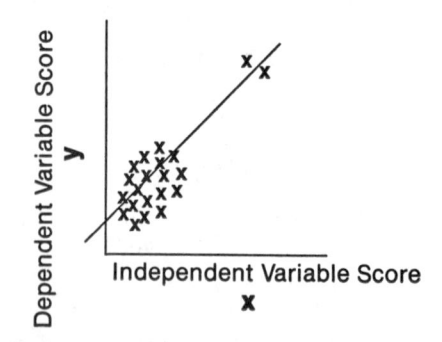

FIGURE 5.1 Extreme Cases Distorting Pearson's r^2

into thinking there was an overall relationship between X and Y if you just calculated an r^2. You always need to examine a plot of the cases on the two variables and look for such outliers.

If they are there, you can, possibly, gather more cases that have scores which will fill in the range of the independent variable so that you can see how other cases would fall. Also consider these other possibilities. You can examine whether some kind of coding or data entry error made those cases extreme and fix the error. You can discard the outliers on the grounds that they are too odd to consider. Or you can argue that, if you had more cases to fill in the gap, they would probably fall along the line anyway; thus, your argument would continue, the inflated r^2 is representative of what you would get if you had more cases. Obviously, the last strategy is risky and depends on a very good theoretical argument.

Just as a high Pearson's r^2 usually suggests either of two possibilities in the data—a strong, meaningful, linear relationship or a measure inflated by outliers—a low or near zero Pearson's r^2 can result from more than one condition of the data. The most obvious possibility is that the two variables are not related. Another is that the two are related but in a curve. Another possibility is that the variance in one of the variables was low; if there's little variance on a variable (i.e., if the cases are fairly homogeneous on one of the variables), the r^2 can be lower than it would be if you had been able to get cases much more heterogeneously spread out along a greater range of the variable. Think back to your plot in Exercise 2 of Chapter 4. Imagine you had only the six cases that were lowest on X—i.e., that the variance in X was very low. With only those cases, you would not be able to discern any relationship between the two variables.

When you get a low r^2, it's a good idea to examine a bivariate plot of the cases, looking for evidence of a curved relationship, and to examine the plots or the standard deviations, looking for overly homogeneous cases, before deciding that the hypothesized relationship doesn't exist. If the problem is in low variance, the solution may be to go back to the operational definition of the concept to construct a measure with more variance. Or maybe you don't have cases for study that have all the possible scores on your variable; perhaps you can collect a greater variety of cases on that variable. If the concept *itself* doesn't imply much variance, you may just be stuck with a low r^2.

There are other reasons for getting a low r^2. One is that there are so many other "causes" of the dependent that you can't see much association with your independent variable; the other causes are making cases vary all over the place. Another possibility is that some single other variable is suppressing the real relationship between your independent and dependent variable. Analyzing these possibilities will have to wait until we get to Chapters 12 and 13. Finally, measurement error can contribute to low correlations—a reason always to measure as precisely as possible.

INTERPRETING PEARSON'S r, THE CORRELATION COEFFICIENT

As indicated above in the discussion of the formula, when you have a negative relationship, the numerator of r^2 is negative before you square it. While no sign is used on r^2, the sign *is* used when Pearson's r (the square root of r^2) is reported. The correlation coefficient, r, is not as neatly interpretable as r^2, but you will frequently see it in the literature, especially because it can indicate a positive or negative relationship. $+1.0$ on r is a perfect positive relationship; -1.0 is a perfect negative relationship; and 0 is indicative of no linear relationship between the variables at all. Remember, however, it is r^2—not r—that is interpreted as the proportion of variation in the dependent variable which is explained by the independent variable and the straight-line relationship.

About the only way to interpret the r (not r^2) between 0 and 1 is to say things like "moderate relationship," "strong relationship," "weak relationship," etc. Such interpretations are clearly judgment calls and depend on the kind of data you have and many other factors. Unless you need a statistic that has a clear positive or negative sign, it's easier to use r^2 so that you can talk about proportion of explained variation.

What constitutes a moderate, a strong, or a weak relationship? Put equivalently in r^2 terms, how great a proportion of explained variation constitutes a weak explanation as opposed to an adequate explanation? Unfortunately, there is no easy answer to this, and all the complex answers boil down to whether you and your scientific colleagues, as experienced researchers with thorough knowledge of the literature and past practice, are satisfied that the statistic you got represents a weak, moderate, or a strong relationship.

There are some rules-of-thumb to guide you. (1) Individual level data will generally yield lower correlations than aggregate data. (*Aggregate data* are variables measured at the group level—like median income of a county or percent literate in a country—rather than measured on individuals—like individual income or whether the individual is or is not literate.) (2) Smaller groups of cases generally require higher measures of association before a relationship is considered strong than would larger groups of cases. (3) Data with a great deal of measurement error in them will generally yield lower measures of association than will data with less measurement error.

These rules-of-thumb, however, are just that—guidelines. In Chapter 18, you will learn how to tell if a particular correlation coefficient (r) is likely to be due to chance, but that statistical procedure will not relieve you of the burden of making the determination that a particular correlation coefficient (or its square, the proportion of variation explained) is *worth* interpreting. That judgment about the substantive importance of a particular correlation will be an informed one, made in the light of knowledge of theory and literature, but it is a judgment call just the same.

CALCULATING THE REGRESSION COEFFICIENT (SLOPE) AND INTERCEPT

Now that you know how to calculate the measure of the *strength of association* between the two variables, we can turn to the calculation of the statistics that describe *the form of the pattern in which the two variables are associated*—statistics that will locate that straight line which best describes the relationship. Ninety percent of the calculating has already been done; you'll just have to plug already calculated figures into formula.

EXERCISE 2 Calculating the Regression Statistics

All you need in order to draw the best-fitting straight line through the points is to know two things: how much to increment the line as you go across and where to start. Following the two formulae below will give you those two quantities that will determine the straight line which reduces the summed squared distance between the points and the line to a minimum—and that is our definition of "best fitting." It is the straight line that will allow us to guess the scores on the dependent variable with less error than with any other straight line. (In the same way, the mean allowed us to guess the dependent scores with less error than would have accumulated in guessing any other single value, as you saw in Chapter 2.)

How much to raise or lower the line for each one-unit increase in the value of the independent variable as you go across is called the *slope* or the *regression coefficient* and is designated "b." It is probably the most important statistic we have in political science research because it summarizes the linear effect that one variable has on another. It describes the form of any linear relationships between the variables in the hypotheses we are testing and the explanations of phenomena we are trying to construct. Since we are describing a straight line, the b is the same all across the range of the independent variable under consideration. A one-unit change in the independent variable has the same effect, regardless of whether it is in the low range of X or in the high range of X.

In Formula 5.2, you will once again see that we are measuring the covariation of X and Y—how much X and Y vary together. We also get the direction of that covariation—positive or negative—because, unlike the measure of the strength of association r^2, the covariation is not squared; thus, we don't lose the sign that indicates the direction of the relationship. Therefore, b will tell you how much to go up (or down) across the plot as you go up each unit on the independent variable.

FORMULA 5.2 The Regression Coefficient (Slope)

$$b = \frac{\Sigma(X_i - \bar{X})(Y_i - \bar{Y})}{\Sigma(X_i - \bar{X})^2}$$

Where to start the line on the Y axis (the vertical axis that represents values on the dependent variable) is called the "Y intercept" and is designated "a." Formula 5.3 shows the calculation of a.

FORMULA 5.3 The Intercept

$$a = \frac{\Sigma Y_i - b\Sigma X_i}{N} \quad \text{or} \quad a = \bar{Y} - b\bar{X}$$

Now compute a and b for the data you used to compute r^2. Notice that to compute b you will use many of the same quantities you used to compute r^2. Show all the steps on the calculations as you go along so that your instructor can check to make sure you are doing the substitutions into the formulae correctly.

VISUAL PRESENTATIONS OF THE BEST-FITTING LINE

EXERCISE 3 Drawing Slopes from the Statistics

While you need to compute b in order to figure out a, once you've got the intercept figured out, drawing the line in can be done more easily than incrementing it by b units of Y for each unit of the independent variable. It happens that the "best-fitting" line, under the definition of best fitting used above, will pass through the point that represents the mean of X and the mean of Y. If you have calculated the intercept, and if you locate the point represented by the two means, you have the two points necessary to draw a straight line.

Now, use another piece of graph paper (or paper that you have made into graph paper) such as the type you used in Chapter 4, and draw an X and Y axis for each of the relationships for which you calculated the intercept and slope. There is no need this time, however, to plot the scores of the cases on the two variables. Label the axes with the variable names; indicate several values along the scale on each axis. (Use the same scale—i.e., draw the axes for the plots—the same way you did for the plots in the last chapter).

For each of the relationships, locate the position of the intercept (a) on the vertical axis, and mark it. Mark the position of the X mean on the horizontal axis and the position of the Y mean on the vertical. Going up from X and across from Y, find the place where they intersect and mark it. With a ruler, connect the intercept (a) and the point at which the means intersect.

INTERPRETING THE INTERCEPT AND SLOPE

These two statistics, a and b, give us a more exact way of predicting the dependent value for any given value of the independent variable than from just reading it off the line. For any given value of X, you can predict what value that case will have on Y from the formula for the predicted value of Y (Y_p): $Y_p = a + bX + e$.

That equation simply means that the best guess for any case's score on Y can be found by adding the value of the intercept to the product of the regression coefficient (slope) and the case's X score, expecting some residual error ($+ e$). Since b represents how much the line goes up each time X goes up by one point, bX indicates that Y has gone up X times from zero, going up b amount for each of those X increments. Since Y was greater than zero when X was zero—a represents how much greater Y was than zero—that a amount has to be added to the bX; that is, when Y started going up, it was already at a.

Notice that, when the relationship between the two variables is negative, as it was in relationship 2 in the exercises, the slope has a negative sign, and the formula becomes:

$$Y_p = a - bX + e.$$

Notice as well that, when there is no linear relationship, the value of the regression coefficient (slope) is at or near zero just as the measure of association, r^2, was. In such a case, the bX quantity will also be at or near zero, and the formula will become: $Y_p = a + e$.

Or, if we look back a minute at the formula for a ($a = \overline{Y} - b\overline{X}$), we can see that, when there is no linear relationship, $Y_p = \overline{Y}$. If there is no linear relationship between the two variables, we cannot improve our prediction by using the independent variable over just predicting the mean. The intercept will be at the mean, and the line will go through the mean of Y; that is, the line will be flat.

You will not get a numeric value for e in the formulae above. It is there to remind you that the predicted values will not be exact, that there are other "causes" of the dependent variable you are interested in or error of other kinds in your predictions; e indicates that you ought to expect residual error in any prediction.

EXERCISE 4 Locating Predicted Values of Y

Go back now to the graphs on which you drew in the regression lines, knowing only the intercepts and the means of the independent and dependent variables. For the relationship indicated by each of them, pick three scores of the independent variable—any scores in the range of X scores; they don't even have to be scores that any of your cases actually had.

Use each of the scores you have picked to predict the score on the dependent variable you would expect a case with that score on the independent variable to have. To do that, create your own $Y_p = a + bX + e$ equation for each graph, putting the values you have calculated for a and b in that relationship into the proper positions. Then substitute the first score you have selected for the independent variable in place of X in the first prediction equation. Solve for Y_p, and repeat the process for each of three scores on the independent variable represented on the first graph. Then repeat the process for the scores you have picked for the independent variable on the second graph.

Now plot the independent variable score and the predicted dependent score on the graphs of the regression lines. Notice how the line and the equation give you the same predicted score on Y from any particular value of X. Later on, we will be using just the equation to predict the scores on Y, but always remember that there is that straight-line relationship underlying all the analysis we do with the slope, intercept, and r^2 statistics.

SOME CHARACTERISTICS OF a, b, AND r

We will be calling attention to more characteristics of these two statistics as we go along, but there are a few important things to note right now. This may be one of those sections to which you will want to return as you get more practice with regression. While it may be a bit advanced, in part, for so early in the course, the ideas in it logically fit into a discussion of bivariate regression. It is probably a good idea for you to begin to get a handle on some of these ideas. At least, read through this section and know that these things are explained here.

Then you can return to it as you need the information.

1. The intercept, a, tells us the value of Y when X is equal to zero. You can interpret it as how much Y we would expect, perhaps from other causes, before the influence of X begins (although you need to be cautious about "cause" in the absence of good theory). One can also interpret it as a kind of "base level" of Y.

Notice how much the value of a depends on how the dependent variable is measured. If your dependent variable is, say, "income," a is going to be quite different if income is measured in dollars as compared to when it is measured in thousands of dollars. (The measure of association, r or r^2, however, stays the same, regardless of the scale on which the variables are measured.)

2. There are conditions under which the intercept is not very interpretable and may be very confusing. If there is a large gap between the value zero and the lowest value present in the sample on the independent variable, a can appear to have rather mysterious values. This sometimes happens when the independent variable is "year" measured in its usual calendar designation (1980, 1982, 1984, etc.) and when the first data point is at 1896 rather than at zero. In such a case, the a value is likely to be quite negative when the relationship is positive or apparently "super high" when the relationship is negative.

The easiest solution for this mysterious intercept is to subtract a constant from the values of the independent variable so that the lowest value is 1. In the example of the years, I'd subtract 1895 from every value on the independent variable so that my lowest value would be 1. The year 1900 would then be represented by a value of 5, the year 1910 by a value of 15, and so forth. Doing this will make the calculated value for the intercept much more interpretable. (Policy analysts and others who frequently use "year" as an independent variable should especially take note of this particular problem.)

3. The regression coefficient (slope), b, tells us how many units of change in the dependent variable to expect with each one-unit change in the independent variable: "As I go up one unit on X, I expect b units of change in Y." Notice how much this depends on how the variables are coded in your data set (unlike r or r^2, the measure of association, which does not change with these kinds of measurement changes). If your independent variable is income measured in single dollars (i.e., $1 is recorded as 1, $2 is recorded as 2, etc.), you will expect a much smaller slope than if income is measured in thousands of dollars (i.e., $1,000 is recorded as 1, $2,000 is recorded as 2, etc.). Simply speaking, you don't expect much change in a dependent variable when your independent variable changes by one unit that represents a single dollar. You do, however, expect much change in a dependent variable when your independent variable changes by one unit that represents $1,000. Similarly, if the *dependent* variable is income, you'll expect a bigger slope when income is measured in dollars because a unit increase in the *independent* variable may change income by lots of single dollars but very few thousands of dollars.

4. The regression coefficient (slope), b, measures how much change to expect in Y for each one-unit increment in X. The correlation squared (r^2) measures how much error there would be in those expectations. These two statistics are similar (after all, their numerators are identical), but it is important to keep them straight.

Given that there are many reasons for variation in almost every variable we care to explain, cases are always going to lie off the prediction line; other things that "cause" cases to be high or low on the dependent variable will be pushing them up or down. Various kinds of errors in our measurement will make cases lie off the prediction line.

It's the correlation coefficient, r, that measures how far off the line cases tend to be. However, from situation to situation—sample to sample, time to time, country to country—the error in measurement will vary, as will the other things related to variation in the dependent variable. The errors in prediction won't be constant across situations. Because of this, r isn't very useful across situations. If you're trying to determine whether an independent variable has the same effect in two different situations, r won't tell you much. You'll know how much error of prediction you'd make in each situation, but error and effect aren't the same. In both situations, the independent variable could be having the *same* effect, but in one situation other "causes" of variation in the dependent variable could be adding lots of error (deflating the value of r). In another case, the independent variable could be having quite different *effects* on variation in the dependent variable. Yet, you might be able to explain the variation equally well in both. Pearson's r measures *how well* you can explain but *not* how much effect X has on Y.

Thus, when comparing across situations, you'll need to use the slope to get at whether the effects of X on Y are the same or different for two different situations. The slope, however, changes with measurement—independent or dependent. If the measurement of X isn't identical in both situations, the meaning of "a one-unit increment in X" changes.* If the measurement of Y isn't identical, the meaning of "how much change to expect" changes. Thus one slope isn't comparable to another slope in another situation *unless* the measurement of the variables is the same.

Still, the fact that slopes are more comparable across situations (as long as measurement is the same) is very important to us. The multiple causes of the variation in the phenomena we want to explain and the various other causes of prediction error have much less effect on the slope than on the correlation coefficient. Even if other causes of variation are affecting the slope, there are ways to compensate partially (we'll get to those in Chapter 10, in which the ways are referred to as statistical controls or multivariate analysis). If we only had constant measurements to use in situation after situation, we'd be in fairly good shape. (However, even such things as Gross National Product are measured differently from country to country.)

This regression coefficient is, remember,

---

*You also need to worry about the range and measurement precision of X, not just measurement intervals.

probably the most important statistic we have going for us in political science. It comes closer than any other statistic to being a precise statement of the linear relationship between two variables—*not the strength* with which they are related but the *way* in which they are related. If all our hypotheses could be stated in such a way as to use the slope as the statistic for testing those hypotheses, we'd be much further along in developing precise, clear, exact explanations of the phenomena we are trying to explain. Unfortunately, for the slope to be at its most informative, we need interval data; and many political science concepts are not yet measured at that level.

5. It is very important to know that r, the correlation coefficient, is a *symmetrical* measure and that b, the regression coefficient, is an *asymmetrical* measure. r measures scatter around the line, regardless of whether the independent variable is on the vertical or horizontal axis and of whether the dependent variable is on the vertical or horizontal axis. In other words, it doesn't matter which variable you treat as independent; r will stay the same. (Note in the formula that variation in both the horizontal *and* vertical variable are in the denominator; r^2 is covariation relative to total variation.) In the formulae we have been using, b measures how much effect to expect in the *vertical Y* variable from a one-unit increase in the *horizontal X* variable. b will be very different, depending on which variable you take to be independent (X/horizontal) and which you take to be dependent (Y/vertical). Notice that variation in only the X/horizontal/independent is in the denominator of b; it is this fact that makes so very much difference in whether you take one or the other variables as the *independent* variable. (b measures covariation relative to variation in only one of the two variables.)

Remember from Chapter 1 that we usually consider as independent the variable that

1. "Causes" the dependent, or
2. Is prior in time to the dependent, or
3. Is theoretically prior in time, even if the two are measured simultaneously, or
4. Is "more basic" theoretically, or
5. Is a "given" for a case, while the dependent is more transient, etc.

6. Most of the problems in the data that can distort r^2 can also have some effect on the slope because of the similarity of their calculations. For example, if you have severe outliers in the data, they may be distorting the slope. If you remember the diagram that showed no relationship in a large group of cases, but which yielded a fairly high r^2 because of the outliers, you can imagine how a fairly flat slope could be distorted. Those strange cases "pulled" the slope up to themselves.

As another example, if you have only very limited variance on the independent variable, you can picture yourself calculating a slope that reflects the data you have but only a narrow band of the data that might potentially be available on the independent variable. You cannot know, if you don't have good variance on the independent variable, whether any linearity you see of the b would continue across all the value of the independent variable or not. Nor can you know whether any apparent absence of relationship would continue outside that limited range.

Thus, for a slope, just as for the measure of association, it is important to examine a scatterplot of your data before you rely on the calculated statistics. You could be misleading yourself and your readers if you don't *look* at the data, in addition to calculating the summary statistics. Remember, all the statistics are just ways to describe and summarize the form and strength of the relationship that exists in the data. You need to look at the scatterplot to see if they are accurate summaries.

Now it is time to test your understanding of r^2, a, and b by letting the computer do the busy work and letting you do the thinking. If you don't feel quite secure with these statistics yet, don't worry too much. You'll get more practice with these (and the ones in earlier chapters) as we go along. And you will want to review the material in this chapter as you do the exercises in the next chapter and several times later as well.

SUGGESTED READINGS

AGNEW, NEIL MCK., and SANDRA W. PYKE. *The Science Game*, 4th ed. (Englewood Cliffs, NJ: Prentice-Hall, 1987), pp. 180–184.

BLALOCK, HUBERT M., JR., *Social Statistics*, 2nd ed. (New York: McGraw-Hill, 1972), Ch. 17. This chapter may still be a bit difficult. Don't worry if it's not 100% clear to you yet.

BOWEN, BRUCE D., and HERBERT F. WEISBERG, *An Introduction to Data Analysis* (San Francisco: Freeman, 1980), pp. 142–150.

DRAPER, N. R., and H. SMITH. *Applied Regression Analysis* (New York: Wiley, 1966). Chapter 3 is a good source for understanding what various patterns in the residuals mean.

JOHNSON, JANET BUTTOLPH, and RICHARD A. JOSLYN. *Political Science Research Methods* (Washington, DC: Congressional Quarterly Press, 1986), Ch. 12. Review, especially, the section on regression.

KOHOUT, FRANK J. *Statistics for Social Scientists* (New York: Wiley, 1974), Unit IV.

NACHMIAS, DAVID, and CHAVA NACHMIAS, *Research Methods in the Social Sciences*, 2nd ed. (New York: St. Martin's, 1981), pp. 348–357.

OTT, LYMAN, WM. MENDENHALL, and RICHARD LARSON. *Statistics: A Tool for the Social Sciences*, 2nd ed. (North Scituate, MA: Duxbury, 1978), Ch. 11.

SHIVELY, W. PHILLIPS. *The Craft of Political Research*, 2nd ed. (Englewood Cliffs, NJ: Prentice-Hall, 1980), pp. 110–131.

ZISK, BETTY H. *Political Research* (Lexington, MA: D.C. Heath, 1981), pp. 237–247.

ARTICLES

BURG, STEVEN L., and MICHAEL L. BERBAUM. "Community, Integration, and Stability in Multinational Yugoslavia," *American Political Science Review*, 83 (June 1989), 535–554. Explains the proportion of self-declared "Yugoslavs" in each county as a function of material development, delivery of social services, political socialization levels, intergroup contact, and generation. Aggregate-level analysis. Table 1, univariate and regional analysis of predictor variables. Table 2, bivariate correlations by region. Table 3, multivariate regression; standardized regression coefficients.

CAMPBELL, JAMES E. "The Revised Theory of Surge and Decline," *American Journal of Political Science*, 31 (February 1987), 965–979. Clear statement of the original theory, challenges to it, and revised theory. Good statement of different conclusions from aggregate vote results and analysis of composition of electorate. Bivariate *r* and *b*; aggregated survey data. Plots reproduced.

HIBBING, JOHN R. "On the Issues Surrounding Economic Voting: Looking to the British Case for Answers," *Comparative Political Studies*, 20 (April 1987), 3–33. Table 1 is bivariate plot of percent vote for party in power regressed on "misery index." Plots printed for aggregate data relationships. Discussion of using ordinary least-squares regression (as presented in this text) with a dichotomous dependent variable. Considers individual-level as well as aggregate-level relationships. (Continues with multivariate analysis.)

KAY, SUSAN ANN. "Feminist Ideology, Race, and Political Participation: A Second Look," *Western Political Quarterly*, 38 (September 1985), 476–484. Introductory remarks (pp. 476–477) and conclusion (pp. 483–484) discuss the problems of applying linear regression to a relationship that may not be linear. At this point, the material in between may be too complex.

MCCRONE, DONALD J., and JAMES H. KUKLINSKI. "The Delegate Theory of Representation," *American Journal of Political Science*, 23 (May 1979), 278–299. Using only bivariate correlation and regression statistics (r^2 and *b*), article assesses conditions that improve a representative's (California legislator's) perception of constituency opinion and enhance roll-call voting on the basis of that perception. Reviews whether representative considers self a delegate and whether constituency sends a consistent message. (Don't worry now that the article uses factor analyses to show that referenda results used to measure constituency opinion were a single dimension.)

MCCRONE, DONALD J., and WALTER J. STONE.

"The Structure of Constituency Representation: On Theory and Method," *Journal of Politics*, 48 (1986), 956–976. Up to page 963, this article presents an argument for a nonlinear test of the relationship between constituency opinion and roll-call vote that should be intelligible at this point. Also see Figure 4, which compares linear and nonlinear relationships.

PUTNAM, ROBERT D., ROBERT LEONARDI, and RAFFAELLA Y. NANETTI. "Attitude Stability among Italian Elites," *American Journal of Political Science*, 23 (August 1979), 463–493. Based on a six-year panel survey of 95 Italian political leaders. Good consideration of meaning of response stability—absolute versus correlational/relative—including examples. Presents r, gamma, and absolute stability in subsequent analyses. Considers partisan orientations, ideological positions, attitudes toward conflict, democracy, and regionalism. (Continues with path analyses; see later chapters). Measurement is occasionally based on coding open-ended items.

SCHNEIDER, WILLIAM. "Democrats and Republicans, Liberals and Conservatives," in Seymour Martin Lipset (ed.), *Emerging Coalitions in American Politics* (San Francisco: Institute for Contemporary Studies, 1978), pp. 183–265. Uses aggregate-vote returns for states to correlate results of one presidential election with another in order to examine stability and change in vote results (pp. 186–190). Then turns to factor analysis (an extension of regression techniques), which may be somewhat confusing at this point.

SEGAL, JEFFREY A., and ALBERT D. COVER. "Ideological Values and the Votes of U.S. Supreme Court Justices," *American Political Science Review*, 83 (June 1989), 557–565. Measures judicial ideology from content analysis of newspaper editorials from time president nominated justice until Senate confirmation. Uses that information to explain judicial voting on civil rights and liberties issues. Bivariate correlation; plot shown.

TEDIN, KENT L. "Assessing Peer and Parent Influence on Adolescent Political Attitudes," *American Journal of Political Science*, 24 (February 1980), 136–154. Good discussion of effect of choice of statistic in determining whether influence exists from parent or peer to adolescent; compares correlation coefficients and percentage agreement. Attention to conditions under which relationships are stronger or weaker (interaction). Data from high school seniors, parents, and peers in Iowa City, Iowa.

USEEM, MICHAEL. "Government Mobilization of Academic Social Research," *Policy Studies Journal*, 4 (1976), 274–280. Based on a questionnaire distributed to social scientists in several disciplines, the article first uses simple correlation coefficients (r) to assess the impact of the social scientist's contribution to the discipline and contribution to public policy on the receipt of federal funds. Continues with multiple regression.

CHAPTER
6

USING PEARSON'S *r* WITH REAL DATA: HYPOTHESES, INDICES, AND THE RELIABILITY OF MEASURES

This chapter will seem long because you will be working with new data, a new measurement technique, and new commands as well as reviewing many of the ideas introduced earlier. First, you will be learning how to work with real data that are already set up in an SPSS file. Although you will have to spend some time getting acquainted with the data files available here, the fact that they are already set up for you will save you considerable time in the long run. Second, you will be learning one way of building an *index*—creating a single new variable out of several old ones; this is one way of turning our ordinarily nominal or ordinal measurements into almost interval ones. Third, you will be learning two ways of making the SPSS package do Pearson's correlations for you.

ABOUT PREVIOUSLY CONSTRUCTED SPSS FILES

The file you're going to be working with is just a more elaborate version of the kind of file you created in Chapter 3. Entering the numeric values for each case on each variable, naming each variable, indicating the location of each variable, and even labeling the values of each variable are already all complete and stored for you. In the data sets you will be using, any case that does not have usable information on a variable has been given a special numeric value, and the computer has been instructed (through a MISSING VALUES command) to drop any case with that value from any analysis.

Since the file is already set up and stored, you get to skip all those steps that related to putting your data in a form usable by SPSS in your last computer run—steps such as specifying the DATA LIST, BEGIN DATA, and END DATA commands, as well as the data themselves. You will retrieve the stored file and then jump right into SPSS procedure commands. (If this paragraph seems a bit fuzzy, you might want to stop here and do a quick review of Chapter 3.)

Data Codebooks

Right now, take a look in the appendices at the codebooks for the data sets that accompany this text. You will be using these data sets frequently in later chapters. They are typical of those that political scientists generally use in their research.

Thumbing through this text's codebooks will help you familiarize yourself with working with real ones. The codebook is a very important part of each research project. It is, essentially, the "official record" of the data as they were collected and coded. If the researcher needs to check certain information, the codebook is the official map of the data and their locations. When researchers share their data with other researchers, the codebook is the only "key" the second person has to making good use of the data.

In a codebook, you'll almost always find:

1. An exact, clear, precise statement of the content of each variable.
2. All possible valid codes for that variable—that is, every number or letter that may mean something when it shows up in the field which is reserved for that variable on each record.
3. A "missing data" code—numbers or other symbols that are used in the field on a record reserved for that variable when a "real" piece of information could not be found or recorded.
4. The record and field onto which that variable was coded/recorded on each case. (Omitted in the appendices, this is less likely to appear when the data are already in a file—like an SPSS file—than when the data are just "raw," with no naming or labeling information.)
5. An SPSS name for the variable, if the data are in SPSS format.
6. Sometimes, you will also find a univariate frequency distribution for each variable, especially for nominal and ordinal ones.

Be sure you can find each of these pieces of information in the codebooks in the appendices. Don't expect each and every codebook to have the information in exactly the same place. Just know that all of this information is likely to be there—preserved in a clear, readable, permanent format.

EXERCISE 1 Testing a Hypothesis with PLOT

Let's start off doing almost exactly what you did by hand in the last chapter: getting the computer to draw a scatterplot that shows the relationship between two variables and getting it to calculate the statistics you have learned to do for Pearson correlation and regression—a, b, r, and r^2.

Stating the Hypothesis

First, make up a hypothesis that posits a relationship between two of the variables in one of the data sets. Looking through the codebooks should give you some ideas. (You should realize, however, that research usually goes the other way: you state a hypothesis and then find the variables. But these are just exercises; besides, sometimes research projects can emerge from this kind of "fishing.") If you have trouble with a hypothesis, some suggestions are given with the exercises at the end of the chapter as examples and guides, but you'll learn more—and have more fun—if you also try to launch out on your own.

Try to state your hypothesis so that it follows all the guidelines for "good" hypotheses (see Chapter 1). Also try to use variables in your hypothesis that are as close to interval-level measurement as possible (review Chapter 1) because the statistics you're using here really require interval data. Write your hypothesis and also write the SPSS names of your independent and dependent variables.

Setting Up a PLOT Job with a Previously Constructed SPSS File

Your instructor will tell you how to retrieve the data sets that have been stored for your use. Essentially, after you connect with the computer and begin to construct your SPSS setup, you will first probably type—

```
GET FILE = 'name'.
```

For name, you will put, with apostrophes, the name of the file given you by your instructor. You may have another line preceding this one. Right after these lines, you get immediately to standard SPSS procedures to begin asking for a plot of the relationship between the two variables in your hypotheses.

To get all the same statistics and associated information you've been calculating in Chapter 4, you need two things: a request for a scatterplot on which you indicate the *names* of the variables you want plotted (listing the one you want to be on the vertical axis—the dependent variable—first) and a request for all statistics associated by SPSS with scatterplots. You do both with the command PLOT and the two subcommands, FORMAT and PLOT, like this:

```
PLOT FORMAT = REGRESSION/PLOT =
   vertname WITH horzname.
```

Substitute, in the PLOT subcommand, the SPSS name of your *dependent* variable just as it is spelled in the codebook where *vertname* is indicated and the SPSS name of your *independent* variable where *horzname* is indicated. Then put in FINISH., if necessary for batch, and you're ready to submit your job, just as you did before. That's it. Here's an example, but note that you'll be using the SPSS variable names you selected for your hypothesis when you do the exercise.

```
PLOT FORMAT = REGRESSION/PLOT =
   CARTHERM WITH INCOME.
FINISH.
```

Interpreting the Output

After you submit your job and retrieve your output (and get it finally to come out with zero errors), examine the scatterplot first. One thing you will quickly notice is that most of the points have numbers or letters. These are used instead of a point—the more ordinary way of designating a case's values on the two variables. (You used points in the exercises that you did in the last chapter.) The numbers from 1 through 9 indicate the number of cases that share that point (i.e., number of cases that have identical scores on the independent and dependent variables). Next, you go through the alphabet: *A* = ten cases, *B* = eleven cases, *C* = twelve cases, and so forth. An asterisk indicates that more than 36 cases share that point.

Don't expect the cases to be as tightly clustered around the line as was the case in the hypothetical examples in the previous chapter. The scatter may be so wide that it may be difficult to see a pattern in the scatterplot. As we've indicated before, variation in political phenomena is "caused" by many things. Your independent variable may be only one of many causes of variation; and the scatter above and below the line will, for now, be quite substantial "unexplained" variation that may be attributed to other causes.

Such scatter may also be due to measurement error. If we can't measure exactly the phenomena we're interested in explaining (or the phenomena we use to explain them), cases may lie off the line due to pure error in measuring before we even begin to analyze the data.

One kind of measurement error creeps in when we think we have an interval variable but we really don't. A classic case is "education completed" measured in years. Anyone would think that a year equals a year equals a year; therefore, "education completed" measured in years is interval—the distance between 1 and 2 is the same as between 3 and 4, and so forth. In practical terms, however, the distance between 11 and 12 is much greater than that between 8 and 9. The "distance" between 11 years completed and 12 years completed is probably the difference between not having and having a high school diploma. No such major event is designated by the 8 to 9 year difference. "Education completed" measured in years, therefore, is probably not as interval as we'd like to think, but it also is probably the closest we have to an interval measure of education.

Another example of variables that appear interval, but may not be in practice, is the "thermometer ratings" of candidates and groups that appear in the National Election Study in the appendices. Respondents were asked to respond on a 0- to 100-point scale, depending on whether they were cool or warm toward the candidate or group. Respondents tend not to use all possible intervals on such a scale—so much so that your results using the thermometers may look as if you had used an ordinal variable instead. Yet, since these are as close as we have to interval measurements of some concepts, we tend to treat them as interval and tolerate the discrepancies as just measurement error.

When you're using aggregate data, as opposed to individual-level data, the relationship may appear to be a bit "tighter." When we measure variables at the individual level, all the possible causes (no matter how idiosyncratic) and all contributors to measurement error (inadequate operational definitions, imprecise measuring instruments, mistakes in coding the data, misinterpretations in coding, respondent's confusion in answering questions, etc.) are operative. When we have aggregate-level data (measures computed from groups of people as opposed to measures on individuals—for example, median income for counties rather than respondents' incomes), some of that error is "averaged out," and we get "purer" measurement. You might think, therefore, that aggregate data are preferable, but they have their own problems especially when we're trying to explain individual-level behavior. (Remember, as we mentioned in Chapter 1, that you can't infer that individuals behave as aggregates behave.)

I mention these situations here in order to remind you of reasons why cases may be tightly or loosely scattered about the regression line—reasons which may have nothing to do with whether the hypotheses are correct. You will also want to remember or review the interpretation of r and r^2 in Chapter 5 for other reasons for low correlation.

Having examined your scatterplot, decide whether you think your hypothesis is disconfirmed and write your conclusion after your hypothesis. If the relationship looks positive and your hypothesis predicted a positive relationship, your hypothesis is not disconfirmed. (See Chapter 1.) Similarly, if the relationship looks negative and your hypothesis predicted a negative relationship, your hypothesis is not disconfirmed. Remember, we don't prove hypotheses true or false. We just test them and see whether they can be falsified.

Regression Statistics from PLOT

Don't expect to see the regression line drawn in. SPSS doesn't do that, but it does give you the information necessary to do it.

Let's look at two ways to draw the regression line in. The first is a bit more complicated, but it may help you see better what is going on. For the first way, start by writing out the prediction equation from the statistics you have on the output, substituting the proper values into $Y_p = a + bX + e$ (or $Y_p = a - bX + e$). On the output, you will see the words "intercept" and "slope." Remember that the former is a and the latter is b. You will see another set of numbers in parentheses after both the intercept and slope. For now you can ignore them. Remember that e will not have a value but is there to remind you of the fact that cases will lie off the line for several reasons.

Now, having written out the prediction equation, pick any two scores from the range of X and figure out the expected score of Y for each of those values of X. Just substitute two values of X into the equation and solve for Y_p twice. (Write your substitutions down with the prediction equation.)

Locate your first value of X on the horizontal axis; go straight up from there until you get to the point that represents the value of Y expected for that value of X; mark the point. Repeat the procedure for the second value of X. Also mark the appropriate place for the intercept on the vertical axis. (You could get by with just one point and the intercept, but the second gives you a check.) Use a ruler to connect the intercept and the two points you've located with a straight line. Extend the line across the graph. Now you can visualize the relationship better.

By now you have probably seen the second way to draw in the regression line. SPSS prints R on both the vertical and horizontal axes to represent where the regression line would intersect these axes. You can simply connect them.

Examine the output again to find answers to the following questions. (Review Chapter 5 if they seem tricky.) Write your answers out, labeling them clearly.

1. What is the average (expected) value on the dependent variable when the independent variable has a value of zero?
2. A one-unit increase in the independent variable is associated with how many units increase in the dependent variable?
3. I have reduced my error in predicting the dependent variable by what percent when I know the value of the independent variable as compared to when I didn't know the independent variable value?
4. I have explained what percent of the variance in the dependent variable using the independent variable and assuming a straight-line relationship? (Caution: this is a trick question. The answers to this and the one just above it are the same and are both based on $r^2 \times 100$.)
5. Examining these statistics now rather than the scatterplot, would you say your hypothesis is disconfirmed? Explain any difference between your two decisions about whether the hypothesis is disconfirmed.
6. Can you think of things that might be causing you to get a less than perfect r^2?

If you have time, you may want to state another hypothesis, change the PLOT procedure to reflect the new hypothesis, and answer the questions about the second hypothesis as well. The more you practice, the easier both the statistics and the computer use will be.

COUNT AND CORRELATIONS PROCEDURES

EXERCISE 2 Uses of Pearson's Correlation in Assessing Inter-item Reliability

Don't worry if this exercise seems complicated—just read it several times. There are several new ideas to learn in it, and they will all be useful to you in the future.

Why Use Multi-item Indices?

Researchers frequently operationalize their concepts by using an *index*—a single, composite measure that combines several separate variables which the researcher either considers parts of the concept or indicators of that concept. (You have already seen several of these in the hypothetical operationalizations in the exercises.)

You can probably imagine several phenomena in which political scientists are interested that are made up of several aspects. Political participation is usually defined as whether a person engages in several different activities. The level of violence in a society is frequently defined by something like a summation of how many riots, how many assassinations, etc. The percentage of time that a member of Congress votes with a particular interest group is calculated from that member's yes or no votes on several bills. These would all probably be measured with multi-item indices.

We also have to deal with the situation in which we have to use multiple *indicators* of our concepts. As we mentioned in Chapter 1, we often have ideas (concepts) in our theories on which we cannot gather data directly because those concepts are not tied to clear, empirical phenomena that we can simply observe. We can often, however, get data on empirical phenomena that our theory tells us will be caused by the concept. We can use those things that we can measure as indirect measures (indicators) of the concept when we cannot measure the concept itself.

The idea is that the unobserved variables are correlated with several observed ones. Because of that covariance, we can measure the observable ones and make inferences to the others. Given that there may be several causes of any single empirical indicator, using more than one that should theoretically be affected by the unobserved variable makes us surer that we are measuring, if indirectly, the concept.*

Whether the researcher considers the variables being combined into an index to be parts of a concept or indicators of it, a reason for

---

*Note that it is "surer"—not certain. We tend to go on with our research arguing that we must operationalize the concept as well as we can and get on with it. Only by going on with the research and sharing the results with others can our theories and tests be scrutinized. It is principally that criticism from other practitioners in the scientific community that can help us assess whether we are on the right track.

using multiple items in an index is to increase the reliability of the concept's measurement. As Chapter 1 suggested, researchers want operationalizations that are reliable.

One meaning of *reliability* is precision of measurement. Precision here suggests that cases can be distinguished from each other rather finely—not by grouping cases into categories but by being able to identify rather accurately where cases stand relative to each other. Combining variables that all measure aspects of the same thing may be a way to get more precise measurement. Each separate variable alone may be yes/no—a dichotomy—and have only two possible values. When we combine the variables, however, we may be able to come up with a scale that has 10 or 20 possible values. We may, thus, be able to construct something closer to interval measurement and gain a greater ability to distinguish among cases.

A related meaning of reliable measurement is that which has as little error as possible. Usually we can decrease the error of measurement using an overall, composite index compared to the error that would be present if we were using the separate variables. Whatever error there is in *each* variable may be "averaged out" in the construction of the overall index.

Basically, we're saying that a single variable can have error in it for many different reasons. The interviewer may have marked the wrong box; the coder may have slipped up deciphering the data; a respondent may not have really given the correct answer; something other than our theoretical concept may be causing the indicator to vary. If we have *only* that one variable, many cases will be misclassified relative to other cases. If we have many variables, however, each of which measures an aspect of the same thing, a case's position on the single scale, which results from combining those variables, will be a truer representation of that case's position relative to all the other cases.*

Think of it this way. Imagine we are trying to operationalize "pays attention to media."

If we had, for example, a yes/no answer to a question on whether a person reads *Newsweek* as our only indicator of "pays attention to media," our operationalization has the potential for a great deal of error. Any miscoding that makes the case a "yes" rather than the "no" it truly is (or a "no" rather than the "yes" it truly is) has the case completely wrong. The case is being treated as if it belongs to the completely opposite category of cases.

But now consider what would happen if we had ten different yes/no answers to ten questions about whether a person pays attention to each of ten magazines or newspapers, and if our operationalization of "pays attention to media" required us to give a person one point for each "yes" answer. If there is miscoding on one variable here, the case would be only one point off where it truly belonged on a zero-to-ten index (0 = reads no newspaper or magazine . . . to 10 = reads all ten newspapers and magazines). A case might be scored 3 instead of 4 on the "pays attention to media" index, or a 6 instead of a 5, but the case would only be off a bit from where it belonged. There would be only a little error rather than a complete misclassification of the case with its opposites. Thus, the multi-item index would be more reliable than the single-item indicator.

Reliability of the Individual Variables

Before you construct the multi-item index, however, you need to make sure—as sure as you can—that all the separate variables are measures of the same phenomenon. For example, we might think that political participation is comprised of several different activities: whether the person voted, wore a campaign button, tried to convince someone else how to vote, etc. But we would not want race or sex as variables included in our index. While those might *explain* who does or does not participate, they aren't themselves either part of political participation or empirical indicators of the concept "political participation."

Similarly, we wouldn't want to include whether the person goes to movies as a variable in an index that will measure political partici-

---

*This, of course, assumes that the error in the individual measures is random and not systematically biased in one direction or the other.

pation. Nor would we want to include whether the person runs in marathons as a variable. While these might indicate activity, they are clearly not *political* activity, nor are they indicators of that concept. When you select a set of variables to construct a measure of a concept, go over the set carefully, discarding any variables that aren't clearly either part of or indicators of the concept you are interested in.

Another step in trying to determine whether all the variables measure the same thing is to examine the way those variables are coded. Always check whether the variables are coded in such a way that they all are measuring the concept in "the same direction." For example, if you were trying to measure political participation, you might find 1 = yes and 5 = no for giving money to a party, while 1 = no and 5 = yes for "ran for office." In the first example, *low* values (1s) stand for *high* participation. In the second example, *low* values (1s) stand for *low* participation. They'd cancel each other out if your overall index just counted the number of ones coded. In this instance, you'd need *either* to recode one or the other variable so that low values always stand for low participation *or* to remember and take into account this discrepant coding when you are constructing the overall index.

In most data sets, coding is consistent; however, it's possible that the original authors had a different principle in mind than you do. Thus, it's a good idea to check whenever you are using someone else's data set, and it's something to remember when you set up your own data.

There is a way to be surer that pairs of variables measure the same concept than just discarding those that obviously don't fit, after you've checked the direction of coding. One way is to look for fairly strong correlation between pairs of variables. If two variables measure the same concept, they should be correlated—positively, if the coding is such that larger numbers mean the same thing on both indicators; negatively, if the larger numbers mean opposite things on the two indicators. You expect error in both variables, however, so you don't expect the correlation to be perfect. At least, however, you expect them to be correlated in the right direction and reasonably strongly if they measure the same concept.

The problem with the argument that high correlation suggests two variables measure the same concept is that many things can result in two variables being correlated—chance or their both having the same cause, for example. Looking for correlation alone, therefore, won't tell us for sure that the two variables measure the same concept. We also have to look for indication that they're not measuring the same concept; that is, we look for instances of very low, near zero correlation between two variables. If the variables are not correlated, they can't be measuring the same concept.

Therefore, even if you haven't proved they *are* measuring the same concept when a correlation shows up, at least you can get rid of variables that tell you by very low correlation that they are probably *not* measuring the same concept. You will drop from the index any variables that have very low correlation with variables that are fairly strongly correlated in other pairs.

Selecting Variables for an Index

Search through one of the codebooks and try to find several variables that all seem to be measuring the same concept—a concept you'd like to use as either the independent or dependent variable in a hypothesis. (The suggestions given in the exercise section may serve to stimulate your imagination. You may use those or, better, create your own.)

For the purposes of this exercise, make sure that the variables are dichotomies (have only two scores) or are, at least, ordinal in their measurement levels; don't use any nominal variables other than dichotomies. Write the name of the concept and the SPSS names of all the variables you think may measure that concept. Check the codes on all the variables while you are at it to see whether the variables are coded in the same direction (i.e., whether high values consistently stand for the same—either high or low—levels of the concept, while low values represent the opposite level of the concept.) It's probably a good idea to note the codes and their meanings along with the variable names.

Another thing to be aware of is the distribution of the variables you are thinking of combining into the index. Look at the variation on each item by looking at how the cases are clustered or spread out over the possible codes for the variable. If the cases are fairly homogeneous and cluster up on one or a few of the possible values, the variation is low. This will have two consequences.

First, it may make the correlation between that variable and other variables low, even if they are measuring the same concept. You may want to keep such an item in the index, even if its correlation with the other items is not very high.

Second, if the variation is very low on each variable and in the same direction, you could end up with an index with very low variance. For example, consider again the index suggested above for "pays attention to the media." If almost all the respondents in the sample don't read any of the indicated magazines, and if you are totaling up the number of magazines read by each respondent for your new index, you could end up with most of your cases scored zero. That will then play havoc with any statistical analyses that require variance on the variables. Sometimes there's nothing you can do about this problem. (The variables just naturally have low variation.) Sometimes, however, you can pick the most variable indicators on purpose in order to improve the variance on the index.

Determining Whether the Variables All Measure the Same Concept

Now that you have selected your items, you will do the preliminary step before combining them into an index. You will need to check whether all pairs of these indicators are correlated. This time we aren't particularly interested in the plot of the scatter we would get from PLOT. Rather, we just want to make a quick check on a measure of association—correlations that will suggest the degree to which a set of variables seem to be measuring the same concept in order to reduce overall error. Therefore, we'll just use the CORRELATIONS procedure, which only prints out the correlation statistics, rather than the PLOT procedure, which prints a plot and the regression statistics as well.

Here's the form:

```
CORRELATIONS VARIABLES =
   name name name name.
```

Just use the command CORRELATIONS and, after the subcommand VARIABLES, the names of all the variables you want to check for correlations. Put this command in place of the PLOT command in the setup you used for Exercise 1 above. Submit your job and examine the output.

If you want to be able to examine the mean and variation on each variable, you can add a STATISTICS subcommand to the CORRELATIONS command.

```
For SPSS/PC+:
CORRELATIONS VARIABLES =
   name name name/
   STATISTICS = 1.
For SPSS-X:
CORRELATIONS VARIABLES =
   name name name/
   STATISTICS = DESCRIPTIVES.
```

In order to show the inter-item correlation, construct a *correlation matrix*. Just list the names of all the indicators across the page and list the names down the side as well. In the space indicated by the intersection of column and row, put the Pearson r between those two variables. Notice that what you are looking at is r not r^2. The r is the first entry in each group of numbers on the output. Do not be misled by the p. The p is not a measure of association but an indication of statistical significance. You won't get to this until Chapter 18. (It's a measure of how likely you are to have gotten your Pearson's r by chance.) Under the r, you also

Table 6.1 A Correlation Matrix

	VARONE	VARTWO	VARTHR
VARONE	1.0		
VARTWO	.70	1.0	
VARTHR	.25	.67	1.0

will see the number of cases on which a correlation is calculated.

Since the square matrix represents each correlation twice, you only have to do one-half of it. For example, if you have three variables and the first and second are correlated at .70, the first and third at .25, and the second and third at .67, the matrix would look like Table 6.1.

Scan your matrix to make sure the Pearson's correlation between each variable and every other variable is in the direction you'd expect, given the coding for that pair and "reasonably high." There's no exact cutoff point. You probably want something larger than .10 or .20 or .30, at least. You'd like correlations in the neighborhood of .3 or .4 with individual-level, survey data—higher with aggregate data. You will drop from the final index any items that don't pass whatever level you set for this test.

You also probably don't want to keep in your index both variables in any pair that have near perfect correlations (1.0) with each other. If you have perfect 1.0 correlation between two variables, you might as well use only one of the two. You're not adding anything by using both. This process of checking the correlations between variables that are about to be combined into an index is called testing for *inter-item reliability* (or item-to-item reliability). It is a way to determine whether we are likely to be creating an index that has relatively little error in it.

If we were methodologists doing really serious scale construction, we would want a more exact statistic to report the reliability we are trying to assess. And there are other statistics that more precisely indicate the degree of reliability in the variables which are combined into an index. Here, however, you need primarily to learn the principles of index construction and to practice with various forms of Pearson's *r*. This exercise attempts to do both so that you can get the ideas down. Some of the suggested readings will take you on the next step of assessing reliability with more precise statistics.

Now that you have checked the correlations, mark the names of the variables on your list that seem to be measuring your concept (all of the variables you used for CORRELATIONS that are related in the direction you expected and that also have reasonably high correlations). You are now finally ready actually to construct the index itself.

Building the Index Using the COUNT Procedure

An easy way to get all these items into a single index is to use COUNT. (You'll learn other ways later.) First you have to imagine that each variable is a dichotomy, even if it is not naturally one; that is, you have to decide which values on each variable stand for "presence" of the concept and which indicate "absence," or which values indicate that a case should be considered "high" or "low" on the concept. We want to count up the number of times on all the variables where a case has the scores that represent presence or high levels of the concept.

Let's use an example here. Imagine that a teacher has given five exams, each exam having ten points on it. In the data file, each student has a grade on each of five exams. The teacher isn't interested in the exact total score each student has on all the exams taken together. The teacher is interested in a new variable called "how many tests child passed."

The teacher decided that a passing grade on the first exam was 5 correct out of 10; on the second exam, passing was 7 out of 10; on the third, 4 out of 10; on the fourth, 5 out of 10; and on the fifth, 8 out of 10. The teacher wants to count the number of times a student scored *at or above* 5, 7, 4, 5, 8 on the five exams; that is, the teacher wants to count how many exams the student passed.

Assuming the teacher had the data in an

SPSS file, a COUNT command could be used in the following form:

```
COUNT NEWSCALE = TEST1 (5 THRU
  10) TEST2 (7 THRU 10) TEST3
  (4 THRU 10) TEST4 (5 THRU 10)
  TEST5 (8 THRU 10).
```

This would give the teacher a new variable that represents the number of tests a student passed. A student whose original scores were 4, 8, 3, 6, 9 on the five tests would have a score of 3 on the new variable (three tests passed). A student whose original scores were 4, 6, 3, 4, 7 would have a score of zero on the new variable (no tests passed). A student whose original scores were 6, 7, 9, 8, 10 would have a score of 5 on the new variable (all tests passed).

Or, for another example, imagine we had asked survey respondents whether they read each of eight magazines or newspapers. We recorded eight variables as follows:

Reads *Time*
  1 = yes
  0 = no

Reads *New York Times*
  1 = yes
  0 = no

Reads *Nation*
  1 = yes
  0 = no

Reads *National Review*
  1 = yes
  0 = no

Reads *Ms*.
  1 = yes
  0 = no

Reads *Mother Jones*
  1 = yes
  0 = no

Reads *Washington Monthly*
  1 = yes
  0 = no

Reads *Washington Post*
  1 = yes
  0 = no

We might then want a multi-item index that represents how many magazines and/or newspapers the respondent reads. Assuming the eight variables were in an SPSS file, we could:

```
COUNT NREAD = TIME, NYTIME,
  NATION, NATREV, MS, MJ,
  WMONTH, WPOST (1).
```

A respondent who was coded yes (1) on *Nation*, *Ms.*, and *Washington Post* and no (0) on the others would have a score of 3 on the new variable NREAD. A respondent who was coded yes (1) only on *National Review* would have a score of 1 on the new variable NREAD, and so forth. After NREAD has been constructed using COUNT, it can be used as a variable in subsequent SPSS procedures like PLOT or DESCRIPTIVES, etc., just by putting "NREAD" in the proper position for the variable on the procedure command.

For creating your own index, follow the general format:

```
COUNT newname = name (n or
  n,n,n)
  name (n or n THRU n) name (n)
  name (n)/QMISS = name name
  name
  name(MISSING).
```

Where there is "newname" above, put in a name (up to eight characters) of what you want to call your index. This name must be unique; it cannot be the same as the name of a variable in the file already.

Where "name" is above, put in the names of the variables you want to combine into an index; each name goes on the command twice—once after "newname" and once after QMISS. Where there is "n," put in the value on the variable that is to be counted into the index. Or, if you need more than one value counted in, put in several values, as in (n,n,n) or a range, as in (n THRU n). Basically you are creating a new variable that will reflect the total number of times the particular value or set of values appears on all the separate variables. (The examples in the exercises may make this clearer and will indicate some shortcuts.)

One problem arises when some of your cases don't have data on the variables you are combining into an index. You saw in the codebooks that a special number is entered in the place of a case's value on each variable where the case could not be given a real score for one reason or another. Those special numbers were declared "missing values" when the data sets were constructed. You don't want cases that didn't have real scores on any one of the variables that make up an index to get a score for the overall index. Whenever a case is missing a true code on any single variable, we want to drop that case from the overall index we are creating because we don't know where it would fit if we had all the data on it.

The QMISS on the command above is a way to deal with this problem. With the QMISS inserted as it is on the COUNT procedure, you are creating an *additional new variable* named QMISS, the scores on which will be a count of the number of times a case has a "missing value" code on any of the separate indicators. If this new variable, QMISS, is greater than zero, we know that the case was missing on at least one of the separate items.

Since QMISS will give us an indication of which cases have some missing scores on the variables, we can declare those cases missing on the overall index. We do this by adding two lines after the COUNT.

```
IF (QMISS GT 0)newname=999.
MISSING VALUES newname(999).
```

Fill in the name of the multi-item index from the COUNT command where "newname" is indicated above. The IF statement tells the package to give a case a different score on your new index whenever that case has a value on QMISS that is greater than 0—whenever, that is, the case had missing values on any variable. The MISSING VALUES command then tells the package to drop from any later analyses those cases that were missing values on any of the indicators.

Using the Index in Analysis

Notice that we are creating an almost interval-level measurement for a concept out of noninterval variables by constructing a new variable that counts the number of times a certain score shows up on the constituent variables of the index. Therefore, you can use your new variable to test a hypothesis using interval-level statistics like Pearson's r and regression.

Write a new hypothesis that uses the concept which is measured by your new variable. Submit a new PLOT job that has the COUNT, IF, MISSING VALUES, and a command for a new PLOT. Remember that the name of the newly created variable comes before the WITH if it is dependent and after WITH if it is independent. Your whole set of commands would be in this order *after* the lines necessary to access the stored SPSS file:

```
COUNT newname = name(n) name
   (n)
   name (n)/QMISS = name name
   name (MISSING).
IF (QMISS GT 0)newname=999.
MISSING VALUES newname(999).
PLOT FORMAT = REGRESSION/PLOT
   vertname WITH horzname.
FINISH.
```

Examine your output and write out your answers to the following questions about it, labeling the answers clearly:

1. A one-unit increase in the independent variable named _____ is associated with a _____ unit increase in the dependent variable named _____.

2. If I were trying to predict a case's score on the dependent variable, knowing its value on the independent variable, I'd use the following equation:
    Dependent variable name = $a + b$ (Independent variable name) $+ e$, where $a = $ _____, and $b = $ _____.

3. Using the independent variable and assuming a straight-line relationship, I can explain

_____% of the variance in the dependent variable.

Compare your output to that of other class members and try to determine why they got higher or lower correlations. If any of you had more nearly ordinal than interval variables, that correlation will almost certainly be pretty low; ordinal measurement can be thought of as interval measurement with a lot of error in it, and measurement error decreases correlation. (Think about it.)

Did any of you get a scatter that suggested a curvilinear relationship? Since we measure how close the cases lie to a straight line with the kind of statistics we've been using, curved relationships will yield low measures of association because the curve displaces cases farther off a straight line; the more curved, the lower the measure of association.

Were any of you using the same kinds of data? If someone used survey data and another used aggregate data, the strengths of the correlations will be different, probably, all other things being equal.

Did any of you have variables with more or less variance in them? Remember the consequences of low variance on the independent and/or dependent variables on correlational statistics.

Finally, did any of you have a hypothesis whose independent variable was more probably the single "cause" of the dependent? Anyone who did will have higher correlations (all other things being equal).

EXERCISE 3 Another Kind of Reliability Test Using CORRELATIONS

Sometimes reliability is assessed by correlating a measurement with the same measurement done at another time (*test/retest reliability*). If we take a measurement of a variable at two different times on the same cases and correlate those two measurements, a high positive correlation will indicate good reliability. The measurement will be shown to rank the same cases relatively high at two different times, relatively low at two different times, and relatively medium at two different times.

When we are assessing over-time reliability, we assume no events intervened to change cases' relative positions on the measure in the meantime. If intervening events moved all cases either up or down while preserving their locations relative to each other, the measure can still be considered reliable, and the statistic we calculate for that will still be high.

See if you can find, in one of the codebooks, two variables that represent the same thing measured the same way at two different times and correlate them using the CORRELATIONS procedure to assess the reliability of the measure. (Suggestions are outlined in the exercises for this, but you aren't limited to the suggestions.)

When you get your output, write the answers to the following questions:

1. What is the Pearson's r that represents the correlation between the two measurements of the same variable at two times? For reliability tests, r is ordinarily used rather than r^2. For reliability tests, we're only interested in correlation—not in explained variance.

2. Do you think this is a reliable measure? Why or why not?

There's no *exact* correlation we look for to say we've got reliable measurement, but we want it to be high. As a rule-of-thumb, we want it to be above .70, at least, for individual-level survey data and above .90 for other kinds of data, although the longer the time lag between measurements, the lower the correlation is likely to be. For test-retest reliability, there are more precise statistics, just as there are for inter-item reliability. For those, consult the suggested readings.

Notice the difference between the correlation required for test/retest reliability and that for inter-item reliability. Here in test/retest reliability, correlating a measure with itself, we expect very high correlation (little error). In inter-item reliability, items might be measuring slightly different aspects of the same concept, or each might be caused by some other things than just the underlying concept; thus, the expected correlations in inter-item tests will be lower, even if the items are reliable indicators.

Also write an answer to this question: What events might have intervened between the two times to change a case's *relative* position on values of the variable? If there are no such events, we have to assume that any differences in the relative positions of cases on the variable are error and indicate unreliability. If we can identify reasons for change, we may have reliable measures that are getting at that real change.

Remember what you've learned in this rather complicated chapter. You now know two analysis procedures in SPSS you didn't know before—PLOT and CORRELATIONS. Although we'll leave them for a while, they're basic to much research work.

You are also beginning to learn the COUNT procedure, one of the many ways you can manipulate and combine data. There are many more. We began with index creation because that really gets you into many measurement questions fast. Some researchers forget these basics—like reliability tests and checking the directions variables are coded—and their analyses are mush as a result.

And you're practicing with real data. These aren't hypothetical data. They're real—with all the problems real data have. You're learning to interpret statistics *within* the context of the data to which they're applied.

Next we turn to even more problems of real data—how to handle noninterval measurement. You may, by this time, think noninterval data are the only kinds we political scientists have, and that's not too much of an overstatement. Even so, it is enormously important to learn the interval statistics. Statistics at other measurement levels were constructed to emulate interval statistics. We frequently apply interval statistics to noninterval data (and you need a feel for the consequences of that). And we really are getting better and better at measuring.

EXERCISES

EXERCISE 1 Suggestions for Completing the Exercise

Use income (almost interval in this coding) to explain evaluation of a candidate on a feeling thermometer.

Use a respondent's feelings about one party on the thermometer to explain feelings about the other party on the thermometer.

Use age or education to explain feeling thermometer reactions to a group or candidate.

Use feelings about one group to explain feelings about another group—both measured on the thermometers.

EXERCISE 2 Suggestions for Completing the Exercise

Measure efficacy by counting the number of efficacious responses on GOVTSAY TO PARTINT. (They are all consecutive in the file, so the TO notation saves you the trouble of writing them all out.) If you say COUNT EFFICACY = GOVTSAY TO PARTINT (5), you will end up with an efficacy measure that is a score of 0 for all cases who gave no efficacious responses to any of the six items, a score of 1 for only one efficacious response in the six items, a score of 2 for two efficacious responses, up to a score of 6 for six efficacious answers. Because the value that represents the efficacious response on all six items is the same (5), you can enter it just once at the end of the variable list, rather than repeating it after every variable name on the COUNT command. (Don't forget the QMISS, IF, and MISSING VALUES.) This efficacy measure isn't much of an interval variable. Expect low correlations because it is practically ordinal. Also notice on your scattergram how the cases are piled up at each score rather than spread out.

Or try creating a measure of political participation by counting the number of acts performed on INFLUEN TO MONEYPAC. Note here that the value which means "did do it" is 1, so 1 goes into the parentheses in COUNT PARTIC= INFLUEN TO MONEYPAC (1). Again, don't forget the QMISS, IF, and MISSING statements; you can use the same list format INFLUEN TO MONEYPAC after QMISS that you used after COUNT PARTIC= .

EXERCISE 3 Suggestions for Completing the Exercise

Party identification (ordinal, but sometimes treated as interval) is measured both before and after the election.

Evaluations of candidates are measured on thermometers, both before and after the election.

SUGGESTED READINGS

Plot and Correlations and Using an SPSS File

BERENSON, MARK L., DAVID M. LEVINE, and MATTHEW GOLDSTEIN. *Intermediate Statistical Methods and Applications: A Computer Package Approach* (Englewood Cliffs, NJ: Prentice-Hall, 1983), Ch. 8. This material may be too advanced yet; if you don't feel comfortable with it, don't worry.

NORUSIS, MARIJA. *SPSS/PC+* (Chicago: SPSS, Inc., 1988). Chapters 12 and 13 in Part B are statistical discussions of PLOT, CORRELATIONS, and the regression statistics. The commands are in C-116 — C-121 for PLOT and in C-28 — C-30 for CORRELATIONS.

SPSS-X User's Guide, 3rd ed. (Chicago: SPSS, Inc., 1988). Chapter 24 is CORRELATIONS, pp. 418-427. Chapter 41 is PLOT, pp. 788-803.

Count, Multiple Indicators, Measurement, and Reliability

BABBIE, EARL L. *The Practice of Social Research*, 3rd ed. (Belmont, CA: Wadsworth, 1983), pp. 113-119; 129; 367-378.

BOWEN, BRUCE, and HERBERT F. WEISBERG. *An Introduction to Data Anaylsis* (San Francisco: Freeman, 1980), pp. 106-114.

CARMINES, EDWARD G., and RICHARD A. ZELLER. *Reliability and Validity Assessment*, # 17 in series, *Quantitative Applications in the Social Sciences* (Beverly Hills: Sage, 1979). Perhaps too advanced for this stage of the game, it—will be of use to you later.

JOHNSON, JANET BUTTOLPH, and RICHARD A. JOSLYN. *Political Science Research Methods* (Washington, DC: Congressional Quarterly Press, 1986), pp. 77-81.

KIDDER, LOUISE. *Selltiz, Wrightsman and Cook's Research Methods in Social Relations*, 4th ed. (New York: Holt, Rinehart and Winston, 1981), pp. 126-129; 199-202.

NACHMIAS, DAVID, and CHAVA NACHMIAS. *Research Methods in the Social Sciences*, 2nd ed. (New York: St. Martin's, 1981), pp. 146-151; 391-392.

NORUSIS, MARIJA. *SPSS/PC+* (Chicago: SPSS, Inc., 1988), pp. C-31 — C-32 for COUNT.

SPSS-X User's Guide, 3rd ed. (Chicago: SPSS, Inc., 1988), Section 7.37, pp. 132-133 on COUNT. The example "pays attention to media" and the NREAD index in the text parallel the SPSS example closely.

ZELLER, RICHARD A., and EDWARD G. CARMINES. *Measurement in the Social Sciences: The Link Between Theory and Data* (New York: Cambridge University Press, 1980). This may be too advanced for right now. Save the reference for later.

Aggregate Data

ZISK, BETTY. *Political Research* (Lexington, MA: D.C. Heath, 1981), Ch. 3.

CHAPTER

7

EXPLAINING VARIATION IN AN INTERVAL DEPENDENT VARIABLE WITH A NOMINAL/ORDINAL INDEPENDENT VARIABLE

Less than Interval Measurement

Up to this chapter, you have been using interval (or almost interval) measurement of the concepts. As you have probably figured out, however, there are many concepts in political science which are not measured that precisely, even if we sometimes think of them in interval terms in our theories. Some of our most important concepts are measured at only the ordinal or nominal level. (Review Chapter 1 if these words are giving you trouble.)

Think about party identification, for example. We ask survey respondents in the U.S. whether they consider themselves Democrats or Republicans or independents. We then ask Democrats and Republicans whether they consider themselves strong or weak, and we ask independents whether they lean toward a party or not. These questions allow us to code people as 0 for strong Democrats, 1 for weak Democrats, 2 for independents who lean toward the Democrats, 3 for really independent independents, and so on, up to 7 for strong Republicans. On such a measure, we know that people coded 5 are "more Republican" than people coded 4, that people coded 4 are "more Republican" than those coded 3, and so on; but we don't have any way of knowing exactly how much more Republican they are. This measurement is ordinal, not interval.*

Or think about measures of democracy. We might construct a democracy index giving countries one point for each of the following characteristics: a free press, peaceful turnover of offices, more than one political party, universal suffrage, etc. We'd be able to say that countries scored 4 were more democratic than countries scored 2 and that countries scored 2 were more democratic than countries scored 0; but we wouldn't be able to say how much more because this measure is ordinal, not interval.

As a review, imagine how you would construct this democracy index using the COUNT procedure in SPSS. In your data set, you would need a variable for each characteristic—free press, peaceful turnover, multiple parties, universal suffrage—scored, perhaps, 1 = yes, the characteristic is present; or 0 = no, the characteristic is not present; or 9 = missing, whether the characteristic is present cannot be ascertained. To make the democracy index, you'd use the following statements:

---

*For some of the controversy over this measure see: Shively, 1980.

```
COUNT DEMINDEX = PRESS,
  TURNOVER, PARTIES, SUFFRAGE
  (1)/QMISS = PRESS, TURNOVER,
  PARTIES, SUFFRAGE (9).
IF (QMISS GT 0) DEMINDEX=99.
MISSING VALUES DEMINDEX(99).
```

Then you would be ready to do any analysis procedure with DEMINDEX as a variable. SPSS would drop from the analyses any countries on which you didn't have information on all four indicators of democracy.

Many concepts are measured at the even lower nominal level. Take religion, for example. We might give Protestant respondents a score of 1, Catholic respondents a score of 2, and Jewish respondents a score of 3; but the numbers might as well be *a, z, e* for all the meaning they have relative to one another. The numbers just "stand for" a word. They don't mean even "more than/less than." They are nominal, not ordinal.

Other important nominal variables and examples of the codes they might be given include sex of respondent (1 = male / 2 = female), or region in which a state exists (1 = North / 2 = South, or 1 = North / 2 = East / 3 = South / 4 = West), or country in which a respondent lives, or governmental form of a country (1 = parliamentary / 2 = presidential/ 3 = combination).

Using Nominal/Ordinal Independent Variables with Regression and Pearson's Correlation

Sometimes you will see ordinal *independent* variables used in regression analyses, especially if the researcher can imagine that the order of the codes represents an interval-level measurement she or he just can't get at very precisely. The researcher probably believes that the concept is theoretically interval but that the measurement skills for empirical data just haven't developed that far yet.

For example, how intensely a respondent feels about a particular candidate might, at the theoretical level, be conceptually interval; that is, we can imagine it as an interval scale—with equal increments up a scale from -100 = intense dislike, through 0 = neutral, to +100 = intense like. But we might only be able to get at order in our measurement and not at the equal increments; that is, we might be able to measure only 1 = dislike, 2 = neutral, 3 = like.

In this case, we might argue that the ordinal measurement of the variable is just an interval one with a lot of error in it, use the variable as an independent variable in regression or correlation, and expect very low correlations because of the very wide scatter that would result from the error. For an example, let's use "response to candidate" given above: with an interval measurement, according to our theory, we ought to be able to distinguish 201 different degrees of dislike from -100 to +100. In reality, where we only have an ordinal measure, all those cases that, in theory, ranged from -100 to -1 are lumped together in one category on our ordinal measurement and scored 1. All those cases that, in theory, ranged from +1 to +100 are lumped together in another category and scored 3. Those at zero are considered to be in another category and are scored 2. The degree of precision we lose using ordinal rather than interval measurement is the degree to which we fail to distinguish between a -50 and a -75, for example, or between +21 and +38. This lack of precision is the error that is in the ordinal measurement but which wouldn't have been there with better measurement.

A scatterplot would look something like Figure 7.1 if a nine-value ordinal independent variable were used. Cases are spread out vertically on the interval dependent variable but are clustered on the ordinal independent variable above each of the ordinal numbers. Notice that the cases are not in every location along the horizontal scale. They are confined to the ordinal positions—not spread out horizontally as they would be with interval measurement.

Regression may reasonably be used to describe such a relationship but only if the interval dependent variable is linearly related to the ordinal independent, as in Figure 7.1. The regression line would go through the middle of each category of cases. If you take a ruler and draw in what looks like the best-fitting line,

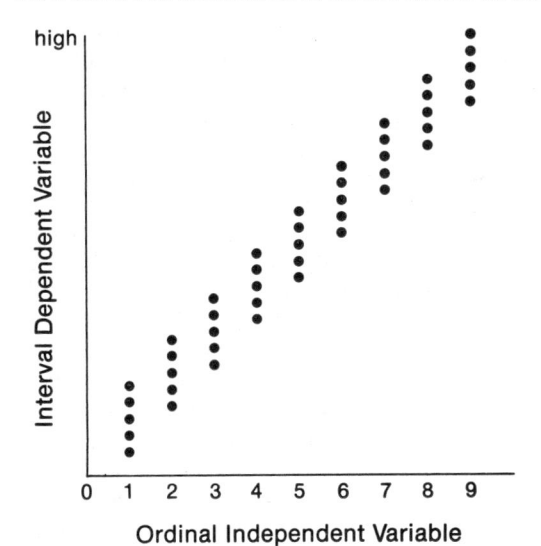

FIGURE 7.1 Scatterplot with an Ordinal Independent Variable

you can easily imagine measuring error off this line and getting a measure of explained variation, an interpretable slope, and intercept.

Think, however, what would happen in Figure 7.2 if you drew a straight line trying to come as close as possible to all the points.

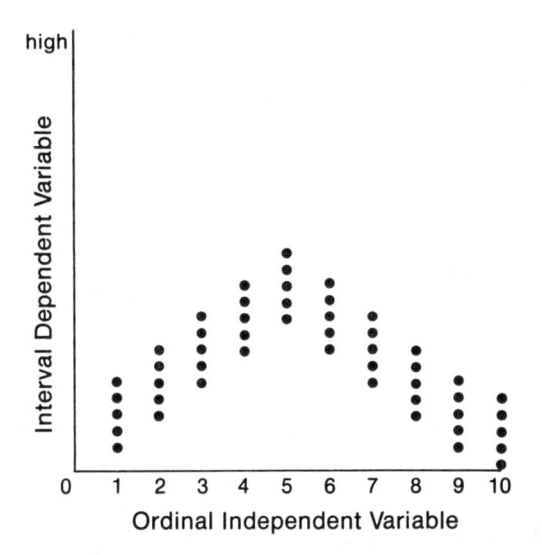

Figure 7.2 Scatterplot, Ordinal Independent Variable, Curvilinear Relationship

In that plot, there is a curved relationship—a straight line won't describe the relationship well at all. Neither the strength of the relationship nor the form of the relationship can be measured using straight-line statistics. If you use linear regression to get the best-fitting straight line, that line will be flat. The slope will be zero, and the scatter off the straight line would reduce the correlation coefficient to near zero.

Think through that a minute. Linear regression involves calculating the best-fitting *straight* line. The slope (b) of the line is constant across the entire range of the independent variable. Regardless of which one-unit increment in X you are talking about, the expected increase (decrease) in Y is the same.

The best-fitting slope for the curved relationship in Figure 7.2 is zero, which will draw a flat line at the mean of the dependent variable. Such a flat line at the mean is the only one that will minimize the squared distances from the data points to the line. For r^2, the error is measured off that best-fitting straight line, but there will be just as much error from the data points to the line as from the data points to the dependent variable mean. And that yields a correlation of zero. None of the variation around the mean is explained by a straight-line description of a curved relationship, like that given in the example.

On the other hand, with the earlier example, in which the relationship was not a curved one, the error from data points to the line was less than from the data points to the overall mean of the dependent variable. Some variation was explained, even though there was ordinal rather than interval measurement of the independent variable. The Pearson correlation would be pretty high. In that previous case, error came from the error in the independent variable (and, of course, from unexplained variation in the dependent variable) but not from the curve of the relationship. The lack of precision (cases are not spread out between 1 and 2 or between 5 and 6 but are lumped up at the ordinal values 1, 2, 5, 6, etc.) in ordinal measurement there adds error and reduces correlation. It does not, however, completely rule out the use of regression because the *relationship* is linear.

More severe problems arise with *nominal* independent variables. You can't talk about an "increase" on a nominal variable because "to increase" has no meaning when the numbers merely stand for unordered variables. Consider religion, for example, with Protestant = 1, Catholic = 2, Jew = 3. An increase of one unit has no meaning because there is no way that one "increases" from Protestant to Catholic. A decrease of one unit has no meaning because there is no way that one "decreases" from Jew to Catholic or from Catholic to Protestant.

Nor does "linear" relationship have any meaning when the numbers on the values have no inherent relationship to each other but could be shifted around the various values of the variable without consequence. The means on some dependent variable might progress upward as categories on an independent changed from Protestant to Catholic to Jew (1 to 2 to 3); but if another researcher had chosen to code 1, 2, 3 as Protestant, Jew, and Catholic, the means on that dependent would no longer progress neatly upward.

When an independent variable is nominal measurement with more than two values, therefore, regression is ordinarily useless, and a Pearson correlation won't tell you anything. A slope in regression represents how much a dependent variable increases for each unit increase in the independent variable; with nominal measurement, the concept of "unit increase" is meaningless. The correlation coefficient measures scatter off a straight line; with nominal measurement, the relation may or may not be straight, depending on what order the values happen to be coded. (In Chapter 16 you will learn a way to salvage nominal variables with more than two values for use in regression.)

But sometimes, if the nominal independent variable is a dichotomy (a variable that has only two values), you will find regression and Pearson correlation used. The cases in the scatterplot will "pile up" on the dependent variable above the codes on the dichotomy, as they do in Figure 7.3, and just as they piled up over the values of the ordinal independent variable, except that here there are only two values of the independent variable.

Remember that ordinarily the slope (b) is interpreted as how much increase is expected in Y for every one-unit increase in X. If the independent variable dichotomy is coded so that its values have a one-unit difference (i.e., 0/1, 1/2, 5/6, 7/8, *not* 8/12, 1/5), the regression slope (b) can be interpreted as the difference of means on the dependent variable of the two groups defined by the independent variable. As you go up one unit on the independent variable (which, with a dichotomous independent variable, means as you go from one group to the second group), the dependent variable increases an average of so many points (b, the slope).

The value of the slope, as you go up one unit on the dichotomous independent variable, takes you from the dependent variable mean of one group of cases to the dependent variable mean of the other group of cases. Since the mean of the dependent variable is the "best

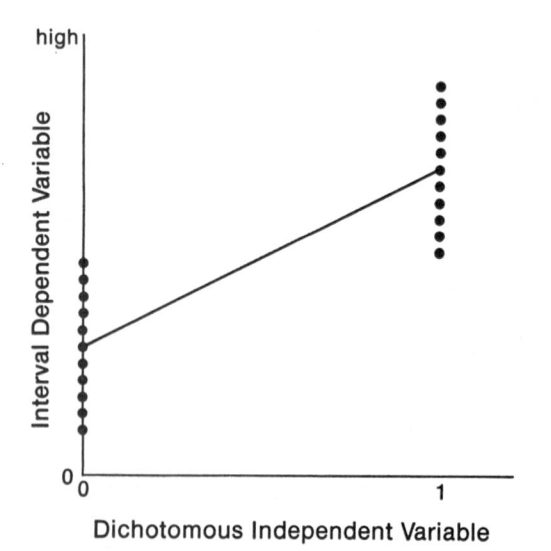

FIGURE 7.3 Scatterplot with Dichotomous Independent Variable

fit" within each group (the value to guess to reduce error in a group to a minimum), connecting the two means gives the best-fitting line for all the cases.

If the dichotomy is scored 0/1, a (the intercept) is the mean score for the group scored 0, and b (the slope) is how much you increment (or decrement) a to get to the mean of the second group. You can figure this out if you remember the equation for the straight line, the best guess in regression: $Y = a + bX + e$. The predicted value of Y is a when $X = 0$; i.e., $Y_p = a + b(0) + e$; the predicted value of Y is $a + b$ when $X = 1$; i.e., $Y_p = a + b(1) + e$. Therefore, the intercept, a, = mean of Y for the group coded zero on independent; and $a + b$ = mean of Y for the group coded 1 on independent. The r^2 in this situation is still how much variation is explained by the independent variable.

Until you really know what you are doing, the safest rule is never to use regression with less than interval measurement on the *dependent* variable. (See the Suggested Readings for solutions, or recode your independent variable into categories and use the tabular analysis presented in Chapter 8.) Still, you can see that regression is easy to use and to interpret, when the independent variable is a dichotomy. It can be cautiously used and interpreted when the independent variable has several ordinal codes and the relationship is linear. It cannot be used at all with several ordinal codes on the independent variable and a nonlinear relationship or, ordinarily, with several nominal codes on the independent variable. (Remember, however, that there is an exception to the rule about using regression with nominal independent variables of more than two codes; this will be covered in Chapter 16.)

If regression won't work, we have to think about another statistic when we have measurement problems on the independent variable or when we have a curvilinear relationship; for example, what do we do when we have ordinal or nominal codes on the independent variable and interval measurement on the dependent variable or when we have a relationship that is not a straight-line one? One solution is to use a procedure called analysis of variance, which is analogous in its interpretation to the correlations examined in the last chapter.

ANALYSIS OF VARIANCE

Imagine now a situation in which you have an interval dependent variable and an independent variable with, say, four values. The values of the independent variable can represent either nominal or ordinal measurement. The statistic we are about to examine does not take any notice of whether the scores on the independent variable have any order to them. That makes the statistic useful when we want to ignore the order in the values of an independent variable so that we can describe a curvilinear relationship which doesn't progress neatly and linearly as we go up or down the scale of order on the independent variable. It also makes a useful statistic for variables on which the values are merely nominal, standing for categories rather than a particular order or interval.

The Strength of the Relationship

You want to explain the variation in the dependent variable. Without knowledge of a case's score on the independent variable, your best guess of each case's value on the dependent variable is the overall mean of the dependent variable for all the cases. (Remember Chapters 2 and 4.) You make the smallest error with that guess—i.e., $\Sigma (Y_i - \overline{Y})^2$ is smaller when the mean is the value to which the actual score is compared than it would be with any value other than the mean.

How can you improve the guess (i.e., reduce the error), knowing the independent variable score for each case? Examine the situation pictured in Figure 7.4, in which I want you to imagine many cases at each dot. A dot represents the dependent variable, Y, score of all the cases in a particular category. What category a case is in is determined by the case's score value on the independent variable.

86 EXPLAINING VARIATION IN AN INTERVAL DEPENDENT VARIABLE WITH A NOMINAL/ORDINAL INDEPENDENT VARIABLE

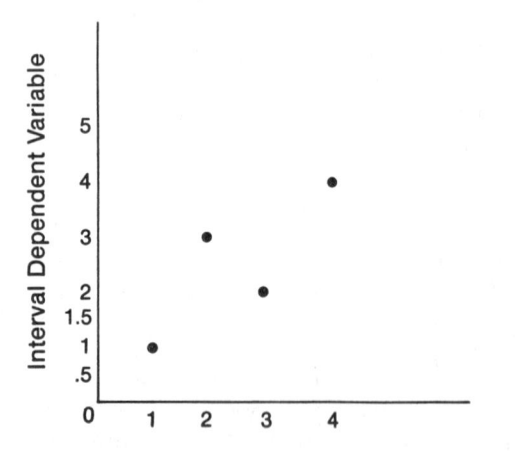

FIGURE 7.4 Hypothetical Distribution of Scores for Analysis of Variance

FORMULA 7.1 The PRE Measure of Association

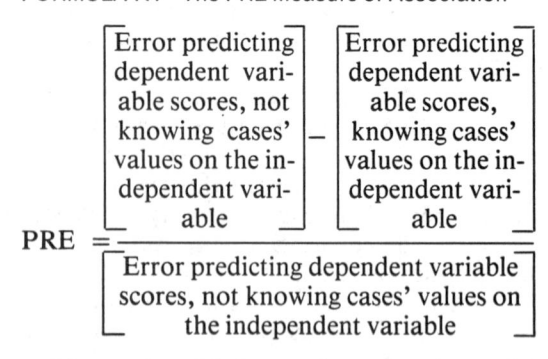

$$PRE = \frac{\begin{bmatrix} \text{Error predicting} \\ \text{dependent vari-} \\ \text{able scores, not} \\ \text{knowing cases'} \\ \text{values on the in-} \\ \text{dependent vari-} \\ \text{able} \end{bmatrix} - \begin{bmatrix} \text{Error predicting} \\ \text{dependent vari-} \\ \text{able scores,} \\ \text{knowing cases'} \\ \text{values on the in-} \\ \text{dependent vari-} \\ \text{able} \end{bmatrix}}{\begin{bmatrix} \text{Error predicting dependent variable} \\ \text{scores, not knowing cases' values on} \\ \text{the independent variable} \end{bmatrix}}$$

Notice that this is exactly analogous to the correlation (Pearson's r^2) you learned in Chapter 4—a PRE statistic to describe the strength of a relationship between two variables. However, here you have another rule for guessing. Guess the category mean rather than basing your guess on the straight line, that is, rather than guessing the score predicted by $Y = a + bX + e$. The changed rules represent changes in the measurement levels of the variables.

If all cases in each category of the independent variable had the same dependent variable score right at the mean of the dependent variable, knowing a case's category on the independent variable would allow you to predict its score on the dependent variable exactly. If a case were in category 1 of the independent variable (had a score or value of 1 on the independent variable), you'd predict 1 for the dependent; if it were in category 2 of the independent, you'd predict 3 for the dependent, etc. And you'd make no error.

Each case is exactly at the dependent variable mean for all cases that fall into the particular category defined by the value on the independent variable. Therefore, subtracting the dependent variable mean for cases in that category from each case's score would leave zero error: $\Sigma (Y_i - \overline{Y}_j)^2 = 0$. Here j means category and $\overline{Y}_j$ means category mean.

In this case, knowing the independent variable's value for each case would allow you to reduce your error by 100%. You would have explained 100% of the variance in the dependent variable. The PRE statistic (the measure of association) to indicate this relationship is shown by Formula 7.1. In Figure 7.4, it would be 1.0.

What if not all the dependent variable scores fall exactly at the mean of the dependent variable for cases in each category of the independent variable (just as not all scores fell exactly on the regression line), as is shown in Figure 7.5? You'd still guess the category

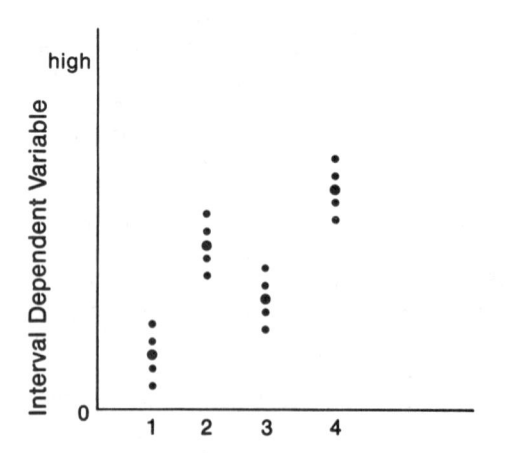

FIGURE 7.5 Hypothetical Distribution of Scores for Analysis of Variance

mean. By guessing $\bar{Y}_1$ when the case is in the X_1 category defined by a score of 1 on the independent variable, $\bar{Y}_2$ when the case is in the X_2 category defined by a score of 2 on the independent variable, $\bar{Y}_3$ when the case is in the X_3 category defined by a score of 3 on the independent variable, etc., you'd reduce your error to its smallest possible amount.

The amount of scatter and error around each category mean $\Sigma (Y_i - \bar{Y}_j)^2$ can then be summed for all categories to give a measure of the amount of unexplained variation—that which we still cannot explain knowing the independent variable score. You would subtract that unexplained variation from the overall variation in the dependent variable and divide by the overall variation to get the proportion of variation in the dependent variable that can be explained by the independent variable.

Now we can state Formula 7.2 in notational terms to summarize our measure of strength of association (the proportion of explained variation) when the independent variable is categorized and the dependent variable is interval. This is exactly the same formula as Formula 7.1; here, however, it is in the kind of notation that may make the new guessing rules clearer.

FORMULA 7.2 E^2, a PRE Measure of Association, Interval Dependent Variable and Categorized Independent Variable

$$E^2 = \frac{\Sigma (Y_i - \bar{Y}..)^2 - \Sigma\Sigma (Y_i - \bar{Y}_j)^2}{\Sigma (Y_i - \bar{Y}..)^2}$$

where:

$\Sigma \Sigma (Y_i - \bar{Y}_j)^2$ says to sum the error $(Y_i - \bar{Y}_j)^2$ around the dependent variable mean for all the cases in each category of the independent variable and then sum those totals for all the categories

$\bar{Y}..$ is the overall (grand) mean of the dependent variable calculated in the usual way by adding up all the cases and dividing by the total number of cases

$\bar{Y}_j$ is the dependent variable mean within each category of the independent variable

Although this isn't the formal notation usually seen in statistics books, it does make clear what is going on in this measure of association, which we call E^2 or the *correlation ratio* to differentiate it from the r^2 (the correlation coefficient), which implies interval data and a linear relation.

As you go piece by piece through the formula, you can see that we first have a measure of overall variation in the dependent variable—the amount of variation there is to be explained. This is the amount of error we'd make guessing the mean as the predicted score of each case on the dependent variable without regard to the cases' scores on the independent variable. We symbolize this variation as $\Sigma (Y_i - \bar{Y}..)^2$, which is exactly the same as the variation you saw in Chapter 2 (except here we use Y to show we are talking about the dependent variable) and in Chapter 4. We change the designation of the Y mean from $\bar{Y}$ to $\bar{Y}..$ to clarify that we are now referring to the dependent variable mean for all the cases (the grand mean), not the mean for a particular category of cases. To calculate that overall variation, take the grand mean of the dependent variable from each case's score on the dependent variable, square the difference, and add the squared differences up for all the cases, just as you learned to do in Chapter 2.

Second, subtracted from the overall variation in the dependent variable, we have a measure of how much variation in the dependent variable we cannot explain when we know into which independent variable category a case falls. That is $\Sigma \Sigma (Y_i - \bar{Y}_j)^2$ in the formula. It represents the scatter around the mean of the dependent variable within each category of the independent variable, which is then added to the scatter around the dependent variable means of the other independent variable categories. To calculate that, the dependent variable mean for all cases in a category is subtracted from the true dependent variable scores of all cases in that category. The differences are each squared $(Y_i - \bar{Y}_j)^2$. After the differences are squared, they are added up in each category: $\Sigma (Y_i - \bar{Y}_j)^2$. Then the sums for each category are added together: $\Sigma \Sigma (Y_i - \overline{Y}_j)^2$.

The numerator of the statistic thus represents how much variation was explained by the independent variable. You have the total variation minus that variation left unexplained by the independent. The difference is the amount explained.

The denominator, once again, represents the total variation. Thus, when numerator is divided by denominator, you get a measure of the proportion of the total variation explained by the independent variable.

There is another way of thinking about the strength of relationship between the categorized independent variable and the interval dependent variable, which is equivalent to the one we have just gone through. Instead of focussing as we have above on how much error remains in the guesses from the category means, you can think of how different the distributions of the dependent variable are within the categories defined by the independent variable.

Remember how we described distributions in Chapter 2? Recall that we were talking about the average score on a variable and the distribution of scores around that average.

Think now about a distribution of scores around the mean of the dependent variable within each category of the independent variable. If the independent and the dependent variables were not related, the means on the dependent variable within categories of the independent variable would be the same as the overall, grand mean of the dependent variable. And the variations of the dependent variable within the categories would be the same as the variation in the dependent variable for the total group of cases. With no relationship, knowing what category a case belonged in on the independent variable would not help you predict a value for it on the dependent variable.

The more different those dependent variable distributions are from each other, the more likely you are to be able to predict, with relatively little error, a dependent variable value for a case, knowing its independent variable value. Thus, the more different those distributions are, the greater the proportion of the variation in the dependent variable that you can explain with the independent variable and the greater the E^2. You can compare the distributions in Figure 7.6 (a–b) to see what this means.

In the distributions on Figure 7.6(a), knowing that a case had a score of 1 on the independent variable would allow you to predict its score on the dependent variable rather exactly. The distributions of Y in the various categories of the independent variable don't overlap;

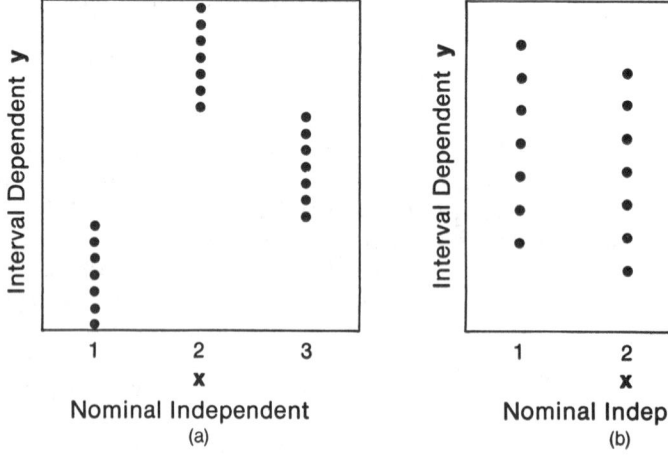

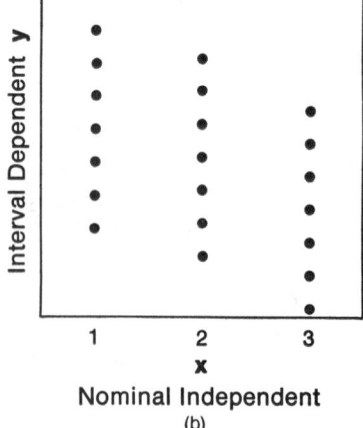

FIGURE 7.6 Two Distributions of Hypothetical Data for Analysis of Variance

their means are quite distinct. The case you are looking at with a score of 1 on the independent variable would not, in reality, have a dependent variable score that would place it in the range of the dependent variable for any of the other categories of the independent variable. An analysis of variance for these data would yield a rather high E^2.

However, in the distributions on Figure 7.6(b), which are less distinct, knowing that a case had a score of 2 on the independent variable would not allow you to predict its dependent variable score with any degree of accuracy. Cases that have different scores on the independent variable might frequently have the same scores on the dependent variable. An analysis of variance for these data would yield a rather low E^2.

The Form of the Relationship

Remember that E^2 is a measure of the strength of the relationship, not of the form of the relationship. There is no equivalent in analysis of variance to the intercept or the slope, which we used to describe the form of the relationship in regression. When we are using analysis of variance, we lack the kind of data that make them meaningful. With analysis of variance, remember, you cannot talk about an "increase of one unit" in an independent variable, which is assumed to be, at best, ordinal. Thus, there is no "slope."

However, you can describe the form of the relationship by reporting the dependent variable means within the categories defined by the independent variable. For example, if your independent variable is "region" and your dependent variable is "political participation," you can say something such as Westerners average 5 acts of political participation per year, Southerners average 4.3 acts, and Northerners average 6.2 acts. The differences among the means of participation for the three regions indicate the effect of region on participation. Those means, thus, are the best statistic you have for reporting the form of the relationship between X and Y.

EXERCISE 1 Computing E^2

It's your turn to try your hand at computing E^2. For comparison purposes, we are going to use exactly the same data as you used for regression in Chapters 4 and 5. (You may want to look back and re-examine the relationships there.) We will leave the scores on the *dependent* variable just as they were there. Remember the *dependent* has to be as interval as possible for analysis of variance.

However, we will change the interval *independent* variable scores into three categories. This has already been done for you in the reproduction of the data in the exercise section of this chapter; but, were you doing it yourself, you would simply find the lowest four scores on each *independent* variable and change each of those four scores on each independent variable to 1. Next you would find the middle four scores on each *independent* variable and change each of those four scores to 2. Finally, you would find the top (highest) four scores on each *independent* variable and change each of those four scores to 3. Given those new scores, you can divide your cases into categories on the basis of their scores on the independent variable—category 1 or 2 or 3.

You have already calculated the total variation in Y when you computed r^2 for these data in Chapter 5. There is no need to recalculate it here as you now follow Formula 7.2 in order to calculate four E^2s for the relationships between each of the independent variables you have just recoded into categories and the dependent variable you have not changed. Just follow the steps of the formula to compute measures of association for the same four relationships for which you estimated r^2 in Chapter 4. (You actually calculated at least two of the r^2s in Chapter 5.) Be sure to write out all your calculations and label them clearly.

Note: Cases are placed into categories on the basis of their *independent* variable values. For calculating the E^2 to examine a relationship between an independent and a dependent variable, you must examine *cases*, category by category. For the error within categories of the independent variable, you will take cases in one category and examine the dependent variable values only for cases in that category to calculate a category mean of the dependent variable; you will subtract that particular category mean from only the dependent variable scores of cases in that category; square and sum. Then you take cases in another category and do the same thing—and so forth, category by category. Note that this will require sorting cases into categories differently, based on independent variable scores for the four different relationships on which you are calculating an E^2.

This notion of sorting the cases on the basis of the independent variable score seems to throw some people until they get used to the logic of it. As a way of getting an understanding, you may want to try actually, physically sorting the cases as outlined here. If you follow these steps, you will have calculated an E^2 for each relationship by Formula 6.2.

Begin by photocopying the page with the data for this exercise at the end of this chapter. Cut the cases apart so that you have separate pieces of paper for each of the twelve people represented here.

Now, for the first relationship, sort the cases into three piles on the basis of their scores on the independent variable for the first exercise. It is the *second* entry following the case number on each case.

1. Take just the four cases that are scored 1 on the first independent variable. Calculate their *dependent* variable mean. The dependent variable is the first entry on each case. Subtract that mean from each of their individual dependent variable scores, square each difference, and add the squared differences for the four cases. $\sum (Y_i - \overline{Y}_j)^2$ for category 1.
2. Take just the four cases that are scored 2 on the first independent variable. Calculate their *dependent* variable mean. Subtract that from each of their individual dependent variable scores, square each difference, and add the squared differences for these four cases. $\sum (Y_i - \overline{Y}_j)^2$ for category 2.
3. Take just the four cases that are scored 3 on the first independent variable. Calculate their *dependent* variable mean. Subtract that from each of their individual dependent variable scores, square each difference, and add the squared differences for these four cases. $\sum (Y_i - \overline{Y}_j)^2$ for category 3.
4. Add the sums of the squared differences from steps 1, 2, and 3 above. This is the *unexplained* variation around the category means that cannot be explained by the independent variable, $\sum \sum (Y_i - \overline{Y}_j)^2$.
5. Subtract the unexplained variation from the overall, total variation $\sum (Y_i - \overline{Y}..)^2$, which you have already calculated in Chapter 5 for this *dependent* variable, and divide the difference by that same total variation in the dependent variable. The result is E^2.
6. Now sort the cases *again* on the basis of the second independent variable (the *third* entry following the case number on each case), and repeat each step for the E^2 for the second relationship.
7. Sort the cases *again* on the basis of the third independent variable (the *fourth* entry following the case number on each case), and repeat each step for the E^2 for the third relationship, and so on, for the fourth relationship.

Comparing E^2 and r^2

Compare your E^2 for each hypothesis to the r^2 you calculated for the same data in Chapter 5. (If you only calculated two of the correlation coefficients there, you can get the other two from a classmate for the comparison requested here.) Generally speaking, the E^2 should be a little bit lower *if* there was a *linear* relationship in the data for the regression because you have added error by categorizing the independent variable, losing the precision of the interval measurement and considering all cases in a category to be the same. Thus, the explanation will be a bit weaker. (Note that, if you used exactly the same independent variable measurement for the r^2 and the E^2, using the categorized independent variable for r^2, the resulting statistics would be identical if the relationship were linear.)

If, however, the original relationship based on interval data happened to have some curve

EXPLAINING VARIATION IN AN INTERVAL DEPENDENT VARIABLE WITH A NOMINAL/ORDINAL INDEPENDENT VARIABLE **91**

to it, the E^2 here may be a bit higher than the r^2 you calculated in Chapter 5. If the means on Y within the categories give you better prediction than $Y = a + bX$ did in the regression, the variation you explain using analysis of variance can be quite a bit larger than the variation explained in regression.

Consider the diagram of a curvilinear relationship between two variables shown in Figure 7.7.

Fitting a straight line to that curved relationship leaves you with quite a lot of error. Imagine how far off the line those cases at the top of the curve would be and how poorly predicted they would be by the line. However, if you categorized the independent variable as indicated in Figure 7.8 and used analysis of variance, you would be measuring how far the cases are vertically off the category mean of the dependent variable (indicated with a circle).

You would *lose* the distinction and precision of interval measurement on the independent variable—indicated by the arrows shown moving cases to the right or left to get them all together at low or medium or high. However, you would *increase* your ability to predict the dependent variable score because you have reduced the distance between predicted score (which here is the category mean of the dependent variable rather than the regression line in the previous diagram) and the actual score. Thus, sometimes the complexity of the analysis of variance allows you to describe the relationship more accurately than a regression would.

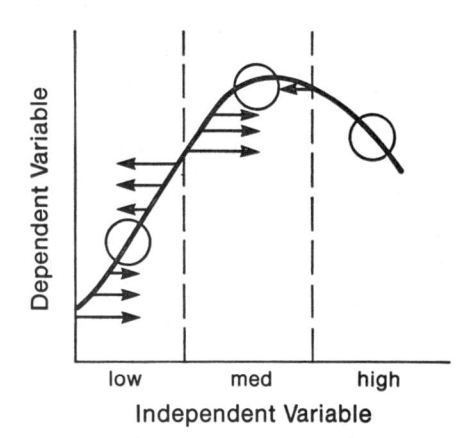

Figure 7.8 Hypothetical Curvilinear Relationship between a Categorized Independent and an Interval Dependent Variable

Let's be really clear on how analysis of variance is more complex than regression by reiterating earlier comments on the form of the relationship. On the one hand, to describe the form of a relationship when the independent variable is categorical, you have to have one descriptive statement for each category:

When the independent variable is _____, the average dependent variable score is _____; but

When the independent variable is _____, the average dependent variable score is _____; and so forth, for each and every value on the independent variable.

On the other hand, the description of the form of a linear relationship, when the independent variable is interval, can be very simple. It is the straight line defined by $a + bX + e$. One statement and the whole relationship is described. To get the average dependent variable score for cases with any value on the independent variable, the same statement applies: multiply that score on the independent vari-

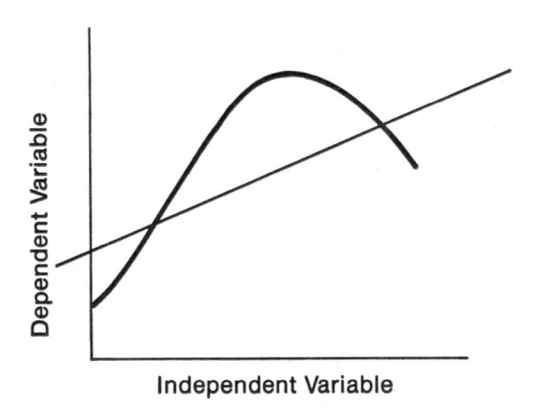

Figure 7.7 Hypothetical Curvilinear Relationship between Two Interval Variables

able by b and add a. There is no need to have a separate descriptive statement for *each* value of the independent variable.

This question of "whether it's worth the complexity" is an important one and not limited just to E^2 versus r^2. In science, we try to explain phenomena. We want good, reasonably thorough explanations but also clear, simple explanations.

We know we'll never be able to explain every bit of variation in the phenomena we're interested in. Nor do we really want to. If we did, we'd have to proceed on a case-by-case basis and never develop any general explanations that apply to wide ranges of cases.

Since we don't particularly desire to explain every last bit of variation, we want simple, parsimonious explanations. We want to explain as much variation as we can and still retain the simplest, clearest, most general explanation possible.

Thus, in seeking the most elegant, most general, simplest explanation, we want to use the statistics that let us proceed toward that goal. Unless a complex model (here analysis of variance) allows us a much better understanding of a phenomenon than a simple model (here regression), we'd just as soon use the simpler one. The comparison between E^2 and r^2 helps us make that decision.

EXERCISE 2 Comparing r^2 and E^2

For each one of the relationships on which you calculated an E^2, write whether you think there was very much curve in the relationship by comparing the regression and analysis of variance. Consider the proportion explained by the predictions based on category means (E^2) as compared to the proportion explained by the prediction based on the linear model ($Y = a + bX + e$), that is, r^2. Is the complexity of the analysis of variance procedure worth it in your opinion? (In Chapter 18, you'll learn a statistic to help you form an opinion. Right now, just answer in terms of whether that difference in proportions seems important to you.)

EXERCISE 3 Making the Computer Do the Work

SPSS Setup with the Data. Now let's see how to do the same analysis by computer using SPSS. You will be using MEANS, another SPSS procedure, on either the data from Chapter 4 or the equivalent data from this chapter. If you use those data from Chapter 4, you will get to learn more about recoding variables, a very useful thing to know.

First, you will need to make an SPSS file for the five variables. You set up a file exactly as you learned to do in Chapter 3. Start with the DATA LIST command, on which you name and tell the location of each variable, but this time name and indicate a location for each of the five variables in the preceding exercises. Then use the BEGIN DATA. command followed by one line for each case's data. Copy the data exactly from either Chapter 4 or this chapter. Then you put in the END DATA. command.

Recoding a Variable. If you are copying the data as they appeared in Chapter 4, you will need a RECODE command to get the independent variables into categories. Back in Chapter 4, remember, the independent variables were treated as interval; but, for the analysis of variance you are about to do, you need to get the independent variables into categories. If you are using the data as they appear in this chapter, the independent variables are already in categories, and you can skip down to the MEANS procedure.

The RECODE command takes one of the following three forms:

```
RECODE varname (x,x,x,x = 1)
   (y,y,y,y = 2) (z,z,z,z = 3).
RECODE varname (x THRU x = 1)
   (x THRU x = 2)
   (x THRU x = 3).
RECODE varname (LO THRU x = 1)
   (x THRU x = 2)
   (x THRU HI = 3).
```

Whichever form you use, just put the name of the variable you want recoded into the example where "varname" is. In the first format, put the existing values on that variable which you want to combine into the first category in place of the "x's." Put the existing values on that variable which you want to combine into the second category in place of the "y's." Put the existing values on that variable which you want to combine into the third category in place of the "z's."

You can also use the words LO (LOWEST), HI (HIGHEST), and THRU in order to combine a whole range of values into fewer categories. To do this, use the second or third format.

You can recode more than one variable on a single RECODE command. If the variables are to be recoded differently, place a slash after you finish indicating the recodes on one, and continue after the slash with the next variable name and its recodes. Indent any additional lines if you have to go beyond one line. Here is an example.

```
RECODE varname1 (x THRU x = 1)
    (x THRU x = 2)
    (x THRU x = 3) /varname2
    (x THRU x = 1)
    (x THRU x = 2)
    (x THRU x = 3)
    (x THRU x = 4)
```

If several are to be recoded in exactly the same way, with the same existing values being changed into the same new values for all of the several variables, the variable names can go in a list, and the recodes can be indicated just once. Here is an example of that.

```
RECODE varname1, varname2,
    varname3, varname4
    (x THRU x = 1)
    (x THRU x = 2)
    (x THRU x = 3).
```

Beware: When you are recoding data that are more complicated than those for this exercise, avoid including any codes that indicate missing values in one of the ranges of values which get recoded. For example, we might want to recode an age variable into three groups. For that we might say:

```
RECODE AGE (LO THRU 30 = 1)
    (31 THRU 50 = 2) (51 THRU HI
    = 3).
```

Age would then be ready for any analysis that required an ordinal variable of a very few codes. However, if the missing data code on AGE happened to be 99, all the cases with missing data on AGE would also be included in the third group. We might even get some young ones in that group by mistake just because their ages were not ascertained and, as a result, were given the missing data code. To avoid this, we'd say (51 thru 98) rather than (51 thru HI) on the RECODE command. That would get all the highest age group into one category without including the cases missing on the variable being recoded.

Also Beware: When you are using data already set up in a file and stored on tape or disk, the fact that you have recoded the values on a variable will not change any labels that may be attached to those values in the data set. For example, male respondents might be coded 1 on the variable "sex." If the label "male" was attached to the value of 1 on that variable when the data set was created, each time the variable is used, it will have the word "male" printed next to the value 1 on all printouts. If, for some reason, you recoded the variable "sex" so that women were coded 1, the printout would still have the word "male" attached to that value. You can change the value labels every time you recode (consult the SPSS manual), but you may find that more trouble than just remembering this problem.

The MEANS Procedure. After the recode, if you need it, you're ready to do the analysis of variance with a procedure command and subcommands like this:

```
MEANS TABLES=depvarname BY
    indvarnam1, indvarnam2,
    indvarnam3/STATISTICS = ALL.
FINISH.
```

On the MEANS command, put the name of your dependent variable where it says "depvarname" and the names of your independent variables where it says "indvarnam1, indvarnam2, indvarnam3" in the example above. Assemble and submit your job.

Examine the output and write down the proportion of the variation in the dependent variable that you explain using each of the four independent variables. Remember that the statistic which gives you that information is E^2.

It is important, as well, to determine the form of the effect of the independent variables on the dependent variable. Write out sentences that describe the effect of each of the independent variables on the dependent variable. Remember that the statistics which give you this kind of information are the dependent variable means within the categories of the independent variable. You compare those means for all the categories of an independent variable in order to see the effect of X on Y.

Did you get the same answers using the computer that you did by hand (within the bounds of some rounding error)? If not, something is wrong. Try to figure out what, and fix it. If you need help, see the instructor.

Note what you get on your output in addition to E^2 (the strength of the relationship) and the dependent variable means—for each category of cases defined by the independent variable (the form of the relationship).

For one thing, you get a test of linearity that (in addition to some tests you won't see until Chapter 18) shows you what r^2 would be calculated from the same data on which E^2 was calculated. This is not the same as the r^2 you calculated earlier in Chapter 5 with the interval form of the independent variables. There, you had the full precision of the measurement before it was recoded into categories. Here, it is the r^2 calculated on the categorized independent variables using the numbers that represent those categories as if they were interval scores. If the r^2 and E^2 are very close, you can assume the relationship was linear. If they are different, the relationship must have had some curve in it.

Another part of the output worth noticing is the number of cases in each category. When you are doing your own analyses, as you will see, you will want to make sure you have a substantial number of cases in each category.

EXERCISE 4 Analysis of Variance on Real Data

The Hypothesis. Now make up a hypothesis that posits a relationship between two concepts which can be operationalized with the variables in any one of the data sets whose codebooks are in the appendices.

Choose an independent variable that is nominal or ordinal with only 2, 3, or 4 possible values. (It gets hard to interpret many more values than this number.) Or you can choose an independent variable that can be recoded into 2, 3, or 4 categories, perhaps a multi-item index that you want to construct, using the same procedure that you learned in Chapter 6, and then recode. Make sure your dependent variable is as interval as possible; a multi-item index is a possibility, but there are also interval or near-interval variables in the data sets.

As you are selecting variables or deciding how to recode those independent variables that you have already selected, be sure to examine the distributions on those variables. You need a fairly good number of cases in each category of the independent variable for the analyses of variance. You want the dependent variable mean you calculate for each group to be a rather good estimate of what the dependent variable mean would be if you had even more cases that shared the same category on the independent variable. Moreover, you do not want one or two cases with extremely different scores on the dependent variable to be able to distort the mean of all the others in that category.

Unless the dependent variable is badly skewed, the more cases you have in each category of the independent variable, the surer you are that the mean is a pretty good description of where the cases actually are. While we cannot be exact about how many is enough, it does make some sense to shoot for about 15 to 20 cases per category—more if you have a large number of cases.

If there are categories that don't have many cases, think about recoding them to the missing data code so that they will be dropped from the analysis. Alternatively, consider whether categories with small numbers of cases might not logically be recoded to be combined with other categories. As long as they seem to have similarities on the independent variable, that is sometimes a solution.

Now, write your hypothesis, paying attention to good form in hypothesis writing. Indicate, rather completely, how you will operationalize the two concepts. Include the variables selected, how they are to be combined if you are using an index, and how they are going to be recoded if that is necessary.

For *nominal* independent variables, making a clear statement of a hypothesis is sometimes difficult because you can't say, "The greater the X, the greater the Y." You'll have to say something like: "Compared to a's, b's are greater on Y"; or, "a leads to higher Y than does b." Be sure to get the comparisons into the statement of the hypothesis, however. Comparisons are the essence of any hypothesis and of science more generally.

For *ordinal* independent variables, you can still say, "As X goes up, Y goes up," because you still have a greater-than/lesser-than measurement in ordinal data. You do have to be careful to look at the means of the dependent variable to make sure they are going up or down as you hypothesized. You might get a strong E^2 but a different *form* of the relationship than you expected. Therefore, don't just look at the strength (E^2) of the relationship. Look at the form as well.

SPSS Setup

Now let the computer and SPSS do the statistics for you to test that hypothesis. You can use the same basic setup you used in Chapter 6. You'll need exactly the same commands that you received from the instructor for the exercises in Chapter 6 to access the stored data sets. If you want to use a multi-item index either as the independent (if you recode it into a few categories) or as the interval dependent variable, you'll need next the same commands you learned to use in Chapter 6:

COUNT command
IF statement
MISSING VALUES command

Now if you need to recode a variable in the stored data file or one you have constructed with the COUNT procedure for use as an independent variable, you next need a—

RECODE command

Remember that you may be recoding in order to reduce the number of categories on the *independent* variable, to combine similar categories of the independent variable for purposes of increasing the number of cases in each remaining category, or to break an interval independent variable down into categories. Remember that you do *not* recode the *dependent* variable because it has to stay as interval as possible. (You may want to review the recode section above, especially if you didn't need to use it on Exercise 3.)

Finally, you get to the procedure command for doing the analysis of variance:

```
MEANS TABLES=depvarname BY
    indvarname/STATISTICS = ALL.
FINISH.
```

Interpreting Analysis of Variance. Submit your job, make sure it has run correctly by examining your output, and answer the following questions:

1. What percentage of the variation in the dependent variable does the independent variable explain?
2. What are the means of the dependent variable within each category?
3. Is the hypothesis consistent with the pattern you see in the different category means?
4. What other variables do you think could be caus-

ing variation in your dependent variable? Explain.

Compare your results with those of your friends in class. Try to figure out why some of the E^2 statistics are higher/lower than others.

Before you go on, let me mention that analysis of variance is frequently thought of in connection with experiments. The independent variable in an experiment would be "group" with, for example, two codes: 1 = experimental group; 0 = control group. The experimental group would be the one exposed to whatever "treatment," the effects of which the researcher was assessing. The control group would be the one not exposed. You will see more detail on experimental design and analysis in Chapter 11.

Given that many political science concepts are not amenable to experimentation, analysis of variance isn't seen as frequently in political science literature as one might expect. This is not, however, an indication that it is not a most useful technique for types of data other than experiments. Certainly you should add it to your reservoir of skills; it will come in handy.

Indeed, in political science, you frequently see analyses that revolve around the differences between means of two groups, and there are statistical tests to assess how different two means really are. Analysis of variance is equivalent to an assessment of the difference of means between two *or more* groups simultaneously; and it gives a measure of explained variation (association) that the difference of means statistics do not.

EXERCISES

The data for the Exercises 1 and 3 in this chapter are exactly the same as those for Chapter 4, except that each independent variable below has been recoded into categories. The lowest four scores on each have been recoded to 1; the middle four scores on each have been recoded to 2; and the highest four scores on each have been recoded to 3.

Case Number	Var 1 Efficacy	Var 2 Years Involved	Var 3 Social Distance	Var 4 Income	Var 5 Knowledge
1	6	1	2	1	1
2	9	1	2	1	3
3	6	1	3	3	3
4	9	1	3	2	1
5	11	2	1	2	1
6	8	2	3	2	1
7	12	2	1	2	2
8	9	2	3	3	3
9	14	3	1	1	2
10	11	3	2	1	3
11	14	3	2	3	2
12	13	3	1	3	2

SUGGESTED READINGS

Recode, Means

BOWEN, BRUCE D., and HERBERT F. WEISBERG. *An Introduction to Data Analysis* (San Francisco: Freeman, 1980), pp. 103–106.

NORUSIS, MARIJA J. *SPSS/PC+* (Chicago: SPSS, Inc., 1988). Discussion of the statistics, pp. B109–B115. Commands for MEANS, pp. C89–C91. Commands for RECODE, pp. C123–C124.

SPSS-X User's Guide, 3rd ed. (Chicago: SPSS, Inc., 1988). MEANS, Chapter 34, pp. 642–654. RECODE, Section 8.5, p. 143.

Analysis of Variance

Do not focus on significance tests (F); keep your eye on difference of means at this point.

BLALOCK, HUBERT M. *Social Statistics*, 2nd ed. (New York: McGraw-Hill, 1972), Ch. 16.

BOWEN, BRUCE D., and HERBERT F. WEISBERG. *An Introduction to Data Analysis* (San Francisco: Freeman, 1980), pp. 179–185.

IVERSON, GUDMUND R., and HELMUT NORPOTH. *Analysis of Variance*, #1 in series, *Quantitative Applications in the Social Sciences* (Beverly Hills: Sage, 1976), pp. 7–39. This may be too complicated yet; nevertheless, you will want to become familiar, eventually, with this fine series.

JOHNSON, JANET BUTTOLPH, and RICHARD A. JOSLYN. *Political Science Research Methods* (Washington, DC: Congressional Quarterly Press, 1986), pp. 287–291.

KOHOUT, FRANK J. *Statistics for Social Scientists* (New York: Wiley, 1974), Unit VI.

OTT, LYMAN, WM. MENDENHALL, and RICHARD LARSON. *Statistics: Tool for the Social Sciences*, 2nd ed. (North Scituate, MA: Duxbury, 1978), Ch. 12.

Party Identification

SHIVELY, W. PHILLIPS, "The Nature of Party Identification: Review of Recent Developments," in John C. Pierce and John L. Sullivan (eds.), *The Electorate Reconsidered* (Beverly Hills: Sage, 1980), pp. 219–236.

Dichotomous Dependent Variables

ALDRICH, JOHN H., and FORREST D. NELSON. *Linear Probability, Logit, and Probit Models* (Beverly Hills: Sage, 1984).

KLECKA, WILLIAM R. *Discriminant Analysis*, #19 in series, *Quantitative Applications in the Social Sciences* (Beverly Hills: Sage, 1980).

KLEINBAUM, DAVID G., *Applied Regression Analysis and Other Multivariable Methods* (North Scituate, MA: Duxbury, 1978), Ch. 22.

Also see: Hibbing and Welsh cited in the articles list in Chapters 5 and 16, respectively.

ARTICLES

GITELSON, IDY B., and ALAN R. GITELSON. "Adolescent Attitudes Toward Male and Female Political Candidates: An Experimental Design," *Women and Politics* (Winter 1980–81), 53–64. A more complicated analysis of variance than the bivariate ones in this chapter, this one has two independent variables used simultaneously. Nevertheless, you can focus on the means in Table 1, for example, and see the effects of sex of candidate in the ratings of those candidates given by men and women. Don't worry yet about F, df, and p; they come later.

KAY, SUSAN ANN. "Socializing the Future Elite: The Nonimpact of Law School," *Social Science Quarterly*, 59 (September 1978), 347–354. Table 3 shows 13 simple analyses of variance that compare three classes of law students on their ratings of various considerations in deciding to appeal a case.

CHAPTER
8

READING TABULAR DATA

RELATIONSHIPS BETWEEN ORDINAL VARIABLES

Now we need to move to variables with lower measurement levels—ordinal on both the independent and dependent variables. With no interval data at all, we can no longer use measures of relationship that call for adding and subtracting values; we'll only be able to use measures that rely on counting how many cases are in higher or lower categories.

In order to understand the statistics we will be using to describe the relationships between variables, we need to start by looking at the relationships we are trying to communicate, just as we started the discussion of correlation coefficients by plotting the cases on two variables. Data for relationships between ordinal variables are usually presented in tabular form, so we will start with reading tables. Measures of association for ordinal variables will wait for the next chapter.

REVIEW: SIMILARITIES BETWEEN TYPES OF ANALYSES

Let's look back a minute so that we can get a picture of how similar all these analyses of relationships are—regardless of the level of measurement of the variables. First, we measured relationships between interval-level variables by how closely cases were tied to the straight line that predicted a dependent variable score from the independent variable value, as shown in Figure 8.1.

Then, almost as if we were breaking the horizontal axis into categories, we measured the relationships by how closely cases were tied to the dependent variable means, as you can see diagramed in Figure 8.2. We predicted separate dependent variable values for each of the categories of the independent variable when

FIGURE 8.1 Relationship between Interval-Level Variables

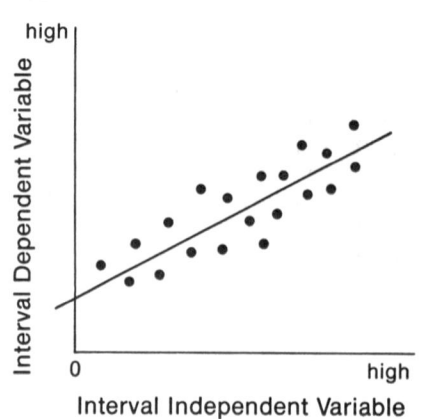

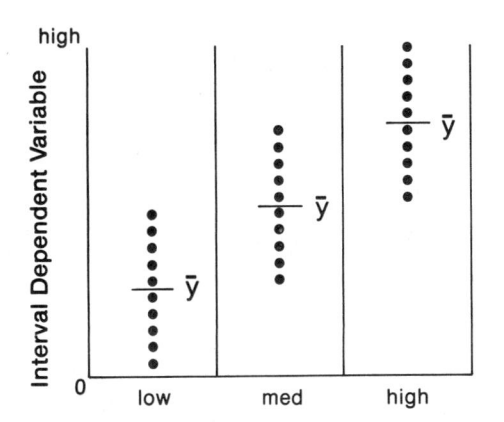

FIGURE 8.2 Relationship between a Nominal Independent Variable and an Interval Dependent Variable

we had categories on the independent variable and interval measurement on the dependent variable.

Now, we will also divide the vertical axis into categories, as in Figure 8.3. How strong the relationship is will be measured by how closely cases cluster together in the particular categories of the dependent variable predicted from their categories of the independent variable.

In both regression and analysis of variance, we began with a description of the distribution of the dependent variables. For that description, we calculated the mean and variation in

FIGURE 8.3 Relationship between Two Ordinal Variables

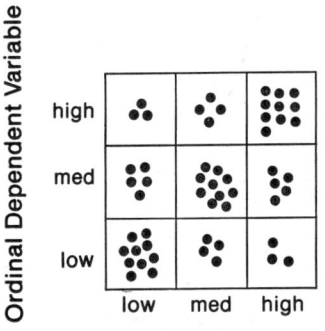

the dependent variable. (See Chapter 2, if necessary.) Then we used an independent variable to see how much of that variation could be explained. We saw that, if two variables are not related to each other, the variation in the dependent variable is the same, knowing the independent as it was before we knew the independent variable. We saw that when two variables are related, the mean of the distribution of the dependent variable is different, depending on the value of the independent variable; we can explain some of the original variation in the dependent variable.*

This is to say that the scores predicted by the line (in regression) or by the category means (in analysis of variance) represent the mean of the distribution on the dependent variable for all cases that share a particular score on the independent variable. When two variables are unrelated, the predictions about the dependent variable are all the same, regardless of the scores on the independent variable. The regression line is flat all across the range of X; and, in analysis of variance, the dependent variable means within the categories of the independent variable are all the same as the overall mean. When two variables are related, the predictions about the dependent variable (the means of the distributions) are different at different levels of the independent variable. The more different the predicted (mean) scores and the more tightly cases are arrayed around the predicted scores (the less variation around predicted scores), the better we are able to predict cases' dependent variable scores, knowing their independent variable scores, and the more variation we can explain.

We will do something similar here with ordinal data. We will describe the distribution on the dependent variable of all the cases first. Then we will see whether the distributions of the dependent variable within categories of the independent variable are similar to the overall

---

*For reasons that won't be clear until Chapter 18, we hope the variances of the distributions of Y at various values of X will *not* be different. The relationship between X and Y shows up in changes of means of Y at various levels of X, not in changes of variance.

distribution. If they are, we know that the independent variable doesn't help us to explain any of that overall variation; the two variables are unrelated. The independent is not causing any difference in the dependent variable.

However, if those distributions of the dependent variable are different in each of the categories of the independent variable, we know that the independent variable is affecting the dependent variable; the two variables are related. The more different the distributions of the dependent variable are as we look from one category of the independent variable to another, and the more different they are from the overall dependent variable distribution for all the cases, the more related the two variables are. When two variables are strongly related, we will be able more accurately to predict cases' dependent variable scores, knowing their independent variable scores.

Let's look back again to regression to clarify this. Remember that you sketched the dependent variable values on the vertical axis as a way of representing the distribution on the dependent variable for all the cases, as in Figure 8.4.

Then you plotted those same values against values of the independent variable (as in Figure 8.5) as a way of examining the distribution on

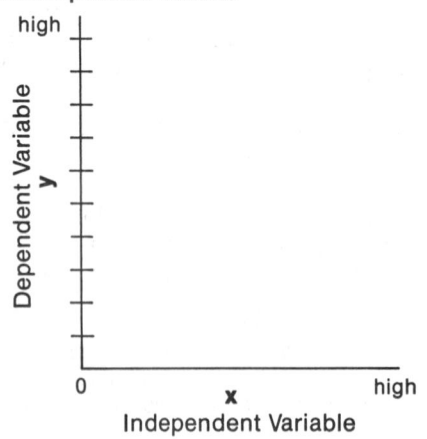

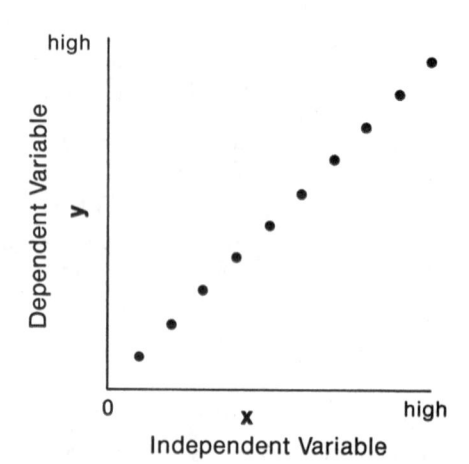

FIGURE 8.5 Review of Plotting Cases for Regression

the dependent variable for cases at a given value of the independent variable.

You can see that the scores on the dependent variable are different for each value on the independent variable when the variables are related. Were there a lot more cases, as Figure 8.6 shows, it would be clear that the distribution of the dependent variable (not just

FIGURE 8.6 Scatterplot of Scores of Two Interval Variables

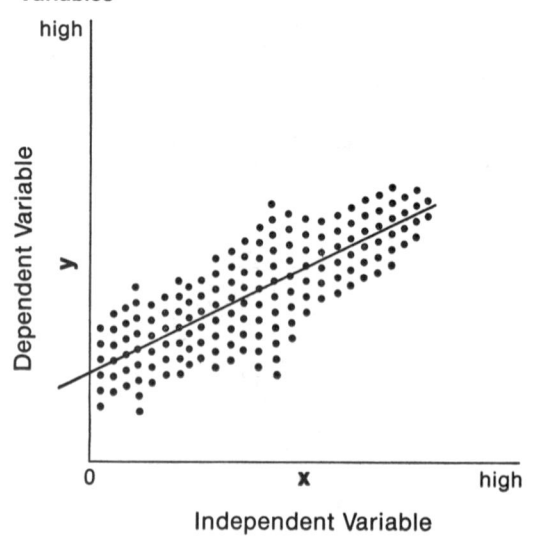

FIGURE 8.4 Review of Plotting Scores of an Interval Dependent Variable

the score of a single case) is different for each value of the independent variable. The dependent variable would have a different mean for each different value of the independent variable.

Also remember, when there was no relationship, that the distribution of the dependent variable was similar for each value of the independent variable. The dependent variable mean of all the cases at any particular independent variable value was not much different from the dependent variable mean for cases at any other independent variable value, as in Figure 8.7.

Similar things happened with analysis of variance. When the variables were related, the means of the dependent variable were different for cases in different categories of the independent variable; i.e., the distributions of the dependent variable differed across categories of the independent variable, as they do in Figure 8.8.

When there was no relationship, the distributions across categories of the independent variable were pretty much alike, as they are in Figure 8.9.

DESCRIBING DISTRIBUTIONS OF ORDINAL VARIABLES

With ordinal variables, we will be using similar

FIGURE 8.7 Scatterplot of Scores of Two Unrelated Interval Variables

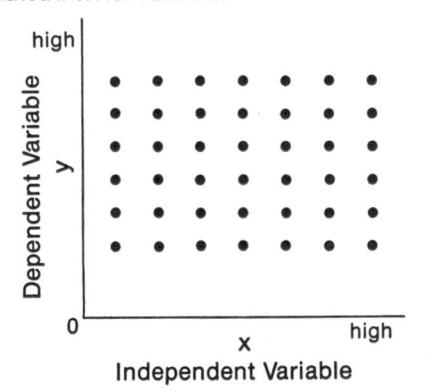

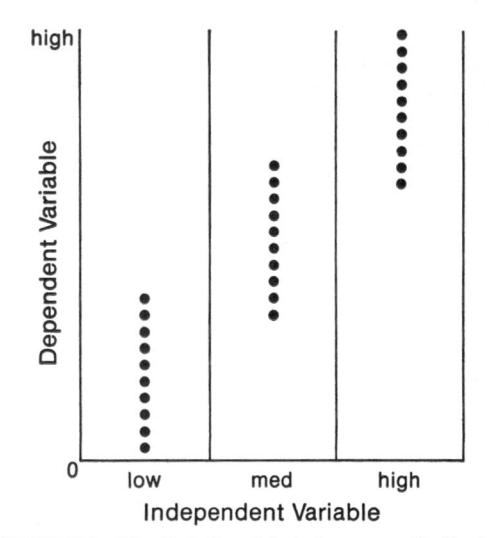

FIGURE 8.8 The Relationship between an Ordinal Independent Variable and an Interval Dependent Variable

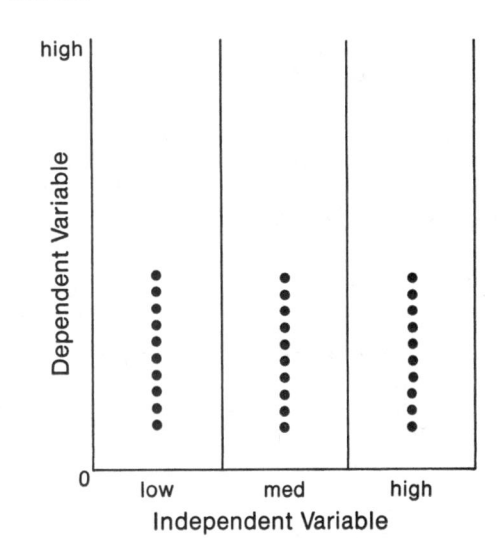

FIGURE 8.9 An Indication of No Relationship between an Ordinal Independent Variable and an Interval Dependent Variable

concepts to talk about relationships, but we cannot describe the distributions the same way. We can't calculate a mean because that requires adding up the scores; and we can't add ordinal scores because we don't know that the distance from 1 to 2 is the same as the distance from 2 to 3. We can't use variation because that requires subtracting the mean from each value; and we can't subtract when we don't know that the distance from one score to the next is the same all along the scale.

However, there is a way to describe the distribution of an ordinal variable by saying what percentage of cases falls into each category of the variable; and there is a way to look at the distribution of an ordinal dependent variable within every value of an independent. Therefore, although our way of describing the distributions will change for ordinal measurement level, the interpretations we will use are much the same. When the distributions of the dependent variable change as the values of the independent variable change, we will say that we have explained the dependent variable.

EXERCISE 1a   Describing the Overall Distributions of Ordinal Variables

In the exercise section at the end of the chapter, you'll find a list of cases and their values on four variables. Begin by examining the independent and first dependent variables and by considering the hypothetical operationalizations attached to them.

Write a hypothesis that posits a relationship between the two variables, and draw up a blank table of three rows and three columns. For now, rather than worry about proper table form, use something like the form in Figure 8.10.

Now, in order to describe the distribution on the dependent variable, follow these steps:

1. Count the number of cases that are high on the dependent variable.
2. Write that number to the right of the table, below the word "totals," and to the right of the row marked "high" for the dependent variable.
3. Count the number of cases that are medium on the dependent variable.
4. Write that number to the right of the first table, below the word "totals," and to the right of the row marked "medium".
5. Count the number of cases that are low on the dependent variable and write that number in the remaining space.
6. Now calculate a percentage that will describe the relative sizes of the high/medium/and low dependent variable categories, and write those percentages next to the numbers in the "totals" column. (Take the number "high" and divide by the total number of cases; this is the *proportion* that is high; multiply that answer by 100 to get the percentage high. Then take the number "medium" and divide by the total number of cases; multiply by 100; that is your percentage medium.

Ordinal Independent Variable

	low	med	high	Totals
high				
med				
low				
Totals	100%	100%	100%	

(Ordinal Dependent Variable)

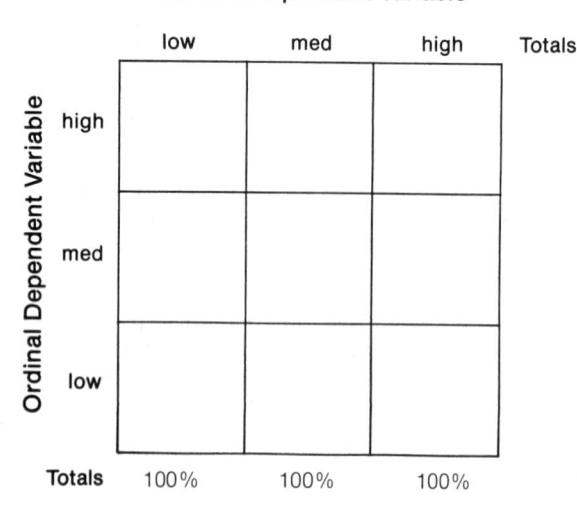

FIGURE 8.10   Sample Table for Exercise 1

Repeat for low. Round each to the nearest whole percent. The three percentages should add to 100% unless there is some rounding error, which may make the total 101% or 99%.)

This set of percentages describes the distribution of the dependent variable—tells how clustered the cases are in which categories or how spread out they are across categories. If roughly one-third of the cases fall into each category of a three-value dependent variable, the cases are spread out. This result is analogous to having a large standard deviation and lots of variation. The only way the cases could be more spread out is to have them begin to cluster in both of the two extreme categories. The more the cases cluster up in one category so that category begins to contain a number closer and closer to all the cases, the closer you get to a very narrowly distributed variable—analogous to a very small standard deviation that we'd interpret as very low variation.

EXERCISE 1b Describing Conditional Distributions of Ordinal Variables

The next task is to describe the distributions of the dependent variable *within* each category of the independent variable in order to see how they differ from the overall distribution. To do this for the first relationship under consideration here, examine the independent variable and the first dependent variable at the same time.

On the blank table you created above, put a number in each cell to indicate how many cases have the values both on the independent variable and on the dependent variable indicated for that cell. For example, in the upper left cell, put the number of cases that are low on the independent variable *and* high on the dependent variable; in the lower right cell, put the number of cases that are high on the independent variable *and* low on the dependent; in the center cell, put the number of cases that are medium on the independent variable *and* medium on the dependent variable; and so forth, until all the cells have a number for the cases that have the designated values. Then add up the number of cases that share each value of the independent variable; that is, add the numbers of cases in each column, and indicate this total at the bottom of each column below the 100% label.

As a check, look to make sure that the numbers of cases in the cells in each row add up to the total you had indicated earlier for that row. Moreover, make sure that the numbers of cases in the column totals add up to the total number of cases overall (here 50). If the numbers in the cells don't add up across a row to the total number of cases that is supposed to be in a row, or if the columns totals don't add up to the total number of cases, something is wrong. Figure out what, and fix it.

Some people find this counting procedure easiest if they go case by case and put a mark for each case into the appropriate cell. They examine a case on the independent variable to determine what column the case is going to go in (high, medium, or low on the independent variable). Then they examine that same case on the dependent variable to determine what row to put it in (high, medium, or low on the dependent variable). Having figured out the appropriate column and row for the case, they put a mark in the cell. Then they turn to the next case and repeat the procedure.

When you have finished figuring out how many cases there are in each cell, describe the distribution of the dependent variable *within* each category of the independent variable, just as you did for the overall distribution. Working one column at a time (that is, working with cases scored alike on the independent variable):

1. Divide the number of cases in the top cell (high on the dependent) by the total number of cases *for that value of the independent variable* (the number of cases scored low on the independent variable—the number in the first column of cases); multiply the result by 100.
2. Divide the number of cases in the middle cell (medium on the dependent) by the total number of cases for that value of the independent variable (low); multiply the result by 100.

3. Repeat for the number of cases in the bottom cell.
4. Repeat steps 1, 2, and 3 for the second column—cases scored medium on the independent variable.
5. Repeat steps 1, 2, and 3 for the third column—cases scored high on the independent.

Enter your results in the cells of the table, along with the number of cases that fell into that cell. Make sure the columns total to 100% (within the limits of some rounding error, as you make percentages equal to the nearest whole percentage). Make sure the table is clearly labeled.

You have now described three *conditional* distributions—distributions of the dependent variable within the conditions laid out by the values of the independent variable. Unlike the marginal distribution of the dependent variable that doesn't take into account the values of the independent, each conditional distribution indicates the distribution of Y when X is a certain value. If X is low, then the distribution of Y looks like that in the first column; if X is medium, then the distribution of Y looks like that in the second column; if X is high, then the distribution of Y looks like that in the third column. In short, these distributions of Y depend on (are conditional on) the values of X.

Another way to construct the tables may help you examine the distribution of the dependent variable within categories of the independent variable. It's similarity to one of the analysis of variance exercises may indicate to you how the two procedures are similar and different.

Go to the 50 cases scored on the four variables you use for Exercises 1 through 3 and photocopy them. Cut them into strips so that you have 50 pieces of paper—one for each person represented. On each strip, you find four entries. The first entry after the case number of each strip is the independent variable value for the case followed, in turn, by the dependent variable values for each of three exercises. For Exercise 1, you need to look at the independent variable and the first dependent variable.

Follow these directions. Sort the 50 pieces into three piles, based on their values on the independent variable. Take the pile of cases that are scored low on the independent variable; sort them into 3 piles on the basis of their values of the first dependent variable; count how many are high, how many are medium, and how many are low on the dependent variable; and enter those three numbers of cases into the low X column of a blank table such as the one you constructed before. Take the pile of cases that are scored medium on the independent variable and do the same things, entering the appropriate numbers of cases into the medium X column of the table. Finally, take the pile of cases that are scored high on the independent variable and do the same things, entering their numbers into the high X column of the table. Now, percentage the tables the same way as indicated above in the earlier instructions. The results are identical.

Interpreting the Conditional Distributions. Examine each of those three conditional distributions (being sure to focus on the percentages, which are comparable to each other, and not on the raw numbers, which are not comparable to each other). Compare them to each other and to the total distribution in order to see how different they are. The more different they are, the more related the two variables are, and the more knowing the independent would improve your ability to predict the dependent variable.

Are the distributions within categories of the independent variable different from the total distribution of the dependent variable? Are the two variables related? Write a brief answer to those two questions under the table you have been working on.

EXERCISE 2 Building and Interpreting Tables

Now move on to the second dependent variable and, using the same independent variable, do the same things. Remember to start by writing a hypothesis that posits a relationship between the independent and dependent variables and drawing up a table to fill in.

Are the distributions within categories of the independent variable different from the overall distribution of the dependent variable, which is usually called the "marginal distribution"? Are the two variables related? Write the answers under the second table.

EXERCISE 3 Reading Tables for Strength and Form of the Relationship

Now move on to the third dependent variable and do the same things (still using the same independent variable and remembering to write a hypothesis and draw up a table for the results). Are the distributions of the dependent variable within categories of the independent variable different from the marginal distribution of the dependent variable? Are the two variables related? Write these answers as well.

On which of the three exercises are the variables most strongly related? (That is, on which of the exercises are the conditional distributions most different from the marginal distributions.) On which are they hardly associated at all? (Write strongest and weakest near the appropriate tables.)

On which exercise is the form of the relationship positive? To answer that, look for the table in which cases that have higher values of the independent variable show higher distributions of the dependent variable. Compare the distribution of the dependent variable when X is low to the distribution of the dependent variable when X is medium to the distribution of the dependent variable when X is high. Does the distribution of Y get higher? If so, the relationship is positive. Write "positive" next to the table that has a positive relationship in it.

On which exercise is the relationship negative? Make the comparisons of the distributions of Y as you did above. If the distribution of Y gets lower as you move from low to medium to high X cases, the relationship is negative. Write "negative" next to the table that has a negative relationship in it.

You will learn statistics in Chapter 9 that will help you describe the strength of the relationships you have been examining. However, as you will see, statistics to indicate the form of the relationship between ordinal variables are somewhat lacking. When you talk about the form of the relationship between ordinal variables, you will be more or less confined to descriptive words like "positive" and "negative." Moreover, although you will have a statistic with a sign on it to help you repeat that form, you will have to rely on your own ability to see the positive or negative relationship in a table.

HELP IN READING TABLES

To examine the relationship, we percentage *within* categories of the independent and *compare across* categories of the independent. As you look at each conditional distribution (the distribution of the dependent variable *within* a category of the independent), visualize a distribution of cases. You may want to think in terms of a bar chart.

For example, if we had the relationship shown in Table 8.1, you might imagine three different distributions of the dependent variable, as shown in Figure 8.11: one, when the independent variable is low; one, when the independent variable is medium; and one, when the independent variable is high.

Notice how the distribution of Y changes as X goes up. When X is low, the distribution of Y is also low. (The cases are more at the low end of the scale.) When X is medium, the dis-

Table 8.1 Example of a Positive Relationship between Ordinal Variables

		Independent		
		Low	Medium	High
	High	9%	27%	66%
Dependent	Medium	18%	55%	21%
	Low	73%	18%	13%
	Totals	100%	100%	100%

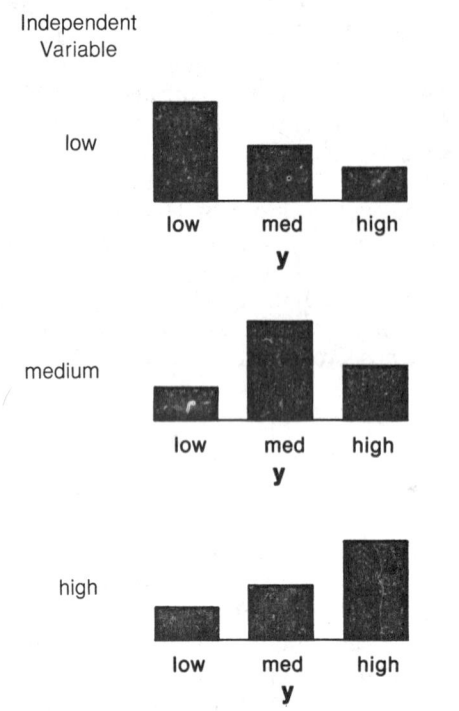

Figure 8.11 Bar Charts to Represent Conditional Distributions of the Dependent Variable

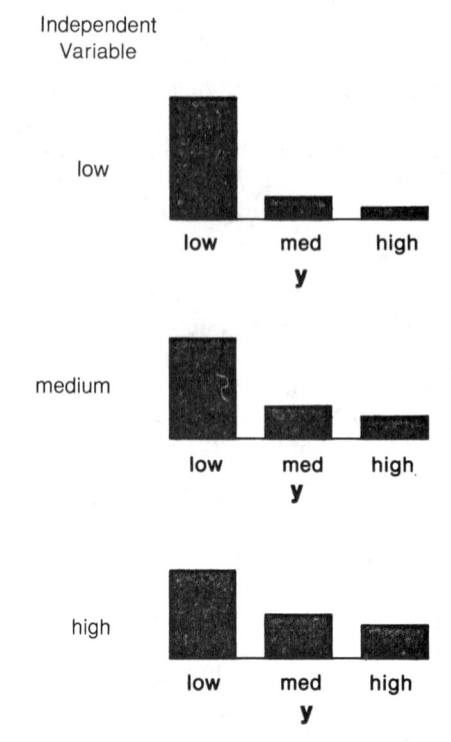

Figure 8.12 Bar Charts to Represent Conditional Distributions of the Dependent Variable

tribution of Y is more evenly distributed but with the cases more toward the middle category. When X is high, the distribution of Y is also high. (The cases are more at the high end of the scale.) This is a positive relationship: as X increases, Y increases.

For another example, imagine the distributions of the dependent variable in Table 8.2. And consider the three bar charts that would

Table 8.2 Example of a Positive Relationship between Ordinal Variables

		Independent		
		Low	Medium	High
	High	2%	9%	11%
Dependent	Medium	3%	15%	28%
	Low	95%	76%	61%
	Totals	100%	100%	100%

show the conditional distributions of Y within the various values of X that are shown in Figure 8.12.

This is another example of a positive association. As X goes from low to medium to high, the distribution of Y gets *higher*. Notice that we can't say that *most* cases are high on Y when X is high. We can't even say that a majority of cases are high on Y when X is high. It is indeed true that a majority of the cases are low on Y when X is high. But none of that interferes with the fact that the *distribution* of Y is *higher* when X is high than when X is low.

As you encounter tables elsewhere, practice thinking about how the distribution of Y changes as X changes. In both these examples, the distribution of Y gets higher as X goes from low to medium to high. In the first example, however, you see a stronger XY relationship. The conditional distributions are more different from each other than the conditional distributions in the second example are. In that second example, there is still a positive relationship, but it is much weaker. The conditional distributions are more alike than in the first example.

This is very important to remember. The more different the conditional distributions are from each other, the stronger is the relationship between the two variables.

SPSS TABLE CONSTRUCTION

EXERCISE 4   CROSSTABS

Let's turn to the computer now. Examine the variables in the codebooks in the appendices. Pick an ordinal independent and an ordinal dependent variable, or pick two interval variables that can be recoded into ordinal categories. Write their names and a hypothesis that predicts a relationship between them.

Now set up a computer job to test the hypothesis. Use the same method for accessing the stored data sets that you've been using before. You will need a RECODE command if there is an unmanageable number of codes on your variable(s) that needs reducing to a smaller number. (See heading below on recoding.) You will also need a RECODE command if some of your categories don't have enough cases. (See heading below on number of cases.) Then add a CROSSTABS command like this:

```
CROSSTABS TABLES=depvar BY
    indvar/OPTIONS=4.  (SPSS/PC+)
CROSSTABS TABLES=depvar BY
    indvar/CELLS=COLUMN. (SPSS-X)
```

Substitute the name (from the codebook) of the dependent variable where it says "depvar" on the CROSSTABS command; substitute the name of the independent variable (from the codebook) where it says "indvar" on the CROSSTABS command above. The OPTION and CELLS subcommands above will cause the computer to print the column percentages you need, in addition to the cell frequencies it ordinarily prints. End with the FINISH. command, if necessary, and submit the job.

Now draw the table that SPSS has produced for you. Make sure, however, that you set up the table as you have been doing in this chapter. Make sure the cell representing the lowest values on the two variables is in the lower left corner and that the cell representing the highest values on the two variables is in the upper right corner. (And make sure that the other cells graduate up to that one in logical order.) SPSS does not construct tables with the cells in that order, but the interpretation of tables is easier if you keep them somewhat analogous to regression plots, as we have been doing in the examples in this chapter.

Now, interpret your table by answering the following questions. Are the two variables related? Are they related in the positive/negative direction you hypothesized? Would you say the association is pretty weak or pretty strong? (More on this in the next chapter.)

RECODING FOR CROSSTABULAR ANALYSIS

Recoding for Clarity of Interpretation

Generally speaking, it is pretty hard to interpret a table if the variables have more than three to five values each. We start finding it increasingly difficult to read differences in the various distributions of the dependent variable as their numbers increase for more values on the independent variable; and differences in the distribution of the dependent variable are easiest to see if there aren't a large number of values on it. If your independent or dependent variable has too many codes, you may want to reduce the number of values by combining some of the categories with a RECODE command.

When you recode to combine categories, have a good reason for putting values on that variable together. Remember that you are saying that cases that share a value on a variable are alike in rather important ways and are different from cases that have a different value on that variable.

For example, on a variable that measures education, you might want to combine the values that represent the first eleven years of school into a value of 1, change the value for the twelfth year of school to 2, and combine all the codes for post-high school into 3. This would mean you saw something similar, theoretically, about all the people who had no school or some school (0 through 11); something similar about all the people who had a high school diploma that differentiated them from those with less school and those with more; and something similar about all those who had some training beyond high school that differentiated them from those with less. Just remember to have some good reason for combining the values on a variable into fewer codes.

Remember also that all measurement must have mutually exclusive and exhaustive values: *mutually exclusive* means that each case may have one and only one value; *exhaustive* means that all cases must have some value on the variable even if it is a value that represents missing data. Your recoded variable is no exception; its values must be mutually exclusive and exhaustive.

Recoding in Order to Have Enough Cases for Analysis

Crosstabulation tables require a rather large number of cases overall, and they require a substantial number of cases in each row and column. The reason for this lies in the accuracy of what we communicate to ourselves and to our readers.

When we describe the conditional distributions of the dependent variable, we want there to be enough cases so that the description is a fairly accurate one. We want those percentages to be based on a fairly large number of cases so that the percentages are fairly resistant to error. We don't want the percentages to communicate something different if one case happens to be miscategorized because of error. Imagine the distributions in Table 8.3.

Table 8.3 Hypothetical Distributions of Two Groups on an Ordinal Variable

High	20%	High	30%
Medium	70%	Medium	50%
Low	10%	Low	20%

On the face of it, you'd probably say that the group represented by the first distribution on the left is quite a bit more moderate (medium) than the group represented by the second distribution on the right. Yet, if the first group has just one person that ought to be coded "high" who is coded "medium" instead—because of some error or another—and has just one person that ought to be coded "low" who is coded "medium" instead, and if the first group has only 10 people in it, its real distribution would be identical to that of the second group as Table 8.4 shows.

Now, consider the second group in Table 8.3. If it had one case miscoded "high" and one case miscoded "low" and both should have been coded medium and if the second group had 100 people in it, its real distribution shown below in Table 8.5 would hardly be different from the one with the error that you saw on the second group in Table 8.3 above.

Therefore, you can see, the larger the N, the

Table 8.4 Hypothetical Distribution of Previous Group on an Ordinal Variable

High	30%	$N = 3$	(from 2 above)
Medium	50%	$N = 5$	(from 7 above)
Low	20%	$N = 2$	(from 1 above)

Table 8.5 Hypothetical Distribution of Previous Group on an Ordinal Variable

High	29%	$N = 29$	(from 30 above)
Medium	52%	$N = 52$	(from 50 above)
Low	19%	$N = 19$	(from 20 above)

more stable the percentages. The larger the N, the more resistant our results are to error. But how large is large enough? N should be large enough so that those distributions communicate accurately to you and to your reader.

Let me recommend an absolutely arbitrary guideline. In Chapter 10 you will learn to tell, by looking at the marginal distributions on the independent and dependent variables, how many cases would be in each cell if the two variables were unrelated. If you could expect more than about 10 cases in each cell if the variables were unrelated, you probably have enough cases.

When you are planning your own research and data collection, and planning to use tabular presentations of your data, there are two things to keep in mind: (1) the more values you plan to have on the independent variable in your table, the larger the number of cases you will need to get a good number of cases in each of the conditional distributions; (2) the more skewed you expect the distributions on either variable to be, the more cases you will need for analysis. If you expect that most of your cases will be rather homogeneous and will have the same one or two values on either variable, that means that there will be relatively few left for the other categories. (On those other categories, it will be hard to get an accurate description of the distributions because you won't have enough cases unless you collect a very large number of cases overall.)

If you are analyzing data already collected, as you are for the exercise here, you should look at the distributions of the variables and think about recoding to combine the values that are represented by very few cases. That way, instead of several values with only a few cases on each, you can sometimes create one value with enough cases for analysis. Usually the codebook will give you the distribution on the variables you are thinking of using. If not, you can get it with a FREQUENCIES procedure.

When you find values that have very few cases, think about how your conditional distributions are likely to be affected. And think about recoding.

Remember, when you are recoding to try to get enough cases for analysis, that the recoded values must be theoretically meaningful. You only want to combine those values on the variable that can be meaningfully combined. Those cases that share a value on the variable must be somehow alike. If you cannot meet this requirement, it is better to drop those values that have only a few cases from the analysis. Do that by recoding that value to the missing data code.

Other Considerations in Recoding

Remember that there was a fairly long discussion of recoding in Chapter 7, which you may want to review for this exercise. (And remember that the forms for RECODE commands were given there.) One warning that is worth reiterating here is that the labels on variables in SPSS files do not move when you recode that variable. Whatever label was attached to a number in the original file stays with that number unless you change it with a VALUE LABELS command. Thus, the labels on a table that is constructed using recoded variables may be meaningless.

Another warning from that chapter also worth reiterating is the warning not to include the missing data code in a category you are creating with a recode. You would just be putting cases about which we have no meaningful information into a category for analysis. But the other side of that warning is: don't recode meaningful values to the missing data code unless you want cases with that value dropped from the analysis. Anytime you change a value to the code that has been designated missing data when the SPSS file was set up, the cases that have that value will be dropped. (A good thing to check when you suddenly see that you don't have all the cases you thought you should have.)

EXERCISES

You can think of the first dependent variable as representing *political efficacy*. Imagine that we posed three efficacy questions, using phrasing from the National Election Studies, asking people to agree or disagree to statements like:

1. People like me have no say about how the government runs things.
2. Voting is the only way people like me have a say in politics.
3. Government officials don't care what people like me think.

We then gave people one point for each item on which they disagreed. That left us with a scale that ranged from zero to three. Seeing that we had few people in the zero category, we recoded the efficacy scale so that either no or one efficacious answer was considered low (1), two efficacious answers were considered medium (2), and three efficacious answers were considered high (3). (See questions in Appendix A.)

The second dependent variable can be thought of as a measure of "political misinformation." Imagine that we had asked a series of ten knowledge questions, ranging from which party was in control of Congress to the names of state legislators. Further imagine that we counted the number of wrong answers people gave us. We ended up with a scale of misinformation, on which values ranged from 0 to 10. Having too many categories, we recoded the misinformation scale into three categories: 0 through 2 wrong answers were considered low (1) misinformation; 3, 4, 5, or 6 wrong answers received a score of medium (2) misinformation; and 7, 8, 9, or 10 received a score of high (3) misinformation.

The third dependent variable can be thought of as a measure of concern over the outcome of an election. For that, we asked respondents, "How much would you say you cared about who wins the election next week? A lot (3), some (2), or not very much (1)?"

The independent variable can be considered a measure of education. Imagine that we had "years of schooling" and recoded it so that everything below twelve was considered low (1); twelve years completed was considered medium (2); and anything beyond twelve was considered high (3).

Hypothetical Data for Crosstabular Analysis

Case Number	Independent Education	Dependent 1 Efficacy	Dependent 2 Misinformation	Dependent 3 Concern
1	1	1	1	1
2	3	3	1	3
3	2	2	2	3
4	3	3	1	3
5	1	1	3	3
6	2	3	3	2
7	1	1	1	1
8	3	3	1	2
9	3	3	1	2
10	3	3	3	3
11	2	2	2	2
12	3	3	1	2

Case Number	Independent Education	Dependent 1 Efficacy	Dependent 2 Misinformation	Dependent 3 Concern
13	2	2	2	2
14	1	1	1	1
15	3	3	3	2
16	3	3	1	1
17	1	1	3	3
18	2	2	3	2
19	2	2	2	3
20	2	2	2	1
21	3	3	1	1
22	2	2	3	3
23	2	1	2	2
24	1	1	3	1
25	1	1	3	2
26	1	1	1	1
27	1	2	3	3
28	1	1	1	1
29	3	1	2	1
30	2	2	2	1
31	3	3	1	1
32	3	3	3	2
33	1	1	1	2
34	1	3	3	3
35	2	2	2	1
36	1	1	3	3
37	2	2	1	1
38	2	2	2	1
39	1	1	2	2
40	3	3	2	3
41	3	3	1	1
42	1	1	3	2
43	3	3	2	3
44	2	2	2	3
45	1	1	3	3
46	2	2	1	3
47	3	3	2	2
48	2	2	2	1
49	1	1	3	2
50	2	2	3	3

SUGGESTED READINGS

SPSS Crosstabs

NORUSIS, MARIJA J. *SPSS/PC+* (Chicago: SPSS, Inc., 1988). Chapter 9 is "Crosstabulation and Measures of Association," pp. B92—B107; commands are on pages C-33—C-36.

SPSS-X User's Guide (Chicago: SPSS, Inc., 1988), Ch. 25, pp. 428-445.

Crosstabulation of Ordinal Data Generally

BABBIE, EARL. *The Practice of Social Research*, 3rd ed. (Belmont, CA: Wadsworth, 1983), pp. 355-360.

BOWEN, BRUCE D., and HERBERT F. WEISBERG. *An Introduction to Data Analysis* (San Francisco: Freeman, 1980), Ch. 6.

JOHNSON, JANET BUTTOLPH, and RICHARD A. JOSLYN. *Political Science Research Methods* (Washington, D.C.: Congressional Quarterly Press, 1986), pp. 269-287.

KOHOUT, FRANK J. *Statistics for Social Scientists* (N.Y.: Wiley, 1974), Unit III to p. 84.

ARTICLES

ABRAMSON, PAUL R. "Intergenerational Social Mobility and Partisan Choice," *American Political Science Review*, 66 (December 1972), 1291-1294. Table 1 is simple crosstabulation between social mobility and party preference. Table 2 is a multivariate table (father's preference controlled) but can be read as a series of bivariate tables. British survey data.

CASSEL, CAROL A., and DAVID B. HILL. "The Decision to Vote," in Normal R. Luttbeg (ed.), *Public Opinion and Public Policy*, 3rd ed. (Itasca, IL: Peacock, 1981), pp. 46-53. Clear statements of operationalizations (mostly in footnotes). Tables which show that the relationships between various psychological variables and voting participation in the 1970s are similar to those first found in the 1950s; also that strength of these relationships is similar for a presidential and congressional election. Text discusses degree to which absolute levels of the psychological variables changed from 50s to 70s.

DEKKER, PAUL, and PETER ESTER. "Working-Class Authoritarianism: A Re-examination of the Lipset Thesis," *European Journal of Political Research*, 15 (1987), 395-415. Dutch survey data (1975-85) used to reassess Lipset's work. Tables 1 and 4 are percent agreement by class with F (fascism) scale items and other measures of authoritarianism.

JAMES, PATRICK, and JONATHAN WILKENFELD. "Structural Factors and International Crisis Behavior," *Conflict Management and Peace Science*, 7 (Spring 1984), 33-53. Unit of analysis is the group of states that are involved in a conflict. Analysis of effects of nature of the source of crisis, size of group, and homogeneity of outlook in group on five different types of outcomes of conflict. Crosstabulation tables with percentages. Chi-square used unmodified as significance test not measure of association. (See chi square in Chapter 10.)

KAY, SUSAN ANN. "Sex Differences in the Attitudes of a Future State," *Women and Politics*, 1 (Fall 1980), 35-48. Table 1 is a simple crosstabulation table. Author asked an open-ended question about things a respondent considers when deciding to appeal a case, categorized responses into five types, and considered differences between genders in their responses.

POLSBY, NELSON W., and AARON WILDAVSKY. *Presidential Elections*, 5th ed. (New York: Scribner's, 1980), p. 200. Table there is a good example of using simple percentages distribution for a variable to show change or absence of change across repeated surveys.

POMPER, GERALD M., with SUSAN LEDERMAN. *Elections in America*, 2nd ed. (New York: Longman, 1980), pp. 198-199. Table 9.5 assesses the difference in segregationist attitudes (for candidates and elected governors) between the peripheral and deep South in two periods, 1954-65 and 1966-73. A good example of the decline in absolute levels of segregationism but with a simultaneous strengthening of the relationship between region and segregationism.

SAINSBURY, DIANE. "Class Voting and Left Voting

in Scandinavia: The Impact of Different Operationalizations of Working Class," *European Journal of Political Research*, 15 (1987), 507–526. Study of the operationalization of "working class" and the implications of various operationalizations for the measurement of class-voting cross-nationally. Deals with way line is drawn between classes, treatment of pensioners, and classification of married women by own or husband's class. Considers implications for Alford index (percentage of left voting in working class minus that in middle class) of various operationalizations. Data analysis is Alford index across time and percent voting left in working/middle class across time. Also considered are age and sex and women's occupational classification.

WEEDE, ERIC. "Preventing War by Nuclear Deterrence or by Détente," *Conflict Management and Peace Science*, 6 (Fall 1981), 1–18. Bivariate crosstabulations between the presence of deterrence and war, 1962–1980. Unit of analysis is the dyad, a two-nation pair. Discussion of which pairs are relevant to the analysis.

CHAPTER
9

MEASURES OF THE STRENGTH OF ASSOCIATION BETWEEN ORDINAL VARIABLES

Now that you have learned to tell when two ordinal variables are related, we can go on to measures that can be used in addition to or in place of tabular displays in order to communicate how strong the association is. Frequently you will have so many tests of hypotheses to discuss in a research project that to display all the tables is impractical. A measure of association can serve as a shorthand to a tabular display, providing a description in a single statistic of what the relationship looks like. Moreover, you may have so many values on each variable that a tabular display is difficult to read. A measure of association can communicate much the same information to a reader.

Perhaps you want to measure inter-item reliability of two ordinal variables before constructing an index. A measure of association can help you assess that reliability. Perhaps you have two coders making judgments on where cases fit on an ordinal scale. Correlating one coder's judgments with those of another can help you assess inter-coder reliability. A measure of association can communicate such reliability to a reader easily and quickly.

The measures you are going to calculate range from -1.0 for a perfect negative relationship, to 0 for no association between the variables, to $+1.0$ for a perfect positive relationship. They also have somewhat the same interpretation we have seen for r^2 and E^2—the percentage by which the error has been reduced, knowing the independent variable as compared to the error made not knowing it. Since the rules for "guessing" are based on pairs of cases rather than on individual cases, however, they aren't completely analogous to those we have used for r^2 and E^2; thus, we will jump right into the statistics rather than spelling out how their interpretation is linked with regression and analysis of variance.

UNDERSTANDING THE LOGIC OF THE MEASURES OF ASSOCIATION BASED ON PAIRS OF CASES

The measures of association we will examine for ordinal data are all based on the notion of "excess of concordant over discordant pairs of cases" (positive relationship) or "excess of discordant over concordant pairs of cases" (negative relationship). Having only ordinal data and, therefore, not being able to add and subtract scores, we are limited to comparing pairs of cases and how they are ordered on two variables.

If a case is higher on both variables than another case, or if it is lower on both variables than another case, the two cases constitute a *concordant* pair—a pair of cases on which the variables are positively associated. If a case is higher on one variable and lower on the other variable than another case, the two cases constitute a *discordant* pair—a pair of cases on which the variables are negatively associated. If two cases are the same on either variable, that pair can't tell us anything about the direction of a relationship between variables because, with the same scores on the two cases, no comparison of different values on the variable across cases is possible. (This is similar to earlier notions that variables must vary before we can tell anything about relationships; here they much vary across *pairs* of cases.) Thus, we will focus primarily on sets of cases that differ on the values of the two variables.

Let's get straight what we mean by concordant first. Imagine we have two cases and that each is scored (has a value of) high, medium, or low on each of two variables. Let's compare two cases:

Case No.	Variable 1	Variable 2
1	High	Medium
2	Low	Low

Note that case 1 is *higher* than case 2 on the first variable. Case 1 is also higher than case 2 on the second variable. This pair of cases is *concordant* on the two variables. Now look at these cases:

Case No.	Variable 1	Variable 2
2	Low	Low
3	High	Medium

Note that case 2 is *lower* than case 3 on *both* variables. This pair (2 and 3) is *concordant* on the two variables.

However, look at this pair:

Case No.	Variable 1	Variable 2
3	High	Medium
4	Low	High

Case 4 is *lower* than case 3 on the first variable *and higher* on the second variable. This pair of cases (3 and 4) is *discordant* on these two variables.

What about cases 1 and 3? They have the same value on the first variable and also on the second variable. *Either* variable being the same gets us into the problem of our not being able to compare the two cases in order to find any evidence of a positive or negative relationship. We consider such a pair *tied* on a variable. Cases 1 and 3, thus, are a pair that can't tell us anything about the direction of a relationship. It is, for the moment, an irrelevant, tied pair.

EXERCISE 1 Counting Concordant and Discordant Pairs of Cases

Here are the previous cases and some additional ones. Examine them and answer the questions below.

Case No.	Variable 1	Variable 2
1	High	Medium
2	Low	Low
3	High	Medium
4	Low	High
5	Low	Low
6	Medium	Low
7	Medium	Medium
8	Medium	High

Write whether each pair indicated is concordant (*C*), discordant (*D*), or tied (*T*). Don't forget to notice how many nonredundant pairs there are. Once case 1 has been paired with each case that has a higher number, then case 2 must be paired with each case of a higher number, and so on, until case 7 is paired with case 8. (Once you have paired case 1 with case 5, for example, you don't then turn around and also compare case 5 with case 1; that would be counting redundant pairs, and you only want the nonredundant ones.)

Did you get 10 concordant pairs, 6 discordant pairs, and 12 tied pairs? If not, reread the explanation, re-examine the data, and check yourself. If you still have problems, check with your instructor or lab assistant before you continue.

GAMMA

With no more than the number of concordant and discordant pairs, we can now construct a measure of association based on the excess of concordant or discordant pairs as a proportion of untied pairs. The measure is called "gamma" and considers only untied pairs to be relevant. It is calculated as in Formula 9.1.

FORMULA 9.1 Gamma

$$\text{Gamma} = \frac{C - D}{C + D}$$

where:
C = Number of concordant pairs
D = Number of discordant pairs

For our example, it is: $(10 - 6)/(10 + 6) = 4/16 = .25$.

As we will discuss a little later, sometimes gamma reports a stronger relationship than you can see in reading the tables. Sometimes it also does not give you the best measure of the relationship you are trying to describe. It is best, therefore, to be a little suspicious of strong gammas when you haven't seen the distributions laid out in tables.

Extending the Logic to Tabular Displays of Ordinal Variables

Let's apply this logic about pairs of cases to the tables you constructed in Exercises 1, 2, and 3 of Chapter 8. You constructed tables that looked like Table 9.1 when you put *numbers* of cases (*not* percentages for the purposes of the calculations here) in the cells.

How would you draw all possible non-redundant pairs of cases out of this table and examine their values on two variables? Doing it as described above would take forever, but there is a shortcut.

All pairs that could be made between a case and any other case in the same column or same row are tied on either the independent, the dependent, or both variables. Those pairs that share the same value on one or both variables (whether they share high, medium, or low—i.e., pairs from within the third column *or* within the second column *or* within the first column; pairs from within the third row *or* within the second row *or* within the first row) are irrelevant, for the moment. They are irrelevant because, if the pair of cases is tied on either or both of the variables, it cannot tell us anything about the direction of the relationship between them.

This leaves us with pairs of cases that *differ* on *both* the independent and dependent variables—pairs that would come from *different* rows *and* columns in the table. Imagine, for example, that you wanted to pair up all the cases that are low on both variables with all the cases that are medium on both variables—i.e., cases from cells 3 and 5: (Look at Table 9.1; verify that cell 3 represents cases "low" on both variables and cell 5 represents cases "medium" on both variables.)

Table 9.1 Example Table for Counting Concordant and Discordant Pairs

		Ordinal Independent Variable		
		Low	Medium	High
Ordinal Dependent Variable	High	n_1	n_4	n_7
	Medium	n_2	n_5	n_8
	Low	n_3	n_6	n_9

Cell No.	Variable 1	Variable 2
3	Low	Low
5	Medium	Medium

You can figure out how many pairs that would be by multiplying the number of cases in cell 3 by the number of cases in cell 5. That would tell you how many pairs could be made from cases in cells 3 and 5; all those pairs would be concordant because of the direction of the values—i.e., the second case of each pair is always higher on both variables.

If you wanted to pair all the cases low on both variables with all those medium on the independent and high on the dependent—i.e., cases from cells 3 and 4—

Cell No.	Variable 1	Variable 2
3	Low	Low
4	Medium	High

you would multiply the number of cases in cell 3 by the number of cases in cell 4. All those pairs would be concordant.

In fact, the cases in any cell will make *concordant* pairs with all the cases in all the cells *above and* to the *right* of the cell you are starting with. Therefore, to get the concordant pairs *in a table set up like the one above*, where cases with low values on both variables are in the lower left-hand cell, multiply the number of cases in a cell by the number of cases in all cells above *and* to the right of it, and add the results.

Concordant pairs in the above table can be calculated this way:

$$[n_3 \times (n_5 + n_4 + n_8 + n_7)]$$
$$+ [n_2 \times (n_4 + n_7)]$$
$$+ [n_6 \times (n_8 + n_7)]$$
$$+ [n_5 \times (n_7)]$$

Please study this a while before you go on. You are working cell by cell, multiplying the number of cases in each cell with the number in each cell above *and* to the right.

If you wanted to pair each case that was medium on both variables with each case that was low on the independent and high on the dependent—i.e., cases from cell 5 with those in cell 1—

Cell No.	Variable 1	Variable 2
5	Medium	Medium
1	Low	High

you could do it by multiplying the number of cases in cell 5 by the number of cases in cell 1. All of those pairs would be discordant. If you wanted to pair each case that was medium on the independent and low on the dependent with each case that was low on the independent and medium on the dependent—i.e., cases from cell 6 with those from cell 2—

Cell No.	Variable 1	Variable 2
6	Medium	Low
2	Low	Medium

you could do it by multiplying the number of cases in cell 6 by the number of cases in cell 2. All of those pairs would be discordant.

In fact, the cases in any cell will make *discordant* pairs with all the cases in all the cells *above and* to the *left* of the cell you are starting with. Therefore, to get the discordant pairs *in a table set up like the one above*, multiply the number of cases in a cell by the number of cases in all the cells above *and* to the left of it and add the results. Discordant pairs in the above table can be calculated this way:

$$[n_6 \times (n_2 + n_1)]$$
$$+ [n_5 \times (n_1)]$$
$$+ [n_9 \times (n_5 + n_2 + n_1 + n_4)]$$
$$+ [n_8 \times (n_4 + n_1)]$$

Please study this a bit before you go on. Can you see what discordant and concordant pairs would be calculated differently for a table set up differently, say, like Table 9.2?

Table 9.2 Example Table for Calculating Gamma with Different Counting Rules

		Ordinal Independent Variable		
		High	Medium	Low
Ordinal Dependent Variable	High	n_1	n_4	n_7
	Medium	n_2	n_5	n_8
	Low	n_3	n_6	n_9

In this table, look at the relationship of cells 3 and 5:

Cell No.	Variable 1	Variable 2
3	High	Low
5	Medium	Medium

Here, given the way the table is set up, cell 3 makes *discordant* pairs with cell 5. In every possible pair, the case from cell 5 will be lower on variable 1 and higher on variable 2 than the case from cell 3. Given the way the earlier table was set up, pairs from the same lower-left and middle cells made concordant pairs. Thus, you can see that, if you follow the above-right/above-left rule blindly without looking at how the table is set up, you may end up with pairs erroneously counted as concordant or discordant. Then you may end up with a sign on the gamma that does not reflect the true direction of the relationship.

Whether a relationship is positive or negative, however, is a question that shouldn't depend on how a table is set up. You may have to revise calculating rules for tables set up in a different way in order to get the sign of $C - D$ in the direction the data clearly indicate. (High values on one variable linked with a higher distribution on another variable means positive relationship, regardless of whether the rows and columns are ordered from low to high or from high to low.) Just remember that "above and right = concordant," while "above and left = discordant" won't always work with all tables.

Also note that you are taking *nonredundant* pairs. If you go up and right to get the concordant pairs, and if you go up and left to get the discordant pairs, you don't then go down at all. To make pairs with cells that are below the ones you started with would count those pairs twice; they would be redundant pairs.

EXERCISE 2 Calculating Gamma

Go on now and calculate gamma for the tables in Exercises 1 through 3 of Chapter 8. Write out all the steps.

Now answer the following questions about your gammas. On which of the three tables is the gamma largest, indicating the strongest relationship? On which of the tables is the gamma closest to zero, indicating the weakest relationship? On which of the tables is the gamma (and relationship) positive? On which of the tables is the gamma (and relationship) negative? Notice that, by looking at gamma, you get the same answers to these questions that you got earlier from examining the tables themselves.

Interpreting Gamma

Gamma has a PRE interpretation. We can say, if we ignore ties, that we have reduced our error in predicting order 25% by knowing the independent variable over not knowing it; but we have to talk about error in predicting order on *paired* cases, not error in predicting individual cases, and we have to say that ties are not relevant.

It may seem strange to be talking about predicting pairs of cases when our hypotheses are about collections of individual cases, but that is a problem which stems from having to build statistics from ordinal data. When the level of measurement does not permit adding and subtracting the values on the variables, the statistics have to be built on what is allowed—comparisons of more than/less than. Thus, the ordinal character of the data leaves us with a statistic that does not quite match our usual sense of what hypotheses are about. But we put up with it.

Gamma sometimes gives an indication of a perfect relationship (1.0) when there are still cases you might consider error as far as your hypothesis is concerned. Look at Table 9.3, for example, where $n =$ some cases and $0 =$ no cases in a particular cell. In Table 9.3, there are no discordant pairs, so gamma would be 1.0; yet, the relationship isn't as "perfect" as that in Table 9.4.

This is not just a problem of gamma giving you a 1.0 in cases like Table 9.3. If it were, it would be an easy matter just to look for empty cells in a certain pattern. It is also a problem

Table 9.3 A Table That Would Give an Inflated Gamma

	Low	Medium	High
High	0	0	n
Medium	0	n	n
Low	n	n	0

Table 9.4 A Table That Shows a Perfect Relationship

	Low	Medium	High
High	0	0	n
Medium	0	n	0
Low	n	0	0

when your cases are predominantly concentrated in the cells marked with an *n* but when you have a few cases in the cells indicated as zero, as in Table 9.3. That situation will give you very few discordant pairs and will inflate the gamma, even though it will not go all the way up to 1.0. Although such a pattern might result from the nature of the relationship in the data, it might also arise if you didn't have many cases in the low independent variable category or in the high dependent variable category; that is, if your marginals were very skewed, gamma could be distorted.

It is important, therefore, to examine the table to make sure gamma is communicating what you want it to before using the measure of association alone without displaying the table.

KENDALL'S TAU$_b$

Gamma ignores information that we frequently want to use in building a measure of association. By focussing on only the concordant and discordant pairs, gamma is using information from only those pairs of cases that can tell us something about the direction of the relationship—whether it is positive or negative. Pairs of cases that do not reveal anything about the positive or negative form of the relationship still may be of interest to us because they can tell us something about the strength of the relationship. When some of those pairs of cases that are tied on one or the other or on both variables are considered evidence that the independent variable cannot fully explain the dependent variable, we want a measure of association to take them into account. And there are statistics other than gamma that do look at some of those ties as error—cases that are not where they ought to be if our hypotheses were completely consistent with the data.

One is called Kendall's tau$_b$, which you can use if you have the same number of values on both variables, a square table. (Its value is somewhat reduced on nonsquare tables.) Tau$_b$ defines error very strictly as any cases that do not fall into the cells of the main diagonal of the table.

Tau$_b$ uses the same numerator as gamma, as you can see in Formula 9.2: the excess of concordant or discordant nonredundant pairs.

FORMULA 9.2 Tau$_b$

$$\text{Tau}_b = \frac{(C - D)}{\sqrt{1/2\, N(N-1) - R}\sqrt{1/2\, N(N-1) - C}}$$

where:
$R = 1/2 \Sigma [r \times (r-1)]$
$C = 1/2 \Sigma [c \times (c-1)]$
r = Number of cases in a row
c = Number of cases in a column

Notice, however, the difference in the denominator. Gamma's denominator had in it only the total number of concordant and discordant pairs (the untied pairs) with no mention of any of the other possible pairs of cases. That is what it means to say that gamma considers tied pairs irrelevant and ignores them. Gamma is not based on all possible pairs of cases in the table—only on the untied pairs.

Tau$_b$, however, is based on more of the possible pairs than gamma is. What you see in the denominator is the total number of possible nonredundant pairs minus one particular kind of tied pair.

With a perfect relationship (and equivalent marginals on both variables), every case would fall into one of the diagonal cells. Pairs of cases drawn from each of those cells would be tied on both X and Y, but these pairs don't indicate any lack of relationship between X and Y. Their ties can be attributed to the measurement level of the variables. The kind of ordinal data you have been using here groups lots of cases into a single value of a variable—low, medium, or high. The measurement does not have the potential to spread cases uniquely over many values as an interval scale might. Since you do not want the measure of strength of association to be reduced because of that kind of tied pair, the maximum possible number of such ties, given the distributions, is taken out of the total number of possible pairs for the denominator.

A second kind of tied pair, however, you leave among the relevant pairs in the denominator of tau_b. The second kind of tied pair is not considered to be a result of the level of measurement; it is considered error that ought to reduce the measure of association. These are the pairs, tied on one or both variables, made by cases that are not in the diagonal. Thus, the denominator of tau_b is the total number of nonredundant pairs minus the number of pairs that would be tied on both variables with a perfect relationship.

The calculation of the denominator is fairly straightforward.

1. First you need the number of nonredundant pairs that would be tied on Y, even if the relationship were perfect. To get that, take each row total and multiply it by that same row total minus one, $[r \times (r - 1)]$. Sum Σ those results for all the rows, and divide the total by two. That gives you the value for R in the formula above.
2. Now do all the parts of step 1 again, but use the column totals. That will give you the value for C in the formula above.
3. Subtract the results of steps 1 and 2 (R and C) separately from the total number of possible nonredundant pairs, $[1/2\, N(N - 1)]$.
4. Take the square roots of the two results of step 3.
5. Multiply the two square roots together.

EXERCISE 3 Computing Tau$_b$

Now calculate tau$_b$ for all three tables in Exercises 1 through 3 of Chapter 8. (Remember you already have $C - D$ from gamma above.)

Interpreting Tau$_b$

Notice that tau$_b$ is *lower* than gamma for the same table. This is because gamma considers ties irrelevant, but tau$_b$ takes some of those tied pairs to be an indication of *remaining error* that has not been explained by the independent variable. For tau$_b$, any distribution of cases that is not in the cells of the diagonal of the table is considered error.

Notice the similarity between tau$_b$ and r^2. Tau$_b$ is less than 1.0 to the degree that cases are not in the cells on the diagonal; r^2 is less than 1.0 to the degree that cases are not on the regression line. Being in cells other than those on the diagonal is considered unexplained error in the calculation of tau$_b$. Being off the regression line is considered unexplained error in the calculation of r^2.

Tau$_b$, like r^2 and like gamma, has a PRE interpretation. It can be read as: the proportion by which you have reduced the error in predicting order on pairs of cases, knowing the independent variable compared to not knowing it, and taking into account ties on both variables.

SOMER'S d_{yx}

While gamma ignores ties and tau$_b$ takes ties on both the independent and dependent variables into account very strictly as evidence of error in the relationship, there is another measure that considers the only relevant ties to be those on the dependent variable. Somer's d_{yx} (Y dependent on X) takes into account the ties in Y, as shown in Formula 9.3.

FORMULA 9.3 Somer's d_{yx}

$$d_{yx} = \frac{C - D}{C + D + T_y}$$

where:

T_y = Number of pairs tied on Y but not on X

The numerator of d_{yx} is the same as we have seen for gamma and tau$_b$. The denominator is the familiar $C + D$ *plus* the number of pairs tied on the dependent, but not on the independent, variable.

In order to figure the number of pairs tied on the dependent but not on the independent variable, you have to imagine picking up those pairs of cases you did not use in the calculation of gamma because they shared the same row. Remember that pairs of cases that are made from the same row are tied on the dependent variable; but you can ignore pairs of cases made from the same cell here because they are also tied on the independent, and you only want to include here those pairs tied on Y but not on X. If you go back to Table 9.1, you can imagine figuring the number of nonredundant pairs the cases in each cell could make with other cells in the same row. Thus—

$$\begin{aligned}T_y = &\; n_1(n_4 + n_7) \\ &+ n_4(n_7) \\ &+ n_2(n_5 + n_8) \\ &+ n_5(n_8) \\ &+ n_3(n_6 + n_9) \\ &+ n_6(n_9)\end{aligned}$$

What you put in the denominator as the relevant cases under consideration is the total number of concordant pairs, discordant pairs, and pairs tied on Y but not on X. That means that you are considering relevant all those pairs that can tell you something about what happens to Y as X changes. The concordant pairs can be interpreted as X having a positive effect on Y; the discordant pairs can be interpreted as X having a negative effect on Y. The pairs tied on Y, but not on X, can be interpreted as instances of X changing and there being no effect on Y.

For d_{yx}, you aren't interested in pairs of cases that share the same score on the independent variable. Those pairs can't tell you anything about X's effect on Y because the independent variable does not change from one case of the pair to the other. Even if Y is different across the pairs, the absence of change in X means you can't tell anything about its effect. You don't want these kind of pairs to reduce your measure of association, so you leave them out of the denominator.

You keep your focus on those pairs in which X changes—pairs where you can observe the effect of the independent variable; and your resulting measure of association becomes the excess of concordant or discordant pairs as a proportion of the pairs of cases that differ on X. Remember that you can get a low measure of association both by having the number of concordant and discordant pairs cancel each other out *and/or* by having a large number of pairs on which Y doesn't change. A Y's not changing when X does is counted as error and reduces the measure of association.

Interpreting d_{yx}

Somer's d_{yx} has a PRE interpretation. It can be read as the proportion by which error in predicting order on pairs of cases has been reduced by knowing the independent over not knowing it when ties on the dependent variable have been taken into account.

Somer's d_{yx} will usually be between gamma and tau$_b$. Gamma is the highest because it considers relevant only the concordant and discordant pairs; the pairs of cases tied on either variable are not considered to represent error that ought to reduce the measure of association. Somer's d_{yx} reduces gamma to indicate the degree to which X's changes do not always change Y; pairs of cases tied on the dependent but not the independent variable are considered to be error that has not been explained by the independent variable. Tau$_b$ is the lowest because it has the strictest definition of error;

any case off the main diagonal, therefore, can make pairs that are considered error with cases from other cells.

EXERCISE 4   Calculating d_{yx}

Now calculate d_{yx} for the three tables you constructed for the first three exercises in Chapter 8.

DECIDING WHICH STATISTIC TO USE

How do you know whether to use gamma or tau_b or d_{yx} to indicate the strength of the relationship between the variables? Four considerations are important.

The most important consideration is your hypothesis. What do you expect to be happening between these variables? You want a measure of association that will increase when your expectations are met and decrease to the degree that they are not. This is also the most important question when you are using the measure of association to help you assess various kinds of reliability. There you would ask yourself what kinds of error you are interested in reducing, and you would pick a measure of association that matched your conception of what kind of error was important.

At the one end of a continuum, gamma is probably the choice if you hypothesize just a weak, monotonic relationship between X and Y, that is, if your hypothesis suggests that, as X increases, Y will either increase or stay the same. Gamma is symmetrical; it doesn't matter which variable you consider independent or dependent when you calculate it. If you expect X, as it increases, to increase Y, and vice versa, but you do not expect any very clear pattern other than monotonicity to that increase, gamma may be your measure. (More on monotonicity below.)

At the other end of the continuum, tau_b is likely to be your choice if you expect a far more precisely clear-cut relationship similar to the kind of linearity we saw in interval-level relationships measured by r^2. Here the hypothesis would be that, as X goes up, Y goes up, and the reverse is also true. As you can see, tau_b is symmetrical.

In between the two extremes, d_{yx} measures, asymmetrically, the existence of a monotonic relationship when X is independent and Y is dependent. Your hypothesis would be that, as X changes, Y changes but not necessarily vice versa. Since it is asymmetric, it may be your choice when you are looking for a test of a causal hypothesis and not just a measure of relationship, especially when you do not predict the kind of linearity presumed for tau_b.

Second, look at your marginal distribution. For the example of Table 9.1, which had cells designated n_1, n_2, n_3, etc., compare:

$(n_1 + n_4 + n_7)$ = Total cases that are high dependent
to $(n_2 + n_5 + n_8)$ = Total cases that are medium dependent
to $(n_3 + n_6 + n_9)$ = Total cases that are low dependent

and

$(n_1 + n_2 + n_3)$ = Total cases that are low independent
to $(n_4 + n_5 + n_6)$ = Total cases that are medium independent
to $(n_7 + n_8 + n_9)$ = Total cases that are high independent

Are your cases pretty evenly spread across all categories of your independent and dependent variables? If so, gamma is appropriate. If not, gamma may be inflated. When one or both distributions are skewed (a few cases in one or a few categories compared to many cases in most of the categories), use tau_b, if you have a square table.

Third, think about the size of your table. Tau_b is (usually) only for square tables. Gamma and d_{yx} can be used on tables of any size.

Finally, you may want to think about your measurement, although this criterion is certainly more debatable. Let's say that you have a hypothesis that suggests a monotonic, linear relationship between X and Y. And let's say that you want your measure of association to reflect how strong you think the relationship really is without the measure's being deflated for the kind of measurement error that results when cases are grouped into the kind of ordinal categories we have been working with rather than being spread out over the more precise codes of many more categories.

If, on the one hand, you can say, "If only I had ten codes on each variable rather than three, I bet all the cases would show up clearly on the diagonal—a perfect relationship—and someday I'll have that more precise, if still ordinal, measurement," then use gamma. The "error" that you can clearly see in your relationship may be considered somewhat less relevant because, you can assert, it's probably a function of measurement imprecision, not the hypothesis. The imprecision of your measurement has lumped cases together in "low" that should have been considered "extra low," "low," and "not very low." If you had that more precise measurement, you can argue, there would be very few cases tied on either of the variables.

On the other hand, if you've measured the variables as well as can be expected—if your theoretical concepts are themselves ordinal and your empirical measurement matches your theoretical concepts fairly well—and if both variables have the same number of ordinal categories, then use tau_b. The error you can see in the table is really error in the relationship (cases that don't fit the hypothesis) and should be reflected in a lower measure of association.

In between, if you consider error on X irrelevant, but error on Y important enough to consider, use d_{yx}. This can happen if you think you have the dependent variable measured so precisely that ties on it should be considered error while you also think that your measurement of the independent variable could be improved. In such a case, ties on the dependent ought to reduce the measure of association because they are considered error in the hypothesis. Ties on the independent variable, however, are ignored because they are considered merely measurement error.

Now take all four criteria under consideration at the same time. Don't rely on just one criterion when deciding which measure of association to use. What would you do if the criteria contradict each other? (1) Consider which one you think best represents what you see in the table, reading it for yourself; or (2) use tau_b because it is the most conservative and you won't mislead either yourself or your reader into thinking your hypothesis reflects the data very well when it may not.

Tau_c

One final measure is necessary. When tables aren't square (that is, when the two variables don't have the same number of values), tau_b is depressed. If you cannot use gamma because of the marginal distributions and cannot use d_{yx} because one variable is not being thought of as dependent on the other, you need another measure, tau_c.

The numerator is the same as that of the others, but the denominator is based on the number of rows and columns—not on the number of pairs. It is shown in Formula 9.4.

FORMULA 9.4 Tau_c

$$Tau_c = \frac{C - D}{1/2 N^2 [(m - 1)/m]}$$

where:
$m =$ Whichever is smaller—
the number of rows *or*
the number of columns

To calculate the denominator, square the number of cases and divide by 2. Multiply that result by the quantity in brackets, substituting for m, in both places, the smaller of the number of rows or the number of columns.

Since tau_c is based on rows and columns, clear interpretation breaks down somewhat. You can't say, anymore, the excess of concordant (discordant) pairs *as a proportion of "rel-*

124 MEASURES OF THE STRENGTH OF ASSOCIATION BETWEEN ORDINAL VARIABLES

evant" pairs. You can only say that .75 on one table is stronger than .56 on another *same-sized* table. Thus, even though it is easy to calculate, you probably won't want to use it unless you have nonsquare tables that don't meet the criteria for the other measures.

MONOTONICITY AND LINEARITY

All of these—gamma, the tau's, and d_{yx}—measure *monotonic* relationships, so don't use them if your hypothesis specifies a nonmonotonic relationship. In a monotonic relationship, the relationship continues to go either up or down but does not reverse itself as in the examples pictured in Figure 9.1.

Compare those to the following two examples of nonmonotonic relationships shown in Figure 9.2.

If your hypothesis specifies a monotonic relationship, these measures of association we've been discussing are fine *even if your data reveal nonmonotonicity.* Any nonmonotonicity is error when the hypothesis suggests monotonicity. Under such a circumstance, a lower figure on the measure of association appropriately reflects error. If, however, your hypothesis suggests a nonmonotonic relationship, your best bet is probably a nominal measure of association (which you will learn in Chapter 10) rather than one of these.

Remember, however, that tau_b measures more than monotonicity. Tau_b is the measure

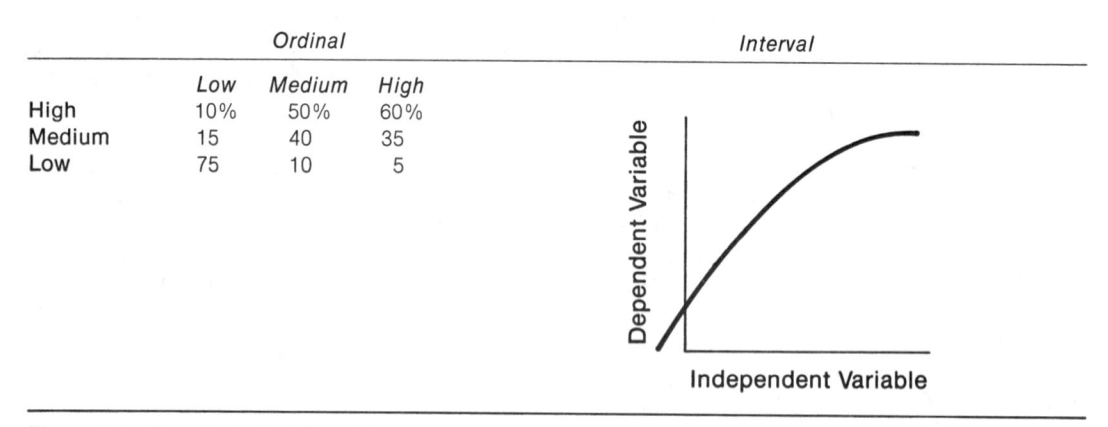

Ordinal

	Low	Medium	High
High	10%	50%	60%
Medium	15	40	35
Low	75	10	5

Interval

Figure 9.1 Monotonic Relationships

Ordinal

	Low	Medium	High
High	10%	75%	15%
Medium	15	15	75
Low	75	10	10

Interval

Figure 9.2 Nonmonotonic Relationships

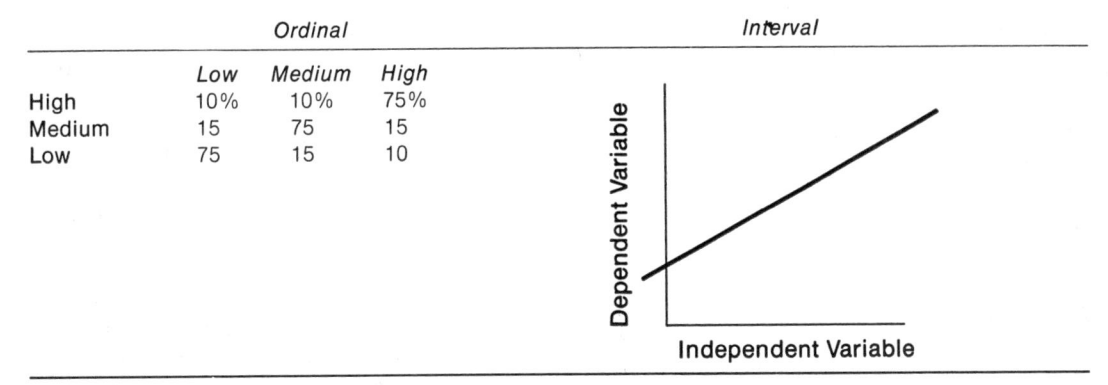

	Ordinal		
	Low	Medium	High
High	10%	10%	75%
Medium	15	75	15
Low	75	15	10

Figure 9.3 Monotonic Linear Relationships

for the ordinal equivalent of linearity, as shown in Figure 9.3. Therefore, it should ordinarily be used if you have hypothesized that the variables are as linearly related as we can measure with ordinal data.

You should be alerted that other ordinal measures of association exist. By now, you should be able to consult statistics books and uncover whatever you need. There is Spearman's rho and Kendall's tau_a for fully ranked data. If you have as many values as cases (for example, ten ranks for ten cases with no or few ties), one of those may serve your needs. Even those, however, are for monotonic relationships.

COMMUNICATING THE FORM OF THE RELATIONSHIP

Remember that gamma, d_{yx}, and the tau's are all measures of the *strength* of the association. They do not directly communicate the form of the relationship, except by their signs. If the relationship is a positive one (as X increases, Y increases), only the sign really tells you that form. Similarly, if the relationship is negative, only the sign tells you that.

If you want to say that the relationship is monotonic, or the ordinal equivalent of linear, you have to look at the table itself in order to know whether this is true. The measure of strength of association cannot tell you that. Although it will be lower as the data deviate from the form supposed (e.g., as the data deviate from monotonic, gamma gets smaller), it could also be low just because the relationship is weak.

This is one more instance of not having a simple statistic to communicate the form of the relationship when the data are less than interval. You can talk about the distribution of Y getting higher or lower as X increases, but the simplicity of $Y = a + bX + e$ and of knowing you could report the slope as a single summary statistic for the form is lost with less than interval data.

SPSS ORDINAL MEASURES OF ASSOCIATION

EXERCISE 5 Computer Generated Statistics

Now make the machine calculate some ordinal measures of association for you. Decide on two hypotheses to test with the data from one of the codebooks. Use the same SPSS setup you used earlier in Chapter 8. Remember the RECODE if you need it for combining categories. On the CROSSTABS command, put in a subcommand for the ordinal measures of association like this:

```
CROSSTABS TABLES = depvar1 BY
    indvar1/depvar2 BY indvar2/
    OPTIONS=4/STATISTICS 6 7 8 9.
                            (SPSS/PC+)
CROSSTABS TABLES = depvar1 BY
    indvar1/depvar2 BY
    indvar2/CELLS=COLUMN/
    STATISTICS=BTAU CTAU GAMMA D.
                              (SPSS-X)
```

Where the command says "indvar1, indvar2," put in the names of the independent variables for each of your two hypotheses. Where the command says "depvar1, depvar2," put in the names of the dependent variables for each of your two hypotheses.

Write your hypotheses and draw up the tables you get from your output. Indicate the values gamma, tau_b, tau_c, and d_{yx}. Be sure to get the right values on d_{yx}. SPSS prints out one for the row variable taken as the dependent and another for the column variable taken as the dependent. Be sure to examine your tables as well as the statistics to make sure any signs on the statistics reflect what is really happening in the data. Spell out which statistic you would choose to represent the relationship in the table and why. Write out a sentence that describes the relationship between X and Y for each table.

SUGGESTED READINGS

Measures of Association for Ordinal Data

BABBIE, EARL R. *The Practice of Social Research*, 3rd ed. (Belmont, CA: Wadsworth, 1983), pp. 411–413.

BLALOCK, HUBERT M., JR. *Social Statistics*, 2nd ed. (N.Y.: McGraw-Hill, 1972), pp. 421–426.

BUCHANAN, WILLIAM. "Nominal and Ordinal Bivariate Statistics: The Practitioner's View," *American Journal of Political Science* 18 (1974), 625–646.

KOHOUT, FRANK J. *Statistics for Social Scientists* (N.Y.: Wiley, 1974), Section VII.3. Good on deciding which measure to use; interpretation.

NACHMIAS, DAVID, and CHAVA NACHMIAS. *Research Methods in the Social Sciences*, 2nd ed. (N.Y.: St. Martin's, 1981), pp. 339–348.

OTT, LYMAN, WM. MENDENHALL, and RICHARD LARSON. *Statistics: A Tool for the Social Sciences*, 2nd ed. (North Scituate, MA: Duxbury, 1978), Ch. 10. Especially clear on all the PRE measures.

SHIVELY, W. PHILLIPS. *The Craft of Political Research*, 2nd ed. (Englewood Cliffs: Prentice-Hall, 1980), pp. 135–137. On gamma: calculating, interpreting.

A More Sophisticated Approach to Choosing Appropriate Measures

WEISBERG, HERBERT F., "Models of Statistical Relationship," *American Political Science Review*, 68 (December 1974), 1638–1655.

ARTICLES

BRENNER, SAUL. "Issue Specialization as a Variable in Opinion Assignment on the U.S. Supreme Court," *Journal of Politics*, 46 (1984), 1217–1225. Uses opinion assignment ratios (number of times a justice is assigned the writing of a majority decision out of total times that justice is available) to look for issue specialists on the Warren Court. Also uses the gamma, which indicates the correlation between one justice/all other justices and assignment/nonassignment, where times available are taken as the units of analysis. Also uses scale scores on issue indices to compare specialists to Warren in order to show that specialists were ideologically close to the Chief Justice. May be a bit confusing because unit of analysis is unconventional.

ERICKSON, ROBERT. "The Relationship between Public Opinion and State Policy: A New Look Based on Some Forgotten Data," *American Journal of Political Science*, 20 (February 1976),

25-35. Uses large sample public opinion data from the 1930s aggregated to measure state-level support for three issues, either as a continuous variable for Pearson's r (and biserial r) or as a dichotomy for Q, phi, gamma, and tau$_c$. Dependent variables include whether a state allowed capital punishment, ratified the child labor amendment, and allowed female jurors. Good discussion of early survey-sampling techniques. Considers alternate explanations for the discovered correlations.

FRASER, JOHN. "Validating a Measure of National Political Legitimacy," *American Journal of Political Science*, 18 (1974), 117-133. Mentioned first in Chapter 2. Right now, do not worry too much about the factor analysis (an extension of regression) to ascertain which of several measures of support were similar enough to combine into multi-item indices or the factor scores used to construct new multi-item indices. Uses regression to analyze their relationship to legitimacy measure. Uses the legitimacy measure, dichotomized to explain several other support measures in crosstabulation tables with the statistics. Finally, shows that national legitimacy is separable from state or university legitimacy.

JOHNSON, DONALD BRUCE, and JAMES R. GIBSON. "The Divisive Primary Revisited: Party Activists in Iowa," *American Political Science Review*, 68 (March 1974), 67-77. This was listed in Chapter 1. It is relevant here for the crosstabulations and gammas.

KENSKI, HENRY C. "Partisanship and Ideology in the Revenue Act of 1978," *Policy Studies Journal*, 9 (Autumn 1980), 74-81. Roll-call analysis of the proposed amendments to the 1978 Revenue Act. Conservative coalition support and opposition scores used to measure ideology. Simple, bivariate percentage tables and gammas.

KENSKI, HENRY C., and MARGARET C. KENSKI. "Partisanship, Ideology, and Constituency Differences in Environmental Issues in the U.S. House of Representatives: 1973-78," *Policy Studies Journal*, 9 (Winter 1980), 325-335. Uses League of Conservation Voters index of environmental voting as dependent on ideology (conservative coalition support and opposition), partisanship, and constituency characteristics (region, rural/urban). Analysis based on means and gamma. Attention to problems in use of roll-call data.

NIE, NORMAN, SIDNEY VERBA, and JOHN R. PETROCIK. *The Changing American Voter*, enlarged edition. (Cambridge, MA: Harvard University Press, 1979), pp. 148-150. Authors correlate responses to one "issue position" item on a survey to another "issue position" item. Both items have the same response scale from "agree" to "disagree." Thus, for each pair of items, there is a square table on which a gamma is calculated. (If people are consistent in their responses for the two items, gamma = +1.0.) Gammas are averaged across a large number of sets of items and presented for each presidential election year from 1956 through 1972 to demonstrate changes in consistency.

PALUMBO, DENNIS, and RICHARD A. STYSKAL. "Professionalism and Receptivity to Change," *American Journal of Political Science*, 18 (1974), 385-394. Mentioned first in Chapter 2. Tables 1 and 2 compare school board members and principals or different classes of respondents using percentage distributions and differences of means. Also used is correlation of a measure of professionalism with change orientation as well as Yule's Q to assess alternate hypotheses. Limited sample.

CHAPTER 10

MEASURES OF RELATIONSHIP FOR NOMINAL VARIABLES

The only level of measurement for which we have not examined a measure of association is nominal measurement. Remember that nominal measurement is merely naming, categorizing cases according to some concept.

For example, male/female are two values of the variable "sex," but there's no "more than/less than" meaning to the numbers when 1 stands for male and 2 for female. As another example, Protestant, Catholic, Jewish, Other/None might be four values on the variable "religion." It wouldn't matter, however, whether Protestant was coded 1 or 4 because there's no conceptualization of more or less religion. The values on the variable merely name the categories of the concept "religion."

Because the values on nominal variables cannot be manipulated arithmetically, the measure of association we use must be built on counting cases in categories. We can't even examine pairs of cases to see whether one case is higher/lower on two variables than another case because the values on a nominal variable don't even imply order.

We will examine two kinds of measures of association. Two of the measures of association have a proportionate reduction of error (PRE) interpretation that makes them cousins (if distant ones, given the nature of the measurement) to a Pearson's r^2. The other measures of association have less clear interpretations but are frequently seen in the literature. They are chi-square-based measures of association.

For the PRE measures, we will guess all the cases' values on the dependent variable and see how much error we make. Then we will guess all the cases' values on the dependent variable, knowing each case's value on the independent variable, and see how much error we make. The proportionate reduction of error knowing the independent variable value over not knowing it is the measure of how associated the two variables are. Notice how similar this interpretation is to r^2 and E^2.

TWO PRE MEASURES OF ASSOCIATION

Lambda, A Measure Based on the Modal Category

Let's begin with a table that looks like Table 10.1.

To see how the statistic works, imagine that you are given another 100 cases and told that the dependent variable is distributed the same as the distribution above. You are to guess the values on the dependent variable for your new 100 cases and make as few errors as possible, just as you guessed the mean for Pearson's r^2

MEASURES OF RELATIONSHIP FOR NOMINAL VARIABLES   129

Table 10.1

		Nominal Independent Variable		
	1	2	3	Totals
Nominal	3			33
Dependent	2			34
Variable	1			33
	Totals			100

Table 10.2

		Nominal Independent Variable		
	1	2	3	Totals
	3	25	4	4	33
Nominal				
Dependent 2	6	10	18	34
Variable				
	1	2	20	11	33
	Totals			100

or for E^2 in analysis of variance; but you don't have a mean here. Values on a nominal variable cannot be added up as required for a mean, remember. Therefore, there must be a rule other than "guess the mean."

One rule for guessing a case's value on the nominal dependent variable is to guess the *mode* of the variable for all cases. (The mode, remember from Chapter 2, is the category that has the largest number of cases, and with nominal data we *can* count the number of cases in each category.) Here you would guess 2 for each of your 100 new cases because 2 is the mode of the distribution of the dependent variable.

How many errors would you make if your new 100 cases were distributed just as the 100 in the table? If you said 66, you're right. Assuming the new 100 cases were distributed the same as the cases on the above table, 34 really would have a value of 2, and the other 66 would be wrong—errors.

Now suppose you could find out the independent variable value on your imaginary 100 new cases, and you are told the dependent variable is distributed within independent variable categories, just the same as the original 100 were. Table 10.2 shows how the original 100 cases distributed within categories of the independent variable.

For all your new cases with an independent variable value of 1, you'd guess the value that represents the mode of the original dependent variable distribution within independent variable category 1. Therefore, for all your new cases that are 1 on the independent variable, you'd guess a value of what of the dependent variable? If you said 3, you are set to go on. If not, reread.

How many errors would you make on independent variable category 1? The correct answer is 8. Of the 33 cases coded 1 on the independent, 25 really have a value of 3 on the dependent; the other 8 don't and are errors.

Now go to the new cases that are coded 2 on the independent variable. If they are distributed on the dependent variable exactly as were the old cases that were scored 2 on the independent, what is your best guess of the dependent variable value on this batch of new cases? The dependent variable mode of independent variable category 2 is 1, so 1 is your best guess. How many errors do you make? Here, the answer is 14.

Now go to your new cases that are scored 3 on the independent variable. 2 is the mode of the dependent variable for cases scored 3 on the independent variable, so 2 is the best guess. And you will make 15 errors.

Now you are ready to construct the measure of association. When you did not know the value of the independent variable for each case, you made a total of 66 errors in guessing the dependent. When you did know the value of the independent variable for each case, you made 8 for the first category of the independent variable, 14 for the second, and 15 for the third, that is, 37 total errors.

The PRE measure of association (called "lambda" for these particular procedures) is given in Formula 10.1. For our data, it works out to $(66 - 37)/66 = .44$. We have reduced our error 44% by knowing the independent over not knowing it.

FORMULA 10.1 PRE Measure of Association

$$\frac{\text{Errors not knowing independent} - \text{Error knowing independent}}{\text{Error knowing independent}}$$

Notice that the PRE measure stays the same as it was for r^2 and for E^2, but that the rules for guessing the dependent variable change for the different measurement levels.

If two variables are not associated, remember, the conditional distributions of the dependent variable *within* categories of the independent are the same as the marginal (*overall*) distribution of the dependent variable. (Review Chapter 8 on table reading if this seems unclear. Reading nominal variable tables is very much like reading ordinal variable tables, except that higher/lower doesn't make sense anymore.) If the conditional distributions *are* the same as the marginal distributions, we'll make just as much error knowing the independent as not knowing it, and the measure of association will be close to zero.

Look at Table 10.3 where there is practically no relationship between the variables. We'd make 66 errors guessing the dependent variable value of 100 new cases distributed the same way, not knowing the independent. We'd make 21 errors guessing the dependent in category 1 of the independent; 22 errors in category 2 of the independent; and 21 errors in category 3 of the independent, for a total of 64 errors, knowing the independent. The measure of association would be $(66 - 64)/66 = .03$.

Make sure you understand exactly how that was computed. When the conditional distributions (the distributions of the dependent variable within categories of the independent variable) are very much alike, there is little to no association, and a low measure of association results.

Notice that lambda is *asymmetric*. Whether you consider the row variable or the column variable to be independent can make a big difference. The way you have been instructed to calculate the measure assumes that the *row* variable is *dependent* and that the *column* variable is *independent*.

To change the procedure in order to do the calculations so that the *column* variable is taken as the dependent variable, work from the distribution of cases at the bottom of the table for the errors not knowing the independent variable. Then work from the conditional distributions of cases within the rows for the errors knowing the independent variable.

EXERCISE 1 Calculating Lambda

It happens that Tables 10.2 and 10.3 work out the same, whether you consider the columns or rows to be dependent, but that won't always be the case. For example, consider Table 10.4 below.

Compute lambda for this table, considering

Table 10.3

		Nominal Independent Variable			
		1	2	3	Totals
Nominal Dependent Variable	3	12	11	10	33
	2	11	11	12	34
	1	10	12	11	33
	Totals				100

Table 10.4

		Nominal Independent Variable			
		1	2	3	Totals
Nominal Dependent Variable	3	25	6	2	33
	2	12	19	3	34
	1	13	5	15	33
	Totals	50	30	20	100

the *column* variable to be the independent variable. Then, compute lambda for the same table, but consider the *row* variable to be the independent variable. Be sure to write out all your work.

If you percentage the table with the columns totalling to 100%, treating the column variable as the independent variable (as in Table 10.5), and then percentage the table so that the rows total to 100%, treating the row variable as the independent variable (as in Table 10.6), you can see the difference in the two relationships.

First read across the columns when the column variable is treated as independent. Then read across the rows when the row variable is treated as independent. (Either way you are varying the independent variable and observing the distribution of the dependent variable.) You will see that the former is the stronger relationship. You will see that the lambdas that you calculated are larger or smaller, depending on the strength of the relationship when different variables are treated as independent, just as the distributions on the two tables are different when different variables are treated as independent.

Goodman and Kruskal's Tau, A Measure Based on the Whole Distribution

When we have the same dependent variable mode for each of the two categories of a two-value (dichotomous) independent variable or when the marginal distributions on a table are very uneven, lambda can have a value of zero, even when there really is some association between two variables. In such a case, there is another PRE measure of association for nominal variables. The guessing rules are somewhat changed for this measure of association, which is called Goodman and Kruskal's tau. (Note: this is not the same tau you used for ordinal variables, which was Kendall's tau.)

EXERCISE 2 Lambda on Misleading Data

Let's first examine how lambda can be misleading before we go on with calculating Goodman and Kruskal's tau.

Consider Table 10.7. If we percentage the table, we see there is a fairly strong relationship between the independent and dependent variables, as shown in Table 10.8.

Table 10.5

		Column Variable Independent		
		1	2	3
Row Variable Dependent	3	50%	20%	10%
	2	24	63	15
	1	26	17	75
	Totals	100%	100%	100%
	Read ──────────────►			

Table 10.6

		Column Variable Dependent			
		1	2	3	Totals
Row Variable Independent	3	76%	18	6	100%
	2	35%	56	9	100%
	1	39%	15	45	99%
					Read

Table 10.7

		Nominal Independent Variable		
		1	2	Totals
Nominal Dependent Variable	3	45	12	57
	2	3	10	13
	1	2	8	10
	Totals			80

Table 10.8

		Nominal Independent	
		1	2
Nominal Dependent Variable	3	90%	40%
	2	6%	33%
	1	4%	27%
	Totals	100%	100%

Compute a lambda on Table 10.7 (the raw, unpercentaged table) and see why we frequently need another measure of association to convey the strength of some associations between nominal variables. (Write out each step of your work.) Lambda cannot always communicate clearly what we easily see is going on in the table.

EXERCISE 3 Calculating Goodman and Kruskal's Tau

The changed guessing rules for Goodman and Kruskal's tau will correct this problem. It tells us to guess the overall distribution—not just the mode. Assume we are given the Table 10.7 below. This is the same table, remember, that gave us the zero lambda.

Let us imagine we are given 80 new cases and told to guess their values on the dependent variable without knowing their values on the independent variable, but we are told they are distributed just as in the original table. We'd

Table 10.7

		Nominal Independent Variable		
		1	2	Totals
Nominal Dependent Variable	3	45	12	57
	2	3	10	13
	1	2	8	10
	Totals			80

guess that 57 cases (any random 57) were scored 3 on the dependent variable; 13 cases (any random 13) were scored 2; and 10 cases (any random 10) were scored 1.

How many errors would we make? Well, if we distributed our new cases randomly, part of the cases would really be what we guessed them to be, and part would not. Of the 57 for which we guessed a score of 3, a fraction of 57/80 would in all probability really belong there, but a fraction of 13/80 and 10/80 would really be either 1 or 2. Therefore, for those 57 cases we make $(13 + 10)/80$ errors.

Similarly, for the 13 we guessed to be 2, a fraction—13/80—would probably be right, but another fraction—$(57 + 10)/80$—would be wrong. For the 10 we guessed to be 1 on the dependent variable, a fraction—10/80—would probably be right, but another fraction—$(57 + 13)/80$—would be wrong.

Our total errors guessing the dependent while not knowing the independent would be:

$$57 \times 23/80 = 16.39$$
$$13 \times 67/80 = 10.89$$
$$10 \times 70/80 = \underline{8.75}$$
$$36.03$$

Before going on, study the table and these calculations long enough to see exactly how the guesses were made and the errors calculated.

Now, imagine you are told which 50 new cases are scored 1 on the independent variable, that they are distributed on the dependent variable the same as similarly scored cases on the independent variable on the original table, and that you are to guess the dependent variable value. Of those cases scored 1 on the independent, you'd take a random 45 cases and guess them to be 3; a random 3 cases and guess them to be scored 2; and a random 2 cases and guess them to be scored 1. How many errors would you make?

$$45 \times 5/50 = 4.50$$
$$3 \times 47/50 = 2.82$$
$$2 \times 48/50 = \underline{1.92}$$
$$9.24$$

And now imagine you are told which 30 of your new cases have a value of 2 on the independent variable and that they are distributed the same as cases scored similarly on the independent variable in the original table. You guess their dependent variable scores randomly and make the following errors:

$$12 \times 18/30 = 7.20$$
$$10 \times 20/30 = 6.67$$
$$8 \times 22/30 = \underline{5.87}$$
$$19.74$$

Knowing the independent variable, you would make 9.24 errors for the first value of the independent plus 19.74 errors for the second value or a total of 28.98. Remembering the 36.03 errors made not knowing the independent, you'd construct the PRE measure shown in Formula 10.2, the same PRE measure as you have seen all along since Chapter 4 but with different rules to reflect the different measurement levels. Tau = (36.03 − 28.98)/36.03 = .19.

FORMULA 10.2 PRE Measure of Association

$$\frac{\text{Errors not knowing independent} - \text{Error knowing independent}}{\text{Error not knowing independent}}$$

We've reduced our error 19% knowing the independent over not knowing it. For practice, now compute tau on Table 10.4.

EXERCISE 4 Tau as It Reflects Strong and Weak Relationships

When the relationship is perfect, tau will be 1.0. When there is no association, tau will be zero. Now, for Exercise 4, compute tau for both the following tables. Remember to use raw numbers in your calculations of tau; but you can calculate the percentages for the table as well, if that will help you to see the relationship. Write out all your work.

Notice that the tau you get is zero when there is no association (Table 10.10) and that it

Table 10.9

		Nominal Independent Variable		
	1	2	3	Totals
Nominal Dependent Variable 3	30	0	3	33
2	2	2	29	33
1	1	31	1	33
Totals				99

Table 10.10

		Nominal Independent Variable		
	1	2	3	Totals
Nominal Dependent Variable 3	11	11	11	33
2	11	11	11	33
1	11	11	11	33
Totals				99

gets larger as the relationship gets stronger (Table 10.9). Compare the taus to the percentage tables you may have constructed; they will show you the same relationship.

EXERCISE 5 Calculating Tau, Treating Row Variable as Independent

Tau is *asymmetric*, as is lambda. It matters which variable you consider to be dependent. The tau you have been constructing is tau$_b$, which takes the row variable as the dependent variable. For Tables 10.9 and 10.10, the taus which take different variables as independent are the same, but this is not always the case. For Exercise 5, compute a tau for Table 10.7, considering the row variable to be the independent variable. You will come up with something different from the .19 we got when we considered the column variable to be the independent one. When the row variable is the independent variable, the overall distribution of the dependent variable, which you need in order to guess the values of the dependent variable without knowledge of the independent, is at the bottom of the table—the overall distribution of the column (now dependent) variable. The conditional distributions of the dependent variable, which you need in order to guess the values of the dependent variable, knowing the value of the independent on each case, are now in the rows of the table.

MEASURES OF ASSOCIATION BASED ON CHI SQUARE

Some measures of association for nominal data are based on chi square. Chi square *itself* is not a measure of the strength of an association between two variables. Instead, it is a measure of how likely an association was to have happened by chance. You will run into chi square and several other such tests in Chapter 18.

Right now, however, you need to meet measures of association based on chi square because they are very common in the literature. Unfortunately, you have to learn to calculate chi square itself before you can get to the measures of association. For that you have to imagine how different your table is from one that would show no real relationship between the variables—a table whose cell entries happened purely by chance, given the marginal distributions of the two variables.

For example, let's imagine that you have a hypothesis which suggests that the method of political participation people prefer varies by the region of the country in which they live. In your sample, you find 20 people whose preferred political activity is partisan, 35 who prefer interest-group activity, and 15 who prefer communicating with officials. You also find that these 70 people include 30 Northeasterners, 25 Westerners, and 15 Southerners. In short, you have marginal distributions that look like those in Table 10.11.

If nothing but chance were operating to distribute cases in the cells of the table (that is, if there were no "real" effects of region on pre-

Table 10.11 Preferred Political Activity by Region

Preferred Activity	North-eastern	Western	Southern	Totals
Partisan				20
Interest Group				35
Communicating				15
Totals	30	25	15	70

ferred mode of political activity), you would expect the 30 Northeasterners to be distributed across the categories of participation in roughly the same way as participation is distributed overall. Similarly, the Westerners and the Southerners should be distributed across the participation categories in roughly the same way as participation is distributed overall.

So if 20 out of 70 prefer partisan activity in the overall group, the same fraction (20/70) of the Northeasterners should prefer that form of activity. What number of 30 people represents the same fraction as 20 of 70 people?

$n/30 = 20/70; n = (30 * 20)/70;$
$n = 8.57$
(Keep the decimals—imagine part people.)

Just remember a bit of basic arithmetic here to figure that out. If $n/30 = 20/70$, you can isolate n on one side of the equals mark by multiplying both sides of the equation by 30. Thus: $n/30 \times 30 = n$, and $(20/70) \times 30 = (20 \times 30)/70 = 8.57$.

However, there's a simpler way to think of it. You multiply the two marginals that correspond to the cell you are estimating and divide by the total N. Therefore, if 35 out of the total sample prefer interest-group activity, what number of the 30 Northeasterners would prefer interest-group activity by chance? Multiply the two marginals that correspond to the cell you are estimating and divide by the total N, that is, (30 × 35)/70 or, in words, the 30 Northeasterners times the 35 who prefer interest-group activity divided by the total number of cases that is 70. You will find that the answer is 15.

EXERCISE 6 Calculating Expected Frequencies and Chi Square

Draw the table above and fill in the other seven cells, just as we have figured the two above. And, just so you can see for yourself that this procedure gives you cell entries that would occur if there were no relationship at all, create the percentage table that results from the estimation of cell entries you have just completed. Consider "region" to be the independent variable and "preferred activity" to be dependent on it as you construct your table. Now you can see that there is no relationship between region and preferred political activity when the cell values expected by chance are percentaged. The distributions of preferred participation activity among Northeasterners, Westerners, and Southerners are the same as the distribution for the participation variable in the whole group.

Now that you have seen what the table would look like if only chance were operating, we can go on to compute a statistic which measures how different our real results are from those. The chi square statistic compares the numbers (not percentages) we actually got in our data to those numbers (not percentages) we would have expected to have occurred by chance were the marginals the same but the variables unrelated. For example, imagine we actually got Table 10.12 from our data.

Just so you can see the relationship clearly, draw a percentage table for these data, treating region as the independent variable. The percentages show clearly that there is a fairly strong relationship between the two variables from the initial hypothesis.

Now let's proceed to compare the *obtained frequencies* (those that actually turned up in the cells of the table) to the *expected frequen-*

Table 10.12 Preferred Political Activity by Region

Preferred Activity	North-eastern	West-ern	South-ern	Totals
Partisan	17	2	1	20
Interest Group	8	17	10	35
Communi-cating	5	6	4	1
Totals	30	25	15	70

cies (those you got by estimating them from the marginals). Do notice that you must use frequencies, not percentages. The percentage tables were only for helping you see the relationship or absence of a relationship.

This comparison forms the basis of the chi square statistic, which is shown in Formula 10.3.

FORMULA 10.3 Chi Square

$$\text{Chi square} = \Sigma \frac{(f_o - f_e)^2}{f_e}$$

To use the formula, you work cell by cell.

1. Take the observed frequency in the cell and subtract from it the expected frequency in that cell, $(f_o - f_e)$.
2. Square the result of step 1, $(f_o - f_e)^2$.
3. Divide the result of step 2 by the expected frequency for that cell, $(f_o - f_e)^2 / f_e$.
4. Repeat steps 1 through 3 for each cell.
5. Sum the results of step 3 for all the cells, $\Sigma[(f_o - f_e)^2 / f_e]$.

Now, compute chi square for Table 10.12, the "obtained" table. Write down each step of your work. For each cell, show the frequency observed minus the expected frequency, square the result, and divide by the expected frequency. Total all the $(f_o - f_e)^2 / f_e$ calculations for each cell. That total is the chi square statistic; label it clearly on your work.

That number gets larger and larger as the relationship gets more and more different from chance. Unfortunately, it can get very much above 1.0 and, therefore, doesn't fit very well with our notion of what a measure of association ought to look like. It also, unfortunately, varies with the number of cases. In fact, keeping the strength of the relationship the same, chi square will double if the number of cases doubles. That, too, violates our notion of how a measure of association ought to behave.

Because of these problems of interpreting chi square itself, it is frequently manipulated to force it to behave like a measure of association. There are several ways to do this. We will look at only two. The first is shown in Formula 10.4; it is called phi.

FORMULA 10.4 Phi

$$\text{Phi} = \sqrt{\frac{\text{Chi square}}{N}}$$

Phi is used on a 2 × 2 or 2 × k table. (2 × k means that one variable is a dichotomy, while the other can have any number of categories.) For no relationship, it is 0; for perfect relationship, it is 1.0. On larger tables, it can exceed 1.0 and, thus, loses comparability to other measures of association.

Another possibility, this one useful for any sized table, is Cramer's V, defined as in Formula 10.5.

FORMULA 10.5 Cramer's V

$$\text{Cramer's V} = \sqrt{\frac{\text{Chi square}}{N \min (r - 1, c - 1)}}$$

Here the denominator refers to whichever is smaller, the number of rows or the number of columns (i.e., pick *either* the number of rows *or* the number of columns, depending on which is smaller; subtract 1 from that; multiply by N).

EXERCISE 7 Calculating the Chi-Square-Based Measures of Association

Now, for practice, calculate V for the table you've been working on and phi for Table 10.7. Label them clearly on your work sheets.

INTERPRETING THE CHI-SQUARE-BASED MEASURES OF ASSOCIATION

None of the chi-square-based measures of association is great. You can't do much comparison of how strong a relationship is in one group of cases compared to the strength in another group because each of these measures gives greater weight to columns or rows with small N's (as opposed to those with large N's). Thus, to compare strengths of relationships across samples, you need samples that have the same marginals.

These measures are also arbitrary; that is, none has a clear interpretation as PRE statistics do. You will eventually get used to calling the results strong, moderate, or weak, but you will not be able to use these measures of strength of association to say by what percentage you reduce your error, knowing the independent variable as compared to not knowing it.

You should also be aware of a few more things about these chi-square-based statistics. First, this method of calculating chi square requires quite a few cases. No cell should have an *expected* frequency of less than five. A correction should be made when small numbers of cases in some categories lead one to *expect* (not achieve) fewer than five cases per cell. (See Blalock in the suggested readings; SPSS will make that correction for you.)

And, secondly, chi square is *symmetrical*. It doesn't matter which variable you assume to be independent and which dependent; the resulting statistic will be the same.

If all you need is a quick-and-dirty check to see if two variables are symmetrically correlated, the chi-square-based measures will work fine. They are acceptable to use for rough reliability checks, etc., and you do sometimes see them in the literature.

As you will see in Chapter 18, there are other uses for chi square that make learning to calculate it worthwhile—even if you don't ordinarily want to use the measures of association that are based on it.

THE FORM OF RELATIONSHIPS BETWEEN NOMINAL VARIABLES

When you have nominal variables, the concept of monotonic relationship no longer makes sense. One can relocate columns at will because the numbers have no inherent relationship to each other. The important thing is that knowing into what independent variable category a case falls lets you predict into which dependent variable category a case will fall.

This makes writing hypotheses somewhat tricky because you are deprived of the chance to say, "The greater the X, the greater the Y," as you can with ordinal monotonic relationships. You also cannot say, "As X goes up one unit, Y goes up b units," as you can with interval linear relationships. You will have to say things like: "Men are more likely to support peace movements than women are"; or, "Parliamentary countries are more likely than presidential countries to respond to public opinion." You have to compare one independent variable category explicitly to the other or others in the hypothesis, naming each independent variable category and predicting where those cases will fall on a dependent variable.

This same interchangeability of columns, however, makes these nominal measures of association useful to communicate the strength of nonmonotonic ordinal associations. Even though a relationship does not keep going up (or down) as it would in a monotonic ordinal relationship, you may be able to predict a dependent variable category, knowing the independent variable category. Therefore, in those situations, nominal measures of association may be useful. (Cf. the use of analysis of variance to measure strength of association when a relation is curved and linear regression is inappropriate; see Chapter 7.)

Gamma for Nominal Variables

Let's discuss one more quick measure before we leave nominal measures. If you have two dichotomies, Yule's Q is appropriate. (Dichotomies are variables that have only two values. They may be thought of as nominal or, if the underlying concept is measured as more than/less than, they may be thought of as ordinal; as you will see later, we sometimes even treat them as interval.)

Yule's Q is gamma for nominal data, and it is interpreted much the same way as gamma in the last chapter. (It has a PRE interpretation if you talk about reducing error in predicting pairs of cases.) It is just quicker to compute. Imagine a table such as Table 10.13 in which the numbers of cases in the cells can be thought of as a, b, c, d.

Given such a table, Yule's Q can be defined as in Formula 10.6.

FORMULA 10.6 Yule's Q

$$Q = \frac{ad - bc}{ad + bc}$$

To compute it: (1) take the number of cases in cell a times the number in cell d; (2) then take the number of cases in cell b times the number in cell c; (3) for the numerator, subtract step 2 from step 1; (4) for the denominator, add step 2 and step 1.

Table 10.13

	Independent Variable 1	2
Dependent Variable 1	a	b
Dependent Variable 2	c	d

Table 10.14

		Independent Variable	
		1	2
Dependent Variable	1	32	41
	2	14	76

EXERCISE 8 Computing Yule's Q

Try it on Table 10.14.

SPSS AND NOMINAL MEASURES OF ASSOCIATION

EXERCISE 9 Using the Computer for Tables and Nominal Measures of Association

Now write up two hypotheses using nominal variables from the codebooks in the appendices. Run CROSSTABS and ask for STATISTICS =1 2 4 (for SPSS/PC+) or STATISTICS = CHISQ PHI LAMBDA (for SPSS-X).* Interpret your tables and tell why lambda, tau$_b$, Yule's Q, or one of the chi square-based measures would be more appropriate for each table. Remember, when deciding what measure is appropriate, to consider the following: (1) whether you need a PRE measure; (2) distributions of the variables; (3) table size; (4) and whether an asymmetric or symmetric measure is appropriate (see below).

Note: statistic 2 gives you phi for 2 × 2 tables and V for larger tables. You have seen that neither phi nor V has the relatively clear PRE interpretation of lambda or Goodman and Kruskal's tau, or Yule's Q. Of these latter statistics, SPSS only calculates lambda; and it gives you both the asymmetric one we've been using here and a symmetric one for which it doesn't matter which variable is considered independent. And, if you have two dichotomies, you can ask for and read the gamma you'd get from GAMMA or STATISTICS number 8 for Yule's Q. If you need one of the other statistics, you can let SPSS construct your tables, and then you can calculate the statistics by hand. Since they are relatively simple, that's not much of a problem.

Asymmetric versus Symmetric Measures

How should you choose an asymmetric or symmetric measure of association? It depends on what you are doing. If you are assessing a hypothesis, the asymmetric measure is appropriate; one variable precedes the other or "causes" the other in the hypothesis. If you are doing reliability tests or something else where you care only about correlation and not about "causation," symmetric measures are appropriate.

PREPARATION FOR THE NEXT STEP

Just because we've been through measures of association for all measurement levels, don't assume your job is over. Your next step is twofold: (1) trying out other reasons that you found or didn't find an association; and (2) trying to refine and improve the initial hypothesis/explanation.

Both procedures involve adding additional independent variables to your hypothesized relationship. In other words, you move from assessing bivariate relationships into assessing multivariate relationships. The next several chapters will take you through the process of basic multivariate analysis for variables at each level of measurement.

MEASUREMENT VALIDITY

As you are moving into a more sophisticated level of analysis, this seems an appropriate

---

*Note: the same precautions about having only a few values on each variable and many cases in each category apply to nominal as well as to ordinal tables. RECODE if necessary.

place for a warning about measurement. All the statistics in the world can neither help us to know what is "really" going on nor help us to explain phenomena satisfactorily if our measurements are not valid. Validity means that we are measuring what we think we are measuring.

Basically, there are four ways to assess whether an operationalization of a concept is a valid measurement. The simplest is *face validity* (sometimes called *content validity*). This, in effect, means that measures are valid "on their faces." If trained researchers look at an operationalization and say, "For sure; that does seem to measure the concept," you can assert content validity.

A more exact way of assessing the validity of an operationalization depends on the prior existence of a valid measurement. If your operationalization and the old operationalization are both measured on the same subjects and are highly correlated, you have *concurrent validity*.

Another way to assess validity is if your operationalization is highly correlated with some standard of its success in the future. This is called *predictive validity*.

The most scientific assessment of validity is *construct validity*. This means that your operationalization behaves as it should, given the expectations of well-established theory. In any good theory, there are predictions about what causes a phenomenon and about what its effects are. If your measurement is highly correlated in the right direction (as specified by theory) with its causes and effects, you can assert that your measurement has construct validity.

It is very important to note that validation must be done *separately* from the research hypotheses you are testing. If your research hypothesis is that $a \rightarrow b \rightarrow c$, you cannot use correlations between a and b between b and c to assert construct, predictive, or concurrent validity. You must have separate hypotheses and separate variables for your validation tests.

Validation is much more important than the short treatment here seems to imply. You can read more in the works listed in the suggested readings, and you can begin to remember to ask yourself at every analysis, "What does this variable *really* measure?"

SUGGESTED READINGS

Measures of Association for Nominal Data

BABBIE, EARL R. *The Practice of Social Research*, 3rd ed. (Belmont, CA: Wadsworth, 1983), pp. 410–411.

BLALOCK, HUBERT M., JR. *Social Statistics*, 2nd ed. (NY: McGraw-Hill, 1972), pp. 291–303. Blalock covers the corrections necessary for chi square when you have fewer than five expected cases per cell.

KOHOUT, FRANK J. *Statistics for Social Scientists* (NY: Wiley, 1974), Section VII.4.

NACHMIAS, DAVID, and CHAVA NACHMIAS. *Research Methods in the Social Sciences*, 2nd ed. (NY: St. Martin's, 1981), pp. 334–339.

OTT, LYMAN, WM. MENDENHALL, and RICHARD LARSON. *Statistics: A Tool for the Social Sciences*, 2nd ed. (North Scituate, MA: Duxbury, 1978), Ch. 10. Especially clear on all the PRE measures.

SHIVELY, W. PHILLIP. *The Craft of Political Research*, 2nd ed. (Englewood Cliffs, NJ: Prentice-Hall, 1980), pp. 138–142.

ZISK, BETTY. *Political Research* (Lexington, MA: D.C. Heath, 1981), pp. 232–237.

Measurement Validity

BABBIE, EARL R. *The Practice of Social Research*, 3rd ed. (Belmont, CA: Wadsworth, 1983), pp. 116–119.

BOWEN, BRUCE D., and HERBERT F. WEISBERG. *An Introduction to Data Analysis* (San Francisco, CA: Freeman, 1980), pp. 11–12.

CARMINES, EDWARD G., and RICHARD A. ZELLER. *Reliability and Validity Assessment*, # 17 in series *Quantitative Applications in the Social Sciences* (Beverly Hills, CA: Sage, 1979).

ZELLER, RICHARD A., and EDWARD G. CARMINES. *Measurement in the Social Sciences: The Link between Theory and Data* (Cambridge: Cambridge University Press, 1980).

A More Sophisticated Approach to Choosing Appropriate Measures

WEISBERG, HERBERT F., "Models of Statistical Relationship," *American Political Science Review*, 68 (December 1974), 1638-1655.

ARTICLES

DIEHL, PAUL F., and GARY GOERTZ. "Territorial Changes and Militarized Conflict," *Journal of Conflict Resolution*, 32 (March 1988), 103-122. Uses crosstabular analysis to assess whether violence results from changes of territory, depending on size, contiguity, whether the gaining/losing side was major/minor power, and type of change. Tau_b, Cramer's V. Chi square used as significance test, not as measure of association.

DUBOIS, PHILIP L. "The Illusion of Judicial Consensus Revisited: Partisan Conflict on an Intermediate Court of Appeals," *American Journal of Political Science*, 32 (November 1988), 946-967. Using the California appeals courts (three judges) as units of analysis, shows effect of partisanship of the panel on conservatism or liberalism of decisions, effect of split partisanship on unanimity, effect of partisanship of opinion author in conservatism or liberalism of opinion. Bivariate crosstabulation. (Chi square used as test of significance, not modified into a measure of association.)

KUECHLER, MANFRED. "Maximizing Utility at the Polls? A Replication of Himmelweit's 'Consumer Model of Voting' with German Election Data from 1983," *European Journal of Political Research*, 14 (1986), 81-95. Maybe slightly difficult to follow at this early stage, especially those sections on measurement. Defines which party survey respondents are closest to by creating an index (basically) of the intensity and frequency that each party opposed an issue the respondent thought bad and supported an issue the respondent though good across fourteen issues. Tables 2, 3 and 4 are crosstabulations (Cramer's V) of the "closest party to respondent" and the vote, once modified by whether person expected that party to be represented, and once modified by criterion that a minor party be much closer in order to be considered "closest." Continues with multivariate analysis using weighted least-squares regression.

MUNDT, ROBERT J., and PEGGY HEILIG. "District Representation: Demands and Effects in the Urban South," *Journal of Politics*, 44 (1982), 1035-1047. Mentioned in Chapter 1; uses crosstabulation tables, chi-square, and Cramer's V.

PORTNEY, KENT E. "State Tax Preference Orderings and Partisan Control of Government," *Policy Studies Journal*, 9 (Autumn 1980), 87-95. Uses Cramer's V and Contingency Coefficient to measure the strength of relationship between types of partisan control of governorship/legislature and the order in which various taxes are adopted.

SHARP, ELAINE B. "Citizen Perceptions of Police Service Delivery: A Look at Some Consequences," *Policy Studies Journal*, 9 (Summer 1981), 971-981. Assesses the effects of perceived inequality and dissatisfaction with police service delivery on alienation, complaining, fear of crime, and failure to contribute to the public good. Crosstabulation, Cramer's V, Contingency Coefficient, phi, survey data.

CHAPTER
11
INTRODUCTION TO CONTROL VARIABLES

GOALS OF MULTIVARIATE ANALYSIS

The next chapters revolve around the process of "controlling" variables that may interfere with our understanding of a basic bivariate relationship and around the process of adding more independent variables that may improve our understanding and explanation. We will be:

1. Adding additional independent explanatory variables in order to improve explanation of a dependent variable
2. Removing the effects of a third variable in order to determine whether the original bivariate relationship was real or in order to determine whether the original absence of a bivariate relationship was real
3. Controlling the effects of a variable that intervenes between the independent and dependent variables in order to assess the process by which the independent variable influences the dependent variable
4. Controlling the effects of a variable that may specify when the original bivariate relationship holds or fails to hold or is stronger or weaker

Let's discuss each of these possible effects of adding additional independent variables before going forward.

Improved Explanation

In order to improve your explanation of a dependent variable (Y), you may want to use two independent variables (X, Z) that separately explain it. Although each separately explains some of the variation in Y, taken together they explain more of the variation in Y.

Figure 11.1 shows the situation in an arrow diagram where the arrow between Z and Y suggests that those two variables are correlated, the arrow between X and Y suggests that those two are correlated, and the absence of an arrow between X and Z indicates that they are not correlated.

The directions of the points of the arrows are determined by your theoretical understanding of what is causing what. Remember that you can observe whether two variables are correlated but cannot observe whether one causes the other; you infer causation from what you see and what your theories and common sense tell you is reasonable. (See Chapter 1 on causation, if necessary.)

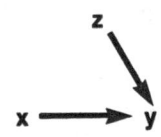

Figure 11.1 Explanation Improved with Two Independent Variables

142 INTRODUCTION TO CONTROL VARIABLES

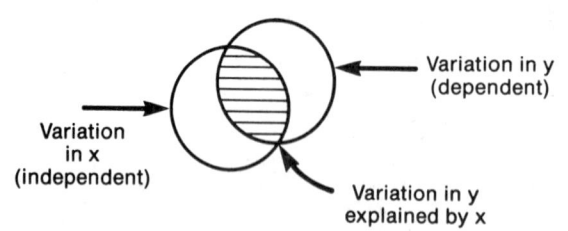

Figure 11.2 Diagram of Bivariate Correlation

Imagine that the variation in a variable can be represented by a circle. The correlation between X and Y can be represented by the overlap between two circles, such as that shown in Figure 11.2. The overlapped part is the explained variation in whichever is taken to be dependent.

If the additional independent variable, Z, also explains part of the variation in Y, you have the situation shown in Figure 11.3.

You can explain more of the variation in Y using both X and Z as independent variables than you can by using either alone. As long as X and Z are not correlated with each other, you can easily talk about the separate effects of X and Z: how much does X explain of Y versus how much does Z explain of Y; and what is the form of the relationship between X and Y or between Z and Y. Such an analysis would not be very different from doing two bivariate analyses.

For example, you might want to explain U.S. political participation. You might be able to explain part of the variation in participation using "region" as the independent variable if, say, Southerners participate less than do people from other regions. You also might be able to explain part of the variation in participation using "age" as the independent variable if young people participate less than their elders.

Using both region and age to explain participation would give you a more complete explanation than either taken alone; moreover, you would be able to assess readily which was the better explanation of participation and what forms their separate impacts took because there probably wouldn't be any (or much) correlation between region and age to worry about. Southerners probably don't tend to be much older or younger than people from other regions.

When X and Z are correlated, you can probably still explain more of the variation in Y using both than using either alone; however, it becomes somewhat more difficult to know which independent variable is doing what part of the explaining. Consider the diagram of this situation in Figure 11.4.

When X and Z are correlated, as they are in Figure 11.4, we just can't separate the effects of X from the effects of Z as clearly as we can when they are not correlated. X is explaining a portion of the variation in Y, and Z is explaining a portion of the variation in Y; but X and Z are themselves correlated as represented by their own overlap, part of which also overlaps Y and is represented by a cross-hatched portion. Either X or Z may explain that cross-hatched portion of Y, but we don't know

Figure 11.4 Diagram of Correlated Independent Variables

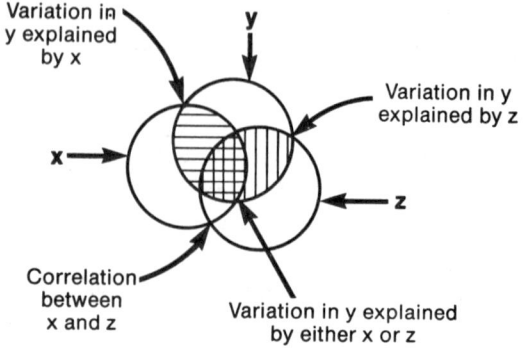

Figure 11.3 Diagram of Two Independent Variables (Uncorrelated)

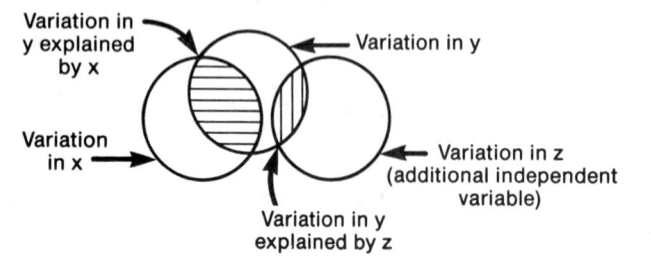

which. We do know that, taken together, X and Z explain more than either separately, but we can only cautiously assess the strengths and, perhaps, the forms of the separate relationships between the two independent variables and the dependent variable because we do not know to which to attribute that portion of Y that either could be explaining.

For example, if you want to know whether educational level or income level has more to do with whether people participate in politics, it may be a difficult analysis to undertake. As educational level goes up, income tends to go up; the two are correlated. You may know that educated people participate more than their income would predict, that is, education has some effect of its own on participation; but it is difficult to know how much effect to attribute to each of the two explanatory factors. What you can find out, without much question, is whether knowing both people's incomes and their educational levels lets you explain their participation better than either variable separately does.

In the most extreme case of almost perfect correlation between the two independent variables, you might as well drop one or the other because they tell you very little more together than either does separately. Consider Figure 11.5 in which X and Z are so correlated that the circles representing them are very overlapped. That makes the cross-hatched part of Y's circle—the part that could be explained by *either* X or Z—almost as large as the area that shows how much X and Z *together* explain.

Figure 11.5 Diagram of Highly Correlated Independent Variables

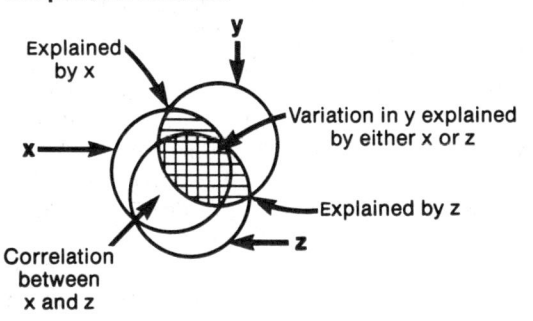

For example, if the cases you had to work with were in a situation where how much education a person had was very closely tied to what kind of job a person could get and where the kind of job determined the amount of income a person had, trying to disentangle the effects of education and income on political participation would be impossible. There would be no people with low education and high income to compare to people with low education and low income in order to examine the effects of income level among those with low education; nor would there be cases who had high incomes and low education to compare to those with high incomes and high education in order to see the effects of educational level among those with high incomes.

As you can see, correlated independent variables (a condition called *multicollinearity*, which you will meet again in the next chapter) are a problem for some kinds of analyses in political science. They make it hard to determine which are the most important causes of a dependent variable. They sometimes make it hard to know the exact form of the relationship between any one of the independent variables and the dependent variable in multivariate analysis.

When researchers are interested in how much variation in a dependent variable can be explained by each of two independent variables separately or what the form of the relationship is between an independent and a dependent without interference from a third variable, it is worth having the two independent variables uncorrelated. Yet, political researchers frequently find their independent variables are naturally correlated in the kinds of data they have to deal with.

And, as you will discover below, when we are assessing chains of causality from A to B to C or more complicated sets or causal relationships among several variables, it is the relationships among these variables that constitutes part of what we want to understand; that is, such correlation between our independent variables is theoretically interesting even if sometimes statistically problematic.

Many of the statistical problems of correlated independent variables can be mitigated by large samples and very good measurement, but whenever you do analysis with more than one independent variable, you will need to be alert to the possibility that correlation among your independent variables can affect your interpretations.

Assessing a Spurious Correlation in the Bivariate Relationship

Sometimes when you get a correlation between an independent and a dependent variable, there is a third variable that you haven't taken into account that is causing that correlation. (Such a third variable is called an *extraneous* variable because it is outside the relationship that is initially under consideration and is, frequently, irrelevant or not pertinent to the theory you are using.)

If there is such a third variable that is related positively to both the independent and dependent variables (or negatively to both), you may see a positive bivariate relationship between the independent and dependent variables, which would not exist without the effects of that third variable.

In either of the situations in Figure 11.6, for example, Z, the extraneous variable, is causing high values of X to occur at the same time as high values of Y. Unless these effects of Z in the two examples are removed (controlled), any bivariate correlation coefficients figured between X and Y in either situation will be positive, even though there may be no real association between them.

Z doesn't even have to be causally related to X for this to occur; it merely has to be positively correlated with X for whatever reason. When X and Z are positively correlated, and Z

Figure 11.6 Spurious Positive Correlations Caused by Extraneous Variables

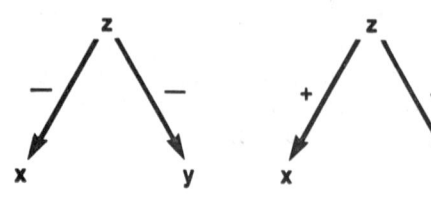

Figure 11.7 Spurious Negative Correlations Caused by Extraneous Variables

is positively correlated with Y, your examination of the XY relationship is going to look like a real positive correlation unless you remove the effects of Z.

Similarly, an extraneous variable related in opposite directions to an independent and dependent variable (as in Figure 11.7) can give evidence of a negative bivariate correlation unless the effects of the extraneous variable are controlled.

In either of the situations in Figure 11.7, a Z that is outside the basic XY relationship under consideration is operating to drive up one variable and simultaneously drive down another. Unless the effects of that Z are identified and taken into account in the analysis, the independent and dependent variables will look negatively correlated when the only reason for that correlation is the effect of Z operating on them both.

Again in this situation of a negative spurious correlation, Z does not have to be "driving up" one variable and "driving down" the other; Z may be causally related to X, but it may just be correlated with it for whatever reason. Either way, if you examine just the XY relationship, it will look correlated until you remove the effects of Z.

Imagine something like the diagram in Figure 11.8 in which X and Y are not overlapped at all, except where Z overlaps them both. Starting from the top circle, Z is shown to be causing X to vary on the left and causing Y to vary on the right, but there is no shared XY variation, except that which is caused by Z—using "cause" rather lightly. Therefore, once the effects of Z on both X and Y are removed, there is no XY connection.

Let's look at two hypothetical examples of a spurious correlation. In the first, we will exam-

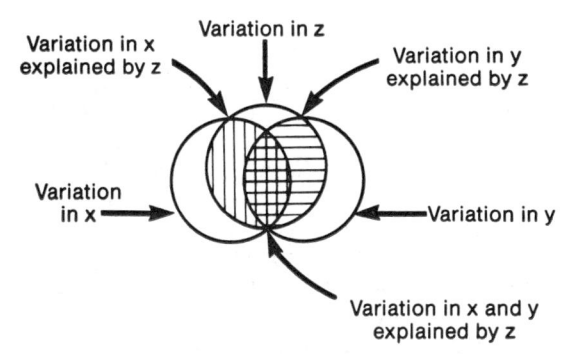

Figure 11.8 Diagram of a Spurious Relationship

ine a situation in which the extraneous variable theoretically could be causing the independent and dependent variables.

We might find, for example, a negative bivariate correlation between people's sense of identification with the Democratic Party and their participation in politics: the more they identified with the Democrats, the less they were likely to participate in politics. Yet, if we controlled the effects of the extraneous variable, income, we might find that the higher their income, the less they identified with the Democratic Party (a negative correlation); and, at the same time, the higher their income, the more they participated in politics (a positive correlation).

In such a situation, if income is explaining both the sense of identification with the Democrats and the level of participation, there might be no real relationship left between identification with the party and political participation. If that is the case, after we have controlled the effects of income, we will see no correlation between party identification and participation.

For a second example, let's look at a case of a spurious relationship in which the extraneous variable can be interpreted as merely correlated with the independent variable rather than causing it. Suppose that we find a negative relationship between age and political participation. Before we conclude that aging makes people participate less in politics, we may want to control for level of education. Our theory tells us that education is probably positively related to participation; our knowledge of history tells us that age is probably negatively associated with level of education because older people grew up in an era when higher levels of education were not so readily available.

It may be, when we control the effects of education, that we have no correlation left between age and participation. But is education "causing" age? No. Should the causal arrow point in the other direction; i.e., does theory tell us that the older you get, the less educated you get? No. That negative correlation is a product of when currently alive people were born. What we have here is probably just a correlation, not a causal link (although a definitive answer to whether the link is causal or not depends on your theory and on what concept "number of years old" is meant to measure). The extraneous variable does not have to be causing the independent variable in order to be considered to be extraneously causing a spurious correlation.

When you have a hypothesis that suggests that X leads to Y, you don't want to rest your test of that hypothesis on a correlation that was caused by another variable. Only by knowing, measuring, and controlling the effects of the extraneous variable can you get at a better description of the "real" relationship between X and Y.

As a researcher, you are obligated to rule out as many as possible of these alternate explanations for the relationships you find. While you will never be able to prove that you have isolated the "true cause" of your dependent variable, you will at least be able to rule out many of the possible alternate reasons for having found a correlation between X and Y and, as a result of such analyses, strengthen your theoretical argument that you have found a cause of the dependent variable.

Assessing a Spurious Noncorrelation or a Distorted Correlation

The extraneous variable may have the effect of counteracting, covering up, or exacerbating the real relationship between the independent and dependent variables. It may be producing enough spurious correlation between X and Y to counteract a relationship in the other direction between X and Y. In such a case, without controlling the effect of Z, you would see a zero or near zero correlation in the bivariate analysis.

Similarly, a very strong spurious correlation may cover up or distort a weaker, real relationship. Unless the effects of the extraneous variable are removed, you may be misled as to the strength and maybe even the direction of the real bivariate relationship.

When Z is suppressing or distorting the XY relationship, we will find that X is exerting some independent effect on Y even after Z is controlled, as is suggested by Figure 11.9. In the circles of Figure 11.9, you can imagine this situation as very much like that in Figure 11.8, which showed a completely spurious correlation, except that here not all the overlap between X and Y is attributable to Z. In this situation, again imagining from the top, Z can be seen to cause X on the left and to cause Y on the right. However, even after removing Z's effects, X is overlapped with ("causing") Y independently of any effects of Z. In this situation, controlling the effects of Z would leave evidence of an effect of X on Y beyond that which could be explained by the effects of Z.

Think of a more concrete example. You can probably imagine a situation in which you are trying to relate involvement in politics (independent variable) to faith in the political system (dependent variable). You may come up with a positive correlation between the two:

Figure 11.9 Independent Effect of an Independent Variable

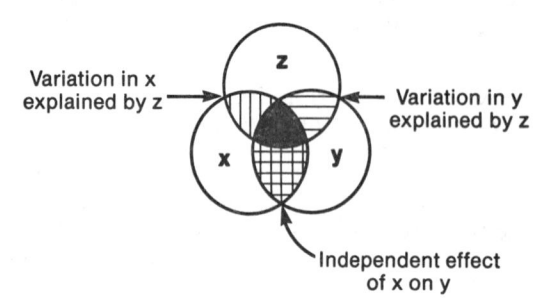

the more involved people are, the more faith they are likely to have in the system. Imagine, however, controlling for education, which is likely to be positively correlated with both the other variables. It conceivably could be so strongly positively correlated with both involvement and faith in the system that it could cover up, unless you removed its effects, a negative relationship between the two variables you were initially interested in. It is just possible that the more people get involved, the more they see whatever problems exist, and the less faith they have in the system; but you wouldn't see that until the effects of education were removed.

Assessing the Effects of Intervening Variables

Frequently in theory, we assert that X causes Z which, in turn, causes Y. We are frequently asserting that if, and only if, the *antecedent* variable (the one that comes first in the causal chain we are interested in) causes the intervening variable to, in turn, lead to the dependent variable does any correlation exist between the antecedent and the dependent variables, that the impact of X on Y is an indirect one that happens through Z. Figure 11.10 shows the arrow diagram for Z as a variable that intervenes between X and Y, a causal chain.

In such a situation, we begin with a bivariate correlation between X and Y. When the effects of Z are included in a multivariate analysis and controlled, the correlation between X and Y will be reduced to near zero. Think of it as variation in X which produces variation in Z that then produces variation in Y, as in the diagram in Figure 11.11.

You can start reading the figure on the left and can think of variation in X, the left circle, causing variation in Z, represented by the middle circle. The variation in Z then causes part

Figure 11.10 An Indirect Relationship with an Intervening Variable

$$x \longrightarrow z \longrightarrow y$$

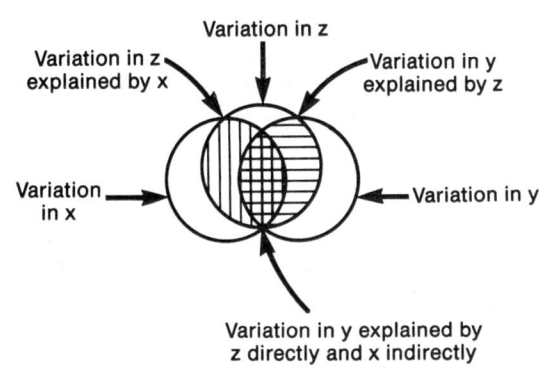

Figure 11.11 Diagram of an Indirect Relationship with Intervening Variable

of the variation in Y, represented by the right circle. The correlation between X and Y represented by the cross-hatched overlap of their two circles can be seen to be completely due to Z. There is no XY overlap otherwise. (Notice that this diagram is exactly like Figure 11.8 on extraneous variables, except for the labels. That is intentional, and we will return to it later.)

You can probably think of many situations in which we argue that X leads to Z which, in turn, leads to Y. For example, it is likely that there is a bivariate correlation between social class and political participation; as social class increases, participation in the political system increases. However, it is somewhat unlikely that social class has this effect directly; rather, it is more likely to act by creating in people certain attitudes about their responsibility to participate and beliefs about their own effectiveness at participation; it may be those attitudes and beliefs, therefore, that directly influence participation. To test that notion of how the causation works, we can develop measures of class, participation, and the attitudes and beliefs we think intervene between them. We can then correlate class and participation to see if we get the expected bivariate correlation; then we can control for the attitudes and beliefs. If they are, indeed, intervening, we will see a zero correlation between class and participation when the attitudes and beliefs are controlled.

Figure 11.12 Direct and Indirect Effects through an Intervening Variable

Frequently we may argue that the antecedent variable has its own causal effect on the dependent variable as well as causing the dependent variable indirectly through the intervening variable. The arrow diagram for this situation is shown in Figure 11.12.

In pictures, you can imagine something similar to the diagram in Figure 11.13, which looks very much like the preceding one, except that the circle representing variation in X overlaps the circle representing variation in Y *apart from* the circle representing variation in Z. In this case, X is shown to have a direct effect on Y not just an effect through the intervention of Z. (The fact that this diagram is identical, except for the labels, to that in Figure 11.9, the distorter/suppressor variable, is not an accident; we will return to this later.) In this situation, controlling Z, while relating X and Y, would yield a correlation between X and Y that is greater than zero.

We can return to the social class/political participation example above in order to examine this possibility. If the correlation between social class and political participation were greater than zero when we controlled for political attitudes and beliefs (even though class was positively correlated with the attitudes, and the measure of the attitudes was positively correlated with participation), we would prob-

Figure 11.13 Diagram of Direct and Indirect Effects

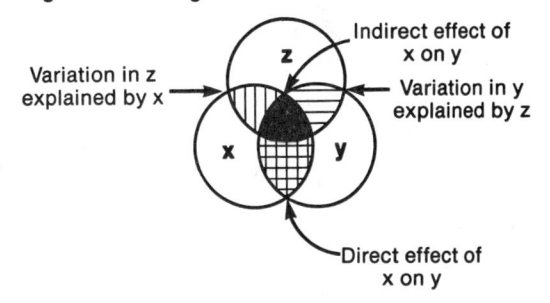

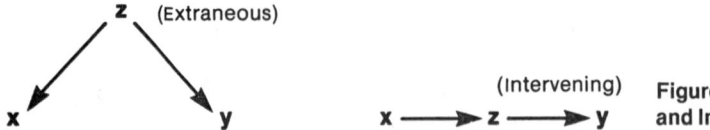

Figure 11.14 Comparing Extraneous and Intervening Variables

ably argue that class had some independent, direct effect on participation in addition to the effect it had through attitudes—perhaps because people in higher social classes have greater leisure and resources for participation.

It is very important to note that arithmetically controlling for extraneous and intervening variables can produce the same result—a near-zero correlation between X and Y—just as the two circle diagrams (11.8 and 11.11) for extraneous and intervening variables were the same. The statistical similarity between the extraneous and intervening variables in the two diagrams in Figure 11.14 means that in both cases the correlation between X and Y will, when the effects of Z are controlled, be zero.

Similarly, if there is some real relationship between X and Y that is not spurious and attributable to Z or if there is some direct effect of X on Y other than that through the intervention of Z, some effect will remain of X on Y when Z is controlled. (You can go back and compare the circle diagram in Figures 11.9 and 11.13 to see the similarities of these two situations.) Figure 11.15 below summarizes them in arrow diagrams.

The only way to tell whether you have an extraneous or an intervening variable is through theory—or at least through a conceptual understanding of what is happening. Causation is inferred—not demonstrated. If Z occurs conceptually prior to X and Y (even though you happen to be measuring them all at the same time), it cannot intervene between them, given our understanding of the theoretical nature of causation. If Z theoretically occurs between X and Y (even if all three are measured at the same time), it cannot be other than intervening.

The difference, diagrammatically and theoretically, between extraneous and intervening variables is only the direction of the arrows indicating causation. And you as researcher draw those arrows theoretically. Statistics won't usually help you; logic will.

Note, however, that your theory building is on much sounder grounds with multivariate analysis than it would be if you stopped with simple bivariate analysis. Only by examining the relationship between X and Y with Z controlled do you get at the "real" form and strength of the relationship. Without removing the effects of the control variable, you might be basing inferences on correlations that are the wrong strength or even the wrong positive or negative form. Only by examining the possibility that a variable intervenes between your independent and dependent variables can you begin to spell out just how one variable influences another and what the intervening mechanisms may be.

Specifying the Conditions under which a Relationship Holds

There are times when a bivariate relationship holds only under certain conditions. Perhaps the direction of the relationship is even reversed under other conditions. Whenever a relationship is different, depending on the level or condition of a third variable, we have *statistical interaction*: one variable interacts with the variables in the relationship and specifies the conditions under which a relationship be-

Figure 11.15 Comparing Partial Spuriousness and Partial Intervention

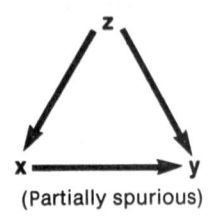

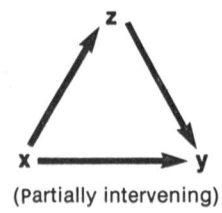

tween other variables exists or in what form it exists.

For example, increasing self-esteem may increase political participation for the educated but not for the uneducated. The variable "education" specifies the condition under which the self-esteem/participation relationship holds. Or education might be positively related to participation in one country but negatively related in another. The variable "country" specifies the condition under which the education/participation relationship is positive or negative. Another possibility is that public opinion might be strongly related to public policy among parliamentary governments and only weakly related in presidential governments. The variable "type of government" specifies the public opinion/public policy relationship.

Sorting out this specification is one of the most exciting theory-building exercises we can do. It is also among the most frustrating. Unfortunately, the specifying variable does not have to be correlated with either the independent or the dependent variable for this statistical interaction to happen. That makes discovering the specifying variable extremely tricky.

Other Reasons for Controlling Third Variables

While the four situations above cover most of the reasons for multivariate as opposed to bivariate analyses, there are others with which you will become familiar as you advance as a data analyst.

It is the purpose of the next few chapters to lead you through the process of using at least one additional independent variable and determining its effects so that you can begin the process of inferring causation with some assurance. You will begin to get the feel for such multivariate analysis *at each level of measurement*. For each of the statistics we have used in the past chapters to describe the basis bivariate relationships, you will now learn a multivariate counterpart.

How will you know which third variables may be intervening or causing spurious correlations, spurious noncorrelations, distortions, or statistical interaction? You never know for sure, and you'll never be 100 percent sure that you have examined all the possibilities. But we are now back to Chapter 1 and the discussion of where to find variables for hypotheses: the literature of your field will suggest possibilities; your own intuition will make you think of others; and, occasionally, blind luck may lead you to others. Just remember that all this needs to be thought out and anticipated, as much as possible, *before* you collect data. After all your data are collected, it may be too late to go out and gather, for the same cases, additional variables in which you may be interested.

EXERCISE 1 Trying Out Multivariate Hypotheses

Before you go on, the important thing now is to make sure you understand the concepts. Therefore, try your hand at speculating on the following questions and writing out your answers. Use your own field of political science for examples.

1. Try to imagine a situation in which a variable might be related to both an independent and a dependent variable in such a way as to make them appear correlated in the bivariate relationship. What would you imagine would be such an extraneous variable? To what independent and dependent variables? Why do you think so? (The "why" can be in the form of testable hypotheses.)

2. Speculate on what variable might intervene between an independent and a dependent variable. Indicate the independent and dependent and explain why you think the intervening variable would do so.

3. What two probably uncorrelated variables might improve explanation of what dependent variable over the explanation provided by either independent alone? Why do you think so?

4. What set of conditions might change the relationship between what independent and what dependent variable? What would you expect the differences in the relationship to be under different conditions? Why?

Although you don't need to write these out, make sure you are beginning to get a clear definition in mind of the following: spurious correlation, extraneous variable, intervening variable, antecedent variable, direct effects, indirect effects, statistical interaction or specification, and bivariate and multivariate analyses.

If you are having any trouble at all with the concept of explained variation or explanation of one variable by another, go back and review—Chapters 4 and 5, especially, although Chapters 7 through 10 also concern those same ideas.

EXPERIMENTAL VERSUS STATISTICAL CONTROL

It may be worth stopping here for a moment to consider how political scientists might be less concerned about some of the statistical problems and manipulations we have just been discussing if we had different kinds of data than we usually have to work with. Maybe going over some of those ideas again in a slightly different way will also help you get a better feel for them.

Political scientists tend not to have very much chance to gather experimental data to test their hypotheses. The essence of experimentation is that the researcher can determine which cases are subjected to what levels or conditions of the experimental variable. In the simplest form of an experiment, this means that the researcher assigns subjects, purely by chance, to an experimental or control group. The experimental group receives the "treatment," whatever it may be, while the control group does not. Any differences between the experimental and control groups are then attributed to the effects of the treatment.

Many of our hypotheses are not amenable to experimental testing. We cannot "age" people, for example, to test whether aging causes people to grow more conservative politically. Many other hypotheses probably could be tested but not without violating our ethical standards. We wouldn't deprive people of an education to see whether that affected their political participation, for example. Nor would we likely convince one group of nations to build up their stockpiles of arms in order to determine whether other nations followed suit.

Inferring Causation

Let's start with the major question we dealt with above—making inferences about causation—and see how differently we would proceed if we were able to engage in experiments rather than trying to infer causation from nonexperimental data. With nonexperimental data, we have to rule out alternative explanations of our correlations statistically before we can argue that they substantiate an inference that the independent variable caused the dependent.

If we could design experiments to test all our hypotheses, we could be somewhat surer about what causes what because we could potentially be in physical control of almost every competing explanation of apparent change. (Doing this is much more complicated than we have room for here; consult one of the sources in the suggested readings to see how complicated it can be.)

As an example, let's imagine that we believe seeing a certain film will make respondents give more conservative responses on a political questionnaire. In ordinary, nonexperimental political science research, we would do a survey, ask whether the respondent had seen the film (independent variable scored yes/no), and compare the conservative responses on a questionnaire (dependent variable) of those who had seen the film with those who had not.

Let's imagine that those who had seen the film were, indeed, more conservative. What problem do we have in asserting that the film "caused" more conservative responses and how would an experiment solve that problem?

It is possible that primarily higher income people (who tend to be more conservative) could afford to see the film. The film, then, might not be the "cause" of more conservative attitudes. Seeing the film and being more con-

Income
z
↙ ↘
x   y
Seeing   Conservatism
film

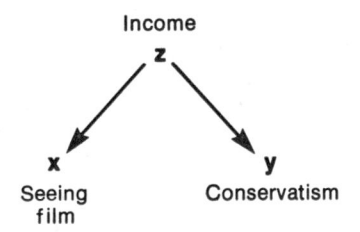

Figure 11.16 Example of a Spurious Relationship

servative could both be results of higher income, as shown in Figure 11.16 above.

In an experiment, however, the experimenter assigns subjects to one of two groups strictly by chance (randomly). The experimenter then is able to assume that the groups are equal because, if only chance were assigning the subjects, conservatives and liberals, rich and poor, or any other characteristics that might affect conservatism would be spread equally over the two groups. Random assignment should equalize the groups on *any* variables relevant to the experiment not just on income or attitudes.

One group will be shown the film; one will not (as diagramed in Figure 11.17). If the former group is more conservative on a measure taken after the film/no film condition, the researcher will assert that the film "caused" conservatism.

As the two groups are assumed to be equal on *everything* except seeing the film, *only* the film could have caused any difference on the measure of conservatism between the two groups—that is, only the film *or* something that happens or doesn't happen in conjunction with the film but about which the experimenter has neither knowledge nor any means to knowledge. As only the presence/absence of the film differentiates the groups (varies across groups), only it could cause any difference in attitudes. Remember: No variation → No relationship → No causation.

If there is any doubt that the groups are equal before the film, the experimenter can give the two groups a pretest of attitudes (as shown in Figure 11.18). The pretest should establish that the two groups are equal on whatever variables are measured.

If there is any suspicion that the pretest will somehow affect the results—perhaps by sensitizing subjects so that the effects of the film are more powerful—the researcher can add two more groups (as shown in Figure 11.19) but pretest only two of the resulting four groups.

The researcher will use groups 1 and 2 to demonstrate that the assignment process equalized the groups on measured variables by showing that groups 1 and 2 are equal on the pretest. The researcher will then assume that groups 3 and 4 are equal as well because they were assigned by the same process. Then dif-

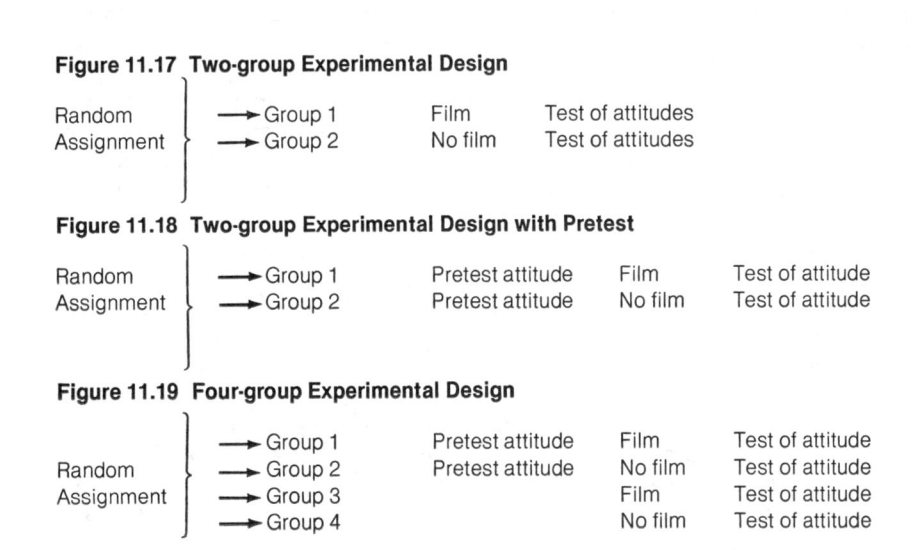

Figure 11.17 Two-group Experimental Design

Random Assignment	→ Group 1	Film	Test of attitudes
	→ Group 2	No film	Test of attitudes

Figure 11.18 Two-group Experimental Design with Pretest

Random Assignment	→ Group 1	Pretest attitude	Film	Test of attitude
	→ Group 2	Pretest attitude	No film	Test of attitude

Figure 11.19 Four-group Experimental Design

Random Assignment	→ Group 1	Pretest attitude	Film	Test of attitude
	→ Group 2	Pretest attitude	No film	Test of attitude
	→ Group 3		Film	Test of attitude
	→ Group 4		No film	Test of attitude

ferences in the post-test of attitudes between groups 3 and 4 will be attributed to the film.

Any differences between groups 1 and 3 and between groups 2 and 4 on the post-test of attitudes will be attributed to the sensitizing effects of the pretest; if no sensitizing effects can be seen, groups 1 and 3 can be combined into one group and groups 2 and 4 can be combined into another group; then differences between the two groups must be due to the film, assuming good experimental design of the procedures and conditions under which the experiment was administered.

The experimental design, therefore, fairly well eliminates the possibility that higher income (or anything else because *all* variables are assumed to be equalized by the random assignment) caused whatever results are found when the experimenter shows the film to Groups 1 and 3 and does not show it to Groups 2 and 4.

The experimenter will measure attitudes of all four groups after showing (or not showing) the film. If group 1 is more conservative than group 2, and if group 3 is more conservative than group 4, the experimenter will assert that the film "caused" a difference in attitude.

In survey analysis, in contrast to the experimental situation, the researcher must *statistically* control income (or anything else that could cause a correlation between seeing the film and conservatism) which, in the experimental design, was controlled by the experiment itself. The survey analyst would (in one form of control) break the sample into several groups, each of which contained people who were alike on income. If the relationship between having seen or not seen the film and being more conservative held *within* the income groups, the survey analyst would know that income level was not the cause of both seeing the film and being conservative. Within each income group, income would be constant enough not to be affecting the other variables. Within an income group, everyone is alike on income; if income doesn't vary, it cannot be causing anything else.

The survey researcher, however, cannot be sure that variables other than income are controlled as well. She or he would have to control other variables statistically in a fashion similar to breaking the sample into groups on the basis of income. Each income group would itself be broken into groups on the basis of another variable. The film/conservatism relationship would then be examined within each group defined by income and the other variable. The survey researcher would have to have a very large number of cases for those simultaneous controls. And she or he would still be less sure of having controlled everything than the experimenter is as a result of random assignment.

In some circumstances, survey researchers may have a better than usual handle on inferences about causation, and we shouldn't overlook those. When survey researchers can follow the same people over time and gather longitudinal data, they can sometimes get a firmer grasp on the direction of causality than can researchers working with cross-sectional data gathered on a group of people at one point in time. Let's use the film example again. In a survey taken at just one time asking whether people saw the film or not, it is possible that people in the sample "self-selected" themselves into film audiences. If a film were widely touted as one that would appeal to conservatives, it is possible that conservatives were more likely, in the first place, to see the film. With a survey and a cross-section, when we just correlate having seen the film with conservative attitudes, there is no way to determine whether, on the one hand, seeing the film made people more conservative or, on the other, conservatism led people to see the film. We couldn't decide between: Conservatism → Seeing film and Seeing film → Conservatism. The correlation would give us no hint as to the direction of causation.

If we were following the same people over time, however, we could get a little closer to the experimental situation. With longitudinal data, the analyst could measure how conservative people were *before* the film was released. The analyst could then statistically control the level of pre-film conservatism when later measuring the differences between those who saw and didn't see the film. Those differences after the film was shown might still be due to something besides the film; but there is, at least, a firmer grasp on time sequence and, as a consequence, the potential for causation. Even then, however, note that the experimenter can make cleaner inferences about causation than can the survey researcher in the field because the experimenter has more control over other possible causes.

Statistical Interaction and Specification

We discussed above that sometimes one variable seems to set the conditions in which a relationship between two other variables is positive or negative, strong or weak. Sometimes an experiment can allow us to sort out those kinds of effects better than the kinds of statistical analyses we usually use. For example, the experimenter may, on occasion, be able to turn a pretest into a condition that may affect the relationship between an independent and dependent variable and proceed to test that effect.

Going back to the film, for example, perhaps an experimenter suspected that awareness of political events might specify the relationship between seeing the film and conservatism. The hypothesis might be that the film would make for more conservative attitudes only among those aware of certain political events. The experimenter could use something like a pretest to *make* groups 1 and 2 (in Figure 11.19 above) aware of the events before showing the film. Then he or she could measure the difference the film made between the aware groups 1 and 2 as compared to the difference between the unaware groups 3 and 4. If the relationship between seeing the film and conservatism were different among those who were aware of the events (compared to the relationship between seeing the film and conservatism among those unaware of the events), the experimenter would argue that being aware of certain political events specified the effect of the film on political attitudes.

The survey analyst, in contrast, would have to measure awareness, separate the respondents into the aware and the unaware, and relate having seen the film to the conservatism of attitudes *within* groups that differ on the awareness measure. The survey analyst would, at the same time, have to control for income and whatever other variables might be influencing the relationship. The survey analyst, therefore, must deal with far more variables simultaneously and must rely on finding sufficient numbers of cases with all combinations of the characteristics in a sample. The experimenter can generally design research so as only to have to deal with one or two at a time.

The Problem of Multicollinearity

Let's turn now to the difficulties of analyzing the separate effects of correlated independent variables, one of the problems we discussed above, and see how experimental data would alleviate that concern. We mentioned above that researchers who use nonexperimental data frequently find their variables naturally correlated. Experimenters, in contrast, can simply design their experiments so that the independent variables are not correlated.

By designing the experiment so that subjects are randomly (by chance) assigned to groups that will be subjected to two sets of experimental conditions (independent variables), the researcher can assure him or herself that the two independent variables are uncorrelated. Consider the experimental situation outlined in Figure 11.20.

The researcher wants to examine the separate effects on a dependent variable of two experimental variables and plans to administer high, medium, and low levels of each experimental variable. In order to assess the effects of the two independent variables, equal num-

Figure 11.20 Two-variable Experimental Design

Experimental (Independent) Variable 2	Experimental (Independent) Variable 1		
	High	Medium	Low
High	Group 1	Group 4	Group 7
Medium	Group 2	Group 5	Group 8
Low	Group 3	Group 6	Group 9

bers of experimental subjects are randomly assigned to each of nine groups defined by combinations of the levels of the two variables *and then* subjected to one of nine sets of conditions.

There is no way a high value on one independent variable consistently goes with a high value on another independent variable or that a low value on one variable consistently goes with a low value on another because the researcher sees to it that subjects are randomly and equally distributed into the various conditions on the two variables. As a result, those who are to receive each level of one variable are distributed equally into each level of the other variable. The distributions of one variable are thus no different across the categories of the other variable; that is, the two experimental variables are uncorrelated.

The researcher doesn't have to worry, as he or she would in analyzing nonexperimental data, that so many cases high on one independent variable would show up also high on the other that it would be impossible to know which of the two independent variables was having what effect on the dependent variable. Thus, the experimenter has relatively little problem in assessing how much variation in the dependent variable is explained by each of the independent variables acting separately, and relatively little problem in assessing the forms of the relationship, although there still might be statistical interaction to worry about.

Even if one of the two independent variables is fixed and not under the control of the experimenter (like sex of subject), the experimenter can still keep it uncorrelated with another independent variable by randomly assigning the subjects with fixed characteristics to groups that are then subjected to the experimental (other independent) condition. If the distribution of males and females is the same within each of the conditions of the experimental variable, sex and the experimental variable are, by definition, uncorrelated. This is diagrammed in Figure 11.21.

Since the two independent variables are uncorrelated, it is fairly easy to say how much variation in the dependent is caused by sex and

Figure 11.21 Experimental Design with One Fixed Variable

Independent Variable 2 (Fixed)	Experimental (Independent) Variable 1		
	High	Medium	Low
Female	Group 1	Group 3	Group 5
Male	Group 2	Group 4	Group 6

how much by the experimental variable in order to talk about the strength of the two relationships. Since the cases don't cluster up due to correlation, there are enough cases in each group to give a fairly reliable assessment of effects (forms) of relationships as well.

Don't get the idea from the above discussion that we only have to worry about statistical controls with *survey* data. Using the survey example was merely a convenience. We have to worry about causal inference, multicollinearity, statistical interaction in much the same way, regardless of what kind of nonexperimental data we have to work with.

Don't get the idea from this chapter that, if we political scientists just had experimental data, all our problems would be solved, and we could pretty much rely on the simpler kinds of analyses you learned in the first nine chapters. The point is that, lacking experimental data, political scientists generally have to "tease out" statistically evidence of the relationships between independent and dependent variables, and political scientists must infer causation from less evidence of cause than an experimenter would have when she or he has more physical control of the setting and the administration of the independent variable.

Furthermore, we do have some situations in which experiments are appropriate. Don't get the idea that we *cannot* experiment. It's just that many of our questions are not amenable to such treatment. There are also *advantages* to nonexperimental data, which you can read about in the sources listed in the suggested readings. Other advantages you will pick up as you go along. (One obvious advantage is that our situations are usually far less artificial than those in real experiments.)

SUGGESTED READINGS

Beginning Multivariate Analysis

BABBIE, EARL R. *The Practice of Social Research*, 3rd ed. (Belmont, CA: Wadsworth, 1983), Ch. 16.

JOHNSON, JANET BUTTOLPH, and RICHARD A. JOSLYN. *Political Science Research Methods* (Washington, D.C.: Congressional Quarterly Press, 1986), Ch. 13.

NACHMIAS, DAVID, and CHAVA NACHMIAS. *Research Methods in the Social Sciences*, 2nd ed. (NY: St. Martin's, 1981), Ch. 14.

ROSENBERG, MORRIS. *The Logic of Survey Analysis* (NY: Basic, 1968). Much more than the logic of survey analysis, this is the logic of multivariate analysis spelled out clearly and simply. Examples are dated now, but text is excellent. The presentation in the chapter you have just finished parallels Rosenberg's work.

SHIVELY, W. PHILLIP. *The Craft of Political Research*, 2nd ed. (Englewood Cliffs, NJ: Prentice-Hall, 1980), Ch. 6.

ZISK, BETTY. *Political Research* (Lexington, MA: D.C. Heath, 1981), pp. 247–252.

Going on with Multivariate Analysis

BENSON, OLIVER. *Political Science Laboratory* (Columbus, Ohio: Merrill Publishing, 1969), Ch. 9. Benson uses crosstabulation tables to show all the arithmetic possibilities of adding control variables. Do not confuse his arithmetic approach with Rosenberg's outline of all the theoretical possibles; rather, work at integrating the two.

BLALOCK, HUBERT M., JR. *Social Statistics*, 2nd ed. (New York: McGraw-Hill, 1972), Part 19.3. You will want to read this now and return to study it later.

BOWEN, BRUCE D., and HERBERT F. WEISBERG. *An Introduction to Data Analysis* (San Francisco: Freeman, 1980), Ch. 8.

KOHOUT, FRANK. *Statistics for Social Scientists* (New York: Wiley, 1974), Section III.3.2.

SCHROEDER, LARRY D., DAVID L. SJOQUIST, and PAULA E. STEPHAN. *Understanding Regression Analysis: An Introductory Guide*, # 57 in series, *Quantitative Applications in the Social Sciences* (Beverly Hills, CA: Sage, 1986). A good review for you at basic regression and a good introduction to multivariate regression. For now, ignore F and T tests; you won't need those until Chapter 18.

Experimental Design

AGNEW, NEIL MC.K., and SANDRA W. PYKE. *The Science Game*, 4th ed. (Englewood Cliffs, NJ: Prentice-Hall, 1987), Part III and Ch. 13.

CAMPBELL, DONALD T., and JULIAN C. STANLEY. *Experimental and Quasi-experimental Designs for Research* (Chicago: Rand McNally, 1963). This is a classic on experimental design. Good on how to be as sure as possible that the experimental variable—and not something else—"causes" the dependent. Doesn't take much translation to make their work applicable to nonexperimental research as well.

JOHNSON, JANET BUTTOLPH, and RICHARD A. JOSLYN. *Political Science Research Methods* (Washington, D.C.: Congressional Quarterly Press, 1986), Ch. 5.

SPECTOR, PAUL E. *Research Designs*, # 23 in series, *Quantitative Applications in the Social Sciences* (Beverly Hills, CA: Sage, 1981).

ARTICLES

IYENGAR, SHANTO, and DONALD R. KINDER. *News That Matters* (Chicago: University of Chicago Press, 1987), Ch. 2, pp. 6–15. Provides a nice description of an experimental design in political science; concern over internal validity and generalizability discussed.

JAROS, DEAN, and GENE L. MASON. "Party Choice and Support for Demagogues: An Experimental Examination," *American Political Science Review* 63 (March 1969), 100–110. An experiment within a survey.

CHAPTER 12

MULTIPLE CORRELATION AND REGRESSION I: MULTIVARIATE ANALYSIS WITH INTERVAL INDEPENDENT AND DEPENDENT VARIABLES

CONTROLLING THE EFFECTS OF A THIRD VARIABLE: THE PARTIAL CORRELATION COEFFICIENT

As a first step in multivariate statistics, we will begin "controlling" the linear effects of a third interval variable as we examine the relationship between an interval independent and an interval dependent variable. This is just an extension of Pearson correlation and regression covered earlier, especially in Chapters 4 and 5 but also in Chapter 6. If you need a refresher on how variance in one variable is explained by another, using an interval independent variable to predict interval values on the dependent variable, you should do that review now before going on.

The Concept of Control Variables

Actually, the word "control" is a bit misleading. As you could see in the previous chapter in the discussion of the difference between experimental and other kinds of data, we do not have actual, physical control over the variable at all.

Lacking that ability to manipulate the variables, we will sometimes separate cases into groups that are alike on the control variable and examine the relationship between X and Y within each group. Such strategies are examined in Chapters 16 and 17, for example. In this chapter, where we have interval measurement on all the variables, we will examine a strategy to remove the linear effects of the control variable from the scores of both X and Y and see what's left. Let's work through the ideas behind this procedure with some pictures first.

Imagine we have variation in a dependent variable Y, and we let a control variable Z explain all it can of that dependent variable Y, as shown in Figure 12.1. We then let that same control variable Z explain all it can of the independent variable X, as shown in Figure 12.2. Then, having let Z explain all it can in both the independent and dependent variables, we let *what's left* of X explain what it can of *what's left* in Y, as in Figure 12.3.

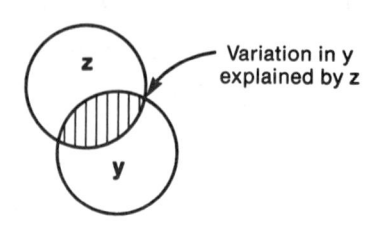

Figure 12.1 Control Variable Explaining Dependent

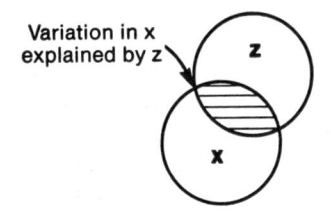

Figure 12.2 Control Variable Explaining Independent

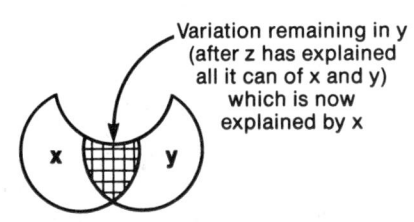

Figure 12.3 Independent Variable Explaining Dependent after the Control Has Explained All It Can of Both

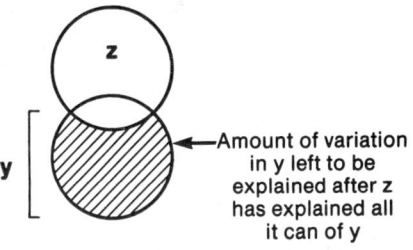

Figure 12.4 Control Only Slightly Correlated with Dependent

In Chapter 5, you learned Pearson's r^2—a measure of the proportion of variation explained in one variable by another variable. In the example here, you could calculate one r^2 for the proportion of Y explained by Z and another r^2 for the proportion of X explained by Z. Either would be a bivariate r^2—a measure of the proportion of variation in one variable explained by one other variable.

Now, you will learn how to calculate a first-order partial r^2—a measure of the proportion of one variable explained by one other variable *after* a third has explained all it can in the first two. *First-order partial* means that one variable is "controlled." A *second-order partial* would refer to two variables controlled, etc. (*Zero-order* correlation means no controls, by the way—the kind of Pearson's r you calculated in Chapter 5.)

Notice that the amount of variation in Y to be explained by the independent X is *different* in the partial correlation from that in the bivariate, zero-order correlation. In the bivariate analysis, you examine *all* of the variation in Y and see what proportion X can explain. In the partial r^2, you examine the variation in Y that is *left* after the control Z has explained all it can; then you see what proportion of the variation that is left can be explained by what is left of X after Z has explained as much of X as it can as well.

The amount of variation in Y left to be explained may be great if the control is not very correlated with the dependent, and explaining 50 percent of that remainder would mean explaining a lot of variation, as in Figure 12.4.

Or the amount of variation in Y left to be explained can be very little if the control is more highly correlated with the dependent; in which case, explaining 50 percent of the remainder would mean that not much more has been explained than that already explained by Z, as in Figure 12.5. Thus, our interpretations of the partial r^2 must be very cautious ones—always keeping in mind how much variation was left by the control to explain. (Such caution is always necessary with all correlations.)

Just as we used both r and r^2 in earlier chapters, we will be using both the partial r ($r_{xy \cdot z}$) and partial r squared ($r^2_{xy \cdot z}$) here. The squared version is the measure of proportion

Figure 12.5 Control Very Correlated with Dependent

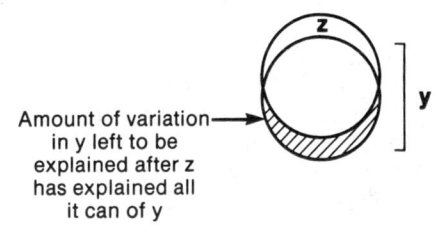

of explained variation. We will use it when we need a measure of "what proportion of the variation in Y can be explained by X after Z has explained all it can of both of them, assuming linear relationships between each pair of variables."

The unsquared version is also a measure of the strength of association between X and Y once the effects of Z are removed, but it doesn't have as clear an interpretation as the proportionate one of the partial r^2. The partial r, however, has the advantage of being able to indicate either positive or negative directions of the relationship between X and Y, once the effects of Z are removed.

Note: Read $r_{xy \cdot z}$ as "the correlation between X and Y controlling for Z." The letter after the dot represents the control variable. On the partial r statistic, the order of the X and Y subscripts, before the dot, is irrelevant, since the correlation is a symmetric measure for which it doesn't matter whether X or Y is considered dependent.

We will examine the partial r when we are trying to determine whether the XY relationship is a spurious one that occurs because the extraneous variable Z causes variation in both X and Y. If the XY correlation is completely spurious, the partial $r_{xy \cdot z}$ will be zero; that is, the partial $r_{xy \cdot z}$ will be zero if Z is the cause of all the relationship between X and Y. The partial will be greater than zero if there is some real XY relationship in addition to that caused by Z.

Similarly, the partial r will help assess whether a variable intervenes between X and Y. If Z intervenes between X and Y, such that the XY correlation is completely due to the fact that X leads to Z, which in turn leads to Y, the partial $r_{xy \cdot z}$ will be zero. If X has some direct effect on Y and some indirect effect through Z, the partial will be greater than zero; that is, if X leads to Y both directly and indirectly because X leads to Z, which in turn leads to Y, the partial will be greater than zero. Remember: whether a variable intervenes between or is an extraneous cause of both X and Y can only be determined by theory; the statistical results of the control are the same.

Controlling Z may also allow us to examine a partial relationship in the $r_{xy \cdot z}$ that was masked before the effects of Z were removed. The partial may show either a positive or a negative relationship between X and Y and either a weak or a strong relationship between X and Y—once the effects of Z are removed. Uncontrolled, Z could have suppressed the XY relationship or distorted it.

If it is not already clear, we should note that we are typically dealing with variables that have multiple causes. (Review Chapter 1 and the pictorial representations in Chapter 11.) Thus, variables will typically not explain all of the variation in other variables. In the case of an extraneous or intervening variable, removing its effects will still leave some variation in both the independent and dependent variables to be examined in the partial. In the rare case when an independent is perfectly correlated with the control, there is no way to sort out which of the two is causing the dependent because there will be no variation left in X to examine after the effects of Z are removed.

The Arithmetic Logic of the Partial $r_{xy \cdot z}$

It is important to work through the operations of the control conceptually before proceeding to the formulas. First, we would take the distribution of dependent variable scores, shown at the left in Figure 12.6, and regress the dependent variable on the control variable (using the control as an independent variable in the regression), as shown on the right of Figure 12.6, in order to let the control variable explain all it can in the dependent variable.

Figure 12.6 Regressing the Dependent Variable on the Control Variable

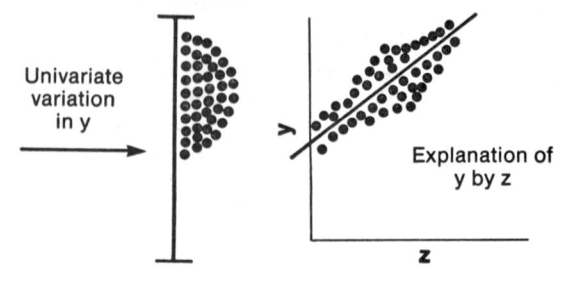

In this example, you can see that the control variable is linearly related to the dependent variable; it explains some of the variation in the dependent variable Y but not all of it. The scatter of cases around the regression line indicates variation in Y that is still unexplained by Z. The *distance* between the actual value (score) on Y and the value predicted for that case by Z (the point on the regression line at a particular value of Z) is *unexplained* by Z. Remember that this distance from the predicted value to the actual value is called the *residual*. It represents that part of a case's score on the dependent variable that is not explained by the independent variable. Later we will want to see whether any of the unexplained variation, the residuals, can be explained by X.

As a second step, we must first let the control variable Z explain all it can of the independent variable X, as shown in Figure 12.7. We will regress X on the control variable, just as we previously regressed Y on the control variable, here treating the control as if it were the sole independent variable, just as if we were doing bivariate regression.

Figure 12.7 Regressing the Independent Variable on the Control Variable

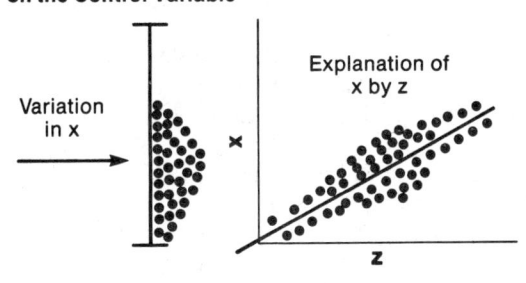

Now you can see that the control (Z) is also linearly related to X; it explains some, but not all, of the variation in X. That leftover variation is not explained by Z. The scatter around the line—the distance between the actual value of the independent variable for each case and that predicted for it by the control variable—is variation in X that Z won't explain. The distance between the X score predicted for each case by Z, the point on the line above a case's value on Z, and the actual X score of that case is the residual—that part of the X score on each case that Z cannot explain. It is that remaining variation in X, the residuals, that we will use to determine whether X (after Z has explained all it can of X) can predict/explain Y (after Z has explained all it can of Y).

In effect, we will create new scores on X and Y that represent that part of each that Z cannot explain. We will let Z explain all it can of each and remove the linear effects of Z from each. For each case, the new score on X is the *difference* between the actual X score and that predicted by Z (i.e., it is the distance off the line when X is regressed on Z). For each case, the new score on Y is the difference between the actual Y score and that predicted by Z (i.e., it is the distance off the line when Y is regressed on Z).

These *new* scores on both X and Y are what's left of the original X and Y scores that have not been explained by Z—the residuals. We will then correlate the *new* scores, the residuals of X and Y, to get the partial r, controlling Z. The partial r will give us a measure of how correlated X and Y are after Z has linearly explained all it can of both.

It is important to note that the procedures we have to work with take out the *linear* effects of Z on the other two variables. We are adjusting the scores on X and Y to delete the linear effect of Z from them. However, if Z is related to X and Y in some other fashion, this procedure won't get rid of its effects. You have to argue that Z is linearly related to *both* X and Y in order to use this procedure; if it is not, you will get misleading results.

Note: if Z is *not* correlated with X, the "new score" on X will simply be the distance of that case above or below the mean of X, because, in this case of no correlation, $X_p = \overline{X}$. Similarly, if Z is not correlated with Y, the "new score" on Y will simply be the distance of that case above or below the mean of Y because, when $r_{zy} = 0$, $Y_p = \overline{Y}$. If we then correlated the *new* X scores ($X_i - \overline{X}$) with the new Y scores ($Y_i - \overline{Y}$) when Z is correlated with neither X nor Y, we would have the exact equivalent of the zero-order r. In calculating r (remember or review the formula), deviations from the mean of X are multiplied by deviations from the mean of Y. Therefore, if Z is correlated with neither X nor Y, calculating a partial will yield a measure exactly the same as the zero-order r.

EXERCISE 1   Calculating the Partial Correlation Using the Residuals and the Formula for Pearson's r (bivariate)

In the exercise section of this chapter, you will find three examples for relating an independent to a dependent variable controlling for a third variable. Unless your instructor tells you to do all three examples (or unless you feel you need the practice), do only one example for this exercise. If you work in teams with two of your colleagues, each of the three of you can do a different example. Then you can compare results on all three examples. (All members of a team should turn in their work together.)

Now, just follow each of the steps, 1 through 4, below. They will lead you through the process of constructing a partial correlation coefficient by the method I have just described.

1. Let the control variable (Z) explain all it can of the independent (X), and create a new set of scores for the adjusted X variable by following (and thinking about) steps a through c below.
   a. Make your best guess about (predict) a value for each case on X using the equation gained from regressing X on Z, $X = a + bZ$. That regression has already been done for you using exactly the same method you learned in Chapter 5. The equation with the proper values for a and b appears after the data in the exercises. On each case, examine the score on the Z variable. Multiply the value on the Z variable by the value of b and add the value of a to the product. This gives you the X score predicted from that case's Z value.

      Note that you need the intercept (a) from the equation in which X is dependent on Z and the slope that represents the X variable being treated as dependent on Z (b_{xz}). The order of the subscripts on b is important. Whichever variable is being treated as dependent is listed first, X given Z, because the slope is asymmetric. It matters which variable is considered independent and which dependent.
   b. For each case, subtract the value you have predicted for X (X_p) from the actual value of X (X_i).
   c. Write the results clearly. These are your new X scores, the residuals from regressing X on Z.
2. Let the control variable (Z) explain all it can of the dependent variable (Y), and create a new set of scores for the adjusted Y variable by following steps a through c below.
   a. Predict (make your best guess about) a value for each case on Y using the prediction equation gained from regressing Y on Z: $Y = a + bZ$. Just as you did above, examine a case's score on Z. Multiply that score by b and add a to the product. This gives you the Y score predicted from that case's value on the Z variable. The a and b values are calculated for you (and listed in the exercise section) using exactly the same formulas you used in Chapter 5 for the intercept and the slope.

      Note that you need the slope that represents Y being treated as dependent on Z (b_{yz}) and the intercept (a) from that same equation.
   b. For each case, subtract the predicted Y value (Y_p) from the actual Y value (Y_i).
   c. Write these results—the residuals of Y being regressed on Z, your new Y scores—next to the new X scores for each case.
3. You now have two new sets of scores. You have taken the linear effects of Z out of the X scores; you have also taken the linear effects of Z out of the Y scores. What you are left with are the residuals in X and Y, two sets of scores with the linear effects of Z "adjusted out."

   In order to *see* what's happening, *plot* these *new* scores. Draw an X axis and a Y axis, putting numbers on them in appropriate locations. (Since you will have a mixture of positive and negative numbers, you will have to start working with axes that cross at zero so that you can accommodate both the positives and negatives.) For each case, plot the Y residual and the X residual so that you can see the correlation between X and Y with the linear effects of Z removed.

4. You are now ready to calculate the correlation between the residuals in order to have a measure of what the partial correlation is (having adjusted/removed/controlled the effects of Z). To do this, use the formula for Pearson's r (not r^2) that is given in Formula 12.1 below, just as you learned to do in Chapter 5 for the bivariate correlation, but correlate the *residual scores* now rather than the scores before the effect of Z was removed. (Since the mean of residuals is zero, except for rounding error, you don't have to subtract it from each score.)

FORMULA 12.1   Pearson's Correlation (r)

$$r = \frac{\Sigma (X_i - \bar{X})(Y_i - \bar{Y})}{[\Sigma X_i - \bar{X})^2][\Sigma Y_i - \bar{Y})^2]}$$

While you are calculating, remember to notice how much more the extreme scores are contributing to the measure of association than would seem to be "their fair share." As we discussed in Chapter 5, this is the case with all forms of Pearson correlation and the statistics in regression (a and b). Extreme cases can make slopes seem higher and correlation seem stronger than your eyeballing of the scatterplot would suggest. That's one more reason for always checking the scatterplots—to see if there are *really* extreme cases (oddball cases that don't seem to fit with the rest). They can give very misleading results.

What partial correlation did you get? Remember this is the *correlation* between X and Y adjusting out the effects of Z. To get the *proportion* of the variance in Y explained by X, controlling the effect of Z, square the number you got for the correlation. What percent of the variance is explained? Record your answers and label them clearly.

EXERCISE 2   Computing Formula for the Partial

It is easier, now that you see what's going on, to use the computing formula (Formula 12.2) for the partial correlation ($r_{xy \cdot z}$—the relation between X and Y controlling for Z). And here, examining the computing formula may help to show what's going on; it isn't just a simplified calculation.

FORMULA 12.2   Computing Formula for First-order Partial Correlation Coefficient

$$r_{xy \cdot z} = \frac{r_{xy} - (r_{xz})(r_{yz})}{\sqrt{1 - r_{xz}^2} \sqrt{1 - r_{yz}^2}}$$

Before going on, examine the formula intuitively. The denominator is a measure of how much variation in X and Y is not explained by Z. There is $1 - r_{xz}^2$ the proportion of variation in X not explained by Z. There is $1 - r_{yz}^2$, the proportion of variation in Y not explained by Z.

The numerator has a measure of how correlated X and Y are in the bivariate case (r_{xy}) *minus* the variation Z can explain in X (r_{xz}) and in Y (r_{yz}). Therefore, the whole numerator is the XY correlation after Z has explained all it can in both X and Y. That then is divided by the variation in X and Y that is left after Z has done all the explaining it can.

The overall partial $r_{xy \cdot z}$ is—when squared—the proportion of variation in Y explained by X when the effects of Z are adjusted out.

In the exercise section, you will find, already calculated for you, all the zero-order correlations necessary to figure the first-order partial you just computed in Exercise 1 by correlating the adjusted scores (residuals). Do the proper substitutions into the computing formula for the partial, continuing with the same example you have been working on, just to make sure you can follow the process.

After you have learned to get these statistics from the computer, we will turn to interpreting what you have calculated.

EXERCISE 3 Using the Computer for Partial Correlations

The computer setup for getting the computer to do partial correlations is fairly simple. First, you will need to set up a file (data and information regarding their locations) using the ten cases' scores on all nine variables in the exercise section of this chapter. Remember that, for data coming into the computer with the job, you will need:

> A DATA LIST—naming (uniquely) and indicating the locations of your variables. (To help you and the instructor interpret your output, please call your variables VARX1, VARY1, VARZ1, VARX2, VARY2, VARZ2, VARX3, VARY3, VARZ3, or just X1, Y1, Z1, X2, Y2, Z2, X3, Y3, Z3.)
> The BEGIN DATA command.
> All the data on the nine variables on each of the ten cases.
> The END DATA command.
> A procedure (see below).
> The FINISH command, if necessary.

Also, review Chapter 3 (or, better, the SPSS manuals) for details of this setup, if necessary.

The PARTIAL CORR Procedure. If all you need is a quick look at the partial correlations, the easiest *procedure* to use is PARTIAL CORR if you are using SPSS-X. If you are using SPSS/PC+, you will need to use REGRESSION. Although REGRESSION is somewhat more complicated, it is well worth learning, as you will begin to see in subsequent chapters. Let me alert you that you will be using the same data in the next chapter. After you have set up the computer job for this exercise, you will want to save it so that you won't have to set up the file again.

The PARTIAL CORR command is followed by the names of the independent and dependent variables separated by the word WITH. Then comes the word BY, followed by the name of the control variable. To indicate that you want first-order partials, put a (1) after the name of the control variable. Requests for additional partials can follow after a slash, as shown below:

```
PARTIAL CORR name WITH name BY
  name(1)/name WITH name BY
  name(1)/
STATISTICS = CORR
DESCRIPTIVES.
```

By adding a STATISTICS subcommand, you can get the zero-order correlations, and the mean, standard deviation, and number of nonmissing cases for each variable. The zero-order correlations (which will be called zero-order partials on the printout) will help you interpret the causal processes—to see, for example, whether a bivariate correlation goes to near zero in the partial, or whether a near-zero bivariate is greater than zero in the partial, or whether the direction of the bivariate correlation changes, etc. The remaining statistics are useful in describing the distribution of each variable—to see, for example, whether a low correlation might be due to low variance rather than the absence of a relationship and for checking to make sure there are as many cases as you think there should be.

Don't forget to complete your job with a FINISH. command, if you need it. When you see your output, the partial *r* between two variables will be the first number in a set of three. The second number is degrees of freedom, and the third is the significance. You don't have to worry about the latter two until Chapter 18.

The REGRESSION Procedure. If you are using SPSS/PC+, you will need to go ahead and use REGRESSION to get your partials. This will also work for SPSS-X.

In its simplest form, you'll need the REGRESSION command followed by subcommand VARIABLES = with a list of variables. Then you will ask for the bivariate (zero-order) correlation and the mean and standard deviation for each variable with a DESCRIPTIVES subcommand. You then have a STATISTICS subcommand in order to get the partial r. Finally, for every partial you want, you'll issue a DEPENDENT = subcommand and use the ENTER subcommand to indicate the independent and control variables. Here's an example:

```
REGRESSION VARIABLES = X1 Y1
  Z1 X2 Y2 Z2 X3 Y3 Z3/
  DESCRIPTIVES/
  STATISTICS = ZPP/
  DEPENDENT = Y1/ENTER X1 Z1/
  DEPENDENT = Y2/ENTER X2 Z2/
  DEPENDENT = Y3/ENTER X3 Z3.
```

Of course, you will be using the variable names from your DATA LIST.

When you get your output, you'll first see the result of the DESCRIPTIVES subcommand—the means and standard deviations of the variables and the zero-order, bivariate correlations. Some of the correlations will be irrelevant because you will get bivariate r between *each* pair of variables on the VARIABLES = list, whether they are involved in a partial correlation in which you're interested or not.

After the descriptives, you will see the output for each of your three sets of variables. For the moment, skip everything until you see the heading, "Variables in the Equation." Under it, you will see the names of your two independent variables. By the name of each, in a column marked "Partial," you will find the partial r between that variable and the dependent variable *controlling* for the other independent variable.

You are interested in the partial in the same lines as X1, X2, and X3 (or whatever you named your three independent variables). Those will be the partials between X1 and Y1 controlling Z1, between X2 and Y2 controlling Z2, etc.

Under the column labeled "Correl," you will find the bivariate, zero-order correlation between the variable named to the left and the dependent variable. This information is redundant to that you received from the DESCRIPTIVES subcommand.

Don't be sidetracked by the column labeled "Part Cor," for it is a part correlation—not the partial correlation we are studying here.

Now, set up and run your partial correlation job for the data in the exercise section so that you can get r_{xy}, r_{xz}, r_{yz}, $r_{xy \cdot z}$, and N for each example. Write out each of those statistics for each of the three exercises, thinking about the operationalizations of the variables and what the correlations are telling you about their relationships, as you do so. Compare the results on the output to the results in the example you have been working on in order to make sure they are the same. If they aren't, correct whatever is wrong. (See the instructor if you can't figure it out.)

Interpreting the Partial Correlation Coefficient

It's worth recalling Formula 12.2 for the partial correlation coefficient at this point.

FORMULA 12.2 The Partial Correlation Coefficient

$$r_{xy \cdot z} = \frac{r_{xy} - (r_{xz})(r_{yz})}{\sqrt{1 - r_{xz}^2} \sqrt{1 - r_{yz}^2}}$$

If Z explains all or almost all the XY correlation, the numerator and fraction will be close to or at zero. This will indicate either that Z was extraneously causing the spurious XY zero-order correlation or that Z is an intervening variable between X and Y. If Z was completely suppressing the XY correlation so that, before the control, the bivariate XY relation was close to zero, the partial r between X and Y will be larger than zero.

If Z is merely adding additional explanation to Y, and is uncorrelated with the independent variable, the partial r between X and Y controlling Z will be at least a bit higher than the zero-order XY correlation. That's because some of the variation in Y is removed by adjusting for the explanatory power of Z; i.e., after Z has explained all it can, X has a smaller amount of variation in Y to explain, so the proportion it explains is higher.

Sometimes you can have a "some of one, some of another" situation. As was indicated in Chapter 11, an XY bivariate, zero-order correlation can be partly spurious. If the partial r is not close to zero, some of the relationship between X and Y, but not all, may be explained by the extraneous variable Z. Or if the partial is not close to zero, Z may well partially intervene between X and Y but leave X to have some direct effect on Y.

The situations are not necessarily clear-cut. In the non-clear-cut situations, much of your interpretation of the partials will depend on your understanding of what's happening both in the theory and in the statistics. For now, just keep in mind that (unless the partial goes to near zero where there has been a bivariate correlation or appears as greater than zero where there has been a zero bivariate correlation) you cannot really talk about the relationship between X and Y increasing or decreasing when the effects of Z are removed. The partial is not directly comparable to the zero-order correlation because the amount of variance in the dependent variable is not the same when the independent explains it in the bivariate and when the control has explained part before the independent goes to work in the partial.

Later on, you'll learn how to rely on the slopes of the equation in these non-clear-cut situations. For now, just try to puzzle them through by examining the operationalizations and trying to figure out what is likely (theoretically) to be happening.

EXERCISE 4 Interpreting the Partial r

Start drawing diagrams as aids in thinking about the causal processes involved. Remember that only you, on the basis of theory and

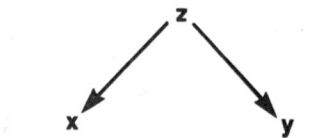

Figure 12.8 Extraneous Control Variable

literature and common sense, can decide to which direction causal arrows point. Statistics can reveal correlation for you—one necessary ingredient in trying to demonstrate causation—but only you can assert (not prove) what is probably causing what.

After you study the operationalizations, draw arrow diagrams for each of the three examples to indicate your hypotheses of what will happen in the test. Draw both the bivariate and the control situation. With arrows, indicate the direction you suspect causation is operating. For example, each example begins with a test of $X \rightarrow Y$; then each adds a control variable.

If you suspect the control variable is extraneous and causing a spurious correlation (positive or negative) between X and Y, the diagram would be as in Figure 12.8. The absence of an X to Y arrow would diagram the expectation that, when Z is controlled, the XY correlation will be near zero.

Similarly, if Z is suspected of intervening, the diagram would be as in Figure 12.9, and the absence of an X to Y arrow would indicate the expectation that the partial r controlling Z would be near zero. In either of the above two cases, for there to be a substantial positive bivariate r between X and Y reduced to near zero in the partial, the bivariate r_{xz} and r_{yz} correlations would both have to have the same sign (either both positive or both negative). For

Figure 12.9 Intervening Control Variable

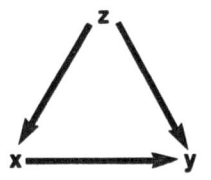

Figure 12.10 Spurious Noncorrelation

there to be a substantial negative bivariate r_{xy} reduced to near zero in the partial, the bivariate r_{xz} and r_{yz} would have to have opposite signs.

If there is a near-zero bivariate r between X and Y (i.e., $X \to Y = 0$) and the control for Z indicates a substantial correlation in the partial, several things could be going on in the bivariate relations, as long as they are strong enough to cover up any XY relationship: that is, X and Y could be positively related but have that counteracted by Z acting positively on one of them and negatively on the other; X and Y could be weakly negatively related but have that covered up by Z acting strongly positively on both of them; etc. The bivariate near-zero relationship between X and Y would be a case of spurious noncorrelation, and you could diagram the finding, as in Figure 12.10.

If you hypothesize a "some of one, some of the other situation," in which Z operates to suppress or distort the XY correlation before it is controlled, there will be an arrow between X and Y, even in the multivariate situation. If you hypothesize that the XY correlation is partly spurious due to the effects of Z, the diagram would look like that in Figure 12.8 but with an arrow between X and Y. Similarly, if you hypothesize that Z partially intervenes in the XY relationship, the diagram would look like that in Figure 12.9 but with an arrow between X and Y.

Now check the relevant correlations from the output to make sure that the model you hypothesize corresponds to the data. Then, having drawn the two diagrams for each example, put on the *bivariate* diagrams the bivariate r with its sign to indicate the uncontrolled r_{xy}. Put the partial $r_{xy \cdot z}$ on the *multivariate* diagrams between X and Y to indicate the relationship between X and Y with Z controlled.

Write below each diagram a description of the processes you infer from the data and operationalizations (i.e., name the control variable and suggest whether it is extraneously causing the other variables you name or whether it intervenes between the others, etc.). Briefly indicate what you saw in the data to make you come to that conclusion.

Cautions about Using the Partial Correlation Coefficient

It is important to understand that a partial correlation coefficient is inappropriate if the control variable *specifies* the relationship between X and Y; that is, if the relationship between X and Y is different for different levels of the control, a single number *cannot* summarize the XY relationship with the effects of Z removed.

Imagine, for example, that X and Y are positively related when Z is low and negatively related when Z is high. A single measure of partial correlation cannot reveal this. You'd have to report one correlation coefficient between X and Y for each level of Z.

Before calculating and reporting a partial r, therefore, one really should separate the cases into several categories on the basis of their scores on Z and calculate r_{xy} for each category of Z, just to make sure they are the same.

It's also very important to remember that Pearson's r is a measure of *linear* association. And so is the partial. That means that *all* the relationships must be linear: r_{xy}, r_{xz}, r_{yz}. One really should check the bivariate scattergrams before calculating and reporting a partial.

You aren't through with multiple independent variables in correlation and regression yet. Now you will need to learn a measure of the total explained variance and how to interpret the whole regression equation when there are multiple independent variables.

EXERCISES

Data for Calculating Partials

Let me give you some situations which will make the hypothetical data below a bit more realistic.

EXAMPLE 1

The bivariate r_{xy} (.08) makes it appear that there is virtually no relationship between the independent and dependent variable. Just for the sake of an example, imagine our ten cases are from a country where the government decides who gets to pursue education and where the government is rather corrupt to boot.

Now imagine our independent variable (X) is a measure of knowledge about politics. We've given our people ten questions, decided whether the answers were correct or incorrect, and scored the variable with the "number of correct responses out of ten."

Further imagine that the dependent variable (Y) is a measure of "support for the political system." We gave our people 12 statements and asked them to agree or disagree with each. On each statement, an "agree" indicated support for the system. The dependent variable, then, is a count of the number of "agree" responses.

When we correlate knowledge and support for the system, we find that knowing about politics is not at all ($r = .08$) related to support for the system. We suspect something is fishy here. Therefore, we control for education (here measured as number of years completed past elementary school). It is clear that education and knowledge are correlated (+.60). As might be expected when the government is deciding who gets to go to school, education and support for the system are correlated (+.84).

But what happens to the relationship between knowledge and support when the effects of education are removed? That's your task to figure out with a partial r.

EXAMPLE 2

This looks like a pretty clear-cut U.S. election example. We have a measure of income for the independent variable X, but here we have measured income as the percent gained or lost in real dollars over the past four years. Someone who stayed even in real dollars is scored zero; someone who gained 5 percent in real dollars is scored +5; someone who lost 3 percent in real dollars is scored -3, etc.

Our dependent variable, Y, is a measure of support for a Republican candidate. We handed respondents a card with a picture of a ladder. The rungs of the ladder were numbered from 1 to 25. We asked the respondents how far up the ladder they would place the Republican candidate relative to other candidates for president in the past few elections.

Not surprisingly, the better the economic gains, the more support for the Republican candidate ($r_{xy} = .58$), but we want to know whether the link between economic well-being and support for a Republican candidate can be explained by the intervention of beliefs that result from increased economic well-being or whether the effect is a direct one from well-being to Republican support.

One such belief might be "support for poor people trying to get retraining money from the national government." Here we asked our survey respondents a series of 12 questions designed to elicit whether they supported such a policy. We gave them one point each time they did support it, ending up with a potential 0- to 12-point scale.

It is clear that economic well-being makes respondents less supportive of that policy ($r_{xz} = -.67$). It is also clear that the more one supports that policy, the less one supports the Republican candidate ($r_{zy} = -.70$). Is the effect of economic well-being on this belief about policy the only way economic well-being influences support for the Republicans? That's your problem with the partial.

EXAMPLE 3

For the independent variable here, we presented a large number of statements to our respondents. Each statement was designed to indicate some element of conservatism. We asked respondents whether they strongly agreed, agreed, were neutral, disagreed, or strongly disagreed with each statement. For each statement, then, we could score a respondent from 5 down to 1, according to how strongly they agreed. We then summed the responses to the large number of statements, giving us a conservatism scale that, for these respondents, ranged from a low of 50 to a high of 325.

This we correlated with how many hours they spent campaigning for their party. (This is a *very* active group to have spent a low of 44 hours and a high of 267 hours.) We found a very strong correlation ($r_{xy} = .86$) between conservatism and amount of time spent campaigning.

Are we to conclude that conservatives, as a result of their ideology, spend more time campaigning than liberals and that conservatism somehow "causes" one to spend more time campaigning? Maybe.

But what if we control for socioeconomic status? Here, imagine it to be measured on ten indicators. A respondent could get from 0 to 10 points on each indicator, which were then summed across all indicators, yielding an SES measure from 0 to 100. In our sample, the lowest SES is 1, and the highest is 83. Is it possible that the higher the SES, the more time one has to campaign? And the higher the SES, the more conservative? The bivariate correlations suggest this is worth looking into. Conservatism and SES are correlated at .94. SES and time spent campaigning are correlated at .92.

When SES is controlled, is there any real link between conservatism and time spent campaigning? That is the question for you to answer with a partial.

Example 1			Example 2			Example 3		
X	Y	Z	X	Y	Z	X	Y	Z
9	11	10	0	12	8	50	44	07
5	2	3	−4	13	10	110	114	32
4	10	7	1	14	5	325	267	83
3	1	2	−3	15	11	112	67	01
3	9	6	2	16	7	296	156	69
8	6	7	−2	17	9	247	117	50
9	3	6	5	18	6	96	55	15
8	2	5	−1	19	3	101	90	14
6	10	8	3	20	2	165	155	48
2	4	3	4	21	4	98	72	14

Example 1:
$Y_p = a + b_{yz}Z$
$Y_p = -1.66 + 1.31Z$
$X_p = a + b_{xz}Z$
$X_p = 2.03 + .64Z$
$r_{xy} = .08$
$r_{xz} = .60$
$r_{yz} = .84$

Example 2:
$Y_p = a - b_{yz}Z$
$Y_p = 21.03 - .7Z$
$X_p = a - b_{xz}Z$
$X_p = 4.9 - .67Z$
$r_{xy} = .58$
$r_{xz} = -.67$
$r_{yz} = -.70$

Example 3:
$Y_p = a + b_{yz}Z$
$Y_p = 40.7 + 2.19Z$
$X_p = a + b_{xz}Z$
$X_p = 53.36 + 3.2Z$
$r_{xy} = .86$
$r_{xz} = .94$
$r_{yz} = .92$

SUGGESTED READINGS

Partial Correlation

SPSS-X User's Guide, 3rd ed. (Chicago: SPSS, Inc., 1988), Ch. 40, pp. 774–787.

Regression

NORUSIS, MARIJA J. *SPSS/PC+* (Chicago: SPSS, Inc., 1988). Chapter 17, pp. B197–B243, discusses the statistics available in the procedure; pp. C125–C136 contains the commands.

SPSS-X User's Guide, 3rd ed. (Chicago: SPSS, Inc., 1988), Ch. 45, pp. 848–870.

Partial Correlation Coefficient

BLALOCK, HUBERT M., JR. *Social Statistics*, 2nd ed. (New York: McGraw-Hill, 1972), Ch. 19.

BLALOCK, HUBERT M., JR. *Causal Inferences in Nonexperimental Research* (Chapel Hill: Univ. of North Carolina Press, 1964). Although Blalock, in this work, examines situations with more than one control variable, and although the work may be just a little complicated for you at this point, within the next few chapters, this book ought to be accessible to you.

BOWEN, BRUCE D., and HERBERT F. WEISBERG. *An Introduction to Data Analysis* (San Francisco: Freeman, 1980), pp. 154–162.

KERLINGER, FRED N., and ELAZAR J. PEDHAZUR. *Multiple Regression in Behavioral Research* (N.Y.: Holt, Rinehart, and Winston, 1973), pp. 81–93, pp. 97–99. This text is reasonably easy to use and understand at the level at which you are currently working. It does not, however, go into elaborate detail. You may have to labor over each paragraph.

KLEINBAUM, DAVID G., and LAWRENCE L. KUPPER. *Applied Regression Analysis and Other Multivariate Methods* (North Scituate, MA: Duxbury, 1978), pp. 163–168. Includes "significance," which has not yet been covered in your chapters. This reference is especially sparse; nevertheless, you may find insights here.

KOHOUT, FRANK J. *Statistics for Social Scientists* (N.Y.: Wiley, 1974), Unit V. (On page 187, there is a typo in example 1; the denominator ought to read r_{xz}^2 where it says r_{xy}^2.)

WONNACOTT, RONALD J., and THOMAS H. WONNACOTT. *Regression: A Second Course in Statistics* (N.Y.: Wiley, 1981), pp. 179–180. This is a more advanced text. A pretty good reference to have around for all kinds of problems.

ARTICLES

CAMPBELL, BRUCE A. "A Theoretical Approach to Peer Influence in Adolescent Socialization," *American Journal of Political Science*, 24 (May 1980), 324–344. Using survey data from high school seniors in Atlanta, their parents, and their peers, tests hypothesis derived from theory on influence of peers. Tests for spuriousness of the relationships using partial *r* and standardized regression coefficients (Chapter 14). Attention given to differential effects across subgroups and reliability of measurement.

MULLER, EDWARD N., THOMAS O. JUKAM, and MITCHELL A. SELIGSON. "Diffuse Political Support and Antisystem Political Behavior: A Comparative Analysis," *American Journal of Political Science*, 26 (May 1982), 240–264. A somewhat difficult article that deals with very important questions of the reliability and validity of measurement of political support-alienation. Uses partial correlation coefficients to show that correlation between a poor measure of negative evaluation of government and antisystem behavior is completely explained by a better measure of alienation. Uses the means of a measure of aggressive political participation across categories of the trust and alienation measures to demonstrate that the alienation measure can tap the extremes of that concept sufficiently to predict aggressive behavior. Assesses cross-cultural applicability of the measurement of alienation.

ROTHGEB, JOHN M., JR. "Contagion at the Sub-War Stage: Siding in the Cold War, 1959–63," *Conflict Management and Peace Science*, 6 (Spring 1982–83), 39–58. First mentioned in Chapter 2. Analysis of the factors that lead states to participate in conflicts. Two measures of "joining the conflict"—one based on U.N. voting; the other, on frequencies of public expressions of support by decision makers. Explanatory factors include geographic distance, level of interaction, trade relations, diplomatic representation, and being alliance partners. Sample of states in a single conflict analyzed using Pearson's r (logarithmic transformation of one set of scores should not detain you; it is one way of dealing with curvilinear relationship), partial r to test spuriousness.

CHAPTER 13

MULTIPLE CORRELATION AND REGRESSION II: MULTIVARIATE ANALYSIS WITH INTERVAL INDEPENDENT AND DEPENDENT VARIABLES

THE PREDICTION EQUATION AND THE PROPORTION OF EXPLAINED VARIATION

The Two Independent Variable Prediction Equation

When you are explaining an interval dependent variable using two interval independent variables, you have an expanded linear prediction model. It is no longer $Y = a + bX + e$, in which you predict/explain Y as a function (b) of X and unexplained error, as it was in the bivariate case.

It is now $Y = a + b_1 X + b_2 Z + e$, where X represents the first independent variable and Z represents the second. You are now saying that the dependent variable is a linear function not solely of a single independent variable (plus some random, unexplained error) but of two independent variables (plus some random, unexplained error).

In the rare case that the two independents are completely uncorrelated, the slopes on the independent variables in the new expanded multivariate equation are the same as if two separate regressions, one for each independent variable separately, were used. Thus, if $r_{xz} = 0$, considering the slopes in the prediction equation

$$Y_p = a + b_1 X + b_2 Z + e$$

b_1 is the same as the b in the bivariate model $Y_p = a + bX + e$; and b_2 is the same as the b in the bivariate model $Y_p = a + bZ + e$.

When X and Z are uncorrelated (and when there is no statistical interaction), a one-unit increase in X can have nothing to do with whether Z increases or not; a one-unit increase in Z can have nothing to do with whether X increases or not. The effect of X on Y is the same, whether the effect of Z is controlled or not. The effect of Z on Y is the same, whether the effect of X is controlled or not.

When X and Z are even a little correlated, however, we need to know the effect of one when the effects of the other have been adjusted out ("controlled"). When X and Z are correlated, the slopes in $Y = a + b_1 X + b_2 Z + e$ are *not* the same as the two slopes in the two separate bivariate prediction models. In the case of correlated independent variables, when one independent changes, the other does as well. Therefore, we need a slope that reflects the effect of a one-unit change in a dependent without including any effects of concomitant changes in the other independent variable.

What we will do in order control the effects of the independent variables on each other is to let Z explain all it can of X and use the residuals of X as new independent variable scores to explain Y. We will simultaneously let X explain all it can of Z and use the residuals of Z

as new scores on a second independent variable to explain Y. This should sound familiar now because we used the same procedure to adjust the scores of one variable to take out the effects of another in Chapter 12.

The slope on X, then, will be the expected increase in Y for every one-unit change in the new residual X scores—those that have the effects of Z removed. The slope on Z will be the expected increase in Y for every one-unit change in the new residual Z scores—those that have the effects of X removed. Thus, we will not be measuring any of the effects of X that might be attributed either to X or to the fact that Z was making X vary; and we will not be measuring any of the effects of Z that might be attributed either to Z or to the fact that X was making Z vary. The slopes will show us the unique effects of each of the independent variables—not any that might be working through the other independent variable. Luckily, calculation of the slope does not require that we go though each of those steps.

Calculating the Partial Slope. The partial slope is as easy to calculate as the partial r, once you have the requisite bivariate statistics. Notice in Formulae 13.1 and 13.2 that you merely substitute the appropriate bivariate slopes in the appropriate places.

You may remember from Chapter 5 that the bivariate slope calculation is very similar to the calculation of the bivariate r. In fact, r and b had the same numerators; both numerators were measures of covariation in X and Y. The computing formulas for the partial slope and the partial r are more different than that, but do compare Formulae 13.1 and 13.2 for partial slopes to the formula for the partial r that you examined in Chapter 12. Such thinking through the formulae may give you a better grasp of what is going on.

FORMULA 13.1
The Partial Slope for Y Dependent on X with Z Controlled

$$b_{yx \cdot z} = \frac{b_{yx} - (b_{yz})(b_{zx})}{1 - b_{xz} b_{zx}}$$

FORMULA 13.2
The Partial Slope for Y Dependent on Z with X Controlled

$$b_{yz \cdot x} = \frac{b_{yz} - (b_{yx})(b_{xz})}{1 - b_{zx} b_{xz}}$$

We can point to the numerator of $b_{yx \cdot z}$ (the slope that represents Y being treated as dependent on X with Z controlled) as, more or less, a measure of the overall effects of X on Y (b_{yx}) minus the part of X's effect on Y that could be coming through Z's relationship to Y (b_{yz}) when X causes Z to vary (b_{zx}). The denominator is a kind of "leftover" variation in the independent variable, X, after the effects that X and Z have on each other are subtracted out. Since $b_{xz} \times b_{zx} = r^2_{xz}$, you can argue that the denominator is the proportion of variation in X left after Z has explained all it can. You will want to compare this to the formula for the bivariate slope (Formula 5.2). Similar reasoning applies to $b_{yz \cdot x}$ (the slope that represents Y being treated as dependent on Z with X controlled).

Do note the *asymmetric* nature of slopes, both bivariate and multivariate: only the variable or coefficients for variables being considered *independent* appear in the denominator. To regress Y on X (that is, to treat Y as dependent on X) yields a different slope than to regress X on Y (to treat X as dependent on Y). That asymmetry is reflected in the subscripts on the notations for the slopes—b_{yx} and b_{xy} are not the same. In bivariate situations, when predicting Y from X, the prediction model is $Y = a + b_{yx}X$. You read the yx as, "Y regressed on X," or as, "Y given X." When predicting X from Y, the prediction model is $X = a + b_{xy}Y$. You read xy as, "X regressed on Y," or as, "X given Y." The two slopes are not the same. In multivariate situations, the subscripts *before* the dot are read as above. The subscripts *after* the dot are those variables being controlled.

Calculating the Intercept. For the multivariate equation, you need a new formula for the intercept that is also different when there are two independent variables rather than one. However, the intercept is easy enough to get, once you have the partial slopes, as you can see from Formula 13.3 below.

FORMULA 13.3
The Intercept in the Multivariate Prediction Model

$$a_{y \cdot xz} = \bar{Y} - b_{yx \cdot z} \bar{X} - b_{yz \cdot x} \bar{Z}$$

Then the overall multivariate prediction model with the partial slopes in place finally becomes

$$Y = a + b_{yx \cdot z} X + b_{yz \cdot x} Z + e.$$

Extensions to More Independent Variables. You can keep adding independent variables to the prediction equation so that you have three or four or more independent variables. Such a model could look something like—

$$Y_p = a + b_{yx \cdot zwa} X + b_{yz \cdot xwa} Z + b_{yw \cdot xza} W + b_{ya \cdot xzw} A + e$$

Keep in mind, however, that each slope in the equation is the relationship between Y and that slope's independent variable with the linear effects of all the other independent variables in the equation adjusted out. Thus, all the relationships in such a prediction equation need to be linear. Remember as well that no two variables (or two sets of variables) can be perfectly correlated with each other. The implications of some of these reminders may be clearer after you turn to the section on interpreting the slopes, which follows the first exercise.

EXERCISE 1 The Multivariate Model

Now you are ready for calculating the intercept and slopes in a multivariate model. First, using the same data (scores, not residuals) on which you calculated a partial in the last chapter, figure out $a_{y \cdot xz}$, $b_{yx \cdot z}$, and $b_{yz \cdot x}$ for the following model and write the complete model out, substituting the slopes and intercept you calculate in the appropriate places in the prediction equation:

$$Y_p = a_{y \cdot xz} + b_{yx \cdot z} X + b_{yz \cdot x} Z + e$$

Although you will need to calculate one *bivariate* slope (b_{yx}) using the formula you learned in Chapter 5, you already have many of the other bivariate statistics you need to substitute into the formulae given in this chapter in order to calculate all the statistics in the model.

1. You have b_{yz} in the equation $Y = a + b_{yz} Z$, which was given for your example in the exercise section of the last chapter.
2. Similarly, you have b_{xz} in the same place in the equation $X = a + b_{xz} Z$.
3. An easy way to get various slopes (in this case b_{zx}) is to know that the bivariate r^2 is arithmetically equal to the product of the two slopes that relate its variables; thus, $r_{zx}^2 = b_{zx} \times b_{xz}$. And $b_{zx} = r_{zx}^2$ divided by b_{xz}. You are given r_{zx}. It will be easy to get b_{zx}. Or, notice that the denominator of the partial slope formula is the product of two bivariate slopes that equals the square of an r you are given; you can substitute the appropriate r^2 rather than the separate slopes there.

Now let's make sure you can read your completed prediction model before going on. Write out answers to these questions along with your model:

1. When Z is controlled, a one-unit increase in X produces how many units increase in Y?
2. When X is controlled, a one-unit increase in Z produces how many units increase in Y?
3. The predicted value of Y is what, when both X and Z are zero?

INTERPRETING THE PARTIAL SLOPES (REGRESSION COEFFICIENTS)

Remember that slopes are probably the most important statistics that we have to work with. They come closer than most others to being able to measure and describe the "laws" of behavior that we are trying to construct in our theory-building. They give us some precision, as we describe the linear effects of one variable on another. Moreover, the partial slopes we have been examining give us ways to assess whether correlation is or is not a likely indicator of causation; they help us in making causal inferences.

However, we need to be cautious in our interpretations of the slopes, as we would with any statistic. The more we can understand about what is happening statistically, what is influencing the size of those slopes in addition to any underlying causation between the variables, the clearer and better our interpretations can be. That is why we need to spend some time trying to get at the interpretation of the slopes and some of the potential problems of such interpretation.

It is well to remember that the problems we outlined with bivariate slopes appear in the multivariate situation as well. Outliers can distort slopes in both, for example. If you have extreme residuals from the regressions of X and Z on each other, you may have some problems. Thus, you eventually need to learn to examine plots of those residuals as well as the residuals of the overall equation.*

However, there are additional cautions for interpretation in the multivariate situation as well. For example, the partial slopes in the regression equation deny to both independent variables the effects that could be attributed to either. Remember that overlap between the circles when two independent variables are correlated? (You can see it again in Figure 13.2 on p. 179.) Since there is no way to know which independent variable explained that portion of the dependent variable, the formula for figuring out the slopes denies to both independent variables the effect that could be attributed to either. Thus, the partial slope can be interpreted as the effect on the dependent variable of a one-unit increase in that particular independent variable, while controlling the other.

If, hypothetically, we could actually control one variable so that it did not vary, the partial b on the other independent would be the effect of varying it alone. However, since we do not have physical control, think of the partial slope as a measure of the effects of varying one independent with the effects of the other adjusted out. The partial slope is, therefore, a measure of the *direct* effects of that variable which does *not* include any effects that result from its causing the other to vary and, consequently, indirectly causing changes in the dependent.

Notice how this is going to help you in those instances in which the interpretation of the partial *correlation* coefficient is ambiguous. Remember from the earlier consideration of the partial correlation coefficient in Chapter 12 that, when you have bivariate correlation greater than zero and then a partial correlation coefficient at or near zero when a third variable is controlled, you know that you had either of two things going on. Either you started out with a spurious correlation in the bivariate situation that was revealed to be nothing by the partial correlation coefficient, or you had a bivariate correlation only because the independent variable was affecting the dependent variable indirectly; removing the effects of the intervening (control) variable showed you in a zero partial correlation coefficient that the independent had no real, direct effect on the dependent variable. Conversely, when you had a near-zero bivariate correlation and then, when a control variable was added, got a nonzero partial correlation, you knew that the control had been suppressing the original correlation.

However, still remembering from the earlier discussion of the partial correlation, whenever you were dealing with less clear-cut situations (in which the partial correlation was not obviously virtually zero or in which the partial didn't spring from an obviously zero bivariate relationship), the interpretation was more difficult. You couldn't say that a partial correlation was stronger or weaker than the bivariate because they were calculated on different amounts of variance in Y. Therefore, it was hard to talk about a control variable that

---

*The REGRESSION procedure has a subcommand, SCATTERPLOT, for this.

caused only some spuriousness in a bivariate or about a partially intervening variable in a situation where there was some remaining direct effect of the independent variable on the dependent.

With the slopes, on the other hand, it is easier to compare the impact of a variable in the bivariate situation to its impact when the effects of another variable are controlled. The bivariate slope is more comparable to the partial slope than the bivariate r was to the partial r because, with the slopes, you are not dealing with the proportions of explained variance (and figuring the bivariate and the partial proportion of explained variance on different bases), as you were with r. Both the bivariate and the partial slopes are read as, "This is how much change I expect in the dependent variable from a one-unit change in the independent variable." The difference is that the partial slope has the effects of the other independent variable taken out, while the bivariate slope does not.

In the bivariate regression of Y on X, you can read the slope and see what effect a one-unit increase of X has on Y. In that case, you do not know what Z is doing; it may be responsible for the apparent effect of X on Y, or it may not. It is uncontrolled and, as far as you are concerned, hidden. But then you can look at the multivariate regression of Y on X and Z. There, in the slope on X ($b_{yx \cdot z}$), you can see the effect on Y of a one-unit increase of X with the effects of Z adjusted out—the direct effects of X without all the indirect effects of Z through X or X through Z.

Now you can look at the slope in the multivariate equation and compare its size to that in the bivariate equation. If the multivariate one is smaller, then the effect of X on Y must have been partially spuriously due to Z, or Z must be partially intervening between X and Y. If the multivariate one is larger, then Z must have been partially suppressing the XY relationship. You can also examine the signs on the slopes for changes compared to the bivariate situation in order to see if the effects of Z were distorting the bivariate XY relationship.

The slopes in the multivariate give you all the information the unambiguous partial correlation coefficients did as well. If you have a non-zero slope in the bivariate regression of Y on X and if the $b_{yx \cdot z}$ in the multivariate equation is at or near zero, you know that the original XY relationship was either spurious or caused by the intervention of Z. If you have a near-zero slope in the bivariate regression of Y on X and if the $b_{yx \cdot z}$ is greater than zero, you know that Z was acting to suppress the real XY relationship, etc.

Lest you think that the partial slopes solve all problems of interpreting relationships between variables, however, eight more problems need to be mentioned.

First, for theory-building, it is pretty important to get relatively reliable assessments of these slopes. We need to know with some accuracy exactly what the effects of X and of Z are.

Yet, with correlated independent variables, there is that troublesome overlap that represents effects of either X or Z, but we don't know which. The partial slopes, remember, assume that we are interested only in the direct effects of the variable at hand (not the effects of it that could be caused by being correlated with the other and causing, thereby, some indirect effects). The partial slopes have to be interpreted, therefore, as if the effects that could have been attributed to either independent variable belong to neither.

If we want to repeat the study on different samples to make sure we have a good idea of what the effects of X and Z are on the dependent variable, we have some trouble. Our estimates of the slopes will depend on just how correlated X and Z are for the sample at hand, and correlation depends on so many things that the chances are slim of having two samples with the same degree of correlation between independent variables.

The exact sizes of the slopes may vary from sample to sample because of the degree of correlation between the independents *not* because the effects of X and Z are changing from sample to sample. The more correlated the two independents, the worse our problem. We just aren't as sure of our assessments of the effects of X and/or Z.

As was mentioned in the last chapter, this is called the problem of *multicollinearity*. The best bet for getting around part of the problems it causes involves large samples and precise measurement. Lacking those, we must be careful not to attribute too much accuracy to our assessments of the direct effect of each independent variable when they are themselves very correlated.

Second, we ought to mention the most extreme form of multicollinearity—the situation in which one independent variable is perfectly correlated with another independent. In this situation, both partial slopes will be zero. When you adjust for the effects of one independent variable in order to figure the direct effects of the other, there will be no direct effects left to examine if the two independents are perfectly correlated with each other. When you adjust for one, you effectively wipe out the other.

Perfect correlation between two independent variables is easy enough to spot and correct. You just have to look at the bivariate correlations between independent variables. If you have perfect correlation between two, throw one out. It isn't telling you anything unique, anyway.*

However, the problem has an extension. No independent variable can be perfectly correlated with any *set* of independent variables (when you extend your analysis beyond two independent variables) either. Since the partial slope controls for *all* the other independent variables, you have a situation similar to that for two variables. If you can effectively wipe out any effects of a particular variable by adjusting for several others (that is, if the one has a multiple R^2, which you will learn below, of 1.0 using any set of the others as independent variables), the slope will be zero and meaningless. This may sound like an esoteric problem that you are unlikely to meet; but, especially when you have small numbers of cases and a rather large number of variables, it is not as unlikely as you may think.

This is not as easy to spot as perfect correlation between just two variables. You'd have to compute several separate multiple R's, treating each independent variable in turn as dependent on all the others. Nevertheless, it is something to file away to and think about as a potential answer when you have problems computing the slopes for a particular equation.

Third, we should also note another problem, in passing, because it is a kind of multicollinearity problem in disguise. Remember that you are treating Y as if it were "caused" by X and Z and e (some random error). Basically, you are ignoring e and whatever variables might be hidden within it.

As long as e represents just a lot of little things that are unimportant influences on Y, it's no problem. But if you think there is another, single, big, major cause of Y, other than those represented by X and Z, and that e probably is primarily composed of that other cause, you may have problems when that cause is correlated with one of the variables already being used as an independent variable.

Since $Y = a + bX + bZ + e$ basically ignores the influence of any variable represented by e, rather than controlling it, a big uncontrolled influence in e could cause your assessment of the other slopes to be thrown way off. To ignore an e that concealed an important cause would be the equivalent of not controlling an extraneous or intervening variable; the slopes would be just as distorted as those you have been looking at in bivariate relationships that disappear when you control another variable.

The solution is to plan ahead, collect data on what you theorize are all the major causes of Y, and get them all into the equation. Rather than two independent variables, you'd have three or four plus the remaining random error. Then you would have their effects controlled (not distorting the other slopes), rather than ignored and causing trouble. Frequently an analysis of the residuals in regression can help you determine whether your e (error term) is concealing a variable that ought to be

---

*If you drop one variable that is just highly correlated with another, you run into the third problem, which is described in the text.

brought into the analysis. The work required is pretty advanced for this text. If you think it's a problem in things you're working on, consult one of the more advanced texts in the suggested readings.

A fourth problem arises from the fact that the partial slope is a measure of just the direct impact of each independent variable on the dependent. Remember that the calculation of the partial slope controls for all the other independent variables in the equation and denies to all correlated independent variables the effects that could conceivably be attributed to any one of them.

With multiple regression, you are not getting an indication of the total effect that any one independent variable might be having. For example, imagine that an antecedent caused an intervening variable to cause the dependent variable but maintained some direct effect of its own. A multiple regression equation would not give you the total impact that the antecedent had both directly and indirectly. You would get, in the slope on the antecedent, only its direct effect on the dependent variable.

If you need to know the total effect of a variable—rather than just its direct effect—you will need to use path analysis rather than simple multiple regression. Although that technique is beyond the scope of this text, you should be ready to start some reading of it. It is basically just an extension of multivariate regression. Once you understand the prediction equation for each variable in the model as dependent on all those before it in the model, you need only an adjustment of the slopes in order to start to understand path analysis. And you will learn that adjustment in the next chapter.

A fifth problem, though not a large one, can arise from the fact that the slopes in the multivariate equation are dependent on the measurement scale. A one-unit increase in X is not the same as a one-unit increase in Z unless the two happen to be measured on the same scale. Since the units are not the same, it is impossible to say whether X or Z is having more impact on Y.

Remember that the squares of the partial correlation coefficients are just telling you what proportion of the variation in Y can be explained by either X or Z, controlling for the other; they are measures of the strength of a relationship between X or Z and Y after the other independent variable has explained all it can of the variation in Y. The partial correlation coefficients are not measures of the precise form of the relationship (how much change in Y is to be expected with a change in X or Z); therefore, they cannot answer the question of which is having more impact.

If you need to compare the amount of change in Y expected from changes in X and changes in Z, you will need another statistic. Fortunately, that is no problem. An adjustment to the already calculated slopes mentioned above, which you will see in Chapter 14, will handle the problem. The adjustment will give you standardized slopes that are comparable across variables which have different scales of measurement.

The sixth in this list of problems of interpretation is the following: we assume that the relationship (slope) between dependent variable and each independent is the same, regardless of the condition of the other independent variables; that is, we assume there is no statistical interaction—that one independent variable does not specify the relationship between another independent and the dependent variable.

Imagine a situation, for example, in which you are trying to predict political participation from both education and income. If the relationship between political participation and education is negative when income is high, positive when income is low, and zero when income is medium, you cannot get *one* partial slope to summarize those relationships. A single statistic cannot communicate all three relationships. If you went ahead and calculated a partial slope for participation as dependent on education with income controlled, you'd get a single figure that represented a kind of average of all three—in this case, practically zero. Yet, zero does not communicate the relationship that exists.

When there is statistical interaction, you cannot use multiple regression. A solution is to break your sample into groups on the basis of the other independent variable (in the example above, income) and run bivariate regressions within the groups you have created. Then you will get (continuing the example above) three slopes for the effect of education on participation: one for only those cases in which income is high, one for only those cases in which income is low, and one for only those cases in which income is medium.

A seventh consideration—one that cannot be mentioned often enough—is that this is *linear* regression. The statistics are based on linear relationships between every pair of variables. This means that not only do the independent and dependent variables have to be hypothesized to be linearly related but also the independent and the control, as well as the control and the dependent, have to be linearly related. The statistics give us the straight lines that best describe the data; curved relationships are not well represented by them. It is often worth running bivariate scatterplots just to make sure that your data aren't deviating too far from linearity.

Eighth, and finally, you need to have enough cases so that your calculation of the slopes is based upon enough information to make them fairly reliable. Although it is less severe here, this is the same problem you had in crosstabulation tables when you needed enough cases to know that error on one or two was not substantially distorting the percentage distribution. It is the same problem you saw in analysis of variance when you needed enough cases to calculate a fairly reliable mean. Here you probably need to think in terms of around 20 cases per independent variable, perhaps fewer if you are just trying to get the best possible descriptive statement of the relationships in the data, but more if you are trying to make inferences about larger groups from the sample you have at hand. Consult the more advanced texts listed in the suggested readings.

THE MULTIPLE R^2

When you want a measure of the strength of the association to assess what amount of the variation in Y you can explain using the two independent variables, you will use a new proportionate reduction of error (PRE) statistic

called the multiple R^2. It is designated $R^2_{y \cdot xz}$—the proportion of variation in Y explained by X and Z taken together. (The subscript before the dot designates the dependent variable; those after the dot designate the independent variables, and their order after the dot is irrelevant.)

This multiple R^2 is very much like the bivariate r^2 you calculated earlier. (Review Chapters 4 and 5, if necessary.) You first determine how much error you make in guessing the dependent variable *without* knowledge of the independent; that is, you make your best guess for each case, the mean of Y ($\overline{Y}$), just as you did before. Error is defined (as shown in Formula 13.4) as the squared difference between a case's actual dependent variable score (Y_i) and the guess ($\overline{Y}$) summed over all the cases (i.e., variation in Y).

FORMULA 13.4
Error Guessing Dependent with No Knowledge of Independent (Error by Definition 1)

$$\text{Error} = \Sigma (Y_i - \overline{Y})^2$$

You then make the best guess based on the linear prediction model (i.e., knowing both of the independent variables). For each case, you would predict a Y value based on $Y_p = a + b_{yx \cdot z} X + b_{yz \cdot x} Z + e$. Knowing the case's values on X and Z and knowing the value of a and the values of the two b coefficients, you predict a value for Y. Now figure your error again. Error is now defined (Formula 13.5) as the squared difference between a case's actual dependent variable score (Y_i) and the guess (prediction) based on the model (Y_p) summed over all the cases. This is the variation in Y that cannot be explained by X and Z together.

FORMULA 13.5
Error Guessing Dependent from Knowledge of Independents (Error by Definition 2)

$$\text{Error} = \Sigma (Y_i - Y_p)^2$$

Then you construct a PRE statistic, as you have now seen several times and as you see repeated in Formula 13.6.

FORMULA 13.6
PRE Formula: Multiple R^2

$$R^2 = \frac{\text{Error by definition 1} - \text{Error by definition 2}}{\text{Error by definition 1}}$$

As was the case with the zero-order, bivariate r^2, to the extent that two independent variables are linearly correlated with a dependent, the error variation will be reduced in the second calculation of error. In the extreme case in which two variables are able exactly to predict a third, there will be no error left in the second formulation, and the fraction will be 1.0. You will have explained 100% of the variation in Y.

EXERCISE 2 The Multiple R^2

Now figure the multiple R^2 for the prediction equation you were using in the first exercise. You will get a formula for doing this later; but, instead of just going straight to the formula for the multiple R^2, go through the logical steps for the calculation of a PRE statistic.

First, figure out how much total variation in the dependent variable there is to explain, $\Sigma (Y_i - \overline{Y})^2$. Be sure it is clearly labeled on your work. This is the error you'd make guessing the mean for each case in absence of knowledge of the independent variables' values.

Second, knowing each case's values on the two independent variables and the linear prediction model that you have just constructed, make your best guess for each case's value on the dependent variable. For each case, multiply the value on each independent variable by the appropriate slope for that variable; sum the two products and the value for the intercept. Write clearly the predicted value for each case in a column labeled Y_p.

Third, subtract that predicted value from the case's real value on the dependent variable and square the difference. List all those results in a column marked as $(Y_i - Y_p)^2$.

Fourth, sum the squared differences between the predicted and actual values on the dependent variable, $\Sigma (Y_i - Y_p)^2$. This is the unexplained variation in Y—the error you'd still make knowing the values on both independent variables. Label this clearly in your work.

Fifth, follow the formula for the PRE statistic (13.6) and write out the result.

Computing the Multiple R^2

For this statistic, looking at a computing formula may help you see what is happening. In the rare case that the two *independent variables* are completely *uncorrelated* with each other, the multiple R^2 is simply the proportion of the variation in Y explained by X added to the proportion of the variation in Y explained by Z, as shown in Formula 13.7.

FORMULA 13.7
Multiple R^2: Uncorrelated Independent Variables

$$R^2_{y \cdot xz} = r^2_{xy} + r^2_{yz}, \text{ if } X \text{ and } Z \text{ are completely uncorrelated}$$

In terms of the pictures we have been using to illustrate the concepts, refer to Figure 13.1. The two lined portions of Y, if each is figured as a proportion of the total variation in Y, are the proportion explained by X and the proportion explained by Z. Since X and Z are not correlated, you can see that all you would have to do to get the proportion explained by both is to add the two proportions together.

However, when the two independents are at all correlated, there is a proportion of varia-

Proportion of y's variation explained by x (r^2_{xy})
+ **Proportion** of y's variation explained by z (r^2_{zy})
= $R^2_{y \cdot xz}$, if x and z are **not** correlated
(proportion of y's variation explained by x **and** z)

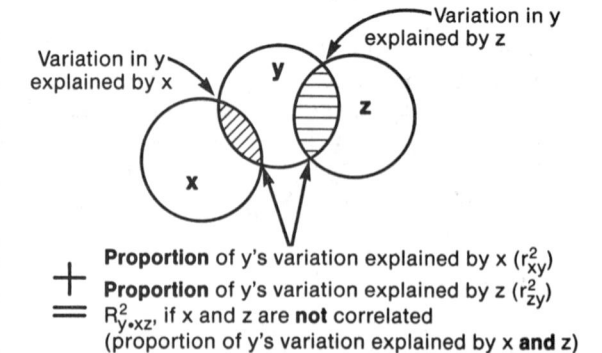

FIGURE 13.1 Diagram of Multiple R^2: Uncorrelated Independents

tion in Y explained by one or the other independent; we don't know which. For the *total* proportion explained, that which is measured by the statistic $R^2_{y \cdot xz}$, it really doesn't matter *which* of the two independents is doing the explaining. The total explained variation is the same, regardless, but for a computational formula for R^2, we need to assign that variation to one or the other independent variable so that it doesn't get counted twice. For computational purposes, let's just give it to X. Then we get the formula for the multiple R^2, as shown in Formula 13.8.

FORMULA 13.8
Multiple R^2: Correlated Independent Variables

$$R^2_{y \cdot xz} = r^2_{xy} + r^2_{zy \cdot x}(1 - r^2_{xy})$$

Proportion of Y explained by X (including overlap with Z) — Proportion of Y explained by Z after X has explained all it can (i.e., partial r^2 between Y and Z controlling X) — OF — The proportion left unexplained by X

The formula points out that we basically let X explain the proportion (r^2_{xy}) it can of variation of Y and then let Z explain the proportion ($r^2_{zy \cdot x}$) it can *of* the proportion ($1 - r^2_{xy}$) left unexplained by X. Then we add the two proportions together for a measure of the proportion of the variation in Y that is explained by X and Z acting together.

In effect, R^2 is giving us a measure of the proportion of Y covered by the cross-hatched area under variation in both X and Z in the pictorial representation in Figure 13.2.

As you can see, X is correlated with Y in the figure, and Z is correlated with Y. But X and Z are also correlated with each other. The overlap between the part of Y explained by X and the part of Y explained by Z is that portion of Y that could be explained by either of the two independents. We want that to count in the measure of the strength of the relationship only once. Therefore, we consider that area in the proportion explained by X (although it doesn't matter which); then we figure the *extra* proportion explained by Z and add that to the proportion explained by X to get the multiple R^2.

Think through instances in which you might want to report $R^2_{y \cdot xz}$. You might, for example, want to explain the voting turnout of counties as a function of both the median education level and the average distance to voting registration facilities within a county. The first would be positively related to the dependent and would yield a positive *partial r*; the second would be negatively related to the dependent and would yield a negative partial r. By the time we talk about *proportion* explained by both (i.e., the *multiple R^2*), however, the sign is irrelevant. As another example, you might want to explain percentage of national budgets that is committed to defense as a function of both the proximity of threatening neighbors and the level of internal unrest.

Whenever you need to report the proportion of variance explained in a dependent by two (or more) independents, the multiple R^2 is appropriate (with interval measurement and linear prediction models).

This PRE statistic (with multiple interval independent variables, an interval dependent variable, and a linear prediction model) is the multiple R^2—$R^2_{y \cdot xz}$. It tells you, remember, the proportion of variance in Y you have explained with X and Z as independents.

EXERCISE 3 Multiple R^2, Computing Formula

Now, assure yourself that the computing formula for $R^2_{y \cdot xz}$ (which you were given in Formula 13.8 above) gives you the same results as

Shaded area, when figured as a proportion of variation in y = $R^2_{y \cdot xz}$

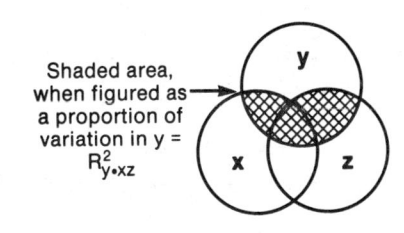

FIGURE 13.2 Diagram of Multiple R^2: Correlated Independents

the more conceptual way of figuring the multiple R^2, which you did for the second exercise. Write it out and show your substitutions into it. You'll have to calculate a partial r, but you are given, in the exercise section of the previous chapter, all the necessary bivariate r statistics to substitute into Formula 13.9 below for the appropriate partial.

FORMULA 13.9
The Partial Correlation Coefficient:
the Relationship between Z and Y with X Controlled

$$r_{zy \cdot x} = \frac{r_{zy} - (r_{xy})(r_{xz})}{\sqrt{1 - r_{zx}^2} \sqrt{1 - r_{yx}^2}}$$

Remember that the *order* of the subscripts is irrelevant on the bivariate r because it is symmetric. On the partial r, the order of the subscripts before the dot on the subscripts is also irrelevant; after the dot, however, is the variable whose effects are controlled. Which letter comes after the dot is not irrelevant. Notice that the partial r you are using here is the correlation between Z and Y with the effects of X removed. Compare that to the formula for the partial given earlier (Formula 12.2), which was for the relation between X and Y with the effects of Z removed. Be sure you understand how they are different.

Interpreting Multiple Regression

Before you go on to the computer exercises, be sure to compare your results on all the above exercises with those of people who chose other examples, so you can get a clear idea of what's happening. Also, compare the analyses in this chapter with those in the last chapter.

Particularly, note that when a partial r (between two variables controlling for a third) is zero, the corresponding slope is as well. When you're trying to assess whether a control variable is extraneous to a relationship or intervenes between the variables of a relationship, the partial slope (of Y dependent on X controlling for Z) gives the same interpretation as the partial r (between X and Y controlling for Z). When you are dealing with less clear-cut situations, the partial slopes give you more information.

Also note that both the partial r (not partial r^2) and the partial slope can tell you the direction of a relationship when another variable's effects are controlled. Is X positively related to Y when Z is controlled? Either $r_{xy \cdot z}$ or $b_{yx \cdot z}$ will tell you.

Otherwise, remember a partial slope and a partial r give you different kinds of information. The slope $b_{yx \cdot z}$ is a measure of the *amount* of effect on Y that a one-unit increment of X has with Z controlled and is thus interpreted in light of the measurement scale of Y, as is the case with any slope. The partial $r_{yx \cdot z}$ is a measure of strength of relationship between X and Y with Z controlled and is not dependent on the scale of measurement.

Finally, note how the multiple R^2 can give you a measure of the proportion of variation in Y explained by both X and Z acting together.

USING THE COMPUTER FOR MULTIPLE REGRESSION

EXERCISE 4 The REGRESSION Procedure

You will be using the data from the last chapter here. If you saved the file you set up for that chapter, just access it and make the changes indicated below. If you didn't, you will first need to set up a file. Remember that, for data coming in to the computer with the job, you will need:

A DATA LIST, naming (uniquely) and indicating location of your variables. (To help you and the instructor interpret your output, please call your variables VARX1, VARY1, VARZ1, VARX2, VARY2, VARZ2, VARX3, VARY3, VARZ3, or just X1, Y1, Z1, X2, Y2, Z2, X3, Y3, Z3.)

The BEGIN DATA command.

All the data on the nine variables on each of the ten cases.

The END DATA command.

A procedure (see below).

The FINISH command, if necessary.

Review Chapter 3 for details of this setup, if necessary.

The REGRESSION Procedure

If you want more of the multiple regression and correlation statistics than you can get from PARTIAL CORR, the procedure you need is REGRESSION. As you learn more and more about regression, you will learn how really versatile this procedure is, but for now, we will set it up as simply as possible.

For each regression you are going to run, you will need the following subcommands:

DESCRIPTIVES = gets the bivariate correlations as well as means, standard deviations, and N of cases for each variable; later, there are others you may want to add.
VARIABLES = tells the names of all the variables—independent, dependent, and control—in the particular equation you are setting up.
STATISTICS = can be left out if all you want is the multiple R and R^2, the regression coefficients, and the intercept (as well as some things we haven't talked about yet). But to get the multiple R and R^2, the slopes, the bivariate correlations between independents and dependents, and the partials between each independent and the dependent controlling the other independent, plus some things we haven't talked about, specify R, ANOVA, CHA, COEFF, ZPP. (Although this list will get you several statistics we haven't gotten to yet, getting them now will allow you to use this output in Chapter 18.)
DEPENDENT = tells which variable from the particular variable list is to be considered dependent for the particular equation being set up.
ENTER = is a "method" subcommand and tells the package to calculate the statistics using the same calculation method you did in this chapter. We will use it twice: first, to get the bivariate equation and, second, for the multivariate equation—for comparison.

REGRESSION commands and subcommands for all the statistics in this chapter would look like the command that follows this paragraph. On the REGRESSION command, you see "dep, ind, con." On the first REGRESSION command, after the first VARIABLES subcommand, substitute the names of all three variables for the first example in place of "dep, ind, con," just as they were spelled on your DATA LIST. Where you see the "dep" after the subcommand DEPENDENT, you insert the name of the variable, from the previous list of three, that is to be dependent. After the first ENTER subcommand, you substitute the name of your first independent variable for "ind." After the second ENTER subcommand, you substitute the name of your control (second independent) variable for "con." Do the same things on the second and third REGRESSION commands, but use the names of the variables for your second example in the appropriate slots on the second procedure and the names of the variables for your third example in the appropriate slots on the third procedure.

```
REGRESSION DESCRIPTIVES =
  MEAN, STDDEV, CORR,
  N/VARIABLES =
  dep1, ind1, con1/STATISTICS =
  R ANOVA CHA COEFF
  ZPP/DEPENDENT =
  dep1/ENTER=ind1/ENTER=con1.
```

Continue with a second and third REGRESSION command for the next two exercises.

There are abbreviations for the subcommands: VARIABLES = VARS; DEPENDENT = DEP; STATISTICS = STATS. Use the abbreviations, if you like.

Set up the regression job and run it either as three separate REGRESSION jobs, if you are working interactively, or all at once in batch. After you get your output, write the following statements with the blanks filled in on a separate sheet of paper. As you are answering the questions, try to remember the interpretation of each statistic and how you would use it. (Help in reading the output follows the questions.)

Example 1

$Y_p = \underline{\qquad} + \underline{\qquad} X + e$

$r^2_{xy} = \underline{\qquad}$

$Y_p = \underline{\qquad} + \underline{\qquad} X + \underline{\qquad} Z + e$

$R^2_{y \cdot xz} = \underline{\qquad}$

$r_{xy} = \underline{\qquad}$

$r_{xz} = \underline{\qquad}$

$r_{zy} = \underline{\qquad}$

$r^2_{xy \cdot z} = \underline{\qquad}$

Example 2

$Y_p = \underline{\qquad} + \underline{\qquad} X + e$

$r^2_{xy} = \underline{\qquad}$

$Y_p = \underline{\qquad} + \underline{\qquad} X + \underline{\qquad} Z + e$

$R^2_{y \cdot xz} = \underline{\qquad}$

$r_{xy} = \underline{\qquad}$

$r_{xz} = \underline{\qquad}$

$r_{zy} = \underline{\qquad}$

$r^2_{xy \cdot z} = \underline{\qquad}$

Example 3

$Y_p = \underline{\qquad} + \underline{\qquad} X + e$

$r^2_{xy} = \underline{\qquad}$

$Y_p = \underline{\qquad} + \underline{\qquad} X + \underline{\qquad} Z + e$

$R^2_{y \cdot xz} = \underline{\qquad}$

$r_{xy} = \underline{\qquad}$

$r_{xz} = \underline{\qquad}$

$r_{zy} = \underline{\qquad}$

$r^2_{xy \cdot z} = \underline{\qquad}$

After you've filled in those blanks, put the numbers of the following phrases next to the appropriate statistics in Example 1 in order to practice your interpretations of these statistics.

1. When both X and Z are zero, this is the expected/predicted value of Y.
2. The proportion of variance in Y that can be explained by X and Z together.
3. The proportion of variance in Y that can be explained by X, once Z has explained all it can.
4. A one-unit increase in X, controlling Z, is related to this many units of increase in Y.
5. A one-unit increase in Z, controlling X, is related to this many units of increase in Y.
6. The proportion of variation in Y explained by X, ignoring (not controlling) the effects of Z, is described by this.
7. The bivariate relationship between Z and Y is given here.
8. The bivariate relationship between Z and X is given here.

Even if you ran REGRESSION in Chapter 12, you may have a little trouble recognizing things on this output at first. The first thing you will see for each example is the set of "descriptive" statistics. Here you are getting the univariate statistics on each variable in the example—means and standard deviations—as well as the bivariate correlations between each pair of variables, which are in a matrix right after the means and standard deviations.

It is always a good idea to see how many cases are being read and processed. Sometimes you may find that you have entered data incorrectly, and the correct number of cases cannot be read. Sometimes you may have recoded in such a way as to lose cases. You can check the N of cases right after the means and standard deviations.

Next, notice that the output with the regression information itself is in two "blocks." The first block has everything you need to set up the bivariate equation. In that block, only the first independent variable is explaining the dependent; only the variable you have told the program to enter first is in the prediction equation here.

The second block has everything you need to set up the multivariate equation. Here, both the variable entered for the first block *and* the second independent (control) variable, which was entered by the second ENTER subcommand, are in the prediction equation. It is in the second block that you are explaining the dependent variable using both the two independent variables.

Within the appropriate block, the intercept (*a*) is after the word "Constant," which is in parentheses. It looks as if it is in a column of slopes, but it shouldn't be thought of as one. That line is just a convenient place on the output in which to put the intercept.

The slopes you need for the prediction equation *are* in the column of slopes, headed by the letter B. The coefficient for X is next to the name of the X variable. In the first block, it is b_{yx}; in the second block, in that same location, it is $b_{yx \cdot z}$. The coefficient for Z ($b_{yz \cdot x}$) is next to the name of the Z variable but only in the second block where it is in the equation.

The *bivariate* correlations between each independent variable and the dependent (in addition to being with the descriptive statistics above) are also in a column headed "Correl." These, remember, are without controls.

The partial correlations between *each* independent and the dependent *controlling* for the *other* independent are in a column headed "Partial." To get $r^2_{xy \cdot z}$, *you* have to square it. (Do not be confused by "Part Cor"; it does not stand for the partial.)

The multiple R and multiple R2 are labeled in the MULTIPLE REGRESSION part of the output, after the descriptive statistics and above the slopes. These, remember, relate to variation in the dependent explained by all the independent variables in the equation. Therefore, in the first block, they are the bivariate r and r 2. In the second block, they are the multiple R and R2.

Now that you are beginning to be able to read the output, you are ready to move on to multiple regression on real data in Chapter 14.

SUGGESTED READINGS

See the suggested readings for the previous as well as the next chapters, in addition to those cited below.

Multiple Regression

ASHER, HERBERT B. *Causal Modeling*, #3 in series, *Quantitative Application in the Social Sciences* (Beverly Hills, CA: Sage, 1980). This goes into path analysis, which is somewhat beyond what is being done in this textbook; nevertheless, the leap from this book to such analysis is not so great that you will find Asher's work impossible.

BERENSON, MARK L., DAVID M. LEVINE, and MATTHEW GOLDSTEIN. *Intermediate Statistical Methods and Applications: A Computer Package Approach* (Englewood Cliffs, NJ: Prentice-Hall, 1983), Ch. 10. (You may need to review Chapter 9 first to understand 10.)

DRAPER, N.R., and H. SMITH. *Applied Regression Analysis* (N.Y.: Wiley, 1966), Chs. 3-4. This is helpful in examination of residuals, a topic only hinted at in this textbook.

HANUSHEK, ERIC A., and JOHN E. JACKSON. *Statistical Methods for Social Scientists* (N.Y.: Academic Press, 1977), Chs. 4-5. This text is rather advanced compared to what you have been doing; nevertheless, it is useful and especially good in its coverage of problem areas.

KERLINGER, FRED N., and ELAZAR J. PEDHAUZER. *Multiple Regression in Behavioral Research* (N.Y.: Holt, Rinehart, and Winston, 1973), Chs. 1-5.

KLEINBAUM, DAVID G., and LAWRENCE L. KUPPER. *Applied Regression Analysis and Other Multivariable Methods* (North Scituate, MA: Duxbury, 1978), Chs. 10-11.

LEWIS-BECK, MICHAEL S. *Applied Regression: An Introduction*, #22 in series, *Quantitative Applications in the Social Sciences* (Beverly Hills, CA: Sage, 1980).

SPSS Regression

NORUSIS, MARIJA J. *SPSS/PC+* (Chicago: SPSS, Inc., 1988). Chapter 17, pp. B196-B243 discusses the statistics available in the procedure; pp. C125-C136 contains the commands.

SPSS-X User's Guide, 3rd ed. (Chicago: SPSS, Inc., 1988), Ch. 45, pp. 848-870.

ARTICLES

Many of these use standardized slopes, which you will learn in Chapter 14. Here you can get by with knowing that standardized slopes are interpreted as if all the variables were measured on the same scale; thus, one unit on any variable is the same size as one unit on any of the variables in that equation. This lets you compare which independent variable has the greatest effect on the dependent in terms of which one causes the most difference in the dependent when the independents each change one unit, controlling the other independents.

BENTON, J. EDWIN. "Policy Responses to Citizen Attitudes," *Policy Studies Review*, 2 (May 1983), 615-630. Unit of analysis is the decision-maker, here the property appraiser. Survey data are aggregated by county to get a measure of citizen attitudes for each decision-maker; that is used as independent variable to explain decisions of the appraiser with attitude of the appraiser considered intervening, controlling two measures of appraiser's cynicism. Considers conditions that enhance the impact of citizen attitudes on decision-maker behavior (specification variables). Multiple regression interpreting standardized and unstandardized partial slopes. Diagram of basic model.

BROOKS, GARY H., and WILLIAM CLAGGETT. "Black Electoral Power, White Resistance, and Legislative Behavior," *Political Behavior*, 3 (Spring 1981), 49-68. Attempts to explain legislative roll-call behavior with aggregate constituency characteristics. Begins with test of simple, additive model that assumes legislator will be more responsive to blacks as their electoral power increases, as white resistance decreases, and as the legislature is from a new generation. Finding that the additive model explains little, proceeds to test an interactive model that shows different effects of the independent variables under different conditions of black electoral power and white resistance. To read this, understand that b_0 is authors' indication of the intercept; then try writing out the model: Payoffs = a + b Electoral Power + b White Resistance + b Generation for each of the four combinations of electoral power and resistance. Look at the slopes in the four to see the different effects.

BURG, STEVEN L., and MICHAEL L. BERBAUM. "Community, Integration, and Stability in Multinational Yugoslavia," *American Political Science Review*, 83 (June 1989), 535-554. Mentioned first in Chapter 5; Table 3 uses multivariate regression with standardized regression coefficients.

CAPUTO, DAVID A. "New Perspectives on the Public Policy Implications of Defense and Welfare Expenditures in Four Modern Democracies: 1950-1970," *Policy Sciences*, 6 (1975), 423-446. Listed first in Chapter 2. Country by country regression (simple and multiple) in which annual percentage change in health or education expenditures is treated as dependent on annual percentage change in health or education expenditures, defense expenditures, all expenditures, and national income. Betas (standardized regression coefficients) examined within country to assess most important correlates. Graph of the data for each country is presented. Finally, data for all countries are combined and analyzed under varying defense and economic conditions. A case for analysis is a year for a country. Attention given to problems of cross-cultural reliability of measurement.

HIBBING, JOHN R. "On the Issues Surrounding Economic Voting: Looking to the British Case for Answers," *Comparative Political Studies*, 20 (April 1987), 3-33. Mentioned first in Chapter 6, uses multiple regression analysis (standardized and unstandardized slopes) at both the aggregate and individual levels to assess the impact of economic variables on vote choice.

KUGLER, JACEK, and MARIANA ARBETMAN. "Exploring the 'Phoenix Factor' with the Collective Goods Perspective," *The Journal of Conflict Resolution*, 33 (March 1989), 84-112. Although the operationalizations of the variables may seem complex, they are carefully explained. The multiple regression is straightforward. Explains "whether domestic political and economic levels of destruction account for the ability of developed nations to recover within two decades...from war," (p. 84).

MLADENKA, KENNETH R. "Blacks and Hispanics in Urban Politics," *American Political Science Review*, 83 (March 1989), 165-191. Explanation of black and Hispanic share of total jobs, officials/administrators, professionals, and protective service workers using demographic, political power, political structure (e.g., reform/unreformed), region, and workforce composition variables in 1,224 cities. Considers interaction effects of region and political structure. Multiple regression.

SAVAGE, JAMES. "Postmaterialism of the Left and Right: Political Conflict in Postindustrial Society," *Comparative Politicial Studies*, 17 (January 1985), 431–451. Mentioned first in Chapter 2, article concludes with multiple regression to predict left- versus right-wing postmaterialism and right-wing materialism versus right-wing postmaterialism on basis of church attendance, party identification, age, education, and occupation.

USEEM, MICHAEL. "Government Mobilization of Academic Social Research," *Policy Studies Journal*, 4 (1976), 274–280. Mentioned first in Chapter 5, article uses multiple regression (standardized partial slopes) to assess relative importance of several independent variables within disciplines on receipt of public funds.

CHAPTER 14

MULTIPLE REGRESSION III: NEW OPERATIONALIZATIONS AND STANDARD SLOPES

OPERATIONALIZING WITH STANDARDIZED VARIABLES

Problems With COUNT

Before we turn to multiple regression on real data, we will examine another way of operationalizing a concept by constructing a scale from multiple indicators of the same concept. You've done something like this once in Chapter 6 using the COUNT procedure.

A problem with COUNT is that it only allows you to increment the scale by one point each time a case meets a criterion on one of the constituent variables. In effect, COUNT treats each indicator as if it were a dichotomy (the case either meets or doesn't meet the criterion), and you count up the number of times a case has a particular value on the dichotomies.

When your indicators aren't actually dichotomies, you can lose an enormous amount of precision. If you have cases spread out over 5, 15, or even 50 values, you can discriminate between cases rather readily. You sacrifice much of that ability to discriminate when you dichotomize the scores in order to create an index using the COUNT procedure.

Perhaps an example will clarify this criticism of indices based on dichotomous indicators. Would you rather have a "pass" or a B for a course grade? The pass treats everyone from 70 through 100 as though they were all alike. The B indicates very good performance indeed. If I had received a B, I'd rather have it recorded than the pass, since it communicates more precisely about my performance and lets someone know that I didn't just squeak into the passing range. It can discriminate between my grade and that of the person who did not do nearly as well.

The COUNT way of creating an index is little more than adding up how many courses you passed. It cannot do much to indicate how well you passed them. The procedure you're about to learn carries more precision—more like a grade-point average, which indicates how well you did in all your courses on average.

The procedure presented here will allow you to take advantage of the full differentiation of cases provided by indicators that have multiple ordinal or interval values. You will learn a way to combine several indicators in order to get the benefit from multi-item indexing while, at the same time, retaining all the information from the full range of scores on the variables that make up the scale.

Why Standardize?

The simplest way of creating a more precise index would be to find several indicators of the same concept all measured on the same interval scale. Then you could add a case's values on those indicators to get an overall scale score. This would be the equivalent of constructing your overall grade-point average by saying: every course has a grade measured on a zero to 4 scale; let's just add the F(0) you got in P.E. to the A(4) you got in research methods to the B(3) you got in Russian and conclude that your g.p.a. for those courses is 7. This approach has some shortcomings.

The most obvious problem is that each indicator of the concept "grade point" is given the same weight. A P.E. course is probably one credit hour, research methods three, and Russian perhaps 5. Yet, by adding 0 to 4 to 3 for "g.p.a.," we counted each equally. The solution to that is obvious. *Weight* the indicators. Multiply the value on each indicator by the credit hours.

$$
\begin{aligned}
0 \times 1 &= 0 \\
4 \times 3 &= 12 \\
3 \times 5 &= \underline{15} \\
\text{g.p.a.} &= 27
\end{aligned}
$$

It is then easy to deal with the other shortcoming such as everyone having a different number of hours. You can divide the weighted summed indicators by the number of hours: 27/9 = 3.0. Now you've got the concept "g.p.a." operationalized in a fairly precise, reasonably accurate way that allows some discrimination among students.

There are subtler problems we have to worry about in research, but one is not unlike the problem of weighting mentioned above. In the grade-point example, we wanted to make sure that a four-hour course counted into the average four times as heavily as a one-hour course. When we have several equivalent indicators of a concept, we want to make sure that each counts equally in the overall scale. Even with indicators measured on the same scale, however, we cannot be sure they will count equally in the overall index after we have added them up.

The problem of weighting here stems from the fact that, even though two indicators have the same measurement scale, they are unlikely to have the same variance. The indicator with the larger variance (when added to an indicator with smaller variance) will have greater "weight" in determining the final ranking of cases on the combined index.

An example may clarify this. Suppose an instructor has given three exams during the semester. She plans to add the grades together at the end of the term and use the resulting sum to rank-order the students. She then plans to give the top 10 percent of the students As, the next 20 percent Bs, and so on. Suppose that, on the first exam, grades ranged pretty evenly from the 50s to the 100s. On the second exam, almost everyone got above 90. On the third exam, almost everyone got between 80 and 90. Once the grades are summed, the relative ranking of students is far more influenced by the first exam than by the second and third exams. The exam with the greatest variance was most important in determining the final ranking of students. Think about it. In order for each indicator to have the same weight in the overall index, we must make them all have the same variance.

At least the instructor with the three exams has three indicators all measured on the same scale (0–100), but we political scientists frequently don't have several indicators (of the same concept) measured on the same scales. Therefore, even if we can weight scores to take into account unequal variance, we still have to worry about different scales. We might have several 0–100-point scales, a few dichotomies, several things measured on five-point scales, and a few more measured on seven-point scales.

Surely you wouldn't want two five-point exams on which you did well and a 100-point exam on which you did poorly simply to be added together for your final grade. You'd want the two five-point exams to have their scales translated into the 0–100-point scale before adding them to the 100-point exam. If the scores were simply summed, your two perfect fives would only bring your 50 up to 60—the same score as a person who made two zeros on the five-point exams and only ten points better than you on the 100-point exam.

Combine the variance problem and the scale problem and you see what you face in political research. We may have a whole set of indicators that indicate, say, approval of the Democratic Party and its symbols. But two are 0–100 thermometers, one measuring attitudes toward a candidate almost everyone likes (small variance) and one measuring attitudes about a candidate on which people feel strongly either way (big variance). And two are seven-point approval of Democratic policy questions we want to combine with the thermometers. We want each item to count equally in the overall index. What do we do?

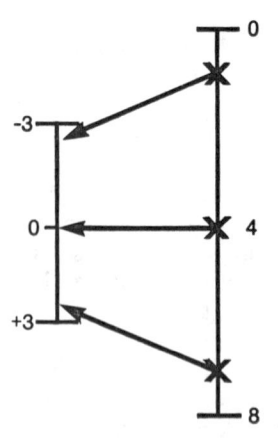

FIGURE 14.1 Changing One Scale into Another

Procedure for Standardizing

The solution is to get all indicators both onto the same scale and into the same variance. Let me try to draw a picture of getting various indicators onto the same scale. Let's say we want all indicators to end up on a scale that ranges from −3 to +3. The variable we want to transform into this new −3 to +3 scale happens to be a nine-point scale ranging from 0 to 8—"strongly disagree" to "strongly agree," say. We can simply pair up the −3 to +3 and the 0 to 8 scales and figure out what the equivalent points are on them. Then we basically match cases values on the old 0 to 8 scale with their equivalent values on the −3 to +3 scale—maintaining their locations relative to other cases (keeping them ranked the same and preserving the relative degrees of difference between them), as is shown graphically in Figure 14.1.

However, we also need to get the various indicators to all have the same variance. Obviously, if the scores on one indicator (for example, a thermometer question that asks how warm or cool do you feel toward _____) are distributed like those in Figure 14.2, indicating that sizable groups of respondents both approve and disapprove of the object being evaluated, and if scores on another indicator are distributed like those in Figure 14.3, indicating that respondents cluster more around neutral in their responses to the object being evaluated, the two indicators don't have the same variance. (Review the concept of variance in Chapter 2, if necessary.)

We have to manipulate the scores so that they come up with the same variance as well as the same scale. We do this by translating the variance into 1.0 in much the same way we translated the scores into a new scale—preserving the cases' *ranking* relative to one another and the degree of differentiation between them.

Both things (scale and variance transformations) can be accomplished at the same time by standardizing the variables. We can transform any distribution of a variable into a new scoring system. Regardless of the old scale, mean, and variance, our transformation can give us a variable whose distribution has a mean of 0

FIGURE 14.2 A Bimodal Distribution, High Variance

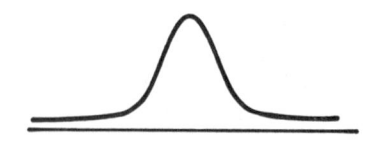

FIGURE 14.3 A Unimodal Distribution, Low Variance

and a variance of 1.0. In effect, we create a new set of scores that indicate how far above or below the mean of the variable a case is *in standard deviation units*. (Review standard deviation in Chapter 2, if necessary.)

We create this new scoring system on each variable by subtracting the mean of a variable from each case's actual score on that variable and dividing by the standard deviation of that variable: $(X_i - \overline{X})/s \cdot d$. The result is a new variable that is equivalent to the old one except that its scale and variance are standardized. Each case now has a score on this new variable that can be used in further analyses.

Recall that in Chapter 2 you worked with standard deviations; you laid out the scores of a variable along a line, drew the distribution of the variable similar to that shown in Figure 14.4, and marked the points on the scale where 1 s.d. above and below the mean would be.

Once you have gone through the process of standardizing scores, you can begin to talk in terms of standard deviation units rather than in terms of the actual scores of the variable, as if you were looking at those distributions in Chapter 2 and seeing standard deviation units as the scales of measurement rather than scores. Rather than giving the actual score of a case, you could say that it was 1.3 s.d. units above the mean or .5 s.d. below the mean. You wouldn't even have to know the actual range and distribution of scores to get an idea of where that case lay relative to other cases.

Talking in terms of standard deviation units also lets you compare variables that may have very different scales and talk about a case's relative position on several variables of different scales. A case could be 1.5 s.d. units above the mean on one variable and .2 s.d. units below the mean on another. That case's standard score (in standard deviation units) is +1.5 on the first variable and −.2 on the second. Those scores let you know that the case is relatively high, compared to other cases, on the first variable and a bit lower than most cases on the second variable.

However, this standardizing process won't get you a distribution of scores that is nicely symmetrical and smooth unless you start out with a distribution that is. The process merely pushes and pulls the scores so that you get a mean of 0 and a variance of 1.0. If you start out with a skewed set of scores, you will end up with one. If you start out with a dichotomy, you will end up with one.

What you gain are equal variances and equivalent scales of measurement and comparability. You don't gain more precision or a more symmetrical distribution. Be careful lest you trick yourself into thinking you have worked magic rather than just a data manipulation.

Creating a Scale

Once the standardizing is done for every indicator you wish to combine into a multi-item index, all the variables have the same scale (roughly from −3 to +3), and all have the same variance, 1.0. You can then add up the scores on all the standardized indicators, which will now have equal weight, to give each case a score on a new overall index that measures the overall concept.

Now think through what you need to do:

1. Find multiple indicators of the concept.
2. Make sure they are all correlated in the "right" direction so that you are at least partially sure the indicators are all measuring the same concept. [Sometimes you will find high scores on one indicator and low scores on another indicating the same "end" of the concept. For example, you might have two items on which people are asked to answer from "agree strongly" to "disagree strongly" on a 1 to 5 scale. On one item, agreeing strongly might indicate support for something while, on another item, support for the same thing might be indicated by disagreeing strongly. One or the other of these will need to be recoded

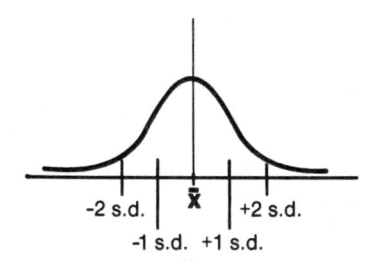

Figure 14.4 Distribution of Standard Scores

so that all indicators have high scores, indicating high levels of the concept. *Without* such recodes, prior to checking the correlations, some correlations will be negative; and, *without* such recodes prior to adding the variables into the index, you will be subtracting when you think you are adding, and vice versa. The only way to avoid such recoding is to *subtract* the reversed concepts rather than to add them. This can confuse you; and I recommend the recodes.

3. Get means and standard deviations on each indicator.
4. Construct standard scores on each indicator.
5. Add standard scores together for the overall index.

We are assuming that each case was measured on every variable to be added up for the overall index (i.e., you have no missing data). If you do have data missing for some cases, two solutions are possible: (1) average the indicators (as we did in the grade-point example when not everyone had the same number of hours) by dividing the total of the scores for each case by the number of indicators on which that case was measured; or (2) drop any case on which not all indicators were measured from any analyses which use this index.

Generally speaking (unless there are reasons for trying to save every possible case in research involving small numbers of cases), it is preferable to drop the case that has missing data on one or more indicators. We simply don't know whether it would be similar on the unmeasured indicators to its score on the measured indicators. Thus, we probably avoid more error by dropping the case.

STANDARD SCORES AND STANDARDIZED SLOPES

Now that you have a handle on standard scores, we can go back and talk about standardized slopes in a regression analysis—something that was hinted at in Chapter 13.

Whenever you want to talk about which independent variable has more or less effect than other independent variables on a dependent variable, you need to get the independent variables measured on the same scale so that you can compare their effects on the dependent variable. Unless you can, comparing the two slopes would be like comparing a one-dollar increase to a one-year increase.

Fortunately, you don't even have to standardize your variables to get comparability. You can standardize the slopes themselves, so they reflect what would happen if the measures were standardized—the effects of a one-standard-deviation-unit change in X compared to a one-standard-deviation-unit-change in Z.

Standard partial slopes (sometimes called *beta weights*) are calculated by the formulae in 14.1 below:

FORMULA 14.1
Standardized Partial Slopes

$$b^*_{yx \cdot z} = b_{yx \cdot z} \frac{S_x}{S_y} \qquad b^*_{yz \cdot x} = b_{yz \cdot x} \frac{S_z}{S_y}$$

In other words, the standard partial slope equals the partial slope multiplied by the ratio of the standard deviations of the independent to the dependent variable (both standard deviations uncontrolled).

The standardized partial slope gives the relationship of two variables (controlling others) *in terms of* standard-deviation units. When you go up one standard-deviation unit on X, how many standard deviation units of change do you expect in Y when other variables are controlled? Remember that, to get slopes in terms of what happens to a dependent variable when an independent increases by one standard-deviation unit, you don't have to standardize the scores themselves. Standardizing the slopes gives you the same effect.

Two words of caution are in order. First, when there are correlated independent variables, the regression process denies to either independent the effect that could be caused by either; that is, the slope (or standardized slope) represents only the *direct* effect of that variable not any indirect effects. Thus, when you say that one has more or less effect than the other, make sure you are clearly saying that one has more or less *direct* effect.

Second, you can compare standardized effects of independent variables only within a single sample. You can't say (using a standardized slope) that one independent variable has more effect in one sample than in the same analysis for another sample.

It is standardizing by the standard deviations (and, thus, variances) in a sample that keeps these standard slopes from being comparable across samples; variances are too different across samples to allow these to be comparable. Remember that there's a similar problem with correlation coefficients. They are, in effect, standardized to sample variance and aren't comparable from one sample to another. Remember the interpretation of the formula for the correlation coefficient in Chapter 5—how much of the variation in X and Y is covariation. It is unlikely that we can find samples that have the same amounts of variation in the variables; and, as a result, it is not possible to say that an r of a certain value in one sample is the same as an r of the same value in another sample. Similarities and differences may owe as much to the amount of variance as to the relationship of the variables.

If you need to compare effects of an independent variable across samples, use the unstandardized slope and make sure your measurement scale is the same in both samples. Since the unstandardized slopes depend only on the variances in the independent variable, they are less subject to comparability problems, especially when your measurement of the independent is as precise as possible.

You don't have to calculate any standard slopes for this chapter. Just learn to find them on REGRESSION output and to interpret them. They are in a column (like slopes) labeled Beta.

EXERCISE 1 Creating and Using Multi-indicator Indices Composed of Standardized Variables

For this chapter's exercises, think of a hypothesis that uses two independent variables (or one independent and a control variable) whose concepts can be operationalized using variables from one of the data sets that accompany the text. For at least one of the operationalizations, look for indicators you can combine into a single measure. The indicators to be combined must technically be interval but ordinal will do. The other two variables should be as close to interval as possible; that is, you are to construct a three-variable hypothesis and model—one dependent and two other variables. At least one of these must be operationalized as a multi-item index; the other two may be single-item indicators but must be as close to interval as possible.

Write the hypothesized relationships among the three variables. Pay attention to stating the form of the relationship; write so as to make the independent variable clear and distinct from the dependent variable; write in the plural; and imply whether it is a cross-sectional or a longitudinal test.

Now that you have multiple independent variables, some indication of how those two work together should be indicated in the hypothesis even if it takes you two sentences to get it all in. Examples follow: (intervening), as X increases, Z increases as a result, in turn increasing Y; (spurious), Z increases both X and Y, which are not themselves directly related; (two independent explanatory variables), X decreases Y, while Z independently increases Y.

Remember that, for regression to provide an appropriate statistical test of your hypotheses, *all* the relationships implied must be linear. The uncontrolled relationship between X and Y must be linear; the uncontrolled XZ and YZ relationships must be linear. The partials between each pair of variables controlling for the third must by hypothesized to be linear.

And you really ought to argue and/or show that there is no statistical interaction before interpreting partial slopes or partial correlations. You may skip demonstrating this step for this practice exercise, but do not here or anywhere apply multiple regression of the sort we have been discussing if you *hypothesize* that the XY relationship is specified by Z.

(You will learn how to test for this specification in Chapter 16.)

Write down your operationalization of each variable from the hypotheses, listing the indicator or set of indicators that you will use to measure the concepts suggested by the conceptual variables in the hypotheses. Remember that a good operationalization is so clear that another political scientist could pick it up and use it with no more information than you supply in the description of the measurement.

Now run CORRELATIONS to make sure all the variables in *each* potential multi-item scale are correlated appropriately. (Review Chapter 6, if necessary, for this test that approximates a measure for inter-item reliability.)

While you are at the computer, also use DESCRIPTIVES for all variables in all your multi-item indices to get the means and standard deviations you will need. You are going to standardize the variables themselves because you want to add them up into a single index for use in REGRESSION as an independent, a dependent, or a control variable. While the REGRESSION output gives you a standardized slope, it is important to remember that the standardized slopes are interpreted in terms of standard deviation units of the variables *in* the regression equation (*not* of all the indicators that were combined for those variables). You still get stuck standardizing the indicators themselves when what you are doing is building an index (rather than interpreting regression equations).

You are using the SPSS file already set up for you; remember the commands you need:

The relevant accessing information
RECODE, if necessary
CORRELATIONS (refer to Chapter 6 or the SPSS manual)
DESCRIPTIVES (refer to Chapter 3 or the SPSS manual)

Are the items appropriately correlated for multi-item scales? From the CORRELATIONS output, write out the matrix for the correlations among the items for the multi-item scale or scales you are using. Circle any items you will not use and indicate why.

Examine the means and standard deviations for each variable from the DESCRIPTIVES output. You will need them for the next part of the exercise.

Now, using just the indicators that fit the criteria for a multi-item scale, set up another computer run, construct the multi-item indices, and run the regression necessary to test your hypotheses. To do this, use the same accessing information and any necessary recodes (such as you used above) to get file variables coded in the right direction.

Then, after the recodes, you need to construct a COMPUTE statement for each indicator to be standardized. The COMPUTE statement outlined below does the standardizing for you. Where it says "newname," invent a new, unique variable name for the new standardized form of your old variable. Substitute the name of the variable to be standardized and the mean and standard deviation from the DESCRIPTIVES output for that variable. Where it says "name1," put in the name of your first variable; for "name2," put in the name of your second variable, etc. Where it says "mean1," put in the mean of your first variable, etc. Where it says "s1," put in the standard deviation of your first variable, etc.

```
COMPUTE newname1 = ((name1 -
    mean1)/s1).
COMPUTE newname2 = ((name2 -
    mean2)/s2).
```

Add another line for each additional variable to be standardized.*

When I use COMPUTE statements for such standardizing, I always stop here and run DESCRIPTIVES to make sure all my variables now have mean = 0 and variance = 1. That's

---

*DESCRIPTIVES will calculate the standardized scores for you, and in the future, you may want to take advantage of that. Doing it yourself here will help you see what is going on and will introduce you to COMPUTE statements.

because I don't trust my typing and copying. You can just go on if you feel secure.

Now add an additional COMPUTE statement to add up the standardized indicators on each scale you are constructing, remembering to add up the standardized rather than the unstandardized variables. Make up a name for each index you are computing and put it in place of "scalename."

```
COMPUTE scalename1 =
  (newname1 +
  newname2 + newname3, etc.).
COMPUTE scalename2 =
  (newname4 +
  newname5 + newname6, etc.).
```

Add a new line for each scale whose components must be summed. You don't have to worry about cases that are missing on one of the indicators. SPSS will automatically drop them out (declare them missing) on the overall index.

Now add the necessary subcommands on a REGRESSION command to test your hypothesis (review Chapter 13 or the SPSS manual). The variables on the variable list are: (1) the new scale names you invented for the multi-item indices; and (2) any names of single items you have used to operationalize your concepts.

To summarize this computer run, you need—

The accessing information

Any RECODE statements necessary

As many COMPUTE statements as necessary, (1) to standardize indicators for multi-item indices, and (2) to add up indicators for multi-item indices

A REGRESSION command

And a FINISH command, if necessary

Finally, interpret what you've got by answering the questions below. Write your answers after your hypotheses and operationalizations. Then, be sure to compare your work to that of colleagues working on different variables. You might find it helpful to tell each other what your hypotheses were, why you operationalized the variables as you did, and what you found in the analyses.

In answering the questions that follow, use the names of your variables where you would ordinarily use X, Y, or Z to designate them or where you would ordinarily call them the independent, dependent, or control variable. Also, instead of just writing out the value of the statistic for each question, write the names of the relevant variable and the relevant statistic name. For example, don't just put in the value of r^2; say, "The Pearson r^2 between efficacy and participation is .25." Having the names of the statistics and the names of your variables rather than the other designations will make checking your answers easier.

1. What is the strength of the bivariate correlation between the independent and the dependent variables? What is the form of the effect of the independent variable on the dependent variable?

2. What is the strength of the bivariate correlation between the independent variable and the control variable? What is the form of that relationship?

3. What is the strength of the partial correlation between the independent and dependent variables when the second independent/control variable is controlled? What is the form of the direct effect of the independent on the dependent variable?

4. What is happening between the independent and the dependent when the effects of the other variable are controlled? (Is XY found to be spurious? Is Z intervening between X and Y? Was Z suppressing the XY relationship? Are both X and Z contributing to explanation of Y? Or what?) How do you know? Be sure to refer to the partial slopes as well as the partial correlation coefficients in your answer.

5. How would you draw the linkages between your independent, dependent, and control variables in a three-variable diagram to show what is going on in the multivariate analysis? Put signs on the arrows on diagrams.

6. If you were predicting values on the dependent variable from scores on the two independent variables, what equation would you use?

7. What proportion of the variation in the dependent variable is explained by both the independent variables?

8. Controlling for one independent variable, a one-standard-deviation-unit increase in the other independent variable produces how many standard-deviation-units increase in the dependent variable.
9. Controlling for the other independent variable, a one-standard-deviation-unit increase in the first independent variable produces how many standard-deviation-units increase in the dependent variable.
10. Which independent variable has the more important impact on the dependent? What do you look at to tell?

SUGGESTED READINGS

SPSS References on Regression, Compute, and Standard Scores

NORUSIS, MARIJA J. *SPSS/PC+* (Chicago: SPSS, Inc., 1988). Chapter 4, pp. B24–B37 discusses data transformation; Section 4.6 and following is on COMPUTE. The commands for COMPUTE are on pp. C24–C27. Regression is covered in Chapter 17, pp. B196–B243, and pp. C125–C146. DESCRIPTIVES is in Chapter 8, pp. B80–B91, and pp. C50–C53.

SPSS User's Guide, 3rd ed. (Chicago: SPSS, Inc., 1988). Section 7.11 and following is on COMPUTE, p. 117; Chapter 45 is on REGRESSION, pp. 848–870; Chapter 26 is on DESCRIPTIVES, pp. 428–453; Section 26.4 is on Z scores.

Standard Scores

BOWEN, BRUCE D., and HERBERT F. WEISBERG. *An Introduction to Data Analysis* (San Francisco: Freeman, 1980), pp. 117–118.

BLALOCK, HUBERT M. *Social Statistics*, 2nd ed. (NY: McGraw-Hill, 1972), pp. 99–101.

Note: Both of the above deal with standard scores (Z scores) in the context of the normal distribution, which has not yet been discussed. (Don't worry about it.)

KOHOUT, FRANK. *Statistics for Social Scientists* (N.Y.: Wiley, 1974), pp. 50–53.

Multiple Regression

ACHEN, CHRISTOPHER. *Interpreting and Using Regression*, # 29 in series, *Quantitative Applications in the Social Sciences* (Beverly Hills, CA: Sage, 1982).

BABBIE, EARL R. *The Practice of Social Research*, 2nd ed. (Belmont, CA: Wadsworth, 1979), pp. 499–507.

BERENSON, MARK L., DAVID M. LEVINE, and MATTHEW GOLDSTEIN. *Intermediate Statistical Methods and Applications: A Computer Package Approach* (Englewood Cliffs, NJ: Prentice-Hall, 1983), Chs. 13 and 14. These chapters are rather advanced; the first is on evaluating various models, and the second is on violating the assumptions.

BERRY, WM. D., and STANLEY FELDMAN. *Multiple Regression in Practice*, # 50 in series, *Quantitative Applications in the Social Sciences* (Beverly Hills, CA: Sage, 1985).

BLALOCK, HUBERT M., JR. *Social Statistics*, 2nd ed. (N.Y.: McGraw-Hill, 1972), Ch. 19.

BOWEN, BRUCE, and HERBERT F. WEISBERG. *An Introduction to Data Analysis* (San Francisco: Freeman, 1980), pp. 157–63.

DRAPER, N.R., and H. SMITH. *Applied Regression Analysis* (N.Y.: Wiley, 1966), Ch. 4.

HANNUSHEK, ERIC A., and JOHN E. JACKSON. *Statistical Methods for Social Scientists* (N.Y.: Academic Press, 1977), Ch. 5. A more advanced text. You may find it either quite useful or quite confusing.

KERLINGER, FRED N., and ELAZAR J. PEDHAZUR. *Multiple Regression in Behavioral Research* (N.Y.: Holt, Rinehart, and Winston, 1973), Part I.

KLEINBAUM, DAVID G., and LAWRENCE L. KUPPER. *Applied Regression Analysis* (North Scituate, MA: Duxbury, 1978), Chs. 10–12.

SHIVELY, W. PHILLIPS. *The Craft of Political Research*, 2nd ed. (Englewood Cliffs, NJ: Prentice–Hall, 1980), pp. 145–150.

WONNACOTT, Thomas H., and Ronald J. Wonnacott. *Regression: A Second Course in Statistics* (N.Y.: Wiley, 1981), Ch. 3.

Index Construction—
More Advanced Considerations

KRUSKAL, JOSEPH B., and MYRON WISH. *Multidimensional Scaling*, # 11 in series, *Quantitative Applications in the Social Sciences* (Beverly Hills, CA: Sage, 1978).

LODGE, MILTON. *Magnitude Scaling*, # 25 in series, *Quantitative Applications in the Social Sciences* (Beverly Hills, CA: Sage, 1981).

McIVER, JOHN P., and EDWARD G. CARMINES. *Unidimensional Scaling*, # 24 in series, *Quantitative Applications in the Social Sciences* (Beverly Hills, CA: Sage, 1981).

SULLIVAN, JOHN L., and STANLEY FELDMAN. *Multiple Indicators*, # 15 in series, *Quantitative Applications in the Social Sciences* (Beverly Hills, CA: 1979).

ARTICLES

Many of these articles make use of path analysis, an extension of multivariate regression and standardized slopes. Path analysis uses standardized partial slopes, controlling for all prior and intervening variables in a model, to measure the direct effect of one variable on another. After computing that standardized partial slope for every two-variable linkage in the model, the researcher can assess total (direct plus indirect) effects of one variable on another.

ERIKSON, ROBERT S. "Constituency Opinion and Congressional Behavior: A Re-examination of the Miller-Stokes Representation Data," *American Journal of Political Science*, 22 (August 1978), 511-535. May be difficult. An extension of multiple regression. First, shows that correlation between actual population characteristics of congressional districts and those one would assume from usual national survey results broken down into aggregate measures for congressional districts are low; suggests survey results don't reliably measure opinions of congressional districts. Second, uses regression to predict individual-level opinion on basis of several independent variables. Third, uses those same independent variables measured at the aggregate level to estimate aggregate opinion in congressional district. Fourth, uses estimated (simulated) opinion to assess, with path analysis, the congressional district opinion link with roll-call behavior of members of Congress.

PUTNAM, ROBERT D., ROBERT LEONARDI, and RAFFAELLA Y. NANETTI. "Attitude Stability among Italian Elites," *American Journal of Political Science*, 23 (August 1979), 463-493. First mentioned in Chapter 5; uses path analysis to assess degree to which stability is due to partisanship.

SPALDING, NANCY L. "Providing for Economic Human Rights: The Case of the Third World," *Policy Studies Journal*, 15 (September 1986), 123-134. Uses path analysis. Article explains "well-being" in a country as dependent on political as well as economic factors. Clear operationalizations and concern for measurement. System-level measurement.

THOMAS, DAN, and LARRY A. BAAS. "Presidential Identification and Mass-Public Compliance with Official Policy: The Case of the Carter Energy Program," *Policy Studies Journal,* 10 (March 1982), 448-465. Attempt to sort out contributions of self-interest, identification with president, and diffuse system support in people's energy-saving efforts. Clear statement of theoretical rationale for explanatory factors. Indices created from summed standard scores, for the measure of diffuse support, from intra-individual correlations on respondents' assessment of Carter and own ideal self on 50 personality items, from simple addition of items measuring attitudinal and behavioral support for conservatism policies, and from addition of weighted items measuring support for resource development. Simple Pearson correlation and multiple correlation. Standardized regression coefficients. Sample recognized as limited.

CHAPTER 15

TWO-WAY ANALYSIS OF VARIANCE

ANALYSIS OF VARIANCE WITH UNCORRELATED INDEPENDENT VARIABLES

A Regression Interpretation

When you have less than interval independent and control variables explaining an interval dependent variable, one appropriate technique is analysis of variance. When there are only two independent variables (or an independent and a control), the technique is called two-way analysis of variance, but the logic can be extended to more than two explanatory factors.

An easy way to consider two-way analysis of variance is to think of it in terms of regression. That keeps the relationship between the two techniques clear and lets you review multiple regression as you learn the new procedure. It also prepares you for the next chapter.

I'm going to ask you to think, for the moment, in terms of two dichotomous *independent variables* that are *uncorrelated* with each other. Think of explaining a dependent variable using a dichotomous independent variable and then improving that explanation by adding a second one.

The dichotomies might be two treatments in a two-variable experimental design, or they might include many of the concepts we ordinarily use in political science, as in the following examples:

Sex, where 1 = male and 0 = female
Region, where 1 = non-South and 0 = South
City government form, where 1 = manager and 0 = mayor
National government form, where 1 = authoritarian and 0 = democratic

The dependent variable might be any interval variable thought to be affected by, caused by, or dependent on the two independent variables.

Since we are thinking in terms of *uncorrelated* independent variables (with no interaction), we can think of doing two separate, bivariate regressions to analyze the separate effects of the independent variables. We can then combine the results of those two analyses to see what proportion of the variation in the dependent variable we can explain with both independent variables. Let's start by working with just one dichotomy (scored zero and one).

If we regressed an interval dependent variable on a dichotomous independent variable, a plot of the relationship would look something similar to the plot in Figure 15.1. A bivariate regression procedure would get us the intercept and slope in the model $Y_p = a + bX + e$. The

FIGURE 15.1 Interval Dependent Plotted on Dichotomous Independent Variable

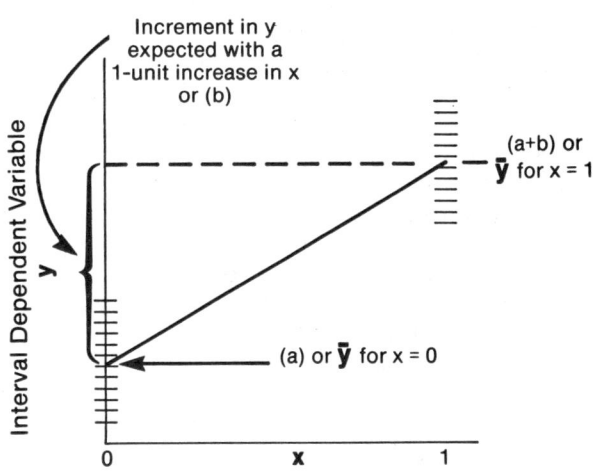

FIGURE 15.2 Interpretation of Slope with Dichotomous Independent Variables

slope, b, represents the amount that the predicted value of Y is incremented for every one-unit increase in X. But with a dichotomous independent variable, there is only the increment from 0 to 1; X doesn't have any other values. If you were predicting values on the dependent variable from cases' values on the independent variable, there would only be two possible predictions: $a + b(0)$, where the product of the slope and 0 drops out because b times 0 is 0, or $a + b(1)$. Thus, the intercept, as always, is the predicted (mean) dependent variable score for all those cases scored 0 on X, and $a + b$ is the predicted (mean) dependent variable value for all those cases that have a score of 1 on X, as is illustrated in Figure 15.2.

Thus, the form of the relationship between X and Y is described by the slope, as it ordinarily is in a regression. With a dichotomous independent variable, however, we can also think of that slope as representing the difference of dependent variable means for the two different groups of cases defined by the independent variable—the difference between a and $(a + b)$.

For the strength of the relationship between X and Y, the r^2 from regression will give us the proportion of variation in Y explained by X. Remember that r^2 indicates how closely clustered around the regression line the cases are. Here, as in any regression, the error around the line, which represents variation in Y that cannot be explained by X, is the predicted value of Y taken from the actual value of Y for each case squared and summed across all cases, $\Sigma (Y_i - Y_p)^2$. It's just that now there are only two predicted values ($\overline{Y}_1$ for $X = 0$ and $\overline{Y}_2$ for $X = 1$) to worry about.

If we take that unexplained variation around the line, subtract it from the overall variation in Y, $\Sigma (Y_i - \overline{Y}_{..})^2$, and divide by the overall variation, we have the proportion of variation in Y that is explained by X. (Remember we use $\overline{Y}_{..}$ to emphasize that we are talking about the variation around the mean of Y that is figured on all the cases.) This r^2 is exactly equivalent, as you will see, to an E^2 in analysis of variance.

Now imagine we took another dichotomous independent variable (Z), uncorrelated with the first, and did exactly the same things with it. If we regressed Y on Z in another bivariate regression, we'd get another equation, $Y_p = a + b_2 Z + e$. The intercept would represent the average value of Y for all the cases scored 0 on Z; $a + b_2$ would represent the average value of

198 TWO-WAY ANALYSIS OF VARIANCE

Y for all the cases scored 1 on Z; and b_2 could be interpreted as the difference of means of Y for the categories of Z. And we could again figure the variation around those means, subtract it from the overall variation in Y, and get another r^2_{zy} (identical to E^2_{zy}) for the proportion of variation in Y explained by Z.

Then we could add the two r^2s—from the two separate bivariate regressions—together to get the total proportion of the variation in Y that was explained by both X and Z ($R^2_{y \cdot xz}$), which would be the equivalent to $E^2_{y \cdot xz}$ in analysis of variance terms.

It would be easier to get the forms of the effects of both X and Z on Y, as well as the proportion of variation in Y explained by them both, in a single, multivariate regression rather than doing the separate, bivariate regressions we have been talking about. A single analysis would also give us a chance to look at the effects of the two independent variables at the same time, rather than looking at the differences in Y caused by X and, in a separate analysis, the differences in Y caused by Z. If you will imagine a distribution of cases like that in Figure 15.3, we can see how such a multiple regression would work.*

In Figure 15.3, you can still see the distributions of the scores on Y when X is 0 and when X is 1, just as you saw them in Figure 15.1. A regression on these data would give us a slope that would connect the means of the two Y distributions, just as it did in Figure 15.1.

Here in Figure 15.3, however, you can also see that the top half of the cases in both the Y distributions are cases that are scored 1 on Z. So, in the scatterplot represented by Figure 15.3, you can see that X has an effect in increasing Y but also that Z has a similar effect. We want to be able to describe the effect of X on Y and the effect of Z on Y, simultaneously.

Doing a multiple regression with two dichotomous independent variables and an interval dependent variable will give us the ordinary multivariate prediction equation:

$$Y_p = a + b_1 X + b_2 Z + e.$$

We can also show how that equation describes all the data in Figure 15.3.

First, imagine connecting the mean of the Y scores when X is 0 and Z is 1 to the mean of the Y scores when X is 1 and Z is 1. That would give you the top slope in Figure 15.4. If you could get a statistic to describe that line, it would represent the difference in the predicted Y scores between cases scored 0 on X and cases scored 1 on X. (Z is not varying for those two sets of cases, so it can be having no effect.)

Next, imagine connecting the mean of the Y scores when X is 0 and Z is 0 to the mean of the Y scores when X is 1 and Z is 0. That would give you the bottom slope in Figure 15.4. If you could get a statistic to describe that line, it would represent the difference in the predicted Y scores between cases scored 0 on X and cases scored 1 on X. (Z is not varying for those two sets of cases, so it can be having no effect here either.)

Notice that the effect of X on Y is the same,

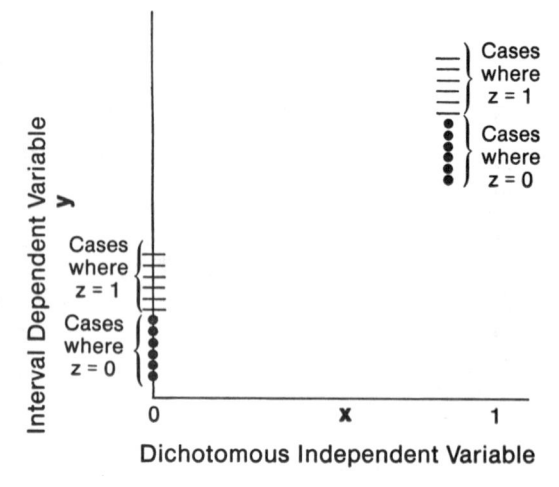

FIGURE 15.3 Scatterplot of Two Dichotomous Independent Variables and an Interval Dependent Variable

---

*Notice that there are the same numbers of cases for $Z = 1$ and $Z = 0$ for both 0 and 1 X. This is evidence that X and Z are uncorrelated.

TWO-WAY ANALYSIS OF VARIANCE   199

Figure 15.4 Scatterplot of Two Dichotomous Independent Variables and an Interval Dependent Variable with Slopes

regardless of whether Z is 1 or 0. The slopes are parallel. When you go up one unit on X, the effect on Y is the same when Z is 0 as when Z is 1. (That is what we mean when we say that there is no interaction.) It means that b_1 from the multiple regression equation represents that effect of X on Y that we want described in Figure 15.3—the difference in the means of Y comparing those cases scored 0 on X with those scored 1 on X.*

Next, we need the effects of Z on Y. For that, imagine yourself comparing the Y mean for those cases scored 0 on Z to the Y mean for those cases scored 1 on Z in Figure 15.3. Do that both for the cases where $X = 0$ (and does not vary, so it cannot be affecting Y for these cases) and the cases where $X = 1$ (and again is not varying, so it cannot be affecting Y). You can see that more clearly on Figure 15.4, where you can see the difference in the two intercepts on the Y axis and the difference between the two points indicated by the other ends of the slopes.

---

*Were X and Z correlated, the slopes might still be parallel, if there were no interaction, but there would be unequal numbers of cases for Z_1 across X_0 and X_1 and for Z_0 across X_0 and X_1.

You need a statistic to describe this effect of Z. Think through the comparison you just made: you varied Z from 0 to 1 (both when X was 0 and when X was 1) and looked at the effect of varying Z on the predicted value of Y. The effect was the same, regardless of the value of X; the distance between the two means of Y when X was 0 was the same as when X was 1. The effect on Y of a one-unit increase in Z is represented by b_2 in the multiple regression equation and can be interpreted as the difference of dependent variable means when Z is 1 compared to when Z is 0. (That the effects of Z are the same, b_2, regardless of value of X, is another indication of what we mean by there being no statistical interaction.)

If we take the multiple regression equation apart, you can see more clearly that there are within it two prediction equations—one that describes the bottom line for those cases scored 0 on Z and another that describes the top line for those cases scored 1 on Z. When $Z = 0$, the multivariate regression equation might as well be $Y_p = a + b_1 X + e$ because zero (the value of Z) times $b_2 = 0$, and that term drops out of the prediction.

When $Z = 1$, that equation might as well be $Y_p = a + b_1 X + b_2 + e$ because Z doesn't vary; it takes on only a value of 1, and b_2 times $1 = b_2$. This means that the slope attached to Z can be simply added in as a constant every time Z equals 1, so we can simply rewrite the equation for cases where $Z = 1$ as $Y_p = (a + b_2) + b_1 X + e$.

The only difference between the two equations

$Y_p = a + b_1 X + e$ (when Z is 0), and
$Y_p = (a + b_2) + b_1 X + e$ (when Z is 1)

is that the intercept is higher in the second. Thus, we are saying that the effect of Z is to increase Y by the difference in the two intercepts (b_2); on average, cases scored 1 on Z are b_2 units higher than are cases scored 0 on Z. And it is that difference of intercepts that you can see in Figure 15.4.

Because X and Z are uncorrelated and there

is no interaction, the multivariate regression gives you exactly the same indication of their effects on Y as the two bivariate regressions did. When you compare the multivariate equation $Y = a + b_1 X + b_2 Z + e$ to the two bivariate equations, you see that the b_1 in the multivariate equation is the same as the slope in the bivariate $Y = a + bX + e$. And b_2 from the multivariate is the same as the slope in the bivariate $Y = a + bZ + e$.

If we need an estimate of what the dependent variable means are for the four groups defined by the two independent variables (rather than just the *difference* of means that we get from the two slopes), we can just plug the relevant values of the two independent variables into the prediction equation, $Y = a + b_1 X + b_2 Z + e$.

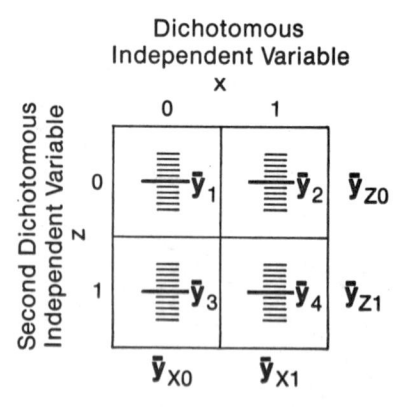

Figure 15.5 Dependent Variable Means within Categories Created by Two Dichotomous Independent Variables

When X is 0 and Z is 0, $Y_p = a$
When X is 0 and Z is 1, $Y_p = a + b_2$
When X is 1 and Z is 0, $Y_p = a + b_1$
When X is 1 and Z is 1, $Y_p = a + b_1 + b_2$

Those values of Y predicted by the two independent variables, then, give us the means. We can compare the actual values of Y for our cases against those predicted values, square the differences and sum them—$\Sigma (Y_i - Y_p)^2$—and determine what proportion of the overall variation in Y—$\Sigma (Y_i - \overline{Y}_{..})^2$—is explained using both X and Z as independent variables.

From the multiple regression analysis, that measure of the strength of the relationship between Y and both X and Z is given by the multiple R^2 ($R^2_{y \cdot xz}$). For uncorrelated independent variables, it is equivalent to the sum of the two bivariate r^2s. And the multiple $R^2_{y \cdot xz}$ is equivalent to the multiple $E^2_{y \cdot xz}$, which you would get from a two-way analysis of variance on the same data.

Thinking about Two-way Analysis of Variance

Now let's work through the same ideas using concepts that are more like analysis of variance and less like regression, so that we can show how similar they are. For the moment, we will still deal with two uncorrelated independent variables (and assume no statistical interaction).

Imagine a distribution of dependent variable scores within the cells created from the values of the two independent variables, such as in Figure 15.5. (Don't confuse this with a crosstabulation table that has counts of cases in the cells. Here, in the cells, we have a *distribution* of scores on an interval dependent variable, Y.)*

First, let's figure the effect of X on Y in a bivariate analysis. To do this, consider all the cases in the first column where $X = 0$ (regardless of whether they are scored 0 or 1 on Z). You figure their mean on Y ($\overline{Y}_{x0}$ in the figure) and how much variation there is around that mean, considering all the cases in that column, $\Sigma (Y_i - \overline{Y}_{x0})^2$. Now take all the cases in the second column where $X = 1$ (regardless of whether they are scored 0 or 1 on Z). You figure their mean on Y ($\overline{Y}_{x1}$ in the figure) and how much variation there is around that mean considering all the cases in that second column, $\Sigma (Y_i - \overline{Y}_{x1})^2$.

---

*That the number of cases in X_0 and X_1 is the same for Z_0 and Z_1 is evidence of the absence of correlation between X and Z.

Add those two variations together, and you have the variation unexplained by X. If you subtract that from the total variation in Y, $\Sigma (Y_i - \overline{Y}_.)^2$, and divide the result by the total variation in Y (just like any PRE statistic), you get E^2_{xy}, the proportion of variation in Y explained by X, the strength of the relationship between X and Y.

The form of the relationship between X and Y is found by comparing the two means of Y—the mean of Y when X is 0 to the mean of Y when X is 1 ($\overline{Y}_{x0}$ compared to $\overline{Y}_{x1}$). The difference between those two means of Y is how much effect X is having on Y.

Second, let's do a bivariate analysis to look at the effect of Z on Y. Here you do exactly the same thing, but you take all the cases in the row indicated as cases scored 0 on Z first (regardless of their scores on X). Figure a mean of Y ($\overline{Y}_{z0}$ in the figure) for all the cases in that row, and compute the variation around the mean for all of them, $\Sigma (Y_i - \overline{Y}_{z0})^2$. Now take all the cases that are scored 1 on Z (regardless of their scores on X), figure a mean of Y ($\overline{Y}_{z1}$) for them, and compute the variation for them, $\Sigma (Y_i - \overline{Y}_{z1})^2$.

If you now add up those two variations, you have the variation in Y that is unexplained by Z. Again, if you follow the ordinary formula for a PRE statistic, you can subtract that unexplained variation in Y from the total variation in Y, $\Sigma (Y_i - \overline{Y}_.)^2$, and divide by the total variation in Y to get the strength of the relationship between Z and Y—the proportion of variation in Y explained by Z, or E^2_{zy}.

The form of the relationship between Z and Y can be seen by comparing the means of Y when $Z = 0$ and when $Z = 1$ (i.e., comparing $\overline{Y}_{z0}$ to $\overline{Y}_{z1}$). The difference between those two means indicates the impact of Z on Y.

It is a simple matter to add the two bivariate E^2 statistics together to get the proportion of the variation in Y explained by both X and Z together, $E^2_{xy} + E^2_{zy} = E^2_{y \cdot xz}$ (because of the uncorrelated independent variables, remember).

Because X and Z are uncorrelated and because there is no statistical interaction, the procedure above—figuring the proportion explained by X and adding it to the proportion explained by Z, as you did in the two bivariate analyses—gives you exactly the same results as you would get if you considered the effects of the two independent variables simultaneously in a multivariate analysis, as you will see next.

If we were trying to examine the effects of X and Z simultaneously, we would look at the means of the dependent variable within the cells rather than the means of the dependent variable first for the categories of X and then, separately, for the categories of Z. We would divide the cases, as you can see in Figure 15.5, into four groups. The first group is all the cases in which both X and Z equal zero; the second is all the cases on which $X = 1$ and $Z = 0$, and so forth.

With the cases in four groups, you can calculate a mean of the dependent variable for the cases within each of the four groups. You can then figure how much variation in Y is still unexplained by X and Z by comparing cases' actual scores on the dependent variable to their mean in the group and summing those variations for all four groups:

$$[\Sigma (Y_{i1} - \overline{Y}_1)^2 + \Sigma (Y_{i2} - \overline{Y}_2)^2 + \Sigma (Y_{i3} - \overline{Y}_3)^2 + \Sigma (Y_{i4} - \overline{Y}_4)^2].$$

That will give you the variation unexplained by *both* X and Z, the variation around the cell means.

The multiple $E^2_{y \cdot xz}$ that is used to describe the strength of the relationship between Y and both X and Z is given by subtracting the unexplained variation figured in the above paragraph from the total variation in Y, $\Sigma (Y_i - \overline{Y}_.)^2$, dividing that difference by the total variation in Y. That is the same form of the PRE statistic that we have been using all along.

The form of the two relationships is easily read from the group means of Y. The effect of X on Y can be seen in the difference between either $\overline{Y}_1$ and $\overline{Y}_2$ or $\overline{Y}_3$ and $\overline{Y}_4$. The two differences are identical, regardless of whether Z is 0 or 1 (because we are assuming no statistical interaction). The effect of Z on Y can be seen in the difference between either $\overline{Y}_1$ and $\overline{Y}_3$ or $\overline{Y}_2$ and $\overline{Y}_4$; those two differences are identical (again, no interaction). And this reading of the effects of X on Y will be the same as in your bivariate analysis above, where you were comparing the means of Y in the columns, just as this reading of the effects of Z on Y will be the same as your comparison of the means of Y in the rows because X and Z are uncorrelated.

Notice now the similarities between the regression approach to this problem of explaining variation in an interval dependent variable using two dichotomous independent variables and the analysis of variance approach to the same task. Regardless of whether we take a regression approach or an analysis of variance approach, the measures of the strength of the relationship are the same.

Moreover, the measures of the form of the relationship are almost the same, whether they come from slopes or differences of means. The four group means that you computed for doing the analysis of variance were the same as the group means you estimated from the regression equation by plugging relevant independent values in the regression equation, assuming there was no interaction.

Those group means that you got from the regression were estimates based on the assumption that there was no interaction. Those you calculated for the analysis of variance were the actual means of the groups. Any difference between the actual calculation and the estimate from the regression can be attributed to statistical interaction. That complication is what we have to turn to next.

STATISTICAL INTERACTION

The Absence of Interaction

Remember that, when there is no interaction, one variable has the same effect on a dependent variable, regardless of the condition of the other independent variable. Another way of saying this is that one variable does *not* *specify* the conditions under which the other has a particular effect; the effect of the other is the same, regardless of what value the first has. Another way of saying this is that the effects of the two variables are *additive*; you can simply add the effects of one to the effects of the other (remember $b_1 + b_2$) to get the effects of both.

If you look at the cell means outlined in Figure 15.5 and remember the regression equations for Figure 15.3, you will see the following similarities between them.

The difference between Y_1 and Y_2 is b_1, the slope on X.

The difference between Y_3 and Y_4 is b_1, the slope on X.

The difference between Y_1 and Y_3 is b_2, the slope on Z.

The difference between Y_2 and Y_4 is b_2, the slope on Z.

Note that the difference between the top two cells is the same as the difference between the bottom two cells, b_1. The difference between the left two cells is the same as the difference between the right two cells, b_2. This shows that X is having the same effect when Z is 0 and when Z is 1, and that Z is having the same effect when X is 0 and when X is 1.

The Presence of Interaction

What if the effects are not additive? Look at the example in Figure 15.6, where you can see an example of statistical interaction. There you can see that the difference between groups 3 and 4 is not the same as the difference between groups 1 and 2, and the difference between groups 3 and 1 is not the same as the difference between groups 4 and 2.

In regression terms, the slope that represents the effect of X on Y is not the same when Z is 1 as it is when Z is 0; the slope that represents the effect of Z on Y is not the same when X is 1 as it is when X is 0. The effects of one independent variable are not the same at all levels of the other independent variable.

When you've got interaction such as that shown in Figure 15.6, the additive multiple re-

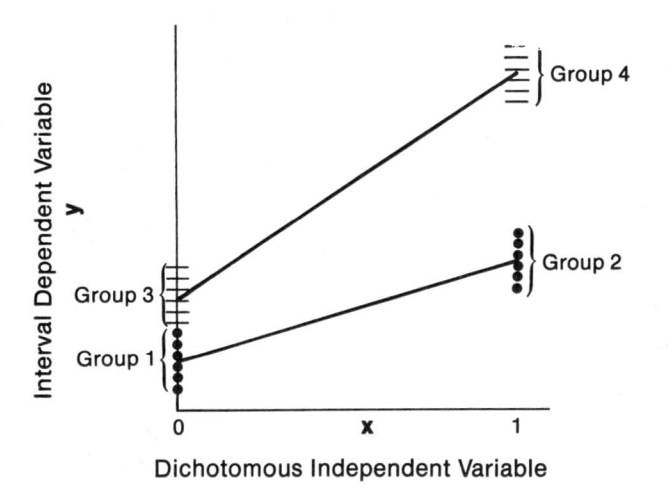

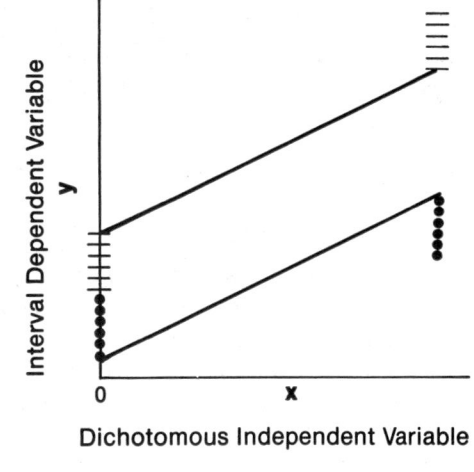

Figure 15.6 Nonadditive Effects of Two Dichotomous Independent Variables

Figure 15.7 Using an Additive Model to Describe Interactive Relationships

gression model we've been using, $Y = a + b_1X + b_2Z + e$, doesn't describe what you can see in the data very well. If you go ahead and apply an ordinary, additive, multiple regression analysis to those data, the "best-fitting" slopes will no longer hit the means of the groups, as they did in Figure 15.3. Because the multiple regression procedure assumes additivity, when you figure out the slopes and intercept in $Y = a + b_1X + b_2Z$, the formulae for calculating the coefficients are going to give you the best-fitting slopes and intercept *within the constraint of additivity*.

You will end up with slopes and intercepts that look something like those in Figure 15.7. Notice that none of the differences of means for any of the pairs of groups is described very well. The single number you get for the slope cannot very well describe both differences of means between groups 3 and 4 and between groups 1 and 2 because those differences are not the same. Nor can a single number describe the differences of means both between groups 1 and 3 and between groups 2 and 4 because those differences are not the same.

If you went on to compute the proportion of variation in Y explained by both X and Z, you would find that proportion very low.

Look at the four groups of cases and where they lie relative to the best-fitting line. Think how much farther they all are off the line than they would be if the line were more in the middle of their respective groups. Think how much variation that leaves unexplained by the line. And you can see the reason for the low multiple R^2.

Similarly, imagine doing an analysis of variance for data in which there was interaction. The differences between the row means would not give you a good description of the effect of Z because its effect (seen in comparing the cell means) would be different depending on the value of X. The difference between the column means would also not give you a good description of the effect of X because the effect of X could not be summarized in a single number; the effect, looking from cell mean to cell mean, would be different depending on the value of Z.

In the analysis of variance, you would also get misleading results about the strength of the relationship between Y and both X and Z if you calculated a multiple $E^2_{y \cdot xz}$ by just adding up the two bivariate E^2s (figured from the row and column means) for the proportions of the variation in Y explained by X and Z separately. When their interaction is taken into account, X and Z together explain substantially more of the variation in Y than the total of their separate E^2s would indicate. Variation around the row and column means is substantially greater than variation around the actual cell means.

Dealing with Interaction

When there is interaction and the difference between the cell means is not the same as the differences between row or column means, you will get a substantially higher $E^2_{y \cdot xz}$ when you subtract the variation around the cell means from the overall variation in Y and divide by the overall variation to get the proportion of variation in Y explained by both X and Z than when you add up the E^2_{xy} and the E^2_{zy}. Working from the column and row means, as you do when you add up the bivariate E^2s, assumes that the effects of X and Z can simply be added up. Working from the cell means allows for the possibility of nonadditivity (interaction).

Thus, if you are doing a two-way analysis of variance when there is interaction, to get a measure of the total proportion of the variation in Y explained by X and Z operating together, you need to take the overall variation in Y that you are seeking to explain, $\Sigma (Y_i - \overline{Y}_.)^2$, and subtract from it the variation around the cell means—the variation that cannot be explained by X and Z acting together—

$$[\Sigma (Y_{i1} - \overline{Y}_1)^2 + \Sigma (Y_{i2} - \overline{Y}_2)^2 + \Sigma (Y_{i3} - \overline{Y}_3)^2 + \Sigma (Y_{i4} - \overline{Y}_4)^2].$$

Then you need to divide by the overall variation in Y.

When you are trying to describe the form of the effect of X on Y or of Z on Y when there is interaction, you will need to have a different statement of the effect of one variable for every condition of the other variable. For example, "When Z is 1, the difference between the means of Y for the two categories of X is _____; when Z is 0, the difference between the means of Y for the two categories of X is _____," etc.

We can also modify the regression model we have been using to do analyses of variance in order to make it give us better descriptions of the relationships in Figure 15.6, where you first saw the interaction. Having described the relationship more accurately, we will be able to get a better measure of the strength of the relationship from the regression procedure as well because the error will be measured off lines that more exactly fit the data.

When we have dichotomous independent variables scored zero and one, the modification of the regression equation is simple. We add another term to the equation, which is simply the product of the first two independent variables. As you will see in a minute, this product will let us describe the nonadditive effects of the two independent variables.

To do this, we create a new variable, which is the *product* of the two independent variables. Let's label it "INTER" for interaction. When we COMPUTE INTER = (X ∗ Z), we get a new variable, which can be treated just like any other independent variable. Each case will get a score on this interaction variable, but that score can only be 0 or 1 depending on that case's values on X and Z. A case will be scored 1 on interaction only when $X \times Z = 1$, that is, when both X and $Z = 1$, as in group 4 in Figure 15.8 below. A case will be scored 0 on interaction when $X \times Z = 0$, that is, when either X or $Z = 0$, as in groups 1, 2, and 3 in Figure 15.8.

Having computed the new variable, we do a REGRESSION with X and Z *and* INTER as independent variables. That will give us all the coefficients for this equation: $Y = a + b_1 X + b_2 Z + b_3 I + e$. These coefficients will help describe the forms of the relationships among data when there is interaction such as you saw in Figure 15.6. (You may want to review that material before going on.)

First of all, look for the coefficients we need in order to be able to describe the bottom line—the relationship between X and Y when

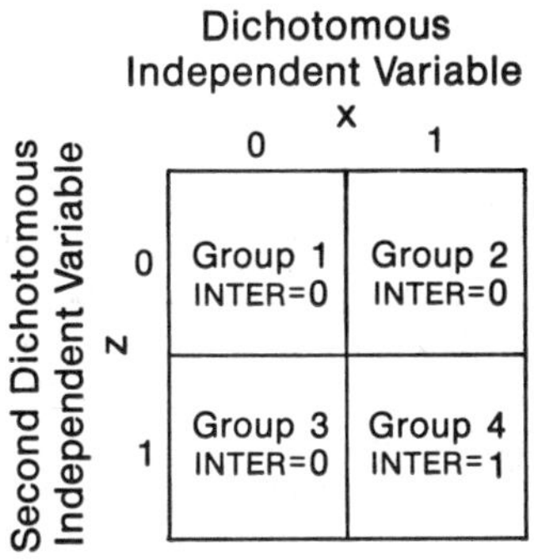

TWO-WAY ANALYSIS OF VARIANCE   205

Dichotomous Independent Variable

	X = 0	X = 1
Z = 0	Group 1 INTER=0	Group 2 INTER=0
Z = 1	Group 3 INTER=0	Group 4 INTER=1

(Second Dichotomous Independent Variable)

FIGURE 15.8 An Interaction Term for Two Dichotomous Independent Variables

$\overline{Y}_1 = a$ $(X = 0; Z = 0; \text{INTER} = 0)$
$\overline{Y}_2 = a + b_1$ $(X = 1; Z = 0; \text{INTER} = 0)$
$\overline{Y}_3 = a + b_2$ $(X = 0; Z = 1; \text{INTER} = 0)$
$\overline{Y}_4 = a + b_1 + b_2 + b_3$ $(X = 1; Z = 1; \text{INTER} = 1)$

Z is 0. We need the intercept (a), the effect of going from 0 to 1 on X (b_1), and that's all. Since Z is 0, both its product with b_2 and its product with X to make the interaction variable will be zero and drop out. This leaves the description of the relationship between X and Y, when Z is 0 as $a + b_1X + e$.

Now, look for the coefficients we need in order to be able to describe the top line—the relationship between X and Y when Z is 1. We need the intercept, the effect of going from 0 to 1 on X, the added-in effect of Z now being 1, and the effect of the interaction variable that—now that both X and Z are scored 1—equals 1. As was the case when we were doing this without interaction, we can combine the intercept and the effect of Z's being one as a kind of increased intercept ($a + b_2$). Here, however, you can see that X has more effect on Y when Z is 1. (The top slope is steeper.) We can represent this by combining the effect of X going from 0 to 1 (b_1) with the additional effect from interaction (b_3). That will give us the following description of the effect of X on Y when Z is 1: $Y = (a + b_2) + (b_1 + b_3)X$.

If we need to get the values of the means of the four groups defined by the two independent variables, we can simply put the values of the combinations of the independent variables in to the multiple regression equation and use the coefficients to figure out the means of the groups as follows:

Because we have allowed for interaction in the regression model we are using, we are no longer forcing the regression to give us the best-fitting, additive model. When we are estimating the group means from the regression equation above, therefore, we will get the actual group means rather than an estimate based on the assumption of additivity. And you can see, the new descriptions of the difference of means are no longer constrained to be the same, regardless of the value of the other variables. Now,

$(\overline{Y}_2 - \overline{Y}_1) = b_1$, while $(\overline{Y}_4 - \overline{Y}_3) = (b_1 + b_3)$
$(\overline{Y}_3 - \overline{Y}_1) = b_2$, while $(\overline{Y}_4 - \overline{Y}_2) = (b_2 + b_3)$

Now that we have allowed the regression model to fit the data more exactly, the measure of the strength of the relationship will be higher than that which took only X and Z separately as explainers of Y. It will be substantially higher if interaction is explaining much of the variation in Y. The regression using X and Z and the interaction as independent variables will give us a multiple $R^2_{y \cdot xzi}$ to indicate the proportion of variation in Y that is explained by X and Z and their interactive effects. This multiple R^2 is equivalent to the multiple E^2 that you got working from the cell means.

The nonadditive, interactive, model is clearly more complex than the additive one, whether you are thinking in analysis of variance or in regression terms. If we can get by with it, given our desire to find parsimonious (and easy) explanations, we'd rather use the additive model. So how do you tell?

When you are thinking in analysis of variance terms, deciding between the additive and interactive models will be a matter of deciding whether you can get by with summarizing the effects of X from the differences in Y means for the columns and the effects of Z from the differences in Y means for the rows or whether you have to make separate statements about the effects of X for every value of Z and the effects of Z for every value of X.

When is the simpler, additive description of the effects of the two independent variables good enough? One way to decide this (although you will learn a more statistical way in Chapter 18) is to compute two multiple E^2 statistics. Compute one based on the Y means in the rows and the Y means in the columns—i.e., assume additivity and just combine the two bivariate E^2s. Compute the other based on the Y means in the cells; i.e., measure the variation in Y that neither X nor Z can explain around the cell means and use that to compute a multiple E^2.

Compare the two. Do you explain enough more of the variation in Y using the more complicated model to make a difference in your thinking about the phenomenon you are trying to explain? Will that additional explained variation be important in your explanation of the dependent variable? When you are trying to state a generalization for your reader that will capture the effects of X and Z on Y, does the reader need to know about the interaction in order to understand what is going on? If your answer to these questions is "yes," go with the more complicated, interactive model. If your answer is "no," opt for parsimony and use the simpler model, even though it increases your error.

When you are thinking in regression terms, deciding between the additive and interactive models will be a matter of determining whether you need that "third independent variable," the interaction term, in the equation or not. You are asking whether a description of the relationships based on parallel lines (like those shown in Figure 15.7) is good enough, even though there is some error in it, or whether you need the complexity of a description that allows those lines not to be parallel (as in Figure 15.6.)

How do you tell? One way, although you will learn a more statistical one for this, too, in Chapter 18, is to look at that slope on the interaction term, b_3. If it is zero or near zero, you know that interaction is nonexistent or not very important; the model might as well be $Y = a + b_1 X + b_2 Z + e$ because cases won't be predicted much better from knowing their values on interaction than from not knowing them. You can just drop the interaction term out, ignoring the interaction and considering it just part of the error. Unfortunately, it is hardly ever going to be exactly zero; and, when it is not zero, you have to decide whether it improves the explanation enough that you want to leave it in. To help you decide, you can run two regressions—once with and once without the interaction term in the multiple regression model.

Compare how much variance you explain with and without taking interaction into consideration. Is it enough more explained variation that you can interpret the difference? Do you explain enough more variation that it is worth stating separate findings dependent on the interaction? Or are you willing to leave interaction out and put up with the additional error? If you are willing to put up with the additional error and, thus, with the lower proportion of explained variation for the sake of parsimony and ease of communication, go with the model, $Y = a + b_1 X + b_2 Z + e$, and with the measure of explained variance, $R^2_{y \cdot xz}$. If you need the interaction in order to describe what you actually see going on, go with the model, $Y = a + b_1 X + b_2 Z + b_3 I + e$, and with the measure of explained variance based on all three independent variables.

Although, as we said earlier, you will discover a more statistical approach to this decision in Chapter 18, it is worth asking yourself first, "Is this interaction meaningful in substantive terms?" Ask yourself whether it's worth including interaction in an explanation; if interaction explains one percent of the variation and you've already explained 97 percent with the two independent variables, this may be an important substantive increase in the thoroughness of the explanation. However, if interaction explains one percent of the variation and you've only explained ten percent with the two independent variables, this may be only a trivial increase in the thoroughness of the explanation unless that interaction is theoretically interesting.

This interaction problem is *not* limited to analysis of variance (and it is not limited to uncorrelated independent variables); it is just easier to see here. If you remember our discussion of the partial r and partial slope in the coverage of multiple correlation and regression, we briefly discussed that, before computing a partial r or partial b, you really ought to break the second independent into several categories and run the regression of Y on X within those categories to make sure the effect of X on Y is the same, regardless of the level of Z. Similarly, you really should break X into several categories and run the regression of Y on Z within those categories to make sure the effect of Z on Y is the same, regardless of the level of X.

Even when X and Z are uncorrelated, it is entirely possible that their effects on Y are not the same under all conditions of the other. And a single partial r or partial b cannot reflect the facts that the relationship between one independent and the dependent may be extremely different—even positive at one level of the other independent and negative at another level. Solutions for the interaction problem in regression are beyond the scope of this text unless you can dichotomize the independents and follow the procedures similar to those in this and the next chapter.

THE ANOVA PROCEDURE IN SPSS

We have gone through a discussion of two-way analysis of variance, both with regression concepts and with analysis of variance concepts with two dichotomous, uncorrelated independent variables, in order to show the relationship between multiple regression and two-way analysis of variance. We have also gone through this so that the choices one must make for the ANOVA procedure in SPSS are clearer.

When you need to do a two-way analysis of variance, you may want to use the ANOVA procedure in SPSS rather than REGRESSION because it is somewhat easier to do when your variables have more values on them than just the dichotomies we have been working with so far. The ANOVA procedure will also get you more information and give you more flexibility than the MEANS procedure you learned in Chapter 7. Moreover, it is generalizable to some of the problems we will turn to in Chapter 16.

If you look at the ANOVA chapter in the SPSS manual, however, you'll likely find it a little intimidating. Perhaps the exercises here can show you that, for relatively simple analyses, you can tackle the ANOVA procedure and not worry about its complexity too much.

ANOVA is operated by an ANOVA command that looks like this:

```
ANOVA VARIABLES = dependent BY
   independent1 (n,n)
   independent2 (n,n).
```

You substitute the SPSS names of your variables for "dependent" and for "independent1" and "independent2." The values in parentheses behind the names of the independent variables represent the low and high possible values of each independent variable and must be there. You just put, in place of the first "n," the lowest score that any of your cases has on that variable and, in place of the second "n," the highest score that any of your cases has on that variable—being sure to put in the lowest or highest *valid* score, not a missing data code.

When using ANOVA rather than REGRESSION to do these procedures, you don't have to compute a separate variable for the interaction term, nor do you mention it in the command; the procedure takes care of that for you.

For the purposes of deciding whether interaction is an interesting addition to your explanation or not, you want to get two separate ANOVA outputs. You want one ANOVA with the interaction considered as a separate explanatory factor (as if the unexplained variation in Y were being calculated from the cell means and not from the column and row means—the analogue to having the third independent variable in the regression model). You want a separate ANOVA where any effects of interaction are considered just part of the error (as if the unexplained variation in Y were being calculated from the row and column means of Y rather than from the cell means—the analogue to the regression model with just the two independent variables).

To get the two different kinds of ANOVA outputs, you need to run two separate ANOVA commands, one with the subcommand MAXORDERS=NONE (in SPSS-X) or OPTIONS=3 (in SPSS/PC+) and the other with no MAXORDERS or OPTIONS mentioned. When the subcommand is on the ANOVA procedure, you are instructing the program to include the interaction effects in the error.

In the *presence* of the subcommand, the procedure assumes you are considering interaction part of the error and adds any of the variation that interaction explains into the error. Thus, the program is assuming an additive model and working from the row and column means of Y. It doesn't have to calculate cell means, so it doesn't; asking for STATISTICS=1 in SPSS/PC+ or STATISTICS=MCA in SPSS-X will get an estimate of what the cell means would be were the effects of X the same, regardless of the value of Z, and were the effects of Z the same, regardless of the value of X.

The *absence* of the subcommand tells the program to separate the interaction effects out as a part of the explanation. It will give you the variation explained by X and that explained by Z, figuring both from the column and row means as if there were no interaction. But then it calculates cell means and uses those to figure the variation explained by X and Z and their interaction. You will explain more variation in Y from the cell means than from the row and column means if there is any interaction at all. The difference between the variation explained by X and Z separately and that explained by X and Z and their interaction will be attributed to interaction and printed out for you. To get those cell means printed out, specify STATISTICS=3 in SPSS/PC+ or STATISTICS=MEAN in SPSS-X.

Now, let's discuss a complicating problem that will show you why the choices you have to make in the ANOVA procedure can seem a bit complex. In the ANOVA procedure, you have to choose between the "classical approach" and the "regression approach." The differences between them have to do with which variable or variables are controlled before assessing the effects of the other variables. As you will see, under some conditions, the choices are pretty much irrelevant.

To get results as close to those of regression as those we have been discussing, you want to use the regression approach in the analysis. The regression approach to an analysis of variance, as done in SPSS, assesses the impact of an independent variable (or interaction) on the dependent variable controlling the other independent variables (and/or interaction if it is considered to be part of the explanation). What you will see printed out is the variation in Y that can be uniquely attributed to the effects of each variable (or interaction). To get this approach, use the subcommand OPTIONS = 9 in SPSS/PC+ or METHOD = UNIQUE in SPSS-X.

Contrast that regression approach with the classical experimental approach that you get by default if you don't specify another optional method. In the classical experimental approach, for the kind of analysis we are doing here, the effect of each independent variable is assessed controlling for the other (as is the case in the regression approach) but *not* controlling for the effects of interaction as would happen in the regression approach. Then the effect of interaction is assessed controlling for the effects of the two independent variables, just as it is in the regression approach.

The differences between the regression approach and the classical experimental approach are minimal, as long as you have only two categorical independent variables, unless interaction is very high. For example, once you have decided that interaction doesn't matter, the choice between the regression and classical approaches is irrelevant; they are identical for the kinds of analyses we have been doing here.

However, if you use the regression approach, the procedure doesn't give you give you the cell means or any other statistics we can use to estimate the cell means; and those means are our most useful interpretive device for assessing the form of a relationship. When you are using the regression approach, the procedure only gives you information on which to calculate the strength of the relationship, i.e., the variation in Y explained by the independent variables, and some tests we haven't come to yet. To get the cell means, you need to run another procedure—perhaps MEANS or another ANOVA approach (being sure *not* to suppress the interaction with OPTIONS = 3 or MAXORDERS = NONE).

As you become more comfortable with the ANOVA procedure, you may want to try everything once, just to see what happens. For now, you may be content to follow the instructions below and let me try to walk you through the output you will get.

EXERCISE 1 Uncorrelated Independent Variables

In order to see these comparisons we've been describing, you will submit three ANOVA commands. On the first two, there will be one without OPTIONS = 3 (or MAXORDERS = NONE) and one with, so you can see what happens when interaction is and is not treated as part of the error; on both you will also use the regression approach so that you can get results most comparable to REGRESSION. You will run a third ANOVA, on which (for SPSS/PC+) you will specify STATISTICS = 1 3 or (with SPSS-X) STATISTICS = MCA MEAN to get information on cell means and correlations. (If you will put no other subcommands on this third ANOVA, the procedure will do the classical experimental method by default and will also separate out the interaction term and consider it part of the explanation.) You will also run REGRESSION to show how it compares to ANOVA.

For data, use those in the exercise section of this chapter. When you get your output, answer the questions that you find in the exercise section. They are designed to guide you through the output. If you have to do any calculating to get the answers, write out those calculations as well.

Here is a summary of the computer assignment.

DATA LIST with names and locations of variables. (Please call them X, Z, Y or some variation like VARX, VARZ, VARY so that they are easy to keep straight.)

COMPUTE INTER = (X * Z), adjusting names to match whatever you have named your two independent variables. (This is for your REGRESSION; were you doing only ANOVA, you wouldn't need it.)

```
BEGIN DATA.
...data...
END DATA.
REGRESSION DESCRIPTIVES =
    MEAN,
    STDDEV, CORR, N/VARIABLES =
    X,
    Z, INTER, Y/STATISTICS = R,
    ANOVA, CHA, COEFF,
    ZPP/DEPENDENT=Y/ENTER=
    X,Z/ENTER=INTER.
ANOVA VARIABLES = dependent BY
    independent1 (n,n)
    independent2 (n,n)/
    OPTIONS = 3 9.      (SPSS/PC+)
    MAXORDERS=NONE/METHOD=
    UNIQUE.             (SPSS=X)
ANOVA VARIABLES = dependent BY
    independent1 (n,n)
    independent2 (n,n)/
    OPTIONS = 9.        (SPSS/PC+)
    METHOD = UNIQUE.    (SPSS-X)
ANOVA VARIABLES = dependent BY
    independent1 (n,n)
    independent2 (n,n)/
    STATISTICS = 1 3.   (SPSS/PC+)
    STATISTICS = MCA MEAN(SPSS-X)
FINISH.
```

When you get your output, several things will have new names other than those we have been using, but they are equivalent or analogous to the terms you already know from regression.

Main effects sum of squares refers to the variation (sum of squares) explained by both X and Z together. Using the classical experimental approach (what you get if you don't specify an optional approach in SPSS/PC+ or another method in SPSS-X), it is the variation explained by X and Z together without any control for interaction. (If you divide this by the total sum of squares, you have a multiple $E^2_{y \cdot xz}$ for the proportion of variation in Y explained by both X and Z.) When you are doing ANOVA with the regression approach, interaction (unless you put it in the error term) is separated out and already controlled before the effects of X and Z together are calculated.

Under the main effects are listed the *sums of squares* (variation) explained by each independent variable—X and Z—in each case controlling for the other (with control for interaction if the regression approach is being used without putting interaction into the error term; without control for interaction if the experimental method is used *or* if interaction is in the error term). As long as X and Z are uncorrelated (when there is no control for interaction), the sum of squares associated with one divided by the total sum of squares will give you the bivariate E^2_{yx}. You could also do two bivariate ANOVA procedures to get the bivariated E^2_{xy} and E^2_{zy}.

Under the independent variables, when the interaction has not been put into the error term, you will see the variation (sum of squares) explained by interaction, controlling for the independent variables. Here the sum of squares explained by interaction is attributed to interaction as if it were a separate explanatory variable just like X and Z. It's not a *main* effect, but it is an *explained* effect.

Next you will see the *explained sum of squares* that is the variation explained by both independents; it may or may not include variation explained by interaction. When interaction is treated as if it were just ordinary error and is put into the error term with OPTIONS = 3 or MAXORDERS = NONE, it is not part of the explained variation. Otherwise, the explained sum of squares is the variation explained by both independents and interaction. Dividing the explained sum of squares by the total sum of squares will get you an $E^2_{y \cdot xzi}$ or $E^2_{y \cdot xz}$, depending on whether interaction is considered explained or not.

The *residual sum of squares* is the unexplained variation. The residual includes the interaction sum of squares if OPTIONS = 3 or MAXORDERS = NONE has been indicated; interaction there is just treated as part of the error, part of what we can't (or don't want to) explain. Otherwise, the residual sum of squares does not contain interaction effects because we are treating them as part of the explanation.

The *total sum of squares* is exactly the same variation in Y you have been calculating since Chapter 2. It represents the total of the squared deviations of all cases' real values from the mean of Y.

You can get the multiple E^2 by dividing:

$$\frac{\text{Total sum of squares} - \text{Residual sum of squares}}{\text{Total sum of squares}}$$

If the interaction sum of squares is in the error term (residual sum of squares), the multiple E^2 given above is the proportion of variation in Y explained by X and Z, $E^2_{y \cdot xz}$. If the interaction sum of squares is in the explained sum of squares (not in the residual, unexplained sum of squares), the multiple E^2 given above is the proportion of variation in Y explained by X and Z and interaction, $E^2_{y \cdot xzi}$.

When you see the output produced by the third ANOVA command, you will see cell means produced by your request for STATISTICS = 3 or STATISTICS = MEAN. These are the actual means of Y in the cells identified on the output.

On the output, you will see three sets of means: (1) the means of the dependent variable within each category of the first independent, within each category of the first independent, disregarding the other independent variable; (2) the means of the dependent variable within each category of the second independent, disregarding the other independent variable; and (3) the means of the dependent variable within the joint categories of both independents. In other words, you get the row means, the column means, and the cell means.

Also on that third ANOVA output, you will see a Multiple Classification Analysis (MCA). Given the way the statistics are calculated for this table, you will want to use it only if you think interaction is unimportant. (MCA is a version of the technique you will learn in Chapter 16.)

On the MCA table, you will find the grand mean for the dependent variable and the deviations from the grand mean for the categories of the variables indicated. These deviations from the grand mean, when added to or subtracted from the overall grand mean, will give you the *estimates* of the cell means, *assuming additivity*. These deviations do not give you the actual means of Y; they give you what the means of Y would be if there were no interaction at all. To use them to estimate the mean of Y when X is 0 and Z is 1, for example, take the grand mean, add/subtract the deviation indicated next to $X = 0$, and then add/subtract the deviation indicated next to $Z = 1$. Use the unadjusted deviations when you have uncorrelated independent variables.

Also on the MCA table, you will find eta (which we have called E) for each independent variable. Remember that its square represents the proportion of variance in the dependent explained by that independent acting alone. It is a bivariate measure of association. You could get the identical information from a bivariate ANOVA or from dividing the sum of squares associated with an independent variable—without controls for interaction—by the total sum of squares, as long as the independent variables were uncorrelated.

In addition, you will see a "MULTIPLE R SQUARED" entry at the bottom of the MCA table. That is the equivalent of the multiple E^2—the proportion of variation in Y explained by both independents. You could have gotten that by dividing the main effects sum of squares—without controls for interaction—by the total sum of squares. When the independent variables are uncorrelated with each other, the squares of the etas will add up to the multiple E^2.

ANOVA WITH CORRELATED INDEPENDENT VARIABLES: MULTICOLLINEARITY REVISITED

Frequently you will need to be able to work with correlated independent variables, especially if you are testing correlations to determine if they are spurious, if you suspect that a second independent variable suppresses or distorts the original relationship between an independent variable and a dependent variable, or if you believe a second independent variable intervenes between two other variables.

In order to make the assessments necessary for these kinds of analyses, you need to be able to examine the form of the relationship between an independent variable and a dependent variable controlling for another variable. You will need a measure of how much variation one variable explains in a dependent variable, controlling for another variable. And you will need a measure of how much the two explanatory variables explain together.

You will use most of the same information you just learned above for getting these statistics from ANOVA or (if you have two dichotomous independent variables) from the REGRESSION we have been using to do analyses of variance without using the ANOVA procedure itself). The bivariate measures of relationship (either the form or the strength of the relationship) between X and Y or Z and Y are the same, regardless of whether you end up with a multivariate analysis or not. Similarly, the measures of the total proportion of the variation in Y explained by X and Z working together are the same whether X and Z are correlated or not. There are, however, a few cautions that have to be pointed out for dealing with correlated independent variables.

Assessing the Forms of the Relationships

Remember from above that, with uncorrelated independent variables and no interaction, you can see the effect of X either in the difference between the column means of Y or in the differences between the cells within one or the other value of Z. Similarly, you can read the effects of Z either in the difference between the row means of Y or in the differences between the cells within one or the other value of X. (Refer back to Figure 15.5, if necessary.)

That set of equalities, between the row or column differences and the corresponding cell differences, won't hold anymore with correlated independent variables. The effects of X on Y that you see in the bivariate relationship may disappear when Z is controlled if Z is either extraneously causing the XY correlation or is intervening between X and Y. Or the effects of X on Y may appear greater or different if Z has been suppressing or distorting the XY relationship. Or the effects of X on Y may be lessened if Z is either partially intervening or if the XY relationship is partially spurious. Everything you learned about interpreting the partial slopes in regression is going to be applicable in your interpretation of analysis of variance with correlated independent variables.

What you *will* see with correlated independent variables, as long as you have additive and not interactive effects, is that the differences between the Y means within categories of X will be the same regardless of their scores on Z. (From Figure 15.5, the difference between $\overline{Y}_1$ and $\overline{Y}_2$ is the same as the difference between $\overline{Y}_3$ and $\overline{Y}_4$; but that difference just won't be the same as the $\overline{Y}_{x0} - \overline{Y}_{x1}$ difference.) Similarly, the differences between the Y means within categories of Z will be the same, regardless of their scores on X. (From Figure 15.5, the $\overline{Y}_1 - \overline{Y}_3$ difference will equal the $\overline{Y}_2 - \overline{Y}_4$ difference, but those will not necessarily equal the $\overline{Y}_{z0} - \overline{Y}_{z1}$ difference.)

All this is to say: without interaction, the effects of one independent variable will be the same, regardless of the level of the other independent variable, but the effects will not be the same as the bivariate relationship when the independent variables are themselves correlated.

So where do you look in ANOVA to find the effect of one variable on another with the third controlled? One answer is to look at the beta that you will see printed out on the MCA table. It can be interpreted as a kind of standardized partial slope. Remember from Chapter 14 that the standardized partial slope gives you, in standard deviation units, the effect on the dependent variable of increasing the independent variable one standard deviation unit, with all the other independent variables controlled.

Since it is standardized and does not depend on the measurement scale of the independent variable for its interpretation, the beta can tell you which of the independent variables is having the greater effect on the dependent, with the other independent variable controlled. Be somewhat cautious with it in an analysis of variance because you don't have the kind of data that would allow you actually to talk about increasing or decreasing a variable; you have nominal data for the independent variables. Also remember that statistics from the MCA table are appropriate only when there is little or no interaction.

If all you need is a partial that will tell you whether the relationship between X and Y is close to zero with Z controlled, the beta is fine. You could use it the same way you used a partial correlation coefficient for assessing spuriousness, intervention, etc.

Another, and more easily interpretable, place to get the effect of one independent variable on the dependent variable when the other independent is controlled is in the means of the dependent variable. This you get by STATISTICS = 3, using SPSS/PC+, or STATISTICS = MEAN, using SPSS-X, with a classical approach ANOVA, which doesn't put interaction into the error term.

For the relationship between an independent and a dependent when the other independent is controlled, you have to look at the means of Y in the cells created by taking the two independent variables jointly, as you did back in Figure 15.5. For the means of Y that show the effects of X, controlling for Z, you look at the means of Y for each category of X but *within* a category of Z. For the means of Y that show the effects of Z, controlling for X, you look at the means of Y for each category of Z but *within* a category of Z.

Those means are the *actual* cell means of Y within the categories created jointly by the two independent variables, so any interaction that is present will show up in those means. The effects of X may not appear to be *exactly* the same, regardless of the value of Z, and the effects of Z may not appear to be exactly the same, regardless of the value of X.

If you need to know what the cell means would look like if the effects of X and Z were purely additive (if there were no interaction at all in the data), you can get this information from the MCA table that you get from STATISTICS = 1, using SPSS/PC+, or from STATISTICS = MCA, using SPSS-X, on a classical ANOVA. Now that you have correlated independents, you look for the *adjusted* deviations for each category of an independent variable and add or subtract them from the grand mean. These deviations are calculated having controlled the other independent variable.

You can compare the cell means you construct from the MCA table to those that really appear in the data. Since the MCA analysis assumes additivity, any difference between it and the actual cell means can be attributed to interaction. If the two assessments of the cell means are only a little different, you will probably want to treat the interaction as error and ignore it. If they are very different, you will need to interpret and report the interaction effects.

If you have dichotomous independent variables and are doing the REGRESSION procedure that we used above to do analyses of variance without the ANOVA procedure, you can also get the actual cell means and the cell means that would be there were there only additive effects by running two regressions, one with and one without interaction as an explanatory variable. From the coefficients provided in the output, you can estimate the cell means both ways. This doesn't change from the situation with uncorrelated independent variables.

What problems are you facing interpreting these means when there are correlated independent variables? The big one is that the more correlated the two independent variables become, the fewer cases you are going to have in some of the cells defined by the two independent variables. Imagine a crosstabulation table, for a minute. The more correlated the two independent variables, the more the cases cluster up in the diagonal cells, leaving the off-diagonal cells getting emptier and emptier. The same thing would show up in Figure 15.5, were the two independents correlated. Cases would begin to fall in the upper left and lower right cells or in the upper right and lower left cells.

In analysis of variance and its regression substitute, you are going to be calculating a mean of the dependent variable on those cases in the sparsely populated cells. And you are going to be comparing that mean to others in order to assess the effect of an independent variable on the dependent.

How sure can you be that the mean of the dependent variable is a good measure of what is going on when it is based on only a few cases? Thus, the more correlated the independent variables are with each other, the less sure you are about the accuracy of your assessments of their effects. If the two are perfectly correlated, you will be left with no cases in two cells on which to calculate a mean. You will be totally unable to assess the separate effects of the two independent variables.

Luckily, when you ask for the means to be printed out, you also get a count of the number of cases in each cell. It is worth looking at those numbers of cases to make sure you have a pretty good number of cases in each. (10, maybe?) Without a good number, you won't be able to be very confident about the difference *between* means (the form of the relationship) because you won't be very sure that the mean itself is reliable in the first place.*

Assessing the Strength of the Relationships

Although you don't usually see the equivalent of a partial r^2 from analysis of variance, you may occasionally need a measure of the proportion of the variation in the dependent variable that is explained by each independent variable controlling for the other, a partial correlation squared. Here you will see another problem you have already met in regression.

The more correlated the two independents are, the less variation in Y each independent can *uniquely* explain. The proportion of the variation in the dependent variable that can be explained by an independent variable, after the other independent variable has explained all it can, may seem to indicate only a little effect from each of the independent variables, while the measure of the strength of association between the two independents and the dependent may show that the two together can do quite a bit of explanation. (Review Chapter 12 on the partial correlation coefficient if this seems vague; the problem is the same in regression and analysis of variance.)

There is not really an equivalent of the partial correlation coefficient squared from ANOVA output to use when you need to know the proportion that can be explained by one independent variable of the variation left in Y after the other independent variable has explained all it can. However, you can do a bit of calculating from the information on the output and construct one yourself.

Use an ANOVA output in which interaction is not controlled when the effects of the independent variables are assessed (i.e., with OPTIONS = 3 or MAXORDERS = NONE on a

regression method or any classical method.) For the equivalent of the partial $r^2_{yx \cdot z}$, take the sum of squares associated with X as the numerator. That is the *amount* of variation explained by X after Z has explained all it can.

For the denominator, first take the main effects sum of squares and subtract from it the sum of squares associated with X. That leaves you with the sum of squares, explained by Z or by either X or Z. Now subtract that difference from the total sum of squares, which will leave you with a denominator that measures the amount of variation in Y after Z has explained all it can.

Divide the numerator by the denominator as indicated in Formula 15.1 and you're left with the equivalent of a partial correlation coefficient squared.

FORMULA 15.1
A Partial E^2 for the Relationship between X and Y with Z Controlled

$$E^2_{yx \cdot z} = \frac{SSX}{TSS - (MESS - SSX)}$$

where: SSX = Sum of squares associated with X
TSS = Total sum of squares
MESS = Main effects sum of squares

If you are doing the REGRESSION substitute for ANOVA, you can look at the partial listed in the row of statistics next to each independent variable. Square it and you get the proportion of variation in Y that is explained by that independent variable after all the other independent variables listed have explained all they can.

All the principles you learned in Chapter 12 about interpreting the partial correlation coefficients compared to the bivariate correlations apply here as well. It is just that now you cannot talk about one variable increasing or decreasing another because you don't have anything more than nominal data.

Remember that the bivariate correlation between each independent variable and the dependent is given on the MCA table. Square the

---

*If you are working with more than two categories on your independent variables, you may be able to increase the numbers of cases in the cells. You can combine some categories of your independent variables if you have two groups that are theoretically fairly similar on one of the independent variables; or you may want to drop from the analysis some of the categories that don't have many cases on one or the other independent variable.

eta there for the proportion of variation in the dependent explained by that independent acting alone. The multiple E and E^2 are also there (called R or R^2); the latter gives you the proportion of variation in Y explained by both independent variables together. You can also get the multivariate E^2 by dividing the explained sum of squares by the total sum of squares.

You may also need to know how correlated your two independent variables are. On the REGRESSION output, you can see that correlation in the descriptive statistics printed at the top of the output, but the correlation between the two independent variables is not given you in one convenient statistic on the ANOVA output. You can look at the numbers of cases given you for each cell when you request STATISTICS = 3 or STATISTICS = MEAN and construct your own crosstabulation table for the relationship between the two independent variables, or you can run a separate CROSSTABS procedure to see whether the two independent variables are correlated.

MULTICOLLINEARITY AND INTERACTION COMPARED

Notice that both multicollinearity and interaction lead to problems of interpretation, but they are two different and separate problems. You don't have to have correlated independent variables to have interaction problems, and you don't have interaction problems every time you have correlated independent variables.

It is useful to remember that we worry about two things—measures of the *strength* of relationships and measures of the *form* of relationships.

In regression, we assess *strength* with various versions of the r^2 statistic. (What proportion of variation in Y are we explaining with a single independent variable or some combination of independent variables?) In analysis of variance, we assess *strength* of relationships with the E^2 statistic and various manipulations of the explained sums of squares. (Again, what proportion of the variation in Y are we explaining with a single independent variable or some combination of independent variables?)

In regression, we examine the *form* of the relationship through the regression coefficient—the slope, b. That tells us what effect a one-unit increase in the independent has on the dependent variable. In analysis of variance, we examine the *form* of the relationship through the difference of means. As we go from one category of the independent variable to another, the difference in dependent variable means shows us the effect the independent variable is having.

Multicollinearity, correlated independent variables, affects both our assessment of the *strength* and the *form* of relationships. When we need to be able to tell which independent explains the most variation, the correlation between them gives us a problem. We have no way to decide which of the two independent variables is responsible for the variation in Y that *either* independent variable could be explaining. Our only evidence is that part of the dependent variable variation is explained by both. There is no *statistical* way to know whether to assign it to one or the other independent variable. The *theory* with which we are working may help, however. There are statistical procedures that we haven't covered, such as hierarchical analysis of variance, which will force the statistical analysis to assign the variation to one or the other independent variable when the theory mandates this.

Multicollinearity also affects our ability to assess the form of the relationship. The problem here, however, lies primarily in the instance when we have a sample and are trying to make estimates about the form of the relationship in the population from which the sample was drawn. The greater the intercorrelation between the independent variables, the less sure we are that the form of the relationship we calculate on the sample data is a reasonably correct description of the population as well. And we have trouble comparing samples because it's so unlikely we'd find another with the same correlation.

Interaction is primarily a problem of assessing the form of a relationship. When a slope changes under different conditions defined by a third variable, describing the form of the relationship between two variables becomes a complex matter, indeed, which means that describing what is going on in plain language (as opposed to statistics) is complicated as well. The greater the interaction (the more different the slope at different levels of the control variable or in different categories of the control variable), the more difficult the problem.

Similarly, in two-way analysis of variance, it is already difficult to describe the effect of an independent variable as a change of the mean of Y from one category of the independent to another, even before introducing the complexity of interaction; but why an independent variable affects a dependent differently in different categories of another variable (i.e., interaction) is really a challenge.

To be sure, interaction affects our ability to assess strength of relationships as well. When there is important interaction, it is useless to calculate a partial correlation measure relating one independent to the dependent controlling another variable because any single such partial is meaningless. Interaction, however, is probably far more important in our understanding of the *form* of relationships. We can, after all, always calculate several bivariate measures of association (strength)—one for each level or category of the control variable.

OTHER COMMENTS AND REMINDERS ABOUT ANALYSIS OF VARIANCE

Unlike the REGRESSION procedure that you used with dichotomous independent variables to perform an analysis of variance without ANOVA procedures, the ANOVA procedure itself isn't confined to dichotomies as independent variables. (Actually, neither is the REGRESSION, as you will see in the next chapter.) Any nominal variables are possibilities.

Also remember that you work in analysis of variance with the variation around means of the dependent variable *within* categories of the independent variables). Since the *order* of the categories of the independent variables doesn't make any difference, you don't *need* ordinal variables; even if you have them, they are treated as nominal, and their order is not taken into account. Since the *distance between* categories of the independent variable(s) doesn't enter into it, you don't need anything like interval *independent* variables; if you are recoding an interval variable down to a few categories, whether the categories are the same distance apart is immaterial.

In analysis of variance, it doesn't matter at all whether the two independent variables have the same number of categories. However, it is usually a good idea to keep the number of categories on each independent variable fairly small. Usually, interpretation is easier if there are only a few possible values on each independent variable. As is the case in crosstabulation, there is a need to keep a good number of cases in each cell that is created by crossing the independents. You can't get a very reliable judgment about a mean with only a few cases. And you can't get a very reliable sense of how much unexplained variation is left around the mean of Y with only a few cases.

Keep analysis of variance in mind when you spot nonlinear relationships in regression scatterplots. Since the independent is not treated as interval or ordinal, analysis of variance can be an alternate analysis method. Just keep the *dependent* interval. Only then can you justify calculating a mean and subtracting it from the individual scores.

EXERCISE 2 Analysis of Variance on Real Data

Turn now to analysis of variance on real data. Write a hypothesis using two nominal or ordinal independents and an interval dependent that can be tested using one of the data sets in the appendices. What does your hypothesis suggest about the three bivariate associations—between X and Y, between Z and Y, and between X and Z? What do you expect to happen to the *XY* relationship when *Z* is controlled?

As you are operationalizing the concepts in your hypothesis, remember that you know two ways to construct multi-item indices; you may want to use those to construct the dependent variable.

Now set up the following ANOVA programs for your hypothesis. You will run two two-way ANOVAs. One will separate out interaction from the rest of the error so that you can assess how important it is. The other is there in case you decide to disregard any interpretation of interaction and to consider it part of the unexplained (residual) error. In anticipation of not very impressive interaction, run the classical approach rather than the regression approach. If interaction is very small, there's no particular point in controlling it, as the regression approach does. Besides, if you use the classical approach, you can get the cell means and an MCA table easily.

For the classical approach, you will need the following:

The accessing information to get to the data set

Any COUNT or COMPUTE commands (and any necessary accompanying commands) to construct your dependent variables, should you decide to use a multi-item index

Any RECODE commands necessary to reduce the number of values on the independent variables or to assure you have enough cases in each category

```
ANOVA VARIABLES = depvar BY
   indvar1 (n,n) indvar2 (n,n)/
   STATISTICS = 3 1.
                      (for SPSS/PC+)
   STATISTICS = MEAN MCA.
                      (for SPSS-X)
ANOVA VARIABLES = depvar BY
   indvar1(n,n) indvar 2 (n,n)/
   (identical to ANOVA
    command above)
   OPTIONS = 3.    (for SPSS/PC+)
   MAXORDERS = NONE.(for SPSS-X)
FINISH.
```

Substitute the SPSS name of your dependent variable *before* the BY where "depvar" is indicated. Substitute the names of your independent variables in the other places "indvar" is indicated. Put the minimum and maximum valid codes for each independent variable in the parentheses in place of the "n."

Submit your job and answer the following questions from your output.

1. Is *X* correlated with *Y* as you hypothesized it would be in the bivariate situation? What do you look at to know? (Remember to consider the form as well as the strength of the relationship.)
2. Is *Z* correlated with *Y*, as you hypothesized it would be, in the bivariate situation? What do you look at to know?
3. What about *X* and *Z*? Are they correlated, as you hypothesized? How do you know?
4. Before moving into the multivariate analyses, ask yourself, "Can interaction can be considered part of the error or does it need to be explained?" What do you consider to tell?
5. Given the decision you make in question 4, which of the two outputs will you use now—the one with interaction as an explanatory variable (without OPTIONS or MAXORDERS) or the one with interaction in the error term (i.e., OPTIONS = 3 or MAXORDERS = NONE)?
6. Now look at the relationship between *X* and *Y* controlling *Z*. What is the form and strength of that relationship? And what are you looking at to give that answer?
7. What proportion of the variation in *Y* is explained by *X* and *Z* acting together? What statistic tells you that?
8. Can you describe the effects of *X* on *Y* controlling *Z* in plain English, succinctly? If interaction is relevant, how does it affect the description you just made?

EXERCISES

Just for the sake of having some feeling for what these variables might be, imagine these hypothetical operationalizations:

X = "Sex," with females scored 0 and males scored 1.

Z = "Partisan orientation," with those who lean more toward the party of the president scored 1 and those who lean more toward the opposition scored 0. Note that Z is the second variable.

Y = A measure of support for the president's policy on which the respondent was presented with a picture of a thermometer that had a low mark of 0 and a high mark of 100. The respondent was told to locate him/herself on the thermometer by how warm or cool he or she felt toward the president's policy. Note that Y is the third variable.

Case No.	X	Z	Y	Case No.	X	Z	Y
1	0	0	8	17	1	0	31
2	0	0	6	18	1	0	28
3	0	0	10	19	1	0	30
4	0	0	12	20	1	0	25
5	0	0	14	21	1	0	26
6	0	0	6	22	1	0	23
7	0	0	6	23	1	0	25
8	0	0	5	24	1	0	27
9	0	1	38	25	1	1	56
10	0	1	40	26	1	1	51
11	0	1	34	27	1	1	56
12	0	1	39	28	1	1	49
13	0	1	38	29	1	1	50
14	0	1	38	30	1	1	55
15	0	1	37	31	1	1	52
16	0	1	33	32	1	1	56

EXERCISE 1 Comparing REGRESSION and ANOVA Procedures in SPSS: Analysis of Variance with Uncorrelated Independent Variables

First look at both the REGRESSION output (left column) and the ANOVA with MAXORDERS = ALL (right column) below in order to decide how important interaction is.

From REGRESSION—
What *extra proportion* of the variance in Y is explained by INTER after X and Z have explained all they can; i.e., compare the percent of variance in Y explained by the two independents and interaction in the step where interaction is considered an explanatory variable to the percent of variance in Y explained by the two independents alone in the step where interaction is not among the explanatory variables. (R^2 change will give this to you.)

From ANOVA with MAXORDERS = ALL—What *extra proportion* of the variance in Y is explained by interaction after X and Z have explained all they can; i.e., divide interaction sum of squares (which is calculated by SPSS controlling X and Z) by total sum of squares.

From REGRESSION—
What *proportion* of the variation in Y left *unexplained* by X and Z is explained by INTER? Find the partial r for interaction and square it.

From ANOVA with MAXORDERS = ALL—What *proportion* of the variation in Y left unexplained by X and Z is explained by interaction? Divide the interaction sum of squares by the total sum of squares minus the main effects sum of squares.

Given the percentage of variation Y explained by interaction, does that seem to be a substantively important amount? Explain very briefly why you say that.

Having made a decision about the *amount* of interaction, we turn to an examination of the *effects* of interaction. Here you will examine the means of the cells defined by the values of the two independent variables in order to see the effects of the independents on the dependents; then you will see how interaction changes those apparent effects.

TWO-WAY ANALYSIS OF VARIANCE

From REGRESSION in which interaction is *not* a separate explanatory variable, what are the estimated means of the four groups? Show the equation first and then your substitutions into it:

when $X = 1, Z = 1, Y_p =$
$X = 0, Z = 0, Y_p =$
$X = 1, Z = 0, Y_p =$
$X = 0, Z = 1, Y_p =$

From REGRESSION in which interaction is treated as a separate explanatory variable, what are the means of the four groups? Show the equation first and then your substitutions into it:

when $X = 1, Z = 1, \bar{Y} =$
$X = 0, Z = 0, \bar{Y} =$
$X = 1, Z = 0, \bar{Y} =$
$X = 0, Z = 1, \bar{Y} =$

From the MCA table, estimate the means of the four groups. To do this, examine the Multiple Classification Analysis. Find the grand mean, which is the overall mean for all the cases. Find the column labeled "unadjusted dev'n." (If X and Z were correlated, you'd use the "adjusted deviations" for this.) There you will see the effect on the grand mean produced by the independents. You add or subtract, as indicated by the sign on the deviation, these values to the grand mean to get the mean when X is either 0 or 1 and when Z is either 0 or 1. Show your calculations. For each of the four groups, you will manipulate the grand mean for the effect of X and then manipulate that answer for the effect of Z.

From the ANOVA with STATISTICS = MEANS look for a title "cell means" and indicate here what the means are. Be sure to get the bivariate classification means (8 cases per cell) rather than the univariate classification means (16 cases per cell).

When $X = 1, Z = 1, Y_p =$
$X = 0, Z = 0, Y_p =$
$X = 1, Z = 0, Y_p =$
$X = 0, Z = 1, Y_p =$

When $X = 1, Z = 1, \bar{Y} =$
$X = 0, Z = 0, \bar{Y} =$
$X = 1, Z = 0, \bar{Y} =$
$X = 0, Z = 1, \bar{Y} =$

The means estimated by the two procedures at the left are *estimates* based on an assumption of additivity (no interaction). The two sets of means on the right are, in the case of the regression, an estimate that allows for interaction or, in the case of ANOVA, a direct calculation of the cell means from the data. If there is any interaction, the left-hand estimates will differ from the right-hand calculations. The effect of interaction can be seen in how different the two sets are.

From the above statistics and from the output, develop an interpretation of the data.

- Which group defined by the two independent variables is most supportive of the president's policy? What do you read in order to be able to say that?
- Do people who lean toward the president's party support the president's policies more or less than those who lean toward the opposition, when controlling sex? How much more or less? What do you read in order to be able to answer those questions?
- Are males or females more supportive of the president's policies controlling partisan orientation? How much? What do you read in order to be able to answer those questions?
- What proportion of the variation in support for the policies can we not explain with sex and partisan orientation? How do you calculate that?
- Which of the independent variables operating alone in a bivariate relation explain the most variation in support for the president's policies? What do you read in order to know?
- Which of the two independent variables controlling for the other has the most effect on the mean support for the president's policies? From what statistic(s) can you assess this? Here, because both independent variables have the same measurement scales, you can get an answer to this from the differences between cell means. Where else?

SUGGESTED READINGS

BERESON, MARK L., DAVID M. LEVINE, and MATTHEW GOLDSTEIN. *Intermediate Statistical Methods and Applications: A Computer Package Approach* (Englewood Cliffs, NJ: Prentice-Hall, 1983), Chs. 5–7.

BLALOCK, HUBERT M., JR. *Social Statistics*, 2nd ed. (N.Y.: McGraw-Hill, 1972), Ch. 16.3.

BOWEN, BRUCE D., and HERBERT F. WEISBERG. *An Introduction to Data Analysis* (San Francisco: Freeman, 1980), pp. 185–194.

BRAY, JAMES H., and SCOTT E. MAXWELL. *Multivariate Analysis of Variance*. # 54 in series, *Quantitative Applications in the Social Sciences* (Beverly Hills, CA: Sage, 1985). More advanced.

COLLYER, CHARLES E., and JAMES T. ENNS. *Analysis of Variance: the Basic Designs* (Chicago, IL: Nelson-Hall, 1986). Ads for this say it contains "analysis of variance with BMDP, SAS, and SPSS-X applications"; appears to describe the more complex designs.

DRAPER, N.R., and H. SMITH. *Applied Regression Analysis* (N.Y.: Wiley, 1966), Ch. 9.

KERLINGER, FRED N., and ELAZAR J. PEDHAZUR. *Multiple Regression in Behavioral Research* (N.Y.: Holt, Rinehart, and Winston, 1973), Chs. 6–8.

KLEINBAUM, DAVID G., and LAWRENCE L. KUPPER. *Applied Regression Analysis* (North Scituate, MA: Duxbury, 1978), Chs. 19–20.

KOHOUT, FRANK J. *Statistics for Social Scientists* (N.Y.: Wiley, 1974), Unit VI.

NIE, NORMAN H., et al. *SPSS: Statistical Package for the Social Sciences*, 2nd ed. (N.Y.: McGraw-Hill, 1975). Chapter 21, "Special Topics in General Linear Models," is worth reading in connection with this and subsequent chapters, even though it is from a manual for an earlier version of SPSS.

NORUSIS, MARIJA J. *SPSS/PC+* (Chicago: SPSS, Inc., 1988). Chapter 15, pp. B164–B175, is on the statistics associated with ANOVA. The command structure is on pp. C17–C21.

SPSS-X User's Guide (Chicago: SPSS, Inc., 1988). Chapter 20 is on ANOVA, pp. 364–377. For more complicated analysis, see MANOVA, Chapter 33.

ARTICLES

FARNSWORTH, DAVID N., and JOHN E. STANGA, JR. "Seniority, Reform, and Democratic Committee Assignments in the House of Representatives," *Policy Studies Journal*, 5 (Summer 1977), 431–436. Creates an index of over- or under-representation on committees in order to examine whether reforms in the 94th Congress changed committee assignments for first-term members compared to other Congresses since the 87th. Then treats seniority converted to Z scores as continuous variable to assess whether exclusive, semi-exclusive, and nonexclusive committees have different levels of seniority across two Congresses. Using what appears to be an independent variable as the interval variable in analysis of variance, authors construct a typology of committee membership more than test hypotheses in the usual sense.

GITELSON, IDY B., and ALAN R. GITELSON. "Adolescent Attitudes toward Male and Female Political Candidates: An Experimental Design," *Women and Politics*, 4 (Winter 1980/81), 53-64. Mentioned first in Chapter 7. High school students' evaluations of hypothetical political candidates assessed, using multivariate analysis of variance, to determine relative contributions of sex of candidates, sex of subject, and success/failure of candidate on student's overall ratings of candidates, their potency, and their activity.

KIM, JOOCHUL. "Characteristics of Migrants within the Framework of Current Migration Direction in the United States: Some Evidence from Micro-Data Analysis," *Policy Sciences*, 12 (1980), 355-370. Using data from a longitudinal, nationwide sample survey subjected to multiple classification analysis, assesses the direction of migration—to urban or rural regions—of various categories of people. Dependent variable constructed to measure degree of urban/rural migration. Clear, easy to understand.

SUEDFELD, PETER, and SUSAN BLUCK. "Changes in Integrative Complexity Prior to Surprise Attacks," *Journal of Conflict Resolution*, 32 (December 1988), 626-635. Focuses more on significance tests than analyses of mean differences; nevertheless, means are given, and you can assess them. Same concept of "integrative complexity," as in their article listed in Chapter 1.

CHAPTER
16

DUMMY VARIABLE REGRESSION AND AN INTRODUCTION TO ANALYSIS OF COVARIANCE

DUMMY VARIABLES

The next procedure you will learn can be thought of in either of two ways. You can think of it as using regression to perform a two-way analysis of variance when the independent variables have more than the two categories of a dichotomy or as a method for using nominal independent variables in regression rather than the interval ones previously demanded.

Understanding this procedure, which is called dummy variable regression, will help with the next step, analysis of covariance, in which interval and noninterval independent variables are combined. Basically dummy variable regression is just an extension of the last chapter; so you can treat this as something of a review before the next step. As you go along, keep in mind that the dependent variable in the analyses must be interval or as close to interval as you can get it. We are going to be doing regression and analysis of variance here; both of them require the interval dependent variable because of the kinds of calculations involved.

Creating a Dummy Variable from a Single Nominal Variable

We can transform any single nominal variable that has multiple codes into a series of dichotomous variables. We will be making one real variable into several dummy variables. Since a concrete example helps, let's imagine we have a single nominal variable called REGION, which is coded as follows:

1 = South
2 = Northeast
3 = Northwest
4 = Southwest

We can't use this as an independent variable in regression as it stands because the category values don't have any particular meaningful order or intervalness. However, we could use the following four dichotomous variables, each of which is scored 0 or 1:

Southness   1 = yes; 0 = no
Northeastness   1 = yes; 0 = no
Northwestness   1 = yes; 0 = no
Southwestness   1 = yes; 0 = no

In order to create the four variables we can use, we simply take our cases and examine their codes on the original variable REGION and give them scores on all four new variables. When a case is scored 1 on the variable REGION, it gets a 1 on the variable Southness and a 0 on the other three variables—

Northeastness, Northwestness, and Southwestness. When a case is scored 2 on REGION, it gets a 0 on Southness, a 1 on Northeastness, and a 0 on both Northwestness and Southwestness, and so forth.

This can be accomplished in SPSS with IF statements; you don't have to do it by hand. You need the following SPSS statements:

```
IF (REGION EQ 1) SNESS = 1.
IF (REGION NE 1) SNESS = 0.
IF (REGION EQ 2) NENESS = 1.
IF (REGION NE 2) NENESS = 0.
IF (REGION EQ 3) NWNESS = 1.
IF (REGION NE 3) NWNESS = 0.
IF (REGION EQ 4) SWNESS = 1.
IF (REGION NE 4) SWNESS = 0.
```

(The last set of two IF statements is later left out, as explained below.) If a case originally did not have its region recorded and was given a missing value in the original data set on the variable REGION, the SPSS IF procedure gives it a missing value automatically for all the new dummy variables.

Using the Dummy Variables in an Analysis

If we were just interested in region as the one independent variable, we could do a regression analysis using the *set* of dummy variables created to represent the original region variable in place of an ordinary independent variable. We would want to compute the values for the coefficients in the equation:

$$Y = a + b_1\text{SNESS} + b_2\text{NENESS} + b_3\text{NWNESS} + e$$

We wouldn't put in the variable for SWNESS because a case's value on that dichotomy can be exactly predicted by knowledge of its values on the other dichotomies in the set of dummy variables. If we knew a case was scored 1 on SNESS and 0 on NENESS and 0 on NWNESS, we'd know it would have to be 0 on SWNESS. In other words, SWNESS is a perfect linear function of the others. As you learned in Chapter 13, regression can't be done when any independent variable is a perfect linear combination of any other independent variable or set of independent variables. In fact, if you happen to leave all the dummy variables in, SPSS will drop one of them out so that it can perform the regression. For myself, I prefer to pick the one that is dropped rather than leaving it to the program, but the outcome is the same either way.

Here's another way to say this: if any independent variable is perfectly correlated with any other one or any set of independent variable(s), no unique effect at all can be attributed to it, and it must be dropped from the equation. If you'll think back to the diagrams of overlapped circles in Chapter 11 and remember the one in which the circles for the two independent variables were very overlapped (Figure 11.5), you'll mentally have a visual representation of this idea. Two perfectly correlated independent variable cannot give you independent information. Their effects cannot be separated. Actually, we don't lose any information when we drop the one dummy variable, as you will soon see.

What would we get out of such a regression? You will get the prediction model: $Y = a + b_1\text{SNESS} + b_2\text{NENESS} + b_3\text{NWNESS} + e$. In it, the intercept, a, is like any other intercept, and the intercept is the predicted mean of Y when all independent variables are 0. Therefore, the intercept equals the mean of Y when a case is not South, not Northeast, and not Northwest. The intercept is the mean of Y, then, for cases in the *Southwest* category of the original REGION variable. (This is the information that is not lost by leaving the perfectly correlated variable out of the equation.)

The slopes are also interpreted in the same way we would interpret any other slopes. B_1 represents the increment in Y that results from a one-unit increase in SNESS on top of the intercept amount. Therefore, when all the independent variables except that which represents being southern are 0, $a + b_1$ equals the mean in Y for the Southern cases. B_2 represents the increment in Y that results from a one-unit

(0 to 1) increase in NENESS on top of the intercept amount. Therefore, when all the other independents are 0, $a + b_2$ equals the mean of Y for the Northeast cases, and so forth.

a = Mean of Y for Southwestern cases
$a + b_1$ = Mean of Y for Southern cases
$a + b_2$ = Mean of Y for Northeastern cases
$a + b_3$ = Mean of Y for Northwestern cases

The R^2 we get from such a regression is the proportion of variation explained by the *set* of dummy variables. It is equal to the proportion of variance explained by the original four-category ordinal independent variable were we using analysis of variance procedures rather than doing analysis of variance through a regression procedure. Thus the R^2 from this regression is equal to the E^2 that represents the explained variation around the four-category means of the REGION variable in an analysis of variance.

EXERCISE 1   One-Way Analysis of Variance; Dummy Variable Regression

Stop now and prove to yourself that analysis of variance with the original nominal variable and regression with a set of dummy variables constructed to represent the nominal variable will give you the same results. Write out a hypothesis that can be tested using data from one of the codebooks in the appendices. Make sure the independent variable in your hypothesis is a nominal variable that has more than two categories. Make the dependent variable one that is as interval as possible. In order to keep in practice, you may want to make your dependent variable one that can be measured with a multi-item index constructed with the COUNT procedure or summed standard scores. Use one of the dependent variables you constructed earlier if you want to.

Consider the Number of Cases Required. Regardless of whether you do this kind of analysis using analysis of variance or regression, you need quite a few cases in each category. To calculate a dependent variable mean on just a few cases can be very misleading. Therefore, before you decide what independent variables to use, examine their distributions in the codebook. Make sure each code has a good number of cases.

If there are so many codes on the nominal variable that some do not have enough cases, you will need to recode the variable first in order to combine the categories (but you want to end up with at least three categories or this won't be any different from the dichotomies you used in Chapter 15).

Were you just going to do a regression analysis here, you could combine categories of the variable when you set up the IF statements to create the dummy variables. For example, here are the statements you would need to combine all Southern cases into one group and all Northern cases into another:

```
IF (REGION EQ 1 OR REGION EQ 4)
  SOUTH = 1.
IF (REGION NE 1 AND REGION NE
  4) SOUTH = 0.
IF (REGION EQ 2 OR REGION EQ 3)
  NORTH = 1.
IF (REGION NE 2 AND REGION NE
  3) NORTH = 0.
```

However, you are also about to do a regular analysis of variance procedure to show that it and the regression using dummy variables give the same results. Therefore, if you are going to combine categories, you will first recode the variable in order to get the number of independent variable codes you want for the analysis of variance. Then you will construct your dummy variables using the recoded form of the nominal variable.

For example, suppose you had the nominal variable RELIGION with the following codes: 1 = Evangelical Protestant; 2 = Mainstream Protestant; 3 = Roman Catholic; 4 = Orthodox Catholic; 5 = Orthodox or Conservative Jew; 6 = Reform Jew; 7 = Oriental Religion; 8 = African Religion; 9 = Other; 0 = None. If you want to run your analysis of variance with just Protestant, Catholic, Jew/Other/

None as the three categories of the independent variable, you will first: RECODE RELIGION (1, 2 = 1) (3, 4 = 2) (0, 5 THRU HIGHEST = 3). That gets RELIGION into the form necessary for analysis of variance. Then you will set up the dummy variables necessary for regression:

```
IF (RELIGION EQ 1) PROT = 1.
IF (RELIGION NE 1) PROT = 0.
IF (RELIGION EQ 2) CATH = 1.
IF (RELIGION NE 2) CATH = 0.
```

There are two chief points to consider here: (1) you need enough cases in every category of the independent variable you are going to use in analysis of variance or in every half of each dichotomous dummy variable you are going to use in a regression for meaningful analysis; and (2), if you are trying to show that analysis of variance with a nominal independent variable gives the same results as regression with dummy independent variables, the categories on the single nominal variable and the set of dummy variables have to match.

Creating the Dummy Variables. If you don't have to worry about recoding categories, just write enough IF statements to create a series of dichotomous variables to represent the same nominal variable that you will use in the analysis of variance. Remember you will need two IF statements for every *value* of the nominal variable minus one value. You will not create a new variable for the last value of the nominal variable.

For this exercise, after your hypothesis, write out each of the values on the nominal variable and the IF statements necessary to transform them into dummy variables. Also write out the operationalization of the dependent variable. (If you are using a multi-item index, you can skip checking inter-item correlation in order to make the exercise shorter. Keep in mind, however, that an assessment of whether the items are measuring the same thing really ought to be done.)

Set up a computer job and run both REGRESSION and ANOVA. On the ANOVA, use the original (or recoded, if necessary) nominal variable to explain the dependent variable. On the REGRESSION, use your new series of dummy variables to explain the same dependent variable. You will need:

The accessing information to get to the stored data set.

The RECODE, if necessary, to combine categories of the independent variable to be used in ANOVA.

Enough IF statements to create the series of dummy variables.

The COUNT or COMPUTE statements necessary for constructing your dependent variable, if you are using a multi-item index (and any of the commands necessary to accompany COUNT).

ANOVA VARIABLES = depvar BY indvar (n,n)/. Here the "depvar" is the dependent variable name, either from the codebook or which results from your COUNT or COMPUTE; the "indvar" name is the SPSS name of the original nominal variable in the data set. (The high and low codes are the recoded values if you have recoded.)

STATISTICS = 1 3.   (SPSS/PC+)
STATISTICS = MCA MEAN.   (SPSS-X)
REGRESSION VARIABLES = name (dependent variable as on the ANOVA command) name, name, name (names from the IF statements for newly created dummy variables, omitting one category)/DEPENDENT = name/ENTER.
FINISH.

Remember the other subcommands on the REGRESSION to get other statistics. Insert DESCRIPTIVES/ before the variable list and the subcommand STATISTICS = R ANOVA COEFF ZPP before the DEPENDENT subcommand. Consult the SPSS manual for the details you may have forgotten.

When you get your output, be sure to examine the number of cases in each category first; this is your check that all is going well and you haven't lost cases somehow in the recoding procedure or the construction of the dummy variables. Then answer the following questions, which should indicate the similarities between analysis of variance and dummy variable regression. If you are not getting identical results, something is wrong. Try to figure out what and fix it. Ask for help if you have trouble.

	Male	Female
Southwest	$\bar{Y}$	$\bar{Y}$
South	$\bar{Y}$	$\bar{Y}$
Northeast	$\bar{Y}$	$\bar{Y}$
Northwest	$\bar{Y}$	$\bar{Y}$

1. What proportion of the variation in the dependent variable is explained by the independent variable in each technique? Here, look for the R^2 in REGRESSION and the E^2 in ANOVA.
2. What are the dependent variable means for the various categories of the independent variable as given by each technique? In REGRESSION, you will need to calculate the dependent variable means by using the regression equation, $Y = a + b_1 X + b_2 Z + b_3 W + b_4 V \ldots$, etc., for each of the dummy variables. You will add the appropriate slope value to the intercept (or use the intercept alone, when that is appropriate) to get the group means. In ANOVA, you can simply read the means printed out with from your request with the STATISTICS subcommand.
3. In words of plain English, describe the effect of the independent variable on the dependent variable and give an indication of how strong the relationship is.
4. Are the data consistent with your hypothesis? Explain briefly. Remember to examine the form as well as the strength of the relationship.

TWO-WAY ANALYSIS OF VARIANCE WITH DUMMY VARIABLES

Now, what if there is another independent variable? Let's keep things simple and consider the second independent a dichotomy, like sex, scored 0 = male and 1 = female, or imagine any variable that might meaningfully be *recoded* into a 0/1 dichotomy. (This procedure described below could also easily be extended to another set of dummies, which would represent another nominal variable with multiple codes; but using the dichotomy keeps the explanation simpler.)

Now we will be looking, as in two-way analysis of variance, at the variation in a dependent variable around the eight cell means defined by categories of the two independent variables:

In regression terminology, we can use a regression equation for—

$$Y = a + b_1\text{SNESS} + b_2\text{NENESS} + b_3\text{NWNESS} + b_4\text{SEX} + e$$

If the model is additive—that is, if there is no interaction—the actual means of the dependent variable within the eight groups defined by the two independent variables will equal the estimates of those means that we can derive from the regression coefficients as follows:

For Southwest males (0 on all independents),
$Y_p = a$
For Southwest females (0 on all but sex),
$Y_p = a + b_4$

For Southern males (0 on all but South),
$Y_p = a + b_1$
For Southern females (0 on all but South and sex), $Y_p = a + b_1 + b_4$

For Northeastern males, $Y_p = a + b_2$
For Northeastern females, $Y_p = a + b_2 + b_4$

For Northwestern males, $Y_p = a + b_3$
For Northwestern females, $Y_p = a + b_3 + b_4$

Now that we have more than one independent variable, however, we must consider the possibility that interaction exists. We will need terms in the equation that will allow the separate mean for each sex/region group to be higher or lower than would be predicted from sex and region additively.

If we compute a set of interaction variables that are the products of each of the dummy variables with sex, we can allow for this. (Before you do this, be sure that the dichotomy is coded 0 and 1 or recode it so that it is.)

```
COMPUTE INTER1 = (SNESS *
   SEX).
COMPUTE INTER2 = (NENESS *
   SEX).
COMPUTE INTER3 = (NWNESS *
   SEX).
```

(SPSS will automatically give a missing value to each of the three interaction terms if a case is missing on either REGION or SEX.)

Examine each of those COMPUTE statements carefully. We have made a new variable called INTER1 that will be coded 1 only for Southern females. It will be 0 for everyone else. We have also created a new variable called INTER2 that will be scored 1 only for Northeastern females. It will be 0 for everyone else, and so on.

Now we can do a regression to get the coefficients for—

$$Y = a + b_1 \text{SNESS} + b_2 \text{NENESS}$$
$$+ b_3 \text{NWNESS} + b_4 \text{SEX}$$
$$+ b_5 \text{INTER1} + b_6 \text{INTER2}$$
$$+ b_7 \text{INTER3} + \text{Error}$$

The variables list on the REGRESSION command will have to include the SPSS names of the dependent variable, the dichotomy, all (except the omitted category) of the dummy variables that represent the nominal variable, and all the interaction terms (as many as included dummies).

Now, remembering on which variables each case is going to be scored 0, you can use the slopes on the output to figure out the means of all the categories created by the dichotomy and the nominal variable taken together. We get the dependent variable mean for each of the categories created by the two independent variables by adding together the relevant effects of region, sex, and interaction. Since we have now allowed for nonadditivity, the estimated means from the regression equation will equal the means really present in the data:

For Southwest males (0 on all independents),
$Y = a$

For Southwest females (0 on all but sex),
$Y = a + b_4$

For Southern males (0 on all but South),
$Y = a + b_1$

For Southern females (0 on all but South, sex, and South interaction), $Y = a + b_1 + b_4 + b_5$

For Northeastern males, $Y = a + b_2$
For Northeastern females,
$Y = a + b_2 + b_4 + b_6$

For Northwestern males, $Y = a + b_3$
For Northwestern females,
$Y = a + b_3 + b_4 + b_7$

The multiple R^2 we get from this regression is the same as the multiple E^2 we'd get from analysis of variance using REGION and SEX as two independent variables considering interaction important enough to treat as an explanatory variable included in the explained variation.

EXERCISE 2 Two-Way Analysis of Variance with Dummy Variables

For this exercise, you will run both a two-way ANOVA and a REGRESSION to see that they are the same and to practice your interpretation of both. Write a hypothesis that uses one dichotomy (or recode something into a 0/1 dichotomy) and one nominal variable (which has more than two values) as independent variables to explain an interval dependent variable. Make sure the hypothesis can be tested with the data from one of the data sets in the appendices. The dependent variable can be a multi-item index, if you like, even one you have used before.

After the hypothesis, write out RECODES, if necessary, and the IF statements for creating the series of dummy variables. Also make sure the categories on the independents all have good numbers of cases. Then write out the operationalization of the dependent variable.

Set up and submit both an ANOVA and a REGRESSION as follows. Examine your output in order to answer the questions that will walk you through the similarities of the two procedures. You'll need—

The accessing information to get to the stored SPSS file.
Whatever COUNT or COMPUTE commands are necessary to create your dependent variable. (Remember the other commands needed in COUNT.)
Whatever RECODE statements you need to (1) get your dichotomy to 0/1 or (2) combine categories on the other nominal variable.
IF statements to create the series of dummies. Remember you need two statements for each value on the nominal variable except one.
Whatever COMPUTES are necessary for the interaction terms.

```
ANOVA VARIABLES = depname BY
  dichname (0,1) indvar (n,n)/
  STATISTICS = 1 3.    (SPSS/PC+)
  STATISTICS = MCA MEAN(SPSS-X)
ANOVA VARIABLES = depname BY
  dichname (0,1) indvar (n,n)/
  OPTIONS = 3.         (SPSS/PC+)
  MAXORDERS = NONE.    (SPSS-X)
REGRESSION VARIABLES =
  depname,
  dichname, dumone, dumtwo,
  dumthree, interone,
  intertwo,
  interthree/DEP =
  depname/ENTER dichname/ENTER
  dumone, dumtwo,
  dumthree/ENTER interone,
  intertwo, interthree.
FINISH.
```

On the REGRESSION command, put the name of the interval dependent variable wherever it says "depname." Put the name of the dichotomy wherever it says "dichname." Put the names of *all* your dummy variables (except the omitted category, remember) from the IF statements where it says "dumone, dumtwo, dumthree." Put the names of *all* your interaction variables where it says "interone, intertwo, interthree." Remember to put the DESCRIPTIVES and STATISTICS subcommands on the REGRESSION command.

On the first ANOVA, you'll look at interaction to see whether it matters, just as you did in Chapter 15. If it doesn't matter, you'll turn to the second ANOVA output on which interaction is treated as error.

The setup above allows you to do much the same thing on REGRESSION output. Notice you now have three ENTER subcommands on that regression statement. The first block of your regression output will have only the dichotomy as an explanatory variable and the statistics associated with that bivariate regression. The second block of the regression output will have the set of dummy variables in addition to the dichotomy as explanatory variables and the statistics associated with that multivariate regression. The third block of the output will have, in addition to the dichotomy and the set of dummy variables, the interaction terms as explanatory variables and the statistics associated with that expanded multivariate regression.

At each block, you will be able to look at the R^2 to see if the additional variable(s) explains much more of the variation in the dependent variable. If interaction doesn't explain much more when it is entered in the third block, you will just consider it part of the error and use the output of the second block, in which interaction is treated as error (because it hasn't been brought in as an explanatory variable yet). The second block is the equivalent of the second ANOVA, in which interaction is treated as part of the error rather than as a part of the explanation. If the dummies added in the second block explained little or nothing, you could just interpret the first block where you have the single dichotomy as the sole independent variable. To have an ANOVA analogous to that, you'd need to run a bivariate ANOVA with the dichotomy as the only independent variable.)

1. First examine the interaction and see if either the ANOVA or the REGRESSION gives you any reason to think it is worth worrying about. What do you look at to tell? What is your decision? Given your decision, which ANOVA output will you be using for the rest of your

interpretation? Which block of the REGRESSION output?
2. What percentage of the variation in the dependent variable is explained by the two independent variables (and their interaction, if it is relevant) in ANOVA? By the set of dummies and the dichotomy (and their interaction, if it is relevant) in REGRESSION? Briefly state what you examine on both outputs to answer that question.
3. What are the forms of the relationships between the independent variables and the dependent variable? Construct tables that show either the means of the dependent variable which are predicted by the additive model in both analysis of variance and regression or the actual dependent variable means. Do the means predicted by the additive model if you have decided that interaction is unimportant. Do the actual means if you have decided it is important.
   a. The dependent variable means predicted for the groups defined by the independent variables can be estimated from the MCA table you get from the ANOVA where you have used the STATISTICS subcommand. Remember that you take the grand mean and add/subtract the two adjusted deviations for each group that is created by values on both your independent variables.
   b. The equivalent information (about the means that are predicted by an additive model) can be gotten from the REGRESSION output by taking the prediction equation in which just the dummy variables and the dichotomy are treated as independent variables from the second block of the output. You use the coefficients there to estimate the means of the groups you have created.
   c. The actual means of the groups can be seen on the ANOVA output in which you requested the means through a STATISTICS subcommand. Be sure you are looking at the means for the groups created by the two independent variables simultaneously—not the groups created by looking at the independent variables one at a time.
   d. Finally, the actual means of the groups can be calculated from the third block of the REGRESSION output by using the full prediction model with all the set of dummy variables, the dichotomy, and all the interaction terms treated as explanatory variables. If a particular interaction term is explaining very little of the variation in Y, it may not appear in the regression model in the third step. (Variables have to have certain explanatory power before they are entered by the SPSS program.) If that happens to you, just consider the slope on that interaction term to be 0. You won't be far off in your estimate of the exact mean of that group, but you may be a little off.
4. Now write out a sentence or two in which you describe, in words, the effect your independent variables (and their interaction, if relevant) are having on the dependent variable.
5. Are the data consistent with your hypothesis? Explain briefly. Remember to consider both the forms of the relationships and their strength.

Having done that, you will now turn to just one final complication before you get back to the somewhat less esoteric area of crosstabulation tables. Don't forget, as you go on, that the technique you have just been using can be used for more than one set of dummies for several nominal variables. The only problem is that all the interaction terms get cumbersome.

COMBINING INTERVAL AND NONINTERVAL INDEPENDENT VARIABLES

The one further complication before leaving regression and analysis of variance is the combination of interval and dichotomous independent variables (or, instead of a natural dichotomy, a nominal variable with several values transformed into dummy variables).

Let's review for a minute what it is we are doing with *all* these exercises that have anything to do with measures of relationship. We are trying to explain variation in a dependent variable—explaining why all cases are not just alike on some phenomenon we are interested in. To do this, we use selected independent variables. Typically, we begin with one independent variable related to the dependent. We then add additional independent variables in order to add explanation, assess whether the original relationship was spurious, clarify the original relationship, determine whether the second intervenes between the independent and dependent variables, or determine under what conditions the original bivariate relationship holds.

We need to have more than one statistical technique for doing this because we have different levels of measurement for different variables. Interval-level dependent variables can be used either with regression or analysis of variance depending on the measurement level of the independent variables.

Each statistic is based on assumptions appropriate to a different level of measurement. Regression assesses the impact on a dependent of any one-unit increase in the independent variable. This assumes that one-unit increments in an independent variable make sense; that is, each unit increment of the independent is an equal distance to any other unit increment, and any unit increment has the same effect as any other unit increment. In short, regression assumes interval independents (or a single unit in a dichotomy) and a linear relationship.

Analysis of variance, on the other hand, assesses the difference of dependent variable means within categories of an independent variable. The distance between categories of the independent variable or the order of categories of the independent variable is irrelevant. It is appropriate, therefore, for nominal or ordinal independent variables.

Still, both regression and analysis of variance essentially do the same thing. They allow us to explain why some cases are above and some below the mean on a dependent variable, and they allow us to explain why some are farther up or down than others. Both techniques allow us to add explanation, assess spuriousness, clarify relationships, examine intervention, and see specification in our data. In both, we can get some measures of both the *strength* and the *form* of relationships.

Many of the same cautions apply to both regression and analysis of variance. If the independent variables are correlated, it is tricky to determine which of the independents is causing that variation in the dependent that could be attributed to either of the independents. Both independents taken together may seem to be important causes, while neither taken separately appears important. (Remember multicollinearity.)

Both techniques, moreover, assume that interaction has been determined not to be an important consideration before a partial of any kind (correlation or slope) is calculated. Remember that a partial correlation or slope is meaningful only if it holds true, regardless of the level (value/score/condition) of the variable being controlled. If a relationship between two variables differs, depending on the level of another variable (if interaction is important), different summary statistics describing the relationship must be presented for each condition of the control. (Remember specification or statistical interaction.)

Pictures and Equations

Interval Independent Variables. Having reviewed what we are about, let's turn to the situation of combining interval and dichotomous independent variables. Let's view the situation in pictures first. Let's say we've done a scatterplot like Figure 16.1. We then run a regression and find the slope as in Figure 16.2.

When figuring how much of the variation in the dependent variable [$\Sigma (Y_i - \overline{Y})^2$] is unexplained by the independent, we measure the distance from each actual point to the line, square it, and sum the results: $\Sigma (Y_i - Y_p)^2$.

Interval Independent, Two Groups, Different Intercept, No Interaction. But imagine that there are two groups of cases in our data, one with a higher average score on the dependent variable than the other, even though the interval independent variable has the same ef-

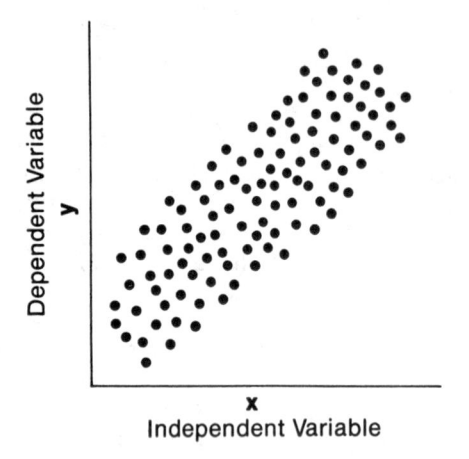

FIGURE 16.1 Scatterplot, Two Interval Variables

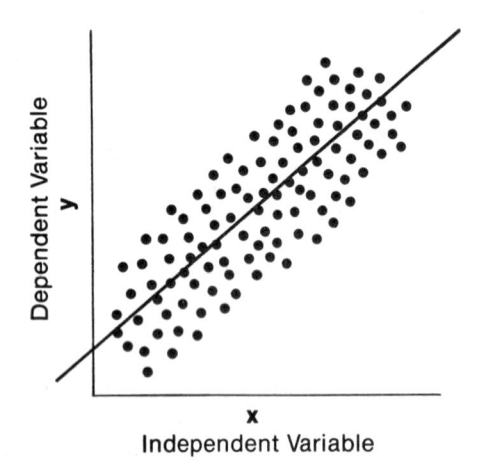

FIGURE 16.2 Scatterplot and Slope, Two Interval Variables

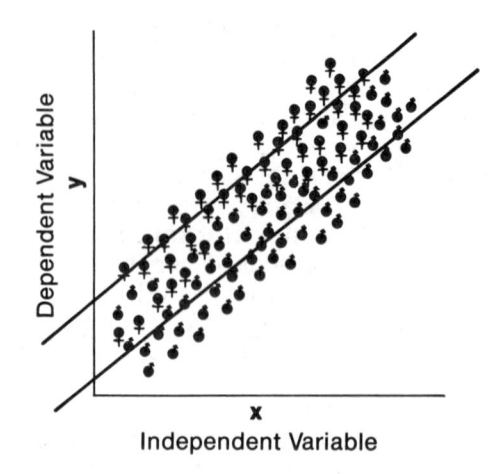

Figure 16.3 Scatterplot and Two Slopes, Two Interval Variables, and a Dichotomy

fect for the two groups. (Because it's easy to label, let's imagine the two groups are males, ♂, and females, ♀.)*

If there were a way, we'd be better off, as we try to explain the variation in Y, drawing in two slopes, as in Figure 16.3. The top slope would represent the effect of X on Y for females; the bottom slope would represent the effect of X on Y for males. Now, rather than measuring error off the single line, we could measure error off two separate lines, which are closer to their respective cases, and reduce the error substantially. Rather than a single predicted value for males and females, both from $Y_p = a + bX + e$, we'd have two different predictions; and the one for females would give a higher prediction for any given value of X. In effect, we'd predict $Y_p = a + bX$, but would *add in* the difference between the male and female means to the prediction for females.

We can get both prediction equations in a single multivariate regression:

$$Y_p = a + b_{yx \cdot z}X + b_{yz \cdot x}Z + e$$

where:
X = The interval variable
Z = Sex, scored 0 for men and 1 for women

Remembering that the slope on a dichotomy represents the *difference of means* between the group scored 0 on that variable and the group scored 1 on that variable, the predicted value of Y for males is—

$$Y_p = a + b_{yx \cdot z}X + e$$

---
*The PLOT procedure in SPSS will produce scatterplots like this, in which a different symbol is used to represent a case's values on a third variable.

For females, it is—

$$Y_p = a + b_{yx \cdot z} X + b_{yz \cdot x} Z + e$$

The error remaining, the variation in Y that is unexplained by X and Z, is simply the cases' actual scores on Y minus their predicted scores, squared, and summed: Error remaining $= \Sigma (Y_i - Y_p)^2$.

The partial slope on X ($b_{yx \cdot z}$) represents the effect on Y of a one-unit increment of the interval variable X, after adjusting out the effects of the dichotomy. The partial slope on Z ($b_{yz \cdot x}$) represents the effect on Y of being in group 1 rather than group 0 on Z, after adjusting out the effects of the interval variable. If X and Z are uncorrelated, those partial slopes would be the same as the bivariate slopes for the XY and ZY relationships.

The partial correlation coefficient squared of X and Y controlling Z ($r^2_{yx \cdot z}$) represents the proportion of variation in Y explained by the interval variable (X), while adjusting for the mean difference between $Z = 0$ and $Z = 1$. The partial correlation coefficient squared of Z and Y controlling X ($r^2_{zy \cdot x}$) represents the proportion of variation in Y explained by the dichotomy (Z), while adjusting for the effects of the interval variable (X).

The multiple $R^2_{y \cdot xz}$ represents the proportion of variation in Y explained by both X and Z—the interval and the dichotomous independent variables.

Interval Independent, Two Groups, Same Intercept, Interaction. But what if the effect of X on Y is not the same for the two categories of the dichotomy? Imagine first regressing Y on X and getting a scatterplot and then deriving its slope, as shown in Figure 16.4.

Again, imagine that two separate groups are concealed in the above scatterplot. If we were able to put in the best slope for each group, we'd get the results in Figure 16.5.

In terms of explaining variation in Y, we would be much better off using these two regression lines rather than the one we started with. This, however, is interaction; the effect

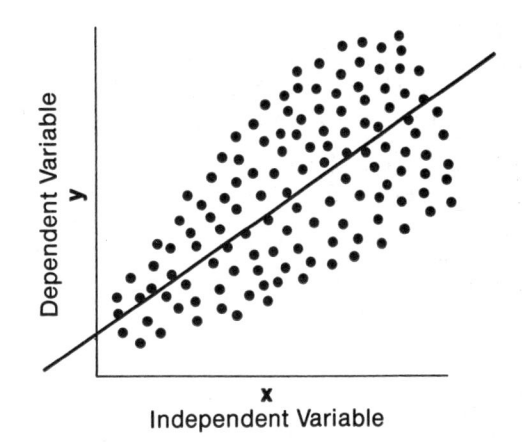

Figure 16.4 Scatterplot and Slope, Two Interval Variables

on Y of a one-unit increment in X is different for one group of cases than for another. Here the effect of X on Y is greater for females than the effect of X on Y for males.

We can handle that with an interaction term in the regression equation. We can compute the product of the interval and dichotomous variables and call it a new variable. We'd then just run a regression with—

$$Y_p = a + b_{yx \cdot zi} X + b_{yz \cdot xi} Z + b_{yi \cdot xz} I + e$$

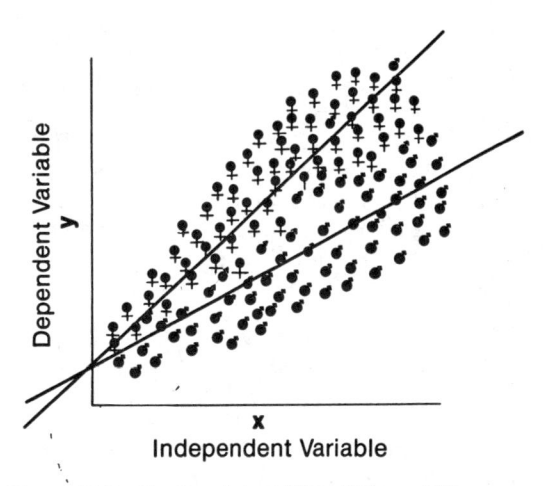

Figure 16.5 Scatterplot and Two Different Slopes, Two Interval Variables, and a Dichotomy

where:

X = Interval independent
Z = Dichotomy scored 0 and 1
I = Product of X and Z

We'd get two predictions models from this multivariate equation. We would get one for cases scored 0 on the dichotomy (and, therefore, 0 also on the variable that represents interaction): When $Z = 0$,

$$Y_p = a + b_{yx \cdot zi} X + e$$

We would get the second for $Z = 1$:

$$Y_p = a + (b_{yx \cdot zi} + b_{yi \cdot xz}) X + b_{yz \cdot xi} Z + e$$

Since the interval independent variable is, in effect, used twice, but with exactly the same value in the model when the dichotomy is scored 1 (i.e., once as X and once in the interaction variable), we can just add the two slopes together—the one for Y regressed on X and the one for Y regressed on the interaction variables—as the slope on X when the dichotomy equals 1. This will get us the steeper slope pictured above for cases scored 1 on the dichotomy.

In this regression, we can talk about the proportion of variation explained by X and Z and interaction using the multiple $R^2_{y \cdot xzi}$. We can indicate a slope for the effect of X on Y when $Z = 1$ and another for the effect of X on Y when $Z = 0$; but we cannot talk about a single partial slope for the effect of X on Y controlling the dichotomy because the effects of X are not the same for the two groups on the dichotomy. Similarly, we cannot talk about a single partial correlation between X and Y controlling the dichotomy because the correlation is not the same for the two groups.

Interval Independent, Two Groups, Different Intercept, Interaction. One more complication. Imagine you relate X and Y and get the bivariate scatterplot and slope in Figure 16.6. Concealed in this bivariate plot, however, you may again have two groups. If you could fit the best-fitting slopes for the two groups,

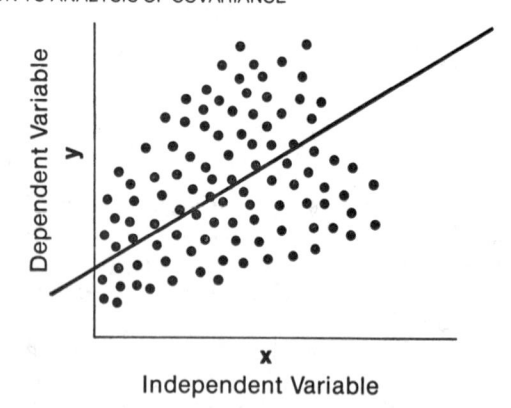

Figure 16.6 Scatterplot and Slope, Two Interval Variables

you'd have two slopes which indicated that the two groups differ not only on the effect of X on Y but also that they differ on the intercepts (average differences), as in Figure 16.7.

This can be represented with exactly the same regression as in the previous example:

$$Y_p = a + b_{yx \cdot zi} X + b_{yz \cdot xi} Z + b_{yi \cdot xz} I + e$$

It turns out that the coefficient on the dichotomy will be 0 in the previous example where the two intercepts coincided but will have a greater numeric value here. If all the difference between the two groups can be represented by the slope differences (no intercept difference),

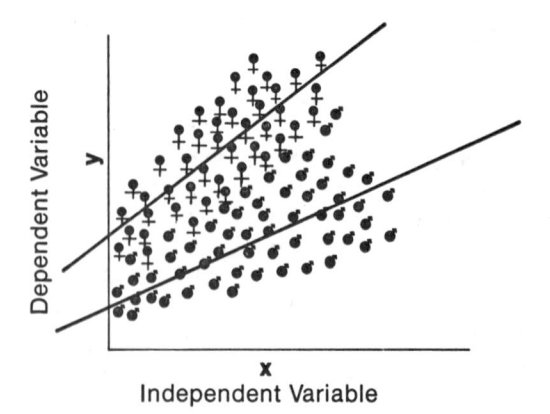

Figure 16.7 Scatterplot and Two Different Slopes, Two Interval Variables, and a Dichotomy

as in the previous picture, the effect of the dichotomy itself will be nil.

If, however, you have both a slope *and* an intercept difference, as you do here, it makes sense to think of some average difference between the groups *as well as* some difference in the effect of the interval variable.

Two prediction models can be extracted from the above model.

When $Z = 1$,

$$Y_p = (a + b_{yz \cdot xi}) + (b_{yx \cdot zi} + b_{yi \cdot xz} X) + e$$

(Since the slope on Z is added in every time $Z = 1$, it may as well be considered part of the intercept, as it is here, and this gets you a statistic that represents the higher intercept in the picture.)

When $Z = 0$

$$Y_p = a + b_{yx \cdot zi} X + e$$

(Note that, when $Z = 0$, the interaction variable is also 0 and, therefore, has no effect.)

Here as in the previous example, the multiple R^2 makes sense, as it normally does. The slopes of Y on the interval variable, however, have to be reported separately for each group on the dichotomy because there is no way to come up with a single number that represents the two effects of X on Y which differ depending on which group on Z is under consideration.

Similarly, the partial correlation coefficient $r_{yx \cdot z}$ doesn't make sense; the correlation between Y and X could be positive for one group and negative for another, and you'd get a near-zero $r_{yx \cdot z}$ despite clear correlation between X and Y when the groups are considered separately.

Remember what we said in Chapter 1: we seek simple and parsimonious explanations. We abstract from the real world rather than trying to represent it in each and every detail. Thus, unless our explanation of Y is substantially improved by the addition of an interaction term or by the addition of the dichotomy,

we'd rather just have the simple XY relationship.

How to tell? At this point, the easiest way is to see whether your explanation is improved enough to convince you that the complicating terms are necessary. Do they let you better understand the phenomenon represented by the dependent variable—enough to justify the complication? If yes, leave them in. If no, use the bivariate.

EXERCISE 3 Combining Interval and Noninterval Independent Variables

1. Select an interval or near-interval independent, interval or near-interval dependent, and a dichotomous independent variable from one of the data sets in the appendices. Write out your hypothesis and operationalizations of your variables.
2. Recode the dichotomy, if necessary, so it's values become 0 and 1. (Watch out! If 0 has been declared a missing value in the stored data set, 0 must be recoded to some other number first; *and*, after the recode, you must put in a missing value statement to declare the new missing value on that variable.)
3. COMPUTE the interaction variable as a product of the interval variable and the dichotomy.
4. Run REGRESSION. On the variable list, indicate the names of the following: the dependent, the interval independent, the dichotomous independent, and the computed interaction variable. Do the ENTER subcommand three times. First, enter the interval independent; next, the dichotomous independent; and finally, the interaction variable.
5. Complete the tasks and answer the following questions:
    a. Write out a prediction model that indicates the additive effects of the independent variable and the dichotomy. Use the form, $Y = a + b_1 \text{ind} + b_2 \text{dichot} + e$, but substitute the proper values for the coefficients and use your own variable names. To do this, you will use the coefficients from block two of the output. Make a summary statement

that describes the additive effects of the independent variables on the dependent variable. Remember to include the direction of the relationship between the interval independent and dependent with the dichotomy controlled, as well as the effects of the dichotomy with the interval indedent controlled.

b. Then, write out two prediction models that allow for interaction—one for the relationship between the independent and the dependent variable when the dichotomy is 0 and another for the relationship when the dichotomy is 1. Use the coefficients from block three of the output; remember that, when the dichotomy is 0, all you will need is $Y = a + b_1\text{ind}$. When the dichotomy is 1, you will need $Y = (a + b_3) + (b_1 + b_4)\text{ind} + e$. Make two summary statements in words that describe the effects of the independent on the dependent variable for the two conditions described by the dichotomy.

c. What proportion of the variation in the dependent variable do you explain using the interval independent, the dichotomy, and the interaction variable? See the multiple R^2 from block three. And what proportion of the variation in the dependent variable is explained by just the interval independent and the dichotomy? See the multiple R^2 at block two. From that comparison, indicate which model you find more satisfactory: the more complicated one with the interaction terms, where you have to have two statements to describe the relationship between X and Y; or the less complicated one without the interaction terms, where one statement summarizes the relationship?

d. Assuming for the moment that interaction is irrelevant, look just at the second block of the output. What proportion of the variation in the dependent variable is explained by the interval independent after the dichotomy has explained all it can? Look for the partial on the line with the name of the interval variable and square it. What proportion of the variation in the dependent variable is explained by the dichotomy after the interval independent variable has explained all it can? Look for the partial on the line with the name of the dichotomy and square it. Which of the independent variables—the interval one or the dichotomy—is the more important cause of the dependent variable? Look at the betas next to the names of each independent variable.

Notice that you have all the information you need to assess whether a bivariate XY relationship was spuriously due to Z, whether Z is intervening in the XY relationship, whether Z is suppressing or distorting the XY relationship, whether the XY relationship is partially spurious or Z is partially intervening, etc. The technique you have just seen is simply one way of combining two different kinds of independent variables in the same analysis.

One extremely important thing about this kind of analysis is how it may let you handle interaction between two interval independent variables. When the relationship between an interval independent variable and a dependent variable differs depending on the level of another interval independent variable, you may be able to dichotomize the second one and use the procedure indicated here. It is even possible to extend the procedure here to more than two nominal categories of the second independent variable. By now, you should at least have the beginnings of a grasp on those possibilities.

You've just begun an understanding of a technique called analysis of covariance. It can take multiple nominal and interval independent variables, but more than one interval independent variable becomes complex indeed. Sometimes it is done using analysis of variance or multiple analysis of variance (MANOVA in SPSS) procedures. In this introduction, however, where the independents are one interval and a dichotomy coded 0/1, the use of regression procedures keeps its ties to the other techniques clearer.

Do remember that the techniques we have been using in this chapter demand interval dependent variables. Like any other analysis of variance or regression, dummy variable analysis has to be able to deal with means on the dependent variable. If you need sophisticated techniques for nominal dependent variables, there are sources listed among the readings for Chapter 7. If you can get by with less sophisticated, crosstabular analyses turn to the next chapter.

SUGGESTED READINGS

Dummy Variables

BERENSON, MARK L., DAVID M. LEVINE, and MATTHEW GOLDSTEIN. *Intermediate Statistical Methods and Applications: A Computer Package Approach* (Englewood Cliffs, NJ: Prentice-Hall, 1983), Ch. 12.

BLALOCK, HUBERT M., JR. *Social Statistics*, 2nd ed. (N.Y.: McGraw-Hill, 1972), pp. 498-502.

BOWEN, BRUCE D., and HERBERT F. WEISBERG. *An Introduction to Data Analysis* (San Francisco: Freeman, 1980), pp. 160-161.

DRAPER, N. R., and H. SMITH. *Applied Regression Analysis* (N.Y.: Wiley, 1966), pp. 134-141.

HANUSHEK, ERIC A., and JOHN E. JACKSON. *Statistical Methods for Social Scientists* (N.Y.: Academic Press, 1977), pp. 101-108, pp. 124-128.

KERLINGER, FRED N., and ELAZAR J. PEDHAZUR. *Multiple Regression in Behavioral Research* (N.Y.: Holt, Rinehart, and Winston, 1973), pp. 72-76, pp. 105-109.

KLEINBAUM, DAVID G., and LAWRENCE L. KUPPER. *Applied Regression Analysis and Other Multivariable Methods* (North Scituate, MA: Duxbury, 1978), pp. 188-208.

SHIVELY, W. PHILLIPS. *The Craft of Political Research*, 2nd ed. (Englewood Cliffs, NJ: Prentice-Hall, 1980), pp. 142-144.

WONNACOTT, RONALD J., and THOMAS H. WONNACOTT. *Regression: A Second Course in Statistics* (N.Y.: Wiley, 1981), pp. 104-119.

IF Statements

NORUSIS, MARIJA J. *SPSS/PC+* (Chicago: SPSS, Inc., 1988). Conditional transformations (IF) are discussed on pp. B33-B37; commands are on C72-C74.

SPSS-X User's Guide, 3rd ed. (Chicago: SPSS, Inc., 1988). See Chapter 9, Conditional Transformation, pp. 154-167.

Combining Interval and NonInterval Independent Variables

BLALOCK, HUBERT M., JR. *Social Statistics*, 2nd ed. (N.Y.: McGraw-Hill, 1972), Ch. 20.

KERLINGER, FRED N., and ELAZAR J. PEDHAZUR. *Multiple Regression in Behavioral Research* (N.Y.: Holt, Rinehart, and Winston, 1973), pp. 265-277.

KLEINBAUM, DAVID G., and LAWRENCE L. KUPPER. *Applied Regression Analysis and Other Multivariable Methods* (North Scituate, MA: Duxbury, 1978), pp. 209-226.

NIE, NORMAN H., et al. *SPSS*, 2nd ed. (N.Y.: McGraw-Hill, 1975). See Chapter 21, "Special Topics in General Linear Models," pp. 368-398. The SPSS procedures in this manual have been updated and are no longer valid, but the discussion of what they do for you is excellent.

WELDT, ALBERT R., and OLLI T. AHTOLA. *Analysis of Covariance*, #12 in series, *Quantitative Applications in the Social Sciences* (Beverly Hills, CA: Sage, 1978).

ARTICLES

DEKKER, PAUL, and PETER ESTER. "Working-Class Authoritarianism: A Re-examination of the Lipset Thesis," *European Journal of Political Research*, 15 (1987), 395-415. Mentioned first in Chapter 8. Dutch survey data. Tables 5 and 6 are multiple regression using, principally, dummy variables and dichotomies.

IYENGAR, SHANTO, and DONALD R. KINDER. *News that Matters* (Chicago: University of Chicago Press, 1987), Ch. 7, pp. 63-72, and Appendix B, pp. 144-147. Experimental design, first mentioned in Chapter 11. This chapter tests the "priming effect"—the degree to which television news can influence the standards against which

KAY, SUSAN. "Feminist Ideology, Race, and Political Participation: A Second Look," *Western Political Quarterly*, 38 (September 1985), 476-484. Uses multiple regression with dummy variable and interaction terms to assess curvilinearity in the relationship between feminism and political participation, as well as differential effects of feminism across racial groups. Attention to measurement problems.

KELLOUGH, JAMES E., and SUSAN ANN KAY. "Affirmative Action in the Federal Bureaucracy: An Impact Assessment," *Review of Public Personnel Administration*, 6 (Spring 1986), 1-13. Multiple regression with interaction terms to assess differences in hiring blacks and women between times before and after Civil Service Commission endorsement of the use of goals and timetables. A "naturally occurring" experimental design using percentage black or female at various grade levels as dependent variable. Four possible patterns of impact are omitted in printing; try to figure out which or write me for the others. Note that the slope for grades 9-11 in Figure 3 is incorrectly printed.

MCCRONE, DONALD J., and WALTER J. STONE. "The Structure of Constituency Representation: On Theory and Method," *Journal of Politics*, 48 (1986), 956-975. Mentioned first in Chapter 5; after page 966, article illustrates one method of handling nonlinear relationships beyond what has been done in this text. Good discussion of limitations of data sources.

ROTHGEB, JOHN M., JR. "Trojan Horse, Scapegoat, or Non-Foreign Entity: Foreign Policy and Investment Penetration in Poor Countries," *Journal of Conflict Resolution*, 31 (June 1987), 227-265. Tests three models "of how foreign investment affects foreign policy behavior in Third World countries (p. 242)." Expectations for the three are clearly spelled out. Foreign policy behavior measured using events data, clearly spelling out operationalization. Multiple regression analysis with dummy variables and interaction terms. Includes time-lagged analyses.

SEROKA, JIM, and ANDREW D. MCNITT. "Energy and Environmental Roll-Call Voting in the U.S. Congress in 1975 and 1979," *Policy Studies Review*, 3 (May 1984), 406-416. Average environmental and energy voting scores analyzed, using multiple regression with interactive terms, to assess impact of party, ideology, regions, and group characteristics. The equation and explanation at the top of page 412 is probably mistyped: b_0 ought to represent the intercept (not party) and X_1 (not b_1) through X_5 (not b_5), then, ought to be indicated as party, seniority, Southern interaction, Northeastern interaction, income interaction.

SHIN, EUI HANG, and IK KI KIM. "Variations in the Duration of Reign of Monarchs," *Comparative Political Studies*, 18 (April 1985), 104-122. Mentioned first in Chapter 2. Table 2 is a bivariate correlation matrix. Balance of the article is based on a dummy variable analysis comparable to, but more complex than, that used in the text. There are four dummy variables (kinship type, causes of removal, period of ascent, and country); also controlled are two interval variables (age at ascent and duration of reign). MCA analysis, assuming additivity, used.

SLOAN, JOHN, and KENT L. TEDIN. "The Consequences of Regime Type for Public-Policy Outputs," *Comparative Political Studies*, 20 (April 1987), 98-124. Uses, in dummy variable form, regime type (carefully operationalized into five types) and years regime has existed to explain various measures of military, economic, and social policies over 20 years for 20 Latin American nations. Also introduces an interaction term. The case under consideration is a country for a year. Authors use generalized least squares regression rather than ordinary least squares taught in this text. GLS is a way of dealing with a problem that frequently occurs in over-time data: the residuals at one time are correlated with those of the next time and interfere with the assessment of error around the slopes. However, the interpretation of the final statistics differs little from OLS. The article should be accessible at this point and offers nice attention to why other authors may have found little effect of regime type.

STONECASH, JEFF, and SUSAN W. HAYES. "The Sources of Public Policy: Welfare Policy in the American States," *Policy Studies Journal*, 9 (Spring 1981), 681-697. Pays close attention to whether the statistical model chosen appropriately matches the theoretical assumptions. Shows previous research to have implicitly assumed (by using additive regression models) that political and economic factors were each sufficient sources of policy. Shows that an interactive model allows one to treat political system and economic factors as necessary but not sufficient sources of policy. Uses cultural characteristics of states as "proxy" or "surrogate" variables for political demands in testing the interactive model with wealth and strength of the governor as the other predictors of AFDC and Medicaid policy. Attention to multicollinearity, deletion of deviant cases from analysis, measurement.

WELSH, SUSAN. "Women as Political Animals? A Test of Some Explanations for Male-Female Political Participation Differences," *American Journal of Political Science*, 21 (November 1979), 711–730. Multiple regression to assess impact of gender on political participation controlling for structural and situational variables. Interprets standardized partial regression coefficient as difference in percent participating or difference in probability of male/female participation in thirteen forms of activity. Note use of unstandardized regression coefficients and interaction terms to calculate absolute means for the groups. Note use of dichotomous dependent variable.

CHAPTER 17

READING MULTIVARIATE TABLES AND CALCULATING PARTIALS FOR NOMINAL AND ORDINAL DATA

Now we turn to what happens when you have nominal or ordinal measurements on the independent, dependent, and control variables. It is important to keep in mind that you are still asking the same kinds of questions you would be if the measurement were more precise.

1. What is the effect of the independent variable on the dependent variable in the bivariate relationship?
2. What is the effect of the independent on the dependent when the control variable is held constant?
3. How strong are the combined or separate effects of the independent and control variables on the dependent variable?

It is also important to remember that the same cautions hold when you are using nominal or ordinal variables as would hold with more precise measurement.

1. The more correlated the independent variable and the control variable are with each other, the more difficult it is to know which is explaining what part of the variation in the dependent variable.
2. When the effect of X on Y is different within different categories of the control variable, a single summary of the effect of X on Y cannot be done; separate statements or statistics are required for each different relationship.

One difference here, where we are dealing with nominal or ordinal data on all the variables as compared to regression or analysis of variance, is that we really hold the control variable constant (statistically, not physically) as opposed to letting it explain all it can before letting the independent variable work on remaining variation. We do not adjust the scores on the dependent variable, taking out the effects of the control variable. We separate the cases into groups on the basis of their scores on the control variable; then we examine the relationship of the independent and dependent variables within categories of the control variable.

AN EXAMPLE

Exercise 1 Table Construction

Constructing a three-variable table at this point is an important first step and will make understanding how to read such tables easier. This procedure will help you get a feel for what's going on. If you feel that you already have a good grip on how to construct tables, you can skip to step 4.

Using the data in the exercise section of this chapter, make one slip of paper for each case. You can do this by photocopying the cases and cutting them up, or you can actually make one piece of paper per case and put on it, in order, the values that case has on each of the three variables. Then construct a table for the relationship of X to Y controlling for Z by following these steps:

1. Sort the cases into piles based on the value of Z. You will have three piles: one for $Z = 1$, another for $Z = 2$, and a third for $Z = 3$. Stop and think a moment: within each pile, Z does not vary. In the first pile, every case has the same value of Z (i.e., $Z = 1$); in the second pile, every case is $Z = 2$; and so on, for each value of the control variable. Since Z is constant *for each pile*, whatever XY relationship we find *within* each pile is the XY relationship *with* Z controlled.
2. Take *each* pile of cases from step 1, in turn, keeping the piles separated. Sort the cases into "subpiles" on the basis of the *independent* variable (X).
3. Now, keeping the control variable values separated and the independent values separated within each value of the control variable, sort the cases within each independent variable value into piles based on the values of the dependent variable (Y).
4. Construct a multivariate table like that in Table 17.1 and fill in the number of cases for each cell, as instructed below. (At the end of the cases in the exercises section, you will find a summary of the cases, which you may use to check your count or to fill in the cells without going through the above sorting procedure.)

    In the part of the table that is labeled $Z = 1$, you will record only the cases in your $Z = 1$ group—i.e., only those cases that have a score of 1 on the control variable. Similarly, on the part of the table labeled $Z = 2$, you will record only the cases in your $Z = 2$ group, and so forth, for the remaining value of the control.

    Therefore, in the part of the table labeled $Z = 1$, put the *number* of cases that are $X = 1$ and $Y = 3$ in the upper left cell; the *number* of cases that are $X = 2$ and $Y = 2$ in the middle cell; the *number* of cases that are $X = 3$ and $Y = 1$ in the lower right cell, and so forth, until all cells are filled in.

    Do the same things for the tables labeled $Z = 2$ and $Z = 3$.
5. Now draw another multivariate table like Table 17.1 and fill in the percentages in each cell. Just percentage each column of the table so that you will be able to see, within each category of Z, the relationship of X and Y with Z controlled.
6. It is sometimes of use in interpreting what is going on to have the *bivariate XY* relationship as well. It cannot be read directly off the multivariate table (Table 17.1), but it can easily be reconstructed from there. In order to recapture the bivariate table from the multivariate one, add the respective cell frequencies (*not* percentages) from the parts of the table under each category of the control variable; that is, begin in the three upper left corners and add all the frequencies that represent cases for which X is 1 and Y is 3; then add the three frequencies that represent cases for which X is 2 and Y is 3 for the middle top-row cell of a bivariate table; and so on, for each of the nine cells of a bivariate table. Enter the frequencies in a bivariate table, like the one shown in Table 17.2.

Then percentage each column so you can examine the bivariate (uncontrolled) relationship between X and Y. (Of course, you could have gotten this bivariate table using the sorting procedure described in Chapter 8.)

TABLE 17.1 Sample Multivariate Table

		Z_1 X				Z_2 X				Z_3 X		
	1	2	3	Total	1	2	3	Total	1	2	3	Total
Y	3				3				3			
	2				2				2			
	1				1				1			
	Total											

TABLE 17.2 Sample Bivariate Table

		X		
		1	2	3
Y	3			
	2			
	1			
	Total			

INTERPRETING THE TABLES

Examining the Bivariate Correlations

The Bivariate Relationship between the Independent and Dependent Variables. Are the independent and dependent variables correlated in the bivariate table? Look to see whether the distributions of the dependent variable in the percentaged *bivariate* table differ as you vary the independent; as you compare one value of the independent to another and another, are the distributions of Y within those categories of X different? Review Chapter 8 on reading tables, if necessary.

The Bivariate Relationship between the Independent and Control Variables. Are the independent and control variable correlated? To answer this question, you have two choices. You can construct a *bivariate* table of the relationship of X to Z; *or* you can see whether you can read the association directly off the control table, essentially constructing the bivariate table for the relationship between X and Z in your mind.

At the *bottom* of the segments of a control table, you will find the distribution of independent variable frequencies for each category of the control variable. Imagine that those raw numbers were percentaged to 100% within each control variable category. Are those percentaged distributions different or the same?

Perhaps an example like Table 17.3 will clarify things. In this example,

When $Z = 1$, X is distributed
$X = 1$ 35   25%
$X = 2$ 76   or   53%
$X = 3$ 31   22%

When $Z = 2$, X is distributed
$X = 1$ 60   24%
$X = 2$ 142   or   56%
$X = 3$ 52   20%

When $Z = 3$, X is distributed
$X = 1$ 105   23%
$X = 2$ 260   or   57%
$X = 3$ 89   20%

A table of that relationship would look like Table 17.4. As you examine the distributions of X and compare the distribution of X for one category of Z to that for another category of Z and so on, you can see that the percentaged distribution of X is virtually the same for each category of the control. X and Z are not correlated.

But now consider Table 17.5. Note that—

When $Z = 1$, X is distributed
$X = 1$ 70   49%
$X = 2$ 41   or   29%
$X = 3$ 31   22%

TABLE 17.3 Relationship between Independent and Control Variables

		Z_1				Z_2				Z_3			
		X				X				X			
		1	2	3	Total	1	2	3	Total	1	2	3	Total
Y	3												
	2												
	1												
	Total	35	76	31		60	142	52		105	203	89	

TABLE 17.4 Relationship between Independent and Control Variables

		Z		
		1	2	3
X	3	22%	20%	20%
	2	53	56	57
	1	25	24	23
	Total	100%	100%	100%

When $Z = 2$, X is distributed

$X = 1$	72		28%
$X = 2$	130	or	51%
$X = 3$	52		20%

When $Z = 3$, X is distributed

$X = 1$	89		20%
$X = 2$	125	or	27%
$X = 3$	240		53%

A table of that relationship would look like Table 17.6.

You can see that the percentaged distribution of X is different when you vary Z by looking first at $Z = 1$ with its distribution of X and then at $Z = 2$ with its distribution of X, and so forth. X and Z are correlated when the distribution of X is different in different categories of Z. The distribution of X is *contingent* on the value of Z; that is, the character of the distribution of X depends on the value of Z.

Notice that, if X and Z were perfectly correlated, all the $Z = 1$ cases would be $X = 3$; all the $Z = 2$ cases would be $X = 2$; and all the $Z = 3$ cases would be $X = 1$. If that happened, X would not be able to vary within categories of Z. If X could not vary, we would not be able to examine its relationship to Y when Z was controlled. Thus, we see that multicollinearity again makes it difficult or impossible to look at the separate effects of two correlated independent variables, while controlling the other. Notice that even with less than perfect correlation between X and Z, you'd start to get very few cases outside $X = 3$ when $Z = 1$, etc. Then your assessment of X's impact on Y wouldn't be very reliable because it would be based on few cases where X was outside 3 when $Z = 1$, or outside 2 when $Z = 2$, or outside 1 when $Z = 3$.

Notice clearly that you *do not* look at the value of Y or the distribution of Y at all when you are trying to figure out whether X and Z are correlated. In the *cells* of the control table, you find the distribution of the dependent variable Y. We didn't even need to fill in the cells in the control tables above to answer the question about the relationship of X and Z.

The Bivariate Relationship between the Control and Dependent Variables. The *bivariate* relationship between the control and dependent variables has to be read from the

TABLE 17.6 Relationship between Independent and Control Variables

		Z		
		1	2	3
X	3	22%	20%	53%
	2	29	51	27
	1	49	28	20
	Total	100%	100%	100%

TABLE 17.5 Relationship between Independent and Control Variables

		Z_1				Z_2				Z_3			
		X				X				X			
		1	2	3	Total	1	2	3	Total	1	2	3	Total
Y	3												
	2												
	1												
	Total	70	41	31		72	130	52		89	125	240	

TABLE 17.7 Relationship between Dependent and Control Variables

		Z_1 X				Z_2 X				Z_3 X		
		1	2	3	Total	1	2	3	Total	1	2	3	Total
Y	3				37				57				101
	2				72				149				267
	1				33				48				86
	Total												

marginals, just as the bivariate XZ relationship does (or from a table separately constructed from a sort on the basis of Z, as if it were independent, and subsequent sorts on Y within each category of Z). But this time you examine the distribution of Y within each category of Z without regard to X. The frequency distribution of Y for each category of Z is found at the *side* of each segment of the control table.

Again, imagine an example like Table 17.7. As you can see,

When $Z = 1$, Y is distributed
$Y = 3$ 37   26%
$Y = 2$ 72   or   51%
$Y = 1$ 33   23%

TABLE 17.8 Relationship between Dependent and Control Variables

		Z		
		1	2	3
Y	3	26%	22%	22%
	2	51	59	59
	1	23	19	19
	Total	100%	100%	100%

When $Z = 2$, Y is distributed
$Y = 3$ 57   22%
$Y = 2$ 149   or   59%
$Y = 1$ 48   19%

When $Z = 3$, Y is distributed
$Y = 3$ 101   22%
$Y = 2$ 267   or   59%
$Y = 1$ 86   19%

Tabling those distributions would give us Table 17.8, in which Y and Z are barely, if at all, correlated.

Consider, however, another example in Table 17.9.

When $Z = 1$, Y is distributed:
$Y = 3$ 73   51%
$Y = 2$ 39   or   27%
$Y = 1$ 30   21%

When $Z = 2$, Y is distributed:
$Y = 3$ 69   27%
$Y = 2$ 134   or   53%
$Y = 1$ 51   20%

TABLE 17.9 Relationship between Dependent and Control Variables

		Z_1 X				Z_2 X				Z_3 X		
		1	2	3	Total	1	2	3	Total	1	2	3	Total
Y	3				73				69				86
	2				39				134				123
	1				30				48				245
	Total												

When $Z = 3$, Y is distributed:

$Y = 3$	86		19%
$Y = 2$	123	or	27%
$Y = 1$	245		54%

Tabling that distribution yields Table 17.10. Clearly, in this example, Z and Y are rather highly correlated.

Notice clearly that, when the bivariate correlation of the control, Z, and the dependent, Y, variables is at issue, the distribution of Y within categories of X—i.e., the distribution in the cells of the control table—is irrelevant. You are only interested here in the joint distributions of Z and Y; the distributions of X don't need to be considered at all.

EXERCISE 2 Bivariate Correlations on the Example Table

For the example table that you constructed earlier, figure out all the bivariate associations. Are X and Y correlated? How about X and Z? And Z and Y? Write out your conclusions on whether a correlation exists between each pair of variables (ignoring—not controlling—the others). Tell what figures you examined to come up with your answer. It will help you understand what is going on in the data if you will refer to the variable names rather than X and Z and Y.

Why Bother with Bivariate Correlations?

If this seems like a lot of trouble, remember that one thing we are trying to do is to sort out causal processes. We are trying to explain why we got or didn't get a bivariate correlation between X and Y. Knowing all the bivariate correlations will go a long way toward helping us understand what's going on.

If X and Z—the *independent and control variables*—are *uncorrelated*, the control variable may: (1) do nothing; (2) add to our explanation of the dependent variable; (3) specify the XY relationship—making the independent/dependent variable relationship different depending on the value of Z; but the control variable cannot be extraneous, antecedent, or intervening. If the control variable is uncorrelated with the independent variable and uncorrelated with the dependent variable, the control variable cannot be adding explanation of the dependent, but it still may specify the XY relationship.

If X and Z—the *independent and control variables*—are *correlated*, the control variable may be: (1) extraneously causing both the independent and dependent variables; (2) antecedent to the independent variable, but then we would not likely be controlling it; (3) intervening between the independent and dependent variables; (4) adding to the explanation of the dependent variable; (5) suppressing or distorting the XY relationship; (6) specifying the XX relationship—making it different for different values of Z. Or the control variable may be doing one of several combinations of these. If the control variable is correlated with the independent variable, but uncorrelated with the dependent variable, the control variable cannot be extraneous, antecedent, intervening, adding, suppressing, or distorting, but it may still be specifying the XY relationship.

Thus, you can see how we can limit the number of possibilities for interpreting a multivariate table by knowing the bivariate correlations first.

Examining the Controlled Correlations

Finally, you are ready to examine the XY relationship controlling for Z. At last, you get to read the *cells* of the multivariate table because it is there that you find the XY relationship *within* each category of Z.

Consider Table 17.11 as an example. Read

TABLE 17.10 Relationship between Dependent and Control Variables

		Z		
		1	2	3
Y	3	51%	27%	19%
	2	27	53	27
	1	21	20	54
	Total	100%	100%	100%

TABLE 17.11 The Relationship between X and Y with Z Controlled (Negative X Y Relationship)

		Z_1 X				Z_2 X				Z_3 X		
		1	2	3		1	2	3		1	2	3
Y	3	52%	22%	12%	3	52%	22%	12%	3	52%	22%	12%
	2	34	61	19	2	34	61	19	2	34	61	19
	1	14	17	69	1	14	17	69	1	14	17	69
	Total	100%	100%	100%		100%	100%	100%		100%	100%	100%

the percentage distributions across categories of X, within each category of Z, in order to see what effect X is having on Y with Z controlled. At this point, what you are doing is reading three separate bivariate relationships: the XY relationship for $Z = 1$, for $Z = 2$, and for $Z = 3$. (Review Chapter 8 if you are having any trouble reading the tables.)

In Table 17.11, Z is controlled; as X increases, Y decreases (assuming both are ordinally measured and we can take the 1, 2, 3 values as an order). That is true for the relationship between X and Y when $Z = 1$, when $Z = 2$, and when $Z = 3$.

The *relationship* between X and Y is exactly the same for each category of Z. Regardless of the category of Z, X is having exactly the same effect on Y. To substantiate this claim, notice that the *differences* in the Y distribution between the $X = 1$ and $X = 2$ columns or between the $X = 1$ and $X = 3$ columns are the same for all values of Z.

Now look at the relationship between Z and Y, the control and dependent variables, when X—the independent variable—is controlled.

Notice that Z is having no effect at all on the dependent variable Y when X is controlled above. To substantiate this claim, compare the distributions of Y in all the $X = 1$ columns. When X does not vary (i.e., when X is controlled/constant at $X = 1$), the distributions of Y, the dependent variable, are identical as you vary Z, the control variable, from 1 to 2 to 3. Then compare the distributions of Y in all the $X = 2$ columns and then in all the $X = 3$ columns. Varying Z from 1 to 2 to 3 is not changing the Y distributions; thus, you can assert that Z is not affecting Y when X is controlled.

Now consider Table 17.12 as the next percentage table example. Here, as X increases, Y decreases (again assuming ordinal measurement), and the *relationship* between X and Y is exactly the same, regardless of the category of Z. Notice the *difference* between the Y distribution for $X = 1$ and $X = 2$ is the same for each of the three values of Z. The *difference* between the Y distribution for $X = 2$ and $X = 3$ is the same for each of the three values of Z.

However, here Z is also affecting the depen-

TABLE 17.12 The Relationship between X and Y with Z Controlled (Negative X Y Relationship; Positive Z Y Relationship)

		Z_1 X				Z_2 X				Z_3 X		
		1	2	3		1	2	3		1	2	3
Y	3	52%	22%	12%	3	72%	42%	32%	3	82%	52%	42%
	2	34	61	19	2	24	51	9	2	18	45	3
	1	14	17	69	1	4	7	59	1	0	3	55
	Total	100%	100%	100%		100%	100%	100%		100%	100%	100%

TABLE 17.13 The Relationship between X and Y with Z Controlled (No X Y Relationship; Positive Z Y Relationship)

		Z_1 X				Z_2 X				Z_3 X		
		1	2	3		1	2	3		1	2	3
	3	46%	46%	46%	3	56%	56%	56%	3	71%	71%	71%
Y	2	29	29	29	2	24	24	24	2	15	15	15
	1	25	25	25	1	20	20	20	1	14	14	14
	Total	100%	100%	100%		100%	100%	100%		100%	100%	100%

dent variable Y when X is controlled. Keeping X constant at 1, notice how the distribution of Y changes as you vary Z from 1 to 2 to 3. As Z goes up, from 1 to 3, Y goes up as well—from 52% high Y when Z = 1, to 72% high Y when Z = 2, to 82% high Y when Z = 3. Or keep X constant at 3 and notice how the percent of cases low on Y goes down from 69% to 59% to 55%, as Z goes up from 1 to 2 to 3.

Now consider another example in Table 17.13. Here, you can see that when Z is controlled, X is having no effect on Y. X and Y are not correlated. Notice that varying X from 1 to 2 to 3 does not change the distribution of Y at all when Z is constant at 1, at 2, or at 3.

Z is affecting Y, however. Notice how the Y distribution changes from one value of Z to the next. With X controlled, as Z increases, Y increases. The percentage of cases in high Y goes from 46% to 56% to 71% as Z goes from 1 to 2 to 3.

Finally, consider Table 17.14. Here, the *XY relationship* is different for different categories of Z. When Z = 1, X and Y are positively related; as X goes up, Y goes up. When Z = 2, X and Y are not related at all; when X goes up, nothing happens to Y. When Z = 3, X and Y are negatively related; as X goes up, Y goes down. Z, in this case, is *specifying* the XY relationship.

The Meaning of the Controlled Relationships

Remember that the effect of X on Y controlling Z is meaningful only within the theoretical context in which you are working. When, after controlling for Z, you find no relationship between X and Y, Z may be considered either an extraneous or an intervening variable. Which of those two Z is considered to be depends on your hypotheses drawn from literature and theory and on your own common sense.

If you find that Z contributes to the explanation of Y, you might consider Z just an additional explanatory variable if X and Z are uncorrelated or if you are just not interested in

TABLE 17.14 The Relationship between X and Y with Z Controlled (Different X Y Relationship in Each Category of Z)

		Z_1 X				Z_2 X				Z_3 X		
		1	2	3		1	2	3		1	2	3
	3	10%	15%	80%	3	15%	15%	15%	3	60%	10%	10%
Y	2	20	60	15	2	60	60	60	2	25	82	15
	1	70	25	5	1	25	25	25	1	15	8	75
	Total	100%	100%	100%		100%	100%	100%		100%	100%	100%

the correlation between X and Z; or you might consider that Z has some direct effect on Y in addition to an indirect effect through X. Much depends on your hypotheses and the analysis you are undertaking.

Do not forget, however, all the interpretations of partials discussed in earlier chapters. Regardless of measurement level of the variables, interpretations of the effects of variables on each other can be very similar.

EXERCISE 3 Multivariate Associations on the Example Table

Using the multivariate percentage table you constructed in the example earlier, examine the various controlled relationships. Describe the XY relationship controlling for Z. Explain how you know that; i.e., what did you read to come to that conclusion? Tell what effect you think Z is having and explain how you know that. Again, you will find it helpful to state the relationships in words that rely on the variable names rather than on X and Y and Z.

MEASURES OF ASSOCIATION

Luckily, measures of association for nominal or ordinal level data displayed in tables are quite easy and straightforward. You calculate the appropriate measure of association for the data *within* each category of the control variable, weight those measures of association by the number of cases in their categories, add up the weighted measures, and divide the sum by total number of cases. The result is a partial measure of association for the relationship between X and Y controlling for Z. That partial measure of association can then be compared to a bivariate measure of association between X and Y in order to make inferences about the causal processes that may be operating.

EXERCISE 4 Measures of Association for Control Tables

Working through an example will help make this clear. Using the example multivariate table (with frequencies, not percentages) you constructed earlier, follow the steps that are listed here.

1. Calculate the same measure of association for each segment of the control table: one measure of the XY relationship for each category of Z. Use gamma for this lesson. In choosing a measure of association, however, you ordinarily have the same considerations as for any nominal or ordinal crosstabulation table. What is your measurement level? How smoothly distributed are the marginals? What is your interpretation of error? You learned to consider these questions in Chapters 9 and 10. Additionally for control tables, you must consider whether the control variable is ordinal or nominal. Only if it is also ordinal is an ordinal partial measure of association appropriate.

2. Having calculated the same measure of association for each category of the control variable, examine both the measures and the tables to make sure there is no important interaction. Make sure that the directions of the relationships are the same in all the subtables and that the relationships between X and Y are not too different. If there is interaction, stop here and report a separate measure of association for each category of the control variable. If there is no substantial interaction, continue.

3. Since we don't want a few cases to contribute more heavily to the overall partial, we will weight each measure of association by the number of cases before combining them into a single measure. Therefore, to construct the partial measure of association, (a) multiply each measure of association by the number of cases in that subtable, (b) sum the resulting products, and (c) divide the sum by the total number of cases. The result is the partial correlation between X and Y controlling for Z. Write out your calculation of the partial gamma for the example table.

In order to interpret the partial, it is necessary to have the bivariate measure of association. From the bivariate frequency (not percentage) table you constructed earlier in this chapter, calculate a bivariate gamma.

Now, interpreting the partial almost like any other partial compared to a bivariate measure of association, write out what would you say about the XY relationship. Again, use the names of the variables in your assessment of the effect of the control variable on the bivariate relationship.

Generally speaking, you'd have to ask whether the partial was near zero when the bivariate measure of association was substantial. If so, the control variable must be either extraneous to or intervening in the XY relationship, and only theory can determine which. Is the partial substantially larger than the bivariate measure of association? If so, the control variable must have been suppressing the original XY relationship. Is the partial measure of association a different sign from the bivariate measure of association? If so, the control variable must have been distorting the original XY relationship. (Remember that only the ordinal measures of association will have signs. For you to see changes in the form, rather than just in the strength, of a relationship between nominal variables, it will be necessary to examine the tables themselves. The statistics will tell you only the strength of the relationship—not anything which would be equivalent to "direction" from an ordinal statistic.)

One nice thing about the ordinal measures of partial correlation is that they are more directly comparable to the bivariate correlation measures than are those for interval data. Since you are controlling, rather than adjusting for, the control variable, you can more easily talk about the relationship getting stronger, weaker, or disappearing under the control without worrying about whether the partial is based on a different amount of variation in Y than the bivariate association.

GETTING SPSS TO DO MULTIVARIATE TABLES

We needn't belabor the partial measure of association because it is so relatively straightforward, but we should indicate how to get the control tables from a computer. You simply add the name of the control variable to the CROSSTABS command you have used before:

```
CROSSTABS TABLES = dependent
   BY independent BY control.
```

If you wish to examine both the bivariate and the control tables, you may get both on one CROSSTABS procedure command:

```
CROSSTABS TABLES = dependent
   BY independent/
   dependent BY
   independent BY control.
```

Substitute the *names* of your various variables in the place of the lowercase letters above on the command; and before the period, remember to add appropriate subcommands. OPTIONS = 4 (in SPSS/PC+) or CELLS = COLUMN (in SPSS-X) will get you the column percentages you need to interpret the table. Asking for STATISTICS = ALL will get you everything, regardless of whether your variables are nominal or ordinal, and you can choose one from among them later.

The control table will not be printed out all in one place. Rather, there will be a separate table for the XY relationship printed for each category of Z. You will have to pull them together.

Similarly, you will not get the partial measures of association. What SPSS will give you are the measures of association for the XY relationship within each category of the control variable. All you have to do is weight them, add them up, and divide by the total number of cases to get the partial.

EXERCISE 5 SPSS Table Construction

Now you do it using data from one of the data sets in the appendices. Write a hypothesis that uses nominal or ordinal variables for independent, dependent, and control variables.

Remember that you may have to recode variables in order to get a manageable number of categories and enough cases in each of them. Then run the SPSS CROSSTABS procedure to get the bivariate and multivariate tables and statistics for your hypothesis.

Draw the bivariate and multivariate tables

for the test of your hypothesis. This time, follow a few rules for good table presentations so that you can practice on the preparation of data for publication. These rules are adapted from the *American Journal of Political Science*. Not all journals will use the same style, but the following rules will produce a clean and easy-to-read table. A summary of these rules appears in Table 17.15 below.

1. You will have one table that draws together all of the XY relationships for the various categories of Z.
2. The table will be clearly titled with words that indicate the relationship which appears in the table.
3. The table will be clearly labeled with indications of the independent, and control variables and their values. SPSS-X variable names (or similar abbreviations) will not be used. The independent variable of most interest—usually the primary independent and not the control—will be nearer the distributions of the dependent than will the other independent.
4. The table will contain enough information that readers can recapture the raw data and repercentage the tables any way they care to, but it will not be cluttered with more information than necessary.
5. The table will not have vertical lines; subtables will be separated from each other with extra space.
6. The table won't have horizontal lines between values of the dependent; in general, horizontal lines will be used sparsely.

Now, read and interpret your table. What is the bivariate effect of X on Y? What is the effect of your control variable on X? On Y? On the XY relationship? State your conclusions regarding your hypothesis. Are the data consistent with it? Can you summarize, in words, the relationship of X to Y and the effect of Z on that?

Do the same interpretation again, but this time base it on the measures of association for the bivariate XY relationship and the partial XY relationship controlling for Z. First, considering your hypothesis, your measurement level, and the distributions of the variables, what is an appropriate measure for the relationship between X and Y? Second, look at that measure of association for all the control tables to make sure there is little or no interaction before you, third, construct the partial measure of association between X and Y controlling Z. Now compare the bivariate measure of association to the partial and state your interpretation of what is happening to the XY relationship when Z is controlled.

TABLE 17.15 The Table Will Be Titled Here with a Phrase that Indicates Y by X Controlling for Z (in Percentages)

	Name of the control
	Values of the control on this line above appropriate subtables
Name of the dependent variable	
	Name of the independent
	Values of the independent on this line, repeated for each subtable
Values of the dependent given on lines here	Percentages only in the cells of the subtables with the percentage sign used only on the first line
N of cases and total % given on these lines	N Total

Any notes go here.

When you have finished these exercises, you are ready to turn to Chapter 18. In this next chapter you will find statistics that help you decide how significant your findings are.

EXERCISES

Hypothetical operationalizations follow these data, which are used in the exercises in Chapter 17. Below the cases, you will find a summary of the values on the cases, which you may use to fill in the table cells without going through the sorting procedure.

Case No.	X	Y	Z	Case No.	X	Y	Z	Case No.	X	Y	Z	Case No.	X	Y	Z
1	1	3	3	38	2	1	3	74	3	3	3	111	1	2	1
2	1	3	3	39	2	1	3	75	3	3	3	112	1	2	1
3	1	3	3	40	2	1	3	76	3	3	3	113	1	2	1
4	1	3	3					77	3	3	3	114	1	2	1
5	1	3	3	41	3	3	3	78	3	3	3	115	1	1	1
6	1	3	3	42	3	3	3	79	3	3	3	116	1	1	1
7	1	3	3	43	3	3	3	80	3	3	3	117	1	1	1
8	1	3	3	44	3	3	3					118	1	1	1
9	1	3	3	45	3	3	3	81	3	3	3	119	1	1	1
10	1	3	3	46	3	3	3	82	3	3	3	120	1	1	1
				47	3	3	3	83	3	3	3				
11	1	3	3	48	3	3	3	84	3	2	3	121	1	1	1
12	1	2	3	49	3	3	3	85	3	2	3	122	1	1	1
13	1	2	3	50	3	3	3	86	3	2	3	123	1	1	1
14	1	1	3					87	3	2	3	124	1	1	1
15	1	1	3	51	3	3	3	88	3	2	3	125	1	1	1
16	2	3	3	52	3	3	3	89	3	2	3	126	1	1	1
17	2	3	3	53	3	3	3	90	3	2	3	127	1	1	1
18	2	3	3	54	3	3	3					128	1	1	1
19	2	3	3	55	3	3	3	91	3	2	3	129	1	1	1
20	2	3	3	56	3	3	3	92	3	2	3	130	1	1	1
				57	3	3	3	93	3	2	3				
21	2	3	3	58	3	3	3	94	3	1	3	131	2	3	1
22	2	3	3	59	3	3	3	95	3	1	3	132	2	3	1
23	2	3	3	60	3	3	3	96	3	1	3	133	2	3	1
24	2	3	3					97	3	1	3	134	2	2	1
25	2	3	3	61	3	3	3	98	3	1	3	135	2	2	1
26	2	3	3	62	3	3	3	99	3	1	3	136	2	2	1
27	2	3	3	63	3	3	3	100	3	1	3	137	2	2	1
28	2	3	3	64	3	3	3					138	2	1	1
29	2	3	3	65	3	3	3	101	1	3	1	139	2	1	1
30	2	3	3	66	3	3	3	102	1	3	1	140	2	1	1
				67	3	3	3	103	1	3	1				
31	2	3	3	68	3	3	3	104	1	3	1	141	2	1	1
32	2	3	3	69	3	3	3	105	1	3	1	142	2	1	1
33	2	3	3	70	3	3	3	106	1	2	1	143	2	1	1
34	2	2	3					107	1	2	1	144	2	1	1
35	2	2	3	71	3	3	3	108	1	2	1	145	2	1	1
36	2	2	3	72	3	3	3	109	1	2	1	146	3	3	1
37	2	2	3	73	3	3	3	110	1	2	1	147	3	2	1

252 READING MULTIVARIATE TABLES AND CALCULATING PARTIALS FOR NOMINAL AND ORDINAL DATA

Case No.	X	Y	Z	Case No.	X	Y	Z	Case No.	X	Y	Z	Case No.	X	Y	Z
148	3	1	1	168	2	3	2	188	2	2	2	208	2	1	2
149	3	1	1	169	2	3	2	189	2	2	2	209	2	1	2
150	3	1	1	170	2	3	2	190	2	2	2	210	2	1	2
151	1	3	2	171	2	3	2	191	2	2	2	211	3	3	2
152	1	3	2	172	2	3	2	192	2	2	2	212	3	3	2
153	1	3	2	173	2	3	2	193	2	2	2	213	3	3	2
154	1	3	2	174	2	3	2	194	2	2	2	214	3	3	2
155	1	2	2	175	2	3	2	195	2	2	2	214	3	2	2
156	1	2	2	176	2	3	2	196	2	2	2	215	3	2	2
157	1	2	2	177	2	3	2	197	2	2	2	216	3	2	2
158	1	2	2	178	2	3	2	198	2	2	2	217	3	2	2
159	1	2	2	179	2	2	2	199	2	2	2	218	3	2	2
160	1	2	2	180	2	2	2	200	2	2	2	219	3	2	2
												220	3	2	2
161	1	2	2	181	2	2	2	201	2	2	2				
162	1	2	2	182	2	2	2	202	2	2	2	221	3	2	2
163	1	2	2	183	2	2	2	203	2	2	2	222	3	2	2
164	1	1	2	184	2	2	2	204	2	1	2	223	3	1	2
165	1	1	2	185	2	2	2	205	2	1	2	224	3	1	2
166	2	3	2	186	2	2	2	206	2	1	2	225	3	1	2
167	2	3	2	187	2	2	2	207	2	1	2				

There are the following number of categorized cases:

5	X_1	Y_3	Z_1		8	X_2	Y_1	Z_1
9	X_1	Y_2	Z_1		1	X_3	Y_3	Z_1
16	X_1	Y_1	Z_1		1	X_3	Y_2	Z_1
3	X_2	Y_3	Z_1		11	X_1	Y_3	Z_3
4	X_1	Y_3	Z_2					
9	X_1	Y_2	Z_2		2	X_1	Y_2	Z_3
2	X_1	Y_1	Z_2		2	X_1	Y_1	Z_3
13	X_2	Y_3	Z_2		18	X_2	Y_3	Z_3
25	X_2	Y_2	Z_2		4	X_2	Y_2	Z_3
					3	X_2	Y_1	Z_3
7	X_2	Y_1	Z_2		43	X_3	Y_3	Z_3
4	X_3	Y_3	Z_2		10	X_3	Y_2	Z_3
8	X_3	Y_2	Z_2		7	X_3	Y_1	Z_3
3	X_3	Y_1	Z_2		3	X_3	Y_1	Z_1
4	X_2	Y_2	Z_1					

Hypothetically, what we have here are 225 instances of anti-government protest demonstrations. On each instance of a demonstration, we have collected various data. Among those data are the three variables represented here.

X is a measure of the number of people involved in each demonstration. We have taken the total number of demonstrators and divided it by the total number of people in a 100-mile radius in order to standardize for population. We have then categorized the cases by whether the proportion of the population involved was high, medium, or low.

Y is a measure of the number of deaths standardized by the number of demonstrators. We divided the number of deaths by the number of demonstrators. On the basis of the results, we categorized the cases into high, medium, and low numbers of deaths.

Z is a measure of the total number of police and military on duty in the immediate area of the demonstration. It, too, has to be standardized to take into account varying sizes of demonstrations. Here we have divided the total number of police and military by the number of demonstrators. Then we divided the cases, on the basis of that figure, into high, medium, and low police involvement.

SUGGESTED READINGS

BABBIE, EARL R. *The Practice of Social Research*, 2nd ed. (Belmont, CA: Wadsworth, 1979), pp. 387-393.

BENSON, OLIVER. *Political Science Laboratory* (Columbus, OH: Bell and Howell, 1969), Ch. 9.

BERENSON, MARK L., DAVID M. LEVINE, and MATTHEW GOLDSTEIN. *Intermediate Statistical Methods and Applications: A Computer Package Approach* (Englewood Cliffs, NJ: Prentice-Hall, 1983). Chapter 17 gives a more sophisticated approach to categorical data analysis than in this chapter.

BOWEN, BRUCE D., and HERBERT F. WEISBERG. *An Introduction to Data Analysis* (San Francisco: Freeman, 1980), Ch. 8.

HILDEBRAND, DAVID K., JAMES D. LAING, and HOWARD ROSENTHAL. *Analysis of Ordinal Data*, # 8 in series, *Quantitative Applications in the Social Sciences* (Beverly Hills, CA: Sage, 1977).

KNOKE, DAVID, and PETER J. BURKE. *Log-Linear Models*, # 20 in series, *Quantitative Applications in the Social Sciences* (Beverly Hills, CA: Sage, 1980). An accessible introduction to this more advanced technique for nominal data.

KOHOUT, FRANK J. *Statistics for Social Scientists* (N.Y.: Wiley, 1974), Section III.3.

LEHNEN, ROBERT G., and GARY G. KOCH. "A General Linear Approach to the Analysis of Nonmetric Data: Applications for Political Science," *American Journal of Political Science*, 18 (May 1974), 282-313. See this article for an example of a more sophisticated approach to the analysis of ordinal and nominal data.

REYNOLDS, H. T. Analysis of Nominal Data, # 7 in series, *Quantitative Applications in the Social Sciences* (Beverly Hills, CA: Sage, 1977).

ROSENBERG, MORRIS. *The Logic of Survey Analysis* (N.Y.: Basic, 1968). Appendix A (by Roberta G. Simmons) is on "Basic Principles of Table Reading"; Appendix B is on "The Arithmetic of Controls."

Computer Applications

NORUSIS, MARIJA J. *SPSS/PC+* (Chicago: SPSS, Inc., 1988). CROSSTABS commands are on pp. C33-C36.

SPSS-X User's Guide (Chicago: SPSS, Inc., 1988), Ch. 25, pp. 428-445.

ARTICLES

CLARKE, JAMES W. "Family Structure and Political Socialization among Urban Black Children," *American Journal of Political Science*, 17 (1973), 302-315. Bivariate table and gamma for relationship between father presence and cynicism. Multivariate table for same relationship controlling age and sex. Bivariate table and gamma for relationship between father presence and integration preferences. Multivariate table controlling that relationship for age and sex. Gammas used to measure internal consistency of index (note 23).

JENNINGS, M. KENT. "Another Look at the Life Cycle and Political Participation," *American Journal of Political Science*, 23 (November 1979), 755-771. Tau_b statistics to assess the impact of parenthood on political participation at national and school-district levels. Does not construct partial tau_b measures of relationship because of statistical interaction; relationship differs by gender and by age. Good attention to definition and to variables not controlled. Uses tau_b on nonsquare tables.

SANDERS, ELIZABETH. "On the Costs, Utilities, and Simple Joys of Voting," *Journal of Politics*, 42 (1980), 854-864. A relatively accessible example of the rational choice literature in political science. Uses a simple multivariate crosstabulation table to demonstrate the effects of costs, duty, benefits, and probability of affecting outcome on voting turnout. Designed to demonstrate importance of costs, which had been downplayed. Needs careful reading of Table 1, given that there are four independent variables, and since the labels of one occupy the usual position for dependent variable labels.

SMITH, RUSSELL L., and THOMAS M. UHLMAN. "Police Policy and Citizen Satisfaction: Evidence from Urban Areas," *Policy Studies Journal*, 7 (Special Issue, 1978), 480-486. Survey data from black and white samples on perceptions and evaluations of police are correlated with "contextual variables" that measure police departments' attempts to improve citizen perceptions controlling for other factors known to influence perceptions. Gamma and partial gammas used to measure strength of relationship.

CHAPTER 18

INFERENTIAL STATISTICS

Before this chapter, we have been asking the same two questions of our data at each measurement level: What is the form of the relationship, and how strong is it? Our goal has been to explain phenomena—to explain why some cases are high, some low, and some in the middle on the distribution of a dependent variable. To do this, we have had to know *how* variables were related (form) and how well we were explaining (strength).

When we had interval data on both the independent variables and the dependent variables and the variables were linearly related, we described the form of the relationship with a slope and the strength of the relationship with R^2.

When we had nominal or ordinal independent variables and an interval dependent variable, we described the form of the relationship by looking at the various dependent variable means within categories of the independent variables. For those data, we described the strength of the relationship with E^2.

When we had ordinal data on both variables, we described the form of the relationship by stating the pattern of percentage distributions on the dependent variable within categories of the independent variable. For those ordinal, tabular data, we described the strength of the relationship with gamma, Kendall's tau$_b$, tau$_c$, or d$_{yx}$, which also have signs to indicate the form of the relationship.

When we had nominal data on both variables, we again had to look at the pattern of percentage distributions on the dependent variable within categories of the independent variable in order to describe the form of the relationship. To describe the strength of the relationship in these data, we used a Goodman and Kruskal's tau, a lambda, or one of the chi-square-based measures of association.

All of the complications of multicollinearity, interaction, nonmonotonicity, nonlinearity, etc., were covered in earlier chapters in order that the form and strength of the relationship might be accurately assessed. All of the reasons and procedures for multivariate analysis can probably be boiled down to procedures that help us explain dependent variables by getting at the form and strength of relationships more accurately.

INFERENCE

There is, however, one question that we have not addressed, although we have alluded to it several times. Whenever we have samples of cases rather than all of the cases in a population, we would like to be relatively sure that our sample is representative of the population. Ordinarily, we would like to argue that the relationships we have found are not limited to our sample but, rather, are characteristic of some larger group of cases. There is a whole body of statistics that allow us to assess the likelihood that our sample results can be safely assumed to be representative of a population.

This same body of statistics can also be used with a slightly different interpretation. Rather than interpreting the results as assessing whether or not a relationship we have found is probably characteristic of a population, we can interpret the results as an assessment of whether a relationship we have found is greater than a zero relationship or is just a product of having chance fluctuation away from zero. Either interpretation is, for practical purposes, equivalent to the other.

A TEST BASED ON THE NORMAL DISTRIBUTION

Imagine now that you have computed a gamma on a two-variable table that you have derived from sample data. You would like to know whether you can assume that a similar relationship exists between the two variables in the population and/or (equivalently) how sure you can be that your sample relationship doesn't represent some chance deviation from what is really no relationship at all.

One way of answering these questions is to know what gammas would probably come from a population. You can imagine that, if you took many, many samples from a population, you would not always get exactly the same gamma. Most gammas calculated on your repeated samples would fall right around whatever the gamma is for the population, but some could be quite different just because you got a really strange sample. If two variables were unrelated in the population from which you were drawing your samples, the gammas calculated for the relationship between those two variables in your repeated samples would cluster around 0, but some would be negative and some positive—even some rather extremely so—just because of the vagaries of sampling. Similarly, if two variables were related positively in the population, most samples would show varying degrees of positive relationship. Moreover, some would show no relationship, and some might even show a strong negative relationship—just by the operation of chance.

Unfortunately, we do not ordinarily know anything about the population from which we draw samples. We cannot even, under ordinary circumstances, draw repeated samples from a population. To know what kind of gammas would ordinarily come from a population, we have to imagine a population and figure out how likely it is that certain gammas would come from that population. Having done that, we can compare our gamma to the gammas from the imaginary population.

If our gamma is *like* those which would ordinarily come from that imaginary population, we will argue that the population from which it did come is like the imaginary one. If our gamma is *not like* those which would ordinarily come from that imaginary popuulation, we will argue that the population from which it did come is different from the imaginary population—more like the sample than like the imaginary population.

How do we know what gammas are likely to come from an imaginary population? If you give statisticians certain assumptions about the statistic in a population (the parameter), about a sampling method, about measurement levels, and about sample size, they can calculate for you what gammas would show up from such a population and how often, just as if repeated samples from that population had been drawn.

It turns out that statisticians can demonstrate that the gammas transformed by some rules into a slightly different statistic (which, as you will see, is a Z score)—calculated on repeated samples larger than ten cases that are randomly drawn from a population in which the two ordinally measured variables are unrelated (i.e., in which gamma = 0)—are distributed in the form of a normal curve. If you calculated this statistic on repeated samples drawn from a population in which gamma was

0, the resulting statistics on an infinite number of samples would be distributed like a normal curve.

We need now to go into a rather lengthy description of what it means to say that a set of numbers (here those transformed gammas) are distributed normally. We will get back to the original question of whether our gamma represents the population a bit later.

A normal curve is a particular form of a symmetrical, smooth curve. Although there are many different normal distributions—one for every combination of mean and standard deviation—we usually use the standard normal distribution that has a mean = 0 and a variance and standard deviation = 1.0.

Any set of values that is already normally distributed can be made into a set of values, called Z scores, which is distributed in a standard normal distribution. The Z scores are in standard deviation units rather than in the original scale of measurements.

Do you remember how you transformed the scores in Chapter 14 into standard scores? You transformed the scores on a variable into Z scores in much the same way that we will transform gammas into Z scores. On every case, you took its score on a variable, subtracted the mean of that variable, and divided the difference by the standard deviation of that variable. You got standard scores that indicated whether a case was, for example, at the mean (0), one standard deviation above the mean (+1.0), or one and one-third standard deviations below the mean (-1.33). Had the distribution of scores been normally distributed before you started on that transformation, the resulting distribution of standard scores would have been standard normal.

In any normal distribution, known proportions of the scores fall between the mean and other given scores. In the standard normal distribution, we know, for example, that the scores of 68.26 percent of the cases fall between -1.0 and +1.0 from the mean; that is, just over 68 percent of the cases fall between one standard deviation unit below the mean ($Z = -1.0$) and above the mean ($Z = +1.0$). Similarly, we know that the scores of 95.46 percent of the cases fall between -2.0 and +2.0 (two standard deviation units below or above the mean of zero). These Z scores are pictured in Figure 18.1.

Recall that in Chapter 2 you drew the distance between the mean of a distribution and one standard deviation unit above and below the mean. In that chapter, you found that roughly two-thirds of the cases were distributed in that range in all but the very odd distributions. Here we can be more precise with stating the proportion of cases that will have scores between the mean and one standard deviation above or below the mean because we are dealing with normal distributions.

The distributions in Chapter 2 deviated from normal; thus, the proportion of scores that fell into particular ranges were just roughly the same as the proportions given here. You can see how different those distributions in Chapter 2 were from normal by looking at the normal curve in Figure 18.1.

Because we know, for any normal distribution of scores, the proportion of cases that will have scores which fall above or below any given standard deviation units (Z scores) in the scale, these proportions can be summarized in a single table. Consider the tabled values for "The Standard Normal Distribution," Table A.1 of Appendix D.

Look for the Z score of .33 (that is, a score that is about one-third of a standard-deviation

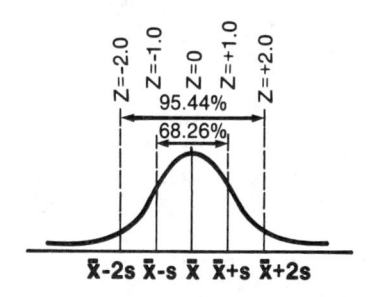

Figure 18.1 Areas under the Normal Curve between Indicated Z Scores*

---

*Figure adapted from Hubert M. Blalock, Jr. *Social Statistics*, 2nd ed. (N.Y.: McGraw-Hill, 1972, p. 99.).

unit above the mean of 0 for the whole distribution) in column A. Column B, next to it, indicates the proportion, .1293, of the scores in a normal distribution that fall between the mean (00) and that Z score. Then Column C indicates the proportion, .3707, of the cases that have scores higher than .33 on the right half of the distribution. (The same proportion of cases, here .3707, has scores lower than −.33 on the left half of the distribution. The left half is not presented in the table because it is just a mirror image of the right half.)

Let's go over another example quickly. Look at a Z score of 2.00. You already know that 95.44 percent of the cases fall between −2.0 and +2.0 on the normal distribution, so you shouldn't be surprised to find in the B column at Z score = 2.00 (the mean plus two standard deviation units) that .4772 is the proportion of cases which has scores that fall between the mean and 2.0—.4772 is half of .9544. To find the proportion of the cases that have scores which fall between the mean minus and the mean plus a score, multiply the tabled proportion by 2; that is, .4772 × 2 = .9544.

It's easy to work the table backwards, too. If you want to figure out what Z score delineates the top 10 percent of the cases, look in Column C until you find the entry closest to .10 (the proportion of the area under the normal curve *beyond* the designated score in Column A). Read across to the left until you find a Z score in Column A of 1.28. That is the designated Z score that separates the bottom .9 proportion of the scores from the top .10 proportion of the scores.

Having looked at the normal distribution, we can now go back to our question of whether your gamma calculated on your sample data can be assumed to exist in the population from which you drew the sample or whether you could get a gamma that large by chance when your sample came from a population in which there was no relationship between the two variables (when all the other sampling and measurement assumptions were met).

As we have said, gammas—modified into Z scores, calculated on repeated random samples of a size greater than ten, from a population in which the two variables are unrelated, and where both variables are measured on an ordinal scale—are normally distributed. From the description of the standard normal curve on Table A.1, we know that only five times out of 100 repeated samples would a Z score greater than +1.64 turn up by chance when the variables are unrelated in the population (and when all the other assumptions are met). Ten times out of 100, a Z score greater in absolute value than −1.64 or +1.64 would show up by chance. Only one time out of 100 repeated samples would a Z score greater than +2.33 turn up by chance. Two times out of 100, a Z score greater in absolute terms than +2.33 or −2.33 would turn up, etc.

In order to decide whether your gamma was a chance occurrence, you will transform it according to Formula 18.1 into a Z score. You don't have to understand what the statistic means at this point; just understand it turns gamma into a Z score.

FORMULA 18.1
The Formula for a Z Score Based on Gamma

$$Z = \text{Gamma} \times \sqrt{\frac{N_c + N_d}{n(1 - \text{Gamma}^2)}}$$

where:
Gamma = Gamma from the sample
N_c = The number of concordant pairs
N_d = The number of discordant pairs
n = Sample size

If the gamma from your sample, transformed by Formula 18.1 into a Z score, exceeds +2.33, you know that only one time in 100 would a gamma that extreme show up in a sample from the kind of population that yields normally distributed gamma/Z scores.

If your gamma is *unlikely* to have come from the kind of population assumed that yields normally distributed gamma/Z scores, you would probably want to assert that it did not come from such a population. Be careful, however, for you could be wrong. Yours could be one of those rare samples that are extremely unrepresentative of the population from which they were drawn. In these rare samples, a strong gamma may show up completely by chance when the variables are unrelated in the population from which the sample is drawn.

If your gamma is *unlikely* to have come from the population assumed that yields normally distributed gamma/Z scores, you probably would want to assert that it, instead, came from a population in which the variables *are* related. But be careful. You have only seen the sample—not the population from which it came. You cannot be sure that correlation in the population produced the correlation in the sample when all you have seen is the sample. Something else could have caused the sample correlation.

Thus, if your Z score shows that your sample was unlikely to have come from a population in which the variables were unrelated (when the other assumptions were met), you can bet there's a relationship in the population, but it's not a 100 percent sure bet.

What if you get a Z score, based on transforming the gamma, of $+.59$? Over one-fourth of the time, you could get a Z score that high or higher by drawing repeated random samples greater than size ten from a population in which gamma equaled 0. Can you say that your sample, therefore, probably came from a population in which the variables were unrelated? Yes, but you have to remember also that you could be in error; having seen only the sample, you cannot assert that low or no correlation in the population caused, as a consequence, low or no correlation in your sample. Other things might cause low or no correlation as well. For instance, this might be the rare sample that would show low or no correlation, even though it was drawn from a population with a very high gamma.

You can see that this procedure of comparing sample results to results from an assumed population is full of logical risks. This procedure can be a guide for you, but it cannot make decisions for you. You have to decide which risks are worth taking and which are not. Moreover, you have a choice of minimizing one or another kind of risk but not both simultaneously.

You can minimize the risk of asserting that your sample *did not come* from a population like one assumed (from which repeated random samples were theoretically drawn to yield the normal distribution of gamma/Z scores) when, in fact, it did. To minimize this kind of risk, just demand that your sample results be *extremely unlikely* to have come from such a population. (Set your standards at one time in 100, or one time in 1,000, or one in 10,000—i.e., proportions in column C of .01 or .001 or .0001 and their corresponding Z scores. See that your sample Z score exceeds those Z scores before asserting that your sample probably didn't come from a population in which the variables are unrelated.)

Or you can minimize the risk of asserting that your sample *probably came* from a population like the one assumed when, in fact, it did not. Just demand that your sample results be extremely *likely* to have come from such a population (i.e., demand that your sample Z score be less than the Z that would be exceeded 20 times out of 100 (.20 in the table, column C), or even more often, before you assert that your sample probably came from a population like that tabled.

Typically, we choose to minimize the former risk. We want to be pretty conservative about asserting that there is a relationship in the population from just our sample results. Therefore, we demand that our sample results be extremely unlikely to have come from a population in which there was no relationship. Such results that are extremely *unlikely* to have occurred by chance are called *statistically significant*. Depending on how sure we want to be, results that would have occurred by chance only five times in 100 or one time in 100 or one time in 1,000 are labeled "statistically significant" at the .05 or .01 or .001 level.

Sometimes we are so conservative that we assert that our gamma probably did not come from a population in which there was no relationship only when a gamma calculated on the sample is greater in absolute value (disregarding the sign) than that which could have happened by chance. For example, a Z score of $+1.96$ or higher could have happened only two and one-half times out of 100 by chance, and a Z score of −1.96 or lower could have happened only two and one-half times out of 100 by chance; thus, a Z score as extreme or more extreme than 1.96 (disregarding the sign) could have happened only five times in 100 by chance. We would then say that a Z greater than 1.96 in absolute value is significant at the .05 level—not at the .025 level; we assert that such an extreme Z score would have been obtained five times out of every 100 by chance (not two and one-half times out of every 100).

On occasion, however, we are less conservative if we have hypothesized the *direction* of the gamma in advance. If we want to argue that our gamma probably did not come from a population in which gamma = 0 (and the other assumptions were met) because a gamma as extreme or more extreme than ours *in the direction* we hypothesized could have happened only five times in 100 by chance, we would look for a Z score greater than +1.64 rather than +1.96. A Z score as or more extremely positive than +1.64 could occur only five times or fewer in 100 by chance when repeated random samples are drawn from a population in which gamma = 0 (when the other assumptions are met).

Thus, when we have a directional hypothesis in advance of our assessment, the gamma itself has to be somewhat less strong before we assert that there is probably some relationship between the variables in the population. This is called doing a *one-tailed test*, since it relies on only one tail or side of the distribution.

When we have not hypothesized the direction in advance, we demand that the gamma has to be stronger before we assert that there is probably some relationship between the variables in the population. This is called doing a *two-tailed test*, since it relies on both tails—positive and negative sides—of the distribution.

Our conservatism about inferring on the basis of sample results that there is a relationship in the population is mitigated by hypotheses from good theory. When we have a strong theoretical reason to expect results to be in a certain direction, we are more willing to make inferences to the population from weaker sample results.

Everything we have said about a significance test for gamma also applies to a significance test for Kendall's tau_b. The only difference is in the formula for transforming tau_b into a Z score. That is more complex. Nevertheless, the principles outlined here are all the same. For the relevant formulas and more information, consult the sources listed in the suggested readings.

EXERCISE 1 Using the Normal Distribution to Test Significance

Before you turn to computer output, make sure you have a grasp on the tabled normal distribution by answering the following questions about the normal curve:

1. What proportion of the cases under a normal curve fall higher than 1.9 standard deviations above the mean?
2. A Z score as high or higher than _____ occurs in only .3 percent (three-tenths of one percent) of the cases.
3. What proportion of the cases under a normal curve fall higher than .05 standard deviations above the mean?
4. Scores lower than +1.05 occur in what proportion of the cases? (Careful: the tabled values represent only half the curve. Column C tells you in what proportion of the total a score greater than +1.05 occurs. Work from that to find the proportion of cases lower than +1.05.)
5. How many times out of 100 would repeated random samples (from a population in which gamma = 0) yield a Z score (calculated from the sample gamma) as extremely negative or more extremely negative than a Z = −2.10 that you get by transforming a sample gamma into a Z score?
6. Is a Z score (calculated from gamma) equal to .71 statistically significant at either the .05 or the .01 level of significance? Explain briefly.
7. Is a Z score (calculated from gamma) equal to 3.09 statistically significant at either the .05 or the .01 level of significance? Explain briefly.

If you'll look now at a piece of SPSS output for gamma and Kendall's tau$_b$, you can see these tests of significance on your own data. If you have kept the output from an assignment in which you correlated two ordinal variables and got gamma and tau, look at that; otherwise, run a CROSSTABS that relates two ordinal variables and ask for the appropriate statistics.

Notice that the *significance* of gamma or tau is printed for you. You do not have to transform gamma or tau into Z scores and then use the table of the normal distribution to look up the significance. If you see that significance = .5000, that means that half the time you'd get a gamma or tau as high as or higher than yours by chance if repeated random samples were drawn from a population in which the variables were unrelated (and the other assumptions were met). If you see that significance = .0000, that means that less than one in 10,000 repeated random samples from a population in which the variables were unrelated would show as much relationship as your sample does.

On your output, circle the significance of gamma and write whether your gamma is statistically significant. Explain your decision briefly.

A SLIGHTLY MORE FORMAL STATEMENT OF THE INFERENCE PROCEDURES OUTLINED ABOVE

A whole set of inferential statistics—not just those based on the normal curve—is available to help you answer the question of how likely your sample results were to have happened by chance. Keep in mind, however, that they are guides, not ways to relieve you of the responsibility for making a judgment about the importance of your findings.

For every one of these statistics, there is a shared logic that is important to understand. Let's review, first, the *distribution of the test statistic*. If you make certain assumptions about a population, about measurement, and about sampling, a statistician can tell you what certain test statistics calculated on samples drawn from that population would look like, as a group, even though the samples are not actually drawn. The statistician can tell you (given a certain kind of population, measurement, and sampling) what proportion of the time you will come up with samples with certain values on those test statistics. For certain sets of assumptions about populations, the proportions of the time that certain statistics will show up in samples have been written down in tables; that is, the distributions of these test statistics have already been drawn for you in tables.

Given the distributions of test statistics in tables, we proceed by examining our sample data for the particular statistic that is set forth in tables by the statistician. If our sample data are unlikely to have come from the population assumed in the construction of those tables, we assert that the population from which our sample came is different from the population assumed by the statistician in constructing the table—different in ways revealed by our sample.

This apparently awkward way of proceeding is necessitated by our need to avoid a logical trap. We cannot proceed more directly without getting ourselves into "the fallacy of affirming the consequent," which we have mentioned in other contexts along the way. We know that certain population characteristics will cause us to get a sample with similar sample characteristics. Observing only the sample characteristics, however, we cannot assert that we know the population characteristics because something else might also have caused us to get a sample with those characteristics.

For example, assume we know that if A occurs, then B, C, D will result. If we observe B, C, and D, we cannot assert that A has occurred. There may have been other possible causes for B, C, and D. If we, on observing B, C, and D, assert that A has occurred, we commit the fallacy of affirming the consequent.

We also proceed in this awkward fashion because we are dealing with probabilities. In our case, certain population characteristics will produce certain sample characteristics only a certain proportion of the time; the population will probably—but not necessarily—produce certain sample characteristics. Thus, no matter what procedure we use, we will never be absolutely certain in this inference business.

Sidestepping problems both of logic and of probability, our procedure is to compare our sample to a hypothetical set of samples drawn from a population with certain characteristics—the distribution of the test statistic. If our sample data are different enough from the characteristics of the hypothetical set of samples so that we think our sample data are *unlikely* to have come from a population like the assumed population, we say that the population from which our sample was drawn is different from the population that was assumed to generate the hypothetical set of samples; that is, we *reject* the population assumptions and so risk error—an error that would happen if our sample happened to be one of the unusual ones from the population assumptions we just rejected. We *fail to reject* the possibility that the population from which our sample was drawn is different from the assumed population and so risk error—an error that would occur if the population from which our sample was drawn were really no different from the population assumptions we rejected.

If the comparison of our sample to the hypothetical set of samples makes it seem *likely* that the sample came from a population like the population that was assumed in order to generate the hypothetical set of samples represented by the distribution of the test statistics, we *fail to reject* the assumptions about the population. We assert that the population from which our sample is drawn is probably like that assumed—taking the risk that our data really did come from a different kind of population.

Thus, there are two kinds of errors. *Type I (alpha) error* is a problem of probability and involves rejecting a true set of population assumptions. If you say that your sample probably didn't come from a population like that assumed for calculating the distribution of the test statistic but it really did, you have committed a Type I error.

Type II (beta) error is a problem of the fallacy of affirming the consequent and involves failing to reject a false set of population assumptions. If you say that your sample probably came from a population like that assumed for the test statistic but it really didn't, you have committed a Type II error.

The possibilities of making Type I and Type II errors cannot be minimized simultaneously. In fact, they are inversely proportional. The more you minimize the chance of making one kind, the more you increase the chance of making the other.

Generally speaking, we want to err on the side of being very conservative about our sample data. We don't want to rush off and proclaim that our sample came from a population different from the assumed population without really good reason. We, therefore, want it to be extremely unlikely that our sample came from one like that assumed by the statisticians before we say it did not and before we infer that our population is, indeed, different. Usually this means that we want our sample outcomes to have been probable from the assumed population only five times in 100, or one time in 100, or one time in 1,000, etc.

Please note that we reject or fail to reject certain assumptions. We do not accept anything as true. That is a problem of philosophy of science and the nature of proof. Hypotheses can only be rejected, never proven true and accepted, because we are never sure we have all the data. Thus, in slightly different terminology, we have the *null hypothesis*, which states the value of the statistic we are assuming for the population (the assumed population parameter) and which entails our assumptions about other population characteristics, measurement levels, and sampling techniques. We also have the *alternative hypothesis* (the research hypothesis), which is the hypothesis that generated the statistic in our sample that we are testing.

If our sample results are likely to have come from the population assumed for the distribution of the test statistic, we say that we reject the alternative/research hypothesis and fail to reject the null hypothesis (and the assumptions it entails). If our sample results are unlikely to have come from the population assumed for the distribution of the test statistic, we say that we reject the null hypothesis and fail to reject the alternative/research hypothesis.

SOME TESTS BASED ON THE F DISTRIBUTION

In order to get another look at all this, we can examine another statistic that is used quite frequently in statistical tests. This statistic is called F, and you don't really need to understand all its meaning right away in order to begin to apply it.*

The F statistic is one that can be calculated for repeated random samples, given certain assumptions about measurement and about the population; its distribution can be written down in a table. We can calculate the same test statistic on our data and compare it to that calculated for the population assumptions to help us in making inferences.

There are many different F statistics, as you will see below, but each of them is a fraction in which the numerator will exceed the denominator and, therefore, have a value greater than 1.0 for a known proportion of the time when F is calculated for repeated samples from a population of certain known characteristics. The F distribution generally looks like that pictured in Appendix D, above Table A.2.

As you can see, most of the time the value of F is more toward zero than toward fractions greater than one when it is calculated on repeated samples drawn from a population of certain (known) characteristics. Sometimes, however, the value of F will fall into the extreme values shown as shaded. The F distribution always has 0 as its lowest possible value, but the other values along the scale are different for different F fractions. Thus the exact value that indicates that shaded region differs for different F statistics.

Crudely put, there are different definitions (as you will see below) for the numerator as well as for the denominator of F, depending on what you are testing; thus, there is a different distribution of the test statistic F for each combination of definitions of numerator and denominator. As a consequence, the value that defines the shaded region is different for each different distribution.

The *critical value*, the exact value that delineates the difference between "extreme" and "not extreme" outcomes, also differs with the definition of extreme. If extreme is defined as an outcome that happens fewer than five times out of 100, the F value that marks the shaded part of the distribution is lower than it would be for an outcome that happened fewer than one time out of 100; and that F value is lower than it would be for an outcome that happened fewer than one time out of 1,000.

Because there are so many different distributions of F—one for each combination of definition of numerator and denominator—and different definitions of what constitutes an extreme outcome, it is not practical to print tables for every different whole distribution as was done for the normal distribution. What you get instead of the whole distribution is just the *value* that delineates the difference between an extreme and a not extreme outcome at a certain definition of extremes.

In Table A.2 in Appendix D, you can see the values of F that mark that extreme point—critical value—for the various distributions. The first half of the table represents a definition of "extreme" as happening by chance only one time or fewer in 100 samples drawn from the population with certain characteristics. The second half defines "extreme" as happening by chance only five times in 100.

To read the tables, you take the "degrees of freedom" that is part of the definition of the numerator of the F you are using for your test and find it across the top. Take the degrees of freedom which is part of the definition of the denominator of the F you are using for your

---

*If you plan to do work that involves serious concerns about statistical significance, you need to go beyond this chapter. Consult the sources indicated in the suggested readings.

test and find it down the side. Now read the number where that row and column intersect. In the first half of the table, for 2 d.f. (numerator) and 20 d.f. (denominator), the critical value of F is 5.849. A value of F this large or larger occurs only one time out of 100 repeated samples from a population with given characteristics.

In the second half of the table, for the same definitions of numerator and denominator (2 and 20 d.f.), you can see that the value is 3.493. A value of F this large or larger would happen fewer than five times in 100 in repeated random samples under the assumptions.

The proper number of degrees of freedom for numerator and denominator will always be given you when you look up test statistics for tests you want to make, so don't worry too much about definition.

For those who want one, degrees of freedom is most easily thought of as, "How many values can I guess at among all the cases and still meet the constraints of the statistics I have calculated?" For example, having calculated a mean, if you were to guess at specific values for all the cases, you could, quite literally, guess any value at all for all the N cases except one and still come up with a set of N values with the same mean. That last case's value, however, would be "fixed" by the constraint of having to have a sum divided by N equal the calculated mean. You'd have $N - 1$ degrees of freedom—that is, freedom to guess and still hit the same mean.

Thus the degrees of freedom associated with the total variation or $\Sigma (Y_i - \overline{Y})^2$ in regression or analysis of variance will always be $N - 1$. You "use up" one degree of freedom having calculated a mean. Similarly, in regression you use up two degrees of freedom: calculating a mean, and the b in the regression equation $Y = a + bX$. Therefore, the degrees of freedom associated with the unexplained variation sum of squares, $\Sigma (Y_i - Y_p)^2$, is $N - 2$; you are free to guess all but two values and have regression come out the same. In analysis of variance, you calculate a mean for every category and the grand mean. There the degrees of freedom associated with the unexplained variation equals $N - k - 1$ (k for the number of categories, and 1 for the grand overall mean).

Rather than worrying about what "degrees of freedom" means, it's better, for the moment, to get on with a concrete example, for you can rest assured that you'll always be able to look up the definition of F and find proper d.f. there.

To get on with our concrete examples of the F test statistic, imagine that you have run a regression and found a correlation between your independent and dependent variables. The question now is whether that correlation exists in the population. Remember, we don't ask the question that way. We ask: How likely is it that I got this correlation in a sample if it doesn't exist in the population? (This is our awkward way of proceeding.)

First, let's list the assumptions about the population, measurement, and sampling that are necessary for a statistician to have in order to calculate the F values that would show up in an infinite number of repeated samples from a population with the following characteristics:

1. In the population:
   a. The variables are not related,
   b. The phenomena are distributed in bivariate normal fashion (defined below),
   c. Variances in Y are equal across all levels of X (homoscedasticity);
2. Measurement is assumed to be interval;
3. Sampling is assumed to be independent random.

Stop here just a second for a few definitions. Remember that normal distributions are basically symmetric (mirror image on both sides) distributions of a particular peakedness—the familiar bell-shaped curve. *Bivariate normal* means that X is normally distributed about Y, and vice versa.* If you have this distribution, you get equal variances in Y for each level of X as a byproduct. Neither of those

---

*Blalock (1972, 369) shows that such a bivariate normal distribution looks something like a firefighter's hat—thinking in the three-dimensional space it takes to show the distribution.

assumptions need detain us too long at this point because regression can tolerate some violations of those assumptions, especially with large samples. *Independent random*, probably more immediately important, means that each case is drawn independently and randomly into the sample. The fact that one case gets in doesn't influence another's getting in.

What you want here is for the residuals in Y regressed on the independent(s) to be independent and normally distributed around the predicted value of Y at each value of X (Berenson, 1983). Over-time data can cause you to violate this assumption because the value of Y for one year is not independent of its value for another year. For example, the number of crimes in cities for one year is highly correlated with the number of crimes in them for previous years. You also don't want a single large cause of Y that is correlated with X to be in the error rather than in the equation.

The second step is to say how unlikely it would have to be that our sample results come from the assumed population before we say that our sample probably came from a different one. This depends on how sure you need to be. For the moment, let's just arbitrarily say we want the results so different that only five times in 100 would repeated samples from the above-described population yield samples that extreme.

Now that the assumptions have been spelled out and our criteria indicated, we are ready to calculate an F based on our sample data. To test a correlation or a slope, the numerator of F is defined as: the explained sum of squares divided by 1 degree of freedom; and the denominator of F is defined as: the unexplained sum of squares divided by $N - 2$ degrees of freedom, as in Formula 18.2.

FORMULA 18.2
F for Testing the Significance of a Correlation or Slope

$$F = \frac{\text{The explained sum of squares} / (1) \text{ d.f.}}{\text{The unexplained sum of squares} / (N - 2) \text{ d.f.}}$$

or

$$\frac{r^2 \times \Sigma(Y_i - \overline{Y})^2 / 1}{(1 - r^2) \times \Sigma(Y_i - \overline{Y})^2 / N - 2}$$

Remember that r^2 = the proportion of explained variation and that $(1 - r^2)$ = the proportion of unexplained variation. Thus, the product of r^2 and the total variation or sum of squares, $r^2 \times \Sigma(Y_i - \overline{Y})^2$, is the explained sum of squares. Similarly, in the denominator, we have $(1 - r^2) \times \Sigma(Y_i - \overline{Y})^2$ or the unexplained sum of squares. Each is divided by the appropriate degrees of freedom—1 for the numerator, and $N - 2$ for the denominator. If you want to know more about the meaning of this statistic and why it will usually be around 0 for samples drawn from a population in which two variables are unrelated, consult some of the sources listed in the suggested readings.

If X and Y are correlated in our sample, the numerator of F (based on the explained sum of squares) will be much bigger than the denominator (based on the unexplained sum of squares). F will then have a value greater than 1.0.

Our final step, then, is to see whether the F based on our sample data is so much bigger than an F would be based on the assumptions (no relation, homoscedasticity, independent random samples, bivariate normality, interval measurement) that we *reject* the notion that our sample probably came from the assumed population and *fail to reject* the notion that our sample came from a population more like our sample.

To do this, we compare the F we got from the sample to the F in the table at 1 and $N - 2$ degrees of freedom (1 across the top; $N - 2$ down the side, finding the column and row intersection). If the F from our sample exceeds the tabled value, we reject the notion that our sample came from the assumed population—*rejecting* the null hypothesis that X and Y are *not* related in the population and *failing to reject* the alternative hypothesis that X and Y *are* related in the population.

If the F from our sample does not exceed

the tabled value, we reject the alternative hypothesis that X and Y are related in the population, and we fail to reject the null hypothesis. We state that we cannot say that X and Y are not unrelated in the population. (This sounds like bad syntax, but it is a close statement to what is happening philosophically.)

Actually, when we reject the null hypothesis (in any significance test, not just with F), we are rejecting the whole set of assumptions—measurement level, sampling, description of the population—and we cannot be absolutely sure that *only* the XY correlation led us to get the large F value. However, we rule out sampling as a possible reason for the large F by good sampling techniques. We rule out measurement as a possible reason by good measurement, and we don't usually worry too much about the rest because of the robustness of the F tests. Therefore, we talk as if we were rejecting only the null hypothesis that X and Y are uncorrelated.

EXERCISE 2 Using the F Test Statistic

Before turning to computer output, make sure you are able to read the F table with facility. Look at Table A.2 in Appendix D and answer the following questions about it.

1. If you are doing an F test for which the numerator is defined as having 2 degrees of freedom (d.f.) and the denominator is defined as having 30 degrees of freedom (d.f.), a _____ value of F will be met or exceeded only one time in 100 repeated random samples from a population whose characteristics are as defined above in the text.
2. At the .05 level of significance, would you reject or fail to reject the null hypothesis that X and Y are unrelated if you calculated an F statistic of 11.08 for a correlation (1 d.f. numerator; $N - 2$ d.f. denominator) found in a sample of 52? Explain your decision very briefly. (Note that you can estimate the critical F value from those around it when the exact critical value you are looking for is not in the table. You have, in the table, the critical value for 1 and 40 d.f. and for 1 and 60 d.f. The critical value for 1 and 50 d.f. is half way in between.)
3. A _____ value of F would occur fewer than five times in 100 repeated random samples drawn from the population assumed for Formula 18.2 when F is defined as having a numerator with 1 d.f. and a denominator with 1,000 d.f.

Stop now and examine a piece of REGRESSION output with more than one independent variable, either newly run or obtained in earlier lessons.

You will find the *F value* and the *significance* of the F for the regression. Circle the value of the F statistic for the regression; put a square around the significance of F for the regression.

The *F value* for the whole regression here is basically the same as if you had calculated F by the above definition. The only difference is that the explained sum of squares in the numerator is that explained by all the independent variables, and the degree of freedom for that explained sum of squares is equal to the number of independent variables; the unexplained sum of squares in the denominator is that variation unexplained by the independent variables in the regression equation, and the degrees of freedom associated with that unexplained sum of squares are equal to N minus 1 minus the number of independent variables.

The *significance* of F is: How likely is it that I would obtain this value of F with repeated random samples from a population in which my independent variable(s) are not related to my dependent variable (and in which other assumptions are met)? If it is .8, that means eight times out of ten you'd get this F value from a population in which the variables are unrelated; if it is .01, one time out of 100; if .002, two times out of 1,000; and if it is .000, less than one time out of 10,000, etc. On your output, write out in a sentence the meaning of the significance of F found there.

Now examine the output again. Can you find how many degrees of freedom are associated with the *explained* sum of squares? Label it on the output. How many degrees of freedom are associated with the *unexplained* sum of squares? Label it on the output. Think this through. The notations used by SPSS are different, but the meaning is the same as the coverage here.

EXERCISE 3 Using the *t* Statistic

Notice that in the statistics associated with each independent variable there is a column labeled "Significance of *t*." It's the far right column usually. *t* is a different inferential statistic that is similar to *F*. What the significance of *t* is telling you is: "How likely is it that I got this partial slope from a population in which **this** independent variable is unrelated to the **dependent variable** *controlling* all the other **independent variables and which meets other criteria** as well?"

As it is printed out, the significance of *t* is for a two-tailed test and is the same as the significance of *F* would be if you used that statistic instead. However, since the distribution of *t* has two tails (like the normal distribution, but unlike the *F* distribution), you can take advantage of this fact for directional tests.

As we said above, if you are interested only in the probability that a statistic (here a slope) as positive or more positive than the one you got could come from a population in which the variables were unrelated, you can look at only one tail of the distribution. Similarly, if you are interested only in the probability that a statistic (again, for example, a slope) as negative or more negative than yours could come from a population in which the variables were unrelated, you can look at only the other tail of the distribution. Rather than splitting the critical proportion (the .05 or .01 or .001 proportion of the distribution) over two tails, you can look at it in one tail of the distribution; as a result, the value of *t* that delineates the critical region of the distribution is lower.

If, because you have hypothesized the direction of the relationship between *X* and *Y* in advance, you are willing to be a bit less conservative than usual about asserting that your sample results indicate a population unlike that assumed for the distribution of the test statistic, you can do a one-tailed test with *t*. All you have to do is divide the significance printed out for *t* by two. Thus, if the significance of *t* is printed out as .1066, the significance for a one-tailed test would be .0533.

Examine the significance of *t* for your first independent variable. If you use the criterion of .05, would you reject the null hypothesis that, in the population, this independent variable is unrelated to this dependent, when all the other independents are controlled? Write your decision on the output. Be sure to indicate whether you are doing a one- or two-tailed test and why you chose the one you did.

If the significance of *t* is .05 or less (either as printed for a two-tailed test or after you divide it by two for a one-tailed test), that means that five times or fewer out of 100 repeated random samples from a population in which that independent (controlling the other independents) was *un*related to the dependent would you get a *t* value such as you obtained. The null hypothesis is "no relation, controlling the other independents." The null hypothesis is rejected if the significance of *t* is .05 or less.

Now look at your second independent variable and its *t* significance (*not* the *value* of *t*, the *significance* of *t*). On the output in the proper place, write whether you would reject the null hypothesis of no relationship (controlling the other independents) at the .01 level of significance. Write a sentence indicating your decision and the reason for it on the output.

STATISTICAL VERSUS SUBSTANTIVE SIGNIFICANCE

Now, before you go any further, look at the R^2 for the regression you examined because we have to talk about a problem: the difference between statistical and interpretive significance. The larger the sample, the more likely *any* correlation is to be significant, statistically speaking. This is true for any of the tests—not just *F*. Given a *large* sample, such as you might have doing survey research, even an $r^2 = .01$ is unlikely to have come from a population in which X and Y are unrelated.

From one perspective, this is intuitively understandable and wonderful. The bigger the sample, the closer we come to getting the whole population in it, and the surer we are we have the correct population value. However, from another perspective, what theoretical meaning do we place on one percent of the variation in a dependent variable being explained ($r^2 = .01$)? What possible theoretical good, in most circumstances that political scientists face, does it do us to explain one percent of the variation in a phenomenon? Yet, it is likely that such an r^2 in a larger sample is statistically significant.

Inferential statistics can guide you. They do not absolve you from making decisions. Only you, the trained and skilled researcher, can decide whether a correlation is worth interpreting—whether it has substantive rather than just statistical significance.

OTHER TESTS BASED ON THE F DISTRIBUTION

Now let's look at some more varieties of the F statistic. As promised in Chapter 15 on two-way analysis of variance, there is a way to help you determine whether interaction makes a difference or should be considered part of the error. You can test the statistical significance of the interaction. We will also show how you can test the significance of the amount of variation explained by the independent variables in a two-way analysis of variance.

Basically, you will be looking at four F statistics. One assesses the effects of interaction; one assesses the effect of one independent variable while adjusting for the other; one assesses the effects of the other independent variable while adjusting for the first; and one assesses the total explanation. Again, you are asking how often an F value for each of the four tests above would show up in repeated random samples from populations in which—

1. The independents are not correlated with the dependent variable; there is no interaction.
2. The variances of Y are equal across all cells defined by the independents.
3. Y is normally distributed in all cells defined by the independents.
4. The dependent is intervally measured.
5. The categories of X and Z represent independent samples.

    (A case having a particular value of X did not influence the selection of a case with another value of X, and the same is true of cases on Z.)

First, you test the significance of the *interaction*. Here F is defined as in Formula 18.3.

FORMULA 18.3
F Test for the Significance of Interaction

$$F = \frac{\text{Sum of squares due to interaction}/(c-1)(r-1) \text{ d.f.}}{\text{Unexplained sum of squares } /(N - cr) \text{ d.f.}}$$

In Formula 18.3, the degrees of freedom in the numerator are $(c - 1) \times (r - 1)$; i.e., the number of *values* (c) on the column variable minus one ($c - 1$) *times* the number of *values* (r) on the row variable minus one ($r - 1$). The degrees of freedom associated with the denominator are $N - cr$, or the total number of cases minus the product of the number of values on both independent variables. (Again, don't worry too much about the degrees of freedom associated with each test. You can find them in any statistics book that you use to look up the formulae.)

We usually want to err in the opposite direction from that usually considered conservative when we test interaction, so we frequently set a high probability at which we would declare it significant. If an F statistic associated with interaction would occur ten times in 100 (significance = .1) from a population in which there was only additivity (no interaction), we sometimes declare it significant and treat it as something more than "error." Certainly, if it is likely only five times in 100 (significance =

.05), we usually treat it as something other than error. Note the qualifiers in the above statement. It still comes down to *your* research judgment (and what the community of scholars in your field have come to accept as reasonable).

EXERCISE 4 Using F Tests in Analysis of Variance

Examine a piece of two-way ANOVA SPSS output in which interaction is considered "explained" variation and is separated from error. Circle the significance of F associated with the sum of squares due to interaction. Is it statistically worth treating separately? Write out a sentence on the output indicating your answer to this and your reasoning.

If interaction is *not* statistically significant, the sum of squares explained by interaction is treated now as error. (The degrees of freedom now associated with error is also the total of those previously associated with error plus those previously associated with interaction.) When you test the significance of one or the other independent variable or the combined independent variables, you must have *first* decided whether interaction is part of the error or not. Which of the next tests you do in order to test the significance of the explanation depends on your decision about interaction.

If interaction is significant and is to be considered part of the explanation, you must use an analysis of variance, on which interaction is separated out and not just lumped in with error. The significances of F for one independent variable and then for the next independent variable, representing significance of each independent variable adjusting for the other (and for interaction if you are using the regression method), are probably not very useful since interaction is significant. The effects of one independent variable really shouldn't be assessed independently of the other. However, do look for the significance of F associated with the explained sum of squares. That is the significance of the proproportion of the variation in Y that is explained by both the independent variables and by interaction. Is the total explanation significant? Write a sentence indicating your decision and reasoning on the output and next to the significance of the total explanation.

If interaction is not significant and is to be considered mere error, look on your ANOVA output (where variation explained by interaction is in the residual) for the significance of first one and then the other independent variable. This is the significance of each taken independently, adjusting for the effects of the other. Draw a box around the significance of F for each independent variable. Write out whether the separate effects of each independent variable are significant.

Then, still using the output on which interaction is treated as error, draw another box around the significance of F associated with the main effects. This is the significance of the variation in Y explained by both the independent variables operating together. Write out your decision about whether the total explanation is significant.

In these F tests you have, in effect, calculated new F statistics defined as in Formula 18.4. Your assessments of each of the independent variables separately would have the sum of squares associated with one of the two variables in the numerator for each assessment of significance. Your assessments of the overall explanations (one with interaction as part of the explanation and one with interaction as part of the error) would have the sum of squares associated with the explanation in the numerator.

FORMULA 18.4
F for the Significance of E^2

$$F = \frac{\text{Explained sum of squares / d.f.}}{\text{Unexplained sum of squares / d.f.}}$$

The only difference between the two tests of the overall explanation is that, in the former case, the interaction sum of squares and its

ANOTHER F TEST

There are many other F tests. One that you can do will help you decide whether a linear model or a curvilinear model better fits your data. Remember when you did regression in Chapters 4 and 5 and, in Chapter 7, trichotomized your independent variable and did analysis of variance on the same data?

Had the data on which you ran the regression been slightly curvilinearly related, as is illustrated in Figure 18.2, fitting a straight line to that relationship (as is shown with the line in that figure) wouldn't get at *all* the relationship. The error off the straight line would be rather high, and R^2 would, therefore, be reduced.

Trichotomizing the independent variable and doing analysis of variance as pictured in Figure 18.3 would probably give you a higher E^2. Error around category means, which do not have to be in a straight line, would be less than error around the straight line.

Whether it is "worth it" to use the more complex analysis of variance model—i.e., whether it allows so much greater explanation that we should keep it and sacrifice the parsimony of the straight-line model—is a matter for your research judgment. An F test, however, can help you decide whether the more complex model explains "statistically significantly" more variation. The test defines an F based on the excess variation in Y explained by

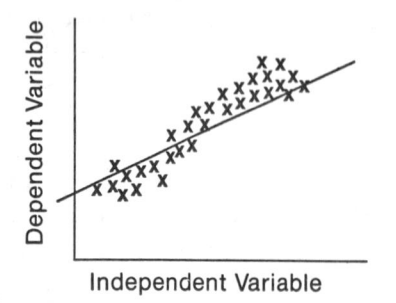

Figure 18.2 Curved Relationship Described by a Straight Line

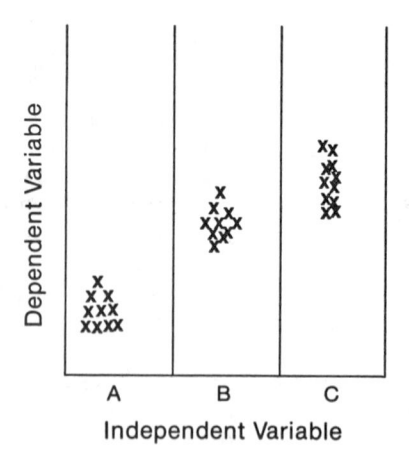

Figure 18.3 Analysis of Variance on a Slightly Curved Relationship

E^2 over R^2 in the numerator, and the variation in Y unexplained by the nonlinear model in the denominator, as you can see in Formula 18.5.

FORMULA 18.5
F Test for Curvilinearity

$$F = \frac{[(E^2 - R^2) \times \Sigma(Y_i - \overline{Y})^2]/(k-2) \text{ d.f.}}{[(1 - E^2) \times \Sigma(Y_i - \overline{Y})^2]/(N-k) \text{ d.f.}}$$

Where:
  k = Number of categories in the independent variable in the analysis of variance

If the resulting F on your sample data is statistically significant, you can reject the null hypothesis that the curvilinear model explains no more than the linear model in the population from which your sample was drawn. Remember, however, that whether you think the excess explanation is *substantively* worth it is another nonstatistical question.

SUMMARY OF F TESTS

To summarize all these F tests without their comprehensive details, let me list the procedure.

1. You first posit a population in which variables are uncorrelated or interaction is insignificant,

or the curved model is no better than a linear one, etc.
2. You look up a definition of F for the test you wish to make.
3. You let a table tell you how likely certain F values are from such a population *and* decide how unlikely your test result will have to be before you reject the notion that your sample came from such a population.
4. You calculate an F statistic on your sample data.
5. You compare your sample F value to the distribution of the F test statistic.
6. You decide whether to—
   a. Reject the notion that your sample came from a population like that assumed for the table and fail to reject the notion that it came from a different sort of population more like your sample; or
   b. Fail to reject the notion that your sample came from a population like that assumed for the table.

Note: remember that you *never accept* a hypothesis that your variables came from or did not come from a population in which variables were correlated or uncorrelated. It is the nature of proof that we can never prove anything. We can only rule out (falsify) other possibilities.

Also note: in some SPSS programs, you don't get all the information we have been discussing for F tests. Only the *probability* of getting the F that would have been obtained is given.

EXERCISE 5 Using Significance Tests on Other Output

Notice your CORRELATIONS output. You will find p = xxx. This is the probability (p) that such a correlation would be found from repeated samples from a population in which the two variables were uncorrelated (plus all the other assumptions necessary for the F test). To see p = xxx is exactly the same as seeing *significance* of F = xxx.

Notice, too, your PARTIAL CORR output, if you ran that in Chapter 12. There, too, you will find p = xxx. That is the probability that such a partial correlation would be found from repeated random samples from a population in which such a partial correlation did not exist (when all the other assumptions necessary for the F test do exist).

Take a piece of CORRELATIONS output. On the output, circle the probability of getting the F that is not, itself, reported. Write whether you would reject the null hypothesis of no correlation. Briefly indicate your reasoning.

Take a piece of PARTIAL CORR output and do the same things to it.

INFERENCE WITHOUT POPULATION ASSUMPTIONS

Some tests do not rely on assumptions about the population, even though they continue to rely on assumptions about measurement and sampling that allow the construction of a distribution of a test statistic. These tests are called *nonparametric*, which means that they don't rely on assumptions about population parameters (the value of the statistic in the population). However, like the tests discussed earlier, they provide a guide to help you assess the likelihood of having gotten your results by chance.

Probably the best known nonparametric test of significance is the chi-square test for independence. You have already learned to calculate the test statistic for this test back in Chapter 10 where you modified it into a measure of association.

When you transformed chi-square into a measure of association, you figured out what the expected frequencies were in each cell, given the marginal distributions. Those expected values are the averages of the values likely to show up in those cells by chance over many, many trials if the marginal distributions shown for the two variables are two independent, unrelated distributions.

Think of it this way. If you had many groups of cases distributed on two variables as indicated in the marginals, and if knowing a case's value on one variable did not help you predict its value on the other variable, the row entries would repeatedly show proportionately almost the same distribution as the horizontal marginal distribution, and the column entries repeatedly would show proportionately almost the same distribution as the vertical marginal distribution.

With only chance operating, sometimes the cell entries would be off the expected values—even, occasionally, way off the expected values. However, over the long run and for many, many groups of cases, chance would distribute the cell entries more or less like the expected values.

Statisticians have calculated and tabled the distribution of a test statistic that basically tells us how often chance will distribute cell entries differently from the expected values and how severely different those distributions will be. The assumptions on which their calculations are based are not, as we have indicated earlier, assumptions about the population. Rather, they have to assume that no more than 20 percent of the cells have expected frequencies of less than five; that no cell has an expected frequency of less than one; and that cases were drawn independently into the sample (the selection of one case did not influence the selection of another case).

We then examine the cell entries in our own data, compare them to those that would be ordinarily expected in a chance distribution, and determine whether our results would be so unlikely, if only chance were operating, that we will reject the null hypothesis that there is no relationship between the variables and fail to reject the alternative hypothesis that there is a relationship between the variables. Should your data happen to violate the assumptions on which the distribution of the test statistic was constructed, you should not use this form of the chi-square test.

You have, in Chapter 10, compared the obtained frequencies to those expected by chance when you calculated the chi-square statistic found in Formula 18.6. Briefly review those calculations now if you don't remember them.

FORMULA 18.6
The Chi-square Statistic

$$\text{Chi-square} = \Sigma \frac{(f_o - f_e)^2}{f_e}$$

After the statistic is calculated, the only thing left to do in the test is to determine whether the comparison of obtained to expected frequencies shows that your results were unlikely to have happened by chance. To do this, you will need to compare the chi-square from your data to those in a table of chi-square values and their likelihood of having been obtained by chance.

Like the distribution of F, the distribution of the chi-square statistic varies with degrees of freedom. While at low degrees of freedom it looks pretty much like the distribution pictured above Table A.3 in Appendix D, the distribution "reaches" out to the right and takes a more "normal" appearance as degrees of freedom increase.

Fortunately, you don't have to worry about what it looks like. You just need to know what value of chi-square marks the point at or above which only 5 percent or 1 percent or .1 percent of the values of chi-square fall by chance. It is those values, for the various degrees of freedom, which are in Table A.3.

To use Table A.3, you need to know two things. First, what are degrees of freedom in this context and, second, what critical region do you need?

Degrees of freedom for tables are figured by multiplying the number of rows in the table minus one times the number of columns in the table minus one: d.f. = $(r - 1)(C - 1)$. Therefore, for a two-by-two table, there is one degree of freedom. For a five-by-four table, there are twelve degrees of freedom, and so on.

You can think of the degrees of freedom this way. If you were given certain set marginals, how many cell entries could you guess at before you were forced, in order to meet the constraints imposed by the marginals, to fill in the remaining cell entries only by subtracting the guessed ones from the relevant marginal number? The number you can guess at is the degrees of freedom. Here again, don't worry much about this; just rely on the $(r - 1)(c - 1)$ definition of degrees of freedom for this use of chi-square.

Asking for the critical region you need is the same as asking how unlikely should the sample results be before rejecting the null hypothesis. Should the sample results be so unlikely they would occur only five times in 100? Only one time in 100? Only one time in 1,000? Values that would be as extreme as only one time in 1,000 are in the next-to-last column of the table (headed 0.1); you divide the heading by 100 for the probability. Values that would be as extreme as only five times in 100 are in the sixth column from the right (headed 5), etc.

Use the table by finding the row appropriate to the degrees of freedom for your table. Find the column for the likelihood you need. The value at the point where the column and row intersect is the value against which you will compare the chi-square value you got from the sample. If the value you calculated is higher than that in the table, you reject the null hypothesis that the variables are unrelated.

EXERCISE 6 Using the Chi-Square Table and Output

Now answer some questions about the chi-square to make sure you can read the table.

1. Look back to Chapter 10 for the chi-square you calculated there. _____ was the value of chi-square before you modified it into a measure of association. _____ were the degrees of freedom for that table. By comparing that chi-square from your table in Chapter 10 to the distribution, decide whether to reject the null hypothesis that X and Y were not related in that table. Write your answer and a brief explanation of it.
2. A chi-square value as high as or higher than 25.00 shows up by chance _____ times out of _____ for a six-by-four table if the assumptions about sampling, absence of relationship, and expected frequencies are met.
3. If you calculated a chi-square statistic for a four-by-three table and got a value of 27.349, assuming the various criteria for sampling and expected frequencies were met, what would be your decision regarding the null hypothesis that the two variables were unrelated if you demanded the probability of your results occurring by chance be .005 or less? Explain briefly why you came to that answer.
4. If you calculated a chi-square statistic for a four-by-four table and got a value of 13.741, would you consider the relationship in your table statistically significant or not? Explain, briefly.

Now examine a piece of SPSS CROSS-TABS output for the tabular presentation of the relationship between two nominal variables. Among the statistics, you will find the *value* of chi-square and the *significance* of chi-square. On the output, circle the value and draw a box around the significance. Notice that you don't have to refer to the table for the distribution of the chi-square test statistic; SPSS has done it for you and with more precision than tables allow. On the output, next to the significance, write out your interpretation in a sentence or two about whether the relationship in the table you are examining is significant or not.

Be sure to examine the strength of the relationship between the variables in the table as indicated by the percentages. Remember that chi-square itself is a measure of statistical significance—not of the strength of the relationship. You may find that a relationship is statistically significant but hardly worth talking about in substantive terms.

Adding to the substantive versus statistical significance problem is the fact that chi-square varies with the number of cases in the table. If you double the sample size, you double chi-square. If you triple the sample size, you triple chi-square, etc. This is intuitively gratifying because you expect that, as the sample gets bigger and bigger, you are surer and surer that you have "real" results and not just some oddball group of cases.

However, while this may be useful as you go from a sample of 50 to a sample of 100, it plays havoc with interpretation of large samples such as those used frequently in survey research. A one- or two-percent difference can be statistically significant with an N of cases that large, but it may be that one or two percent isn't worth interpreting substantively.

Given that almost anything will be statistically significant with a large sample, the burden is right back on you to make decisions based on theory, on your knowledge of the subject matter, and on your own expertise. The statistic won't even provide much of a guide under those circumstances.

On your output near the table, write whether you consider your substantive results different from your statistical results.

This entire chapter has been based on the idea that we are working from sample data to make inferences about how likely we were to have gotten such results by chance, but we have not yet discussed how to get the samples to work from. It is to that question that we turn in Chapter 19.

SUGGESTED READINGS

AGNEW, NEIL MCK., and SANDRA W. PYKE. *The Science Game*, 4th ed. (Englewood Cliffs, NJ: Prentice-Hall, 1987), pp. 185–203.

BABBIE, EARL. *The Practice of Social Research*, 3rd ed. (Belmont, CA: Wadsworth, 1983). See the second part of Chapter 17, pp. 414–428.

BERENSON, MARK L., DAVID M. LEVINE, and MATTHEW GOLDSTEIN. *Intermediate Statistical Methods and Applications: A Computer Package Approach* (Englewood Cliffs, NJ: Prentice-Hall, 1983). Pages 209–211 cover the independence assumptions; pages 225–226 treat how to tell if the assumptions are violated. Their Chapter 14 suggests some ways of dealing with violations.

BLALOCK, HUBERT M., JR. *Social Statistics*, 2nd ed. (N.Y.: McGraw-Hill, 1972). See Part 3 and Chapters 13–15, and the sections of Chapters 16–20 that deal with inference rather than description. This is a very good place to read about the logic of statistical tests; the chapter you have just finished relies heavily on it. Blalock also spells out the meaning of the various F tests.

BOWEN, BRUCE D., and HERBERT F. WEISBERG. *An Introduction to Data Analysis* (San Francisco: Freeman, 1980), Ch. 10.

HENKEL, RAMON E. *Tests of Significance*, # 4 in series, *Quantitative Applications in the Social Sciences* (Beverly Hills, CA: Sage, 1976).

KOHOUT, FRANK. *Statistics for Social Scientists* (N.Y.: Wiley, 1974), Units VIII-XIV.

OTT, LYMAN, WILLIAM MENDENHALL, and RICHARD F. LARSON. *Statistics: A Tool for the Social Sciences* (North Scituate, MA: Duxbury, 1978). See Chapter 5 for the logic of the tests and also 6–8 for several kinds of one- and two-variable tests; Chapters 9 and 10 for nominal and ordinal bivariate tests; and 11 and 12 for regression and analysis of variance. Page 379 gives the test for the significance of tau_b, mentioned in the chapter you have just finished.

ARTICLES

You may want to examine articles listed in other chapters for examples of significance tests. Almost all the articles use them.

CHAPTER
19

A BRIEF INTRODUCTION TO SAMPLING

SAMPLING AND INFERENCE

Tests of statistical significance are most appropriate when you are trying to generalize from a sample to a population—that is, when you have sample results and wish to assert that similar things are going on outside your sample among some larger group of cases. While some researchers argue that you can use the tests when you have data on the whole population to assess such questions as whether your results on any correlation, for example, are significantly different from zero correlation, others insist that the tests should only be applied when you do not have the entire population of cases.

Regardless of which side you take in the argument (about which you can read more in the suggested readings), when you are drawing a sample you must be rigorous in following procedures, or the tests we have been discussing will be somewhat compromised. All the distributions of the test statistics are constructed under certain assumptions about sampling. Although there are others, the ones you have seen above were constructed for *independent random* sampling, in which each element—and each possible combination of elements of the population—has an equal and known chance of being drawn into the sample.

When your sampling method deviates from the one under which the distribution of the test statistic was constructed, you loose the ability to argue that the extremity of your results was due to your sample being from a different population from that assumed for the test statistic (or that the extremity of your results was not due to chance, in the case of chi-square). While the statements could be true, your extreme results might also be due to violating the sampling assumptions of the test.

In ordinary, everyday political research, we probably don't worry enough about violating the assumptions of the test (including the sampling assumption) as long as we aren't doing something completely flagrant.* Our main goals are in explaining phenomena—getting at form and strength of relationships—rather than in assessing statistical significance. Because our goals typically lie elsewhere, we sometimes aren't very sophisticated in our concerns about significance tests.

Perhaps we should be, and, as our measurements improve and our theories become more sophisticated so that we can limit error from those sources, perhaps we will be. It seems

---

*For example, you might want to think about how often you see analyses of only the returned questionnaires from a sample, without great attention paid to whether the returned questionnaires still constitute a rigorous sample of the population. Also, think about how many of our measurements meet the assumption of interval measurement.

that, for many of us, the other sources of error are still so pressing that the effects on significance tests of sampling irregularities or violating other assumptions are not at the center stage.

The best recommendation, for ordinary political scientists who are steeped mostly in questions of theory and measurement, is that they consult a statistician on any complicated sampling questions. Still, you will need to know some basic considerations in sampling before you can ask the right questions.

GOAL OF SAMPLING

Other than to reduce the cost of examining a whole population or to make possible generalizing about a population when it is impossible to study each and every element of it, our goal in sampling is a sample that represents the population we have defined to be of interest. If we very clearly define the population, we can let the laws of chance give us a sample that is *likely* to represent that population.

Of course, there will always be a chance of drawing a strange sample that does not at all seem to be like the population from which it was drawn. However, if we select a *probability sample*—one in which every element has a known chance of being in the sample—we will be able to specify the boundaries of possible error around our findings and the certainty we have that our findings lie within those boundaries. We will be able to make statements such as the following one: if we drew repeated samples from this same population, 95 percent of the time the values of a given statistic in the samples would fall within a certain range around the value of the statistic in the population (the population parameter).

There is a way to narrow the possible error range and to increase the certainty that the samples would fall within that range around the population parameter: increase the size of the sample. Intuitively, it should be clear that, if we increase the sample size enough, we will eventually be assessing the whole population. If we assess the whole population, we are 100 percent sure that our sample statistic accurately represents the true value of the population parameter.

We needn't go so far as to assess the whole population, however, in order to increase the odds that we have accurately measured the phenomenon for the population. Depending on how important the results are to us, we can get 95, 99, or 99.9 percent confidence and 5, 3, or 1 percent likely error range without assessing the entire population. It just depends on how sure you need to be for the project at hand.

SIZE OF SAMPLE

How big does the sample need to be? That depends primarily on four things: how much accuracy you need, how much confidence you need, how homogeneous the population is, and the sampling method. Most people would expect to see the size of the population in that list, but population size has the least to do of any factor with how big the sample is. That fact seems counterintuitive; but you do need almost as big a sample to represent adequately a relatively small population as you would need for a large one. In survey research, for example, you would need almost as large a sample to represent one state (or one congressional district, for that matter) as you would need for the whole United States.

Start first with the question of how accurate your results need to be (how close your estimate has to be to the real population figure) or, in other words, how much *sampling error* you are willing to tolerate. If you are drawing a random sample in order to determine the likely winner of an election, for example, and need to be relatively sure that, when you report the percentage in the sample for a particular candidate, you are going to be off the real population percentage for that candidate by only 1 percent either way, you have to have a sample of around 9,000 people. If you are willing to be above or below the population figure by, potentially, as much as 3 percent, you have to have a sample around 1,000. If you are willing to have potential error of 5 percent either way from the population figure, you need around 400 people.

Notice that you don't just triple the sample size to cut the error down to one-third of its former level. It requires about nine times as many cases to get the error down from 3 percent to 1 percent. (The necessary sample size in these paragraphs presumes that you don't know how to guess the likely vote split in the population; that is, it presumes that you don't know the degree of homogeneity of the population.)

Second, consider the question of how confident you have to be. If you are willing to settle for 95 out of 100 repeated (random) samples falling within specified sampling error ranges around the statistic in the population (parameter), the sample sizes would be those indicated in the paragraphs above. However, if you need much greater confidence, like 99 out of 100 repeated (random) samples falling within the 1 percent error range, you'd need around 16,000 cases instead of around 9,000 cases. If you needed 99 percent confidence in your results being within the 3 percent range of error on either side of the population figure, you'd need around 1,800 cases instead of the 1,000 or so you needed for less confidence. If you needed 99 percent confidence in your results being within the 5 percent range of error, you'd need over 600 cases instead of around 400.

To get the extra 4 percent confidence in your results, you are adding more than half again as many cases. Only you can decide whether the extra confidence merits the extra cost. (The figures in these paragraphs also presume that you don't know anything about the degree of population homogeneity.)

The third consideration is how homogeneous the population is—a slightly more difficult question. To give you a glimpse at this problem, assume that you are trying to describe the dominant groups in the population and think about populations that are less and less homogeneous. In the first, you expect that about 95 percent of the population is alike; in the second, about 85 percent; and in the third, about 70 percent. At the 95 percent confidence level with 1 percent sampling error, you'd need a samples of about 2,000 for the first, about 5,000 for the second, and about 8,000 for the third. With 3 percent sampling error, the equivalent sample sizes would be about 200, something over 500, and almost 900.*

If, in contrast, you are trying to describe the minority groups in the population, the situation is reversed. As the population gets less and less homogeneous on the majority characteristic, the sample can be smaller from which you expect to get enough cases from the minority for analysis. It is very homogeneous populations that require the largest samples *if* you are trying to get enough cases from the nondominant groups for analysis.

This is very closely related to questions we have asked about the data when trying to assess relationships between variables at every level of measurement. Remember that we have asked whether we had cases from the full range of measurement of an independent or dependent variable in regression. Moreover, we asked whether there were enough cases for calculating dependent variable means within each category of the independent variable in analysis of variance; and whether the marginals were smoothly distributed or not for cross-tabulation tables. In homogeneous populations, we have to get rather large samples in order to assure ourselves of enough cases for analysis in the levels and categories we need to assess. In heterogeneous populations, we can assume that the cases in the sample are more likely to spread themselves across the levels and categories we need; therefore, we can worry less about large samples.

As an example of this homogeneity problem, imagine trying to analyze the attitudes of Communist Party members in the U.S. and compare them to other partisans. You are going to need a very large sample in order to get enough Communists for reliable analyses. On the measure you are interested in (Communists versus others), the population is homoge-

---

*The book of tables listed among the readings gives you a good summary of all these considerations and their effects on sample sizes; the discussion above relies on it.

neously non-Communist. However, if you are only trying to compare the attitudes of Democrats to those of Republicans, you are going to get enough of each in a smaller sample. On the measure you are interested in (Democrats versus Republicans), the population is heterogeneous; it has plenty of cases of both.

KINDS OF SAMPLES

The size of the sample also depends on the sampling method you employ. The estimates given so far in this chapter are for simple random samples. Other kinds of probability require more or fewer cases for the same accuracy and confidence.

Basically, there are three kinds of samples you need to know about—random, stratified random, and multistage cluster. All, properly constructed, are probability samples that allow us to estimate accuracy and certainty of our findings. The statistical tests you have examined are all based on random sampling—not on the other kinds of probability sampling. (Tests are available for the other kinds, but they are beyond the scope of this text.)

The simplest sampling procedure is *random sampling*. You number the elements of your population and go to a random numbers table in order to determine which elements to take into the sample. A table of random numbers is simply a list of numbers that bear no mathematical relation to each other, that is, there is no way that knowing one number will help you predict the next (or any other).

If, for example, you have up to 100 elements in the population, you get a table of two-digit random numbers from your library reserve section. (There's also one in the book of tables listed among the suggested readings.) To use it, you'd start anywhere on the table. Go across the rows. For each number you encounter, take the correspondingly numbered element in the population into your sample until you reach your sample size. Discard any numbers higher than your population size. You can use the same table for random numbers from 0–9999. Just combine adjacent two-number sets. So 10 09 becomes 1009, etc.

Again, enter at any point and go systematically across.

There are ways to approximate random samples that don't rely on numbering the population. Telephone surveys, for example, frequently rely on *random digit dialing*. For that, you know the prefixes of the area you're interested in (and the proportion of each prefix). You then use a random numbers table (0–9,999) to supply the last four digits.

Another possibility is *random-start-fixed-interval sampling*. For this, use a list of population elements of approximately known length. Divide the length of the list by the required sample size, which will give you the interval (n). Start blindly at some point on the list and take every nth element into the sample. As long as you don't hit some kind of pattern, the sample is probably reasonably acceptable.

The *stratified random* sample is used primarily when some characteristic is important to your analysis, but not heavily represented in the population, *and* when you know enough about the population to separate it on the basis of that characteristic. Once the population is "stratified"—i.e., separated on that characteristic—you randomly sample within strata but do so more heavily in the small group. Because each strata is more homogeneous than the population as a whole, you can get by with a smaller sample here than with a purely random one.

For example, you might be interested in comparing the attitudes of blacks to those of whites in some population in which blacks are very scarce. In this situation, you'd separate your population on the basis of race, randomly sample blacks fairly densely and randomly sample whites less densely. Then to estimate population attitudes in your analysis, you'd weight the white cases more heavily—i.e., treat each case as if it were two if that was the weight necessary to get the sample proportions back to the population proportions.

A third kind of sample is a *multi-stage cluster*. It is primarily used when no population list can be made and when the population is so spread out that cases drawn into the sample need to be close together for cost effectiveness. This kind of sampling requires larger samples than does random sampling for the same accuracy and certainty because, without larger numbers, you increase the odds of getting a "strange clump" of cases. To do this kind of sampling, you define your population in units and subunits. You sample units and then subunits randomly. Within the remaining subunits, you also sample randomly (or some approximation thereof).

For example, let's say your population is the adult population of the United States. Your units might be congressional districts (relatively equal in size so that each can be in the "pool" just once). The subunits might be precincts—in the pool as many times as necessary to represent their relative populations. In each congressional district, you'd sample precincts. For each precinct, you'd make a list of people and sample those randomly.

A TYPE OF SAMPLE TO AVOID

One kind of sample to avoid is one that, intuitively, looks more representative. Some researchers think that, if they match their samples to known population characteristics, they will have a more representative sample. *Quota samples*, as they are known, seek to get into the sample the same proportion of certain known characteristics as the population.

The problem with quota samples is that a researcher can't be sure that the sample has been matched to the population on *all* the relevant characteristics. There is no way to know what bias may be introduced by this process. Worse, there is no way to estimate certainty or range of possible error. Moreover, our statistics, as you have seen above, aren't usually developed for that kind of sample. You are better off letting chance give you a representative sample.

DEFINING THE POPULATION AND ITS ELEMENTS

It is important to be very clear on what the extent is of the population from which you are drawing your cases. Technically, you will be able to generalize from your sample only to the defined population from which it was drawn. You can avoid misleading yourself into thinking that your results are more widely applicable than they are if you keep a clear definition of the population in mind.

If you are doing survey research, is the population from which you are drawing a sample all adults? All adults who aren't in institutions (jail, college, nursing homes)? All telephones? All telephones listed? Registered voters? If you have drawn your sample from lists of telephone numbers, you cannot generalize confidently even to all adults with phones unless you have somehow controlled who answered the phone and your questions. If you have used phone books for your sample, you can only generalize confidently to a population of people who answer listed phones. If you have sampled from voter registration lists, you can generalize only to registered voters—not to all adults.

If you are sampling court decisions in order to examine changes in decisions over time, is the population from which you will sample all court decisions? All nonunanimous decisions? All decisions with written opinions? Decisions to hear cases argued as well as decisions rendered on cases? And so forth. You can generalize only to the population from which your sample came.

You can also make sure you are getting as wide a range of cases as you need if you spell out clearly the nature of the population from which you are drawing your cases. Remember that independent and dependent variables must vary before you can assess their relationship. Sometimes the reason they don't vary is because of the way the population was conceived and the sampling limited by that conception.

To take an extreme example: if you were trying to test a hypothesis about the differences between teenagers and adults, you could not do it with the usual national election survey. The election survey would have sampled a population of voting-age adults and would not sample from among thirteen- to eighteen-year-olds. Thus, your independent variable (generational cohort) would not vary very much in the data set you were trying to use.

A less extreme example would be trying to test hypotheses about voters and nonvoters by using a sample drawn from voter registration lists. The lists would exclude most habitual nonvoters. If the sample was drawn from the registration lists, you could only generalize about voting and nonvoting among registered voters.

As you spell out the exact boundaries of the population, also keep in mind a clear definition of what constitutes a single element in that population. Thinking clearly about this will help you avoid various kinds of problems later.

Sometimes, for example, people will naively draw samples from a population whose elements are court cases when their hypotheses are really about explaining the voting behavior of judges; and they, therefore, ought to be sampling judges. They then find that they cannot adequately test their hypotheses.

For a less obvious example, think about the time that you might have a population in which the element is defined as (typically) a pair of people. That could happen if you sample student records in order to get a sample of "adults who are interested in public schools," for example. Since many of the records (though not all, certainly) would contain the names of two parents, the record that is the unit of the population represents a pair of adults.

If you then want to test the significance of the difference between female and male opinions about how the school is run, you are in trouble. Many of the significance tests demand that cases be drawn independently into the sample. By sampling records, you drew a pair into the sample—not individuals. Thinking clearly, in advance, about the elements of the population would enable you to avoid that problem. Recognizing the problem would influence your choice of statistics.

The key message here is to think clearly about the definition of the population and its elements. Make sure that the population from which you are sampling is the one you need for testing your hypotheses. Make sure its elements are those on which you wish to measure the variables for the tests of your hypotheses later.

CONTROVERSIES IN SAMPLING

Before we leave the question of sampling altogether, you should know that some methodologists argue that we shouldn't even be terribly worried about representing populations. They would argue that no population in which we might be interested stays put long enough to generalize about: for example, new elements are being born, old elements are dying, all elements are changing through learning, etc., in a human population. These methodologists would say that, since we are really interested in "laws of human behavior" (i.e., the form of relationships between variables), we should focus more on making sure we represent, in our samples, the entire range of an independent variable rather than being so concerned with representing the population as it is (Willer, 1967).

Another argument is that we should test hypotheses first in limited settings and then repeat the tests over and over in slightly different settings to see under what conditions the hypotheses hold and do not hold. When they do not hold, we should add variables to the explanation to account for the differences (Glaser and Strauss, 1967).

Related to this argument is the suggestion that we test hypotheses in extremely different settings. When we find differences in the forms of relationships within the different settings, we should seek variables that will explain the difference (Przeworski and Teune, 1970).

You can read more about these controversies in the suggested readings. Although these controversies are beyond the scope of this text, you should know that they exist. That knowledge should serve to remind you of the underlying philosophical questions not just in sampling but also throughout the topics we have covered. If it serves to remind you that we are not dealing with pat answers, no matter how sophisticated in quantitative analysis we seem to be, it is enough for the moment. You will be able to pursue the questions later at a more sophisticated level.

SUGGESTED READINGS

Sampling in the Social Sciences

BABBIE, EARL. *The Practice of Social Research*, 3rd ed. (Belmont, CA: Wadsworth, 1983), Ch. 7.

BLALOCK, HUBERT M., JR. *Social Statistics*, 2nd ed. (N.Y.: McGraw-Hill, 1972), Ch. 9.5 and Part 5.

BOWEN, BRUCE D., and HERBERT F. WEISBERG. *An Introduction to Data Analysis.* (San Francisco: Freeman, 1980), pp. 9-10, 12-17.

CHEIN, ISIDOR, "An Introduction to Sampling," Appendix A in Seltiz, Wrightsman, and Cook, *Research Methods in Social Relations*, 3rd ed. (N.Y.: Holt, Rinehart, and Winston, 1976).

JOHNSON, JANET BUTTOLPH, and RICHARD A. JOSLYN. *Political Science Research Methods* (Washington, D.C.: Congressional Quarterly Press, 1986), Ch. 7.

KARTON, GRAHAM. *Introduction to Survey Sampling*, #35 in series, *Quantitative Applications in the Social Sciences* (Beverly Hills, CA: Sage, 1983).

KISH, LESLIE. *Survey Sampling* (N.Y.: Wiley, 1965).

Other Views of Sampling and Controversies in Sampling

GLASER, BARNEY G., and ANSELM L. STRAUSS. *The Discovery of Grounded Theory: Strategies for Qualitative Research* (Chicago: Aldine, 1967).

PRZEWORSKI, ADAM, and HENRY TEUNE. *The Logic of Comparative Social Inquiry* (New York: Wiley-Interscience, 1970).

WILLER, DAVID. "Conditional Universals and Scope Sampling," with Judith Willer, *Scientific Sociology: Theory and Method* (Englewood Cliffs, NJ: Prentice-Hall, 1967), Ch. 6.

Controversies in Significance Testing

HENKEL, RAMON E. *Tests of Significance*, #4 in series, *Quantitative Applications in the Social Sciences* (Beverly Hills, CA: Sage, 1976).

MORRISON, DENTON E., and RAMON HENKEL (eds.) *The Significance Test Controversy* (Chicago: Aldine, 1970).

Units and Levels of Analysis

BABBIE, EARL. *The Practice of Social Research*, 3rd ed. (Belmont, CA: Wadsworth, 1983), pp. 76-81, 275.

EULAU, HEINZ. "On Units and Levels of Analysis," in Eulau (ed.), *Macro-Micro Political Analysis* (Chicago: Aldine, 1969), pp. 1-19.

LANGBEIN, LAURA IRWIN, and ALLAN J. LICHTMAN. *Ecological Inference*, #10 in series, *Quantitative Applications in the Social Sciences* (Beverly Hills, CA: Sage, 1978).

Sample Size

ARKIN, HERBERT, and RAYMOND R. COLTON. *Tables for Statisticians*, 2nd ed. (N.Y.: Barnes and Noble, 1963), pp. 145ff.

CHAPTER
20

FORMULATING YOUR OWN RESEARCH DESIGN

Before you begin your own research projects, you'll need a design. By reviewing the elements of such a design here, you can reflect on what you've just learned about data analysis and see what you still need to work on that could not be covered in this text.

REASONS FOR RESEARCH DESIGNS

As you begin to prepare a design, keep in mind where it is you are going. You want a guide for a research project that is so thorough and so complete that another trained political scientist can pick it up, do the research exactly as you planned it, and write up the finished project without any prior knowledge of the specific area in which you are working.

You also want a proposal that will convince a review committee that your research is worth doing and that you have completely thought through each aspect of that research. Convincing a review committee is usually a matter of demonstrating the scientific worth of your project—for example, the need for replication, the need for corrections to earlier work, a theoretical gap to be filled, or a theoretical linkage to be established.

A review committee shouldn't be thought of as your nemesis, by the way. The members will probably think of problems you haven't anticipated or of additional factors your research should take into account. Even though you think you've thought of everything, others' viewpoints can save you headaches in the long run.

The most important goal of a design or research proposal is to keep your own attention focussed. The tendency is to wander afield, forgetting necessary steps toward the goal while gathering side issues. A good proposal will be your own guide through a thicket of possible missteps. Best of all, it will tell you when you're finished.*

THE BEGINNING

Probably the most important paragraphs in a research proposal are the first few paragraphs. It is here that you discuss the phenomenon you wish to explain in the research you propose to do and why you want to explain it.

Identify the phenomenon as clearly and succinctly as you can. This is the primary concept around which all of the rest of the work cen-

---

*A one-page outline of what follows was distributed by Galen Irwin when I took my first research design course. I've been elaborating on that outline for several years as I have worked with students and the problems they encounter in writing designs.

ters. It will be the dependent variable in your hypothesis. Its measurement level has the most impact on the kinds of statistical analysis you will select. Its validity and reliability are the keys to whether your paper is accepted as explanatory or not (without slighting the importance of measurement reliability and validity for *all* variables). The dependent variable is your key to finding literature in which to couch your proposed research. It cannot be stressed strongly enough that what you plan to explain should be the central focus of the rest of the paper.

Next, spell out why research on this phenomenon is worth doing. Keep your focus as scientific as possible. Even though you may want to explain a phenomenon that is of great personal interest to you, the scholarly community is less interested in your personal value structure, except as it may influence your interpretations. Of more interest to the community is whether you've uncovered a single central variable that can unite contradictory bodies of literature, or whether you can measure a phenomenon more simply with as valid results as before. Other areas of interest are whether generally accepted conclusions in the field are invalidated when measurement problems are corrected, or whether generally accepted conclusions stand up to tests on new data or with new measurement or in different circumstances.

The section on why the research is worth doing flows into and may overlap a literature review that itself may flow into and overlap a statement of the theory from which you have derived your hypotheses. The more formal the theory, the more likely it deserves a section of its own for statement in formal terms.

The literature review is sometimes tricky but not if you remember that your focus is on explaining a particular phenomenon. Keep the focus on that phenomenon. It isn't necessary to review *all* the literature in the entire subfield of political science in which you are working. Be selective. Review all the literature that is *relevant* to the task at hand.

Too often, neophytes in research design (and even a few old hands) think that the literature review is just a traditional hurdle to get past or a place to show off the breadth of what they've read. It is neither. The convention of literature review exists for a reason. As long as you keep that reason uppermost in your mind, you can rely on simple deductive logic and, sometimes, inductive logic to get not to a conclusion but to a testable hypothesis. Rules for good, clear writing should do the rest.

In general, this means you will want to review all the studies that have attempted to explain the phenomenon or closely related phenomena you're interested in. Try to group the studies in some way. If there is a clear chronological progression of studies that build one upon another to which your research adds, a chronological examination may suffice. If there are some studies that use one variety of independent variables and some that use another variety, the type of independent variable might be a good way to group the studies. If the studies vary in the levels of analysis used to explain a phenomenon, in some cases focussing on the individual and in others on collections of individuals, the level of analysis might be a good basis for organizing the studies.

Be sure to group the relevant literature in a way that relates to the particular project you are proposing, and make that relationship clear—even if you feel you are writing about the relationship as the introductory sentence of almost every paragraph.

Do not let yourself stray from the focus. You don't have to review every piece of literature that explains an *independent* variable unless you plan to develop a model in the form of a causal chain—one thing causing the next that, in turn, causes the next—or unless it is the measurement of the independent variable in the past that leads to need for replication with new measurement in your research. You aren't usually proposing to explain independent variables; therefore, research on them usually isn't relevant to the literature review.

In effect, you are using the literature (or the theory) as a source of hypotheses, and pure logic plays an important role in this process. You derive your own hypotheses from generally accepted conclusions in the literature. Perhaps you may want to test explanations of anomalies or to resolve contradictions in the literature.

Remember that every piece of literature you cite is in that review for a reason that must be made clear to yourself and a reader. Either you accept what the author did and are using it to build a network of generally accepted explanations from which you'll derive your own hypotheses, or you are critical of a work and cite it to explain how yours improves on the earlier work.

Your literature review establishes where your work fits into the field. It serves to make science more cumulative. It also keeps you from making the same mistakes others have made or from just rehashing what someone else has done. Replication is valuable if done for a reason and with either new measurement or new data or both. But it is a waste of time to do exactly the same thing over again with the same data.

Don't forget proper citations for the works of others. *Every* borrowed idea must have proper noting. All borrowed *words* must be quoted exactly, put in quotations marks, and properly cited. This is true not just in the literature review but throughout the proposal. We don't follow these rules merely because it would be plagiarism not to do so. We follow them because we are seeking to cumulate scientific findings in the community of scientists. We must be able to communicate exactly the roots and sources of ideas and to link one work with the next. Only with proper references can we do this.

Also, we are engaged in an interpretive science. Our data don't speak to us without the potential bias of an observer. We must be able to check and recheck interpretations—and link one interpretation to the next. Without proper references, we cannot do this. Just as we have an obligation to expose our data for reanalysis by others in order to provide a check on our findings and improve on our analysis, we also have an obligation to expose our thought processes as well. Proper references to the sources of our ideas and words—whether those sources are published or unpublished—help us fulfill that obligation.

HYPOTHESES

The statement of the hypotheses that you have derived from the literature and theory of your field is an absolutely crucial part of the design. Hypotheses stated clearly and precisely point the way toward the appropriate statistical analyses and tests.

First, state each hypothesis in the clearest conceptual language you can muster. Explain how your hypotheses are derived from the literature and how they relate to each other, even going so far as to sketch out a model if necessary.

Let's work on further specifying what should be included in the hypotheses.

1. Make sure your language indicates which variable is independent and which is dependent. Some people find if/then language useful: *if* something occurs in the independent variable, *then* something occurs in the dependent variable.

2. Each variable must be conceptually distinct. You cannot use two variables in an explanatory fashion if they overlap conceptually. That would be tautological—definitional—such as giving a synonym for a word. If variables aren't conceptually distinct, you aren't *explaining* variance in one with the other; instead, you are correlating a thing with itself. In short, the hypothesis must be explanatory.

3. Make sure, if you can, that the hypothesis implies the units on which the data are to be gathered and the level of analysis to which the hypothesis relates. Make it as clear as you can what you consider a case. On what unit are the variables to be measured, regardless of what level behavior is eventually to be explained? Also, if you are explaining the behavior of groups or that of individuals, the hypothesis should imply that level of analysis. Although it may be impossible to get all this into the phrasing of the hypothesis, make sure you think it through; and make sure your hypothesis is as close to what you plan to do as possible.

4. Make the hypothesis general enough to cover a

wide range of cases so that, having tested it, you can generalize to enough situations for your findings to be interesting and worthwhile scientifically. It's probably sound theoretically to state the hypothesis in the plural. After all, statistical generalizations are about probabilities among groups of cases, not about individual cases. Pluralizing the hypothesis keeps our own thinking clear. We won't delude ourselves into thinking we have uncovered deterministic laws when we haven't.

5. Try very hard to get a precise form of the hypothesized relationship into the conceptual statement. Don't settle for "is related to," since the phrase is vague and imprecise as compared to "is positively related to." The clearer this statement here, the easier it is to select the correct statistics later.

6. Try to make the language reflect exactly what is to be tested. Don't imply longitudinal change if you plan a cross-sectional test. Don't imply that the independent variable is to be manipulated if, instead, various levels of it are simply to be observed. One way to avoid fallacious reasoning is to state precisely what it is that is being tested and in precisely what way.

   This guideline applies not only here but also to step 3. Avoid the ecological fallacy, the aggregative fallacy, the cross-sectional fallacy, etc., by limiting your hypothesis to exactly the thing being tested. Then, later, don't generalize beyond it unless absolutely necessary.

   Sometimes we have to infer longitudinal change from cross-sectional data, or individual behavior from aggregate data, or the behavior of groups from the behavior of individuals. Every time we do this, however, we are on the brink of slipping into logical fallacy. Try to avoid it.

7. Make sure your language reflects the fact that variables must vary. Only with variation on the dependent variable to explain and variation on the independent variable to use to relate to it can we test any hypothesis. Clear statements at this point can keep you focussed at the later operationalization stage.

8. All of this adds up to one basic point. State the hypothesis so that it can be falsified. Only if it has that potential—and points clearly to the operations necessary to falsify it—does it enable you to make use of the research process to produce some contribution to the cumulation of knowledge.

SECONDARY HYPOTHESES

You still aren't through with hypotheses! If the relationship you expected shows up in the data, you must test every alternative reason for having gotten that relationship—which means more hypotheses that can be falsified in order to rule out all other possible reasons (within the realm of possibility) for having found that relationship.

Let me emphasize that what is being said here is this: Are there other reasons for having found this relationship? This does *not* mean: Are there other causes of the independent variables? Although we sometimes add independent variables in which we have no theoretical interest into explanations (usually to keep the error term in regression from having a single, important cause in it rather than being random error so that slopes can be more accurately estimated), here our focus is *not* just on adding some more independent variables. Although we might be interested in as complete an explanation of a dependent variable as possible and thus add other causes of the dependent variable, here our focus is not just on explaining more variance.

At this stage we focus, instead, on alternative explanations of the *relationship* between the independent and dependent variables. Here you specify all possible extraneous variables that could be causing the original relationship; and you also indicate the hypotheses necessary to show how they could be causing the original *relationship*. For example, "If Z causes X, and if Z causes Y, then I could have gotten an XY relationship when, in fact, it was spurious."

Here you are attempting over and over and over to falsify your own hypothesis. If your best efforts can't falsify it, publish it, and let other people have a try at it. (Don't get so ego-invested in your own hypothesis that you feel hurt if they—or you yourself—falsify it, for this is just the way that science advances.)

Furthermore, you can't stop with just looking for extraneous variables that might have given you a spurious relationship. You've also got to look for all the variables that could have caused your relationship to be distorted (in the opposite direction of what it would be in reality if the distortion were removed). Again, you aren't just haphazardly testing variables that may be related to the independent or dependent variables. You are testing *hypotheses* that might explain why you obtained results that fit your research hypothesis but that should really be interpreted as falsifying your hypothesis. Again, you are trying over and over and over to falsify your own hypothesis, even after you get initially satisfying results.

(If you succeed in falsifying it, take heart. "Science proceeds on the back of falsified hypotheses." However, do keep in mind that we are not absolutely sure we have falsified a hypothesis if we are dealing with probabilistic hypotheses and samples. We may have a situation in which what probably happens did not in this instance; and/or we may have an unusual sample.)

You must also anticipate, at this stage of the design, that your initial test of the research hypothesis may show little or no relationship or may show relationship in the opposite direction. Now you have to worry again about distorter variables, suppressor variables, and about variables that specify relationships. Again, you are not just randomly throwing about variables that might be related to the independent or dependent. You are spelling out very specific hypotheses that might explain why you got little or no or distorted or specified *relationships*. You are stating hypotheses here that may allow you later to salvage the finding of "no relationship" or "weak relationship." All this detailing of alternative hypotheses is not just ivory-tower-feet-on-the-table thinking (although some of it is—called "creativity"). You have the literature to guide you. The literature that substitutes for or relates to a theory provides numerous leads, clues, and outright prescriptions of necessary, secondary hypotheses. And don't forget common sense.

Is all this really necessary before you go through initial tests? Absolutely. Only by thinking about it *and* spelling it out in detail at the design stage can you be sure you will gather data on the necessary variables for all the tests. Once you're at the analysis stage, you can't usually go back and think, "Gee, I'd like to have measured this variable," and be able to go do it. Remember, *all* variables have to be measured on *each* case. Once you've let go of a case, it might be gone for good.

If we did lots of experiments, the proposal might be a bit easier. We'd have a fairly conventional list, found in any experimental design text, of alternative explanations for the change we expect to observe—alternatives to the experimental variable as the cause of change. Each time we designed an experiment, we could just go through the list and show how our particular design had anticipated the alternative possibilities and controlled them.

With nonexperimental data, however, we have to substitute statistical for experimental design controls, and our list of statistical controls necessarily will vary with every project. The best we can do is run through the list: extraneous, distorter, suppressor, specifier. (Note the list here doesn't include "antecedent" or "intervening." Those more properly belong under primary hypotheses in the elaboration of a model or the interrelationship of the various hypotheses.) Make sure, at least, you have thought of as many as possible variables in each category—and also have asked colleagues to think of as many as they can in each category.

IDEAL DESIGN

It is sometimes a very good idea to write down the *perfect* design for testing your hypotheses and the *best* imaginable set of tests for your hypotheses—the most rigorous, most extensive, tests imaginable.

Imagine the most valid, most reliable, most precise measurement possible. Imagine having entire populations and eras at your disposal. Imagine that you are not limited by time, money, energy, or the human life span. Imagine that no government locks up its documents, no officials lie or distort information, no respondents become inarticulate, and no subjects drop out.

Now spell out the tests your hypotheses would stand up to in such a world. What cases would you study? What method will be used to gather data on each case? How would each and every variable be operationalized for maximum validity and reliability? What statistical analyses would be performed?

Don't just stop with a single pass over this ideal design. Work on it and rework it. Talk it out with colleagues. Find, expose, and fix any remaining holes.

This is no fantasy exercise. First, it can help you hone those hypotheses and the secondary hypotheses you wrote above. Second, it gives you a standard against which to judge your real-life test of the hypothesis you are about to propose in the next section.

At every point you find it necessary to compromise the ideal in order to adapt to ethics and real-world constraints, you should stop and ask yourself: "How does this deviate from the best test of the hypothesis? What are the consequences of that deviation? Is there anything I can do to remedy the negative consequences at the design stage? Or must I be content to deal with the problems with very cautious interpretation at the analysis stage? Is the compromise too great for the design to continue to have integrity? Is there a smaller compromise I can substitute? (Just don't compromise your ethics.)

When you get to the real-world design, it may be necessary to go back to the hypotheses and rephrase them so they reflect what you are actually proposing to do, rather than what you had thought you might do. You may have decided, for example, on a cross-sectional rather than longitudinal analysis, on aggregate rather than individual data, or on field studies rather than a controlled experiment.

When you get to the real-world design, compromises you have to make may lead you to revise your literature review. You may, for example, have left out a segment of literature that would be relevant to a compromised design. You may, for example, need to criticize others' compromises in order to demonstrate why yours are better.

PROPOSED DESIGN

Finally you are to the heart of the design, actually proposing step-by-step what you plan to do to test the hypotheses you have laid out. Remember that you have to be so clear at each step that another researcher could carry out your research in your place.

Unit of Analysis

First, you'd better stop, think, and write down just what you consider a case. On what units of analysis are your variables to be measured? Remember that each and every variable must be measured for each and every case for statistical analyses (even if some variables are situational ones shared by several cases—such as "region" or "in/out of experimental group").

For some reason, this trips up many researchers. For parts of their designs, they may write as if nations were cases. They then slip into using years as cases, and then into citing a nation for a year as a case. Sometimes, they start with individuals as cases and then slip into interest groups as cases. They may also start with legislatures as cases, then slip into legislators as cases, and then into bills in the legislature as cases. Avoid confusion over cases.

What is a case? Spell it out. Go back and look at your literature review to be sure it is clearly defined there. Also review your earliest hypotheses and your ideal design for the same definitional clarity.

And now make sure the *same* unit of analysis is in all the sections consistently. Don't move from aggregates to individuals, from documents to leaders, or from years to nations, as you go from section to section. (Actually, the ideal design section may differ a bit. It might be ideal to gather data on individuals, but the rest of the design may reflect your compromise of using aggregates, for example. Just be very clear that this is an instance of the ideal deviating from the real.)

Population

Spell out clearly exactly what population of cases will be studied. The definition of the population must be *operationalized* so that another researcher would include and exclude exactly the same cases from the population to be studied.

Remember that generalizing from a sample to a population is tricky at best and that you cannot generalize from a sample to a population other than that from which the sample was drawn. Thus, the validity of your generalization depends on the clear definition of the population, which will keep you from rashly generalizing to a different population as you write up your conclusions after your analysis.

Sampling

Will the entire population of cases be studied? If not, how will cases be sampled? What sampling goal do you have? Do you plan to sample in order to represent a population? Or sample to represent the full range of an independent variable? What sampling method will you choose? Why? What sample size will you need? Why?

Do these decisions meet or deviate from the ideal? What are the consequences of deviation? Can negative consequences be anticipated and remedied before sampling starts? (Does any sample versus population versus scope-sample question relate back to your criticisms of others in the literature review? If so, refer back to it and cite how your method is as good or better.) You may need to review sampling literature here if you are doing something out of the ordinary.

Data Collection Method

How will data be gathered? Surveys? Experiments? Documents? Content analysis? Field studies? Aggregate data? Statistical abstracts? Or what?

Discuss any necessary literature here on the strengths and weaknesses of the technique. (Such discussion is probably not needed unless you propose something unfamiliar to your readers or unless it guides your own thinking more clearly in executing the project.) How does this meet or deviate from the ideal? How can any negative consequences of deviation be remedied at this time? If any of your arguments in the literature review concern data collection method, refer back to them here. Show how your method is as good or better. (Also check: Are the method and the phrasings of the hypotheses, problems, etc., consistent so that the proposal continues to drive toward a single goal?)

This is the section least covered by this text, although you will have begun to get a handle on it by reading the articles that have shown the statistics in research context and by using the data sets. You will need to read about the techniques of data collection in more specialized sources. A good place to start is in some of the general methodology texts listed in the various suggested readings here. The texts cited have chapters on each technique and, also, bibliographies that will help you find more detailed accounts.

Operationalization

Operationalize every variable in all primary and secondary hypotheses. Spell out precisely the steps one must go through to construct a measure of each and every variable. This operational definition must be so detailed, clear, exact, and precise that another researcher could go out and measure these variables on the cases specified from the instructions themselves.

For example, at the proposal stage, if you do not know what items will eventually make it past various reliability tests into an index, you still must develop the equivalent of a flow chart of operationalization, which might include the following steps:

1. Develop items in the following manner (detail).
2. Subject them to the following tests (detail).
3. Those that pass (define this clearly) will be com-

bined into an index in the following fashion (detail).

If, at the proposal stage, you do not know what categories will eventually be developed for a content analysis, you still must spell out very precisely the steps that will be undertaken to develop the categories. And so forth. The point is to be as clear, exact, specific, and detailed as is humanly possible before pretests of questionnaires, before gathering events data in a presample to see if the definitions work, etc.

In this section, you should criticize other writers' operationalizations (or refer back to your literature review if the operationalization question was important there) to show why you accepted someone else's operationalization, or why your operationalization is as good as or better than the others.

Then you should refer back to the ideal design in order to see how your operationalizations here differ from those. If you anticipate adverse consequences, can those be remedied at this stage of the design? Can the adverse consequences at least be reduced before gathering data? How? Check to see whether that requires modification of your operationalizations or hypotheses.

Be sure to operationalize each variable at the highest possible measurement level. Go back to your hypotheses stated in conceptual form. Are the variables theoretically nominal, ordinal, or interval? Is your operationalization on the same level as the variables are theoretically? Can the operationalization be pushed up as high as the theoretical? If so, change your operationalization to that level. If it cannot be operationalized at as high a measurement level as it is theoretically, can it be measured at any higher level than you have operationalized it so far? If so, change the operationalization. Plan to collect data at the highest possible level. It can always be lowered at the analysis stage if necessary, but data collected at a lower level cannot be elevated.

Now go back to those hypotheses at the conceptual level again. Did you operationalize any variable with a surrogate for the theoretical concept? For example, did you use "sex" when theory suggests "sex-role orientation" is more important? Did you use "year" to substitute for "accumulated social change"? Is there any way to operationalize the theoretical concept rather than using a surrogate variable? If so, change the operationalization. Validity is improved if you measure your concepts as directly as possible.

Reliability and Validity

How will you assess the reliability and validity of your measures? Have other authors tested the reliability or validity of any measures you plan to use? If so, report on that here, but also show how you will test for continuing reliability and validity. (Did your literature review deal with reliability and/or validity? If so, refer back to that here and show how yours is as good or better.)

Can you think of ways to improve the reliability and validity of your operationalizations? Will discussions with your colleagues lead to improvements? If so, go back and improve the operationalizations *before* data collection—i.e., at the proposal stage. Will pretests after the proposal stage and before full-blown data collection improve reliability or validity? If so, spell out the appropriate procedures here. Indicate clearly what steps you will take to modify operationalizations after analyzing the pretest. Don't forget to consider the reliability of your data *sources* as well as the reliability of your own operations on them.

These two areas—measurement and reliability/validity—have not been covered in great detail in the present text. You will need further reading in these areas. Some of the sources in the various bibliographies will start you out.

Statistical Analyses

Think about the following:

1. Measurement levels of operationalization
2. Anticipated distributions on variables

3. Forms of relationships stated in primary and secondary hypotheses
4. Sampling or whole population (refer back to sampling section to make sure you proposed to sample enough cases)

What statistical analyses (descriptive and inferential) will be performed? Why? What results do you expect and how do those bear on the hypotheses being tested?

Do these techniques deviate from the ideal? Can negative consequences of the deviation be anticipated and remedied at the proposal stage?

What if the distributions or forms of relationships don't turn out as you anticipate? What is your fall-back analysis technique? How does it deviate from the ideal? Can any negative consequences be anticipated and corrected at the proposal stage?

Cost Projections

What is all this going to cost? Detail. Think about your time, coder's time, interviewer's time, reproducing documents or interview protocols, data entry personnel, computer time, telephone, various supplies, travel, translators, statistical or other consultation, overhead (typically a research office tells you what to put there), secretarial time, production of illustrative material, publication costs, index and appendix production for books, postage, etc., etc., etc.

Provisions for the Protection of the Rights of Human Subjects

Indicate here for yourself, as well as for review committees, that you have provided adequately for the rights of any human subjects in your research. How is their privacy protected (unless subjects are public officials or candidates being interviewed about their public offices)? How are risks minimized? How is informed consent secured?

Think seriously about these questions even if your research appears to be exempt from formal review. Your university will be able to supply you with guidelines for the protection of human subjects that conform to federal regulations.

Anticipated Results

Summarize here what you propose to do and why it is worth doing. This is a short reiteration of the proposed project and a final "sell" that it is worth doing.

FINISHING THE DESIGN

Now, go back through your proposal and make sure it hangs together as a single design. Obviously, what is spelled out above is a several-draft project. Write this. Then write this. Then see if the first part needs modification. Then write this. Then see if the first two parts need modification. Etc., etc., etc.

Neither to a class nor to a review committee should you turn in an "intellectual history of how I reasoned my way through this." What you turn in is the polished, final product—all of which drives toward the same goal. The report should make a tightly argued statement of why the phenomenon you propose to explain is worth explaining. That argument will lead naturally to a complete but exclusive review and critique of the *relevant* literature and theory.

By the time you explain your hypotheses and how you derived them, you and a reader ought to be set up to exclaim, "Ah, ha! Of course, that logically follows!" The ideal design will be so carefully crafted as a rigorous test of the hypotheses that it will seem as if the hypotheses themselves had dictated the only logical design.

You then will be able to show how your proposed design is almost as good as the ideal and how you have anticipated all consequences of deviating from the ideal. From the hypotheses and the operationalizations, there will appear to be only one logical set of statistical analyses. Even so, you will be prepared with a back-up, just in case. After cost analyses, you will take one more opportunity to reiterate the design and its logic in summary form.

By this point, you will have a step-by-step guide for yourself as you engage in the research. You will know that, if you follow every step exactly as you have spelled it out, you will get a rigorous and thorough test of your hypotheses.

And the final project is practically already written up. Most of the language in the proposal will translate almost exactly into the final article form. Bascially, all you have to do is fill in the real numbers, as they come up in the completed research project.

SUGGESTED READINGS

Units and Levels of Analysis

See the works listed in Chapter 19.

Research Design and Report Writing

AGNEW, NEIL McK., and SANDRA W. PYKE. *The Science Game*, 4th ed. (Englewood Cliffs, NJ: Prentice-Hall, 1987), Ch. 15.

JOHNSON, JANET BUTTOLPH, and RICHARD A. JOSLYN. *Political Science Research Methods* (Washington, D.C.: Congressional Quarterly Press, 1986), Chs. 5-6.

Ethics

AGNEW, NEIL McK., and SANDRA W. PYKE. *The Science Game*, 4th ed. (Englewood Cliffs, NJ: Prentice-Hall, 1987), Ch. 14.

APPENDIX A

A SAMPLE OF CASES AND A SELECTION OF VARIABLES FROM THE AMERICAN NATIONAL ELECTION STUDY, 1980 PRE- AND POST-ELECTION WAVES

This data set represents a 50 percent sample of the respondents in a national sample who were interviewed before and after the presidential election in 1980. The variables in the data set represent only a few of those available in the entire study. These were selected because they are relatively easy to use, have some of the characteristics discussed in the text, do not require long conceptual explanations, and, perhaps, are inherently interesting.

These data were made available by the Inter-University Consortium for Political and Social Research. (ICPSR Study Number 7763.) They were originally collected by the Center for Political Studies of the Institute for Social Research, The University of Michigan, under a grant from the National Science Foundation and the directorship of Warren Miller. Not the Consortium, the CPS, nor the original collectors of the data bear any responsibility for their use or interpretation here.

The codebook that follows is an edited version of selected entries provided in the codebook published by the Consortium. Variable names and value labels in the data set have been constructed by the author as have missing data codes. The distributions have been computed for the cases in the data set.

PRE-ELECTION QUESTIONS

STATE
ICPSR state number

New England
01. Connecticut
02. Maine
03. Massachusetts
04. New Hampshire
05. Rhode Island
06. Vermont

Middle Atlantic
11. Delaware
12. New Jersey
13. New York
14. Pennsylvania

East North Central
21. Illinois
22. Indiana
23. Michigan
24. Ohio
25. Wisconsin

West North Central
31. Iowa
32. Kansas
33. Minnesota
34. Missouri
35. Nebraska

36. North Dakota
37. South Dakota

Solid South
40. Virginia
41. Alabama
42. Arkansas
43. Florida
44. Georgia
45. Louisiana
46. Mississippi
48. South Carolina
47. North Carolina

49. Texas

Border States
51. Kentucky
52. Maryland
53. Oklahoma
54. Tennessee
55. Washington, D.C.
56. West Virginia

Mountain States		Pacific	External States
61. Arizona	65. Nevada	71. California	81. Alaska
62. Colorado	66. New Mexico	72. Oregon	82. Hawaii
63. Idaho	67. Utah	73. Washington	
64. Montana	68. Wyoming		MD None

POPULA
<The actual population of the interview place was coded in thousands rounding to the nearest whole thousand.>

0000. Rural place, no defined census place, census places with less than 500 persons
0001. 500–1499 persons
 .
 .
 .
9999. 9,998,500 and over

MD None
Valid-n = 838 Min = 0 Max = 3367 Mean = 255.3 St.Dev = 659.0

CARTHERM
Q.G1. I'd like to get your feelings toward some of our political leaders and other people who are in the news these days. I'll read the name of a person and I'd like you to rate that person using this feeling thermometer. You may use any number from 0 to 100 for a rating. Ratings between 50 and 100 degrees mean that you feel favorable and warm toward the person. Ratings between 0 and 50 degrees mean that you don't feel too favorable toward the person. If we come to a person whose name you don't recognize, you don't need to rate that person. Just tell me and we'll move on to the next one. If you do recognize the name, but don't feel particularity warm or cold toward the person, you would rate that person at the 50 degree mark. Our first person is Jimmy Carter. How would you rate him using the thermometer?

Q.G1a. Jimmy Carter <Feeling Thermometer>
Actual number is coded.

(34)MD = 997,998,999
Valid-n = 804 Min = 0 Max = 100 Mean = 57.1 St.Dev = 27.1

REGTHERM
Q.G1b. Ronald Reagan <FeelingThermometer>
<See Q.G1 for complete question text>
Actual number is coded.

(45)MD = 997,998,999
Valid-n = 793 Min = 0 Max = 100 Mean = 55.3 St.Dev. = 25.5

MONTHERM
Q.G1h. Walter Mondale <Feeling Thermometer>
<See Q.G1 for complete question text>
Actual number is coded.

(101)MD = 997,998,999
Valid-n = 737 Min = 0 Max = 100 Mean = 55.1 St.Dev = 20.6

BUSTHERM
Q.G1i. George Bush <Feeling Thermometer>
<See Q.G1 for complete question text>
Actual number is coded.

(125) MD = 997,998,999
Valid-n = 713 Min = 0 Max = 100 Mean = 55.0 St.Dev = 18.1

ANDTHERM
Q.G1v. John Anderson <Feeling Thermometer>
<See Q.B1 for complete text>
Actual number is coded.

(126) MD = 997,998,999
Valid-n = 712 Min = 0 Max = 100 Mean = 52.5 St.Dev = 20.3

DEMPARTH
Q.G1o. the Democratic Party <Feeling Thermometer>
<See Q.G1 for complete question text>
Actual number is coded.

(52)MD = 997,998,999
Valid-n = 786 Min = 0 Max = 100 Mean = 61.4 St.Dev = 23.6

REPPARTH
Q.G1p. the Republican Party <Feeling Thermometer>
<See Q.G1 for complete question text>
Actual number is coded.

(54)MD = 997,998,999
Valid-n = 784   Min = 0   Max = 100   Mean = 56.9
St.Dev = 21.7

PARIDPRE
Q.J1x. Summary: R's Party ID
Built from Q.J1, Q.J1a/J1d, Q.J1g/J1n

Q.J1. Generally speaking, do you usually think of yourself as a Republican, a Democrat, an Independent, or what?

If Dem or Rep:
Q.J1a. Would you call yourself a strong Republican or a not very strong Republican?

Q.J1d. Would you call yourself a strong Democrat or a not very strong Democrat?

If ind, no preference, or other:
Q.J1g,n. Do you think of yourself as closer to the Republican party or to the Democratic party?

159	0.	Strong Democrat
196	1.	Weak Democrat
96	2.	Independent-Democrat
110	3.	Independent-Independent
76	4.	Independent-Republican
112	5.	Weak Republican
67	6.	Strong Republican
1	7.	Other, Minor Party, refused to say
20	8.	Apolitical
1	9.	DK, NA

MD = 7,8,9

LIBCON
Q.K1. We hear a lot of talk these days about liberals and conservatives. Here is a seven-point scale on which the political views that people might hold are arranged from extremely liberal to extremely conservative.

Q.K1a. Where would you place yourself on this scale, or haven't you thought much about this?

7	1.	Extremely liberal
47	2.	Liberal
67	3.	Slightly liberal
168	4.	Moderate, middle of the road
114	5.	Slightly conservative
94	6.	Conservative
11	7.	Extremely conservative
274	0.	Haven't thought much
31	8.	DK
25	9.	NA

MD = 0,8,9

FATHPAR
Q.R3e. Did your father (or father substitute) think of himself mostly as a Democrat, as a Republican, as an Independent, or what?

360	1.	Democrat
57	2.	Independent
174	3.	Republican
	4.	Other party, specify
	5.	Not interested in politics
	6.	Wasn't U.S. citizen; no right to vote
	0.	No father or father substitute
	8.	DK
	9.	NA

(247)   MD = 9 [0,4,5,6, and 8 were recoded to 9]

MOTHPAR
Q.R3f. Did your mother (or mother substitute) think of herself mostly as a Democrat, as a Republican, as an Independent, or what?

349	1.	Democrat
48	2.	Independent
187	3.	Republican
	4.	Other party, specify
	5.	Not interested in politics
	6.	Wasn't U.S. citizen; no right to vote
	0.	No mother or mother substitute
	8.	DK
	9.	NA

(254)   MD = 9 [0,4,5,6, and 8 were recoded to 9]

GOVWASTE
Q.U1. Do you think that people in the government waste a lot of money we pay in taxes, waste some of it, or don't waste very much of it?

20	1.	Not very much
148	3.	Some
646	5.	A lot
21	8.	DK
3	9.	NA

MD = 7,8,9

TRUSTGOV
Q.U2. How much of the time do you think you can trust the government in Washington to do what is right—just about always, most of the time, or only some of the time?

20	1.	Always
197	3.	Most of the time
567	5.	Some of the time
32	7.	R Volunteers: None of the time
19	8.	DK
3	9.	NA

MD = 8,9

GOVRUNFR
Q.U3. Would you say the government is pretty much run by a few big interests looking out for themselves or that it is run for the benefit of all the people?

186	1.	For the benefit of all
564	5.	Few big interests
2	7.	Other, depends; both boxes checked; refused to choose
76	8.	DK
10	9.	NA

MD = 7,8,9

SMART
Q.U4. Do you feel that almost all of the people running the government are smart people, or do you think that quite a few of them don't seem to know what they are doing?

281	1.	Are smart people
517	5.	Don't know what they are doing
1	7.	Other; depends; both boxes checked; refused to choose
30	8.	DK
9	9.	NA

MD = 7,8,9

CROOKS
Q.U5. Do you think that quite a few of the people running the government are crooked, not very many are, or do you think hardly any of them are crooked?

79	1.	Hardly any
341	3.	Not many
388	5.	Quite a few
24	8.	DK
6	9.	NA

MD = 7,8,9

AGE
Q.Y1x. Summary: R's age in years

    99.   Ninety-nine years or older

(2) MD = 0
Valid-n = 836 Min = 18 Max = 93 Mean = 44.3
St.Dev = 18.0

MARSTAT
Q.Y2. Are you married now and living with your (husband/wife)—or are you widowed, divorced, separated, or have you never married?

513	1.	Married and living with spouse (or spouse in service)
121	2.	Never married
65	3.	Divorced
29	4.	Separated
97	5.	Widowed
12	7.	Common law marriage; "living together"
1	9.	NA

MD = 9

EDUCA
Q.Y3. What is the highest grade of school or year of college you completed?
[coded in years]

    17.   17 or more years; 5 or more years of college

(4) MD = 98,99

Valid-n = 834 Min = 0 Max = 17 Mean = 12.1
St.Dev = 3.0

UNION
QY50. Does anyone in this household belong to a labor union?

222	1.	Yes
610	5.	No
2	8.	DK
4	9.	NA

MD = 8,9

INCOME
Q.Y52. Please look at this page and tell me the letter of the income group that includes the income before taxes of all members of your family living here in 1979. This figure should include salaries, wages, pensions, dividends, interest, and all other income. (If uncertain: What would be your best guess?)

Responses from Q.52a have been incorporated into the variables so that family income includes data for R's who are only family members.

15	01.	A.	None or less than $2,000
11	02.	B.	$2,00–$2,999
28	03.	C.	$3,000–$3,999
24	04.	D.	$4,000–$4,999
25	05.	E.	$5,000–$5,999
25	06.	F.	$6,000–$6,999
17	07.	G.	$7,000–$7,999
26	08.	H.	$8,000–$8,999
17	09.	J.	$9,000–$9,999
29	10.	K.	$10,000–$10,999
20	11.	M.	$11,000–$11,999
24	12.	N.	$12,000–$12,999
20	13.	P.	$13,000–$13,999
21	14.	Q.	$14,000–$14,999
33	15.	$.	$15,000–$16,999
48	16.	S.	$17,000–$19,999
69	17.	T.	$20,000–$22,999
43	18.	U.	$23,000–$24,999
70	19.	V.	$25,000–$29,999
66	20.	W.	$30,000–$34,999
65	21.	X.	$35,000–$49,999
41	22.	Z.	$50,000 AND OVER
67	98.		R refused to answer
34	99.		NA, DK

MD = 0,98,99
Valid-n = 737 Min = 1 Max = 22 Mean = 14.2
St.Dev = 6.2

CLASS
Q.Y54g. Summary: Social Class
[Built from prior questions that queried whether the person thought in terms of class, with which class he or she would place him or herself, and in which part of the class.]

3	0.	Lower class
315	1.	Average working
6	2.	Working—NA average or upper
86	3.	Upper working
284	4.	Average middle
5	5.	Middle class—NA average or upper
77	6.	Upper middle
	7.	Upper class
7	8.	Refuses to accept the idea of class
45	9.	NA, DK; other

MD = 8,9

RELIGION
Q.Y55.a,b. Religious Preference
[Recoded for this data set from a complex variable that identifies very specific denominational choices.]

534	1.	Protestant (or other non-Catholic Christian)
196	2.	Catholic (inc. Greek-Rite and Orthodox)
23	3.	Jew
77	4.	Other or none
8	999.	Missing or NA

MD = 999

FREQATTN
Q.Y56. (If any religious preference) Would you say you go to (church/synagogue) every week, almost every week, once or twice a month, a few times a year, or never?

201	1.	Every week
115	2.	Almost every week
95	3.	Once or twice a month
236	4.	A few times a year
117	5.	Never
73	0.	Inap.
	8.	DK
1	9.	NA

MD = 0,8,9

SEXPRE
Q.Z1. Respondent's sex is:

353	1.	Male
485	2.	Female
	9.	NA

MD = 9

RACEPRE
Q.Z2. Respondent's race is:

731	1.	White
98	2.	Black
5	3.	American Indian or Alaskan Native
4	4.	Asian or Pacific Islander
	7.	Other
	9.	NA

MD = 9

POST-ELECTION QUESTIONS

PIDPOST
Summary: R's Party ID
[Constructed in the same manner as the pre-election question. See original codebook for details.]

127	0.	Strong Democrat
163	1.	Weak Democrat
74	2.	Independent-Democrat
94	3.	Independent-Independent
81	4.	Independent-Republican
91	5.	Weak Republican
72	6.	Strong Republican
2	7.	Other, minor party, refused to say
18	8.	Apolitical
116	9.	NA, DK; No post election interview

MD = 7,8,9

INFLUEN
R's POLITICAL ACTIVITY
Q.E3. We would like to find out about some of the things people do to help a party or a candidate win an election. During the campaign, did you talk to any people and try to show them why they should vote for one of the parties or candidates?

254	1.	Yes
471	5.	No
	8.	DK
113	9.	NA; No post election interview

MD = 7,8,9

MEETINGS
Q.E4. Did you go to any political meetings, rallies, fundraising dinners, or things like that?

48	1.	Yes
677	5.	No
	8.	DK
113	9.	NA; No post election interview

MD = 7,8,9

WORK
Q.E5. Did you do any (other) work for one of the parties or candidates <during the campaign>?

25	1.	Yes
698	5.	No
	8.	DK
115	9.	NA; No post election interview

MD = 7,8,9

BUTTON
Q.E6. Did you wear a campaign button or put a campaign sticker on your car?

54	1.	Yes
670	5.	No
	8.	DK
114	9.	NA; no post election interview

MD = 7,8,9

MEMBER
Q.E7. Do you belong to any political clubs or organizations?

28	1.	Yes
697	5.	No
	8.	DK
113	9.	NA; No post election interview

MD = 7,8,9

CHECKOFF
Q.E8. Now a few questions about giving money during this last election campaign. First, did you use the one-dollar check-off option on your Federal income tax return to make a political contribution this year?

229	1.	Yes
423	5.	No
3	7.	(R volunteers); don't file federal income tax
65	8.	DK
118	9.	NA; No post election interview

MD = 7,8,9

MONYCAND
Q.E10. What about other political contributions. Did you give any money this year to a candidate running for public office?

41	1.	Yes
683	5.	No
1	8.	DK
113	9.	NA; No post election interview

MD = 7,8,9

MONYPART
Q.E11. Apart from contributions to specific candidates, how about contributions to any of the political parties? Did you give money to a political party during this election year?

31	1.	Yes
692	5.	No
1	8.	DK
114	9.	NA; No postelection interview

MD = 7,8,9

MONEYPAC
Q.E12. Now, what about political action groups such as groups sponsored by a union or a business, or issue groups like the National Rifle Association or the National Organization for Women. Did you give money this election year to a political action group or any other group that supported or opposed particular candidates in the election?

51	1.	Yes
669	5.	No
1	7.	(R volunteers): have only paid union/association dues and have not contributed to any other election funds
3	8.	DK
114	9.	NA; No post election interview

MD = 7,8,9

CARTHPST
Q.G5. I'd like to get your feelings toward some of our political leaders and other people who are in the news these days. I'll read the name of a person and I'd like you to rate that person using this feeling thermometer. You may use any number from 0 to 100 for rating. Ratings between 50 degrees and 100 degrees mean that you feel favorable and warm toward the person. Ratings between 0 and 50 degrees mean that you don't feel too favorable toward the person. If we come to a person whose name you don't recognize, you don't need to rate that person. Just tell me and we'll move on to the next one. If you do recognize [the] name, but don't feel particularly warm or cold toward the person, you would rate the person at the 50 degree mark.

Q.G5b. Jimmy Carter
Actual number is coded.

(126) MD = 997,998,999
Valid-n = 712   Min = 0   Max = 100   Mean = 55.6
St.Dev = 25.8

REGTHPST
Q.G5C. Ronald Reagan—Score on the thermometer
<See Q.G5 for complete question text>
Actual number is coded.

(127) MD = 997,998,999
Valid-n = 711   Min = 0   Max = 100   Mean = 59.5
St.Dev = 24

ANDTHPST
Q.G5h John Anderson—Score on the thermometer
<See Q.G5 for complete question text>
Actual number is coded.

(185) MD = 997,998,999
Valid-n = 653   Min = 0   Max = 100   Mean = 50.2
St.Dev = 20.4

BIGBUSTH
Q.G6. And still using the thermometer, how would you rate the following?
Q.G6a. Big business
Actual number is coded.

(165) MD = 997,998,999
Valid-n = 673   Min = 0   Max = 100   Mean = 52.6
St.Dev = 22.7

POORTH
Q.G6b. Poor people <score on the thermometer>
<See Q.G6 for complete question text>
Actual number is coded.

(149) MD = 997,998,999
Valid-n = 689   Min = 0   Max = 100   Mean = 75.9
St.Dev = 18.0

LIBERTH
Q.G6C. Liberals <score on the thermometer>
<See Q.G6 for complete question text>
Actual number is coded.

(199) MD = 997,998,999
Valid-n = 639   Min = 0   Max = 100   Mean = 51.8
St.Dev = 19.9

SOUTHTH
Q.G6D. Southerners <Rate on the thermometer>
<See Q.G6 for complete question text>
Actual number is coded

(160) MD = 997,998,999
Valid-n = 678   Min = 0   Max = 100   Mean = 67.2
St.Dev = 20.0

ENVIRTH
Q.G6i. People seeking to protect the environment
<score on the thermometer>
<See Q.G6 for complete question text>
Actual number is coded

(152) MD = 997,998,999
Valid-n = 686   Min = 0   Max = 100   Mean = 71.5
St.Dev = 22.3

FEDGOVTH
Q.G6j. The Federal Government in Washington
<score on the thermometer>
<See Q.G6 for complete question text>
Actual number is coded.

(152) MD = 997,998,999
Valid-n = 686   Min = 0   Max = 100   Mean = 52.7
St.Dev = 20.6

GOVTSAY
Q.N3. Now I'm going to read some of the kind of things people tell us when we interview them. As I read, please tell me whether you agree or disagree with each statement.
Q.N3A. People like me don't have any say about what the government does.

274	1.	Agree
436	5.	Disagree
13	8.	DK
115	9.	NA; No post election interview

MD = 7,8,9

VOTONLY
Q.N3B. Voting is the only way people like me can have any say about how the government runs things.
<See Q.N3 for complete question text>

412	1.	Agree
284	5.	Disagree
28	8.	DK
114	9.	NA; No post election interview

MD = 7,8,9

COMPLICA
Q.N3C. Sometimes politics and government seem so complicated that a person like me can't understand what's going on.
<See Q.N3 for complete question text>

507	1.	Agree
200	5.	Disagree
17	8.	DK
114	9.	NA; No post election interview

MA = 7,8,9

OFFCARE
Q.N3D. I don't think public officials care much what people like me think.
<See Q.N3 for complete question text>

379	1.	Agree
308	5.	Disagree
34	8.	DK
117	9.	NA: No post election interview

MD = 7,8,9

LOSETCH
Q.N3e. Generally speaking, those we elect to Congress in Washington lose touch with the people pretty quickly.
<See Q.N3 for complete question text>

509	1.	Agree
165	5.	Disagree
42	8.	DK
122	9.	NA; No post election interview

MD = 7,8,9

PARTINT
Q.N3F. Parties are only interested in people's votes but not in their opinions.
<See Q.N3 for complete question text>

425	1.	Agree
248	5.	Disagree
48	8.	DK
117	9.	NA; No post election interview

MD = 7,8,9

IGNORE
Q.N3G. This country would be better off if we just stayed home and did not concern ourselves with problems in other parts of the world.
<See Q.N3 for complete question text>

118	1.	Agree
566	5.	Disagree
36	8.	DK
118	9.	NA; No post election interview

MD = 7,8,9

DIDVOTE
Q.L1. In talking to people about elections, we often find that a lot of people were not able to vote because (they weren't old enough) they weren't registered, they were sick, or they just didn't have time. How about you—did you vote in the elections this November?

492	1.	Yes, did vote
232	5.	No, did not vote
	6.	R refuses to say whether voted
	7.	Not old enough
	8.	DK
	9.	NA; No post election interview

(114)   MD = 9 (6,7,8 were recoded to 9)

WHOVOTE
Q.L3A/L10A. Who did you vote for <in the election for President?>

232	1.	Reagan
192	2.	Carter
6	5.	Clark
43	6.	Anderson
2	7.	Other, specify
351	0.	Inap., coded 5, 7-9 in Q.L1; coded 5, 8-9 in Q.L3/L10
9	8.	DK; refuses to name candidate
3	9.	NA

MD = 0,8,9

APPENDIX B

A DATA SET BASED ON THE *COUNTY AND CITY DATA BOOK (UNITED STATES), 1983*

The data utilized in this data set were made available by the Inter-University Consortium for Political and Social Research (ICPSR Study Number 8256). The data for *County and City Data Book, 1983*, were originally collected by the U.S. Department of Commerce, Bureau of the Census. Neither the collector of the original data nor the Consortium bears any responsibility for the presentation of the data here. The variables on the presidential vote in 1980 taken from the data set provided by the Consortium are copyrighted by Election Research Center, the publisher of *America Votes*, and are used by permission of the publisher.

Unless otherwise indicated, the data are from 1980, and the number of valid cases is 929. This number represents a 30 percent sample of the counties available.

STATE
State from which data were taken:

01 Ala	15 Haw	25 Mas	35 NMe	46 SDa
02 Als	16 Ida	26 Mic	36 NYo	47 Ten
04 Arz	17 Ill	27 Min	37 NCa	48 Tex
05 Ark	18 Ind	28 Msp	38 NDa	49 Uta
06 Cal	19 Iow	29 Msr	39 Ohi	50 Ver
08 Col	20 Kan	30 Mon	40 Okl	51 Vir
09 Con	21 Ken	31 Neb	41 Ore	53 Was
10 Del	22 Lou	32 Nev	42 Pen	54 WVi
12 Fla	23 Mai	33 NHa	44 RIs	55 Wis
13 Geo	24 Mar	34 NJe	45 SCa	56 Wyo

No missing data

COUNTY
County identification number

No missing data

NAME
Name of the county

No missing data

POP80
Population in the area in 1980

Min = 408   Max = 7,477,503   Mean = 75495.601
   SD = 309,065.998
No missing data

POPSQMI
Population per square mile (to 1 decimal)

Min = .1   Max = 31761.6   Mean = 248.295
   SD = 1614.246
Missing values = −1   (*N* missing = 1)

MEDAGE
Median age of people in the area (to 1 decimal)

Min = 20   Max = 49.8   Mean = 31.000
   SD = 3.939
No missing data

CRIMES
Number of offenses known to the police, per 100,000 population, 1981

Min = 25   Max = 31,640   Mean = 3208.906
SD = 2547.939
Missing values = −1, 0   (N missing = 39)

PERCAPIN
Per capita personal income in dollars

Min = 3913   Max = 23,004   Mean = 8577.838
SD = 2062.825
Missing values = −1   (N missing = 2)

MEDHOUIN
Median household income for 1979 in dollars (no decimal)

Min = 6620   Max = 31,133   Mean = 14,073.578
SD = 3263.294
No missing data

VOTLP80
Party that got the most votes in the area in the 1980 presidential election

1 = Democratic   (N = 276)
2 = Republican   (N = 642)
0 = Missing values (N = 11)

PERLP
Percent of the total vote that was taken by the leading party (1 decimal)

Min = 39.7   Max = 90.4   Mean = 58.492
SD = 8.186
Missing values = −1, 0   (N missing = 11)

POPINC
Percent of population increase from 1970 to 1980

Calculated by subtracting the population in 1970 from that in 1980, dividing the result by the population in 1970, and multiplying by 100

Min = −21.74   Max = 232.03   Mean = 15.196
SD = 20.643
No missing data

URBPER
Percent of the population that lives in urban areas

Calculated by dividing the number of persons in urban areas by the total population of the area and multiplying by 100

Min = .00   Max = 100.00   Mean = 36.103
SD = 29.955
No missing data

WHIPER
Percent of the population that is white

Calculated by dividing the number of white persons by the total population of the area and multiplying by 100

Min = 5.14   Max = 100.00   Mean = 87.823
SD = 16.472
No missing data

BLAPER
Percent of the population that is black

Calculated by dividing the number of black persons by the total population of the area and multiplying by 100

Min = 0   Max = 82.00   Mean = 8.937
SD = 15.287
No missing data

RETPER
Percent of the population that is receiving Social Security Retirement benefits

Calculated by dividing the number of retired persons receiving Social Security by the total population and multiplying by 100

Min = 1.46   Max = 25.92   Mean = 9.531
SD = 3.212
Missing values = System missing   (N missing = 2)

HOUGRO
Percentage growth in housing units between 1970 and 1980

Calculated by subtracting the number of housing units in 1970 from the number in 1980, dividing the difference by the number in 1970, and multiplying by 100

Min = −21.28   Max = 366.83   Mean = 31.818
SD = 26.070
Missing values = System missing   (N missing = 6)

NOPLUMPR
Percentage of the housing units without complete plumbing for exclusive use of the residents of the unit

Calculated by dividing the number of units without plumbing by the total number of units in 1980 and multiplying by 100

Min = .13   Max = 61.72   Mean = 4.095
SD = 5.235
No missing data

HSPER
Percentage of those people twenty-five-years old or older who have completed four years of high school

Calculated by dividing the number of people twenty-five-years old or older who had completed four years of high school by the total number of people that age and multiplying by 100

Min = 25.08   Max = 95.29   Mean = 58.845
SD = 12.670
No missing data

COLPER
Percentage of those people twenty-five-years old or older who have completed four years of college

Calculated as above but with number who had completed four years of college in the numerator

Min = 3.93   Max = 46.16   Mean = 11.424
SD = 5.568
No missing data

FEPERLAB
Female percentage of the civilian labor force, 1980

Calculated by dividing the number of women in the civilian labor force (over sixteen-years old) by the total number of people in the civilian labor force (over sixteen-years old) and multiplying by 100

Min = 19.43   Max = 51.39   Mean = 40.023
SD = 3.893
No missing data

UNEMPPER
Percent unemployment in the area, 1980

Calculated as above but with the total number unemployed in the numerator

Min = .82   Max = 23.81   Mean = 7.023
SD = 3.400
No missing data

EMPMANPR
Percentage employed in manufacturing

Calculated by dividing the number of persons employed in manufacturing by the total number of persons in the area who were employed and multiplying by 100

Min = .40   Max = 57.04   Mean = 20.632
SD = 12.180
No missing data

WMHDFAM
Percentage of the families headed by women

Calculated by dividing the number of families headed by women by the total number of families in 1980 and multiplying by 100

Min = .68   Max = 35.75   Mean = 10.690
SD = 4.479
No missing data

FAMPOVPR

Percentage of families in the area who are below the poverty line

Calculated by dividing the number of families below the poverty line by the total number of families and multiplying by 100

Min = 2.36   Max = 44.77   Mean = 12.937
SD = 6.560
No missing data

WMHDPOV

Percentage of the families below the poverty line that are headed by women

Calculated by dividing the number of female-headed families in poverty by the total number of families in poverty and multiplying by 100

Min = 2.78   Max = 70.00   Mean = 29.508
SD = 12.894
Missing values = 0   (N missing = 2)

POVPER

Percentage of the people in the area who are below the poverty line

Calculated by dividing the number of people in poverty in 1979 by the total population of the area in 1980 and multiplying by 100

Min = 3.07   Max = 52.71   Mean = 15.897
SD = 7.429
No missing data

RURPR

Percentage of the people who live in rural areas

Calculated by dividing the number of people in rural areas by the total population in 1980 and multiplying by 100

Min = 0.0   Max = 58.82   Mean = 9.612
SD = 9.721
No missing data

VOTTURN

Percent voter turnout in the 1980 presidential election

Calculated by dividing the number of people who voted by the total number of people eighteen years of age or older in the area and multiplying by 100

Note: I am suspicious of this variable. The percentages seem high in some cases. Every check I have run indicates that the tape was read correctly. Therefore, I have only declared scores of 100 or higher missing—in addition to the counties missing on numbers of votes cast for President in the CCDB data, of which there were 22 in the total set of U.S. counties.

Min = 24.11   Max = 93.17   Mean = 57.556
SD = 10.745
Missing values = 999   (N missing = 11)

REGPER

The approximate percentage of the two-party vote that went to Reagan in 1980

If the area gave the highest percentage of its votes to the Republican Party, this variable is equal to that percentage.

If the area gave the highest percentage of its votes to the Democratic Party, the area's score on this variable is 100 minus that percentage.

Note: 1980 is a particularly bad year to have to do this estimation. That year, Anderson was a strong third candidate.

Min = 21.50   Max = 90.40   Mean = 54.397
SD = 10.947
Missing values = 999   (N missing = 11)

APPENDIX C

A LEGISLATIVE DATA SET

The data utilized in this data set were made available principally by the Inter-University Consortium for Political and Social Research (ICPSR Study Numbers 7645 and 7803). The data for Voting Studies for Members of the United States Congress, 1945–1982, were originally collected by Congressional Quarterly Inc. Students should check the *Congressional Quarterly Almanac* for more complete definitions than are possible here.

The data for Roster of United States Congressional Officeholders and Biographical Characteristics of Members of the United States Congress, 1789–1984, Merged Data, were originally collected by Carroll McKibbin and the Inter-University Consortium for Political and Social Research. The Fall 1987 version of the data set was used for this codebook.

The data for four variables, the percent of votes in each state taken by each of the two leading presidential candidates in 1976 and 1980, were taken from Michael Barone and Grant Ujifusa, *The Almanac of American Politics, 1982*, published in 1981 by Barone and Company and in subsequent editions by the *National Journal*. They are used with the permission of the authors and publishers. Neither the Consortium nor the collectors of the original data bear any responsibility for the use of those data here.

The data are for the 97th Congress in 1981 and 1982 and are stored in two separate files that are similar but not identical. The Senate file contains background information on the 100 members of the Senate, their voting records on several indices, the two-party presidential votes for their states in 1976 and 1980, and the socioeconomic data on their states which parallels that for counties in Appendix B.

The House file contains information on the 433 members who were eligible either for all the roll-call votes in 1981 or for all the roll-call votes in 1982 (or both). The background information for House members is the same as that for Senators. Their voting records on several indices are conceptually the same but are based on dissimilar numbers of votes, and the state-level data are not provided in the House file.

The two files are set up so that you can add the House cases to the Senate cases if you want to analyze them as one data set on the variables that are shared. The variable names are the same, for example, and there is a variable that designates in which house the Member of Congress serves (PART). Constant within each data set, that variable could serve as a control for the house of a member of Congress in a merged data set.

You will be able to think of many variables that are not included in these data sets, especially in the shorter House version. That is to encourage you to collect some of your own data along the way. The *Almanac of American Politics* contains a wealth of data on members of Congress, as does the *Congressional Quarterly*. You could set up your own data set from data you find from such sources. Perhaps you may be interested in some of the following topics: key votes of members; characteristics of their districts; how close their last election was; other group ratings rather than those given here; how much money members get from political action committees; or, for Senators, how long it is to their next elections. You could use those variables in analyses with the variables already in the data set. If you use SPSS to LIST VARIABLES = MEMBERID NAME. you will see what number you should assign each representative for a MEMBERID variable in your own data set. Then you can merge your data set with this one. (See *SPSS-X User's Guide*, Ch. 6, or *SPSS/PC+*, Ch. 6.) If your university is a member of the ICPSR, you can probably also get access to the full data files. The variables here represent only a part of all the possibilities.

THE SENATE FILE

MEMBERID
ICPSR member number

No missing data

CONGRESS
Number of the Congress

For this data set, it is constant at 97 and, thus, not of any use in analyses. It is included in case you decide to add cases from later Congresses to the file and need an identifier.

Missing data = −1 (0)

STATE
ICPSR state number

No missing data

New England
01. Connecticut
02. Maine
03. Massachusetts
04. New Hampshire
05. Rhode Island
06. Vermont

Middle Atlantic
11. Delaware
12. New Jersey
13. New York
14. Pennsylvania

East North Central
21. Illinois
22. Indiana
23. Michigan

24. Ohio
25. Wisconsin

West North Central
31. Iowa
32. Kansas
33. Minnesota
34. Missouri
35. Nebraska
36. North Dakota
37. South Dakota

Solid South
40. Virginia
41. Alabama
42. Arkansas
43. Florida
44. Georgia

45. Louisiana
46. Mississippi
48. South Carolina
47. North Carolina
49. Texas

Border States
51. Kentucky
52. Maryland
53. Oklahoma
54. Tennessee
55. Washington, D.C.
56. West Virginia

Mountain States
61. Arizona
62. Colorado
63. Idaho

64. Montana
65. Nevada
66. New Mexico
67. Utah
68. Wyoming

Pacific
71. California
72. Oregon
73. Washington

External States
81. Alaska
82. Hawaii

308   A LEGISLATIVE DATA SET

PLNAME
Name of the state represented by the member of Congress

You won't want to use this in any analyses because it is in alphabetic characters. However, you may need it sometime if you decide to print out your results by state.

NAME
Name of the member of Congress

This is alphabetic, too, and is included for reference, should you want to use it.

SEX
Gender of the member of Congress

(98) 1 = Male
(2) 2 = Female

Missing data = 9 (0)

REGION
U.S. region represented by the member of Congress

(12) 0 = Northeast
(8) 1 = Mid-Atlantic
(10) 2 = East North Central
(14) 3 = West North Central
(20) 4 = South
(10) 5 = Border
(16) 6 = Mountain
(6) 7 = Pacific
(4) 8 = External states

Missing data = 9 (0)

BIRTH
State of birth of the member of Congress

See above for codes.

Missing data = 00, unknown or foreign

BIRREP
Is the member of Congress currently representing the state in which she or he was born?

(69) 0 = Yes
(31) 1 = No

Missing data = 9 (0)

RELCONG
Does the member of Congress have relatives who are serving or have ever served in Congress?

(91) 0 = None
(9) 1 = At least one

Missing data = 9 (0)

SECED
What kind of secondary education did the member of Congress have?

(77) 1 = Public school
(12) 2 = Private school

Missing data = 0, 9 unknown (11)

COLLEGE
What kind of college education did the member of Congress have?

(37) 1 = State university
(19) 2 = Ivy League or similar
(44) 3 = Other

Missing data = 9 (0)

MILITARY
What is the military background of the member of Congress?

(26) 0 = None
(38) 1 = Enlisted person
(36) 2 = Officer

Missing data = 9 (0)

OCCUPA
What occupation did the member of Congress have prior to public service?

(6)	1 = Education
(54)	2 = Law
(3)	3 = Professional
(17)	4 = Business
(7)	5 = Agriculture
(7)	6 = Miscellaneous

Missing data = 0,9; none, unknown, no nonpublic service career, retired (6)

AGEELEC
The age of the member of Congress when she or he was first sworn into Congress
Number-of-years-old coded.

Missing data = −1, 0 (0)
Mean = 42.21   S.D. = 8.302   Min = 27   Max = 70

YEARELEC
The year the member was first elected to Congress

This is a three-digit variable that represents the year without the initial "1"; thus, it is effectively Year − 1,000.

Missing data = −1 (0)
Mean = 969.96   S.D. = 9.597   Min = 932
Max = 980

LASTYEAR
The last full year that the member served in Congress

Again, the first digit is deleted from the year. This variable represents the year any members of the 97th Congress left—up to 1987.

Missing data = −1
   999, inappropriate because the member is still serving (74)

SERVED
The number of years served in Congress by the member if he or she had left prior to 1987

Missing data = −1
   9, inappropriate because the member is still serving (74)

WHYLEFT
The reason the member of Congress left

(12)	1 = Defeated in the general election
(0)	2 = Defeated in the primary or not renominated
(2)	3 = Died
(10)	4 = Was not a candidate for re-election
(1)	5 = Elected to other public office
(1)	6 = Resigned

Missing data = −1, 0, unknown
   9, inappropriate because the member is still serving (74)

PART
House in which the member was serving in the 97th Congress

(100)	1 = Senate
(0)	2 = House

Not useful in analysis unless files are merged
No missing data codes

PARTY
Political party affiliation of the member of Congress

(46)	1 = Democratic
(53)	2 = Republican
(1)	7 = Independent

No missing data codes

FIRSTCON
First Congress in which the member was seated

Congress number coded

No missing data codes

ELIG

Eligibility status of the member of Congress for the 1981 Session

(100)   0 = Eligible for all
(0)   1 = Not eligible for all

Missing data = 8, and ge (greater than or equal to) 9

TIMVOT81

The percent of times the member voted in the 1981 session out of 483 roll-call votes

Missing data = 999 (0)
Mean = 93.39   S.D. = 5.772   Min = 62
Max = 100

WITPAR81

The percent of times the member voted with his or her party on 231 party-unity roll calls

Missing data = 999 (9)
Mean = 76.10   S.D. = 14.391   Min = 26
Max = 94

AGNPAR81

The percent of times the member voted against his or her party on 231 party-unity roll calls

Missing data = 999 (0)
Mean = 17.38   S.D. = 12.958   Min = 1   Max = 70

WCONCO81

The percent of times the member voted with the conservative coalition on 104 roll calls

Missing data = 999 (0)

Mean = 61.80   S.D. = 30.575   Min = 3
Max = 100

AGCONC81

The percent of times the member voted against the conservative coalition on 104 roll calls

Missing data = 999 (0)
Mean = 32.52   S.D. = 29.008   Min = 0   Max = 93

WIPRES81

The percent of times the member voted with Reagan on 128 roll calls

Missing data = 999 (0)
Mean = 65.68   S.D. = 18.569   Min = 30
Max = 90

AGPRES81

The percent of times the member voted against Reagan on 128 roll calls

Missing data = 999 (0)
Mean = 28.60   S.D. = 17.358   Min = 5   Max = 63

WITADA81

The percent of times the member voted or announced a position with the Americans for Democratic Action position (liberal) on 20 roll calls selected by that interest group

Missing data = 999 (0)
Mean = 39.47   S.D. = 32.404   Min = 0
Max = 100

WITAFL81

The percent of times the member voted or announced a position with the AFL/CIO (labor) on 19 roll calls selected by that group

Missing data = 999 (0)
Mean = 41.63   S.D. = 33.100   Min = 0
Max = 100

WITACA81

The percent of times the member voted or announced a position with the Americans for Constitutional Action (conservative) on 21 roll calls selected by that group

Missing data 999 (0)
Mean = 52.39   S.D. = 25.884   Min = 0   Max = 95

ELIG82
Eligibility status of the member of Congress for the 1982 Session

(99)   0 = Eligible for all
(1)   1 = Not eligible for all

Missing data = 8, ge (greater than or equal to) 9 (0)
You may want to use this variable to delete this member from analyses of issues on which she or he may not have been able to vote. If so, you can specify

TEMPORARY
SELECT IF (ELIG82 EQ 0)

before any procedures you run that use the 1982 voting scores. This case is *not* missing on the various indices and does have real scores, but was not eligible for all votes. See the *Congressional Quarterly Almanac* for details.

TIMVOT82
The percent of times the member voted in the 1982 session out of 465 roll-call votes

Missing data = 999 (0)
Mean = 93.70   S.D. = 8.252   Min = 27   Max = 100

WITPAR82
The percent of times the member voted with his or her party on 202 party-unity roll calls

Missing data = 999 (0)
Mean = 73.52   S.D. = 16.438   Min = 14   Max = 93

AGNPAR82
The percent of times the member voted against his or her party on 202 party-unity roll calls

Missing data = 999 (0)
Mean = 20.90   S.D. = 14.461   Min = 0   Max = 68

WCONCO82
The percent of times the member voted with the conservative coalition on 94 roll calls

Missing data = 999 (0)
Mean = 60.30   S.D. = 31.111   Min = 0   Max = 99

AGCONC82
The percent of times the member voted against the conservative coalition on 94 roll calls

Missing data = 999 (0)
Mean = 33.41   S.D. = 29.253   Min = 1   Max = 94

WIPRES82
The percent of times the member voted with Reagan on 119 roll calls

Missing data = 999 (0)
Mean = 59.60   S.D. = 19.412   Min = 24   Max = 89

AGPRES82
The percent of times the member voted against Reagan on 119 roll calls

Missing data = 999 (0)
Mean = 35.41   S.D. = 18.622   Min = 8   Max = 71

WITADA82
The percent of times the member voted or announced a position with the Americans for Democratic Action position (liberal) on 20 roll calls selected by that interest group

Missing data 999 (0)
Mean = 44.95   S.D. = 32.123   Min = 0   Max = 100

WITAFL82
The percent of times the member voted or announced a position with the AFL/CIO (labor) on 26 roll calls selected by that group

Missing data = 999 (0)
Mean = 50.36   S.D. = 32.206   Min = 4   Max = 96

WITACA82
The percent of times the member voted or announced a position with the Americans for Constitutional Action Research Institute (conservative) on 21 roll calls selected by that group

Missing data = 999 (0)
Mean = 52.65   S.D. = 25.131   Min = 6   Max = 100

REA80
The percent of vote in the member's state won by Reagan in 1980

No missing data codes
Mean = 52.16   S.D. = 7.273   Min = 37   Max = 73

CAR80
The percent of vote in the member's state won by Carter in 1980

No missing data codes
Mean = 39.16   S.D. = 7.988   Min = 21   Max = 56

FORD76
The percent of vote in the member's state won by Ford in 1980

No missing data codes
Mean = 49.06   S.D. = 5.719   Min = 33   Max = 62

CAR76
The percent of vote in the member's state won by Carter in 1976

No missing data codes
Mean = 48.92   S.D. = 6.504   Min = 34   Max = 67

Note: For variables from here to the end of the Senate file, see Appendix B for more details. Unless otherwise indicated, there are no missing data codes in the file.

POP80
Population of the state from which the member was elected

Mean = 4,518,149   S.D. = 4,691,164
Min = 401,851   Max = 23,667,902

POPSQMI
Population per square mile of the member's state
Missing data = −1 (0)

Mean = 154.37   S.D. = 220.268   Min = .7
Max = 986.2

MEDAGE
The median age of the population of the member's state
Mean = 29.54   S.D. = 1.685   Min = 24.2
Max = 34.7

CRIMES
The number of crimes per 100,000 population in the member's state in 1980

Missing data = 0, −1 (0)
Mean = 5303.64   S.D. = 1368.16   Min = 2580
Max = 8414

PERCAPIN
The per capita personal income of the member's state

Missing data = −1 (0)
Mean = 10,090   S.D. = 1366   Min = 7409
Max = 13,749

MEDHOUIN
The median household income of the member's state

Mean = 16,640   S.D. = 2431   Min = 12,096
Max = 25,414

VOTLP80
Which party had the plurality of the vote in the 1980 presidential election in the member's state?

(12)   1 = Democratic
(88)   2 = Republican

Missing values = −1 (0)

PERLP
The percent of the vote won by the leading party in the member's state

Missing values = −1, 0
Mean = 52.89   S.D. = 6.456   Min = 41.9   Max = 72.8

POPINC
The percent by that the population of the member's state increased between 1970 and 1980

Mean = 16.28   S.D. = 14.317   Min = −.375
Max = 63.79

URBPER
The percent of the population in the member's state in urban areas

Mean = 66.95   S.D. = 14.337   Min = 33.77
Max = 91.29

WHIPER
The percent of the population of the member's state that is white

Mean = 85.71   S.D. = 11.564   Min = 34.41
Max = 99.14

BLAPER
The percent of the population of the member's state that is black

Mean = 9.14   S.D. = 9.174   Min = .22
Max = 35.19

RETPER
The percent of the population of the member's state that is retired and receiving Social Security benefits

Mean = 8.35   S.D. = 1.679   Min = 2.41
Max = 13.25

HOUGRO
The percent growth in the number of housing units in the member's state between 1970 and 1980

Mean = 35.65   S.D. = 19.207   Min = 9.02
Max = 97.01

NOPLUMPR
The percent of the housing units in the member's state that do not have complete plumbing for the exclusive use of the occupants

Mean = 2.29   S.D. = 1.498   Min = .82
Max = 8.40

HSPER
The percent of the residents 25-years-old and older in the member's state who have four years of high school

Mean = 67.47   S.D. = 7.538   Min = 53.13
Max = 82.53

COLPER
The percent of the residents 25-years-old and older in the member's state who have four years of college

Mean = 16.09   S.D. = 2.944   Min = 10.42
Max = 22.96

FEPERLAB
The percent of the civilian labor force (over 16 years of age) that is female in the member's state

Mean = 42.30   S.D. = 1.748   Min = 37.1
Max = 45.76

UNEMPPER
The percent of the civilian labor force (over 16 years of age) that is unemployed in the member's state

Mean = 6.38   S.D. = 1.542   Min = 3.70
Max = 10.95

EMPMANPR
The percent of the labor force employed in manufacturing in the member's state

Mean = 20.25   S.D. = 8.050   Min = 5.44
Max = 32.77

WMHDFAM
The percent of families that are headed by women in the member's state

Mean = 12.64   S.D. = 2.441   Min = 7.53
Max = 17.90

FAMPOVPR
The percent of families that are in poverty in the member's state

Mean = 9.60   S.D. = 2.864   Min = 5.85
Max = 18.69

314 A LEGISLATIVE DATA SET

WMHDPOV
The percent of families below the poverty line that are headed by women in the member's state

Missing values 0 (0)
Mean = 40.57   S.D. = 9.190   Min = 21.39
Max = 59.38

POVPER
The percent of people in the member's state who are below the poverty line

Mean = 12.16   s.d. = 3.363   Min = 7.72
Max = 23.31

RURPR
The percent of people in the member's state who live in rural areas

Mean = 3.563   S.D. = 3.855   Min = .12
Max = 16.34

VOTTURN
Percent voter turnout in the member's state for the 1980 presidential election

Missing data = 999 (0)
Mean = 55.367   S.D. = 7.443   Min = 41.02
Max = 70.66

REGPER
The approximate percentage of the two-party vote that went to Reagan in 1980 in the member's state

Note: see Appendix B for calculation of this estimate.

Missing data = 999 (0)
Mean = 53.226   S.D. = 6.295   Min = 41.9
Max = 72.8

THE HOUSE FILE

MEMBERID
ICPSR member number

No missing data

CONGRESS
Number of the Congress

For this data set, it is constant at 97 and, thus, not of any use in analyses. It is included in case you decide to add cases from later Congresses to the file and need an identifier.

Missing data = −1 (0)

STATE
ICPSR state number

No missing data
Please see codes in the codebook for the Senate file.

NAME
Name of the member of Congress

This is alphabetic, too, and is included for reference should you want to use it.

SEX
Gender of the member of Congress

(414)   1 = Male
(19)   2 = Female

Missing data = 9 (0)

REGION
U.S. region represented by the member of Congress

(24)   0 = Northeast
(80)   1 = Mid-Atlantic
(85)   2 = East North Central
(35)   3 = West North Central
(100)   4 = South
(33)   5 = Border
(19)   6 = Mountain
(54)   7 = Pacific
(3)   8 = External states

Missing data = 9 (0)

BIRTH
State of birth of the member of Congress

See Senate file codebook for codes.

Missing data = 00, unknown or foreign

BIRREP
Is the member of Congress currently representing the state in which she or he was born?

(318)   0 = Yes
(115)   1 = No

Missing data = 9 (0)

RELCONG
Does the member of Congress have relatives who are serving or have ever served in Congress?

(417)   0 = None
(16)   1 = At least one

Missing data = 9 (0)

SECED
What kind of secondary education did the member of Congress have?

(334)   1 = Public school
(44)   2 = Private school

Missing data = 0,9 unknown (55)

COLLEGE
What kind of college education did the member of Congress have?

(17)   0 = None
(155)   1 = State university
(46)   2 = Ivy League or similar
(215)   3 = Other

Missing data = 9 (0)

MILITARY
What is the military background of the member of Congress?

(181)   0 = None
(166)   1 = Enlisted person
(86)   2 = Officer

Missing data = 9 (0)

OCCUPA
What occupation did the member of Congress have prior to public service?

(41)   1 = Education
(188)   2 = Law
(37)   3 = Professional
(91)   4 = Business
(20)   5 = Agriculture
(28)   6 = Miscellaneous

Missing data = 0,9; none, unknown, no nonpublic service career, retired (28)

AGEELEC
The age of the member of Congress when she or he was first sworn into Congress

Number-of-years-old coded.

Missing data = $-1, 0$ (1)
Mean = 40.76   S.D. = 7.7575   Min = 25
Max = 71

YEARELEC
The year the member was first elected to Congress

This is a three-digit variable that represents the year without the initial "1"; thus, it is effectively Year − 1,000.

Missing data = -1 (0)
Mean = 972.55   S.D. = 7.795   Min = 936
Max = 982

LASTYEAR
The last full year that the member served in Congress.

Again, the first digit is deleted from the year. This variable represents the year any members of the 97th Congress left—up to 1987.

Missing data = −1, 999, inappropriate because the member is still serving (283)

SERVED
The number of years served in Congress by the member if he or she had left prior to 1987

Missing data = −1, 999, inappropriate because the member is still serving (283)

WHYLEFT
The reason the member of Congress left

(43) 1 = Defeated in the general election
(10) 2 = Defeated in the primary or not renominated
(11) 3 = Died
(44) 4 = Was not a candidate for re-election
(38) 5 = Elected to other public office
(4) 6 = Resigned

Missing data = −1, 0, unknown
              9, inappropriate because the member is still serving (283)

PART
House in which the member was serving in the 97th Congress

(0) 1 = Senate
(433) 2 = House

Not useful in analysis unless files are merged.
No missing data codes

PARTY
Political party affiliation of the member of Congress

(243) 1 = Democratic
(190) 2 = Republican

No missing data codes

FIRSTCON
First Congress in which the member was seated

Congress number coded.

No missing data codes

ELIG
Eligibility status of the member of Congress for the 1981 Session

(428) 0 = Eligible for all
(4)   1 = Not eligible for all
(1)   8 = Not a member

Missing data = 8 or ge (greater than or equal to) 9 (0)

You may want to use this variable to delete any members who may not have been able to vote all the time. If so, you can specify,

TEMPORARY
SELECT IF (ELIG EQ 0)

before any procedures you run that use the 1981 voting scores. The four cases are *not* missing on the various indices and do have real scores, but the cases were not eligible for all votes. See the *Congressional Quarterly Almanac* for details.

TIMVOT81
The percent of times the member voted in the 1981 session out of 353 roll-call votes

Missing data = 999 (1)
Mean = 91.09   S.D. = 7.722   Min = 50   Max = 100

WITPAR81
The percent of times the member voted with his or her party on 132 party-unity roll calls
Missing data = 999 (1)
Mean = 71.31   S.D. = 16.341   Min = 6   Max = 95

AGNPAR81
The percent of times the member voted against his or her party on 132 party-unity roll calls

Missing data = 999 (1)
Mean = 21.48   S.D. = 15.792   Min = 1   Max = 81

WCONCO81
The percent of times the member voted with the conservative coalition on 75 roll calls

Missing data = 999 (1)
Mean = 57.39   S.D. = 30.198   Min = 0   Max = 99

AGCONC81
The percent of times the member voted against the conservative coalition on 75 roll calls
Missing data = 999 (1)
Mean = 36.19   S.D. = 29.261   Min = 0   Max = 96

WIPRES81
The percent of times the member voted with Reagan on 76 roll calls
Missing data = 999 (1)
Mean = 53.63   S.D. = 17.344   Min = 14   Max = 83

AGPRES81
The percent of times the member voted against Reagan on 76 roll calls

Missing data = 999 (1)
Mean = 39.75   S.D. = 16.65   Min = 11   Max = 76

WITADA81
The percent of times the member voted or announced a position with the Americans for Democratic Action position (liberal) on 20 roll calls selected by that interest group

Missing data = 999 (1)
Mean = 40.11   S.D. = 32.595   Min = 0   Max = 100

WITAFL81
The percent of times the member voted or announced a position with the AFL/CIO (labor) on 15 roll calls selected by that group
Missing data = 999 (1)
Mean = 49.90   S.D. = 33.168   Min = 0   Max = 100

WITACA81
The percent of times the member voted or announced a position with the Americans for Constitutional Action (conservative) on 24 roll calls selected by that group

Missing data = 999 (1)
Mean = 49.54   S.D. = 30.342   Min = 0   Max = 100

ELIG82
Eligibility status of the member of Congress for the 1982 Session

(429)   0 = Eligible for all
(4)   1 = Not eligible for all

Missing data = 8 or ge (greater than or equal to) 9 (0)
You may want to use this variable to delete members from analyses of issues on which they were not eligible to vote. (See ELIG above.)

TIMVOT82
The percent of times the member voted in the 1982 session out of 459 roll-call votes

Missing data = 999 (0)
Mean = 88.72   S.D. = 11.674   Min = 25   Max = 100

WITPAR82
The percent of times the member voted with his or her party on 167 party-unity roll calls

Missing data = 999 (0)
Mean = 70.46   S.D. = 18.926   Min = 3   Max = 100

AGNPAR82
The percent of times the member voted against his or her party on 167 party-unity roll calls

Missing data = 999 (1)
Mean = 20.12   S.D. = 17.028   Min = 0   Max = 93

WCONCO82

The percent of times the member voted with the conservative coalition on 73 roll calls

Missing data = 999 (2)
Mean = 54.11   S.D. = 29.557   Min = 1   Max = 100

AGCONC82

The percent of times the member voted against the conservative coalition on 73 roll calls

Missing data = 999 (2)
Mean = 37.94   S.D. = 28.717   Min = 0   Max = 96

WIPRES82

The percent of times the member voted with Reagan on 77 roll calls

Missing data = 999 (0)
Mean = 49.81   S.D. = 18.556   Min = 0   Max = 90

AGPRES82

The percent of times the member voted against Reagan on 77 roll calls

Missing data = 999 (0)
Mean = 40.70   S.D. = 17.539   Min = 1   Max = 100

WITADA82

The percent of times the member voted or announced a position with the Americans for Democratic Action position (liberal) on 20 roll calls selected by that interest group

Missing data = 999 (3)
Mean = 43.49   S.D. = 33.172   Min = 0   Max = 100

WITAFL82

The percent of times the member voted or announced a position with the AFL/CIO (labor) on 20 roll calls selected by that group

Missing data = 999 (3)
Mean = 53.49   S.D. = 36.986   Min = 0   Max = 100

WITACA82

The percent of times the member voted or announced a position with the Americans for Constitutional Action Research Institute (conservative) on 23 roll calls selected by that group

Missing data = 999 (4)
Mean = 48.53   S.D. = 31.78   Min = 0   Max = 100

APPENDIX D

STATISTICAL TABLES

TABLE A.1 The Standard Normal Distribution

Column (A): Z (A normal variable with mean 0 and variance 1.)
Column (B): Proportion of area between mean and Z.
Column (C): Proportion of area "beyond" Z.

(A) z	(B)	(C)	(A) z	(B)	(C)	(A) z	(B)	(C)
0.00	0.0000	0.5000	0.40	0.1554	0.3446	0.80	0.2881	0.2119
0.01	0.0040	0.4960	0.41	0.1591	0.3409	0.81	0.2910	0.2090
0.02	0.0080	0.4920	0.42	0.1628	0.3372	0.82	0.2939	0.2061
0.03	0.0120	0.4880	0.43	0.1664	0.3336	0.83	0.2967	0.2033
0.04	0.0160	0.4840	0.44	0.1700	0.3300	0.84	0.2995	0.2005
0.05	0.0199	0.4801	0.45	0.1736	0.3264	0.85	0.3023	0.1977
0.06	0.0239	0.4761	0.46	0.1772	0.3228	0.86	0.3051	0.1949
0.07	0.0279	0.4721	0.47	0.1808	0.3192	0.87	0.3078	0.1922
0.08	0.0319	0.4681	0.48	0.1844	0.3156	0.88	0.3106	0.1894
0.09	0.0359	0.4641	0.49	0.1879	0.3121	0.89	0.3133	0.1867
0.10	0.0398	0.4602	0.50	0.1915	0.3085	0.90	0.3159	0.1841
0.11	0.0438	0.4562	0.51	0.1950	0.3050	0.91	0.3186	0.1814
0.12	0.0478	0.4522	0.52	0.1985	0.3015	0.92	0.3212	0.1788
0.13	0.0517	0.4483	0.53	0.2019	0.2981	0.93	0.3238	0.1762
0.14	0.0557	0.4443	0.54	0.2054	0.2946	0.94	0.3264	0.1736
0.15	0.0596	0.4404	0.55	0.2088	0.2912	0.95	0.3289	0.1711
0.16	0.0636	0.4364	0.56	0.2123	0.2877	0.96	0.3315	0.1685
0.17	0.0675	0.4325	0.57	0.2157	0.2843	0.97	0.3340	0.1660
0.18	0.0714	0.4286	0.58	0.2190	0.2810	0.98	0.3365	0.1635
0.19	0.0753	0.4247	0.59	0.2224	0.2776	0.99	0.3389	0.1611
0.20	0.0793	0.4207	0.60	0.2257	0.2743	1.00	0.3413	0.1587
0.21	0.0832	0.4168	0.61	0.2291	0.2709	1.01	0.3438	0.1562
0.22	0.0871	0.4129	0.62	0.2324	0.2676	1.02	0.3461	0.1539
0.23	0.0910	0.4090	0.63	0.2357	0.2643	1.03	0.3485	0.1515
0.24	0.0948	0.4052	0.64	0.2389	0.2611	1.04	0.3508	0.1492
0.25	0.0987	0.4013	0.65	0.2422	0.2578	1.05	0.3531	0.1469
0.26	0.1026	0.3974	0.66	0.2454	0.2546	1.06	0.3554	0.1446
0.27	0.1064	0.3936	0.67	0.2486	0.2514	1.07	0.3577	0.1423
0.28	0.1103	0.3897	0.68	0.2517	0.2483	1.08	0.3599	0.1401
0.29	0.1141	0.3859	0.69	0.2549	0.2451	1.09	0.3621	0.1379
0.30	0.1179	0.3821	0.70	0.2580	0.2420	1.10	0.3643	0.1357
0.31	0.1217	0.3783	0.71	0.2611	0.2389	1.11	0.3665	0.1335
0.32	0.1255	0.3745	0.72	0.2642	0.2358	1.12	0.3686	0.1314
0.33	0.1293	0.3707	0.73	0.2673	0.2327	1.13	0.3708	0.1292
0.34	0.1331	0.3669	0.74	0.2704	0.2296	1.14	0.3729	0.1271
0.35	0.1368	0.3632	0.75	0.2734	0.2266	1.15	0.3749	0.1251
0.36	0.1406	0.3594	0.76	0.2764	0.2236	1.16	0.3770	0.1230
0.37	0.1443	0.3557	0.77	0.2794	0.2206	1.17	0.3790	0.1210
0.38	0.1480	0.3520	0.78	0.2823	0.2177	1.18	0.3810	0.1190
0.39	0.1517	0.3483	0.79	0.2852	0.2148	1.19	0.3830	0.1170

Table A.1 is reprinted from Basil P. Korin, *Statistical Concepts for the Social Sciences* (Cambridge, MA: Winthrop Publishers, 1975), pp. 364-366.

TABLE A.1 (Continued)

(A) z	(B)	(C)	(A) z	(B)	(C)	(A) z	(B)	(C)
1.20	0.3849	0.1151	1.60	0.4452	0.0548	2.00	0.4772	0.0228
1.21	0.3869	0.1131	1.61	0.4463	0.0537	2.01	0.4778	0.0222
1.22	0.3888	0.1112	1.62	0.4474	0.0526	2.02	0.4783	0.0217
1.23	0.3907	0.1093	1.63	0.4484	0.0516	2.03	0.4788	0.0212
1.24	0.3925	0.1075	1.64	0.4495	0.0505	2.04	0.4793	0.0207
1.25	0.3944	0.1056	1.65	0.4505	0.0495	2.05	0.4798	0.0202
1.26	0.3962	0.1038	1.66	0.4515	0.0485	2.06	0.4803	0.0197
1.27	0.3980	0.1020	1.67	0.4525	0.0475	2.07	0.4808	0.0192
1.28	0.3997	0.1003	1.68	0.4535	0.0465	2.08	0.4812	0.0188
1.29	0.4015	0.0985	1.69	0.4545	0.0455	2.09	0.4817	0.0183
1.30	0.4032	0.0968	1.70	0.4554	0.0446	2.10	0.4821	0.0179
1.31	0.4049	0.0951	1.71	0.4564	0.0436	2.11	0.4826	0.0174
1.32	0.4066	0.0934	1.72	0.4573	0.0427	2.12	0.4830	0.0170
1.33	0.4082	0.0918	1.73	0.4582	0.0418	2.13	0.4834	0.0166
1.34	0.4099	0.0901	1.74	0.4591	0.0409	2.14	0.4838	0.0162
1.35	0.4115	0.0885	1.75	0.4599	0.0401	2.15	0.4842	0.0158
1.36	0.4131	0.0869	1.76	0.4608	0.0392	2.16	0.4846	0.0154
1.37	0.4147	0.0853	1.77	0.4616	0.0384	2.17	0.4850	0.0150
1.38	0.4162	0.0838	1.78	0.4625	0.0375	2.18	0.4854	0.0146
1.39	0.4177	0.0823	1.79	0.4633	0.0367	2.19	0.4857	0.0143
1.40	0.4192	0.0808	1.80	0.4641	0.0359	2.20	0.4861	0.0139
1.41	0.4207	0.0793	1.81	0.4649	0.0351	2.21	0.4864	0.0136
1.42	0.4222	0.0778	1.82	0.4656	0.0344	2.22	0.4868	0.0132
1.43	0.4236	0.0764	1.83	0.4664	0.0336	2.23	0.4871	0.0129
1.44	0.4251	0.0749	1.84	0.4671	0.0329	2.24	0.4875	0.0125
1.45	0.4265	0.0735	1.85	0.4678	0.0322	2.25	0.4878	0.0122
1.46	0.4279	0.0721	1.86	0.4686	0.0314	2.26	0.4881	0.0119
1.47	0.4292	0.0708	1.87	0.4693	0.0307	2.27	0.4884	0.0116
1.48	0.4306	0.0694	1.88	0.4699	0.0301	2.28	0.4887	0.0113
1.49	0.4319	0.0681	1.89	0.4706	0.0294	2.29	0.4890	0.0110
1.50	0.4332	0.0668	1.90	0.4713	0.0287	2.30	0.4893	0.0107
1.51	0.4345	0.0655	1.91	0.4719	0.0281	2.31	0.4896	0.0104
1.52	0.4357	0.0643	1.92	0.4726	0.0274	2.32	0.4898	0.0102
1.53	0.4370	0.0630	1.93	0.4732	0.0268	2.33	0.4901	0.0099
1.54	0.4382	0.0618	1.94	0.4738	0.0262	2.34	0.4904	0.0096
1.55	0.4394	0.0606	1.95	0.4744	0.0256	2.35	0.4906	0.0094
1.56	0.4406	0.0594	1.96	0.4750	0.0250	2.36	0.4909	0.0091
1.57	0.4418	0.0582	1.97	0.4756	0.0244	2.37	0.4911	0.0089
1.58	0.4429	0.0571	1.98	0.4761	0.0239	2.38	0.4913	0.0087
1.59	0.4441	0.0559	1.99	0.4767	0.0233	2.39	0.4916	0.0084

TABLE A.1 (Continued)

(A) z	(B)	(C)	(A) z	(B)	(C)	(A) z	(B)	(C)
2.40	0.4918	0.0082	2.75	0.4970	0.0030	3.10	0.4990	0.0010
2.41	0.4920	0.0080	2.76	0.4971	0.0029	3.11	0.4991	0.0009
2.42	0.4922	0.0078	2.77	0.4972	0.0028	3.12	0.4991	0.0009
2.43	0.4925	0.0075	2.78	0.4973	0.0027	3.13	0.4991	0.0009
2.44	0.4927	0.0073	2.79	0.4974	0.0026	3.14	0.4992	0.0008
2.45	0.4929	0.0071	2.80	0.4974	0.0026	3.15	0.4992	0.0008
2.46	0.4931	0.0069	2.81	0.4975	0.0025	3.16	0.4992	0.0008
2.47	0.4932	0.0068	2.82	0.4976	0.0024	3.17	0.4992	0.0008
2.48	0.4934	0.0066	2.83	0.4977	0.0023	3.18	0.4993	0.0007
2.49	0.4936	0.0064	2.84	0.4977	0.0023	3.19	0.4993	0.0007
2.50	0.4938	0.0062	2.85	0.4978	0.0022	3.20	0.4993	0.0007
2.51	0.4940	0.0060	2.86	0.4979	0.0021	3.21	0.4993	0.0007
2.52	0.4941	0.0059	2.87	0.4979	0.0021	3.22	0.4994	0.0006
2.53	0.4943	0.0057	2.88	0.4980	0.0020	3.23	0.4994	0.0006
2.54	0.4945	0.0055	2.89	0.4981	0.0019	3.24	0.4994	0.0006
2.55	0.4946	0.0054	2.90	0.4981	0.0019	3.25	0.4994	0.0006
2.56	0.4948	0.0052	2.91	0.4982	0.0018	3.30	0.4995	0.0005
2.57	0.4949	0.0051	2.92	0.4982	0.0018	3.35	0.4996	0.0004
2.58	0.4951	0.0049	2.93	0.4983	0.0017	3.40	0.4997	0.0003
2.59	0.4952	0.0048	2.94	0.4984	0.0016	3.45	0.4997	0.0003
2.60	0.4953	0.0047	2.95	0.4984	0.0016	3.50	0.4998	0.0002
2.61	0.4955	0.0045	2.96	0.4985	0.0015	3.60	0.4998	0.0002
2.62	0.4956	0.0044	2.97	0.4985	0.0015	3.70	0.4999	0.0001
2.63	0.4957	0.0043	2.98	0.4986	0.0014	3.80	0.4999	0.0001
2.64	0.4959	0.0041	2.99	0.4986	0.0014	4.00	0.49997	0.00003
2.65	0.4960	0.0040	3.00	0.4987	0.0013	∞	0.50000	0.00000
2.66	0.4961	0.0039	3.01	0.4987	0.0013			
2.67	0.4962	0.0038	3.02	0.4987	0.0013			
2.68	0.4963	0.0037	3.03	0.4988	0.0012			
2.69	0.4964	0.0036	3.04	0.4988	0.0012			
2.70	0.4965	0.0035	3.05	0.4989	0.0011			
2.71	0.4966	0.0034	3.06	0.4989	0.0011			
2.72	0.4967	0.0033	3.07	0.4989	0.0011			
2.73	0.4968	0.0032	3.08	0.4990	0.0010			
2.74	0.4969	0.0031	3.09	0.4990	0.0010			

TABLE A.2 Critical Values of F at .01 and .05

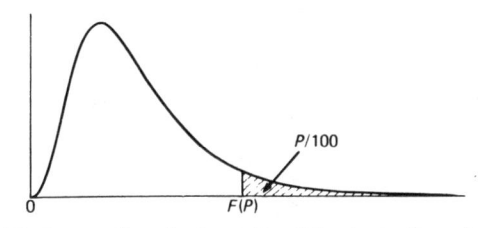

(This shape applies only when $v_1 \geq 3$. When $v_1 < 3$ the mode is at the origin.)

$v_1 =$	1	2	3	4	5	6	7	8	10	12	24	∞
$v_2 = 1$	4052	4999	5403	5625	5764	5859	5928	5981	6056	6106	6235	6366
2	98·50	99·00	99·17	99·25	99·30	99·33	99·36	99·37	99·40	99·42	99·46	99·50
3	34·12	30·82	29·46	28·71	28·24	27·91	27·67	27·49	27·23	27·05	26·60	26·13
4	21·20	18·00	16·69	15·98	15·52	15·21	14·98	14·80	14·55	14·37	13·93	13·46
5	16·26	13·27	12·06	11·39	10·97	10·67	10·46	10·29	10·05	9·888	9·466	9·020
6	13·75	10·92	9·780	9·148	8·746	8·466	8·260	8·102	7·874	7·718	7·313	6·880
7	12·25	9·547	8·451	7·847	7·460	7·191	6·993	6·840	6·620	6·469	6·074	5·650
8	11·26	8·649	7·591	7·006	6·632	6·371	6·178	6·029	5·814	5·667	5·279	4·859
9	10·56	8·022	6·992	6·422	6·057	5·802	5·613	5·467	5·257	5·111	4·729	4·311
10	10·04	7·559	6·552	5·994	5·636	5·386	5·200	5·057	4·849	4·706	4·327	3·909
11	9·646	7·206	6·217	5·668	5·316	5·069	4·886	4·744	4·539	4·397	4·021	3·602
12	9·330	6·927	5·953	5·412	5·064	4·821	4·640	4·499	4·296	4·155	3·780	3·361
13	9·074	6·701	5·739	5·205	4·862	4·620	4·441	4·302	4·100	3·960	3·587	3·165
14	8·862	6·515	5·564	5·035	4·695	4·456	4·278	4·140	3·939	3·800	3·427	3·004
15	8·683	6·359	5·417	4·893	4·556	4·318	4·142	4·004	3·805	3·666	3·294	2·868
16	8·531	6·226	5·292	4·773	4·437	4·202	4·026	3·890	3·691	3·553	3·181	2·753
17	8·400	6·112	5·185	4·669	4·336	4·102	3·927	3·791	3·593	3·455	3·084	2·653
18	8·285	6·013	5·092	4·579	4·248	4·015	3·841	3·705	3·508	3·371	2·999	2·566
19	8·185	5·926	5·010	4·500	4·171	3·939	3·765	3·631	3·434	3·297	2·925	2·489
20	8·096	5·849	4·938	4·431	4·103	3·871	3·699	3·564	3·368	3·231	2·859	2·421
21	8·017	5·780	4·874	4·369	4·042	3·812	3·640	3·506	3·310	3·173	2·801	2·360
22	7·945	5·719	4·817	4·313	3·988	3·758	3·587	3·453	3·258	3·121	2·749	2·305
23	7·881	5·664	4·765	4·264	3·939	3·710	3·539	3·406	3·211	3·074	2·702	2·256
24	7·823	5·614	4·718	4·218	3·895	3·667	3·496	3·363	3·168	3·032	2·659	2·211
25	7·770	5·568	4·675	4·177	3·855	3·627	3·457	3·324	3·129	2·993	2·620	2·169
26	7·721	5·526	4·637	4·140	3·818	3·591	3·421	3·288	3·094	2·958	2·585	2·131
27	7·677	5·488	4·601	4·106	3·785	3·558	3·388	3·256	3·062	2·926	2·552	2·097
28	7·636	5·453	4·568	4·074	3·754	3·528	3·358	3·226	3·032	2·896	2·522	2·064
29	7·598	5·420	4·538	4·045	3·725	3·499	3·330	3·198	3·005	2·868	2·495	2·034
30	7·562	5·390	4·510	4·018	3·699	3·473	3·304	3·173	2·979	2·843	2·469	2·006
32	7·499	5·336	4·459	3·969	3·652	3·427	3·258	3·127	2·934	2·798	2·423	1·956
34	7·444	5·289	4·416	3·927	3·611	3·386	3·218	3·087	2·894	2·758	2·383	1·911
36	7·396	5·248	4·377	3·890	3·574	3·351	3·183	3·052	2·859	2·723	2·347	1·872
38	7·353	5·211	4·343	3·858	3·542	3·319	3·152	3·021	2·828	2·692	2·316	1·837
40	7·314	5·179	4·313	3·828	3·514	3·291	3·124	2·993	2·801	2·665	2·288	1·805
60	7·077	4·977	4·126	3·649	3·339	3·119	2·953	2·823	2·632	2·496	2·115	1·601
120	6·851	4·787	3·949	3·480	3·174	2·956	2·792	2·663	2·472	2·336	1·950	1·381
∞	6·635	4·605	3·782	3·319	3·017	2·802	2·639	2·511	2·321	2·185	1·791	1·000

Tables A.2 and A.3 are reprinted from D.V. Lindley and W.F. Scott, *New Cambridge Elementary Statistical Tables* (Cambridge, England: Cambridge University Press, 1984), pp. 41, 51, 53, with the permission of the publisher.

TABLE A.2 (Continued)

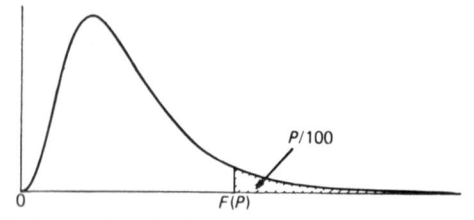

(This shape applies only when $v_1 \geqslant 3$. When $v_1 < 3$ the mode is at the origin.)

$v_1 =$	1	2	3	4	5	6	7	8	10	12	24	∞
$v_2 = 1$	161.4	199.5	215.7	224.6	230.2	234.0	236.8	238.9	241.9	243.9	249.1	254.3
2	18.51	19.00	19.16	19.25	19.30	19.33	19.35	19.37	19.40	19.41	19.45	19.50
3	10.13	9.552	9.277	9.117	9.013	8.941	8.887	8.845	8.786	8.745	8.639	8.526
4	7.709	6.944	6.591	6.388	6.256	6.163	6.094	6.041	5.964	5.912	5.774	5.628
5	6.608	5.786	5.409	5.192	5.050	4.950	4.876	4.818	4.735	4.678	4.527	4.365
6	5.987	5.143	4.757	4.534	4.387	4.284	4.207	4.147	4.060	4.000	3.841	3.669
7	5.591	4.737	4.347	4.120	3.972	3.866	3.787	3.726	3.637	3.575	3.410	3.230
8	5.318	4.459	4.066	3.838	3.687	3.581	3.500	3.438	3.347	3.284	3.115	2.928
9	5.117	4.256	3.863	3.633	3.482	3.374	3.293	3.230	3.137	3.073	2.900	2.707
10	4.965	4.103	3.708	3.478	3.326	3.217	3.135	3.072	2.978	2.913	2.737	2.538
11	4.844	3.982	3.587	3.357	3.204	3.095	3.012	2.948	2.854	2.788	2.609	2.404
12	4.747	3.885	3.490	3.259	3.106	2.996	2.913	2.849	2.753	2.687	2.505	2.296
13	4.667	3.806	3.411	3.179	3.025	2.915	2.832	2.767	2.671	2.604	2.420	2.206
14	4.600	3.739	3.344	3.112	2.958	2.848	2.764	2.699	2.602	2.534	2.349	2.131
15	4.543	3.682	3.287	3.056	2.901	2.790	2.707	2.641	2.544	2.475	2.288	2.066
16	4.494	3.634	3.239	3.007	2.852	2.741	2.657	2.591	2.494	2.425	2.235	2.010
17	4.451	3.592	3.197	2.965	2.810	2.699	2.614	2.548	2.450	2.381	2.190	1.960
18	4.414	3.555	3.160	2.928	2.773	2.661	2.577	2.510	2.412	2.342	2.150	1.917
19	4.381	3.522	3.127	2.895	2.740	2.628	2.544	2.477	2.378	2.308	2.114	1.878
20	4.351	3.493	3.098	2.866	2.711	2.599	2.514	2.447	2.348	2.278	2.082	1.843
21	4.325	3.467	3.072	2.840	2.685	2.573	2.488	2.420	2.321	2.250	2.054	1.812
22	4.301	3.443	3.049	2.817	2.661	2.549	2.464	2.397	2.297	2.226	2.028	1.783
23	4.279	3.422	3.028	2.796	2.640	2.528	2.442	2.375	2.275	2.204	2.005	1.757
24	4.260	3.403	3.009	2.776	2.621	2.508	2.423	2.355	2.255	2.183	1.984	1.733
25	4.242	3.385	2.991	2.759	2.603	2.490	2.405	2.337	2.236	2.165	1.964	1.711
26	4.225	3.369	2.975	2.743	2.587	2.474	2.388	2.321	2.220	2.148	1.946	1.691
27	4.210	3.354	2.960	2.728	2.572	2.459	2.373	2.305	2.204	2.132	1.930	1.672
28	4.196	3.340	2.947	2.714	2.558	2.445	2.359	2.291	2.190	2.118	1.915	1.654
29	4.183	3.328	2.934	2.701	2.545	2.432	2.346	2.278	2.177	2.104	1.901	1.638
30	4.171	3.316	2.922	2.690	2.534	2.421	2.334	2.266	2.165	2.092	1.887	1.622
32	4.149	3.295	2.901	2.668	2.512	2.399	2.313	2.244	2.142	2.070	1.864	1.594
34	4.130	3.276	2.883	2.650	2.494	2.380	2.294	2.225	2.123	2.050	1.843	1.569
36	4.113	3.259	2.866	2.634	2.477	2.364	2.277	2.209	2.106	2.033	1.824	1.547
38	4.098	3.245	2.852	2.619	2.463	2.349	2.262	2.194	2.091	2.017	1.808	1.527
40	4.085	3.232	2.839	2.606	2.449	2.336	2.249	2.180	2.077	2.003	1.793	1.509
60	4.001	3.150	2.758	2.525	2.368	2.254	2.167	2.097	1.993	1.917	1.700	1.389
120	3.920	3.072	2.680	2.447	2.290	2.175	2.087	2.016	1.910	1.834	1.608	1.254
∞	3.841	2.996	2.605	2.372	2.214	2.099	2.010	1.938	1.831	1.752	1.517	1.000

TABLE A.3 The Chi-square Distribution

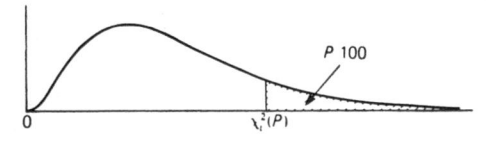

(The above shape applies for $\nu \geqslant 3$ only. When $\nu < 3$ the mode is at the origin.)

P	50	40	30	20	10	5	2.5	1	0.5	0.1	0.05
$\nu = 1$	0.4549	0.7083	1.074	1.642	2.706	3.841	5.024	6.635	7.879	10.83	12.12
2	1.386	1.833	2.408	3.219	4.605	5.991	7.378	9.210	10.60	13.82	15.20
3	2.366	2.946	3.665	4.642	6.251	7.815	9.348	11.34	12.84	16.27	17.73
4	3.357	4.045	4.878	5.989	7.779	9.488	11.14	13.28	14.86	18.47	20.00
5	4.351	5.132	6.064	7.289	9.236	11.07	12.83	15.09	16.75	20.52	22.11
6	5.348	6.211	7.231	8.558	10.64	12.59	14.45	16.81	18.55	22.46	24.10
7	6.346	7.283	8.383	9.803	12.02	14.07	16.01	18.48	20.28	24.32	26.02
8	7.344	8.351	9.524	11.03	13.36	15.51	17.53	20.09	21.95	26.12	27.87
9	8.343	9.414	10.66	12.24	14.68	16.92	19.02	21.67	23.59	27.88	29.67
10	9.342	10.47	11.78	13.44	15.99	18.31	20.48	23.21	25.19	29.59	31.42
11	10.34	11.53	12.90	14.63	17.28	19.68	21.92	24.72	26.76	31.26	33.14
12	11.34	12.58	14.01	15.81	18.55	21.03	23.34	26.22	28.30	32.91	34.82
13	12.34	13.64	15.12	16.98	19.81	22.36	24.74	27.69	29.82	34.53	36.48
14	13.34	14.69	16.22	18.15	21.06	23.68	26.12	29.14	31.32	36.12	38.11
15	14.34	15.73	17.32	19.31	22.31	25.00	27.49	30.58	32.80	37.70	39.72
16	15.34	16.78	18.42	20.47	23.54	26.30	28.85	32.00	34.27	39.25	41.31
17	16.34	17.82	19.51	21.61	24.77	27.59	30.19	33.41	35.72	40.79	42.88
18	17.34	18.87	20.60	22.76	25.99	28.87	31.53	34.81	37.16	42.31	44.43
19	18.34	19.91	21.69	23.90	27.20	30.14	32.85	36.19	38.58	43.82	45.97
20	19.34	20.95	22.77	25.04	28.41	31.41	34.17	37.57	40.00	45.31	47.50
21	20.34	21.99	23.86	26.17	29.62	32.67	35.48	38.93	41.40	46.80	49.01
22	21.34	23.03	24.94	27.30	30.81	33.92	36.78	40.29	42.80	48.27	50.51
23	22.34	24.07	26.02	28.43	32.01	35.17	38.08	41.64	44.18	49.73	52.00
24	23.34	25.11	27.10	29.55	33.20	36.42	39.36	42.98	45.56	51.18	53.48
25	24.34	26.14	28.17	30.68	34.38	37.65	40.65	44.31	46.93	52.62	54.95
26	25.34	27.18	29.25	31.79	35.56	38.89	41.92	45.64	48.29	54.05	56.41
27	26.34	28.21	30.32	32.91	36.74	40.11	43.19	46.96	49.64	55.48	57.86
28	27.34	29.25	31.39	34.03	37.92	41.34	44.46	48.28	50.99	56.89	59.30
29	28.34	30.28	32.46	35.14	39.09	42.56	45.72	49.59	52.34	58.30	60.73
30	29.34	31.32	33.53	36.25	40.26	43.77	46.98	50.89	53.67	59.70	62.16
32	31.34	33.38	35.66	38.47	42.58	46.19	49.48	53.49	56.33	62.49	65.00
34	33.34	35.44	37.80	40.68	44.90	48.60	51.97	56.06	58.96	65.25	67.80
36	35.34	37.50	39.92	42.88	47.21	51.00	54.44	58.62	61.58	67.99	70.59
38	37.34	39.56	42.05	45.08	49.51	53.38	56.90	61.16	64.18	70.70	73.35
40	39.34	41.62	44.16	47.27	51.81	55.76	59.34	63.69	66.77	73.40	76.09
50	49.33	51.89	54.72	58.16	63.17	67.50	71.42	76.15	79.49	86.66	89.56
60	59.33	62.13	65.23	68.97	74.40	79.08	83.30	88.38	91.95	99.61	102.7
70	69.33	72.36	75.69	79.71	85.53	90.53	95.02	100.4	104.2	112.3	115.6
80	79.33	82.57	86.12	90.41	96.58	101.9	106.6	112.3	116.3	124.8	128.3
90	89.33	92.76	96.52	101.1	107.6	113.1	118.1	124.1	128.3	137.2	140.8
100	99.33	102.9	106.9	111.7	118.5	124.3	129.6	135.8	140.2	149.4	153.2

INDEX

a. See Intercept
Additive model. *See* Model, additive
Aggregate-level data. *See* Data, aggregate
Analysis of covariance. *See also* Regression; REGRESSION
  defined, 223
  logic of, 231-35
  with MANOVA, 236
Analysis of variance. *See also* ANOVA; E^2
  compared to regression, 231
  compared to regression and tabular analysis, 98-102
  dichotomous independents and regression, 196-200
  with dummy variable regression, 224-30
  experiments, use in, 96
  interpretation, 210-16
  logic of, 200-202, 231
  PRE measure, 197
ANOVA. *See also* Analysis of variance; E^2; MCA
  approach, classical vs. regression, 208
  command form, 207, 217
  compared to regression with dummy variables 226, 228-30
  compared to tables and regression, 98-99, 101
  eta, 211
  output, 210-15, 229
  subcommands, 208, 217
  test of significance, 269
Arithmetic mean. *See* Mean

Asymmetrical vs. symmetrical measure of association 64, 138
Average deviation, 25

b. See Slope
Barchart, from FREQUENCIES, 40
Batch processing, 37
BEGIN DATA. *See* SPSS file
Best guess (PRE measures)
  interval, bivariate, 46-48
  interval dependent only, 84, 85-87
  interval, multivariate, 177
  interval, univariate, 24, 42, 45
  nominal, 128-29, 132
Beta (beta weights). *See also* Regression; REGRESSION
  comparison within/across samples, 176, 191
  formula, 190
  interpretation, 190-91
Beta (from ANOVA)
  as partial "slope," 212

Case
  in research design, 287-88
  in sampling, 280
  variables measured on, 2-3, 11-12
Causation
  assessment of, 143 ff.
  and asymmetric measures, 64, 122, 138
  chain, causal, 146-48
  and experiments, 150-53

and independent variable, 3, 64
  as reason for covariation of index items, 73
  and spuriousness, 145
  as theoretical concept, 3
Chi square. *See also* Phi; V
  calculating, 135
  from CROSSTABS, 273
  formula, 135, 272
  logic of, 134-35
  test of independence, 271-73
Codebooks
  coding of values in, 73
  description of contents, 67-68
Column, 32. *See also* Data, coding
Command terminator, 38
COMPUTE
  command form, 192
  interaction terms, 204, 228
  summed standard scores, 193
Concordant pair, defined, 114
Confidence, certainty (in sampling), 276, 277
Content analysis. *See* Data, collection methods
Control variables. *See* Variables, control
Correlation. *See also* Variables; names of specific measures of association
  distorted, 145-56
  spurious, 144-45
Correlation matrix, 74-75
Correlation ratio. *See* E^2
CORRELATIONS
  command form, 74
  correlation matrix from, 74-75

INDEX 327

subcommands, 74
test of significance, 271
COUNT, 75-77, 81-82
  command form, 76
  missing data with, 76
  problems of indices constructed with, 186
  recoding index from, 95
Covariation
  of index items, 71
  and interpretation of r, 56
  and interpretation of slope, 60, 64
Cramer's V. See V, Cramer's
Critical value in F tests, 263
CROSSTABS. See also Tables
  command form, 107, 249
  measures of association in,
    ordinal, 125-26
    nominal, 138
  output, 107, 249
  partials from, 249
  subcommands, 107, 125-26, 138
  tests of significance, 261, 273

Data
  coding, 32-33, 73
  collection methods, 12, 288
    experiment compared to survey, 150-53
    effect on size of correlation, 59, 78
  types
    aggregate vs. individual, 6, 59, 70
    cross-sectional, 6, 285
    longitudinal, 6, 285 and F test, 265
    and measurement error, 70
DATA LIST. See SPSS file
Degrees of freedom
  chi square, 272-73
  F test, 263-64
Description, compared to explanation, 1
DESCRIPTIVES
  command form, 36
  for standard scores, 192
  subcommands, 36
Dichotomy. See Values
Discordant pair, defined, 115
Dispersion. See also Distribution
  analysis of, reason for, 17
  diagram, 19
Distorted correlation. See Variables, distorter
Distribution. See also Dispersion; Variance; Variation

bimodal, 23-34
bivariate normal, 264
conditional distribution
  within analysis of variance
    categories, 88-89
  nominal, 128-30
  ordinal, 103-7
  in tables, 100, 242-47
describing, 16-28
marginal
  effect on
    choice of measures, 122
    comparison of measures across samples, 136
  in multivariate tables, 243-45
normal, 257-58
of standard scores, 189
of test statistics, 261
univariate
  analysis of 16-18, 24-25, 39
  in codebooks, 68
  on index items, 74
  ordinal, 99-100, 102-4
  visualizing, 39
Dummy variables. See also Analysis of variance; Regression; REGRESSION; Model
  creating, 223-24, 226
d_{yx}, Somer's, 120-22
  compared to gamma and tau$_b$, 122-25
  and form of relationship, 125
  formula and calculation, 121
  interpretation, PRE, 121-22
  partial, 248

E^2 (correlation ratio). See also
  Analysis of variance;
  ANOVA
  calculating, 89-90
  compared to
    r^2, 90-92, 94
    R^2, 197-98, 200, 228
    eta (from ANOVA), 211
  formula, 87
  interpreting, 95-96
  logic of, 85-89, 200-202
  from MEANS, 93-94
  means as form of relationship, 200-202, 205
  partial, formula for, 214
  PRE formula for, 86, 201
  test of significance, 269-70
  linearity, 270
Effects
  and ANOVA output, 210
  direct, 147, 158, 173, 190
    multicollinearity and, 175
  indirect, 147, 158, 165

END DATA. See SPSS file
Equation, prediction. See Model
Error
  coding, effect on distributions, 108
  measurement
    aggregate data as reduced, 70
    effect on choice of measure, 123
    lower level as increased, 82
    in regression, 59, 69-70
    reliability as lack of, 72
    sources of, 69
  proportionate reduction of, defined, 48-49
  random, in measurement, 72
  reduction of, regression, 45
  sampling, 276-77
  term, correlated with independents, 175
  types of
    alpha, type I, 262
    beta, type II, 262
  variation as, 48
Eta (from ANOVA), 211. See also E^2
Ethics, 287
Expected frequencies, 109, 134-35
  correction of, 136
Experiment. See also Data collection method
  and alternative explanations, 286
  with analysis of variance, 96
  compared to statistical control, 150-53
  as data collection technique, 288
Explanation. See also Generalization; Hypotheses; names of specific measures of association
  alternative, 145, 150
  defined, 7
  as goal of science, 1-3
  improved by multiple independents, 141-42
  parsimony in, 52, 92, 205
  of variation, 42, 48, 141 ff. See also PRE statistics

Fallacy, 285
  affirming the consequent, 8, 261
Falsification, 5, 70, 262, 285-86
Field, 32, 35, 68. See also Data, coding
File. See SPSS file

FINISH. *See also* SPSS file
differences in batch and interactive processing, 38
Form of relationships. *See also* Slope; Means, difference of; Interaction; Multicollinearity
bivariate regression, 42–43, 60
defined, 5
nominal variables, 137
ordinal variables, 105–7, 125
Formula, defining vs. computing, 18
FREQUENCIES
as aid in recoding, 109
command form, 36–37
as error check, 40–41
histograms and barcharts from, 40
F test, 263–67, 268–71
from ANOVA, 269
assumptions, 264, 268
for correlation or slope, 265, 270
curvilinearity, 270
description, 263–64
for E^2, 269
for interaction, 268–69
for partial r, 270
from REGRESSION, 266

Gamma
calculating,
fully ranked data, 114–16
tables, 116–18
compared to d_{yx}. tau$_b$, 119, 122–25
and form of relationship, 125
formula, 116
limitations of, 118–19
logic of 114–16
for nominal data. *See* Q
partial, 248–50
PRE interpretation, 118
test of significance, 255–60
formula for Z, 258
Generalization, 284–85. *See also* Explanation
explanations, simple, 92
from sample to population, 288
GET FILE, 68
Goodman and Kruskal's tau. *See* Tau, Goodman and Kruskal's

Histogram, from FREQUENCIES, 40
Homoscedasticity, 264
Hypotheses. *See also* Explanation; Generalization

alternative, 7, 262
in analysis of variance, 94–95
in bivariate regression, 68
criteria for, 4–7, 284–85
effect on choice of ordinal measure of association, 122, 124–25
in F test, 265–66
and literature review, 283–84
in multiple regression, 191
null, 7, 262
secondary, in research design, 285–86
using indices in, 77

IF
command form, 224
Index construction. *See also* Indicators, Operationalization
with COUNT, 75–77, 81–82
defined, 67
dichotomies in, 73
nominal variables in, 73
reasons for, 71
selecting variables for, 72–74
standardization of index items, 186–89
summed standard scores, 189–90
Indicators, 8, 71. *See also* Operationalization; Index construction
Interaction
in analysis of
covariance, 233–35
variance, 202–4, 206, 208, 228–29
compared between analysis of variance and regression, 231
compared to multicollinearity, 215–16
defined, 148
effect on
form of relationship 216–17
partial r, 165, 207
slope, 176, 207
strength of relationship, 216
in experiments, 153
in multiple regression, 191, 236
in multivariate tables, 240, 247
solutions for 176–77, 204–7, 236
and theory building, 149
Interactive processing, 37
Intercept. *See also* Regression; REGRESSION
formula
bivariate, 60
multivariate, 172

interpretation, 61, 62–63, 171–72
in analysis of covariance, 232–35
from PLOT, 70
from REGRESSION, 183

Kendall's tau. *See* Tau, Kendall's

Lambda
calculating, 128–31
formula, 130
logic of, 128
with misleading data, 131–32
PRE interpretation, 130
Level of analysis. *See also* Data, types
implied in hypothesis, 284
as organization for literature review, 283
Linearity
and choice of statistic, 85, 216
diagram, 125
F test for, 270
and multiple regression, 177
test for with MEANS, 94
Literature review, 283–84

MANOVA, 236
Marginals,
defined, 16
reading in multivariate tables, 242–45
MCA (table from ANOVA), 211–14
Mean
calculation, 18
definition, 18
difference of as form of relationship
analysis of variance, one-way, 89, 99, 224–25
analysis of variance, two-way, 200–202, 205, 212, 227
regression, 99
from dummy variables, 227
formula, 18
interpretation, 19
properties of, 23–34
from SPSS output
ANOVA, 210–12
DESCRIPTIVES, 39
MCA (ANOVA), estimate, 211
MEANS, 94
REGRESSION, 163
use of, 23

MEANS
  auxiliary to ANOVA, 209
  command form 93, 95
  output, 94, 95
Measurement. See also Index construction; Operationalization; Reliability; Validity; Values
  defined, 10
  indirect, 71
  levels of, defined, 11
    effect on regression of, 81-85
  mutually exclusive and exhaustive categories, 108
Measurement error. See Error, measurement
Measures of association based on chi square. See Phi; V
Measures of association for interval data. See E^2, R^2
Measures of association for nominal data, 128-39. See also Lambda, Phi, Q, Tau, V
  partials, 248-49
  from SPSS, 138, 249
Measures of association for ordinal data, 114-26. See also d_{yx}; Gamma; Tau
  choice of, 122-25
  logic of 114-15
  partials, 248-49
  from SPSS, 125-26, 249
  uses of 114
Measures of central tendency. See Mean; Median; Mode
Median
  calculating, 21
  definition, 21
  from FREQUENCIES, 39
  interpretation, 21
  use, 23
Missing data
  codes, 68
  and COMPUTE, 193, 228
  and recoding, 93, 109
MISSING VALUES
  command form, 77
  with COUNT, 76
  in stored file, 67
  use of, 41
Mode
  bimodal distributions, 23-24
  definition, 22
  use, 23
Model
  additive
    complexity compared to interactive, 205-6
    with dummy variables, 227

in two-way analysis of variance, 202-3
prediction
  in analysis of variance with dichotomies, 196-200
  dummy variables, 224
  dummy and dichotomous variables, 227
  in bivariate regression, 70
  with interval and dichotomous or dummy independent variables, 232-35
  multivariate, regression, 170, 172
Monotonicity
  and choice of statistic, 122-25, 137
  diagram, 124
Multicollinearity. 174-75. See also Error, term
  in analysis of variance, 211-14
  compared with interaction, 215-16
  effect on
    form of relationship, 215
    strength of relationship, 215
  experiments as remedy for, 153-54
  mitigating, 144, 175
  separate effects and, 142-43, 231
  in tables, 240, 242-43
Multivariate analysis
  defined, 138
  goals of, 141 ff., 240

Noncorrelation, spurious, 145-46
Normal curve, 256
  characteristics of, 257-58
  diagram, 257
Notation, statistical. See also individual statistical formulae
  how to read, 18
Number of cases needed for
  analysis of variance, 94-95, 213-14
  dummy variable regression, 225
  multiple regression, 177
  sample, 109, 276-77
  tables, 108-9

Operationalization (operational definition). See also Index construction; Indicators; Reliability; Validity
  defined, 7
  examples of, 8-9, 29, 53-54, 71-72, 110, 166-67, 218, 252

multi-item indices, 71-78, 186-90
and research design, 288-89
of sampling population, 279, 288
Outliers
  defined, 58
  effect on
    r^2, 58
    slope, 64, 173
Output, reading, 38-39. See also individual SPSS procedure names

p (probability, on CORRELATIONS output), 74
Package, statistical, computer, 31
Paired cases 114-18. See also Measures of association for ordinal data
Parsimony. See Explanation
Part Cor (REGRESSION output), 163, 183
PARTIAL CORR
  command form, 162
  subcommands, 162
  test of significance, 271
Partial r, r^2. See also Regression; REGRESSION
  in analysis of
    covariance through regression, 233-35
    variance through regression, 233, 35
  calculating, 160-61
  compared to partial ordinal measures, 249
  compared to partial slope, 173-74
  formulae
    X controlled, 180
    Z controlled, 161, 163
  interpretation of, 157-58, 161, 163-65
    cautions about, 165
  logic of, 156-60
  order of, 157
Partials. See Partial r; name of bivariate statistic
Path analysis, 176
Pearson's r. See r
Phi. See also Chi square
  formula, 136
  interpretation, 136-37
  partial, 248-49
Plot
  of bivariate relationships, 43-45, 51
  of residuals, 160, 173

INDEX

PLOT, 68-69, 232. *See also* r
  subcommands, 69
  regression statistics from 70
Population
  defining in research design, 288
  in sampling, 279-80
Prediction equation. *See* Model
PRE statistics, defined, 48-49.
  See also names of individual statistics (R^2, E^2, gamma, d, tau, lambda)
Probability
  and tests of significance, 261-62
Procedure commands, 36. *See also* names of individual SPSS procedures

Q, Yule's, 137

r, Pearson's. *See also* CORRELATIONS; PLOT; Regression; REGRESSION
  definition, 59
  formula, 161
  interpretation, 59-60
  in reliability tests, 74-75
  (bivariate r squared). *See also* PLOT; Regression; REGRESSION
  in analysis of variance, 197
  calculating, 56-58
  compared to E^2, 90-92, 94
  with curves, 51-52
  formula, 55
  interpretation of, 55-56, 58-59, 63-64
    reasons for high/low, 58-59, 69-70
  limitations and uses, 51
  logic of, 45-48
  PRE formula for, 48
    calculating, 49
    interpretation, 49-50
  across samples, 63
  test of significance for, 266
  curvilinearity, 270
R^2 (multiple R squared). *See also* Regression; REGRESSION
  in analysis of covariance, 233, 235
  computing, 178-79
  diagrams of, 178-79
  in dummy variable analysis, 225, 228
  formulae
    correlated independents, 179
    uncorrelated independents, 178
  interpretation of, 178-79
  logic of, 177-78
  PRE formula for, 178
  test of significance, 266
  uses for, 179
Randomization of subjects, 151, 154
Range. *See also* Variation
  defined, 17
  from DESCRIPTIVES, 39
  effect of low in regression, 58, 64
RECODE. *See also* Recoding
  to combine categories, 225-26
  command form, 92-93
  with missing data, 93, 109
  and value labels, 93, 109
Recoding. *See also* RECODE
  and mutually exclusive and exhaustive categories, 108
  reasons for, 94-95, 107-8, 225
Record, 35, 68. *See also* SPSS files
Regression. *See also* REGRESSION; names of individual statistics from regression (intercept, slope, beta, r, partial r, R)
  analysis of covariance, use of for, 231-37
  analysis of variance, use of for, 196-200
  compared to tables and analysis of variance, 98-102, 231
  dichotomous dependent variables in, 85
  dichotomous independent variables, 84-85
  with dummy variables, 223-30
  interpretation, 180
  logic of, 231
  ordinal independent variables, 82-83
  PRE logic in, 42-43
REGRESSION. *See also* Regression; names of individual statistics from regression (intercept, slope, beta, r, partial r, R)
  command form, 162-63, 181
  with dummy variables, 209, 213, 216, 225-30
  interaction terms with, 204
  output, 163, 182-83, 211, 213-15, 229
  standard slopes in, 192
  subcommands, 162-63, 181
  test of significance, 266-67
Regression coefficient. *See* Slope
Relationship. *See also* Explanation
  defined, 3
  ordinal independent/interval dependent, 85-89
    curved, 83, 91-92
  two interval variables
    curved, 51-52, 58, 78
    defined, 3
    direction, 43-45
    form and strength, 43
    nonlinear and analysis of variance for, 216
  two ordinal variables, 98 ff.
    direction in tables, 118
Reliability. *See also* Error, measurement; Operationalization
  defined, 10
  of dependent variable measurement, 283
  of individual indicators, 72
  inter-item (item-to-item), 72, 75
    compared to test-retest, 78
  and multi-item indices, 72
  and ordinal measures of association, 114
  in research design, 289
  test-retest, 78-79
Replication, 284
Residuals
  analysis of for correlated error term, 175-76
  concept, 47-48
  defined, 50
  in F test assumptions, 265
  plotting, 160
  sum of squares, 210
  as that which is explained for partial r, 159, 170
Rho, Spearman's, 125
Right justified, 32. *See also* Data coding

Sample, sampling
  cluster, multi-stage, 278
  confidence, certainty, 277
  controversies, 280
  defined, 12
  error, 276
  and F tests, 266
  goal of, 276
  independent random, 264, 275
  population definition, 279-80
  probability sample, 276
  quota sample, 279
  random, 278

relation to statistical inference, 255–56
and research design, 288
and significance tests, 275
size of sample, 109, 276–77. *See also* Number of cases
stratified random, 278
Scatterplot
defined, 44
interpretation, 69
with noninterval variables, 83–84
from PLOT, 68
SCATTERPLOT. *See also* PLOT; Scatterplot subcommand of REGRESSION, 173
Significance. *See also* Tests of significance
substantive vs. statistical, 267–68, 273
Skewness
definition and interpretation, 22
effect on sample size, 109
from SPSS, 39
Slope. *See also* Regression; REGRESSION
formula, bivariate, Y dependent, 60
interpretation, 61, 63–64
as difference of means, 84–85, 197–98, 213
partial slope
calculation, 170
compared to bivariate slope, 174
compared to partial r, 173–74
formula, 171
interpretation of 171, 172–77
in analysis of covariance, 232, 233, 235
in analysis of variance, 197–99, 231–35
in dummy variable regression, 224
logic of, 170–71
from PLOT, 70
problems comparing across samples, 63, 174, 191
Somer's d_{yx}. *See* d_{yx}
Spearman's rho. *See* Rho
Specification. *See* Interaction
SPSS. *See also* individual procedure and data manipulation (e.g., RECODE) names
batch processing, 37–38
description, 31
files, 33–36, 67
interactive processing, 37–38
output, 38–39
procedures, use of, 36–37
retrieving of stored files, 68

Spurious correlation. *See* Correlation, spurious; Noncorrelation, spurious
Standard deviation. *See also* Variance; Variation
calculating, 26
formula, 26
interpretation, 27–28
ordinal analogue to, 103
Standard deviation units
in measurements, 189
in normal curve, 257–58
in standard slopes, 190
Standardization of items, 186–89
Standard scores. *See also* Index construction
logic of, 186–88
procedure, 189–90
Standard slopes. *See* beta
Statistical interaction. *See* Interaction
Strength of relationship, measure of, 45. *See also* names of individual measures of association (R^2, E^2, gamma, tau, etc.); Interaction; Multicollinearity
Subcommands. *See* SPSS procedure names
Subjects, human, rights of, 290–91
Sum of squares
and ANOVA output, 210
Surveys, 16. *See* Data, collection method
Symmetry in measures of form and relationship
defined, 64, 130, 133, 136, 171

Tables. *See also* CROSSTABS
compared to analysis of variance and regression, 98–102
construction, 103–5, 240–42
effect of on measures of association, 117–18
interpretation
form of relationship, 105–7
multivariate, 242–48
strength of relationship, 104–7
rules for presentation, 250
Tau, Goodman and Kruskal's
Calculating, 132–34
Interpreting, 133
PRE formula for, 133
Tau, Kendall's
tau_a, 125
tau_b
calculation, 120

compared to gamma, d_{yx}, 119, 122–23
compared to r^2, 120
and form of relationship, 125
formula, 119
interpretation, 120
pairs/ties in, 119
partial, 248
PRE interpretation, 120
test of significance, 260, 261
tau_c, 123–34
formula, 123
Tautology, defined, 5
Tests of significance, 255–74. *See also* Significance; names of individual statistics
nonparametric, 271
one-tailed vs. two-tailed
with normal distribution, 260
with t, 266
Theory, 7
and choice of ordinal statistics, 123
in research design, 283
as source of hypotheses, 2
Tied pair, defined, 115
t statistic, 267
Typical case. *See* Mean; Median; Mode; Univariate analysis
Choice of measures to describe, 23

Units of analysis. *See* Case
Univariate analysis
defined, 16
for interval data, 16–28

V, Cramer's. *See also* Chi square
formula, 136
interpretation, 136–37
partial, 248–49
Validity. *See also* Measurement; Operationalization
defined, 10
of dependent variable in design, 283
and research design, 289
types of, 138–39
Value, critical, 263
Values, of variables. *See also* Measurement
defined, 2–3
dichotomous, defined, 72, 131, 137
mutually exclusive and exhaustive, 9
Variables
antecedent, 146–47, 245

Variables (cont.)
　control, logic of, 141–49, 156, 231
　correlated independent, 245
　　in analysis of variance, 211–15
　　possible effects of, 245
　　See also Multicollinearity
　dependent
　　defined, 2
　　importance in design, 283
　distorter, 145–46, 245, 286
　dummy. See Dummy variables
　extraneous, 144, 164, 245, 285–86
　　compared to intervening, 148, 158
　independent
　　defined, 3
　　function of in regression, 42
　　in literature review, 283
　　ordinal in regression, 82
　intervening, 146–47, 164, 245
　　compared to extraneous, 148, 158
　specifier, 145, 245, 286
　suppressor, 59, 145–46, 158, 245, 286
　uncorrelated independent, effects of, 142, 245
　　in analysis of variance, 196–211
　　on multivariate slope, 170
Variance. See also Standard deviation; Variation
　definition, 26
　formula, 26
Variation. See also Standard deviation; Variance
　formula, in regression, 46
　low, effect of in regression, 58, 64, 78
　necessity for
　　in inference to population, 18
　　in tests of hypotheses, 3, 17, 285
　ordinal analogue to, 103, 115
　and PRE in regression, 48–49
　that which is explained, 2–3, 45–46, 48, 56, 85–88, 99, 156–57, 177, 230–31, 255
　and sample size, 109, 277–78
　and scale construction, 74, 187–88

Weights
　of cases in ordinal partials, 248
　of indicators in indices, 187–88

Yule's Q. See Q

Z score
　formulae
　　standard score, 189
　　transforming gamma, 258
　for index construction, 188–89
　for test of gamma's significance, 256–60